# DELIVERING
# BUSINESS
# INTELLIGENCE

with **Microsoft® SQL Server® 2012**

## About the Author

**Brian Larson** served as a member of the original Reporting Services development team as a consultant to Microsoft. In that role, he contributed to the original code base of Reporting Services. Brian is currently the Vice President of Technology for Superior Consulting Services in Minneapolis, Minnesota, a Microsoft Managed Partner.

Brian has presented at national conferences and events, including the SQL Server Magazine Connections Conference, the PASS Community Summit, and the Microsoft Business Intelligence Conference, and has provided training and mentoring on business intelligence across the country. He has been a contributor and columnist for *SQL Server Magazine*. In addition to this book, Brian is the author of *Microsoft SQL Server 2012 Reporting Services* and co-author of *Visualizing Data with Microsoft Power View,* both from McGraw-Hill Professional.

Brian is a Phi Beta Kappa graduate of Luther College in Decorah, Iowa, with degrees in physics and computer science. He has 26 years of experience in the computer industry, and 22 years of experience as a consultant creating custom database applications. Brian is an MCITP: Business Intelligence Developer 2008 and a Microsoft Certified Database Administrator (MCDBA).

Brian and his wife Pam have been married for 26 years. Pam will tell you that their first date took place at the campus computer center. If that doesn't qualify someone to write a computer book, then I don't know what does. Brian and Pam have two children, Jessica and Corey.

## About the Technical Editors

**Dan English**, MVP, MCITP, is a Microsoft SQL Server MVP, an MCITP Business Intelligence Developer for Microsoft SQL Server 2005 and 2008, and an MCTS for Microsoft Office SharePoint Server 2007 – Configuring. Dan is a Principal BI consultant at Superior Consulting Services. He currently helps to lead the Minnesota Business Intelligence User Group and is an avid blogger (http://denglishbi .wordpress.com), Microsoft forums helper, and tweeter (@denglishbi).

**Paul Purington**, MCITP, is a partner and member of the management team at Superior Consulting Services. As a BI consultant, Paul has experience with both large- and small-scale business intelligence environments.

# DELIVERING BUSINESS INTELLIGENCE

with **Microsoft® SQL Server® 2012**

## Third Edition

**Brian Larson**

New York   Chicago   San Francisco   Lisbon
London   Madrid   Mexico City   Milan
New Delhi   San Juan   Seoul   Singapore
Sydney   Toronto

The McGraw·Hill Companies

**Cataloging-in-Publication Data is on file with the Library of Congress**

McGraw-Hill books are available at special quantity discounts to use as premiums and sales promotions, or for use in corporate training programs. To contact a representative, please e-mail us at bulksales@mcgraw-hill.com.

**Delivering Business Intelligence with Microsoft® SQL Server® 2012, Third Edition**

34567890   QFR QFR   109876543

ISBN        978-0-07-175938-0
MHID        0-07-175938-7

**Sponsoring Editor**
Wendy Rinaldi

**Editorial Supervisor**
Patty Mon

**Project Managers**
Harleen Chopra and Ridhi Mathur,
Cenveo Publisher Services

**Acquisitions Coordinator**
Joya Anthony

**Technical Editors**
Dan English
Paul Purington

**Copy Editor**
Lisa McCoy

**Proofreader**
Carol Shields

**Indexer**
Ted Laux

**Production Supervisor**
Jean Bodeaux

**Composition**
Cenveo Publisher Services

**Illustration**
Cenveo Publisher Services

**Art Director, Cover**
Jeff Weeks

**Cover Designer**
Jeff Weeks

*This book is dedicated to my parents. To my father, Robert, who even after 40-plus years as a junior high mathematics teacher and computer instructor, has a love of teaching. He has shown me a real commitment to sharing knowledge with others. To my mother, Beverly, who was my first editor, coaching me through elementary school papers on this state or that president. She taught me the value of sticking with a job and seeing it through to the end. I owe them both a debt of love, caring, and support that can never be adequately repaid.*

# Contents at a Glance

# Contents

## Part IV     Working with a Tabular BI Semantic Model

### Chapter 13     Setting the Table—Creating a Tabular BI Semantic Model  . . . . . . . . . . **501**

### Chapter 14     A Fancy Table—Tabular BI Semantic Model Advanced Features  . . . . . . . . **551**

## Part V    Mining

# Acknowledgments

No project of this size is the work of a single person. I need to thank a number of people for their assistance, professionalism, dedication, and support. So, a *ginormous* thank you…

To Wendy Rinaldi, who allowed me to lean on her as part editor, part coach, part literary agent, and part psychoanalyst. Her professionalism, humor, understanding, and faith truly made this project possible.

To Dan English and Paul Purington, co-workers who make Superior Consulting Services a fun, exciting place to work. Their technical expertise, constructive feedback, and tireless work were vital to the success of this and other SQL Server 2012 projects.

To the rest of the McGraw-Hill Professional staff, who saw it through to the end and made sure there really was a book when all was said and done.

To John Miller, who founded Superior Consulting Services as a place where people can grow and learn, produce solid technology solutions, serve customers, and have a good time to boot.

To Jessica and Corey, my children, who allowed me time to pursue this passion.

To my wife, Pam, who continues to be gracious in her understanding of my affliction with the writing bug. She has given generously of her time to proof and review this book and its Learn By Doing exercises. Her incredible attention to detail has made this a better product.

Last, but certainly not least, to you, the reader, who plunked down your hard-earned cash for this purchase. I hope you view this as a helpful and informative guide to all of the truly exciting business intelligence features in SQL Server 2012.

All the best,
Brian Larson
blarson@teamscs.com

## The Maximum Miniatures Databases and Other Supporting Materials

All of the samples in this book are based on business scenarios for a fictional company called Maximum Miniatures, Inc. You can download the data, image files, and other supporting materials from the book's webpage on the McGraw-Hill Professional website. This download also includes the complete source code for all of the Learn By Doing activities and the applications demonstrated in the book.

The download is found on this book's webpage at www.mhprofessional.com. Search for the book's webpage using the ISBN, which is 0071759387. Use the "Sample Code" link to download the Zip file containing the book's material. Follow the instructions in the individual Zip files to install or prepare each item as needed.

# Part I

# Business Intelligence

# Chapter 1

# Equipping the Organization for Effective Decision Making

## In This Chapter

▶ **Effective Decision Making**

▶ **Keys to Effective Decision Making**

▶ **Business Intelligence**

*"Would you tell me please, which way I ought to go from here?" asked Alice. "That depends a good deal on where you want to get to," said the Cat. "I don't much care where," said Alice. "Then, it doesn't matter which way you go," said the Cat.*

*Alice's Adventures in Wonderland*

—Lewis Carroll

Life is filled with decisions. Should I have the burger and fries or the salad for lunch? Should I get my significant other that new watch they've had their eye on, or should I buy them a new vacuum cleaner? Do I invest my holiday bonus or head for the casino? Should I buy this book or go browse the comics section? (Here is your first bit of business intelligence: buy this book!)

The choices we make can have life-changing consequences. Even seemingly trivial decisions can have big consequences down the road. It's like your parents always told you: the key to success in life is to make good choices!

# Effective Decision Making

Good decision making is as important in the working world as it is in the rest of our lives. Every day a number of decisions must be made that determine the direction and efficiency of the organizations we work for. Decisions are made concerning production, marketing, and personnel. Decisions are made affecting costs, sales, and margins. Just as in our personal lives, the key to organizational success is to make good choices. The organization must have effective decision making.

## Who Is a Decision Maker?

Just who is it that must make good choices within an organization? At first blush, it may seem that only the person at the top, the chief executive officer (CEO), the president, or the chairperson needs to be an effective decision maker. If that person makes appropriate strategic decisions, the organization will succeed!

Unfortunately, it is not that easy. There are countless examples throughout history where absolutely brilliant strategic plans went awry because of poor decisions made by those responsible for their implementation. As emperor and leader of "La Grande Armée," Napoleon Bonaparte had a fairly decent strategic plan for his campaign in Belgium. However, due to some poor decision making by his marshals, Napoleon suffered a major defeat at a little place called Waterloo.

Given this, perhaps it is important for the next level of management to be effective decision makers as well. The chief financial officers (CFOs), chief information officers (CIOs), vice presidents, assistant chairpersons, and department heads (and marshals of the army) must make good choices when creating the policies and setting the priorities to implement the strategic plan. With all of upper management making effective decisions, the organization is guaranteed to go places!

In fact, success is not even assured when this is true. Effective plans and policies created at the top of the organization can be undone by poor decisions made further down as those plans and policies are put into action. The opposite is also true. Good decisions made by those working where the rubber meets the road can be quickly overwhelmed by poor decisions made further up the line.

The answer, then, is to have effective decision makers throughout an organization. Those lower down the organizational chart will have much better morale and will invest more energy in an activity if they have some assurance that their efforts will not be undone by someone higher up. In addition, the success of the person in the corner office is, in large part, simply a reflection of the effective decisions and successes of the people who report to them. Effective decision making at every level leads to success.

## What Is an Effective Decision?

The organization that has the desired products or services, provided in the proper place, at the correct time, produced at the appropriate cost, and backed by the necessary customer support will be successful. This, of course, is fairly obvious. Any business plan or mission statement worth its salt professes to do just this.

What is not so obvious is how an organization goes about making sure it provides what is desired, proper, correct, appropriate, and necessary. The answer, as we learned in the last section, is to have people making effective decisions at all levels of the organization. But what exactly is an effective decision?

### DEFINITION

Effective decisions *are choices that move an organization closer to an agreed-on set of goals in a timely manner.*

An effective decision moves an organization toward its goals in a timely manner. This definition is extremely broad. In fact, this makes a good slogan, but is too broad to be of much use in day-to-day operations. Using this definition, however, we can define three key ingredients necessary for making effective decisions:

▶ First, there must be a set of goals to work toward.

▶ Second, there must be a way to measure whether a chosen course is moving toward or away from those goals.

▶ Third, information based on those measures must be provided to the decision maker in a timely manner.

This information serves as both the foundation for the initial decision making and as feedback showing the results of the decision. Defining effective decision making is the easy part. Taking this rather nebulous definition and turning it into concrete business practices requires a bit more work.

**DEFINITION**

Foundation information serves *as the basis for making a particular decision as that decision is being made.*

**DEFINITION**

Feedback information *is used to evaluate the effectiveness of a particular decision after that decision is made.*

# Keys to Effective Decision Making

In the previous section, we learned that three keys are necessary for effective decision making: specific goals, concrete measures, and timely foundation and feedback information, as shown in Figure 1-1. In this section, we take a detailed look at each of these three keys to learn how to encourage effective decision making.

## Are We Going Hither or Yon?

In Mel Brooks's film, *The Producers,* Max and Leopold set out to stage an absolutely horrible Broadway musical, certain to fail, so they can abscond with the investor's money. Aside from this entertaining exception, organizations do not set out to fail.

**Figure 1-1**    *Three keys to effective decision making*

On the contrary, they come together, raise capital, create organizational charts, draw up business plans, prepare massive presentations, and have endless meetings, all to succeed. The first, largest, and ultimately fatal problem for many of these organizations is they do not define exactly what that success looks like. They don't know what the destination is.

An organization may have some nebulous goals in its mission statement. Phrases such as "superior customer satisfaction," "increased profit margin," or "better meeting our community's needs" grace the reception area, the annual report, and the entryway to the shareholders' meeting. These are great slogans for building a marketing campaign or generating esprit de corps among the employees. They do not, however, make good milestones for measuring business performance.

"Superior customer satisfaction" is a wonderful goal. (The world would be a much happier place if even half the companies that profess to strive toward superior customer satisfaction would actually make some progress in that direction.) The issue is how to measure "customer satisfaction." How do we know when we have reached this goal or if we are even making progress in that direction? What is required is something a bit more concrete and a lot more measurable.

Rather than the ill-defined "superior customer satisfaction," a better goal might be "to maintain superior customer satisfaction as measured by repeat customer orders with a goal of 80 percent repeat orders." This goal may need a few more details filled in, but it is the beginning of a goal that is specific and measurable. We can measure whether our decisions are taking us in the right direction based on the increase or decrease in repeat orders.

"Increased profit margin" makes the shareholders happy. Still, the organization must decide what operating costs impact profit margin and how they are divvied up among a number of concurrent projects. We may also want to state how large the increase to profit margin must be in order to satisfy the investors. Does a 1 percent increase put a smile on the shareholders' faces, or does our target need to be more in the 5 percent range? Once these details are added, we have a specific target to work toward.

"Better meeting our community's needs" is a noble goal, but what are those needs and how can we tell when they are met? Instead, we need to select a specific community need, such as increasing the number of quality, affordable housing units. We can then define what is meant by quality, affordable housing and just what size increase we are looking to achieve.

To function as part of effective decision making, a goal must

▶  Contain a specific target

▶  Provide a means to measure whether we are progressing toward that target

As with the dartboard in Figure 1-2, we need both a bull's eye to aim for and a method for scoring how close we came to that target.

**Figure 1-2** *Required elements of a goal to be used in effective decision making*

## Is Your Map Upside-Down?

Goals are important. In fact, they are essential to effective decision making, as discussed in the previous section. However, goals are useless without some sort of movement toward reaching them. The finish line can only be reached if the ladies and gentlemen start their engines and begin the race.

This is where decision making comes into play. Each decision moves the company in a particular direction. Some decisions produce a giant leap. These are the policy and priority decisions usually made in the upper levels of management. These decisions determine the general course the organization is going to take over a lengthy period, a fiscal year, a school calendar period, or perhaps even the entire lifetime of the organization. It is essential that these decisions point the organization toward its goals if those goals are ever going to be reached.

Some decisions cause the organization to make smaller movements one way or another. These decisions range from workgroup policies to daily operating decisions. It could even come down to the way a particular employee decides to handle a specific customer complaint or which phone number a sales representative decides to dial next. These small variations in the organization's direction, these small steps forward or backward, when added together become a large determinant of whether the organization ultimately reaches its goals. For this reason, effective decision making is needed at all levels of the organization.

But how do we know when a decision moves the organization, either by a leap or a baby step, toward the goal? We need a method of navigation. As shown in Figure 1-3, we need a map or, these days, perhaps a global positioning system (GPS), to tell us where we are relative to our goal and to show us if we are moving in the right direction.

**Figure 1-3**   *Measuring progress toward the goal*

This is the reason why goals must include a means of measuring progress. By repeatedly checking these measures, we can determine whether the organization is making effective decisions. When the measures show we are heading away from the goals, the decision making can be adjusted accordingly. As long as our measures are correctly defined to match our goals, we have a good chance of moving ever closer to those goals.

## Panicked Gossip, the Crow's Nest, or the Wireless

The sinking of the *Titanic* provides a catastrophic illustration of poor decision making. The ship was traveling at high speed in ice-laden waters—an unfortunate decision. This tragedy also provides us with an illustration of how important it is to receive feedback information in a timely manner.

News that there were "icebergs about" reached different people aboard the ship at different times. Most passengers found out about the fatal iceberg through panicked gossip as they were boarding the lifeboats. Of course, the passengers were not in a position to take direct action to correct the situation and, by the time they found out, it was far too late.

The ship's captain got news of the iceberg from the lookout in the crow's nest of the *Titanic*. This warning was received before the collision, and the captain attempted to correct the situation. However, the *Titanic* could neither stop nor turn on a dime so, ultimately, this warning turned out to be too late.

Another warning had been received earlier on board the *Titanic*. The wireless operator received an ice warning from another ship, the *America,* and even passed that warning on to a land-based wireless station. This message was received hours ahead of the collision—plenty of time to take precautions and avoid the tragedy. Because of the large workload on the wireless operator, however, this warning was never relayed to anyone on the *Titanic* with the authority to take those precautions. The feedback information aboard the *Titanic* is shown in Figure 1-4.

In the previous section, we learned about the need to use defined measures to get information to our decision makers. As the story of the *Titanic* illustrates, the timing of this feedback information is as important as its content. Feedback information that does not reach the proper decision makers in a timely manner is useful only to those investigating the tragedy after it has occurred. The goal of effective decision making is to avoid the tragedy in the first place!

As with the passengers on the *Titanic*, information in our organizations may come in the form of panicked gossip among lower-level personnel. Unlike those passengers, these people might even pick up some important information in advance of a calamity. Even if this is the case, these people are not in a position to correct the problem. Furthermore, we need to base our decision making on solid information from well-designed measures, not gossip and rumors.

**Figure 1-4**   *Aboard the Titanic, feedback information was not given to the decision makers in a timely manner.*

Like the captain of the *Titanic*, the decision makers in our organizations often get feedback information when it is too late to act. The information may be extremely accurate, but if it does not get to the decision makers in time to make corrections, it is not helpful. The numbers in the year-end report are not helpful for making decisions during the current year.

Similar to the wireless operator, our organizations often have a person who has the appropriate information at the appropriate time. The situation breaks down when this person does not pass the information along to the appropriate decision maker. This may occur, as in the case of the *Titanic's* wireless operator, because that person is overworked and has too much information to get out to too many people. It may also occur because organizational policies or structures prevent the flow of information. Finally, this may occur because the infrastructure is not in place to facilitate this communication.

# Business Intelligence

The first step in effective decision making is to set specific, measurable goals. As these goals are being set, the objective is to get accurate, useful information to the appropriate decision makers to serve as a foundation for the decision and as feedback on the effectiveness of that decision. Having the foundation and feedback information available at the appropriate time is extremely important. The question becomes: How does an organization go about obtaining and distributing this information? As the title of this book suggests, the answer is through the use of business intelligence. In fact, this objective serves as our definition of business intelligence.

### DEFINITION

Business intelligence *is the delivery of accurate, useful information to the appropriate decision makers within the necessary timeframe to support effective decision making.*

Business intelligence is not simply facts and figures on a printed report or a computer screen. Rows upon rows of numbers showing detailed sales figures or production numbers may be extremely accurate, but they are not business intelligence until they are put in a format that can be easily understood by a decision maker who needs to use them. Concise summaries of customer satisfaction or assembly-line efficiency may be easily understood, but they are not business intelligence until they can be delivered in time to meaningfully affect daily decision making.

We also discovered earlier in this chapter that effective decision making is important at all organizational levels. Timely foundation and feedback information is needed as part of that effective decision making. Therefore, we need to make business intelligence available throughout our organizations.

# Business Intelligence and Microsoft SQL Server 2012

Fortunately, Microsoft SQL Server 2012 provides tools to support all aspects of business intelligence. Integration Services enables us to create automated processes to cleanse data and move it into a business intelligence warehouse, when necessary, to ensure we have accurate information available in a timely manner. Numerous online analytical processing (OLAP) features, such as key performance indicators (KPIs), multidimensional expression (MDX) queries and scripts, and the BI Semantic Model (BISM), enable us to slice, dice, and summarize information so it can be presented in a meaningful manner. Data mining permits us to find and present patterns and behavior predictors that might not otherwise be found in the data. Finally, Reporting Services (along with other Microsoft end-user tools) facilitates the delivery of this information to decision makers throughout the entire organization.

In Chapter 2 of this book, we learn more about the concepts used when creating and delivering business intelligence. We see the types of questions business intelligence can help us answer. We also examine the kinds of information and the timeliness of that information required at various levels within an organization.

Finally, we become acquainted with Maximum Miniatures, Incorporated, the sample company we use throughout the remainder of the book. To make the business intelligence features of SQL Server 2012 easier to understand, we perform several hands-on exercises to create business intelligence solutions. Rather than looking at code snippets without any business context, we use the business needs of Maximum Miniatures. The goal of this book is not to enable you to use this or that feature of SQL Server 2012, but to help you understand how to use these features to meet business needs.

# Chapter 2

# Making the Most of What You've Got—Using Business Intelligence

## In This Chapter

▶ **What Business Intelligence Can Do for You**

▶ **Business Intelligence at Many Levels**

▶ **Maximum Miniatures, Inc.**

▶ **Building the Foundation**

*Out of clutter find simplicity. From discord find harmony.*

—Albert Einstein's First Two Rules of Work

I n the previous chapter, we discussed the importance of effective decision making to the success of any organization. We also learned that effective decision making depends on specific goals, concrete measures to evaluate our progress toward those goals, and foundation and feedback information based on those measures. The latter two items, concrete measures and foundation/feedback information, we referred to as business intelligence.

In this chapter, we take a look at the types of questions this business intelligence can help us answer. We also discuss the types of business intelligence that are needed at various levels of an organization. The chapter ends by talking about Maximum Miniatures, Incorporated, the company we are going to use for our examples throughout the book.

# What Business Intelligence Can Do for You

In Chapter 1, we saw how business intelligence is used to support effective decision making. It provides foundational information on which to base a decision. Business intelligence also provides us with feedback information that can be used to evaluate a decision. It can provide that foundational and feedback information in a number of different ways.

## When We Know What We Are Looking For

In some cases, we know what information we are looking for. We have a set of particular questions we want answered. What is the dollar amount of the sales or services our organization is providing in each region? Who are our top salespeople? In some of these situations, we not only know what we are looking for, but we also have a good idea where to find the information when we design the business intelligence solution.

### Layout-led Discovery

When we know the question we want answered and have a good idea where that answer is going to be found, we can use reports to deliver our business intelligence. This is the most common form of business intelligence and one we are all familiar with. For many situations, this format works well.

For example, if we want to know the dollar amount of the sales or services provided in each region, we know where to find this information. We can design a report to retrieve the information, and the report will consistently deliver what we need. The report serves as an effective business intelligence tool.

This is an example of *layout-led discovery*. With layout-led discovery, we can only learn information that the report designer thought to put in the report layout when it was first designed. If the information wasn't included at design time, we have no way to access it at the time the report is run.

Suppose our report shows the dollar amount for a given region to be unusually low. If the report designer did not include the supporting detail for that region, we have no way to drill into the region and determine the cause of the anomaly. Perhaps a top salesperson moved to another region. Maybe we have lost a key client. The report won't give us that information. We quickly come to a dead end.

## Data-led Discovery

In some cases, we know the question, but we don't know exactly where to look for our answer. This often occurs when the information we initially receive changes the question slightly. As in the example from the previous section, an anomaly in the information may cause us to want to look at the data in a slightly different way. The unusually low dollar amount for sales or services provided in a specific region led us to want detailed numbers within that region.

In other cases, we know where to look, but it is not practical to search through all of the detailed information. Instead, we want to start at an upper level, find a number that looks interesting, and then drill to more detail. We want to follow the data that catches our attention to see where it leads.

This is *data-led discovery:* The information we find determines where we want to go next. The developer of this type of solution cannot know everywhere the report user may want to go. Instead, the developer must provide an interactive environment that enables the user to navigate at will.

To implement data-led discovery, we need some type of drilldown mechanism. When we see something that looks interesting, we need to be able to click that item and access the next level of detail. This is, of course, not going to happen on a sheet of paper. Data-led discovery must be done online.

## Discovering New Questions and Their Answers

In some cases, our data may hold answers to questions we have not even thought to ask. The data may contain trends, correlations, and dependencies at a level of detail that would be impossible for a human being to notice using either layout-led or data-led discovery. These relationships can be discovered by the computer using data mining techniques.

 **DEFINITION**

Data mining *uses a complex mathematical algorithm to sift through detail data to identify patterns, correlations, and clustering within the data.*

Where layout-led discovery and data-led discovery usually start with summarized data, data mining works at the lowest level of detail. Highly sophisticated mathematical algorithms are applied to the data to find correlations between characteristics and events. Data mining can uncover such nuggets as the fact that a customer who purchased a certain product is more likely to buy a different product from your organization (we hope a product with a high profit margin). Or, a client receiving a particular service is also likely to need another service from your organization in the next three months.

This type of information can be extremely helpful when planning marketing campaigns, setting up cross-product promotions, or doing capacity planning for the future. It can also aid in determining where additional resources and effort would produce the most effective result.

# Business Intelligence at Many Levels

In Chapter 1, we discussed the fact that business intelligence should be utilized at all levels of an organization to promote effective decision making. While it is true that business intelligence is useful throughout the organization, the same type of information is not needed at each level. Different levels within the organization require different types of business intelligence for effective decision making.

As we look at what is required at each level, keep in mind the Effective Decisions Triangle from Figure 1-1. We will transform that triangle into a pyramid as we examine the specific goals, concrete measures, and the timing of the foundation and feedback information required at each level. (See Figures 2-1, 2-2, and 2-3.)

**Figure 2-1**    *Specific goals at each level of the organization*

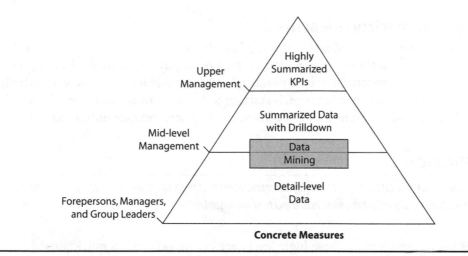

**Figure 2-2**    *Concrete measures at each level of the organization*

## The Top of the Pyramid

Decision makers at the upper levels of our organizations must look at the big picture. They are charged with setting long-term goals for the organization. Decision makers need to have a broad overview of their area of responsibility and not get caught up in the minutiae.

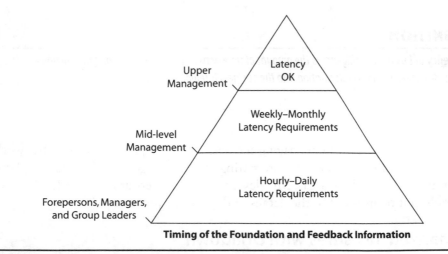

**Figure 2-3**    *Timing of the foundation and feedback information at each level of the organization*

## Highly Summarized Measures

The business intelligence utilized at this level needs to match these characteristics. The measures delivered to these decision makers must be highly summarized. In many cases, each measure is represented, not by a number, but by a status indicator showing whether the measure is in an acceptable range, is starting to lag, or is in an unacceptable range. These highly summarized measures are known as key performance indicators.

**DEFINITION**

Key performance indicators *(KPIs) are highly summarized measures designed to quickly relay the status of that measure. They usually reflect the most vital aspects of the organization.*

KPIs are used to provide these high-level decision makers with a quick way to determine the health of the essential aspects of the organization. KPIs are often presented as a graphical icon, such as a traffic light or a gauge, designed to convey the indicator's status at a glance. We discuss KPIs in greater detail in Chapter 10 of this book.

## Higher Latency

Because these upper-level decision makers are dealing in long-term policies and direction, they do not need up-to-the-minute business intelligence. Another way to state this is to say they can have more *latency* in their business intelligence. These decision makers need to see downward trends in time to make corrections. They do not need to see the daily blips in the organization's operation.

**DEFINITION**

The latency *of business intelligence is the amount of time between the occurrence of a transaction and the loading of that transaction's information into the business intelligence system.*

# Mid-Level

Mid-level decision makers are managing the operation of departments and other working units within the organization. They are setting short-term goals and doing the planning for the functioning of these areas. Mid-level decision makers are still at a level where they should not be involved in the details of day-to-day processes.

## Summarized Measures with Drilldown

These mid-level decision makers need business intelligence that is still summarized, but they often need to drill down into this information to get at more detail. Therefore, these decision makers can utilize reports along with interactive systems, allowing data-led discovery. These decision makers can also make use of information from data mining.

### Some Latency Acceptable

Because these decision makers are closer to the everyday functions, they may require business intelligence with less latency. In some cases, they may need to see measures that are updated daily. In other cases, these decision makers are looking for trends discernable from weekly or monthly loads.

## The Broad Base

At the broad base of our business intelligence pyramid are the forepersons, managers, and group leaders taking care of daily operations. These people are setting daily operational goals and making decisions on resource allocation for the next week, the next day, or perhaps the next shift. They are planning the next sales campaign or maybe just the next sales call. These decision makers usually need business intelligence systems with high availability and high responsiveness.

### Measures at the Detail Level

These decision makers are dealing with the details of the organization's operations. They need to be able to access information at the detail level. In some cases, the work groups these decision makers are responsible for are small enough that they can see the detail for the work group directly without being overwhelmed. In other cases, measures need to be summarized, but drilldown to the detail level will probably be required. These decision makers may utilize some forms of data mining to help discern trends and correlations in daily information.

### Low Latency

Because these low-level decision makers are managing day-to-day operations, they need to react quickly to changes in feedback information. For this reason, they can tolerate little latency. In some cases, these decision makers require data that is no more than one day old, one hour old, or even less.

---

## Maximum Miniatures, Inc.

Throughout the remainder of this book, Maximum Miniatures, Incorporated serves as the basis for all of our examples. Maximum Miniatures, or Max Min, Inc., as it is referred to by most employees, manufactures and sells small, hand-painted figurines.

It has several product lines, including the Woodland Creatures collection of North American animals; the Mythic World collection, which includes dragons, trolls, and elves; the Warriors of Yore collection, containing various soldiers from Roman times up through World War II; and the Guiding Lights collection, featuring replica lighthouses from the United States. The miniatures are made from clay, pewter, or aluminum.

Max Min markets these miniatures through three different channels. It operates five of its own "Maximum Miniature World" stores dedicated to selling the Max Min product line. Max Min also operates MaxMin.com to sell its products online. In addition, Max Min sells wholesale to other retailers.

## Business Needs

Max Min, Inc., has experienced rapid growth in the past three years, with orders increasing by over 300 percent. This growth has put a strain on Max Min's only current source of business intelligence, the printed report. Reports that worked well to support decision making just a few years ago now take an hour or more to print and even longer to digest. These reports work at the detail level with little summarization. Max Min's current systems provide few, if any, alternatives to the printed reports for viewing business intelligence.

In addition, Max Min, Inc., is facing tough competition in a number of its product areas. This competition requires Max Min to practice effective decision making to keep its competitive edge. Unfortunately, Max Min's current business intelligence infrastructure, or lack thereof, is making this extremely difficult.

Because of these issues, Max Min has launched a new project to create a true business intelligence environment to support its decision making. This project includes the design of a data warehouse structure, the population of that data warehouse from its current systems, and the creation of analytical applications to serve decision makers at all levels of the organization.

The new business intelligence platform is based on SQL Server 2012. After an extensive evaluation, it was decided that the SQL Server 2012 platform would provide the highest level of business intelligence capability for the money spent. SQL Server 2012 was also chosen because it features the tools necessary to implement the data warehouse in a relatively short time.

We will examine each step of Max Min's implementation project as we learn about the various business intelligence tools available in SQL Server 2012. Before we begin, let's take a quick look at Max Min's current systems.

## Current Systems

Max Min has five data processing systems that are expected to serve as sources of business intelligence (see Figure 2-4).

## Manufacturing Automation

The manufacturing automation system tracks the materials used to make each product. It also stores which products are manufactured on which production lines. Finally, this system tracks the number of items manufactured during each shift.

The manufacturing automation system uses a proprietary data-storage format. Data can be exported from the manufacturing automation system to a comma-delimited text file. This text file serves as the source for loading the manufacturing data into the business intelligence systems.

## Order Processing

The order processing system manages the inventory amounts for all products. It tracks wholesale orders placed by non–Max Min retailers. The system also records product amounts sold through the Max Min retail stores and the Max Min online store to maintain inventory amounts.

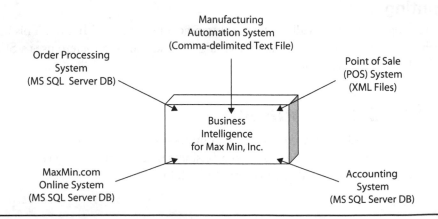

**Figure 2-4**   *Sources of business intelligence at Max Min, Inc.*

The order processing system tracks order fulfillment, including product shipping. It also generates invoices and handles the payment of those invoices. In addition, this system records any products returned from the retailer.

The order processing system uses a Microsoft SQL Server database as its backend.

## Point of Sale

The point of sale (POS) system manages the cash registers at each of the five Max Min–owned retail stores. This system also tracks the inventory at each retail store using Universal Product Code (UPC) barcode stickers placed on each item. The POS system handles both cash and credit card transactions. It also tracks information on any products returned by the customer.

Information from each of the five POS systems is exported to an Extensible Markup Language (XML) file. This XML file is transferred nightly, using File Transfer Protocol (FTP), to a central location. These XML files serve as the source for loading the POS data into the business intelligence systems.

## MaxMin.com

The MaxMin.com online store is an ASP.NET application. It uses SQL Server as its backend database. All sales through the online store are paid with a credit card. All customers of the online store must provide name, address, phone number, and e-mail address with each purchase.

The online store tracks the shipping of orders. It also handles any products returned by customers. Finally, the online store saves information on product promotions and discounts that are run on the store site.

## Accounting

The accounting system tracks all the financial transactions for Max Min, Inc. This includes the purchase of raw materials for manufacturing. The accounting system uses a SQL Server database for its backend.

# Building the Foundation

In Chapter 3, you will learn more about the foundations of our business intelligence systems. We explore possible sources for our business intelligence data. We also look at what the structure of those data sources might look like.

# Chapter 3

# Seeking the Source— The Source of Business Intelligence

## In This Chapter

- ▶ **Seeking the Source**
- ▶ **The Data Mart**
- ▶ **Snowflakes, Stars, and Analysis Services**

*Planning ahead is a good idea. It wasn't raining when Noah built the ark.*

—Anonymous

In the previous chapter, we discussed the various ways business intelligence can aid in making effective business decisions. We also looked at the characteristics of the business intelligence used at different levels within our organizations. Finally, we were introduced to Maximum Miniatures, Incorporated, the source for all sample data in this book.

In this chapter, we begin planning the database structures to serve as the source of our business intelligence. In some cases, we can extract our business intelligence information directly from the same database used to store the data from our daily business operations. In many cases, however, we need to move that data into another location before we can use it as business intelligence. This "other location" is known as a data mart.

## Seeking the Source

We have seen that business intelligence is important for effective decision making in our organizations. This, however, leads to a big question. Just where is this business intelligence going to come from? Is business intelligence a form of corporate espionage? Do we need to send up spy satellites to watch our competitors and tap the phone lines of our clients? Should we be hiring secret agents to infiltrate our rivals' facilities? Of course not!

Does business intelligence require us to take the pulse of the people? Do we need to commission large studies of our potential customers? Do we need to conduct a survey to determine what people are thinking about our products or services? While some business intelligence may come from customer satisfaction surveys or market research, the customer's buying behavior is a better gauge of their tendencies and satisfaction. At any rate, this is not what we are going to focus on in this book.

The bulk of business intelligence for most organizations comes from something they already have: their transactional data.

## Transactional Data

Most organizations need to keep track of the things they do to conduct their business. Orders taken, products produced, services rendered, payments received from clients, and payments made to vendors are all interactions that usually result in one or more entries in some type of data store. Each of these interactions is a business transaction, so we refer to this as transactional data.

**DEFINITION**

Transactional data *is the information stored to track the interactions, or business transactions, carried out by an organization.*

The business transactions of an organization need to be tracked for that organization to operate. Payments must be collected for products and services. Payments must be made for goods and services received. Orders and service requests need to be fulfilled. In general, the organization needs to keep track of what it has done and what it needs to do. When these transactions are stored on and managed by computers, we refer to this as online transaction processing, or OLTP.

**DEFINITION**

Online transaction processing *(OLTP) systems record business interactions as they happen. They support the day-to-day operation of an organization.*

The sum of these transactions stored in OLTP systems is the history of an organization. This transactional data contains the raw numbers necessary to calculate the measures we discussed in the previous chapter. Here, then, is the data we need to create our business intelligence.

## Difficulties Using Transactional Data for Business Intelligence

OLTP systems are the treasure chests holding the raw data we need to calculate measures and create business intelligence. Problems arise, however, when we try to extract these nuggets of raw data from our OLTP systems. Let's take a look at some of the difficulties.

**The Nature of the Beast**   Well-designed OLTP systems are optimized for efficiently processing and storing transactions. This means breaking data up into small chunks using the rules of database normalization. This allows OLTP systems to process a number of transactions at the same time without one transaction getting in another's way. Information of this type is best stored in a relational database.

The measures we are using for business intelligence, on the other hand, are not designed to reflect the events of one transaction, but to reflect the net result of a number of transactions over a selected period. Business intelligence measures are often aggregates of hundreds, thousands, or even millions of individual transactions. Designing a system to provide these aggregates efficiently requires an entirely different set of optimizations.

### DEFINITION

*An* aggregate *is a number that is calculated from amounts in many detail records. An aggregate is often the sum of many numbers, although it can also be derived using other arithmetic operations or even from a count of the number of items in a group. For example, the total amount invoiced to a client in a given year is the aggregate sum of all the invoice amounts for that client in the given year.*

OLTP systems, because of the way they are designed, are usually not good at delivering large aggregates. This is not what they were intended to do. We need to look to a different type of data storage optimization to make these aggregates work efficiently.

**Interfering with Business Operations**   OLTP systems are used by our organizations to support their daily operations. In many cases, the organizations' operation depends on the performance of these systems. If the order processing system or the client management system becomes too bogged down, our organizations can grind to a halt.

We've already discussed the fact that OLTP systems are not good at delivering the aggregates needed for business intelligence. When OLTP systems are called on to produce such aggregates, they typically use a large amount of processing power and take a long time to produce a result. It is also possible that a large number of records will be locked while the aggregate is being produced, rendering those records unavailable to participate in transactional processing. Either of these two events can have a serious impact on transactional processing efficiency.

In other words, requiring an OLTP system to create business intelligence aggregates can tax the system. This can have a detrimental effect on our organizations' daily operations.

**Archiving**   Because OLTP systems are concerned with the day-to-day operations, they aren't too worried about data from the distant past. These systems may only save data for a relatively short time (and/or the data may only represent the current state, such as current quantity in stock). The data may be saved for a year, and then a year-end process may remove it from the database. It may be archived in another format, a text file, or a database backup file; or it might simply be deleted. Whether deleted or archived, the data is no longer easily accessible.

OLTP systems use this archive process to ensure that the system continues to operate efficiently. If a transaction table contains too many records, the OLTP system can become bogged down and begin to operate slowly. Archiving allows an OLTP system to stay lean and mean.

This archiving causes problems for business intelligence. When we are looking for trends in our measures, we want to compare last year's numbers to this year's numbers. We may even want to compare numbers over several years of operation. This is hard to do when the data from past years has been archived or deleted.

**Divided They Stand**   Our organizations probably use a number of different OLTP systems to manage different aspects of their operations. One system is used for order processing, a different system for accounting, another for manufacturing, and still another for personnel. As we saw in the previous chapter, Maximum Miniatures, Incorporated has five different systems that can provide data for business intelligence. Even with the move toward integrated Enterprise Resource Planning (ERP) systems, it is unlikely that all of an organization's transactional data will be in one location.

The measures used to provide business intelligence, on the other hand, do not respect these lines of separation. Instead, they treat the organization as a whole. For example, a reasonable measure to require is the profit margin for a particular product. To calculate this measure, we need the list of raw materials from the manufacturing system, the cost of those materials from the accounting system, the cost of labor required to produce the product from the time entry system, and the amount paid for the product from the order processing system. To calculate this type of measure, then, we need to combine data across systems to get what we need.

Aside from the necessity for communication between systems, this need to cross systems leads to another problem. Each of these systems maintains its own set of product numbering schemes, codes, and calendars. The same product may be known as "12593" in the manufacturing system and "SD125RDS" in the order processing system. The payroll system may work on two-week pay periods, while the accounting system works on fiscal months. When data from these disparate systems is brought together, we need to find some common ground.

# The Data Mart

A number of problems can result when we try to use our organizations' OLTP systems as the source for our business intelligence. What we need to do is take the information stored in these OLTP systems and move it into a different data store. This intermediate data store can then serve as the source for our measure calculations. We need to store the data so it is available for our business intelligence needs somewhere outside of our OLTP systems. When data is stored in this manner, it is referred to as a data mart.

### DEFINITION

*A data mart is a body of historical data in an electronic repository that does not participate in the daily operations of the organization. Instead, this data is used to create business intelligence. The data in the data mart usually applies to a specific area of the organization.*

### NOTE

*In this book, we discuss the creation of data marts rather than the perhaps more familiar term, data warehouse. Data warehouses tend to be large, one-stop-shopping repositories where all the historical data for the organization would be stored. Nothing is wrong with this as a concept; however, attempting to create a data warehouse often led to huge, multiyear technology projects that were never quite finished or were outdated when they finally did get done. In this book, we concern ourselves with creating data marts—smaller undertakings that focus on a particular aspect of an organization.*

## Features of a Data Mart

Because the data mart is meant to serve as a source for business intelligence rather than managing the organization's day-to-day transactions, it is not designed the same as an OLTP database. Instead of being built around the rules of normalization, data marts are built for speed of access. A data mart is still a relational database, but it is designed to require fewer table joins when data is output for analysis and reporting. In a data mart, it is acceptable to have data repeated (denormalized) for the sake of speed.

When designing a data mart, the rules of normalization are replaced by a different method of design organized around "facts." These new design approaches are called stars and snowflakes. We discuss stars and snowflakes in the sections "The Star Schema" and "The Snowflake Schema." Stars and snowflakes may seem like the stuff of children's fantasies, but, in reality, they provide quite grownup and down-to-earth approaches to creating information that is quick and easy to access.

## Not Real-Time Data

OLTP systems store data from business transactions as they occur throughout the day. Data marts, on the other hand, are updated at set intervals. Data is copied from the OLTP systems periodically and written to the data mart. This is known as a *data load*.

Because the data mart exists separately from the OLTP systems, accessing the data mart for business intelligence information does not put any stress on the transactional systems vital to the business's operation. The only exception to this is during the data load. During the data load, the OLTP systems may have to work hard to prepare the data for copying to the data mart. The good news here is the data load is an automated process that can be scheduled to run during off-peak hours.

As we discussed in Chapter 2, information in a data mart has some latency. In most cases, some time elapses between the moment a transaction is completed and the moment when the transaction is copied to the data mart. If a data mart load is scheduled to run each month right after the month-end processing, then the data mart has a latency of one month. If the data load runs nightly, the data mart can have a latency of up to one day.

The latency of the data mart must be set properly to fulfill the business intelligence requirements of that data mart. The information provided by the data mart must be up-to-date enough to facilitate effective decision making. However, the data loads should not occur so often that they cause unneeded stress on the OLTP systems.

## Consolidation and Cleansing

Data from a number of different OLTP systems may be combined into a single data mart. This enables us to calculate some complex measures for our business intelligence. As we discussed earlier, this may also cause problems. Multiple OLTP systems can have different ways of representing data. Inconsistent data types used for the same data, dissimilar unique identifiers used for the same entity, and different time periods and calendar systems can all cause a great deal of difficulty when trying to combine data from heterogeneous systems.

In fact, problems can even arise when using data from a single system. The business rules necessary for a meaningful measure calculation may be stricter than those enforced within the OLTP system itself. If this is the case, some of the data coming from the OLTP system may not meet the stricter rules. Inconsistencies with data types and unique identifiers could also exist within the same system if the database has been poorly designed or poorly maintained.

These problems must be resolved before the data can be stored in the data mart. We must scrub out all the problem data. To do this, the data is put through a data cleansing process.

### DEFINITION

Data cleansing *removes inconsistencies and errors from transactional data so it has the consistency necessary for use in a data mart.*

Data cleansing transforms data into a format that does not cause problems in the data mart environment. It converts inconsistent data types into a single type. Data cleansing translates dissimilar identifiers to a standard set of codes for the data mart.

In addition, it repairs or removes any data that does not meet the business rules required by the measures calculated from this data mart.

Data cleansing is usually done as part of a larger process. This process extracts the data from the OLTP systems and loads it into the data mart. Thus, the entire procedure is known as extract, transform, and load—or ETL.

### DEFINITION

*The* extract, transform, and load (ETL) *process extracts data from one or more OLTP systems, performs any required data cleansing to transform the data into a consistent format, and loads the cleansed data by inserting it into the data mart.*

## Data Mart Structure

The data we use for business intelligence can be divided into four categories: measures, dimensions, attributes, and hierarchies. These four types of data help us to define the structure of the data mart. Let's look at each of these types of data and see how they are stored in the data mart.

### Measures

The measure forms the basis of everything we do with business intelligence. In fact, without measures, there would be no business intelligence. As we learned in Chapter 1, the measures are the whole reason for pursuing business intelligence. They are the basic building blocks for effective decision making.

### DEFINITION

*A* measure *is a numeric quantity expressing some aspect of the organization's performance. The information represented by this quantity is used to support or evaluate the decision making and performance of the organization. A measure can also be called a fact.*

Measures are the facts we use for our foundational and feedback information. Therefore, the tables that hold measure information are known as *fact tables*. Don't let the name fool you, though, Sergeant Friday—fact tables hold more than just the facts.

### Dimensions

Total sales is an example of a measure that is often required for effective decision making. However, it is not often that decision makers want to see one single aggregate representing the total sales for all products for all salespersons for the entire lifetime of the organization. Instead, they are more likely to want to slice and dice this total into smaller parts. Dimensions are used to facilitate this slicing and dicing.

## DEFINITION

*A dimension is a categorization used to spread out an aggregate measure to reveal its constituent parts.*

A dimension enables us to apply a categorization to an aggregate measure. The categorization lets us see the constituent numbers that create the aggregate measure. For example, we can think of the measure of total sales as a single point of information. In geometry, a point has no dimensions.

**Total Sales**

$145,346,834

We can apply a categorization or a dimension to that single point of data to spread it out. In this case, let's spread the total sales out into the total sales for each year.

We now have a line made up of measures of total sales at various points along that line, one point for each year in the dimension. In geometry, a line is a one-dimensional object. Thus, we have added a dimension to our measure: 2008, 2009, 2010, 2011, 2012, and 2013 are each said to be *members* of the year dimension.

We can again spread out the total sales, this time for each product type.

The measures of total sales are now arranged in a square. Because a square is a two-dimensional object, we have added another dimension to our measure. Woodland Creatures, Mythic World, Warriors of Yore, and Guiding Lights are each members of the product type dimension.

Let's spread out the total sales once more—this time by sales region. The measure of total sales has become a cube, which is a three-dimensional object. You can see that each time we add a new criteria to spread out the measure, we increase the dimensionality of our measure, thus, the name dimension.

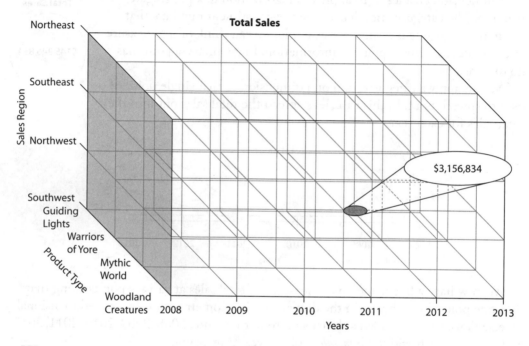

We can continue to spread out the measure using additional dimensions, such as a marketing campaign dimension and a buyer's age bracket dimension, to get a four-dimensional object, and then a five-dimensional object. Even though this becomes difficult to represent in an illustration, it is a perfectly valid thing to do. Also, because we are more familiar with three-dimensional objects than four- or five-dimensional ones, if there is such a thing, we continue to refer to these structures with four, five, or even more dimensions as cubes. We talk more about cubes in Chapter 4.

## The Star Schema

Measures and dimensions are stored in the data mart in one of two layouts, or schemas. First, we look at the star schema. The name of this schema comes from the shape formed by the relational database diagram for the data mart, as we will see in a moment. The star schema uses two types of tables: fact tables and dimension tables.

## DEFINITION

*A star schema is a relational database schema used to hold measures and dimensions in a data mart. The measures are stored in a fact table, and dimensions are stored in dimension tables.*

The center of the star is formed by the fact table. The fact table has a column for the measure and a column for each dimension containing the foreign key for a member of that dimension. The primary key for this table is created by concatenating all of the foreign key fields. This is known as a *composite key*. Fact tables are named for the set of measures they contain, with the word "Fact" added to the end. The fact table for the example in the previous section is shown in Figure 3-1.

The dimensions are stored in dimension tables. The dimension table has a column for the unique identifier of a member of the dimension, usually an integer or a short character value. The dimension table has another column for a description of the member. One dimension is stored in each dimension table, with one row for each member of the dimension. Dimension tables are named for the dimension they contain, with the letters "Dim" added to the beginning. The rows of the DimProductType dimension table would be:

| ProductTypeID | ProductTypeDescription |
|---|---|
| 1 | Woodland Creatures |
| 2 | Mythic World |
| 3 | Warriors of Yore |
| 4 | Guiding Lights |

When we add the dimension tables to the schema, we get the characteristic star design, as shown in Figure 3-2.

| SalesFact |
|---|
| YearID |
| ProductTypeID |
| SalesRegionID |
| MarketingCampaignID |
| BuyersAgeGroupID |
| Total Sales |

**Figure 3-1**    *The SalesFact table*

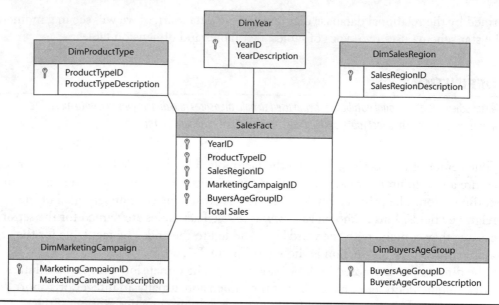

**Figure 3-2**   *The star schema*

Potentially, one row will be in the fact table for every unique combination of dimension members. The word "potentially" is used here because there may be some combinations of dimension members that do not have a value. In some cases, a particular combination of dimension members may not even make sense.

In our example, if History Magazine Spring Ad is a member of the marketing campaign dimension, some of the rows in the SalesFact table would be:

| Year | Product Type | Sales Region | Marketing Campaign | Buyer's Age | Total Sales |
|------|--------------|--------------|--------------------|-------------|-------------|
| 2011 | Mythic World | Northeast | History Mag Spring Ad | 0–25 | 56,342 |
| 2011 | Mythic World | Northeast | History Mag Spring Ad | 25–35 | 104,547 |
| 2011 | Mythic World | Northeast | History Mag Spring Ad | 35–45 | 234,385 |
| 2011 | Mythic World | Northeast | History Mag Spring Ad | 45–55 | 534,532 |
| 2011 | Mythic World | Northeast | History Mag Spring Ad | 55–65 | 829,282 |
| 2011 | Mythic World | Northeast | History Mag Spring Ad | 65+ | 284,540 |

If, in our example, we assume there are eight members of the marketing campaign dimension to go along with six members of the year dimension, four members of the product type dimension, four members of the sales region dimension, and six members of the buyer's age dimension, we have a potential for

$8 \times 6 \times 4 \times 4 \times 6$

or 4608 rows in the SalesFact table. This is not a huge number, but you can see when you have dimensions with tens or hundreds of members, the size of the fact table can grow rather large.

In reality, the fact table should contain the identifiers for the dimension members, rather than their descriptions. This cuts down on the size required to store each fact row. This becomes important in fact tables with a potential for millions or even hundreds of millions of rows.

In addition, a single fact table may contain multiple measures. This can occur when two or more measures use exactly the same dimensions. Putting a number of measures with the same dimensions in the same fact table is also a way to save on storage space required for the data mart.

## Attributes

In some cases, we may want to store additional information about dimension members in our data mart. This helps us further define the members of the dimension. These bits of additional information are known as attributes of the dimension.

### DEFINITION

*An* attribute *is an additional piece of information pertaining to a dimension member that is not the unique identifier or the description of the member.*

Attributes can be used to more fully describe dimension members. They may contain information about a dimension member that the users are likely to want as part of their business intelligence output. Attributes are also used to store information that may be used to limit or filter the records selected from the data mart during data analysis. They are stored as additional columns in the dimension tables, as shown in Figure 3-3.

## Hierarchies

In many cases, a dimension may contain one or more multilevel structures. These structures are known as hierarchies. In our sample, the year, product type, and sales region dimensions each contain hierarchies.

### DEFINITION

*A* hierarchy *is a structure made up of two or more levels within a dimension.*

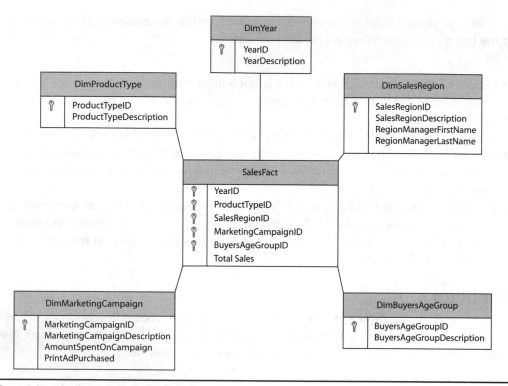

**Figure 3-3** *Attribute columns in the dimension tables*

Hierarchies enable the users to navigate to different levels of granularity within the measures of the data mart. Users can look at the measures at one level of the hierarchy, and then drill into a selected member to see the next lower level. For example, a user can look at the product subtypes within the Mythic World product type. He or she can look at the sales territories within the Northeast sales region. A user can also look at the months within Q1, 2011. In fact, all of these can be combined at once so the user can view the sales totals by the product subtypes of the Mythic World product type, by sales territories of the Northeast sales region, and by months in Q1, 2011. By moving up and down the hierarchy, users can find exactly the right measure to aid in making the decision at hand.

In a star schema, the information about the hierarchies is stored right in the dimension tables, as shown in Figure 3-4. The primary key in each of the dimension tables is at the lowest level of the hierarchy. Because of this, the fact table must be changed so its foreign keys point to the lowest levels in the hierarchies as well. This means, then, the fact table will have one row (and one set of measures) for each unique combination of members at the lowest level of all the hierarchies.

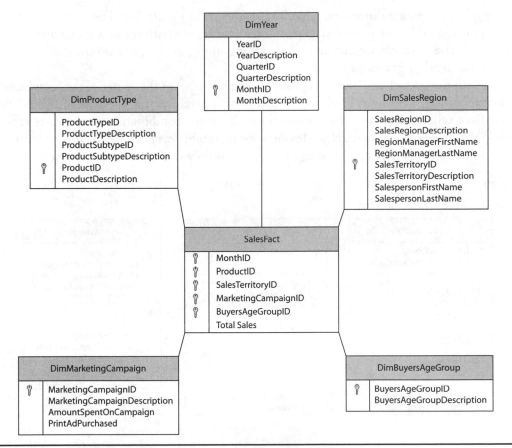

**Figure 3-4**   *A star schema with hierarchies*

Measures for hierarchy levels above the lowest level are not stored in the data mart. Instead, these measures have to be calculated by taking an aggregate of the measures stored at the lowest level. For example, if the user wants to see the total sales for the Northeast sales region, that measure has to be calculated by aggregating the total sales for all of the territories within the Northeast sales region. In this case, the aggregation is the sum of the total sales of the territories.

## The Snowflake Schema

An alternative to the star schema is the snowflake schema. The *snowflake schema* represents hierarchies in a manner that is more familiar to those of us who have been working with relational databases. In a snowflake schema, each level of a hierarchy is stored in a separate dimension table. This is shown in Figure 3-5. These chains of dimension tables are supposed to resemble the intricate patterns of a snowflake. Although the resemblance may not be too strong in Figure 3-5, this is how the snowflake schema got its name.

As with the star schema, the foreign keys in the fact table at the center of the snowflake schema point to the lowest level of each hierarchy. Therefore, the fact table in the snowflake schema also contains one row for each unique combination of members at the lowest level of each hierarchy. Measures for hierarchy levels above the lowest level have to be calculated by taking an aggregate, just as they were with the star schema.

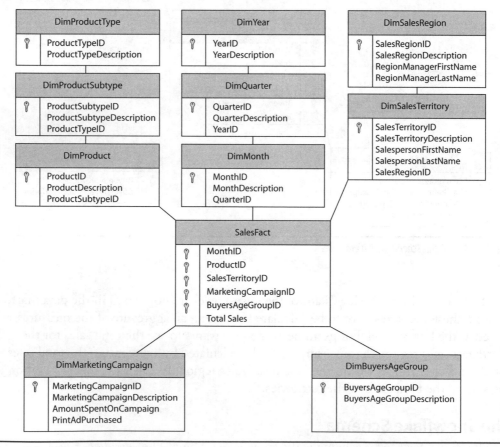

**Figure 3-5** *The snowflake schema*

## Snowflakes, Stars, and Analysis Services

The snowflake schema has all the advantages of good relational design. It does not result in duplicate data and is, therefore, easier to maintain. It also looks more proper to those of us who have been working with relational databases.

The disadvantage of the snowflake design is that it requires a number of table joins when aggregating measures at the upper levels of the hierarchy. In larger data marts or in data marts that experience heavy utilization, this can lead to performance problems.

In both the snowflake and the star schemas, we have to calculate aggregates on the fly when the user wants to see data at any level above the lowest level in each dimension. In a schema with a number of dimensions or with dimensions that have a large number of members, this can take a significant amount of time. The whole idea of business intelligence is to make information readily available to our decision makers.

We could calculate all the measures at every level of our hierarchy and store them in the data mart. However, this would make the data mart much too complex and, therefore, much harder to maintain. How do we get good performance from our data mart at every level of the hierarchy without driving the data mart administrator crazy? The answer is Microsoft SQL Server 2012 Analysis Services, as we see in Chapter 4.

# Chapter 4

# Two, Two, Two Models in One—The BI Semantic Model

## In This Chapter

- ▶ Online Analytical Processing
- ▶ Building OLAP Out of Cubes—The Multidimensional Model

- ▶ Building OLAP Out of Tables—The Tabular Model
- ▶ Choosing an Implementation Method
- ▶ Tools of the Trade

*Snowflakes are one of nature's most fragile things, but just look at what they can do when they stick together.*

–Vesta M. Kelly

In Chapters 1 and 2, we learned how business intelligence can be used to support effective decision making. In Chapter 3, we began the search for the data that serves as the source for this business intelligence. In most cases, the data we need can be found in our online transaction processing (OLTP) systems.

On close examination, we discovered that an OLTP system is not a good candidate for the direct source of business intelligence. OLTP systems are designed for processing business transactions and storing the detail from each of these transactions. They are not optimized for delivering the aggregated information typically required for business intelligence.

The shortcomings of OLTP systems as a source for business intelligence led us to the data mart. The *data mart* is a relational database structure specifically designed for storing large amounts of historical data. Data must be copied from the OLTP systems into the data mart.

At the end of Chapter 3, we were left with a concern about the data mart. Namely, how do we improve performance when the user wants to view aggregate information derived from a large number of detail records? For the answer to this, we look to online analytical processing.

# Online Analytical Processing

In 1993, E. F. Codd, one of the fathers of relational database and OLTP theory, proposed a different type of system that would be tuned to the needs of data analysts. He called this an online analytical processing, or OLAP, system. The criteria Codd originally laid out for an OLAP system were not widely accepted. However, the OLAP name continues to be used for systems designed to quickly provide users with business intelligence.

**DEFINITION**

Online analytical processing *(OLAP) systems enable users to quickly and easily retrieve information from data, usually in a data mart, for analysis. OLAP systems present data using measures, dimensions, hierarchies, and cubes.*

As the first word—online—in the name implies, OLAP is designed to let the user interact with the data during analysis. It is geared toward having the user online with the data, slicing and dicing the data to view it in different ways, drilling down into the data to see more detail. This is a different approach from the static reports produced by most OLTP systems.

## The BI Semantic Model

The Microsoft SQL Server platform provides a tool for facilitating OLAP systems. That tool is SQL Server Analysis Services (SSAS). SSAS hosts one or more data repositories that are optimized for online analytical processing.

To facilitate interactive data exploration, SSAS creates a model of the underlying data. This model presents the data to the user in a manner that more closely matches the way business decision makers think about their business. It provides the business users a more natural way to view the data. This model is referred to as the BI Semantic Model (BISM).

The BI Semantic Model, as implemented in SQL Server Analysis Services 2012, provides two alternative ways of working with the data. The data can be stored and presented to the user in the form of measures, dimensions, attributes, and hierarchies, as we discussed in Chapter 3. This is implemented using the Multidimensional model within SSAS. Data can also be presented in the more traditional form of tables, fields, and relationships. This second format is implemented through the Tabular model within SSAS.

This book looks at both of the technologies available within the BI Semantic Model. Exercises are provided for creating implementations using both the Multidimensional and Tabular models.

# Building OLAP Out of Cubes— The Multidimensional Model

An OLAP system is designed to provide its users with quick and easy access to business data. That data is usually stored in a data mart. The OLAP system simply provides a mechanism for viewing and analyzing the data mart information quickly. When using the Multidimensional model, the business data takes the form of measures, dimensions, hierarchies, and cubes.

In fact, the Multidimensional model focus is on cubes. We briefly discussed cubes in Chapter 3. Before we get into the specifics of the Multidimensional model, let's take a more detailed look at cubes. We again create a cube using the total sales measure. This time, we use month, product, and salesperson as our dimensions. The resulting cube is shown in Figure 4-1.

### DEFINITION

*A cube is a structure that contains a value for one or more measures for each unique combination of the members of all its dimensions. These are detail, or leaf-level, values. The cube also contains aggregated values formed by the dimension hierarchies or when one or more of the dimensions is left out of the hierarchy.*

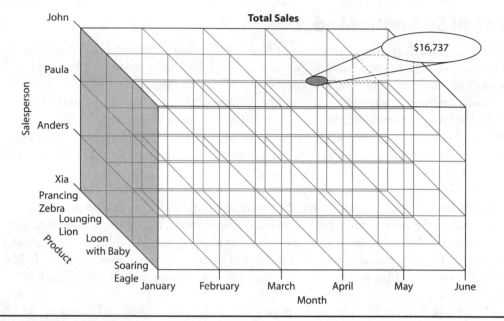

**Figure 4-1** *Total Sales cube*

Within the cube is a measure value for each intersection of members of the three dimensions. Figure 4-1 illustrates the total sales for the Loon with Baby figurine by John in April. Loon with Baby is a member of the product dimension. John is a member of the salesperson dimension. April is a member of the month dimension. The total sales at this intersection are $16,737.

A measure value that exists at an intersection of all of the dimensions is called a *detail*, or *leaf-level, value*. In Figure 4-1, total sales for the Loon with Baby figurine by John in April is an example of a leaf-level value. This is a leaf-level value because members (John, April, and Loon with Baby) are specified for each dimension (salesperson, month, and product).

To determine the total sales by John in April, we need to add together John's total sales of each individual product in April. In other words, John's total sales for April are equal to John's total sales of Soaring Eagle in April, plus his total sales of Loon with Baby in April, plus his total sales of Lounging Lion in April, plus his total sales of Prancing Zebra in April. In OLAP terminology, we aggregate all the leaf-level values from the product dimension using the sum aggregation. This is shown in Figure 4-2.

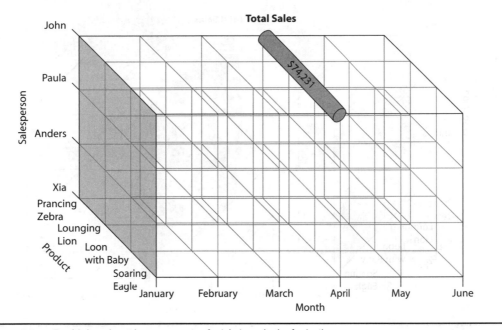

**Figure 4-2**    *Total Sales cube with an aggregation for John's total sales for April*

**DEFINITION**

*An* aggregate *is a value formed by combining values from a given dimension or set of dimensions to create a single value. This is often done by adding the values together using the sum aggregate, but other aggregation calculations can also be used.*

To determine the total sales for April for all salespersons, we need to do another aggregation. This time, we need to aggregate all the total sales for all the salespersons across all the products they sold in April (see Figure 4-3).

We also use aggregate values within the cube when we traverse the hierarchy of one or more dimensions. Recall that salespersons can be grouped, or rolled up, into sales regions; products can be rolled up into product subtypes and product types; and months can be rolled up into quarters and years. Each time one level of a hierarchy is rolled up into a higher level, aggregations are used to combine values from the lower level into the groupings at the upper level. For example, the total sales for the Loon with Baby figurine by John in Quarter 1 would be the total sales for the Loon with Baby figurine by John in January, plus the total sales for the Loon with Baby figurine by John in February, plus the total sales for the Loon with Baby figurine by John in March.

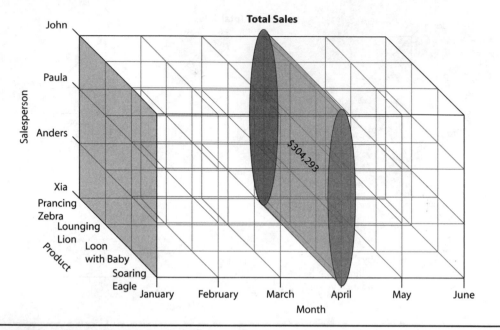

**Figure 4-3**   *Total Sales cube with an aggregation for total sales for all salespersons for April*

You can see that cubes with a number of dimensions and a number of hierarchies require quite a few aggregate calculations as the user navigates through the cube. This can slow down analysis to a large extent. To combat this, some or all of the possible data aggregates in the cubes are calculated ahead of time and stored within the cube itself. These stored values are known as *preprocessed aggregates*.

# Features of a Multidimensional Model Implementation

A Multidimensional model implementation offers many advantages for us as we seek to produce business intelligence. It provides an architecture that is focused on the presentation of information for analysis. This focus makes the Multidimensional model implementation a natural environment for users looking to use information for effective decision making.

## Multidimensional Database

The Multidimensional model implementation is built around data that is structured as measures, dimensions, hierarchies, and cubes. This multidimensional approach makes it easy for users to slice and dice information as needed. Users can use dimensions to view the data in different ways. They can use hierarchies to drill into the data and find more detail when needed.

**DEFINITION**

*A multidimensional database is structured around measures, dimensions, hierarchies, and cubes rather than tables, rows, columns, and relations.*

A multidimensional database is a natural way to store information used for business intelligence, where measures are analyzed by dimensions. Aside from this innate fit, the multidimensional database offers another big advantage. It provides the structure for storing preprocessed aggregates.

## Preprocessed Aggregates

In a data mart, when a decision maker wants to see the value of a measure for a certain set of dimension members, that value must be calculated on the fly. The decision maker must wait while the aggregate value is calculated from all the detail information that rolls up into that aggregate. This can cause a significant delay that distracts from productive research and leads to frustration.

If the goal of an OLAP system is to get the decision maker to interact with the data, then aggregates must be returned quickly. For this reason, Multidimensional model systems preprocess a portion of the aggregates that are found throughout the cube. This preprocessing is done as part of the background task that loads or updates the data in the multidimensional database. Because this is done as part of a background task, the time taken to do the preprocessing does not impact any users. As the aggregates are preprocessed, they are stored within the cube in the multidimensional database.

Now, when a decision maker wants to see the value of a measure for a certain set of dimensional members, that value can be read from the database rather than being calculated on the fly. This greatly improves the responsiveness of the system, which, in turn, encourages online interaction and provides the decision maker with a higher probability of finding the correct piece or pieces of information necessary to make an effective decision.

## Easily Understood

In OLTP systems, the data is normalized and dependencies are represented by complex foreign key relationships; the goal is to reduce redundant data. Any decision maker querying this data must reconstruct the dependencies with the appropriate INNER JOINs and OUTER JOINs. Business rules that define the way a measure is to be calculated are kept in programmatic structures that are used for transaction processing, not reporting. When including a measure, the decision maker must re-create these calculations each time they are used in a report.

Fields and tables in an OLTP system are given names that make sense to the developer, but not necessarily the end user. The database system may impose a limit on the length of a name, or the database administrator may not like typing long names in his or her maintenance scripts. In either case, the result is cryptic abbreviations in field and table names. The decision maker must decipher the code to be sure the correct data is being queried from the tables.

In a Multidimensional model implementation, just the opposite is true. The structure of the data is represented by dimensions and hierarchies. If the Multidimensional model implementation is designed properly, these dimensions and hierarchies should match the structure of the organization. Thus, the data structure is familiar to the decision maker using the system.

The business rules that pertain to each measure in the Multidimensional model implementation are contained within the calculation defined for that measure. The user does not need to re-create this calculation each time that particular measure is used. For example, suppose your organization defines net profit as:

```
Selling Price - (Cost of Materials + Cost of Labor + Sales Commissions)
```

In a relational environment, net profit might be incorrectly reported as

```
Selling Price - (Cost of Materials + Cost of Labor)
```

in one place and as

```
Selling Price - (Cost of Materials + Sales Commissions)
```

in another. This inconsistency can lead to confusion and, worse yet, poor decisions. In the Multidimensional model implementation, the measure for net profit is defined in one place, so it is always calculated properly whether the decision maker is looking at net profit by product, net profit by month, or net profit by sales region.

Finally, because the Multidimensional model implementation exists solely for producing business intelligence, all of the measures, dimensions, and hierarchies are given names that can be easily understood by the decision maker. The Multidimensional model implementation allows additional metadata, such as a long description, to be stored along with the name of the object. This provides the decision maker with enough information to ensure they know exactly what business information they are looking at.

## Architecture of a Multidimensional Model Implementation

The key part of the Multidimensional model implementation is the cube and the preprocessed aggregates it contains. The Multidimensional model uses one of three

**OLAP Architectures**

Figure 4-4    *OLAP architectures*

different architectures for storing cube data. Each architecture has certain advantages and disadvantages. The basics of each are shown in Figure 4-4.

## Relational OLAP

Relational OLAP (ROLAP) stores the cube structure in a multidimensional database. The leaf-level measures are left in the relational data mart that serves as the source of the cube. The preprocessed aggregates are also stored in a relational database table.

When a decision maker requests the value of a measure for a certain set of dimension members, the ROLAP system first checks to determine whether the dimension members specify an aggregate or a leaf-level value. If an aggregate is specified, the value is selected from the relational table. If a leaf-level value is specified, the value is selected from the data mart.

A ROLAP architecture, because of its reliance on relational tables, can store larger amounts of data than other Multidimensional model architectures. Also, because the ROLAP architecture retrieves leaf-level values directly from the data mart, the leaf-level values returned by the ROLAP system are always as up-to-date as the data mart itself. In other words, the ROLAP system does not add latency to leaf-level data. The disadvantage of a ROLAP system is that the retrieval of the aggregate and leaf-level values is slower than the other Multidimensional model architectures.

### Multidimensional OLAP

Multidimensional OLAP (MOLAP) also stores the cube structure in a multidimensional database. However, *both* the preprocessed aggregate values and a copy of the leaf-level values are placed in the multidimensional database as well. Because of this, all data requests are answered from the multidimensional database, making MOLAP systems extremely responsive.

Additional time is required when loading a MOLAP system because all the leaf-level data is copied into the multidimensional database. Because of this, times occur when the leaf-level data returned by the MOLAP system is not in sync with the leaf-level data in the data mart itself. A MOLAP system, therefore, does add latency to the leaf-level data. The MOLAP architecture also requires more disk space to store the copy of the leaf-level values in the multidimensional database. However, because MOLAP is extremely efficient at storing values, the additional space required is usually not significant.

### Hybrid OLAP

Hybrid OLAP (HOLAP) combines ROLAP and MOLAP storage. This is why we end up with the word "hybrid" in the name. HOLAP tries to take advantage of the strengths of each of the other two architectures while minimizing their weaknesses.

HOLAP stores the cube structure and the preprocessed aggregates in a multidimensional database. This provides the fast retrieval of aggregates present in MOLAP structures. HOLAP leaves the leaf-level data in the relational data mart that serves as the source of the cube.

This leads to longer retrieval times when accessing the leaf-level values. However, HOLAP does not need to take time to copy the leaf-level data from the data mart. As soon as the data is updated in the data mart, it is available to the decision maker. Therefore, HOLAP does not add latency to the leaf-level data. In essence, HOLAP sacrifices retrieval speed on leaf-level data to prevent adding latency to leaf-level data and to speed the data load.

## The Parts of a Multidimensional Model Implementation

A Multidimensional model implementation is made up of a number of parts. We look at creating each of these parts in subsequent chapters. For now, we take a quick look at each part and how they fit together.

### Data Sources

A Multidimensional model begins with one or more data sources. A data source stores the information necessary to connect to a database that provides data to the Multidimensional model. The data source includes the server name, database name, and the database logon credentials, among other things. A number of data providers are available for accessing different databases, including Oracle and Microsoft Directory Services.

The database being pointed to by the data source could be a data mart. It could point directly to a table in an OLTP system. When a data source points directly at an OLTP system, the data source view is used to transform the data into more of a star or snowflake structure.

## Data Source Views

Data source views are used to determine which tables and fields in a particular data source are utilized within the Multidimensional model. The data source view can combine tables and fields from a number of different data sources. For instance, tables from the order processing system can be combined with tables from the sales management system so a measure of actual sales versus sales quota can be created.

Once the tables and fields have been added to the data source view, the data source view can then be used to filter out unnecessary items in the database. Only those tables and fields being used to create business intelligence are included in the view. The underlying table structures in the data sources are not changed. The data source view merely controls what is available as building blocks for the next step in the definition process.

This is especially helpful when a data source is a large, highly normalized OLTP system. The data view makes available only those tables that contain the data for the measures, dimensions, and hierarchies we need to define. The same is true within a table. Only those fields that contain required data are visible. All the extraneous tables and fields are filtered out by the data source view.

To make the data view even easier to understand, user-friendly names and descriptions can be assigned to tables and fields. This metadata is used throughout the Multidimensional model. Any measures, dimensions, and hierarchies created from these fields will utilize the user-friendly names.

In addition, we can use the data source view to make virtual additions to the table and field structures. These additions are not made in the database itself, but in the virtual view that exists only in the Multidimensional model. Therefore, we can make these virtual additions without any fear of breaking the OLTP systems that use the relational tables.

One example of these virtual additions is the creation of a relationship between two tables that is not defined in the database itself. Another example is the addition of a calculated field in a database table. For instance, a calculation involving a number of different fields from different tables can be created for use as a measure. Or, a number of strings can be concatenated together for use as a dimension attribute. These calculated fields are given names and descriptions, so they appear just like any other field included in the Multidimensional model.

Once the data source view is completed, its content is used to create measures, dimensions, hierarchies, and cubes.

## Proactive Caching

To obtain maximum performance, a Multidimensional model uses preprocessed aggregates. To facilitate high availability, these preprocessed aggregates are stored in the *proactive cache*.

This structure is referred to as cache because it is created when needed and is changed when the underlying data or the underlying structure changes. It works much the same way as Internet Information Services (IIS) caches web pages, as shown in Figure 4-5. The results of a processed web page are stored in the IIS page cache, so subsequent accesses to that page are faster, as shown in Figure 4-6. When changes are made to the underlying page, that page is deleted and eventually re-created in the page cache, as in Figure 4-7.

The major difference between Multidimensional model caching and other caching mechanisms, such as the IIS example, is summed up in the word "proactive." With IIS, a page is put into cache only after it has been accessed the first time. The first user to request a particular page must wait until the page is read from the disk and processed before the user receives the contents of the page, as you see in Figure 4-5.

The Multidimensional model, on the other hand, can use proactive caching. Items are created in the cache before they have been requested by a user. With the Multidimensional model, the preprocessed aggregates are created automatically, as shown in Figure 4-8. Even the first users receive their requested aggregates from the proactive cache, as in Figure 4-9.

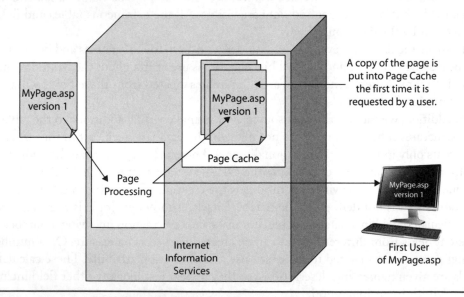

**Figure 4-5**   *Creating a cached web page in Internet Information Services*

**Figure 4-6**    *Retrieving a web page from the Internet Information Services page cache*

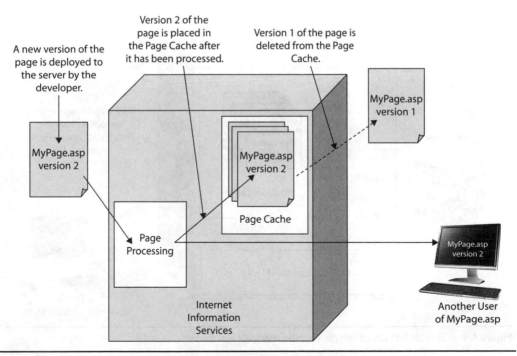

**Figure 4-7**    *Updating the Internet Information Services page cache when a web page is modified*

Aggregates are
preprocessed
automatically and stored
in Proactive Cache.

**Figure 4-8**  *Proactive caching with a Multidimensional model*

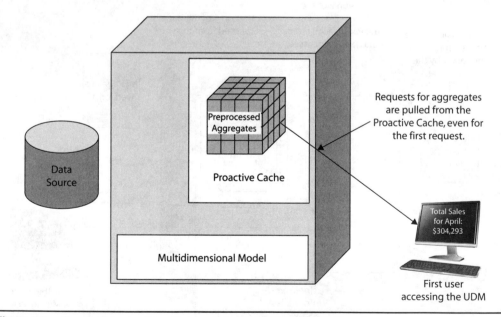

**Figure 4-9**  *Even the first user receives the requested aggregate from the proactive cache.*

The Multidimensional model monitors the data in the data source. As this data is modified, the Multidimensional model checks the options selected for the associated proactive cache. We look at just what these caching options are in Chapter 10. At the appropriate time, as defined by the caching options, the Multidimensional model deletes the current cache and rebuilds it with up-to-date values, as shown in Figure 4-10.

The proactive cache can be built using MOLAP, ROLAP, or HOLAP. The Multidimensional model provides an easy mechanism to assist you in making a decision among these three architectures. It points out the tradeoffs these three architectures make between latency and responsiveness. This enables you to determine which architecture to use based on the business needs without getting lost in the technical details.

## XML Definitions

The definitions of all the objects in the Multidimensional model are stored as XML text files. Each of the data source, data source view, dimension, and cube definitions is stored in its own text file. These XML text files do not contain any of the data for the object—the dimension text file does not contain any of the members of the dimension; the cube text file does not contain any of the preprocessed aggregates. The XML text files simply contain the definitions—the dimension text file tells which table and field

**Figure 4-10**    *The proactive cache is deleted and re-created in response to changes in the data source.*

hold the members of the dimension; the cube text file contains the information on how the preprocessed aggregates will be managed.

Because the definition for each of the objects in the Multidimensional model is stored in its own XML text file, the objects in the Multidimensional model can be managed by a source code utility. The source code utility can track these objects as you develop your Multidimensional model. It can also provide version control in case you need to undo a change to an object's definition and roll it back to an earlier version.

# Building OLAP Out of Tables—The Tabular Model

The Multidimensional model implementation has been highly optimized to efficiently deal with aggregation and exploration of large amounts of data. Its maturity offers a number of compelling features. We will examine those features throughout the Multidimensional model sections of this book.

Advances in computing, including advances in processing power and the wide availability of low-cost memory, have made possible another approach for analyzing a sizeable amount of data in a reasonable manner. This is the Tabular model.

## Features of a Tabular Model

The Tabular model is less complex than the Multidimensional model implementation. Currently, it does not have the breadth of features of a Multidimensional model implementation and cannot work with as large a set of data as a Multidimensional model implementation. That said, a Tabular model provides surprising capabilities with a fraction of the complexity of a Multidimensional model implementation.

### Tabular Structure

The Tabular model does not use the measure, dimension, attribute, and hierarchy structure that we discussed in Chapter 3. Instead, it approaches the data as related tables with fields, just as is done in a relational database. With more and more business decision makers using the data table feature of Excel or having done some basic reporting from a relational database, this tabular approach is more familiar.

### Quick to Implement

Because we do not need to transform the data into measures and dimensions, it may be possible to pull data directly from OLTP systems into a Tabular model. This is one of the ways a Tabular model may enable us to streamline the process of creating a BI system. Of course, considerations such as stress put on the OLTP system by data analysis and the need for data cleansing may still make it desirable to create a data mart as the source for our business intelligence.

As we see when we begin building our Tabular model example, the Tabular model creation process is more interactive and immediate than the creation of a Multidimensional model implementation. Data is available to be viewed in the Tabular model immediately after it is added. This makes it easier to get started and easier to get things right as the implementation progresses.

# Architecture of a Tabular Model

When we looked at Multidimensional models, we saw there were three different architectures that could be utilized: MOLAP, ROLAP, and HOLAP. In the Tabular world, there are two different architectures or modes of operation from which to choose. They are cached mode and direct query mode.

## Cached Mode

When Tabular models were first demonstrated, their capabilities almost seemed like magic—even to us jaded BI professionals. The Tabular model (and the Vertipaq engine that powers it) is not magic, of course. What makes it possible is the in-memory processing of cached mode operation.

When operating in *cached mode*, a Tabular model loads all data into memory. Therefore, having large amounts of memory available and having the 64-bit Windows operating system available to address all that memory make it possible for a Tabular model to do some great things. However, the size of addressable memory does not necessarily define the limit on the amount of data that can be processed.

The Tabular model, operating in cached mode, also applies some extremely effective data compression techniques to the data as it is stored in memory. So, even more data can be crammed into the memory space available. With the data compression techniques in place, the Tabular model squeezes every bit of capability out of the memory provided.

The whole reason for working hard to put massive amounts of data into memory is speed. The processor can read through and analyze data in memory in a fraction of the time necessary to access data stored on a hard drive. Given this inherent speed advantage, the Tabular model can complete the analytical processing by sheer brute force. It doesn't need preaggregates and highly efficient data retrieval methods. It can simply read through the data in memory, looking to match criteria and produce aggregates.

This, then, is the magic.

## Direct Query Mode

A Tabular model has a second mode of operation called direct query mode. When operating in *direct query mode*, the Tabular model does not load any data into memory. Instead, a Tabular model in direct query mode always queries the underlying data sources to get its results. This means, when running in direct query mode, we need to be mindful of the load any queries made through the model are putting on those data sources.

If in-memory processing provides all of the seeming magic for a Tabular model, why then would you ever run in direct query mode? Obviously, performance is going to suffer. Why not query the data directly without the model?

The answer to those questions is twofold. First, when operating in direct query mode, there is no latency to the data. As soon as data is changed in the underlying data source, that change is reflected in queries done through the model. This, then, has the same advantage as querying the data source directly.

Second, the model provides a metadata layer over the top of the underlying data source. This metadata layer, when done properly, exposes the data in a manner closer to the perception of the business user. A business user can query this data through the model without having to write complex SELECT statements. So, a direct query Tabular model still has the advantage of making data accessible to a business user.

## Choosing an Implementation Method

With the Tabular model showing big advantages in simplicity and speed of implementation, why would you want to choose to do a Multidimensional model implementation (and why would I devote so many chapters of this book to telling you about it)? There may be a day when a Tabular model is the right answer for any and all BI needs. That day, however, has not yet arrived.

The Multidimensional model is a mature architecture. Its capabilities have been added to and refined over many years. Quite frankly, there are things that can be done in a Multidimensional model implementation that cannot yet be done in a Tabular model. Those differences are highlighted throughout the remainder of this book.

It is also the case that even with the data compression available within a Tabular model, there are still limits to what can be effectively processed in memory. What that limit is will vary depending on the memory available on the SSAS server and on the content of your data and how well it lends itself to compression.

For these reasons, it is still important to learn how to create both Multidimensional and Tabular models.

## Tools of the Trade

In Chapter 5, we look at the business intelligence tools available in SQL Server 2012. We use two major development and management environments throughout this book. We are introduced to both, SQL Server Data Tools and the SQL Server Management Studio, in the next chapter.

# Chapter 5

# First Steps—Beginning the Development of Business Intelligence

## In This Chapter

▶ **SQL Server Data Tools**
▶ **The SQL Server Management Studio**
▶ **Don Your Hardhat**

*There is a great satisfaction in building good tools for other people to use.*

—Freeman Dyson

Now that we have discussed the basics of business intelligence and the BI Semantic Model, it is time to become acquainted with the tools that we are going to be using. Microsoft has created a special tool for creating and managing business intelligence. This is SQL Server Data Tools.

We begin this chapter with a tour of this tool. SQL Server Data Tools looks familiar to those of you who have used Microsoft Visual Studio as part of front-end or middleware development projects. In fact, SQL Server Data Tools (SSDT) is Visual Studio with some special functionality.

With home improvement, having the right tool for the job makes things faster and easier. The same is true with BI development. Let's see how SQL Server Data Tools can make our job faster and easier.

# SQL Server Data Tools

SQL Server Data Tools is our primary work environment for almost this entire book. All the work we do creating and querying BI Semantic Models, all the work we do building and training data mining models, and all the work we do developing reports will be done in SQL Server Data Tools. Because of this, it is important to become comfortable with the interface and capabilities of this product.

## Visual Studio

SQL Server Data Tools is, in fact, Visual Studio, the same integrated development environment (IDE) used by Visual Basic and C# developers. Visual Studio is also used to author reports for use with SQL Server Reporting Services. Visual Studio provides the business intelligence developer with a robust environment that has been tested and proven by millions of developer hours of use.

## Project Organization

Visual Studio organizes each development effort into projects. Each project produces its own type of output: a Windows application, a web service, or a set of Reporting Services reports. SQL Server provides additional project types: an Integration Services project and an Analysis Services project.

Projects are grouped together in solutions. Each solution represents an answer to a particular business problem. A solution could be an e-commerce website with a Visual Basic web application project to produce the ASP.NET user interface pages and an

Analysis Services project to define the data mining model used to do cross-selling. Another solution might contain a complete business intelligence application, with a C# Windows application project to produce the front-end application, an Analysis Services project to create the BI Semantic Model, and a Reporting Services project that produces reports for presenting the analysis to the user. This grouping of projects into solutions makes it easier to manage software systems built from several different parts.

## Editing and Debugging Tools

Visual Studio also provides a rich set of editing and debugging tools. Some of you may say that color-coded editors and single-step debugging are only for wimps. After all, many of us grew up writing stored procedures in a text editor and debugging them with embedded PRINT statements, and we did just fine. Believe me, once you have these tools available, you will never want to go back!

## Source Code Management Integration

Another benefit of using the Visual Studio environment for BI projects is its ability to integrate with source control. *Source control* copies the source code for your item definitions and report layouts to a central database. Source control then manages access to those definitions and layouts to provide version control and prevent two developers from trying to change the same item at the same time.

Each version of these items is saved. This makes it possible for us to roll back changes if we discover we have gone down the wrong path. It also makes it possible to determine what changed between two versions of an item. This can be helpful when troubleshooting or when copying changes from one server to another.

Source code also enables multiple developers or administrators to work on the same project at the same time without the danger of one person overwriting another's changes. You must check out an item from source control before you can edit it. Only one person can have a given item checked out at a given time. Once changes are made, the item is checked back in for the next person to use.

Visual Studio makes this check-out and check-in process straightforward. In fact, it is simply part of the editing process itself. No additional applications to open. No extra steps writing things out to temporary files.

## Navigating  SQL Server Data Tools

SQL Server Data Tools is found on the Start menu under Microsoft SQL Server 2012, as shown in Figure 5-1. After the splash screen, you see the empty SQL Server Data Tools. No solution has been opened.

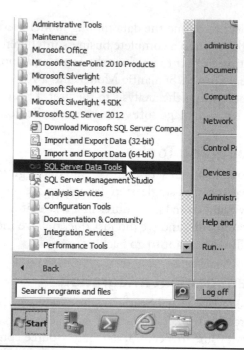

**Figure 5-1**   *SQL Server Data Tools on the Start menu*

In this section, we create a solution and an Analysis Services project within that solution. Then, we explore the menus, toolbar, and windows within SQL Server Data Tools. In the next section, we look at some of the ways to customize this development environment.

## Creating a Solution and an Analysis Services Project

The empty SQL Server Data Tools is not too exciting. Therefore, we begin by creating a solution and an Analysis Services project within that solution. We can then explore all of the windows, menu choices, and toolbar buttons available to us when working in this type of project.

In SQL Server Data Tools, we do not choose to create a solution. Instead, we create a new project. At the same time that project is created, we can create the solution that will contain it.

We can create a new project in SQL Server Data Tools in four ways:

▶   Select File | New | Project from the menu.

▶   Press CTRL-SHIFT-N.

▶   Click the New Project button on the toolbar, as shown in Figure 5-2.

▶   Click the New Project link on the Start Page tab.

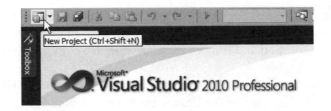

**Figure 5-2**    *The New Project Toolbar button*

No matter how you get there, once you request a new project, you see the New Project dialog box, shown in Figure 5-3. The left side of the dialog box contains a list of the Visual Studio project types installed on your development machine. In this book, we are interested in Business Intelligence Projects. Click this project type to select it, if it is not already highlighted.

The right side of the dialog box displays the various BI projects available to us. These can be displayed as large icons or as small icons, as shown in Figure 5-3. You can toggle between the two sizes using the buttons in the upper-right corner of the dialog box.

**Figure 5-3**    *The New Project dialog box*

The lower portion of the dialog box displays the path and filename for the project we are about to create. Name refers to the name of the new project. Location is the file path where the new solution and project are to be stored. Solution Name is the name of the new solution.

By default, solutions and projects are stored in the Visual Studio 2010 Projects folder under My Documents. You can use the Browse button to navigate to a different folder, if desired. When the Create directory for solution check box is not checked, only one folder is created. Both the new solution files and the new project files are placed in this folder.

When the Create directory for solution check box is checked, two folders are created. One folder is created to hold the solution files, and a second folder is created within this solution folder to contain the project files. By default, the solution folder and the project folder have the same name. You can override this default behavior by entering a unique name for both the Name and the Solution Name. If the solution is going to contain more than one project, it is usually a good idea to keep the solution files and the project files in separate folders.

If source control integration is set up and configured within Visual Studio, we also have the option of placing the project under source control. An Add to source control check box will appear under the Create directory for solution check box. If you are going to use source control for your BI projects, it is a good idea to use this check box to place them under source control right from the start.

To create our empty Analysis Services project, select Business Intelligence | Analysis Services in the Installed Templates area, and select Analysis Services Multidimensional and Data Mining Project in the center area of the dialog box. Click OK.

## SQL Server Data Tools Windows

Now that we have a solution and a project open, SQL Server Data Tools appears as shown in Figure 5-4. We now have some content in the two windows that are open on the right side of the main window. We begin by looking at these two windows, and then at several other windows that are not visible by default.

**Solution Explorer Window**   The Solution Explorer window is visible in the upper-right portion of Figure 5-4. Just as Windows Explorer provides a hierarchical view of the Windows file system, the *Solution Explorer* window in SQL Server Data Tools provides a hierarchical view of your solution and the projects it contains. Both Windows Explorer and the Solution Explorer window use a tree view to let us navigate the hierarchical structure. We can browse through our solution to find and open any item it contains.

Each project node displays the name of the project. Within the project nodes are folders for each type of item the project can create. The number of folders and

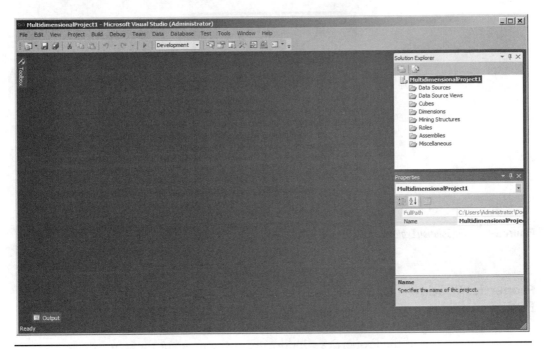

**Figure 5-4**  *SQL Server Data Tools with an empty Analysis Services project*

their labels vary, depending on the project type. In Figure 5-4, you can see that a Multidimensional project contains eight folders, one for each of the eight different types of items it can create.

In addition to the toolbar at the top of SQL Server Data Tools (where we found the New Project button), each window has its own toolbar. The content of this toolbar varies depending on which item or folder is selected. The leftmost toolbar button shown in the Solution Explorer window in Figure 5-4 is the Properties button. If this toolbar button is clicked when a project node is highlighted, the Project Property Pages dialog box is displayed.

Most other items in the solution do not have their own custom property pages dialog boxes. Instead, these items display their properties in the Properties window, which we discuss next. Clicking the Properties button in the Solution Explorer toolbar when any of these other items is highlighted causes the Properties window to gain focus.

The other button shown on the Solution Explorer toolbar in Figure 5-4 is the Show All Files toggle. This toggle causes all the supporting files to be displayed for a project, as shown in Figure 5-5. In most cases, this is not necessary and toggling it on clutters up the Solution Explorer. However, at times, it is helpful to know exactly which files are being used by a project.

**Figure 5-5**    *The Solution Explorer window with the Property and Show All Files Toolbar buttons*

**Properties Window**    Below the Solution Explorer window in Figure 5-4 is the
Properties window. This window displays the property settings of the item highlighted
in the Solution Explorer window or elsewhere in SQL Server Data Tools. The drop-
down list at the top of the Properties window shows the name of the item whose
properties are currently displayed.

The main portion of the *Properties* window is composed of a list with two columns.
The left column shows the name of each property. The right column shows the current
value of that property. If the text in the right column is black, the value of that property
can be changed in the Properties window. If the text in the right column is gray, the
value is read-only.

The lower portion of the screen provides a little more information about the selected
property. The name of the selected property is displayed in bold, along with a description
of this property. This description can often help users understand a property without
having to consult the online help.

There are three buttons on the Properties window toolbar. The left button causes the
properties to be displayed by category. The category headings are shown as light-gray
bands within the properties list. Figure 5-6 shows the properties of the Data Mart data
source. These properties are divided into two categories: Location and Object Model.

The middle button on the Properties window toolbar causes the properties to be
displayed in one continuous, alphabetical list without any grouping. Personally, I never
remember which grouping contains the property I want to see, so I use the alphabetical
list setting. However, you may find it more helpful to have properties grouped. Use
whichever setting works best for you.

**Figure 5-6**    *The Properties window with categorized properties*

The right button on the Properties window toolbar displays the Property Pages dialog box for the selected item. However, only some items have a Property Pages dialog associated with them. Therefore, this toolbar button does not function for all items.

**Toolbox Window**    On the left side of Figure 5-4 is a tab labeled Toolbox. This tab provides access to the *Toolbox* window, which is set to Auto-Hide. The *Auto-Hide* setting causes the window to remain out of the way until it is needed. A window that is set to Auto-Hide can be displayed by hovering the mouse pointer over the window's tab, as shown in Figure 5-7.

The Auto-Hide feature is controlled by the pushpin icon at the top of the window. When Auto-Hide is on, the pushpin is sideways, as shown in Figure 5-7. When Auto-Hide is off, the pushpin is vertical. You can see this at the top of the Solution Explorer and Properties windows in Figure 5-4. To toggle the Auto-Hide setting for a window, click its pushpin icon.

The Toolbox window contains components used to build items in our projects. The contents of the Toolbox window change to match the type of item being built. For example, it contains data transformation tasks when we are creating Data Integration Services packages. The Toolbox window contains report items when we are building Reporting Services reports. The toolbox for report designing is shown in Figure 5-7.

**Opening Windows Not Visible in SQL Server Data Tools**    Any window in SQL Server Data Tools, including the three already discussed, can be closed using the close icon in the upper-right corner of the window. Because this is the case, we obviously need a way to open a window that is not visible on the screen. This is done using the

**Figure 5-7** *Displaying the Toolbox window when it is set to Auto-Hide*

View menu. The Solution Explorer, Properties, and Toolbox windows are available right from the View menu, as shown in Figure 5-8. You may see other windows in the View menu. There are additional windows found in the Other Windows submenu.

In addition to the View menu, windows can be opened directly using buttons on the toolbar. These toolbar buttons are illustrated in Figure 5-9.

**Task List Window**   The *Task List* window can be opened from the View menu. This window provides a convenient place for us to make note of to-do items for this solution. We can assign priorities that are signified by the exclamation point (high priority), blank (normal priority), and down arrow (low priority). When items are completed, they can be checked off. Completed items are displayed with a strike-through. The Task List window is shown in Figure 5-10.

| MultidimensionalProject1 - Microsoft Visual Studio (Administrator) | | |
|---|---|---|
| File  Edit  View  Project  Build  Debug  Team  Data  Database  Test  Tools  Window  Help | | |

| | View menu | |
|---|---|---|
| | Show Deployment Progress | |
| | Solution Explorer | Ctrl+Alt+L |
| | Team Explorer | Ctrl+\, Ctrl+M |
| | Server Explorer | Ctrl+Alt+S |
| | Bookmark Window | Ctrl+K, Ctrl+W |
| | Call Hierarchy | Ctrl+Alt+K |
| | Class View | Ctrl+Shift+C |
| | Code Definition Window | Ctrl+\, D |
| | Object Browser | Ctrl+Alt+J |
| | Error List | Ctrl+\, E |
| | Output | Ctrl+Alt+O |
| | Start Page | |
| | Task List | Ctrl+\, T |
| | Toolbox | Ctrl+Alt+X |
| | Find Results ▶ | |
| | Other Windows ▶ | |
| | Toolbars ▶ | |
| | Full Screen | Shift+Alt+Enter |
| | Navigate Backward | Ctrl+- |
| | Navigate Forward | Ctrl+Shift+- |
| | Properties Window | F4 |
| | Property Pages | Shift+F4 |

Other Windows submenu:

| | | |
|---|---|---|
| | Command Window | Ctrl+Alt+A |
| | Web Browser | Ctrl+Alt+R |
| | Macro Explorer | Alt+F8 |
| | Source Control Explorer | |
| | Document Outline | Ctrl+Alt+T |
| | History | |
| | Pending Changes | |
| | Property Manager | |
| | Resource View | Ctrl+Shift+E |
| | F# Interactive | Ctrl+Alt+F |

**Figure 5-8**   *The View menu*

To add an item to the task list, click the Create User Task button, as shown in Figure 5-10. The Task List window Context menu lets us sort the tasks, control which columns are displayed in the window, copy an existing task, or delete a task. Right-click a task to display the context menu.

Immediate window
Toolbox window
Properties window
Solution Explorer window
Team Explorer window
Start Page
Command window

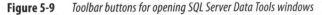

**Figure 5-9**   *Toolbar buttons for opening SQL Server Data Tools windows*

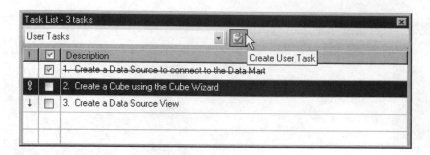

**Figure 5-10**   *The Task List window*

**Error List Window**   The Error List window can be opened from the View menu. In addition, this window automatically opens when we try to build a project or solution and there are problems. The *Error List* window contains an entry for each error, warning, and message that was produced during the build. The Error List window is shown in Figure 5-11.

Double-clicking an entry in the Error List window causes SQL Server Data Tools to open the item that caused the error, warning, or message. This makes it easy to fix a number of build errors that have occurred in various items distributed across several projects. As with the Task List window, right-clicking an entry in the Error List window displays a context menu for controlling the sorting and display columns of the Error List entries.

**Output Window**   The Output window can be opened from the View menu. In addition, this window automatically opens when we try to build a project or solution. The *Output* window contains a narrative of the events that occurred during the most recent build attempt. The Output window is shown in Figure 5-12.

Like the Error List window, the Output window notes errors, warnings, and messages from the last build attempt. Unlike the Error List window, the Output window also notes successful tasks completed. The Output window includes toolbar buttons for clearing its contents and for toggling word wrap within the window.

| | Description | File | Line | Column | Project | |
|---|---|---|---|---|---|---|
| 1 | Dimension 'Store' : The source is not specified. | | 0 | -1 | | |
| 2 | Dimension 'Promotion' : The source is not specified. | | 0 | -1 | | |
| 3 | Dimension 'Product' : The source is not specified. | | 0 | -1 | | |
| 4 | Dimension 'Time' : The source is not specified. | | 0 | -1 | | |

**Figure 5-11**   *The Error List window*

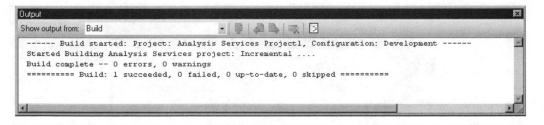

```
Output                                                                    [×]
Show output from:  Build              ▼ | 🗏 | 📄 📑 | 🛒 | 🔁

------ Build started: Project: Analysis Services Project1, Configuration: Development ------
Started Building Analysis Services project: Incremental ....
Build complete -- 0 errors, 0 warnings
========== Build: 1 succeeded, 0 failed, 0 up-to-date, 0 skipped ==========
```

**Figure 5-12**    *The Output window*

**Find Results Windows**    The Find Results windows can be opened from the View menu. In addition, one of these windows automatically opens whenever we perform a Find in Files or a Replace in Files operation. The Find Results 1 window is shown in Figure 5-13.

When we execute a find or replace operation, we can choose to display the results in either the Find Results 1 window or the Find Results 2 window. In this way, we can move between the results of two different find operations. The *Find Results* window contains a list of all of the places where the desired text was found. We can move to any of these locations by double-clicking that line in the Find Results window.

**Designer Window**    All of the windows we have discussed so far are usually found along the left, right, top, or bottom edge of SQL Server Data Tools (although they don't have to be, as we discuss in the next section). That leaves us with the large area in the center. This area is occupied by the Designer window.

The Designer window appears any time we view the code or the design of an item. In fact, the *Designer* window is where most of the work of creating business intelligence gets done. Figure 5-14 shows the Designer window with several designers and source code editors open (note the three tabs across the top). The Cube designer is open for the Min Max Sales cube. The Data Source View designer is open for the Min Max Sales DM data source view. The Dimension source code editor is open for the store dimension. (We can tell this is a source code editor rather than a designer because of the "[XML]" in the tab. We talk more about code editors and designers throughout the rest of this book.)

```
Find Results 1                                                            [×]
🗏 | 📄 📑 | 🛒 | 🔎

Find all "Test", Subfolders, Find Results 1, "Current Project"
C:\Documents and Settings\Blarson\My Documents\Visual Studio\Projects\Analysis Services Project1\Analysis Services Project1\Data M
Matching lines: 1    Matching files: 1    Total files searched: 2
|
```

**Figure 5-13**    *The Find Results 1 window*

**Figure 5-14** *The Designer window with the Dimension, Cube, and Data Source View designers open*

A tab is created each time an item is opened in a code editor or a designer. The tabs enable us to move quickly from one item's designer or source code editor to another item's designer or source code editor with a single click. We can open an item's designer by doing one of the following:

► Selecting the item in the Solution Explorer window, and then selecting View | Designer from the Main menu

► Right-clicking the item in the Solution Explorer window and selecting View Designer from the context menu

► Double-clicking the item in the Solution Explorer window

We can open an item's code editor by doing one of the following:

► Selecting the item in the Solution Explorer window, and then selecting View | Code from the Main menu

► Right-clicking the item in the Solution Explorer window and selecting View Code from the context menu

We can close an item's designer or code editor by selecting the appropriate tab, and then clicking the Close button (the *X*) on the right of the selected tab.

We discuss each designer and code editor as we use them to create and modify the various items in SQL Server Data Tools.

## Window Management

The windows of SQL Server Data Tools can be rearranged any way that we like. This is done by setting various windows to be docked along the sides or bottom, to float, or to Auto-Hide. In this way, each person can arrange the windows to suit their development style.

Each window can be set to one of five states:

▶ Float

▶ Dock

▶ Dock as Tabbed Document

▶ Auto-Hide

▶ Hide

We can set a window's state by selecting that window, and then selecting Float, Dock, Dock as Tabbed Document, Auto Hide, or Hide from the Window menu. Alternately, we can right-click the title bar of a window and set its state using the Context menu. This is shown in Figure 5-15.

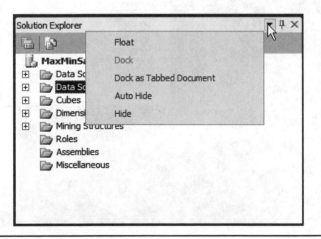

**Figure 5-15**   *Changing a window's state*

**Floating Windows**   When a window's state is set to float, it exists as a separate *floating* window on top of the rest of SQL Server Data Tools windows. A floating window can be moved anywhere around the screen on top of any other part of the user interface. This is shown in Figure 5-16.

**Dockable Windows**   When a window's state is set to *dock,* it is able to dock with the left, right, top, or bottom edge of SQL Server Data Tools. After a floating window's state is set to dock, the window either automatically docks itself or it may be dragged to a docking position. To drag a dockable window (including one that is already docked), click the window's title bar and hold down the left mouse button while you move the window into the appropriate place.

As soon as you begin dragging the window, several docking guides appear on the screen. These docking guides make it easy to dock the window in the desired location. The docking guides are linked to each of the possible docking locations on the screen.

By moving the mouse pointer over one of the docking guides while dragging a dockable window, we can see exactly where that window is going to dock if the mouse button is released at that point. The possible docking location linked to the docking

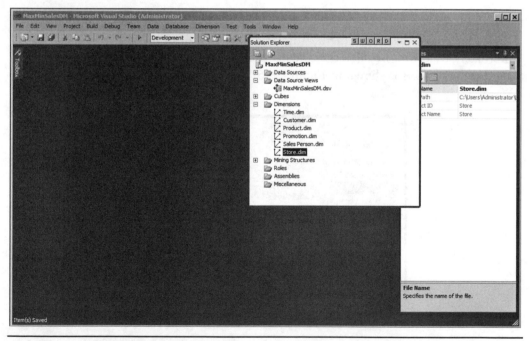

**Figure 5-16**   *The Solution Explorer as a floating window*

guide under your mouse pointer displays as a blue shadow on the screen. If this is not the desired docking location, we can drag the window to another docking guide. When we find the docking guide linked to the desired location, we simply release the mouse button and the window docks in the selected location.

There are docking guides for the top, bottom, left, and right sides of SQL Server Data Tools. Using one of these docking guides, we can dock the window along the entire length of that side. Any other windows that might butt up against that side are moved out of the way. Also, a set of docking guides in the form of a diamond is in the center of the current window. Using one of the docking guides at the points of this diamond docks the window at the side of this current window. As we drag from one window to another, this diamond-shaped docking guide switches so that it is always in the center of the window we are dragging over.

In the center of the diamond is a tabbed-icon docking guide. Using this tabbed-icon docking guide causes the window being docked to fill the current window. The two windows now form a tabbed grouping. Figure 5-17 shows the Properties window

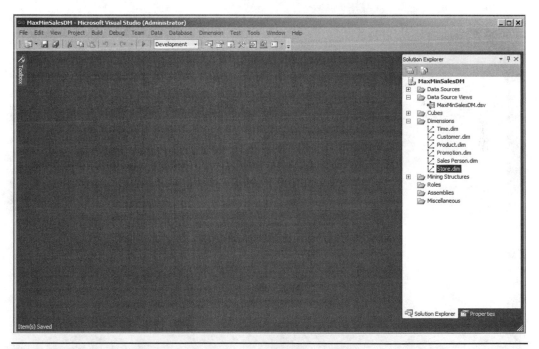

**Figure 5-17**    *The Properties window and the Solution Explorer window combined in a tabbed window*

and the Solution Explorer window combined to create a tabbed grouping. Note the tabs at the bottom of the window for switching between the Solution Explorer and the Properties window. To remove a window from a tabbed grouping, simply click that window's tab, hold down the left mouse button, and drag the window away.

**Tabbed Document**    You can even create a tabbed grouping with the Designer window. In Figure 5-18, the Solution Explorer is part of the tabbed grouping in the Designer window. When this is done, the window's state changes from dock to dock as tabbed document. Remember, this is only true when a window is in a tabbed group in the Designer window. A window in a tabbed group outside of the Designer window continues to have a dock window state.

**Auto Hide**    We have already seen the behavior of an Auto Hide window when we examined the Toolbox window. Note that a window's state cannot be changed to Auto Hide unless it is already docked. A window must have Auto Hide turned off, using the pushpin icon, before it can be changed to another state.

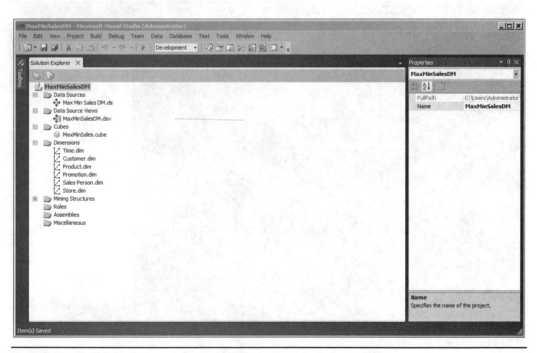

**Figure 5-18**    *The Solution Explorer window in a tabbed grouping on the Designer window*

**Hide**   The final window state is the simplest one of all. This is the hide state. When a window is in the *hide state*, it is closed and no longer appears on the screen. If we want to view a hidden window, we need to use the Window menu or the toolbar, as discussed previously.

# SQL Server Data Tools Options

In addition to the capability to rearrange the windows to our liking, SQL Server Data Tools can be customized using the Options dialog box. The Options dialog box is accessed by selecting Tools | Options from the Main menu. It is shown in Figure 5-19.

The Options dialog box provides the capability to modify a great number of settings for SQL Server Data Tools. We only discuss a few of those settings here. Feel free to explore this dialog further on your own to learn about more of the customization options.

## Fonts and Colors

Further down under the Environment options is the Fonts and Colors entry. This area lets us customize the font and color used for any category of text within SQL Server Data Tools. This is shown in Figure 5-20. The fonts and colors options can be used to

**Figure 5-19**   *The Options dialog box*

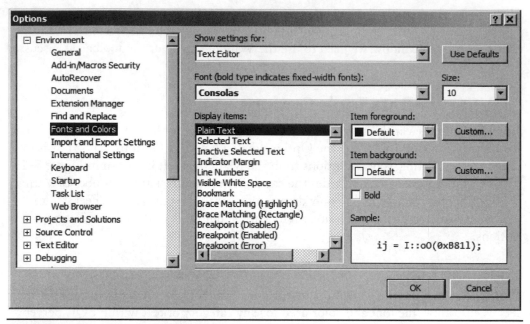

**Figure 5-20**    *Fonts and Colors options*

change font size or typeface to make certain items more readable. They can also be used to change the color of a particular set of text to make it stand out.

To make a change, first make a selection from the Show Settings For drop-down list. Next, select the text we want to change from the Display items list. Finally, make the desired font and color changes, and then click OK to apply the changes.

## Default File Locations

Another area that often needs customizing is the default location for creating solution and project files. This can be changed in the Projects and Solutions area, as shown in Figure 5-21. The path in the Projects location text box is the default location for creating new solutions and projects. To change this, we simply browse to or type in a new path and click OK to apply the changes. Now, whenever the New Project dialog box is displayed, Location shows our updated path. (Refer to Figure 5-3 for another look at the New Project dialog box.)

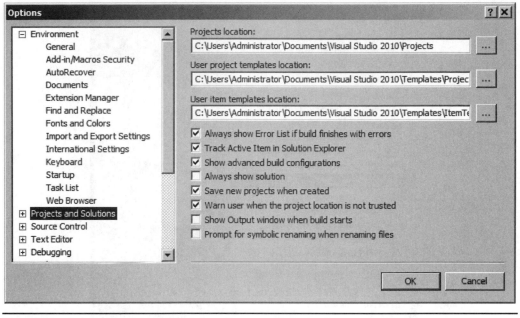

**Figure 5-21**    *Options in the Projects and Solutions area*

# The SQL Server Management Studio

As we have seen in the previous section, we use SQL Server Data Tools to develop BI
Semantic Models. We use another tool to manage our relational and Analysis Services
databases during day-to-day operations. This is the SQL Server Management Studio
(SSMS).

## The SQL Server Management Studio User Interface

The SQL Server Management Studio has a user interface similar to SQL Server Data
Tools. It has the same type of window states (floating, dockable, and so forth), and it
features a tabbed work area. Let's take a quick look at the SQL Server Management
Studio so we have some familiarity with it when it is time to use this tool for managing
databases.

The SQL Server Management Studio is found on the Start menu under Microsoft
SQL Server 2012, as shown in Figure 5-22. When the SQL Server Management
Studio starts up, it attempts to connect to the last server we were working with. The
Connect to Server dialog box is displayed, as shown in Figure 5-23. To connect to
the server, we need to provide logon credentials, if necessary, and then click Connect.

**Figure 5-22** *SQL Server Management Studio on the Start menu*

We can also enter the SQL Server Management Studio without connecting to a server by clicking Cancel.

## The SQL Server Management Studio Windows

By default, the SQL Server Management Studio has one window open, as shown in Figure 5-24. The Object Explorer window is on the left. As with SQL Server Data Tools, additional windows can be displayed when needed using the View menu.

The Object Explorer window functions similarly to the dockable windows in SQL Server Data Tools. We can make them float over other windows or set them to Auto Hide. We can have them form tabbed groupings with other dockable windows or set them to be tabbed documents in the Designer window. The SQL Server Management Studio windows use the same menus, the same docking guides, and the same drag-and-drop functionality.

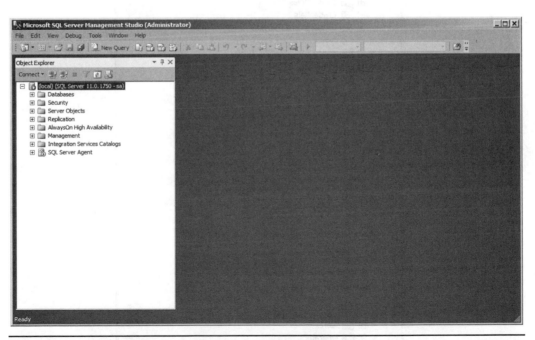

**Figure 5-23**    *Connecting to a server on startup*

**Figure 5-24**    *The SQL Server Management Studio default window layout*

**Object Explorer Window**   The *Object Explorer* window lets us view and manage the objects on a particular server. These objects are displayed in a tree view, as shown in Figure 5-25. In most cases, objects are managed by right-clicking an object to display its context menu and then selecting the appropriate action from the context menu.

**Figure 5-25**   *The Object Explorer window*

We discuss the various objects in the Object Explorer window as we work with them in future chapters.

When the SQL Server Management Studio first opens, the Object Explorer window displays objects for the server you connected to using the Connect to Server dialog box. We can add other servers to the Object Explorer window by clicking Connect in the Object Explorer window toolbar. The servers appear one below the next in the Object Explorer window's tree view.

### Object Explorer Details Window

The *Object Explorer Details* window provides a brief overview of the entry currently selected in the Object Explorer window. If the selected entry is a folder, the Details window shows the contents of that folder. If the selected entry is an object, the Details window shows the current status of that object.

**Query Windows**    One of the functions of the SQL Server Management Studio is the creation and execution of queries. These queries may be Transact-SQL for relational databases, MDX or XMLA for Analysis Services databases, or DMX for data mining. Each type of query has its own specific type of query window. We discuss how to use these query windows throughout the rest of this book.

### DEFINITION

Multidimensional Expression (MDX) *language provides the programming language for BISM Multidimensional navigation.*

### DEFINITION

Data Mining Expression (DMX) *language provides the commands to easily set up and analyze data mining structures.*

### DEFINITION

XML for Analysis Services (XMLA) *is an open, XML-based standard protocol for interacting with Microsoft SQL Server 2012 Analysis Services data over a Hypertext Transfer Protocol (HTTP) connection, such as an intranet or the Internet. XMLA uses the Simple Object Access Protocol (SOAP). (Being an open standard, XMLA is used by other vendors' OLAP tools as well.)*

To create and execute queries, we need to open a query window of the appropriate type. This is done using the query buttons on the toolbar. These buttons are shown in Figure 5-26. The New Query button opens the default type of query window for the database selected in the Object Explorer window. We can also select the specific type

**Figure 5-26**   *The New Query toolbar buttons*

of query window we want to open by selecting the appropriate toolbar button. We can also open a query window by selecting the appropriate option under File | New on the Main menu or by using the context menu for objects in the Object Explorer window. Figure 5-27 shows the SQL Server Management Studio with a SQL Server Query window open in the designer area.

**Figure 5-27**   *The SQL Server Management Studio with a SQL Server Query window*

## The SQL Server Management Studio Projects

The *SQL Server Management Studio* enables us to create solutions and projects to manage and store our queries. Three types of projects are supported: SQL Server scripts, Analysis Services scripts, and SQL Compact Edition scripts. A *script* is simply one or more queries. The SQL Server Management Studio includes a Solution Explorer window and a Properties window to help us manage our solutions and projects. They function in much the same manner as the Solution Explorer window and Properties window in SQL Server Data Tools.

Figure 5-28 shows the same query as Figure 5-27; however, this time, it is part of a solution and a project.

**Figure 5-28**    *The SQL Server Management Studio with a solution and a project*

## Don Your Hardhat

Now that you are familiar with these SQL Server 2012 business intelligence tools, it is time to start building. In Chapter 6, we return to our sample company, Maximum Miniatures, Incorporated. We look at some of their specific business intelligence needs and begin to build the structures to help them meet those needs. Specifically, we build two data marts—one from scratch and one using SQL Server Data Tools Cube Wizard. After these data marts are built, we will determine how to populate them using Integration Services.

Strap on your tool belt and let's go!

# Part II

# Defining Business Intelligence Structures

# Chapter 6

# Building Foundations—Creating Data Marts

## In This Chapter

▶ Data Mart
▶ Designing a Data Mart
▶ Table Compression
▶ The Benefits of Integration

*He who has not first laid his foundations may be able with great ability to lay them afterwards, but they will be laid with trouble to the architect and danger to the building.*

*The Prince*
—Niccolò Machiavelli

Now that you have been introduced to the business intelligence and database management tools in SQL Server 2012, it is time to get to work. The first thing we need to do is lay some foundations. We need to examine our data sources and determine if we need to create one or more data marts.

We look at the criteria to use when determining whether a data mart is needed. Next, we walk through the steps necessary for designing a data mart. Finally, we look at two different methods for creating data marts: using the SQL Server Management Studio and using SQL Server Data Tools.

# Data Mart

In Chapter 3, we were introduced to the concept of the data mart. We learned that a data mart is a repository for data to be used as a source for business intelligence. The data mart is not used as part of day-to-day operations. Instead, the data mart periodically receives data from the online transactional processing (OLTP) systems. The data in the data mart is then made available to Analysis Services for creating BI Semantic Models (BISM). This is shown in Figure 6-1.

## Who Needs a Data Mart Anyway?

In Chapter 4, we learned that it is possible for an Analysis Services BISM to utilize OLTP data without an intervening data mart. Either the Multidimensional or the Tabular model can incorporate data directly from OLTP systems. It is possible to do this in a manner that does not put undue stress on these systems, thus eliminating the need for data marts. This is shown in Figure 6-2.

So, why are we back to talking about data marts? Why don't we skip over all of this and get right to the BISM? The answer is this: Many situations still exist where a data mart may be the best choice as a source for business intelligence data. These situations are shown in Figure 6-3.

## Legacy Databases

The BISM's data sources need appropriate data providers to make a connection to OLTP systems. In many cases, these will be .NET, OLE DB, or ODBC connections. However, some database systems do not have an appropriate data provider to make

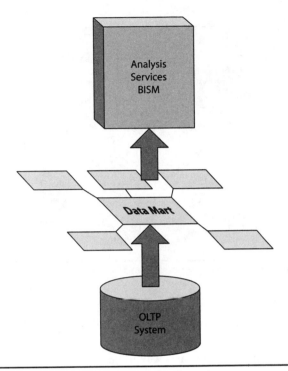

**Figure 6-1**    *An Analysis Services BI Semantic Model receiving data from a data mart*

**Figure 6-2**    *The BISM eliminates the need for a data mart.*

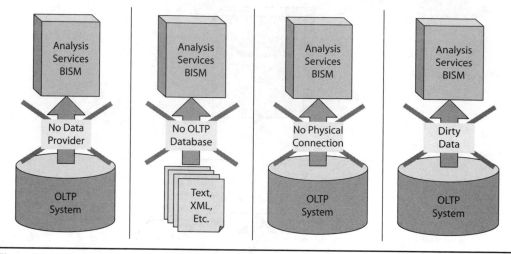

**Figure 6-3**    *Situations where a data mart is advised*

this connection. Either the data provider available does not provide enough speed, flexibility, or reliability, or a data provider does not exist at all. In fact, some systems, especially legacy systems, do not have any way to allow this type of external access.

In these situations, the data must be exported from the legacy system and copied into a database that can be utilized by the BISM. This database is the data mart. The data must be exported from the legacy system into a format that can then be imported into the data mart. Usually, this is in the form of some type of text file: delimited columns, fixed-width columns, or, perhaps, Extensible Markup Language (XML).

Each time the export is run, a text file is created. This text file is then imported into the data mart. The import is accomplished using Integration Services.

## Data from Nondatabase Sources

In some cases, the data needed for business intelligence is not even stored in a database. Production information from the automated manufacturing system could be written to a text file. Customer service call records might be logged to an XML file. Perhaps customer orders only exist on paper forms.

Again, in these situations, we need to import the data into a data mart before it can be utilized by a BISM. The text and XML files can be imported directly by Integration Services. The paper order forms must be scanned in or entered by hand into an electronic format that can be imported into the data mart.

## No Physical Connection

In other cases, the data may exist in an OLTP database that has a data provider but does not have a full-time connection to the location where the business intelligence must be utilized. The BISM requires some type of physical connection that will support the data provider. If there is none, we again need to set up a data mart to serve as a repository for this data at the location where the business intelligence is utilized.

Of course, we also need some way to transport an export file from the OLTP database to the data mart so it can be imported. This might mean performing a File Transfer Protocol (FTP) transfer over a dial-up connection. It could mean putting the export file on a backup tape or burning it on a DVD-R and carrying it or shipping it between the two sites. However the data is transported, it is once again imported into the data mart using Integration Services.

## Dirty Data

Dirty data can also trigger the need for a data mart. If the data in our OLTP systems contains a number of errors, inconsistencies, or duplicate information, we may need to clean the data before we can use it as a source of accurate business intelligence. Because of limitations in the OLTP systems, it may not be possible to properly cleanse the data in the OLTP database. Instead, the data must be exported from the OLTP system and then cleaned up as it is imported into a data mart by Integration Services.

# Designing a Data Mart

Once you establish the need for a data mart, it is time to create a design. As we learned in Chapter 3, a data mart is made up of measures, dimensions organized in hierarchies, and attributes. We begin our design by identifying the information that our decision makers need for effective decision making. We then need to reconcile this with the data we have available from our OLTP systems and organize this data into the data mart components: measures, dimensions, hierarchies, and attributes. When this is complete, we can build the database structure for the data mart using either a star or snowflake schema.

We discuss each step of the data mart design process in the following sections. This is followed by a section called "Learn By Doing." The Learn By Doing section lets you make the concepts more concrete by applying what you just learned to a business scenario from Maximum Miniatures, Incorporated. I encourage you to work through these Learn By Doing exercises to make what can be complex and overwhelming concepts more tangible and straightforward. As Aristotle said, "One must learn by doing the thing, for though you think you know it, you have no certainty until you try."

## Decision Makers' Needs

Business intelligence design should never be done in a vacuum. As we discussed in Chapter 1, the goal of business intelligence is to provide the tools for effective decision making. Therefore, any business intelligence design must start with the decision makers themselves. What foundation and feedback information do they need? How do they need that information sliced and diced for proper analysis? To create truly effective business intelligence, these questions need to be answered by the decision makers themselves.

There are two important reasons to have the decision makers involved in this design process. First, the decision makers are the ones in the trenches. They know the choices that are made each day in the organization's operation. They also have a pretty good idea of what information can aid them in making those choices.

Second, the decision makers are the ones who ultimately determine the success or failure of a project. They do this through their willingness or unwillingness to use the resulting business intelligence tools. Your tool may produce dynamite information, but, ultimately, it is a failure if no one uses that information to produce more effective decisions.

Involving decision makers in the design of the data mart structures distributes the perceived ownership of the project. Most people who get their brainstorming ideas on the whiteboard during a design meeting, or who are allowed to submit a design suggestion via e-mail, feel some sense of having contributed to the project. They feel a small piece of ownership in the project. Just as the owner of a single share in a billion-dollar corporation cares whether the company's stock goes up or down, the person who feels ownership in a project, no matter how small their actual contribution might be, cares about the success or failure of that project. A decision maker who has taken a small piece of ownership in our business intelligence project is far more likely to use the resulting tool and, if appropriate, to push for others to make use of it as well.

So, with the goal of both gaining important insight into the decision makers' needs and creating a sense of ownership among the future users of our business intelligence tool, we need to have our decision makers answer the following questions:

▶ What facts, figures, statistics, and so forth do you need for effective decision making? (foundation and feedback measures)

▶ How should this information be sliced and diced for analysis? (dimensions)

▶ What additional information can aid in finding exactly what is needed? (attributes)

The answers to these questions form half of the required design information. The other half comes from the OLTP data itself.

## Available Data

The input and the ownership buy-in of the decision makers are important to our data mart design. Next comes the reality check. The fact is we cannot place any measures, dimensions, hierarchies, or attributes in the data mart if they are not represented in the OLTP data source.

We need to analyze the data to be received from the data source to make sure that all of the information requested by the decision makers can be obtained from there. Measures and attributes can come directly from fields in the OLTP data or from calculations based on those fields. Dimensions and hierarchies must be represented in the data and relationships contained in the OLTP data.

If a piece of requested information is not present in the OLTP data source, we need to determine if it is present in another data source. If so, data from these two data sources can be joined during the population of the data mart to provide the decision makers with the desired result. If the requested information is unavailable, we have to work with the decision makers to either determine a method to gather the missing information in the future or identify an alternative bit of information already present in the OLTP data source.

## Data Mart Structures

We are now ready to specify the structures that will be in our data mart. These are the measures, dimensions, hierarchies, and attributes. These structures lead us to the star or snowflake schema that is going to define our data mart.

### Measures

We start our data mart design by specifying the measures. The *measures* are the foundation and feedback information our decision makers require. We reconcile these requirements with what is available in the OLTP data to come up with a list of measures, as shown in Figure 6-4.

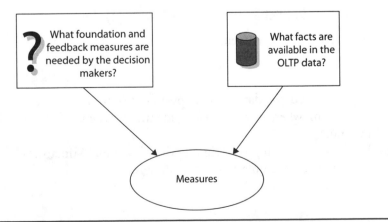

**Figure 6-4**    *Designing the measures in a data mart*

In Chapter 4, we learned measures are numeric quantities. The following are some examples of numeric data that can be used as measures:

### Monetary Amounts

- The cost of raw materials
- The value of a sale
- Operational expenses
- Labor expenses

### Counts

- The number of items produced
- The number of items ordered
- The number of items shipped
- The number of items returned
- The number of calls to customer service

### Time Periods

- The number of minutes or hours required to produce a product
- The number of days required to fill an order
- Mean time between failure of a product

In the design, we need to note the following for each measure:

- Name of the measure
- What OLTP field or fields should be used to supply the data
- Data type (money, integer, decimal)
- Formula used to calculate the measure (if there is one)

As previously discussed, the data cannot appear out of thin air. It must be copied from or calculated from somewhere else. Therefore, identifying the OLTP fields that supply the data is important.

Refer to the "Learn By Doing—Designing the Maximum Miniatures Manufacturing Data Mart" section for an example of measure design.

## Dimensions and Hierarchies

As we learned in Chapter 3, *dimensions* are used to spread a measure into its constituent parts. *Hierarchies* are used to organize dimensions into various levels. Dimensions and hierarchies are used to drill down into a measure to move from more general information to more specific information. While measures define *what* the decision makers want to see, the dimensions and hierarchies define *how* they want to see it.

When the decision makers tell us they want to see "total sales by salesperson by year," they are describing a measure, total sales, and two dimensions: salesperson and date. In discussions with decision makers, dimensions often are preceded with the words "by," "for each," or "for every." When the decision makers tell us they want to be able to "roll up salespersons into sales regions" or "drill down from year into quarter," they are describing hierarchies. The sales region dimension is above the salesperson dimension and the year dimension is above the quarter dimension in the hierarchy they are describing. These are all indications of how the decision makers want to view the measure.

We again reconcile the requested dimensions and hierarchies with what is available from the OLTP data to come up with the list of dimensions and their hierarchies for our design. This is shown in Figure 6-5. In the design, we need to have the following listed for each dimension:

▶   Name of the dimension

▶   What OLTP field or fields are to be used to supply the data

▶   Data type of the dimension's key (the code that uniquely identifies each member of the dimension)

▶   Name of the parent dimension (if there is one)

Refer to the "Learn By Doing—Designing the Maximum Miniatures Manufacturing Data Mart" section for an example of dimension and hierarchy design.

## Attributes

*Attributes* provide additional information about a dimension. They may result from information decision makers want to have readily available during analysis. Attributes may also result from information decision makers want to filter on during the analysis process.

**Figure 6-5** *Designing the dimensions and hierarchies in a data mart*

As before, we need to reconcile the requested attributes with the data available from the OLTP database to come up with the list of attributes in our design. This is shown in Figure 6-6. In the design, we need to include the following for each attribute:

▶ Name of the attribute

▶ What OLTP field or fields are to be used to supply the data

▶ Data type

▶ Name of the dimension to which it applies

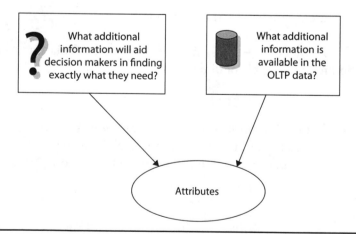

**Figure 6-6** *Designing the attributes in a data mart*

Refer to the "Learn By Doing—Designing the Maximum Miniatures Manufacturing Data Mart" section for an example of attribute design.

## Stars and Snowflakes

Data marts are architected using either a star schema or a snowflake schema. Refer to Chapter 3 if you need a refresher on these two layouts. Our last step is to turn our lists into either a star or a snowflake schema. Figure 6-7 shows a star schema, while Figure 6-8 shows a snowflake schema.

Recall that all the measures are placed in a single table called the fact table. The dimensions at the lowest level of the hierarchies are each placed in their own dimension table. In the *star schema*, all the information for a hierarchy is stored in the same table. The information for the parent (or grandparent or great-grandparent, and so forth) dimension is added to the table containing the dimension at the lowest level of the hierarchy.

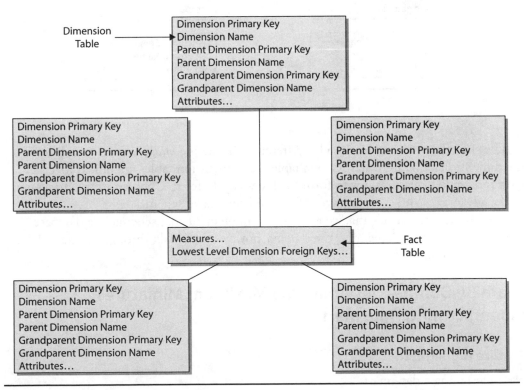

**Figure 6-7**    *A star schema*

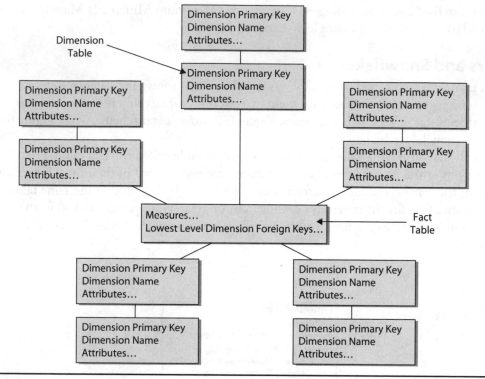

**Figure 6-8**   *A snowflake schema*

The snowflake schema works a bit differently. In the *snowflake schema,* each level in the dimensional hierarchy has its own table. The dimension tables are linked together with foreign key relationships to form the hierarchy. Refer to Chapter 3 for a discussion of the advantages and disadvantages of star and snowflake schemas.

Once we create our schema, we are ready to implement that schema in a database. Before we look at implementing the schema, however, let's walk through an example of data mart design.

## Learn By Doing—Designing the Maximum Miniatures Manufacturing Data Mart

### Feature Highlighted

▶  Designing a data mart

In this section, we apply the knowledge gained in the previous sections to complete a sample task for Maximum Miniatures, Incorporated. In this case, we design the Manufacturing data mart to hold information that is initially logged by the manufacturing automation system in comma-delimited text files.

**Business Need**   The vice president (VP) of production for Max Min, Inc., wants to analyze the statistics available from the manufacturing automation system. He would like an interactive analysis tool, rather than printed reports, for this analysis. In keeping with Max Min's new business intelligence strategy, Microsoft SQL Server 2012 Analysis Services is the platform for this analysis tool. Because the manufacturing automation system does not use a database, logging everything to comma-delimited text files instead, a data mart must be designed and built as a repository for this information.

The manufacturing automation system controls all the machines used by Max Min to create its figurines. Each machine handles all the steps in the manufacturing process of a figurine. This includes the following:

▶   Filling a mold with the raw material (clay, pewter, or aluminum)

▶   Aiding the hardening of this material

▶   Removal from the mold when hardening is complete

▶   Computerized painting of the figurine, if necessary (pewter figurines are not painted)

▶   Curing the paint, if necessary

Multiple painting and curing cycles may be necessary, depending on the intricacy of the paint job required by a product. A quality assurance check is done by the machine operator as the figurine is completed.

Operators log onto a machine. As part of this logon process, the operator tells the manufacturing automation system what product is being produced, along with the batch number of the raw material being used by that machine. The operator also makes an entry in the system when a figurine is rejected.

An interview with the VP of production yielded the following data requirements for effective decision making:

▶   Number of accepted products by batch, by product, by machine, by day

▶   Number of rejected products by batch, by product, by machine, by day

▶   Elapsed time for molding and hardening by product, by machine, by day

▶ Elapsed time for painting and curing by paint type, by product, by machine, by day

▶ Product rolls up into product subtype, which rolls up into product type

▶ Machine rolls up into machine type, which rolls up into material (clay, pewter, or aluminum)

▶ Machine also rolls up into plant, which rolls up into country

▶ Day rolls up into month, which rolls up into quarter, which rolls up into year

▶ The information should be able to be filtered by machine manufacturer and purchase date of the machine

The export file from the manufacturing automation system contains one row for each product produced. Each row includes the following information:

▶ Product

▶ Batch number of the raw material

▶ Machine number

▶ Operator employee number

▶ Start of manufacture date and time (when the batch run begins)

▶ End of manufacture date and time (when the batch run is complete)

▶ Reject flag

### Steps

*In this particular Learn By Doing exercise, you don't have that much to do except follow along and make sure you understand each step. You can use these steps as a guideline when you have to create your own data mart design. Subsequent "Learn By Doing" sections require you to use the SQL Server 2012 tools to create part of a working business intelligence solution.*

1. Prepare a list of the measures requested by the VP of production. This is shown in the Measure column of Figure 6-9.

2. Determine which fields in the OLTP data source supply the data for these measures. This is shown in the OLTP Fields column of Figure 6-9. The Reject Flag field tells us whether a product has been accepted or rejected. This can be used to determine the number of accepted and number of rejected products. The manufacturing system

| Measure | OLTP Fields |
|---------|-------------|
| Number of Accepted Products | Reject Flag |
| Number of Rejected Products | Reject Flag |
| Elapsed Minutes for Molding and Hardening | NOT AVAILABLE |
| Elapsed Minutes for Painting and Curing | NOT AVAILABLE |

**Figure 6-9**    *Requested measures for the Manufacturing data mart*

does not track the time spent in each individual production step. It only tracks the date and time at the start of manufacture and the date and time at the end of manufacture. Therefore, we need to put NOT AVAILABLE for these two items.

3. Resolve any problems with information that is unavailable. In this case, a follow-up interview with the VP reveals he will be satisfied with knowing the elapsed minutes for the entire manufacturing process. When our list is updated with this information, it appears as shown in the Measure and OLTP Fields columns of Figure 6-10.

4. Add the data types and calculations to the list. This is shown in the Data Type and Formula columns of Figure 6-10.

5. Prepare a list of the dimensions requested by the VP of production. This is shown in the Dimension column of Figure 6-11.

6. Determine which fields in the OLTP data source are going to supply the data for these dimensions. This is shown in the OLTP Fields column of Figure 6-11.

7. Resolve any problems with information that is not available. The manufacturing automation system does not include information on the hierarchies within Max Min. To include these hierarchies in the data mart, we need to pull data from another system. It turns out that the accounting system has the data we need. We remove the Paint Type dimension because this data is not available electronically. When our list is updated with this information, it appears as shown in the Dimension and OLTP Fields columns of Figure 6-12.

| Measure | OLTP Fields | Data Type | Formula |
|---------|-------------|-----------|---------|
| Number of Accepted Products | Reject flag | Int | Count when reject flag is false |
| Number of Rejected Products | Reject flag | Int | Count when reject flag is true |
| Elapsed Minutes for Manufacturing | Start of manufacture date and time, End of manufacture date and time | Decimal(6,2) | DATEDIFF(mi, [Start of manufacture date and time], [End of manufacture date and time]) |

**Figure 6-10**    *Finalized measures for the Manufacturing data mart*

| Dimension | OLTP Fields |
|---|---|
| Product | Product |
| Product Subtype | NOT AVAILABLE |
| Product Type | NOT AVAILABLE |
| Batch | Batch |
| Machine | Machine |
| Machine Type | NOT AVAILABLE |
| Material | NOT AVAILABLE |
| Plant | NOT AVAILABLE |
| Country | NOT AVAILABLE |
| Day | Start of Manufacture Date and Time |
| Month | Start of Manufacture Date and Time |
| Quarter | Start of Manufacture Date and Time |
| Year | Start of Manufacture Date and Time |
| Paint Type | NOT AVAILABLE |

**Figure 6-11**   *Requested dimensions and hierarchies for the Manufacturing data mart*

| Dimension | OLTP Fields | Data Type | Parent Dimension |
|---|---|---|---|
| Product | Product | Int | Product Subtype |
| Product Subtype | Accounting System.ProductSubtype | Int | Product Type |
| Product Type | Accounting System.ProductType | Int | None |
| Batch | Batch | Int | None |
| Machine | Machine | Int | Machine Type, Plant |
| Machine Type | Accounting System.MachineType | Nvarchar(30) | Material |
| Material | Accounting System.Material | Nvarchar(30) | None |
| Plant | Accounting System.Plant | Int | Country |
| Country | Accounting System.Country | Nchar(2) | None |
| Day | Start of Manufacture Date and Time | Int | Month |
| Month | Start of Manufacture Date and Time | Int | Quarter |
| Quarter | Start of Manufacture Date and Time | Int | Year |
| Year | Start of Manufacture Date and Time | Int | None |

**Figure 6-12**   *Finalized dimensions and hierarchies for the Manufacturing data mart*

| Attribute | OLTP Fields | Data Type | Dimension |
|---|---|---|---|
| Machine Manufacturer | Accounting.Equipment | Nvarchar(50) | Machine |
| Date of Purchase | Accounting.Equipment | Datetime | Machine |

**Figure 6-13** *Finalized attributes for the Manufacturing data mart*

8. Add the data type of the dimension's key, along with the name of the parent dimension. This is shown in the Data Type and Parent Dimension columns of Figure 6-12.

9. Prepare a list of the attributes requested by the VP of production. This is shown in the Attribute column of Figure 6-13.

10. Determine which fields in the OLTP data source will supply the data for these attributes. Remember, some of this data needs to come from the accounting system. This is shown in the OLTP Fields column of Figure 6-13.

11. Resolve any problems with information that is unavailable. In this case, we do not have any problem attributes, so no changes need to be made to the list.

12. Add the data type of the attribute, along with the name of the dimension it is associated with. This is shown in the Data Type and Dimension columns of Figure 6-13.

13. Turn the lists in Figure 6-10, Figure 6-12, and Figure 6-13 into your choice of a star schema or a snowflake schema. In this case, we use a snowflake schema. Place the measures and their data types in the ManufacturingFact table, as shown in Figure 6-14.

14. Place each dimension into its own dimension table, as shown in Figure 6-15. Include a table name beginning with "Dim" and a primary key designation in each table.

| **ManufacturingFact** | |
|---|---|
| **Field Name** | **Data Type** |
| AcceptedProducts | Int |
| RejectedProducts | Int |
| ElapsedTimeForManufacture | Decimal(6,2) |

**Figure 6-14** *The Manufacturing data mart schema with measures in a fact table*

**ManufacturingFact**

| Field Name | Data Type |
| --- | --- |
| AcceptedProducts | Int |
| RejectedProducts | Int |
| ElapsedTimeForManufacture | Decimal(6,2) |
| DateOfManufacture | DateTime |

**DimMachine**

| Field Name | Data Type |
| --- | --- |
| MachineNumber (PK) | Int |
| MachineName | Nvarchar(50) |

**DimProduct**

| Field Name | Data Type |
| --- | --- |
| ProductCode (PK) | Int |
| ProductName | Nvarchar(50) |

**DimMachineType**

| Field Name | Data Type |
| --- | --- |
| MachineType (PK) | Nvarchar(30) |

**DimProductSubtype**

| Field Name | Data Type |
| --- | --- |
| ProductSubtypeCode (PK) | Int |
| ProductSubtypeName | Nvarchar(50) |

**DimMaterial**

| Field Name | Data Type |
| --- | --- |
| Material (PK) | Nvarchar(30) |

**DimProductType**

| Field Name | Data Type |
| --- | --- |
| ProductTypeCode (PK) | Int |
| ProductTypeName | Nvarchar(50) |

**DimPlant**

| Field Name | Data Type |
| --- | --- |
| PlantNumber (PK) | Int |
| PlantName | Nvarchar(30) |

**DimBatch**

| Field Name | Data Type |
| --- | --- |
| BatchNumber (PK) | Int |
| BatchName | Nvarchar(50) |

**DimCountry**

| Field Name | Data Type |
| --- | --- |
| CountryCode (PK) | Nchar(2) |
| CountryName | Nvarchar(30) |

**Figure 6-15**    *The Manufacturing data mart schema with dimension tables added*

**NOTE**

*The time-related dimensions of day, month, quarter, and year do not need dimension tables. Instead, a single datetime field is placed in the ManufacturingFact table (DateOfManufacture). The entire time-related hierarchy will be extrapolated from this field when we create a cube based on this data mart in a later chapter. This is done using a feature of SQL Server Analysis Services.*

15. Create the dimensional hierarchies by adding foreign keys to the dimension tables. This is shown in Figure 6-16.

16. Link the lowest-level dimensions to the fact table by adding foreign keys to the fact table. Also, add the attributes to the dimension tables. The final Manufacturing data mart schema is shown in Figure 6-17. This may be a pretty funny-looking snowflake, but it is, indeed, a snowflake schema.

The design of the Manufacturing data mart is complete. Next, we learn how to turn that design into a reality.

**ManufacturingFact**

| Field Name | Data Type |
|---|---|
| AcceptedProducts | Int |
| RejectedProducts | Int |
| ElapsedTimeForManufacture | Decimal(6,2) |
| DateOfManufacture | DateTime |

**DimBatch**

| Field Name | Data Type |
|---|---|
| BatchNumber (PK) | Int |
| BatchName | Nvarchar(50) |

**DimMachine**

| Field Name | Data Type |
|---|---|
| MachineNumber (PK) | Int |
| MachineName | Nvarchar(50) |
| MachineType (FK) | Nvarchar(30) |
| PlantNumber (FK) | Int |

**DimProduct**

| Field Name | Data Type |
|---|---|
| ProductCode (PK) | Int |
| ProductName | Varchar(50) |
| ProductSubtypeCode (FK) | Int |

**DimProductSubtype**

| Field Name | Data Type |
|---|---|
| ProductSubtypeCode (PK) | Int |
| ProductSubtypeName | Nvarchar(50) |
| ProductTypeCode (FK) | Int |

**DimMachineType**

| Field Name | Data Type |
|---|---|
| MachineType (PK) | Nvarchar(30) |
| Material (FK) | Nvarchar(30) |

**DimMaterial**

| Field Name | Data Type |
|---|---|
| Material (PK) | Nvarchar(30) |

**DimPlant**

| Field Name | Data Type |
|---|---|
| PlantNumber (PK) | Int |
| PlantName | Nvarchar(30) |
| CountryCode (FK) | NChar(2) |

**DimProductType**

| Field Name | Data Type |
|---|---|
| ProductTypeCode (PK) | Int |
| ProductTypeName | Nvarchar(50) |

**DimCountry**

| Field Name | Data Type |
|---|---|
| CountryCode (PK) | NChar(2) |
| CountryName | Nvarchar(30) |

**Figure 6-16** *The Manufacturing data mart schema with hierarchies added*

# Creating a Data Mart Using the SQL Server Management Studio

Now that we have a design for our data mart based on the decision maker's requests and the data available from the OLTP systems, it is time to turn that design into database tables. We are going to build the relational data mart as shown in Figure 6-18. We use the schema in Figure 6-17 to create a database with a fact table and several dimension tables.

Even though we identified several foreign key relationships among our tables, we are not going to create foreign key constraints in our data mart. Foreign key constraints put a strain on the database engine during a large data load. Large data loads are quite common in the data mart environment. Instead of using foreign key constraints, we will depend on our data extract, transform, and load (ETL) process in SQL Server Integration Services to enforce data integrity. We will see this in action in Chapter 8.

Follow the steps in the "Learn By Doing—Creating the Maximum Miniatures Manufacturing Data Mart Using the SQL Server Management Studio" section to create the Manufacturing data mart.

**Figure 6-17** *The completed Manufacturing data mart schema*

## Learn By Doing—Creating the Maximum Miniatures Manufacturing Data Mart Using the SQL Server Management Studio

### Features Highlighted

- ▶ Creating a data mart database
- ▶ Creating dimension tables
- ▶ Creating a fact table

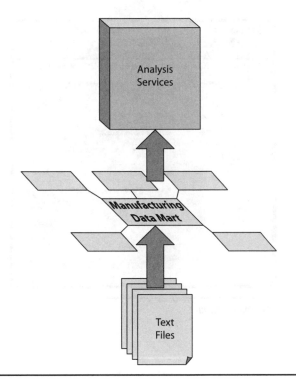

**Figure 6-18**    *Building the relational data mart*

**Business Need**    The business need was stated in the previous Learn By Doing section, where we created the schema for the Manufacturing data mart. In this section, we implement the Maximum Miniatures Manufacturing data mart schema using the SQL Server Management Studio.

**Steps**

1. Open the SQL Server Management Studio, as we discussed in Chapter 5.
2. Connect to a development or test instance of the SQL Server database engine. (Do *not* perform this or any other Learn By Doing activity on a server instance used for production database operations!)
3. Right-click the Databases folder in the Object Explorer window. The context menu appears, as shown in Figure 6-19.
4. Select New Database from the context menu. The New Database dialog box appears, as shown in Figure 6-20.
5. Enter **MaxMinManufacturingDM** for Database name. Select the Options page, and select Simple from the Recovery model drop-down list. Click OK to create the database.

**Figure 6-19** *The Database folder context menu*

### NOTE

*Because this is not a transactional database, there is no need to recover the content of this database to a point in time using the transaction log. The simple recovery model truncates the transaction log on checkpoint, keeping the size of the transaction log small. The Full and Bulk-logged recovery models require a backup of the transaction log before it is truncated.*

6. Expand the Databases folder, and expand the MaxMinManufacturingDM database entry. Right-click the Tables folder, and select New Table from the context menu. A Table Designer tab appears, as shown in Figure 6-21.

7. We use both the Properties window and the Column Properties window as we create our tables. If the Properties window is not visible, as shown in Figure 6-21, select Properties Window from the View menu. Be sure to note whether the entries in the following steps are being made in the Properties window or in the Column Properties window.

8. Begin by creating the DimProduct table from the schema (see Figure 6-17). In the Properties window, enter **DimProduct** for (Name) and **Product Dimension populated from the Manufacturing Automation System export file.** for Description.

### NOTE

*To use a larger editing area when entering the description, click the ellipses button (...) at the end of the Description property entry area. This opens a dialog window with a multiline entry area for typing the description.*

**Figure 6-20**    *The New Database dialog box*

9.  In the first row of the Table Designer tab, enter **ProductCode** under Column
    Name, select int under Data Type, and uncheck Allow Nulls. Click the Set
    Primary Key button in the toolbar to make this the primary key for this table.

10. In the second row of the Table Designer tab, enter **ProductName** under Column
    Name, select nvarchar(50) under Data Type, and uncheck Allow Nulls. (Leave
    Length in the Column Properties window set to the default value of 50.)

11. In the third row of the Table Designer tab, enter **ProductSubtypeCode** under
    Column Name, select int under Data Type, and uncheck Allow Nulls.

12. Click the Save toolbar button to save this table design. This creates the table in the
    database. Click the Close button (the *X* on the right side of the Table Designer tab).

**Figure 6-21** *The SQL Server Management Studio ready to create a table*

13. Next, create the DimProductSubtype table from the schema. Right-click the Tables folder and select New Table from the context menu. In the Properties window, enter **DimProductSubtype** for (Name) and **ProductSubtype Dimension populated from the Accounting System.ProductSubtype table**. for Description.

14. In the first row of the Table Designer tab, enter **ProductSubtypeCode** under Column Name, select int under Data Type, and uncheck Allow Nulls. Click the Set Primary Key button in the toolbar to make this the primary key for this table.

15. In the second row of the Table Designer tab, enter **ProductSubtypeName** under Column Name, select nvarchar(50) under Data Type, and uncheck Allow Nulls. (Leave Length in the Column Properties window set to the default value of 50.)

16. In the third row of the Table Designer tab, enter **ProductTypeCode** under Column Name, select int under Data Type, and uncheck Allow Nulls.

17. Click the Save toolbar button to create the table, and then click the Close button on the right side of the Table Designer tab.

18. Use the same process to create the DimProductType, DimBatch, DimMachine, DimMachineType, DimMaterial, DimPlant, and DimCountry dimension tables based on the schema in Figure 6-17. Be sure to uncheck Allow Nulls for all fields and to enter the appropriate data type along with the appropriate length in the Column Properties window. Also, create a primary key for each field that is followed by a (PK) in Figure 6-17.

19. Right-click the MaxMinManufacturingDM database entry in the Object Explorer window, and select Refresh from the context menu. When you expand the node for columns under each table, the entries should appear just as in Figure 6-22 and Figure 6-23.

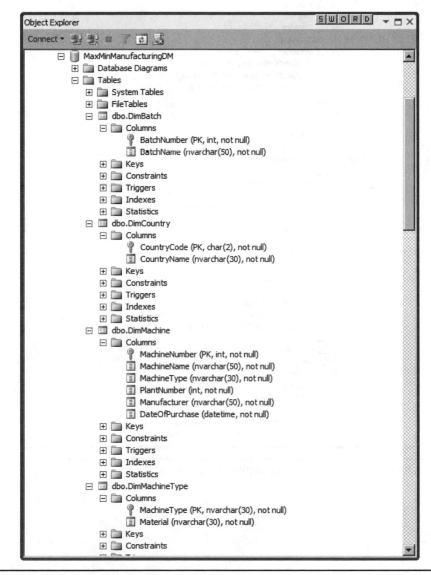

**Figure 6-22**    *The tables in the MaxMinManufacturingDM with columns (Part 1)*

**Figure 6-23** *The tables in the MaxMinManufacturingDM with columns (Part 2)*

**NOTE**

*If you notice any mistakes as you compare Figure 6-22 and Figure 6-23 with your tables, right-click the table that is in error and select Design from the context menu. Make the necessary changes to the table structure to correct the error. Be sure to click the Save toolbar button when you are done. You need to refresh the contents of the Object Explorer window after your changes before again comparing to Figure 6-22 and Figure 6-23. You may need to enable table changes in the SQL Server Management Studio. If you receive an error, select Tools | Options from the main menu. In the Options dialog box, select the Designers | Table and Database Designers page. Uncheck the Prevent saving changes that require table re-creation check box, and click OK.*

20. Now, create the ManufacturingFact table. Right-click the Tables folder, and select New Table from the context menu. In the Properties window, enter **ManufacturingFact** for (Name) and **Manufacturing Fact populated from the Manufacturing Automation System export file.** for Description.

21. Using the schema in Figure 6-17, create the entries for the seven columns in the ManufacturingFact table. When creating the ElapsedTimeForManufacture field definition, select decimal under Data Type, and then enter **6** for Precision and **2** for Scale. (Continue to uncheck Allow Nulls for all fields.)

**NOTE**

*The decimal data type is used to store real numbers. The precision determines the total number of digits contained in the number. The scale tells how many of those digits are to the right of the decimal. The ElapsedTimeForManufacture field has a maximum of six digits, with two of those digits to the right of the decimal. Therefore, the largest number that can be stored in this field is 9999.99.*

22. Click the square to the left of the DateOfManufacture field definition. Hold down SHIFT and click the square to the left of the MachineNumber field definition. This selects these two field definitions and all the field definitions in between, as shown in Figure 6-24. Click the Set Primary Key button in the toolbar to make these four fields a compound primary key for this table.

23. Click the Save toolbar button, and then click the Close button in the Table Designer tab.

We have now manually built the Manufacturing data mart structure using the SQL Server Management Studio. Even though this process took 23 steps, we are only halfway done. In Chapter 9, we complete the other half of the process by creating an Analysis Services BISM that uses this data mart as its data source.

**Figure 6-24**   *Selecting multiple fields to create a compound primary key*

## Creating a Data Mart Using SQL Server Data Tools

In the previous section, we completed the first half of a two-step process for creating a relational data mart and an Analysis Services BISM built on that data mart. This is a long and, as you will see, somewhat redundant process. SQL Server Data Tools comes to our rescue here. We will now use this tool to create the Analysis Services BISM and its underlying relational data mart for the Maximum Miniatures sales data at the same time. This is shown in Figure 6-25. The Cube Wizard creates an Analysis Services cube, and then creates the matching dimension and fact tables in the Sales data mart based on the cube definition.

Follow the steps in the "Learn By Doing—Creating the Maximum Miniatures Sales Data Mart Using SQL Server Data Tools" section to create the Sales data mart through the Cube Wizard.

### Learn By Doing—Creating the Maximum Miniatures Sales Data Mart Using SQL Server Data Tools

#### Features Highlighted

▶   Creating an Analysis Services cube using the Cube Wizard in SQL Server Data Tools

▶   Creating a relational data mart from a cube definition in SQL Server Data Tools

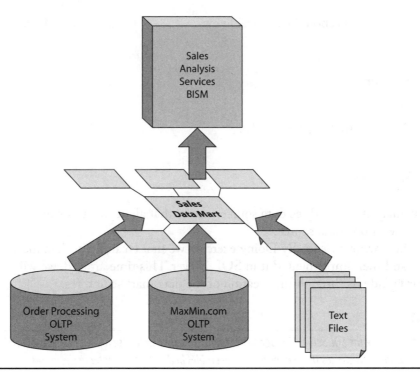

**Figure 6-25**    *Building the Sales relational data mart and the Sales Analysis Services cube*

**Business Need**    The VP of sales for Max Min, Inc., would like to analyze sales information. This information is collected by three OLTP systems: the Order Processing System, the Point of Sale (POS) System, and the MaxMin.com Online System (refer to Figure 2-4). The Order Processing System and the MaxMin.com Online System both use Microsoft SQL Server as their back-end databases. The POS System uses XML files to transfer data from each of the five Max Min–owned retail stores.

Microsoft SQL Server 2012 Analysis Services is the platform for this analysis tool. Because the data must come from three different systems, and because one of these systems is file-based, a relational data mart is created to hold the information that is to serve as the data source for the cube.

The VP of sales would like to be able to analyze the following numbers:

▶    Dollar value of products sold

▶    Number of products sold

▶    Sales tax charged on products sold

▶    Shipping charged on products sold

These numbers should be viewable by:

- ▶ Store
- ▶ Sales Promotion
- ▶ Product
- ▶ Day, Month, Quarter, and Year
- ▶ Customer
- ▶ Salesperson

An analysis of the three data sources shows that all of this information is available from at least one data source.

In the previous Learn By Doing exercise, we first created our data mart structure on paper, and then implemented it in SQL Server. This time around, we will let the Cube Wizard guide us through the creation of the data mart structures.

> **NOTE**
>
> We need to use the SQL Server Management Studio to create a database for our Max Min Sales data mart. SQL Server Data Tools creates the dimension and fact tables in this database later in the process.

**Steps**

1. Open the SQL Server Management Studio and connect to a development or test instance of the SQL Server database engine. Create a new database called **MaxMinSalesDM**, which uses the Simple recovery model. If you have any questions about creating this database, refer to Steps 3–5 in the "Learn By Doing—Creating the Maximum Miniatures Manufacturing Data Mart Using the SQL Server Management Studio" section of this chapter.

2. Close the SQL Server Management Studio.

3. Open the SQL Server Data Tools, as we discussed in Chapter 5.

4. Click the New Project button in the toolbar.

5. Make sure Business Intelligence | Analysis Services is selected in the Installed Templates area, and then select Analysis Services Multidimensional and Data Mining Project from the center area.

6. Enter **MaxMinSalesDM** for Name and set the Location to the appropriate folder. Check Create directory for solution.

**NOTE**

*You should create a folder to hold all of the Learn By Doing activities in this book. Make sure this folder is clearly named so it does not become confused with production source code.*

7. Click OK to create the project.

8. Once the project is open, right-click the Cubes folder in the Solution Explorer, and select New Cube from the context menu. The Cube Wizard dialog box appears.

9. On the Welcome page, click Next.

10. On the Select Creation Method page, select the Generate tables in the data source radio button. Leave (None) selected in the Template drop-down list. Click Next.

11. Click the highlighted cell in the Add new measures grid. Enter **Sales in Dollars** in the Measure Name column.

12. Enter **Sales Information** in the Measure Group column.

13. Select Currency in the Data Type column. Sum should be selected by default in the Aggregation column.

14. Click the cell containing "Add new measure" in the Add new measures grid.

15. Enter **Sales in Units** in the Measure Name column.

16. Make sure **Sales Information** is selected in the Measure Group column.

17. Select Integer in the Data Type column. Sum should be selected by default in the Aggregation column.

18. Click the cell containing "Add new measure" in the Add new measures grid.

19. Enter **Sales Tax** in the Measure Name column.

20. Make sure **Sales Information** is selected in the Measure Group column.

21. Select Currency in the Data Type column. Sum should be selected by default in the Aggregation column.

22. Click the cell containing "Add new measure" in the Add new measures grid.

23. Enter **Shipping** in the Measure Name column.

24. Make sure **Sales Information** is selected in the Measure Group column.

25. Select Currency in the Data Type column. Sum should be selected by default in the Aggregation column. The Define New Measures page should appear as shown in Figure 6-26.

26. Click Next.

27. The Select dimensions from template grid at the top of the Define New Dimensions page will create the Time dimension for us from a time dimension template. Make sure the Time dimension line remains checked.

28. Click the cell containing "Add new dimension" in the Add new dimensions grid.

29. Enter **Customer** in the Name column, and press TAB.

**Figure 6-26**    *After defining the measures in the Cube Wizard*

30. Click the cell containing "Add new dimension" and enter **Product** in the Name column. Press TAB.

31. Click the cell containing "Add new dimension" and enter **Promotion** in the Name column. Press TAB.

32. Click the cell containing "Add new dimension" and enter **Sales Person** in the Name column. Press TAB.

33. Check the box under SCD in the SalesPerson row.

### DEFINITION

*A Slowly Changing Dimension (SCD) varies over time. Of course, the data in many dimensions can change over time. What differentiates an SCD is the fact that the history of that change is important and must be tracked in the business intelligence information. For example, the salesperson dimension changes as salespeople are transferred from one sales territory to another. We need to track which territory a salesperson was in last year versus which territory they are in this year so sales can be rolled up into the correct territory for year-to-year comparisons.*

34. Click the cell containing "Add new dimension" and enter **Store** in the Name column. Press TAB. The Define New Dimensions page should appear as shown in Figure 6-27.

35. Click Next.

**Figure 6-27**   *After defining dimensions in the Cube Wizard*

**36.** The Define Time Periods page enables us to specify range, format, and hierarchy for the time dimension. Select Thursday, January 01, 2009 from the First calendar day date picker. Check Month, Quarter, and Year in Time periods. (Leave Date checked as well.) The Define Time Periods page appears as shown in Figure 6-28.

**Figure 6-28**   *After defining the time periods for the time dimension in the Cube Wizard*

**NOTE**

*If we use week in a time hierarchy, we can specify the first day of the week to use with this dimension. We can also specify the language to use for the members of the time dimension.*

37. Click Next.

38. The Specify Additional Calendars page lets us add calendars other than the standard 12-month calendar to the time dimension. The Specify Additional Calendars page is shown in Figure 6-29. This might include a calendar for a fiscal year that starts on a day other than January 1 or the ISO 8601 standard calendar. Max Min tracks sales based on the standard 12-month calendar, so simply click Next.

39. The Define Dimension Usage page enables us to specify which dimensions are related to each group of measures. The Max Min Sales data mart is only using one group of measures, called Sales Information, so we want all the dimensions to apply to this group. Check the box in the Sales Information column for all of the dimensions, as shown in Figure 6-30. Click Next.

40. The Completing the Wizard page lets us review the cube we defined. Enter **MaxMinSales** for the Cube name.

41. Check Generate schema now. This causes the Cube Wizard to create the relational database to hold the data mart that serves as the source for this cube.

42. We can expand the nodes in Preview to view the measures and dimensions that are to be created in this cube. Note, only the Time dimension has a hierarchy. We add other hierarchies manually. When all the nodes except the Attributes nodes are expanded, the Preview should appear as shown in Figure 6-31. Click Finish.

**Figure 6-29** *Specifying additional calendars in the Cube Wizard*

**Figure 6-30**    *Setting the dimension usage in the Cube Wizard*

**Figure 6-31**    *Completing the cube in the Cube Wizard*

43. Because we checked Generate Schema Now, the Schema Generation Wizard is automatically launched. On the Welcome to the Schema Generation Wizard page, click Next.

44. The Specify Target page enables us to select the database server where the data mart relational database is created. This is done by creating a data source and a data source view. Click New. The Data Source Wizard appears.

45. On the Welcome to the Data Source Wizard page, click Next. On the Select how to define the connection screen, click New.

46. The Connection Manager dialog box lets us define a connection string used to access a database. Provider enables you to select between .NET and OLE DB data providers. In this case, we leave Provider set to Native OLE DB\SQL Server Native Client 11.0. For Server Name, enter the name of the database server where you created the MaxMinSalesDM database in Step 1 of this section.

47. Select Use Windows Authentication under Log on to the server. The Schema Generation process requires Windows Authentication. Make sure that your current Windows credentials have rights to create tables in the MaxMinSalesDM database.

48. Select MaxMinSalesDM from the Select or enter a database name drop-down list. (A valid set of credentials must be specified before the drop-down list is populated.) The Connection Manager will appear as shown in Figure 6-32.

49. Click OK to exit the Connection Manager dialog box.

50. In the Select how to define the connection dialog box, click Next.

51. On the Impersonation Information page, if you are using Windows Authentication in your data connection, select "Use a specific Windows user name and password" and enter a valid Windows user name and password for database access. If you entered a specific SQL Server logon in the data connection, you do not need to worry about impersonation. Click Next. The Completing the Wizard page will appear.

**NOTE**

*Analysis Services needs to access the data mart relational database in order to populate and update the information in the Multidimensional BISM. This is done using the information in the data connection selected in Step 46. The Analysis Services updates may run as a background process. This can be an issue if the data connection specifies Windows Authentication or if the connection is to a file-based database such as Access. In these situations, Analysis Services needs to know what Windows credentials to use when accessing the data source. In other words, it needs to impersonate a Windows identity while accessing the data.*

52. The Completing the Wizard page shows the finished connection string. Click Finish to exit the Data Source Wizard.

53. We are now back to the Specify Target page of the Schema Generation Wizard. Click Next.

**Figure 6-32**  *The Connection Manager dialog box*

54. The Subject Area Database Schema Options page lets us select the operations we want the Schema Generation Wizard to perform. Uncheck the Enforce referential integrity check box. As stated earlier, we will let our ETL process enforce referential integrity. Populate should be selected from the Populate time table(s) drop-down list. Click Next.

**NOTE**

*There are three options for handling the population of the table for the time dimension. The Populate option creates records in the time dimension table for the timeframe specified on the Define Time Periods page in Step 36.*

55. The Specify Naming Conventions page enables us to determine how the tables and fields in the data mart are named. We use all the default settings. Click Next.

56. The Completing the Wizard page provides a summary of the schema generation we defined. Click Finish.

57. The Schema Generation Progress dialog box appears. This dialog box shows each step as the data mart (called the subject area database) is created. When the process has completed, the dialog box should appear similar to Figure 6-33. Click Close.

58. Click the Save All toolbar button.

**Figure 6-33** *The Schema Generation Progress dialog box with a successful process completion*

**NOTE**

*If an error occurs during the process, a red asterisk appears next to the last step, as shown in Figure 6-34. The text next to the red asterisk describes the error. If an error occurs, use the description to determine the cause of the error, click Stop to terminate the process, click Close, and then repeat the process with the problem corrected. The cube and the dimensions may have been created in the Analysis Services project before the error occurred. To restart the entire process, the cube and dimensions need to be deleted from the project. The most common cause of an error is not using Windows Authentication in the data source or being logged onto Windows with credentials that do not have rights to create tables in the MaxMinSalesDM database.*

59. Beyond the basic fields created for us in the Sales data mart, we need to add some fields to hold additional information coming from our data sources. We add these fields using the SQL Server Management Studio. Close SQL Server Data Tools.

60. Open the SQL Server Management Studio, and connect to the instance of the SQL Server database engine hosting the MaxMinSalesDM database.

**Schema Generation Progress**

- Generating Schema and Packages.
  - Start Time:16:51:45
  - Validating cubes and dimensions completed successfully.
  - Updating data source view for subject area completed successfully.
  - Preparing SQL for subject area database.
  - Property Login was not set.

| Show Details | Stop | Close | Help |

**Figure 6-34** *The Schema Generation Progress dialog box after an error has occurred*

61. Expand the Databases folder, and then expand the MaxMinSalesDM database. Finally, expand the Tables folder.
62. Right-click the dbo.Customer table entry, and select Design from the context menu.
63. Add the following columns to the Customer table:

| Column Name | Data Type | Allow Nulls |
|---|---|---|
| Address | nvarchar(50) | Checked |
| City | nvarchar(50) | Checked |
| State | nchar(2) | Checked |
| ZipCode | nvarchar(10) | Checked |
| Homeowner | nchar(1) | Checked |
| MaritalStatus | nchar(1) | Checked |
| NumCarsOwned | smallint | Checked |
| NumChildrenAtHome | smallint | Checked |

64. Close the table design tab. Click Yes when asked if you want to save changes.
65. Right-click the dbo.Product table entry, and select Design from the context menu.
66. Add the following columns to the Product table:

| Column Name | Data Type | Allow Nulls |
|---|---|---|
| RetailPrice | money | Checked |
| Weight | real | Checked |

67. Close the table design tab. Click Yes when asked if you want to save changes.
68. Right-click the dbo.Sales_Person table entry, and select Design from the context menu.
69. Add the following column to the Sales_Person table:

| Column Name | Data Type | Allow Nulls |
|---|---|---|
| Sales_Person_Territory | int | Checked |

70. Close the table design tab. Click Yes when asked if you want to save changes.
71. Right-click the dbo.Store table entry, and select Design from the context menu.
72. Add the following column to the Store table:

| Column Name | Data Type | Allow Nulls |
|---|---|---|
| Store_Type | nvarchar(50) | Checked |

73. Close the table design tab. Click Yes when asked if you want to save changes.

**Figure 6-35**    *The Max Min Sales star schema*

## The Sales Data Mart

We now have a Sales data mart along with an Analysis Services cube built on that data mart. The star schema that defines both the data mart and the cube is shown in Figure 6-35. (Note, the data source view shown in Figure 6-35 does not include the fields we manually added to the tables.) We can tell this is a star schema rather than a snowflake schema because all the levels in the time hierarchy are contained in a single Time table, rather than multiple linked tables. We will add fields to these tables and hierarchies to this cube later.

Also, note the fields in the Sales_Person table. Several fields contain SCD in the field name. These fields are included to help maintain the history of a member of this dimension. We see this in action in future examples.

# Table Compression

Our relational data warehouses may be called upon to store a copious amount of data. This can cause our fact tables and perhaps even some of our dimension tables to grow very large. Fortunately, SQL Server 2012 provides some relief in the form of table compression.

**NOTE**

*The table compression features described in this section require the Developer or Enterprise Edition of SQL Server.*

Table compression modifies the way data is physically stored on the disk drive in order to save space. It does not change the structure of a table, nor does it change the syntax used to SELECT, INSERT, UPDATE, or DELETE data in a table. Table compression is completely transparent to applications making use of the data. It simply makes more efficient use of disk space.

## Types of Table Compression

SQL Server offers two flavors of table compression for us to take advantage of. The first is *row compression*. Row compression works within each row of data.

The second type of table compression is *page compression*. Page compression works within the page structure that SQL Server uses to store data. Let's take a closer look at each of the compression types.

## Row Compression

Row compression reduces the space required to store a row of data. It does this by only using the bytes required to store a given value. For example, without row compression, a column of type int normally occupies 4 bytes. This is true if we are storing the number 1 or the number 1 million. SQL Server allocates enough space to store the maximum value possible for the data type.

When row compression is turned on, SQL Server makes smarter space allocations. It looks at the actual value being stored for a given column in a given row, and then determines the storage required to represent that value. This is done to the nearest whole byte.

Of course, this added complexity adds some overhead as data is inserted or updated in the table. It also adds a smaller amount of overhead when data is retrieved from that table. In most cases, the time taken for this additional processing is negligible. In fact, in some cases, the saving in disk read and disk write time can even be greater than the calculation time required for data compression.

## Page Compression

Page compression takes things a bit further than row compression. In fact, page compression starts by utilizing row compression. It then adds two other compression techniques: *prefix compression* and *dictionary compression*.

Prefix compression looks for values of a given column that have a common beginning within a page of data. If the rows are sorted by account number, then the account number fields that fall within a given page will probably start with the same digits. The same is true if the rows are sorted by last name. The last name fields that fall within a given page are all likely to start with the same characters.

Prefix compression is designed to take advantage of these situations. It determines these common prefixes, and then stores a representative of this common beginning, or prefix, in a reference row in the page header. Rather than storing this repeating prefix data in every row, a pointer to the reference row is used. The pointer to the reference row can even show where a given value diverges from the reference row.

Dictionary compression is applied after prefix compression. This compression scheme looks for repeating values within the page. A representative of the repeated value is placed in the page header. A pointer to the header entry is then used in place of each occurrence of the repeated value.

It is not necessary to understand the technical details of table compression. What is important is to know that we have ways to reduce the storage space required by large tables and, in general, make these tables more manageable. Fortunately, using table compression is much easier than understanding what is happening under the hood.

## Learn By Doing—Enabling Table Compression

### Features Highlighted

▶ Turning on table compression

▶ Using the sp_estimate_data_compression_savings stored procedure

**Business Need**    We want to decrease the disk space required by our fact tables. These tables will grow quite large as we gather a number of years' worth of manufacturing and inventory data for reporting.

**NOTE**

*The Developer or Enterprise Edition of SQL Server is required to complete this Learn By Doing exercise.*

**Steps**

1. Open the SQL Server Management Studio, if it is not already open, and connect to the SQL server hosting the MaxMinManufacturingDM database.
2. Click New Query to open a query window.
3. Select the MaxMinManufacturingDM database from the drop-down list in the toolbar.
4. Execute the following set of statements:

```
ALTER TABLE ManufacturingFact
REBUILD WITH (DATA_COMPRESSION = PAGE)
```

This statement turns on page compression for the fact table in the MaxMinManufacturingDM database.

5. Locate the ManufacturingFact table in the Object Explorer window. Right-click the ManufacturingFact table entry, and select Properties from the context menu. The Table Properties dialog box appears.
6. Select the Storage page of the Table Properties dialog box. Note the Compression type shown near the top of the page. This is shown in Figure 6-36.
7. Click OK to exit the Table Properties dialog box.
8. Click in the Query window, and then select the MaxMinSalesDM database from the drop-down list in the toolbar.
9. Execute the following statement:

```
EXEC sp_estimate_data_compression_savings 'dbo',
                  'Sales_Information', NULL, NULL, 'PAGE'
```

This system stored procedure calculates the amount of space that would be saved if page compression was applied to the Sales_Information table. This stored procedure works by sampling the actual data in the table to estimate compression savings. Of course, because we don't yet have any data in the Sales_Information table, we don't get any meaningful results from the stored procedure. Try executing this stored procedure again after you fill the Sales_Information table with data.

**Figure 6-36**   *The Table Properties dialog box showing page compression turned on*

# The Benefits of Integration

We now have designed two data mart structures to serve as the source for Analysis Services cubes. You might have noticed, however, if you look into either of these data marts, that they are completely empty (expect for the MaxMinSalesDM.Time table). There is not much business intelligence to be gleaned from an empty data mart!

We need to get data into our data marts. This is done using Integration Services. In the next two chapters, we look at the many and varied capabilities of Integration Services. We also develop and utilize some working Integration Services packages to populate our all-too-empty data marts, making them much more useful.

# Chapter 7

# Transformers—Integration Services Structure and Components

## In This Chapter

► **Integration Services**
► **Package Items**
► **Getting Under the Sink**

*There are painters who transform the sun to a yellow spot, but there are others who with the help of their art and their intelligence, transform a yellow spot into the sun.*

—Pablo Picasso

In the previous chapter, we created two data marts on our relational database server. As we pointed out at the end of Chapter 6, these data marts are not much use to us or our decision makers until they contain useful data. Fortunately, SQL Server 2012 has a tool designed for just such a purpose. This tool is Integration Services.

Integration Services enables us to change the location of data by copying it from our online transaction processing (OLTP) databases and other locations into the data mart. As it is being copied, we can also transform the data from the format required by the OLTP systems to the format required by the online analytical processing (OLAP) systems we are creating. Finally, we can verify foreign key values as we load the data. This enables us to implement our data mart database without foreign key constraints.

# Integration Services

Integration Services was introduced with SQL Server 2005. Prior to that, moving data from a data source to a data destination was done with a tool called Data Transformation Services (DTS). DTS offered a limited ability to change data as it was moved from source to destination. Integration Services provides all of the functionality of DTS in an environment that simultaneously offers more capabilities, with less programming and scripting required. In addition, Integration Services offers a large performance boost over DTS. In fact, performance continues to improve with the SQL Server 2012 incarnation of Integration Services.

## Package Structure

Integration Services and its predecessor, DTS, both create structures called packages, which are used to move data between systems. Packages in both tools contain data sources and data destinations. After that, however, the similarities between these two utilities come to an end. Integration Services represents a complete rethinking of Microsoft's approach to data transfer. The result is an easy-to-use, extremely flexible, exceedingly capable, and highly scalable data extract, transform, and load (ETL) tool.

One of the most obvious departures from DTS is in the design of the packages themselves. Where DTS combined control of the package's operation and the mapping of the data flow into one graphical layout, Integration Services splits the two apart. Separating these two related, but ultimately distinct, areas makes Integration Services packages easier to create and certainly much easier to maintain.

A package's overall operation is defined by the control flow. The *control flow* is the sequence of tasks that will be performed by the package. These may be tasks such as transferring a file using File Transfer Protocol (FTP), logging an event, truncating a table in preparation for a data load, or even e-mailing a status message to an administrator. Of course, one of the most-used control flow tasks is the *data flow task,* which moves data from one place to another.

The data flow task provides the plumbing for moving data from one or more sources to one or more destinations. Along the way, the data may be subjected to any number of transformation processes. Data can now be manipulated as it is flowing through "the pipeline" without having to be deposited in a temporary, working table, as in DTS. This capability to massage the data on-the-fly yields a cleaner and more streamlined ETL process and a much more efficient package.

Integration Services packages are created using an Integration Services project in SQL Server Data Tools. When we are working on an Integration Services project, the Designer window contains five tabs, as shown in Figure 7-1. Three of these tabs—the Control Flow Designer tab, the Data Flow Designer tab, and the Event Handlers Designer tab—let us define various types of functionality for the package. The Parameters tab allows us to manage any parameters used to pass information to the package. The Package Explorer tab provides an alternative view of the contents of the package. In addition to the tabs, there is a special area at the bottom of the Designer window for defining Connection Managers, which is called the *Connections tray.*

As stated earlier, each Integration Services package contains a control flow to define the overall operation of the package. This is shown in Figure 7-2. The control flow is defined by dragging items from the SSIS Toolbox onto the Control Flow Designer tab. When the Control Flow Designer tab is selected, only those tasks that can be used on this tab are displayed in the SSIS Toolbox, as shown in Figure 7-1.

An Integration Services package may contain several data flows. Each data flow is represented by a data flow task placed on the Control Flow Designer tab, as shown in Figure 7-2. A data flow task is created by dragging a data flow item from the SSIS Toolbox and placing it in the control flow. We need to drill down into a data flow task to define the contents of that data flow, as shown in Figure 7-3. This is done by double-clicking a data flow task on the Control Flow Designer tab or clicking the Data Flow Designer tab and selecting the correct data flow task from the drop-down list. We can now define the details of the data flow on the Data Flow Designer tab. As might be expected, only Data Flow control items are displayed in the SSIS Toolbox when the Data Flow Designer tab is selected.

Integration Services packages are event-driven. This means we can specify routines to execute when a particular event occurs. An *event* can be the completion of a task or

Control Flow Designer Tab  Data Flow Designer Tab  Parameters Tab  Event Handlers Designer Tab  Package Explorer Tab

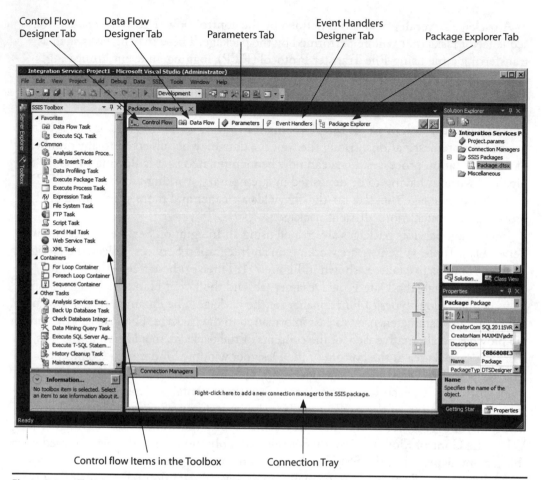

Control flow Items in the Toolbox     Connection Tray

**Figure 7-1**    *The Integration Services package design layout in SQL Server Data Tools*

an error that occurs during task execution. The routine for the event is known as an *event handler* and is defined as a *control flow*. However, event handler control flows are created on the Event Handlers Designer tab rather than on the Control Flow Designer tab, as shown in Figure 7-4.

The same control flow items that can be used on the Control Flow Designer tab can also be used to create event handler tasks on the Event Handlers Designer tab. These might include sending an e-mail to update the administrator on the status of a package or executing an alternative data flow when a task fails. When a data flow task is used in an event handler, the details of the data flow are defined on the Data Flow Designer tab, as shown in Figure 7-5.

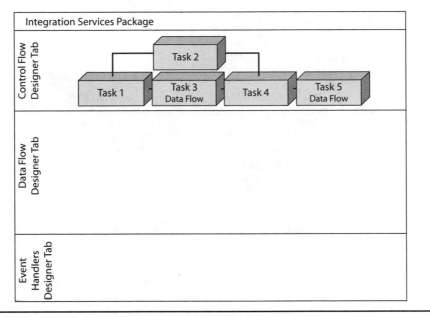

**Figure 7-2**    *The Integration Services package structure Control Flow Designer tab*

**Figure 7-3**    *The Integration Services package structure Data Flow Designer tab*

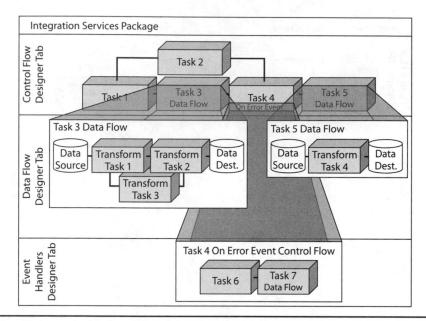

**Figure 7-4**   *The Integration Services package structure Event Handlers Designer tab*

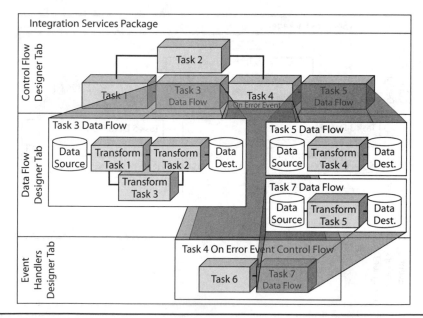

**Figure 7-5**   *Defining a data flow task in an event handler control flow*

The rightmost tab of the Designer window in Figure 7-1 provides access to the Package Explorer. The *Package Explorer* displays all the contents of the Integration Services package in a single tree-view structure. In addition to the control flow tasks, data flow tasks, and event handler tasks, the Package Explorer displays all the parameters and variables available for use in the package. We discuss the use of parameters and variables in Integration Services packages (as well as the Parameters tab) in Chapter 8.

The Connections tray is used to manage all the connections in the package. This includes paths to flat files and connection strings for databases. Rather than having this spread throughout the package, all this connection information is stored in the Connections tray. This makes it much easier to locate and manage the connection information as paths, server names, and login credentials change, or as the package is used in different server environments.

## Drag-and-Drop Programming

Creating nontrivial data transfer packages with DTS usually required someone with a programming background. A certain amount of Visual Basic script or SQL queries were generally required to accomplish even the most straightforward data loading and data cleansing tasks. This blurred the line between database administration tasks and development tasks, while tending to complicate database management.

In a number of cases, the data could not be cleansed prior to loading it into the database. It was just too complicated to implement the aggregations, lookups, and validations as operations in the DTS pipeline. In these situations, the data had to be placed in a staging table in SQL Server. SQL queries would then be developed to do the cleansing tasks, again requiring someone with database development know-how. The SQL queries, not the DTS package, were ultimately responsible for copying the data to its final destination. This has been referred to as ELT (extract, load, and transform) rather than the more traditional, and far more efficient, ETL.

Integration Services is designed to eliminate both the need for a developer and the need for any ELT-mode operations. Integration Services uses a drag-and-drop development style. Task items are dragged from the SSIS Toolbox and placed on the Designer workspace. The behavior of these tasks is controlled by setting properties in the dialog box associated with each task and by connecting the output from one task to the input of another. Some expressions may be required, but these tend to be straightforward, single-line comparison statements, rather than more complicated, multiline programming constructs.

Almost all the data manipulations that required staging tables in DTS can now be done through Integration Services tasks without writing the data to disk. These tasks work with the data in buffers kept in physical memory. Pointers to these memory buffers are passed from one task to another throughout the processing. The only time data is written to disk during a data pipeline process is when it exceeds the size of the physical memory available. All of this makes it easy to develop complex packages while ensuring fast, efficient operation.

## Control Flow Tasks

As we create our Integration Services packages, we use a top-down approach. First, we use the Control Flow Designer tab to define the tasks that the package will perform. Next, we use precedence arrows to define the tasks' order of execution and any dependencies between them. Then, we drill down into each of the data flow tasks to define their operation. Finally, we add any event handlers or other programming needed to get the package functioning in the manner required.

We begin, then, on the Control Flow Designer tab, by specifying the tasks that must be accomplished by the package. We create tasks by dragging Control Flow items from the SSIS Toolbox and placing them on the Control Flow Designer tab. Each item taken from the SSIS Toolbox becomes a control flow task. This is shown in Figure 7-6.

The red circle with the white *X* on the control flow task indicates that the task is in an error state because some of the required properties for the task have not been set or have been set improperly. Hovering the mouse over a task with this symbol displays a message explaining the error. In other situations, a yellow triangle with a black

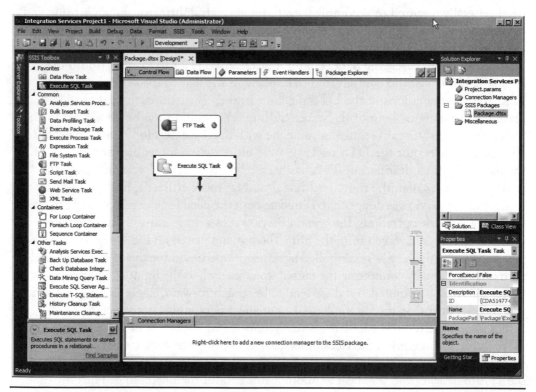

**Figure 7-6**    *Creating control flow tasks from the SSIS Toolbox*

exclamation point appears on a task. This indicates a warning message is associated with this task. Again, hovering the mouse over the task displays the warning message. A task with a warning executes, but a task with an error does not.

We can set the properties of a task by double-clicking the task to display its Editor dialog box. This is shown in Figure 7-7. We can also select the task and modify its properties using the Properties window. We look at the properties of each task in detail in the next section of this chapter.

When creating an Integration Services package, it is important to change the default name for each task that is placed in the package. The names should be changed to a phrase that accurately describes the functionality performed by that task. It is also a good idea to enter a short explanation of each task in the Description property of the task. The description is displayed when we hover over the task on the Control Flow Designer tab. Entering meaningful information for each task makes the package self-documenting and, consequently, much easier to test, debug, and maintain.

**Figure 7-7**    *Setting the properties of a task using the task's Editor dialog box*

## Connection Managers

Any time a control flow task must make a connection to a database or to the file system, this connection information is stored in a Connection Manager in the Connections tray. This makes it easier to move packages from one server to another or from a development environment to a production environment. When database connection information or file system paths need to be modified to work on a different server, we do not need to look for them throughout the package. Instead, they are conveniently located in one place: the Connections tray.

We take a look at creating some of the most commonly used connections in the "Learn By Doing" sections in Chapter 8.

## Precedence Arrows

We control the order in which tasks are executed by connecting the precedence arrow from one task to the task that is to run after it. To do this, we select a task and then click the green arrow that appears below that task. We drag this arrow until the mouse pointer is over the task that should follow during execution. This is shown in Figure 7-8. When we release the mouse button, the green arrow connects the two tasks, as shown in Figure 7-9. This is known as a *precedence constraint* because it constrains one task to run after another.

By default, the precedence arrow is green, meaning the second task will execute only after the successful completion of the first task. This is the "Success" precedence. When we right-click the arrow, a context menu appears, as shown in Figure 7-10. Three options on the context menu—Success, Failure, and Completion—allow us to select the type of precedence the arrow represents.

**Figure 7-8**   *Making a precedence connection between two tasks*

**Figure 7-9**    *The precedence arrow*

## NOTE

*For those with red-green color blindness, you can use Tools | Options on the main menu to display the Options dialog box. In the Options dialog box, go to the Business Intelligence Designers | Integration Services Designers | General page, and select Show precedence constraint labels under Accessibility. This will display a label on each precedence constraint arrow, in addition to the color coding.*

**Figure 7-10**    *The precedence arrow context menu*

When we select Failure from the context menu, the precedence arrow changes from green to red. With "Failure" precedence, the second task executes only after the failure of the first task. When we select Completion from the context menu, the precedence arrow changes to blue. With "Completion" precedence, the second task executes after the first task has completed without regard to whether the first task succeeded or failed.

A single task can have multiple precedence arrows connecting it to other tasks. When we select a task that already has its precedence arrow connected to another task, a second precedence arrow automatically appears. This is shown in Figure 7-11. This second arrow can be connected to another task. When a task has two precedence arrows connected to subsequent tasks, a third arrow appears. And so on. Each of these precedence arrows can be set to Success, Failure, or Completion as appropriate. The result can be a complex sequence of tasks, such as the one shown in Figure 7-12.

We can double-click a precedence arrow or right-click the arrow and select Edit from the context menu to access the Precedence Constraint Editor dialog box, shown in Figure 7-13. The Value drop-down list on this dialog box provides another way to select among Success, Failure, and Completion. If these three options do not provide enough flexibility, we can also attach expressions to a precedence arrow.

If the Evaluation Operation drop-down list is set to Expression, then the contents of the expression must evaluate to true before this precedence path is taken. If the Evaluation Operation drop-down list is set to Expression and Constraint, the contents of the expression must be true and the constraint selected in the Value drop-down list must match the result of the task execution. If the Evaluation Operation drop-down list is set to Expression or Constraint, either the contents of the expression must be true or the constraint selected in the Value drop-down list must match the result of the task execution. We discuss Integration Services expressions in Chapter 8.

The Multiple Constraints section at the bottom of the Precedence Constraint Editor dialog box determines the behavior when more than one precedence arrow connects

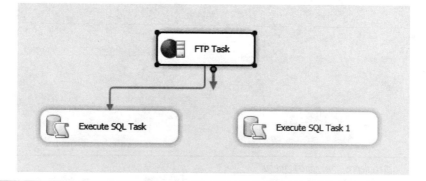

**Figure 7-11** *A control flow task with a second precedence arrow*

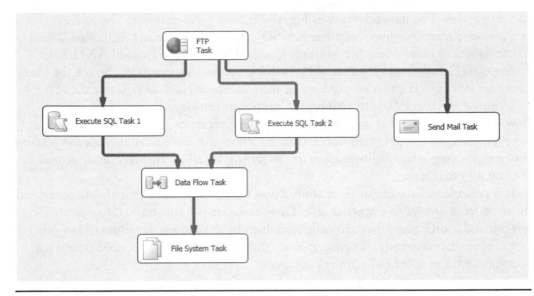

**Figure 7-12**    *Using precedence arrows to make a complex sequence of tasks*

**Figure 7-13**    *The Precedence Constraint Editor dialog box* to a single task. The data flow task in Figure 7-12 is a good example. The Success precedence constraints from both Execute SQL Task 1 and Execute SQL Task 2 lead to the data flow task. When the Multiple Constraints setting is Logical AND, both Execute SQL Task 1 and Execute SQL Task 2 must finish successfully before the data flow task executes. If either one or both of the Execute SQL tasks fails, the data flow task cannot execute. When the Multiple Constraints setting is Logical OR, the data flow task executes if either one or the other of the Execute SQL tasks is successful. Changing the Multiple Constraints setting on any one of the precedence arrows leading into a task changes the Multiple Constraints setting for all of the precedence arrows leading into that task.

It is possible to have one or more control flow tasks in a package that are not connected by precedence arrows to any other task. These tasks are not constrained to execute in any particular order, and they are not constrained by the success or failure of any other task. These disconnected tasks execute every time the package is run, no matter what happens with the other tasks in the package.

## Data Flow

Once we set the precedence constraints for the control flow tasks in the package, we can define each of the data flows. This is done on the Data Flow Designer tab. Each data flow task that was added to the control flow has its own layout on the Data Flow Designer tab. We can switch between different data flows using the Data Flow Task drop-down list located at the top of the Data Flow tab.

The Data Flow SSIS Toolbox contains three types of items: data flow sources, data flow transformations, and data flow destinations. Data flow sources enable us to read data from almost any vendor's relational database, flat file, or Extensible Markup Language (XML) source. Data flow destinations let us write data to these same locations, as well as to certain Analysis Services structures. Data flow transformations operate on the data as it moves through the data flow. In most cases, the transformations change the data to increase its appropriateness for the destination.

Data flow tasks are connected by flow path arrows. These are connected in the same way that control flow tasks are connected by precedence arrows. Green flow path arrows indicate the route that valid data will take through the task. This is the output flow of the task. Red flow path arrows indicate the route that invalid data follow. This is the error flow of the task.

The flow path from a data source to a data destination is called a *data flow segment*. The simplest data flow segment has only a single source and a single destination, connected by a flow path. This type of segment simply copies data from one place to another. Transformation tasks are added to the segment to modify the data as it moves from the source to the destination. In fact, as we see in the sections on data flow, we can do some sophisticated data manipulation using the transformation tasks in Integration Services.

Data flow segments may contain multiple data sources, with the data flow from each source being combined with a merge or union task. Likewise, a segment may have multiple data destinations, with the data flow being divided by an error path, a conditional split task, or a multicast task. We gain even more flexibility with the ability to have multiple, distinct data segments in the same data flow.

When a data flow has multiple segments, the order in which the segments are executed is determined by the execution plan created at run time. This means that we cannot depend on the order in which multiple segments are executed within a single data flow. If the multiple segments are performing independent tasks, such as loading data into different dimensions of a data mart, this is not a problem. However, if these multiple segments are performing dependent tasks, such that one segment must be completed before another segment can begin, the segments should be split up into different data flow tasks. The order of execution can then be enforced by a precedence arrow from one data flow task to the other on the Control Flow Designer tab.

# Package Items

In this section, we take a look at the Control Flow and Data Flow items that can be used in an Integration Services package. We discuss how each item can be used in a package, and we look at the task dialog box provided for configuring each task. Because of the tremendous amount of capability and flexibility available from Integration Services tasks, it would take the remainder of this book, and then some, to provide a complete description. Instead, this section is intended to give you some familiarity with the purpose and capabilities of each task.

## Control Flow

The Control Flow SSIS Toolbox contains three types of objects: Containers, Control Flow tasks, and Maintenance Plan tasks. Each object has a dialog box that lets us configure that component in a straightforward manner. The dialog box is launched by double-clicking the component in the design area or right-clicking the item and selecting Edit from the context menu.

### Control Flow SSIS Toolbox Organization

The Control Flow SSIS Toolbox is divided into several sections: Favorites, Common, Containers, and Other Tasks. These divisions are designed to help you more easily find objects within the SSIS Toolbox. The Favorites section is for the objects you use most often. The Common section is for objects that are used often, but not as frequently as the favorites. Containers are set aside in their own section because they function differently than the other objects. Everything else ends up in the Other Tasks section.

You can move objects between sections to customize the arrangement to suit your tastes. Right-click an object in the SSIS Toolbox to bring up the context menu. Then select the section where you would like the object to be moved. You can expand or hide any of these sections by clicking the triangle to the left of the section name.

## Containers

We begin by looking at the Containers. *Containers* are a special type of item that can hold other Control Flow items and Maintenance Plan tasks. They help us repeat a set of tasks or organize groups of tasks within the package.

**For Loop Container**   The *For Loop Container* enables us to repeat a segment of a

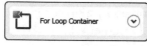

control flow. In this way, it functions much the same as a FOR...NEXT loop in Visual Basic or a *for* loop in C#. The For Loop container in Figure 7-14 executes the Execute SQL task and the Data Flow task multiple times.

The number of times the content of the container is executed is controlled by three properties of the For Loop container: InitExpression, EvalExpression,

**Figure 7-14**   *A For Loop container in a control flow*

**Figure 7-15**    *The For Loop Editor dialog box*

and AssignExpression. These properties are shown in the For Loop Editor dialog box in Figure 7-15. The InitExpression is executed once at the beginning of the loop to initialize the variable (or other item) that is controlling the loop. The EvalExpression is then evaluated. If the EvalExpression evaluates to true, the loop's content is executed. If the EvalExpression is false, the loop is exited. After each execution of the loop's contents, the AssignExpression is evaluated, followed by another evaluation of the EvalExpression.

The For Loop in Figure 7-15 is using a variable called @LoopCounter in the expressions to control the number of times the loop is executed. (We discuss variables and Integration Services expressions in Chapter 8.) We don't need to use an explicit loop counter variable to control the loop. In fact, any valid expression that results in a true value while the loop should continue and a false value when it is complete can be used in the EvalExpression property to control the number of iterations. The InitExpression and AssignExpression properties can be left empty if the mechanism controlling the number of iterations does not require a separate expression for initialization or modification of the counter.

**Foreach Loop Container**    Like the For Loop container, the Foreach Loop container

also provides a way of repeating a segment of a control flow. However, rather than have an expression to control when the loop is exited, the *Foreach Loop container* iterates one time for each item in a collection. The following collections can be used:

- ► Each file in a given folder matching a given file specification
- ► Each row of the first table in an ADO recordset or an ADO.NET dataset
- ► Each row of all tables in an ADO.NET dataset
- ► Each table in an ADO.NET dataset
- ► Each item from a variable that holds a collection
- ► Each node in an XML nodelist
- ► Each object in an SMO collection

Each time the Foreach Loop iterates, it selects a different object from the collection. The name of this object can then be mapped to one or more properties of the control flow tasks inside the container. In this way, the tasks inside the container can operate on each object in the collection.

For example, Figure 7-16 shows the Nightly Transfer package. This package uses FTP to transfer data files from a mainframe to the C:\FTP_RCV directory on the server. Several .dat files may be received by a given transfer. After the FTP transfer is complete, the Foreach Loop processes each of the files that are received. The Collection page of the Foreach Loop Editor dialog box in Figure 7-17 shows the configuration of the Foreach Loop necessary to accomplish this task.

The Data Flow task and the File System task within the Foreach Loop use the Received.DAT Files connection, shown at the bottom of Figure 7-16, to operate on a given data file received from the mainframe. For the Data Flow task and the File System task to operate on each file received, we need a way to change the connection string of the Received.DAT connection for each iteration of the loop. To do this, we first assign the fully qualified filename to a variable. This is done on the Variable Mappings page of the Foreach Loop container as follows:

| Variable | Index |
|----------|-------|
| User::FileName | 0 |

User::FileName is a user variable in the package. The entry in the Index column is an index to the Foreach Loop collection. When used with a collection of files, index 0 contains the file specification and is the only valid index. Next we create an expression in the Received.DAT Connection Manager to assign the value of the User::FileName to its ConnectionString.

**Figure 7-16**  *The Nightly Transfer package using a Foreach Loop container*

**Sequence Container**  Unlike the For Loop and Foreach Loop containers, the Sequence container does not change the control flow. Instead, the purpose of the *Sequence container* is to help organize tasks in a package. The Sequence container can be used to do the following:

▶  Organize a large package into logical sections for easier development and debugging

▶  Manage properties for a group of tasks by setting the properties on the container, rather than on the individual tasks

**Figure 7-17**   *The Collection page of the Foreach Loop container in the Nightly Transfer package*

▶ Allow a group of tasks to be easily enabled or disabled to aid package development and debugging

▶ Provide a variable scope that includes multiple tasks, but does not include the entire package

All of the container objects—For Loop, Foreach Loop, and Sequence—have the capability to hide their content. Figure 7-18 shows two Sequence containers. Sequence Container 2 is hiding its content. The content of a container is hidden or shown by clicking the down arrow, indicated by the mouse pointer in Figure 7-18.

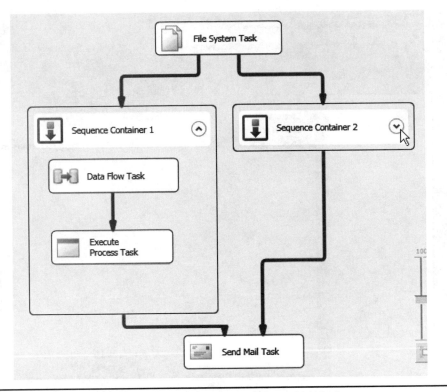

**Figure 7-18**    *Sequence Container 1 is showing its content. Sequence Container 2 is hiding its content.*

## Control Flow Items

Control Flow items implement the ETL process. They enable us to manipulate the source and destination environments to prepare for, execute, and clean up after a data transfer. The Control Flow items include the Data Flow task that implements the actual transfer of data from source to destination.

**Analysis Services Execute DDL Task**    The *Analysis Services Execute DDL task* enables us to run a statement on an Analysis Services server. The statement must be a valid Data Definition Language (DDL) query, which lets us create, modify, delete, and process Analysis Services objects, such as cubes and dimensions. The Analysis Services Execute DDL Task Editor dialog box is shown in Figure 7-19.

**Analysis Services Processing Task**    The *Analysis Services Processing task* enables us to process objects in Analysis Services. This can include cubes, dimensions, and data mining models. This is

**Figure 7-19**   *The Analysis Services Execute DDL Task Editor dialog box*

important after we have made major data changes that affect any of these objects. The Analysis Services Processing Task Editor dialog box is shown in Figure 7-20.

**Bulk Insert Task**   The *Bulk Insert task* lets us rapidly copy data from a text file into a SQL Server table or view. This is equivalent to using the bcp utility program to do a bulk data load. In fact, we can use a bcp format file with the Bulk Insert task. The Bulk Insert Task Editor dialog box is shown in Figure 7-21.

The Bulk Insert task is the fastest way to move large amounts of data into a SQL table. Remember, however, that this data must come from a text file directly and it cannot be transformed as it is being moved. Also, keep in mind that the Bulk Insert task always appends the data to any existing data in the target table.

**Figure 7-20**    *The Analysis Services Processing Task Editor dialog box*

**CDC Control Task**    The *CDC Control Task* is used to implement change data capture for a table within Integration Services. It plays four different roles in the change data capture process. This is determined by the CDC control operation property.

The change data capture process requires two Integration Services packages. The first package is run once to do the initial load of data from the source table to the destination table. This is the Initial Load package. The second package is run periodically to take the incremental changes made to the source table and apply them to the destination table. This is the Incremental Load package.

**Figure 7-21**    *The Bulk Insert Task Editor dialog box*

The CDC Control Task is used in the Initial Load package to record the Log Sequence Number at the beginning of the data load and at the end of the data load. To accomplish this, a CDC Control Task is placed at the beginning of the control flow with the CDC control operation property set to "Mark initial load start." This is followed in the control flow by the Data Flow task that copies the records from the source to the destination. Finally, a second CDC Control Task is placed in the control flow after the Data Flow task. This second CDC Control Task is configured the same as the first CDC Control Task with the exception of its CDC control operation property, which is set to "Mark initial load end."

The CDC Control Task is used in the Incremental Load package in conjunction with the CDC Source in the data flow. The CDC Control Task determines which changes to the source table have not yet been applied to the destination table. The CDC Source uses that information to ensure it only sends the unapplied data changes through the data flow. (More on the CDC Source in the "Data Flow Sources" section of this chapter.) The CDC Control Task is placed at the beginning of the control flow with the CDC control operation property set to "Get processing range." This is followed by a Data Flow task that utilizes the CDC Source to send the unapplied changes to the destination table. Additional control flow tasks may be required to complete the application of the updates and deletes on the destination table. At the end of the control flow, a second CDC Control Task is used to mark the changes as applied. This second CDC Control Task has a CDC control operation property setting of "Mark processed range."

**Data Flow Task**   As was stated earlier, the detail of each *Data Flow task* is configured

using the Data Flow tab. The next section of this chapter contains information about each of the items that may be used on the Data Flow tab.

**Data Mining Query Task**   The *Data Mining Query task* lets us execute a Data Mining Expression (DMX) query against an existing data mining structure. The DMX query enables us to feed parameter values to a data mining model, and then have that mining model make predictions for us based on those parameters. The Mining Model tab of the Data Mining Query Task Editor dialog box is shown in Figure 7-22.

**Figure 7-22**   *The Mining Model tab of the Data Mining Query Task Editor dialog box*

If the selected data mining structure contains multiple data mining models, our DMX query can be run against more than one of these models. The DMX query results are stored in relational database tables. If the result of the DMX query includes nested tables, those tables are flattened before they are stored in the relational database tables. We discuss data mining in Part V of this book.

**Data Profiling Task**     The *Data Profiling task* gathers information about a set of data. This can be used to determine information about a particular set of data we intend to process through an Integration Services package. We can use this information to make intelligent decisions as we design the package that will process this data and the data mart tables that will contain it.

The following profiling operations can be done using this task:

▶ **Candidate Key Profile Request**     Determines whether a column or a set of columns is a unique identifier for the rows in a table. Valid for integer, character, and date/time data types.

▶ **Column Length Distribution Profile Request**     Provides a list of the distinct string lengths present in a column. Valid for character data types.

▶ **Column Null Ratio Profile Request**     Reports the number of NULLS in a column as a percentage of the total number of rows. Valid for all data types.

▶ **Column Pattern Profile Request**     Determines a set of regular expressions that are valid for a specified percentage of the values in a column. Valid for character data types.

▶ **Column Statistics Profile Request**     Finds the maximum, minimum, average, and standard deviation of the data in a numeric column. Finds the maximum and minimum of the data in a date/time column. Valid for numeric and date/time data types.

▶ **Column Value Distribution Profile Request**     Reports the distinct set of values in a column and the number of occurrences of that value as a percentage of the total number of rows. Valid for integer, character, and date/time data types.

▶ **Functional Dependency Profile Request**     Determines how much the value in one column is dependent on the value in another column or set of columns. Valid for integer, character, and date/time data types.

▶ **Value Inclusion Profile Request**     Calculates the commonality of values in two columns or sets of columns. We can use this to determine whether a specific column can be used as a foreign key. Valid for integer, character, and date/time data types.

The Data Profiling Task Editor dialog box is shown in Figure 7-23.

The Data Profiling task outputs its findings to an XML file. This file can be viewed using the Data Profile Viewer. The Data Profile Viewer is run from the Start menu by selecting All Programs | Microsoft SQL Server 2012 | Integration Services | Data Profile Viewer. The Data Profile Viewer is shown in Figure 7-24.

**Figure 7-23**    *The Data Profiling Task Editor dialog box*

**Figure 7-24** *The Data Profile Viewer*

**Execute Package Task** The *Execute Package task* lets us execute a different Integration
Services package. The package containing the Execute Package
task is the parent package, and the package being executed by
that task is the child package. The child package can be stored in SQL Server or in a
structured storage file.

The child package can execute as a separate process by setting the ExecuteOutOfProcess
property to true. Otherwise, it executes in the same process as the parent package.
Executing a child package as a separate process means an error in the child process cannot
crash the parent process. Creating separate processes for each child package does, however,
add some overhead each time a child package is launched.

The Execute Package Task Editor dialog box is shown in Figure 7-25.

**Execute Process Task** The *Execute Process task* enables us to execute a program or
a batch file as part of an Integration Services package. This task
can be used to do such things as unzipping compressed files. The
Execute Process Task Editor dialog box lets us specify the command-line arguments
and working directory, as shown in Figure 7-26. We can also specify variables for the
standard input, standard output, and standard error of the process.

**Execute SQL Task** The *Execute SQL task* enables us to execute SQL statements or
stored procedures. The contents of variables can be used for input,
output, or input/output parameters and the return value. We can

**Figure 7-25**   *The Execute Package Task Editor dialog box*

also save the result set from the SQL statements or stored procedure in a package variable. This result set could be a single value, a multirow/multicolumn result set, or an XML document. The Execute SQL Task Editor dialog box is shown in Figure 7-27.

**Expression Task**   The *Expression task* enables us to assign a value to a variable. Using the Expression Builder dialog box, shown in Figure 7-28, we can build a valid assignment statement in the Expression area. The Evaluate Expression button ensures the assignment statement is valid and shows the resulting value. During package execution, the value that results from the expression at that time will be assigned to the variable specified in the assignment statement.

**Figure 7-26**  *The Execute Process Task Editor dialog box*

**File System Task**  The *File System task* lets us perform one of the following file system functions:

File System Task

▶ Copy a directory

▶ Copy a file

▶ Create a directory

▶ Delete a directory

▶ Delete the contents of a directory

- ▶ Delete a file
- ▶ Move a directory
- ▶ Move a file
- ▶ Rename a file
- ▶ Set the attributes of a directory or file

**Figure 7-27**   *The Execute SQL Task Editor dialog box*

**Figure 7-28**　*The Expression Builder dialog box*

We must create a File Connection Manager in the Connections tray to specify the source and, if necessary, the destination for the file operation. The File System Task Editor dialog box is shown in Figure 7-29.

**FTP Task**　The *FTP task* enables us to perform the following functions on an FTP site:

- ► Send files
- ► Receive files
- ► Create a local directory

- ▶ Create a remote directory
- ▶ Remove a local directory
- ▶ Remove a remote directory
- ▶ Delete local files
- ▶ Delete remote files

We must create an FTP Connection Manager in the Connections tray to specify the address and login credentials for the FTP server. In addition, a File Connection Manager or the content of a package variable is used to specify the local path for the transfer. The FTP Task Editor dialog box is shown in Figure 7-30.

**Figure 7-29**  *The File System Task Editor dialog box*

**Figure 7-30**    *The FTP Task Editor dialog box*

**Message Queue Task**    The *Message Queue task* lets us send a Microsoft Message Queue (MSMQ) message to a different Integration Services package or to the message queue of another application. This messaging can be used to provide coordinated, but asynchronous, processing between various tasks. A message can be any of the following:

▶   A data file

▶   The contents of one or more variables

▶   A string

We must create an MSMQ Connection Manager in the Connections tray to specify the MSMQ queue to use with this task. The Message Queue Task Editor dialog box is shown in Figure 7-31.

**Script Task**    The *Script task* enables us to create .NET code for execution as part of our Integration Services package. The Script task can be used to execute transformations, perform complex calculations, or implement business logic that cannot be created using the other Integration Services tasks. The code resulting from a Script task can be precompiled for superior performance and scalability.

**Figure 7-31**    *The Message Queue Task Editor dialog box*

The Script Task Editor dialog box is shown in Figure 7-32. This dialog box is used to specify the .NET language used to create the script, as well as whether the script is precompiled. When a script is precompiled, the code is compiled as soon as the script is saved in the package. The compiled code is then saved in the package as well. This allows for much faster execution when the package is run. The only disadvantage to this approach is this: the size of the package becomes larger because it contains both the source code and the compiled version of that source code.

The EntryPoint property specifies which method is to be executed first when the Script task is run. The ReadOnlyVariables and ReadWriteVariables properties contain comma-separated lists of variables that are to be made available, either as read-only variables or as read-write variables, within the script. You can type in these variable names or use the ellipses (…) button to select the variables from a scrolling list in the Select Variables dialog box.

**Figure 7-32** *The Script Task Editor dialog box*

Variables are accessed in our script using C# code similar to the following:

```
double GrossSales;

GrossSales = (double)Dts.Variables["GrossSalesAmt"].Value;

Dts.Variables["CurrentAmt"].Value = GrossSales;
```

where "GrossSalesAmt" and "CurrentAmt" are package variables. The equivalent Visual Basic code looks like this:

```
Dim GrossSales As Double

GrossSales = CDbl(Dts.Variables("GrossSalesAmt").Value)

Dts.Variables("CurrentAmt").Value = GrossSales
```

The value of a variable is always returned as a type object and must be cast to the appropriate type. Clicking Edit Script displays the Script Editing window, as shown in Figure 7-33.

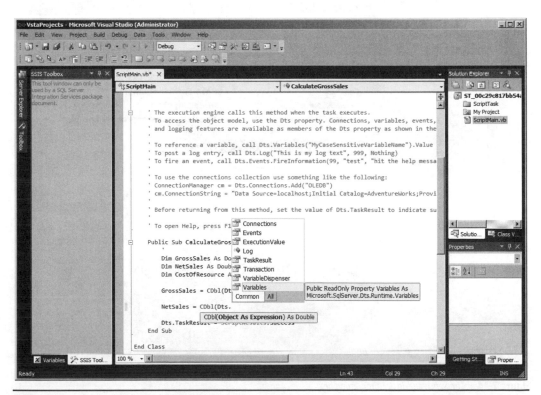

**Figure 7-33**    *The Script Task Script Editing window*

**Send Mail Task** The *Send Mail task* lets us send an e-mail message as part of our Integration Services package. This can be useful for alerting an administrator to an error condition or notifying a key user that a critical process has completed. The Send Mail task uses a Simple Mail Transfer Protocol (SMTP) server to deliver the e-mail. We must create an SMTP Connection Manager in the Connections tray to specify the SMTP server to use with this task. The Send Mail Task Editor dialog box is shown in Figure 7-34.

The content of the e-mail message can come from a file or a package variable, or it can be directly input as a string. If a file is used, we must create a File Connection Manager in the Connections tray pointing to that file. One or more files can be attached by specifying the path to each file in the Attachments property. If multiple files are attached, the paths are separated by semicolons.

**Figure 7-34** *The Send Mail Task Editor dialog box*

### Transfer Database Task, Transfer Error Messages Task, Transfer Jobs Task, Transfer Logins Task, Transfer Master Stored Procedures Task, Transfer SQL Server Objects Task

There are a number of Control Flow items for transferring SQL Server objects from one server to another. The *Transfer Database task* is used to either transfer or move an entire database. Using the *Transfer Error Messages task*, we can copy user-defined error messages. The *Transfer Jobs task* is used to copy SQL Agent Jobs. The *Transfer Logins task* copies one or more SQL logins. Using the *Transfer Master Stored Procedures task*, we can copy user-defined stored procedures between master databases.

The *Transfer SQL Server Objects task* is used to copy any of the following items:

| Object | SQL Server Version |
| --- | --- |
| Tables | 2000, 2005, 2008, 2008 R2, or 2012 |
| Views | 2000, 2005, 2008, 2008 R2, or 2012 |
| Stored Procedures | 2000, 2005, 2008, 2008 R2, or 2012 |
| User-Defined Functions | 2000, 2005, 2008, 2008 R2, or 2012 |
| Defaults | 2000, 2005, 2008, 2008 R2, or 2012 |
| User-Defined Data Types | 2000, 2005, 2008, 2008 R2, or 2012 |
| Partition Functions | 2005, 2008, 2008 R2, or 2012 |
| Partition Schemes | 2005, 2008, 2008 R2, or 2012 |
| Schemas | 2005, 2008, 2008 R2, or 2012 |
| Assemblies | 2005, 2008, 2008 R2, or 2012 |
| User-Defined Aggregates | 2005, 2008, 2008 R2, or 2012 |
| User-Defined Types | 2005, 2008, 2008 R2, or 2012 |
| XML Schema Collection | 2005, 2008, 2008 R2, or 2012 |

### Web Service Task

The *Web Service task* lets us execute a web service method as part of our Integration Services package. We must create an HTTP Connection Manager in the Connections tray to specify the connection to the web service. Once a connection has been specified, a Web Services Description Language file must be located to define the web methods that are available. We can then select the web method we want to execute, along with the parameters to be passed to that web method. This is shown in the Web Service Task Editor dialog box in Figure 7-35. The result returned by the web method call can be stored in a package variable or a file specified by a File Connection Manager in the Connections tray.

**WMI Data Reader Task** The *WMI Data Reader task* enables us to execute a Windows Management Instrumentation (WMI) query to retrieve data about a computer. This could include data from an event log, a list of installed applications and their current versions, or the state of computer hardware. We must create a WMI Connection Manager in the Connections tray to specify the computer that we want to query. The WMI Data Reader Task Editor dialog box is shown in Figure 7-36.

A *WMI query* is used to select the desired information. The output of the WMI query can be returned as a table, a set of property values, or a set of property name/value pairs. The output can be stored in a file, specified by a File Connection Manager, or in a package variable.

**Figure 7-35** *The Web Service Task Editor dialog box*

**Figure 7-36**    *The WMI Data Reader Task Editor dialog box*

**WMI Event Watcher Task**    The *WMI Event Watcher task* lets us wait for a specific computer system event or state before continuing the execution of the Integration Services package. This enables us to do things, such as wait for the server load to drop below a certain level or wait for a file to be copied to a specified folder. We must create a WMI Connection Manager in the Connections tray to specify the computer that we want to watch for the event. The WMI Event Watcher Task Editor dialog box is shown in Figure 7-37.

A WMI query is used to specify the event we want to watch for. We can then specify the desired behavior when the event occurs. The ActionAtEvent property determines if the event is simply logged or if it is logged and, at the same time, fires the Integration Services WMIEventWatcherEventOccurred event. If this Integration Services event is being fired, we can then provide an event handler. (This is covered in Chapter 8.) The

**Figure 7-37** *The WMI Event Watcher Task Editor dialog box*

AfterEvent property determines if this task exits with a success status after the event occurs, exits with a failure status after the event occurs, or waits for another event. If we are waiting for multiple occurrences of the event, the NumberOfEvents property specifies how many occurrences to wait for before exiting the task. The Timeout property lets us specify how many seconds to wait for the event to occur. The ActionAtTimeout and AfterTimeout properties function similarly to their event counterparts.

**XML Task**  The *XML task* enables us to manipulate XML documents. Using the XML task, we can perform the following operations:

▶ Validate an XML document using an XML Schema Document (XSD) or a Document Type Definition (DTD)

▶ Apply an XSL Transformation (XSLT)

▶ Apply an XPath query

▶ Merge two XML documents

▶ Find the difference between two XML documents (Diff operation)

▶ Apply the output of a Diff operation

The XML source document can be supplied from a File Connection Manager in the Connections tray, a package variable, or directly input as a string. The XML document that results from the operation can be saved in a text file specified by a File Connection Manager, saved in a package variable, or discarded. The XML Task Editor dialog box is shown in Figure 7-38.

## Maintenance Plan Tasks

In addition to Containers and Control Flow items, the Control Flow SSIS Toolbox contains Maintenance Plan tasks. The Maintenance Plan tasks, as we might guess from the name, mirror tasks that can be accomplished as part of a database maintenance plan. In fact, when you create a database maintenance plan through SQL Server Management Studio, you are actually creating a SQL Server Integration Services package that utilizes these tasks. The Maintenance Plan tasks can also be used to perform database maintenance as we are loading data. This can be done to ensure that the database is ready for efficient operation at the conclusion of the data load.

Each Maintenance Plan task has a View T-SQL button on its dialog box. This button shows the T-SQL statements that would perform the equivalent operation in a query window. Looking at these T-SQL statements may be helpful to determine exactly how a Maintenance Plan task is operating.

**Figure 7-38**    *The XML Task Editor dialog box*

**Back Up Database Task**   The *Back Up Database task* lets us run a database backup

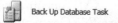

as part of an Integration Services package. This is a wise thing to do just before making major changes to the contents of a database. Often, some type of data load or other operation in an Integration Services package is responsible for these major changes. By using the Back Up Database task in a package, we can create the backup within the same process that makes the changes. We may also find this task useful to create a snapshot of the database contents immediately after a large data load.

Figure 7-39 shows the Back Up Database Task dialog box used to configure the Back Up Database task. The dialog box enables us to back up any combination of databases on a single server. A Full, Differential, or Transaction Log backup can be created. The backup can be stored in a single file or in multiple files, with one file for each database.

---

**Back Up Database Task**                                                                     ✕

Connection:            MaxMinManufacturingDM                          ▼        New...

Backup type:           Full                                                            ▼

Database(s):           Specific databases                                              ▼

Backup component
   ◉ Database
   ○ Files and filegroups:     [                                              ]    ...

☐ Copy-only Backup

☐ For availability databases, ignore Replica Priority for Backup and Backup on Primary Settings

☐ Backup set will expire:
   ◉ After          [ 14 ]  ⇅     days
   ○ On             [ 2/ 4/2012 ] ▼

Back up to:  ◉ Disk   ○ Tape

○ Back up databases across one or more files:

   [                                                        ]        Add...
                                                                     Remove
                                                                     Contents

   If backup files exist:                        [ Append ]                  ▼

◉ Create a backup file for every database
   ☐ Create a sub-directory for each database
   Folder:              C:\Program Files\Microsoft SQL Server\MSSQL11.MSSQLSERVER\MSSQL\Backup   ...
   Backup file extension:                                          [ bak ]

☐ Verify backup integrity

Set backup compression:   [ Use the default server setting ]                        ▼

          OK          Cancel          View T-SQL          Help

---

**Figure 7-39**   *The Back Up Database Task dialog box*

A special type of drop-down box is used to select the databases to be backed up. This is shown in Figure 7-40. This drop-down box contains predefined choices that let us select all of the databases on the server, all system databases on the server (master, msdb, and model), or all user databases on the server. In addition to the predefined choices, we can use the database list at the bottom of the drop-down box to create our own selection of databases using the check boxes.

**Check Database Integrity Task**    The *Check Database Integrity task* lets us check for corruption in one or more databases on a single server. This task executes a

```
DBCC CHECKDB WITH NO_INFOMSGS
```

command against each database specified. This can be a good idea, either right before or right after major changes to the database.

The Check Database Integrity Task dialog box is shown in Figure 7-41. It uses the same database selection drop-down box as the one shown in Figure 7-40 for the selection of the databases to check. We can also specify whether we want indexes included in the integrity check.

**Figure 7-40**    *The database selection drop-down box*

**Figure 7-41**    *The Check Database Integrity Task dialog box*

If the integrity check is successful, the package execution continues with any tasks linked to the Check Database Integrity task, with either a success or a completion precedence constraint. If the integrity check finds database corruption, the package execution continues with any tasks linked to the Check Database Integrity task, with either a failure or a completion precedence constraint.

**Execute SQL Server Agent Job Task**    The *Execute SQL Server Agent Job task* lets us execute a single SQL Server Agent Job as part of a package. A single job can be selected for execution. The Execute SQL Server Agent Job Task dialog box is shown in Figure 7-42.

**Figure 7-42**    *The Execute SQL Server Agent Job Task dialog box*

**Execute T-SQL Statement Task**    The *Execute T-SQL Statement task* enables us to

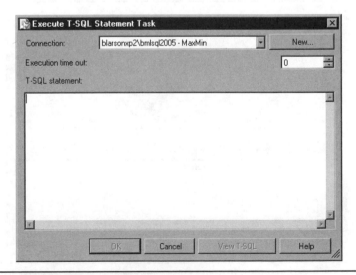 run one or more Transact SQL statements on a SQL server. Anything that can be executed from a query window in the SQL Server Management Studio can be executed here. The Execute T-SQL Statement Task dialog box is shown in Figure 7-43.

Notice there is a task called Execute SQL task in the Control Flow items section of the SSIS Toolbox. The Execute T-SQL Statement task that we are looking at here is simple. It lets us type in T-SQL statements and execute them. The Execute SQL task in the Control Flow items has additional features for creating parameterized statements and dealing with result sets.

**History Cleanup Task**    The *History Cleanup task* enables us to remove historical entries from a database. This includes backup history, SQL Agent Job execution history, and database maintenance plan execution history. We can specify the timeframe for the historical entries we want to keep and, therefore, the timeframe for the historical entries we want to remove. The History Cleanup Task dialog box is shown in Figure 7-44.

**Maintenance Cleanup Task**    The *Maintenance Cleanup task* allows us to remove files created by database maintenance plans and database backups. Specifically, we can remove maintenance plan text reports and database backups. We can remove a single file based on the filename or a number of files with the same file extension from a folder. We can specify the age of the files we want to remove.

**Figure 7-43**    *The Execute T-SQL Statement Task dialog box*

**Figure 7-44** *The History Cleanup Task dialog box*

**Notify Operator Task**    The *Notify Operator task* lets us send a message to one or more SQL Server operators. Operators must be set up in SQL Server before they can be notified using this task. The Notify Operator task dialog box is shown in Figure 7-45.

**Figure 7-45** *The Notify Operator Task dialog box*

**Rebuild Index Task**     The *Rebuild Index task* enables the rebuilding of indexes in one
or more databases. Rebuilding indexes causes SQL Server to drop
the existing indexes and rebuild them. The Rebuild Index task
uses the same database selection drop-down box as the one shown in Figure 7-40 for
the selection of the databases whose indexes are to be rebuilt. We can specify the free
space that should be placed into the rebuilt indexes, along with several other advanced
indexing options. The Rebuild Index Task dialog box is shown in Figure 7-46.

**Reorganize Index Task**     The *Reorganize Index task* lets us reorganize the indexes in
one or more databases. It uses the same database selection drop-
down box as the one shown in Figure 7-40 for the selection of
the databases whose indexes are to be reorganized. The Reorganize Index Task dialog
box is shown in Figure 7-47.

Reorganizing indexes defragments the leaf-level nodes of both clustered and
nonclustered indexes. It does this by reordering the nodes to match the logical order
of the leaf nodes. Reorganizing also compacts the indexes. The reorganization process
does not, however, drop and re-create the indexes as the rebuild process does.

**Figure 7-46**   *The Rebuild Index Task dialog box*

**Figure 7-47**   *The Reorganize Index Task dialog box*

**Shrink Database Task**   The *Shrink Database task* enables the recovery of unused pages
from tables in one or more databases. It uses the same database
selection drop-down box as the one shown in Figure 7-40 for
the selection of the databases that are to be shrunk. We can determine whether these
recovered pages are to be returned to the operating system or remain allocated to the
database. We can also specify how much free space is to be left in the pages allocated to
the database to accommodate future growth. The Shrink Database Task dialog box is
shown in Figure 7-48.

**Update Statistics Task**   The *Update Statistics task* lets us update the statistics in one or
more databases. It uses the same database selection drop-down
box as the one shown in Figure 7-40 for the selection of the
databases whose statistics are to be updated. Because the database statistics are used by
SQL Server to calculate query execution plans, it is important for these statistics to be

**Figure 7-48**   *The Shrink Database Task dialog box*

up-to-date. A large data load can cause the statistics to be inaccurate. Therefore, it is a good idea to use this task to update the database statistics after a major data operation. The Update Statistics Task dialog box is shown in Figure 7-49.

**Custom Tasks** If none of the control flow tasks included with Integration Services fits your needs, it is possible to write your own. You can create a .NET assembly that can integrate seamlessly with both Integration Services and SQL Server Data Tools. Creating a custom task requires a solid knowledge of object-oriented programming in the .NET Framework. Consult the SQL Server Books Online "Developing Custom Objects for Integration Services" topic for more information on developing a custom task.

# Data Flow

The Data Flow SSIS Toolbox contains three types of objects: data flow sources, data flow transformations, and data flow destinations. It also contains two assistants that aid in the process of creating a data flow source or a data flow destination. Each data flow item—source, transformation, destination, and assistant—has an editor dialog box that lets us configure that component or work with the assistant in a straightforward manner.

**Figure 7-49**  *The Update Statistics Task dialog box*

The editor dialog box for a data flow source, data flow transformation, or data flow destination is launched by double-clicking the item in the design area or right-clicking the item and selecting Edit from the context menu. The editor dialog box for the source assistant or the destination assistant is launched by double-clicking the assistant item in the SSIS Toolbox or dragging one of the assistant items onto the data flow design area.

Each of the data flow source, data flow transformation, and data flow destination items also has an advanced editor dialog box. Where the editor dialog box enables us to configure the item for use and make most of the necessary property settings for the item, the advanced editor dialog box contains all of the properties of an item. The advanced editor dialog box lets us set any property for the item. The advanced editor dialog box is launched by right-clicking the item and selecting Show Advanced Editor from the context menu.

## Data Flow SSIS Toolbox Organization

The Data Flow SSIS Toolbox is divided into several sections: Favorites, Common, Other Transforms, Other Sources, and Other Destinations. These divisions are designed to help you more easily find objects within the SSIS Toolbox. The Favorites section is for the objects you use most often. The Common section is for objects that are used often, but not as frequently as the favorites. Everything else ends up in the Other Transforms, Other Sources, or Other Destinations sections.

You can move objects between sections to customize the arrangement to suit your tastes. Right-click an object in the SSIS Toolbox to bring up the context menu. Then select the section where you would like the object to be moved. You can expand or hide any of these sections by clicking the triangle to the left of the section name.

## Data Flow Sources

*Data flow sources* are the starting point of any data flow. This is where the data comes from. Integration Services allows us to pull data from a wide variety of sources.

### ADO.NET Source

The *ADO.NET source* lets us use ADO.NET to connect to a data source. We need to create an ADO.NET Connection Manager in the Connection Managers tray for use with this data source. Once the ADO.NET Connection Manager has been created, it can be selected on the Connection Manager page of the ADO.NET Source Editor dialog box. This is shown in Figure 7-50.

The Connection Manager page is also used to specify whether we are getting our data directly from a table or view, or from a SQL query. If the data is coming from a table or a view, the name of the Table or the View property is used to select a table or view in the database. Alternately, the table or view name can come from a package variable at run time.

**Figure 7-50**    *The ADO.NET Source Editor dialog box*

If the data is coming from a SQL query, we have several ways to specify the content of the query. The simplest method is to type the query into the SQL command text property. This works only if we are comfortable with SQL query syntax and have the database structure memorized or an up-to-date copy of the database schema documentation handy. If this is not the case, we can create the query in the SQL Server Management Studio or some other query-authoring environment and save the completed query to a file. We can then load the query from the file by clicking Browse.

Alternatively, we can click Build Query to create the query using the Query Builder. The Query Builder is discussed later in the "OLE DB Source" section. The Columns and the Error Output pages of the ADO.NET Source Editor dialog box are discussed in the "Flat File Source" section.

### CDC Source

**CDC Source**    The *CDC Source* is used to implement a change data capture processing. The CDC Source works in conjunction with the CDC Control Task. The CDC Control Task and the CDC Source communicate with one another through the variable specified as the "Variable containing the CDC state."

The ADO.NET connection manager utilized by the CDC Source must point to a database that has change data capture enabled. Once this is in place, you can select a CDC–enabled table from that database. Working with the CDC Control Task, the CDC Source provides only that data from the source table that has been modified since the last data load. Each row from the CDC Source has an additional column called "__$operation", which contains a code identifying whether the row has been inserted, updated, or deleted.

The following processing modes can be specified using the CDC processing mode property:

▶ **All**    One row is sent from the CDC Source into the data flow for every change made to a record in the source table. If a given record in the source table was updated three times since the last data load, then that record will be present three times in the data flow. Each row in the data flow will reflect the values of the fields after that particular update was completed.

▶ **All with old values**    One row is sent from the CDC Source into the data flow for every insert and delete made to the source table. Two rows are sent for every update. The first row for each update reflects the values of the fields before that particular update was done. The second row for each update reflects the values of the fields after that update was completed.

▶ **Net**    One row is sent from the CDC source into the data flow for every record that was changed in the source table. If a given record was updated multiple times since the last data load, the record represents the current state of the record after all updates are completed. If a row was updated and subsequently deleted since the last data load, it will not be represented in the data flow.

▶ **Net with update mask**    This is similar to the Net processing mode. One additional column will be added for each column in the source table. These columns are in the format "__${*ColumnName*}__Changed" and indicate whether or not the associated column was changed since the last data load.

▶ **Net with merge**    This is similar to the Net processing mode; however, the updates and inserts are assigned the same code in the __$operation column. This optimizes the data for use with the MERGE T-SQL command.

**Excel Source**    The *Excel source* enables us to utilize data from an Excel spreadsheet.  The Excel Source Editor dialog box is shown in Figure 7-51. We need to create an Excel Connection Manager in the Connection Managers tray for use with this data source. Once the Excel Connection Manager has been created, this Connection Manager can be selected on the Connection Managers page of the Excel Source Editor dialog box. A spreadsheet is then selected from the Excel file pointed to by this Connection Manager. The columns included in the result set are selected on the Columns page of the Excel Source Editor dialog box.

**Flat File Source**    The *Flat File source* lets us utilize data from text files. We need to create a Flat File Connection Manager in the Connections tray for use with this data source. The Flat File Connection Manager

**Figure 7-51**    *The Excel Source Editor dialog box*

requires a bit more configuration than the OLE DB Connection Manager and most of the other Connection Managers. The other Connection Managers deal with specific data formats, so not a lot of configuration is required beyond the connection information. A flat file, on the other hand, can represent, format, and delimit the data in a number of different ways.

The first page of the Flat File Connection Manager, the General page shown in Figure 7-52, enables us to specify the file location in the File Name text box. In addition, we need to tell the Connection Manager how the data is represented with the Locale and Code Page drop-down lists, along with the Unicode check box. Finally, we need to specify how the data is formatted: whether the data is a fixed-width layout or delimited by a comma, tab, or some other separator (Format); if the text is enclosed in some form of quotation character (Text Qualifier); how the header row is delimited (Header Row Delimiter); if there are header rows to skip (Header Rows to Skip); and if the column names are in the first row (Column Names in the First Data Row).

In this example, we are using the ragged-right format. The *ragged-right format* expects fixed-width columns in the text file. This means, for example, that the first 8 characters of each line are always the first column, the next 34 characters are always the second

**Figure 7-52** *The General page of the Flat File Connection Manager Editor dialog box*

column, and so on. The ragged-right format expects some type of end-of-line indicator, such as a set of carriage return and line-feed characters. The *fixed-width format* also expects fixed-width columns, but it specifies the exact number of characters in each line, rather than using an end-of-line indicator. The length of the lines in the ragged-right format can vary because the end-of-line indicator tells the parser where to end one line and begin another. The length of the lines in the fixed-width format must be exactly the same for all lines.

The warning at the bottom of the dialog box in Figure 7-52—"Columns are not defined for this connection manager"—tells us that we are not quite done yet. As soon as we select the Columns page, shown in Figure 7-53, the Flat File Connection Manager uses the information from the General page to access the file. When the delimited format is selected on the General page, the Flat File Connection Manager attempts to figure out what the delimiter is and parse the file accordingly. If the wrong delimiter is chosen, you can edit the delimiter information. When the fixed-width format or, as in our example, the ragged-right format is used, we are given the opportunity to graphically specify the width of each column.

We specify column widths by creating column markers in the Source Data Columns area. The column marker is indicated by the mouse pointer in Figure 7-53. *Column markers* are created by clicking along the bottom of the ruler or below the ruler in the

**Figure 7-53**    *The Columns page of the Flat File Connection Manager Editor dialog box*

sample text area. We can drag the column markers to their appropriate positions, if necessary. We can remove an unneeded column marker by double-clicking it or by right-clicking it and selecting Delete from the context menu.

The Advanced page of the Flat File Connection Manager, shown in Figure 7-54, lets us specify additional information about each column that was defined on the Columns page. We can create, add, and delete column definitions here, as well as on the Columns page. The drop-down list alongside the New button, indicated by the mouse pointer in Figure 7-54, enables us to insert a column definition either before or after the column definition highlighted in the list. We can specify the Name property for each column definition. (If column names are supplied as the first row of the text file, these names appear in the Name property for each column definition.) The *Suggest Types button* instructs the Flat File Connection Manager to suggest a data type for each column definition based on the data in the text file. The final page in the Flat File Connection Manager Editor dialog box lets us preview the data from the text file when it is parsed according to our file layout and column definitions.

Once the Flat File Connection Manager has been created, this Connection Manager can be selected on the Connection Manager page of the Flat File Source Editor dialog box. We can then use the Columns page to specify which columns should be used in

**Figure 7-54**    *The Advanced page of the Flat File Connection Manager Editor dialog box*

the data flow. The Error output page enables us to specify the behavior of the Flat File source when an error or truncation occurs in any given column. We can ignore the failure, direct the row containing the failure to the error output, or cause the process to fail.

**ODBC Source** The *ODBC Source* is used to retrieve data from an ODBC data source. This functionality has been available in prior versions of SQL Server Integration Services through the ADO.NET Source. The ODBC Source in SQL Server Integration Services 2012 provides a more straightforward and more self-documenting version of this data source connection.

**OLE DB Source** The *OLE DB source* lets us utilize data from any source that supports an OLE DB connection. We need to create an OLE DB Connection Manager in the Connections tray for use with this data source. Once the OLE DB Connection Manager is created, it can be selected on the Connection Manager page of the OLE DB Source Editor dialog box. This is shown in Figure 7-55.

The Connection Manager page is also used to specify whether we are getting our data directly from a table or view, or from a SQL query. If the data is coming from a table or a view, the name of the Table or the View property is used to select a table or view in the database. Alternately, the table or view name can come from a package variable at run time.

If the data is coming from a SQL query, we have several ways to specify the content of the query. The simplest method is to type the query into the SQL Command Text property. This works only if we are comfortable with SQL query syntax and have the database structure memorized or an up-to-date copy of the database schema documentation handy. If this is not the case, we can create the query in the SQL Server Management Studio or some other query-authoring environment and save the completed query to a file. We can then load the query from the file by clicking Browse.

Alternatively, we can click Build Query to create the query using the Query Builder. The Query Builder is shown in Figure 7-56. The top quarter of the Query Builder is the Diagram pane. The *Diagram pane* area is used for selecting tables from the database, creating join conditions between tables, and selecting fields to be used in the query, either in the field list or in the filter conditions. The next quarter of the Query Builder, moving downward, is the Grid pane. The *Grid pane* is used to select the fields to be included in the field list (the Output column), as well as for setting the sort order and filter conditions. The next quarter, again moving downward, is the SQL pane. The *SQL pane* shows the SQL SELECT statement that is equivalent to the contents of the Diagram and Grid panes. Changes made directly in the SQL pane are reflected in the Diagram pane and the Grid pane as soon as focus leaves the SQL pane. The bottom quarter of the Query Builder is the *Result pane,* which shows the results of executing the query.

**Figure 7-55** *The Connection Manager page of the OLE DB Source Editor dialog box*

The Columns and the Error Output pages of the OLE DB Source Editor function similarly to their counterparts in the Flat File source.

**Raw File Source**  The *Raw File source* lets us utilize data that was previously written to a raw data file by a Raw File destination. The *raw file format* is the native format for Integration Services. Because of this, raw files can be written to disk and read from disk rapidly. One of the goals of Integration

**Figure 7-56**    *The Query Builder*

Services is to improve processing efficiency by moving data from the original source to the ultimate destination without making any stops in between. However, on some occasions, the data must be staged to disk as part of an extract, transform, and load process. When this is necessary, the raw file format provides the most efficient means of accomplishing this task. The Raw File Source Editor dialog box is shown in Figure 7-57.

**XML Source**    The *XML source* enables us to utilize the content of an XML document in the data flow. The XML document can come from a file or from the contents of a package variable. If the XML document is coming from a file, we can specify the file path at design time or obtain the file path from a

**Figure 7-57** *The Raw File Source Editor dialog box*

package variable at run time. We can also specify the location of an XSD that describes the structure of the XML document. If an XSD is unavailable, click Generate XSD to autogenerate an XSD from the XML document structure. The XML Source Editor dialog box is shown in Figure 7-58.

The Columns and the Error Output pages function similarly to their counterparts in the Flat File source.

**Figure 7-58**    *The XML Source Editor dialog box*

## Source Assistant

The *Source Assistant* aids you in the creation of OLE DB, Excel, and flat file data sources. The dialog box for the Source Assistant is shown in Figure 7-59. The Select source types area has entries for Excel and flat file data sources, as well as an entry for each type of OLE DB provider installed. When "Show only installed source types" is unchecked, entries for some of the other supported OLE DB drives appear in the Select source types area. When one of these types is highlighted, information on where to obtain this OLE DB driver is displayed. This is shown in Figure 7-60.

**Figure 7-59** *The Source Assistant dialog box showing Excel, flat file, and installed OLE DB providers*

The Select connection managers area shows existing Connection Managers of the selected type. Figure 7-59 shows three existing Connection Managers for SQL Server. This can prevent you from creating a duplicate Connection Manager when one already exists for the desired data source. To use an existing Connection Manager, select that Connection Manager in the Select connection managers area and click OK. To create a new Connection Manager of the desired type, select "<New>" in the Select connection managers area and click OK. When creating a new Connection Manager, the Connection Manager dialog box for the selected connection type will be displayed.

When the Source Assistant has completed the process of guiding you through the creation of a data source, the data source item will appear on the Data Flow Designer tab.

## Data Flow Transformations

The *data flow transformations* are used to modify the data as it moves through the data flow. In most cases, the wide array of data flow transformations makes it possible to change the data into the required format without having to save it to a temporary table or utilize large amounts of custom code. This set of powerful transformations lets us take our data from an ugly duckling to a beautiful swan with just a few drag-and-drop operations.

**Figure 7-60**   *The Source Assistant dialog box showing information on additional OLE DB providers*

**Aggregate**   The *Aggregate* transformation enables us to combine information from multiple records in the data flow into a single value. This functions in the same way as aggregation functions and the GROUP BY clause in a SQL statement. The Aggregate Transformation Editor dialog box is shown in Figure 7-61.

We begin by selecting the columns to participate in the aggregation from the Available Input Columns. We then select the operation that is applied to each of the selected columns. A column can either be used as a group by or it can be aggregated. The following aggregations are available:

▶ Average

▶ Count

▶ Count distinct

▶ Maximum

▶ Minimum

▶ Sum

The example in Figure 7-61 calculates the sum of the SalesAmount column for each customer represented by the content of the CustID column.

**Figure 7-61**   *The Aggregate Transformation Editor dialog box*

**Audit**   The *Audit* transformation lets us add columns that contain information about the package execution to the data flow. These audit columns can be stored in the data destination and used to determine when the package was run, where it was run, and so forth. The following information can be placed in audit columns:

- ► Execution instance GUID (a globally unique identifier for a given execution of the package)

- ► Execution start time

- ► Machine name

- ► Package ID (a GUID for the package)

- ► Package name

- ► Task ID (a GUID for the data flow task)

- ► Task name (the name of the data flow task)

- ► User name

- ► Version ID

The Audit Transformation Editor dialog box is shown in Figure 7-62. The information in the columns defined in this dialog box is duplicated for each row in the data flow. In this example, audit columns are being added to the data flow for machine name, package name, execution start time, and execution instance GUID.

**Cache Transform**   The *Cache Transform* transformation enables us to populate a cache that will be subsequently used by a Lookup transformation. Thus, the Cache Transform transformation enables us to apply any of the Integration Services data flow transformations to a set of data before using it as the lookup data set. The Cache Transform transformation can be configured to write the cached data to a cache file using a Cache Connection Manager. This persisted cache can then be used by several lookup transformations in a single package. Only one Cache Transform transformation in a package can write data to a given Cache Connection Manager.

**CDC Splitter**   The *CDC Splitter* transformation is used to implement change data capture processing. The CDC Splitter task works in conjunction with the CDC Source. Each row of data from the CDC Source has an additional column called "__$operation", which contains a code identifying whether the row has been inserted, updated, or deleted. The CDC Splitter data flow transformation is a specialized form of the conditional split transformation designed to work with the codes in the __$operation column.

**Figure 7-62** *The Audit Transformation Editor dialog box*

**Character Map**  The *Character Map* transformation enables us to modify the contents of character-based columns. The modified column can be placed in the data flow in place of the original column, or it can be added to the data flow as a new column. The following character mappings are available:

▶ **Lowercase** changes all characters to lowercase.

▶ **Uppercase** changes all characters to uppercase.

▶ **Byte reversal** reverses the byte order of each character.

▶ **Hiragana** maps Katakana characters to Hiragana characters.

▶ **Katakana** maps Hiragana characters to Katakana characters.

▶ **Half width** changes double-byte characters to single-byte characters.

▶ **Full width** changes single-byte characters to double-byte characters.

▶   **Linguistic casing** applies linguistic casing rules instead of system casing rules.

▶   **Simplified Chinese** maps traditional Chinese to simplified Chinese.

▶   **Traditional Chinese** maps simplified Chinese to traditional Chinese.

Multiple character mappings can be applied to a single column at the same time. However, a number of mappings are mutually exclusive. For example, it does not make sense to use both the lowercase and uppercase mappings on the same column. The Character Map Transformation Editor dialog box is shown in Figure 7-63.

**Figure 7-63**   *The Character Map Transformation Editor dialog box*

The Configure Error Output button displays the Configure Error Output dialog box, shown in Figure 7-64. The *Configure Error Output dialog box* lets us determine the error behavior of this transformation. For the Character Map transformation, the only error condition we need to worry about is a character truncation caused by one of the mappings. For each character mapping, we can choose to ignore truncation, send the row containing the truncation to the error output, or cause the entire transformation to fail.

**Conditional Split**   The *Conditional Split* transformation enables us to split the data flow into multiple outputs. In the Conditional Split Transformation Editor dialog box, shown in Figure 7-65, we define conditions for each branch of the split. When the package executes, each row in the data flow is compared against the conditions in order. When the row meets a set of conditions, the row is sent to that branch of the split.

In Figure 7-65, the conditional split has been defined with three branches. If the content of the SalesAmount column for a given row is less than $10, that row is sent to

**Figure 7-64**   *Configure Error Output dialog box*

**Figure 7-65**    *The Conditional Split Transformation Editor dialog box*

the SmallSales output. If the content of the SalesAmount column is between $10 and $50 inclusive, the row is sent to the MediumSales output. If the content of the SalesAmount column does not fit either of these conditions, the row is sent to the default output, named LargeSales. Figure 7-66 shows the three outputs from the Conditional Split Transformation being routed to three different paths through the data flow.

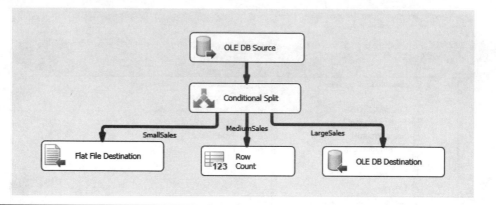

**Figure 7-66**   *A Conditional Split transformation in a data flow*

The Configure Error Output button displays the Configure Error Output dialog box, where we determine the error behavior of this transformation. In addition to truncation, we need to configure the behavior when the condition statement fails during evaluation. For each output column defined, we can choose to ignore an error, send the row containing the error to the error output, or fail the entire transformation.

**Copy Column**   The *Copy Column* transformation lets us create new columns in the data flow that are copies of existing columns. The new columns can then be used later in the data flow for calculations, transformations, or mapping to columns in the data destination. Figure 7-67 shows the Copy Column Transformation Editor dialog box with the SalesAmount column being copied to a new column called SalesAmountForTaxCalculation.

**Data Conversion**   The *Data Conversion* transformation enables us to convert columns from one data type to another. The converted data can either replace the existing column or be added as a new column. The Configure Error Output dialog box functions the same as it does for the Conditional Split transformation.

Figure 7-68 shows the Data Conversion Transformation Editor dialog box with two columns set up for conversion. The currency type contents of the SalesAmount column are converted to a decimal, with two places to the right of the decimal point. The decimal value is placed in a new column called SalesAmountAsDecimal. The Unicode contents of the CustomerPONumber column are replaced by its single-byte equivalent.

**Figure 7-67** *The Copy Column Transformation Editor dialog box*

**Data Mining Query** The *Data Mining Query* transformation lets us execute a DMX query on the data flow. Using the DMX query along with a data mining model, we can make predictions based on the data in each row of the data flow. These predictions can indicate other items that are likely to be associated with the column (that is, other products a customer is likely to purchase based on the current purchase) or the likelihood of a column to fit a certain condition (that is, the likelihood of a prospective client to be interested in a certain service).

The columns that result from the DMX query are added as new columns in the data flow. The new columns can be sent along with the rest of the data to the data destination, or they can be used along with the Conditional Split transformation to

**Figure 7-68** *The Data Conversion Transformation Editor dialog box*

send rows to different data destinations based on the prediction. We discuss DMX queries in Part V of this book. Figure 7-69 shows the Mining Model tab of the Data Mining Query Transformation Editor dialog box.

**Derived Column** The *Derived Column* transformation enables us to create a value derived from an expression. The expression can use values from variables and the content of columns in the data flow. The value can replace the content of an existing column or be added to the data flow as a new column. Figure 7-70 shows the Derived Column Transformation Editor dialog box defining a new column, AmountWithTax, which contains the sum of the SalesAmount and TaxAmt columns. The Derived Column transformation uses the same Configure Error Output dialog box as the Conditional Split transformation.

**Figure 7-69**    *The Mining Model tab of the Data Mining Query Transformation Editor dialog box*

**DQS Cleansing**    The *DQS Cleansing* transformation allows us to use a data quality knowledge base managed by SQL Server Data Quality Services (DQS) to evaluate and cleanse our data. A DQS knowledge base contains information about what does or does not make something a valid bit of data. This might be things like

▶  What are the valid country names

▶  What makes up a valid e-mail address

▶  What are the possible job titles in your organization

Each of these areas within the knowledge base (country names, e-mail addresses, job titles) is known as a domain.

Once we have captured the information about one or more domains in a knowledge base, we can use the DQS Cleansing transformation to apply that captured knowledge to our data. The Connection Manager tab of the DQS Cleansing Transformation Editor

**Figure 7-70**   *The Derived Column Transformation Editor dialog box*

dialog box is shown in Figure 7-71. Here we can create or select a Connection Manager to an instance of SQL Server running Data Quality Services. When a connection has been chosen, we can select one of the knowledge bases on that server. Once the knowledge base is selected, we can see all of the domains within that knowledge base.

On the Mapping tab of the DQS Cleansing Transformation Editor dialog box, shown in Figure 7-72, we select the columns in the data flow to which we apply the knowledge base. For each column selected, we pick a domain from the knowledge base to be used with that column. We also specify the output aliases for the source data, the corrected data, and the status for each column. These are all added as columns to the data flow. In addition to these, a Record Status column is added to the data flow.

The Record Status column, and possibly the statuses for the individual columns, can be used along with a conditional split transformation to determine how to handle each record in our data flow. Figure 7-73 shows one possible way to separate out data coming from a DQS Cleansing Transformation. In this example, data that was deemed correct by the DQS Cleansing Transformation is sent one direction. Data that could be

**Figure 7-71** *The Connection Manager tab of the DQS Cleansing Transformation Editor dialog box*

confidently corrected by the DQS Cleansing Transformation is sent another direction. Data where an autosuggestion was made with a lower level of confidence or where data was deemed to be invalid (no correction or suggestion could be made) is sent a third direction. The configuration of the conditional split to accomplish this is shown in Figure 7-74.

**Export Column** The *Export Column* transformation lets us take the content of a text or image column and write it out to a file. The pathname and filename are specified in a different column in the data flow. In this manner, the content of the text or image column can be written to a different file for

**Figure 7-72** *The Mapping tab of the DQS Cleansing Transformation Editor dialog box*

each row. The Export Column Transformation Editor dialog box, shown in Figure 7-75, can be used to specify whether to truncate the file or append to it if it already exists.

**Fuzzy Grouping** The *Fuzzy Grouping* transformation enables us to find groups of rows in the data flow based on nonexact matches. This is most often used to find possible duplicate rows based on names, addresses, or some other column where the same information may have been entered in different ways. For example, a row for Ms. Kathy Jones, a second row for Ms. Kathryn Jones, and a third row for Ms. Cathy Jones may be three entries for the same person.

The Fuzzy Grouping transformation selects one of the rows in the group as the best candidate for the other rows to be combined into, and this is the *model row*. Once the

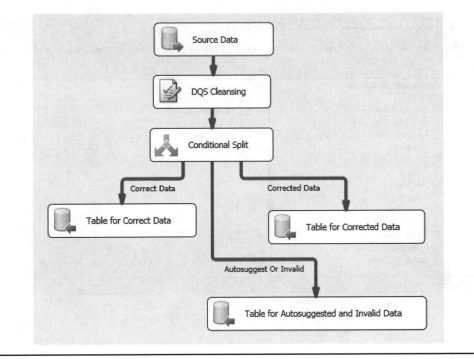

**Figure 7-73**    *A simple SSIS data flow utilizing a DQS Cleansing Transformation*

groups and their model rows have been identified, we can use another transformation to combine any unique information from the nonmodel rows into the model row and delete the nonmodel rows. This removes the duplication from the data. The Fuzzy Grouping transformation identifies row groups and model rows; it does not combine any data or delete any nonmodel rows. This must be done as a separate step in the package or as a manual operation.

Fuzzy Grouping transformation creates similarity scores between strings. This is done by considering the edit distance between two strings. In other words, how many character inserts, deletions, and replacements must be made in one string to produce the other string? Kathy and Kathryn have an edit distance of 2, because we need to insert an *r* and an *n* into the first word to get the second. Kathy and Cathy have an edit distance of 1, because we simply need to replace *K* with *C* in the first word to get the second.

In addition to edit distance, Fuzzy Grouping uses information, such as frequency of character occurrence and the positions of the characters, among other things, to increase its accuracy when creating similarity scores. Fuzzy Grouping is great at detecting character transpositions and other common spelling errors. All of the algorithms that create the similarity scores are language-independent, so Fuzzy Grouping can work with any language we care to throw at it.

**Figure 7-74** *A conditional split based on DQS Cleansing Transformation Record Status output*

**NOTE**

*Fuzzy Grouping assumes a string that is all uppercase is an acronym. Because even acronyms that have a close edit distance, say, FTC and FCC, are not likely to be the same thing, it is unlikely that groups will be identified for strings in all uppercase. If your data was entered in all uppercase (this can be especially true for legacy data), it is important to use the Character Map transformation to change the string to lowercase before trying a Fuzzy Grouping transformation.*

**Figure 7-75**  *The Export Column Transformation Editor dialog box*

On the Columns tab of the Fuzzy Grouping Transformation Editor dialog box, shown in Figure 7-76, we select the columns to use when looking for groupings. These columns can be set for fuzzy matching that uses similarity scoring or for exact matching. In the example in Figure 7-76, the content of the Title column—Mr. or Ms.—must match exactly before we want to even think about trying a fuzzy match on the FirstName and LastName columns. In addition to the exact or fuzzy match setting, we can specify whether leading or trailing numerals (0–9) are significant or should be ignored. (Selecting Leading from the Numerals drop-down list indicates that leading numerals are significant, and so forth.)

**Figure 7-76** *The Columns tab of the Fuzzy Grouping Transformation Editor dialog box*

The columns we select for grouping on the Columns page are automatically passed through to the output of the Fuzzy Grouping transformation. For each of the columns used in the grouping, the Fuzzy Grouping transformation adds a "clean" column to the output. These clean columns contain the values from the row that the Fuzzy Grouping transformation has selected as the model row for that group. In our previous example, if the row containing Ms. Kathy Jones is chosen as the model row for the group, the FirstName_clean column would contain Kathy for the Ms. Kathy Jones row, the Ms. Kathryn Jones row, and the Ms. Cathy Jones row.

We can also select columns to be passed through from the input to the output without participating in the transformation by placing a check mark in the Pass Through column. The Fuzzy Grouping transformation can add three more columns to the output. The default names for these columns are _key_in, _key_out, and _score. We can change the names of these columns on the Advanced tab of the Fuzzy Grouping Transformation Editor dialog box, shown in Figure 7-77.

The _key_in column contains a unique identifier for each field. This unique identifier is generated by the Fuzzy Grouping transformation. If a row is not grouped with any other rows, or if it is the model row for a group of rows, then it has the same identifier in its _key_out column as it has in its _key_in field. If a row is in a group and it is not the model row for that group, then it has the identifier of the model row in its _key_out column.

**Figure 7-77**    *The Advanced tab of the Fuzzy Grouping Transformation Editor dialog box*

The _score column contains the similarity score assigned to the row. The higher the similarity score, the more confidence the Fuzzy Grouping transformation has in the match. A row that is not grouped or that is a model row for a group always has a similarity score of 1. A row that is in a group and is not a model row has a similarity score between 0 and 1, inclusive.

On the Advanced tab of the Fuzzy Grouping Transformation Editor dialog box, we can set the threshold for the similarity score. Similarity scores that fall below the threshold are not used to create groups. A lower threshold allows the Fuzzy Grouping transformation to find more groups of duplicate rows, but also increases the risk of false positives. A higher threshold makes fewer mistakes, but increases the risk that some actual duplicates will not be found. Some experimenting should be done with your data to determine the best threshold for each Fuzzy Grouping transformation.

The Fuzzy Grouping transformation creates a lookup list of items and does fuzzy matching on that lookup list to create the groupings. If we are dealing with the processing of a data flow with a large number of rows, the Fuzzy Grouping transformation may need to write the lookup list to disk. The OLE DB Connection Manager selected on the Connection Manager tab provides access to a tempdb database where this temporary lookup list can be written. Because of this necessity to create a lookup list, the Fuzzy Grouping task can be rather slow.

### Fuzzy Lookup

The *Fuzzy Lookup* transformation lets us look up values using fuzzy matching logic. The Fuzzy Lookup transformation is closely related to the Fuzzy Grouping transformation. In fact, as was noted, the Fuzzy Grouping transformation creates its own lookup list and then does a fuzzy lookup.

The Fuzzy Lookup transformation is extremely useful when the data is moving from a database where a column was entered as freeform text to another database where that same column uses a lookup table and a foreign key constraint. Without the Fuzzy Lookup transformation, any typos in the freeform data leave us with a situation where we cannot determine the appropriate foreign key value to put in the destination table. However, with the Fuzzy Lookup transformation, we can determine a foreign key value even when typos are present.

The Fuzzy Lookup transformation uses an existing table or view as the source for its lookup operation. The transformation creates a copy of the source lookup table to use during the transformation processing. It then creates a second table that holds the information necessary for calculating the similarity score. This second table is called the *match index*. Don't let the name fool you—this is really a table created in the same database that holds the source lookup table.

The copy of the source lookup table and the match index table can be created as temporary tables each time the package is run. This is a good idea if the package performs a one-time data load operation. However, if the package is going to be run frequently, it is more efficient to create these tables as regular tables in the database. This is done using the Store New Index check box on the Reference Table tab of the Fuzzy Lookup Transformation Editor dialog box, as shown in Figure 7-78. For the most efficient operation of the package, we can have the database maintain the match index, so any changes to the source lookup table cause an update to the match index. If a match index already exists in the database, we can use it directly by selecting Use Existing Index and selecting the name of the index table.

Once the match index is configured, we can use the Columns tab to map one or more columns from the data flow to columns in the source lookup table. This is done by dragging a column from the Available Input Columns and dropping it on the corresponding column in the Available Lookup Columns. We can then set the behavior of the transformation using the Advanced tab. The Advanced tab enables us to specify the maximum number of source table records we want the transformation to find for each input row. This is usually one. We can also specify the similarity

**Figure 7-78**   *The Reference Table tab of the Fuzzy Lookup Transformation Editor dialog box*

score threshold for this transformation. This works on the same scale as the Fuzzy Grouping transformation.

The Fuzzy Lookup transformation adds one column to the output for each column from the source lookup table that is used in the lookup. In addition to this, the _Similarity and _Confidence columns are added. The _Similarity column shows the similarity score for the lookup done for that row. The _Confidence column shows how much confidence to place on the lookup that was just completed. Like the similarity score, the confidence figure is a number between 0 and 1, inclusive. A confidence level of 1 represents a near certainty that a value is correct. A confidence level of 0 indicates no confidence in the match at all.

**Import Column**  The *Import Column* transformation lets us take the content of a set of files and insert it into a text or image column in the data flow. The pathname and filename are specified in a different column in the data flow. In this manner, the content of a different text or image file can be written to each row in the data flow. The Input Columns tab of the Advanced Editor for Import Column dialog box is shown in Figure 7-79.

**Figure 7-79**  *The Input Columns tab of the Advanced Editor for Import Column dialog box*

**Lookup**    The *Lookup transformation* works similarly to the Fuzzy Lookup transformation. The difference is the Lookup transformation requires exact matches, rather than using similarity scores. The selection of the source lookup table and the column mapping is done in much the same way as for the Fuzzy Lookup transformation.

One difference between the Lookup transformation and the Fuzzy Lookup transformation is found on the Advanced page of the Lookup Transformation Editor dialog box, as shown in Figure 7-80. When the Lookup transformation executes, by default, it loads the entire source lookup table into cache for faster processing. If the source lookup table is too large to be completely loaded into cache, we can set a restriction on the amount of memory used. In Figure 7-80, the cache memory usage has been restricted to 5MB for both the 32-bit and 64-bit caching.

**Figure 7-80**    *The Advanced page of the Lookup Transformation Editor dialog box*

In addition, if only a portion of the records in the source lookup table is needed to resolve the lookups for a given Lookup transformation, we can load only the required portion of the source lookup table into memory. This is done by modifying the caching SQL statement and adding a WHERE clause. In Figure 7-80 a WHERE clause has been added so only the urban streets in the Street lookup table are loaded into memory. The additional WHERE clause is the highlighted portion of the Caching SQL statement.

The Error Output page of the dialog box lets us determine whether an unresolved lookup is ignored, sent to the error output, or causes the transformation to fail.

**Merge**  The *Merge* transformation merges two data flows together. For the Merge transformation to work properly, both input data flows must be sorted using the same sort order. This can be done by using the Sort transformation in each data flow prior to the Merge transformation. Alternately, if the rows coming from the data source are already sorted by the data provider, you can set the IsSorted property to true for the output of that data provider. The IsSorted property is only available in the Advanced Editor dialog box for the data source. The two data flows are merged together, so the output is sorted in the same manner as the inputs.

Figure 7-81 shows the Merge Transformation Editor dialog box with two lists of street addresses that are being merged together. Each input is sorted first by the street name, and then by the street number. When the records from the two inputs are merged together, the resulting output will also be in street name, street number order.

All of the rows in both of the input data flows are present in the merged output. For example, say 450 rows are in the first input data flow and 375 rows are in the second input data flow. There will be 825 rows in the output data flow.

**Merge Join**  The *Merge Join* transformation enables us to merge two data flows together by executing an inner join, a left outer join, or a full outer join. As with the Merge transformation, both of the input data flows must be sorted. With the Merge Join transformation, both of the data flows must be sorted by the columns to be used as the join condition.

Figure 7-82 shows the Merge Join Transformation Editor dialog box. In this example, an inner join is being used to join the Address Table data flow with the Street Lookup List data flow. The *join key* requires the StreetName column from the Address Table to match the CompleteName column from the Street Lookup List. Because an inner join is being used, only those rows that contain a match are included in the output.

If a left outer join were used in the example in Figure 7-82, all of the columns from the Address Table data flow would be included in the output, even if a matching column in the Street Lookup List data flow was not found. (The Address Table data flow was identified as the left input flow when it was connected to the Merge Join transformation.)

**Figure 7-81**   *The Merge Transformation Editor dialog box*

If a full join were used in the example in Figure 7-82, all of the columns from both the Address Table data flow and the Street Lookup List data flow would be included in the output. The output of the Merge Join transformation is always sorted on the join key column or columns.

**Multicast**   The *Multicast* transformation lets us take a single data flow and use it as the input to several data flow transformations or data flow destination items. The Multicast transformation simply copies the data flow and

**Figure 7-82**    *The Merge Join Transformation Editor dialog box*

sends it in multiple directions. Figure 7-83 shows the Multicast Transformation Editor dialog box. In this example, a data flow containing product information needs to go to the online store database, to the sales processing system, and to the FTP directory, where it can be picked up by distributed point-of-sale (POS) systems.

**OLE DB Command**    The *OLE DB Command* transformation enables us to execute a SQL statement for each row in the data flow. We select an OLE DB Connection Manager to determine where the SQL statement is to be executed. We then enter the SQL statement that is to be executed. Question marks

**Figure 7-83**  *The Multicast Transformation Editor dialog box*

can be used to create a parameterized query, as shown on the Component Properties tab of the Advanced Editor for OLE DB Command dialog box in Figure 7-84. Column values from the data flow can then be fed into these parameters as the SQL statement is executed for each data flow. In the example in Figure 7-84, the retail price of existing product records is updated based on information in the data flow.

**Percentage Sampling**    The *Percentage Sampling* transformation lets us split the data flow into two separate data flows based on a percentage. This can be useful when we want to create a small sample of a larger set of data for testing or for training a data mining model. (We discuss training data mining models in the Part V of this book.) Figure 7-85 shows the Percentage Sampling Transformation Editor dialog box.

**Figure 7-84**    *The Component Properties tab of the Advanced Editor for OLE DB Command dialog box*

Two outputs are created from the Percentage Sampling transformation item. The first output contains the rows that were selected to be part of the sample. In the example in Figure 7-85, 10% of the total rows in the input data flow are selected to be part of the sample. These rows are sent to the first output, called Mining Model Training Output in this example. The second output contains the rows that were not selected for the sample. In this case, the remaining 90% of the total rows in the input data flow are to be sent to the second output, called Mining Model Validation Output.

**Figure 7-85**   *The Percentage Sampling Transformation Editor dialog box*

The Percentage Sampling transformation selects rows at random from the input data flow. This random sampling provides a more representative sample of the entire data flow than simply selecting the top *N* rows. Because of the workings of the random sampling algorithm, the number of rows included in the sample is going to be close to the percentage specified, but it may not hit it exactly.

**Pivot**   The *Pivot* transformation enables us to take normalized data and change it into a less normalized structure. This is done by taking the content of one or more columns in the input data flow and using it as column names in the output data flow. The data in these newly created columns is calculated by taking an aggregate of the contents of another column from the input data flow. An aggregate must be used because a number of rows from the input data flow may define a single row in the output data flow. Figure 7-86 shows the Pivot dialog box.

**Row Count**   The *Row Count* transformation lets us determine the number of rows in the data flow. This count is then stored in a package variable. The package variable can then be used in expressions to modify the control flow or the data flow in the package. All of the columns in the Row Count transformation's input flow are simply passed on to the output flow. The Row Count dialog box is shown in Figure 7-87.

**Figure 7-86**　*The Pivot dialog box*

**Row Sampling**　The *Row Sampling* transformation enables us to split the data flow into two separate data flows based on the number of rows desired. The Row Sampling transformation works in the same manner as the Percentage Sampling transformation. The only difference is the Row Sampling transformation determines the number of rows in the sample based on a requested row count, rather than a requested percentage. The Row Sampling Transformation Editor dialog box is shown in Figure 7-88.

**Script Component**　The *Script Component* transformation lets us create .NET code for execution as part of our data flow. The Script Component transformation can be used as a data source, a data destination, or a data transformation. Our script code could read data from a file format that is not

**Figure 7-87**     *The Row Count dialog box*

**Figure 7-88**     *The Row Sampling Transformation Editor dialog box* supported by any of the Connection Managers, and then expose those rows as its output data flow. In this case, the Script Component item functions as a data source. Our script code could take rows from its input data flow and write data to a file format that is not supported by any of the Connection Managers. In this scenario, the Script Component item functions as a data destination. Finally, the script code could take rows from its input data flow, modify the data in a way not supported by the other data transformations, and then expose those rows as its output data flow. Here, the Script Component item functions as a data transformation.

The data inputs and outputs that are going to be used in the script, even if they are just going to be passed through, must be defined on the Inputs and Outputs page of the Script Transformation Editor dialog box. This is shown in Figure 7-89. Make sure to use different names for the input and output columns. If we use the same name for both an input and an output, only the output column will be visible to the script code.

In the example shown in Figure 7-89, we have street names from a legacy system that were entered in uppercase. We want to change these to title case (sometimes known as proper case; the first character of each word in uppercase, with the remaining characters in lowercase) as part of our Integration Services package. The Copy Column transformation provides translations to lowercase and uppercase, but not to title case. We need to create a custom script to accomplish this task.

Clicking Edit Script on the Script page of the Script Transformation Editor dialog box displays the Microsoft Visual Studio dialog box, where we can edit the script. This is shown in Figure 7-90. The Input_ProcessInputRow method is executed once for each row in the input data flow. The Row object parameter, which is passed to this method, contains the properties that provide access to both the input and output columns defined on the Inputs and Outputs page.

The sample code simply copies the AddressIDIn and StreetNumberIn values from the input data flow to the AddressIDOut and StreetNumberOut columns in the output data flow. The StreetNameIn column is transformed first to lowercase using the ToLower method, and then to title case using the ToTitleCase method. (ToTitleCase does not work on text that is all uppercase, so we need to use the ToLower method first.) The transformed string is then assigned to the StreetNameOut column.

**Slowly Changing Dimension**    The *Slowly Changing Dimension* transformation

> Slowly Changing Dimension

enables us to use a data flow to update the information in a slowly changing dimension of a data mart. This transformation is configured using the Slowly Changing Dimension Wizard. The wizard walks us through the steps necessary to use the input data flow columns to properly update the slowly changing dimension.

**Figure 7-89**    *The Inputs and Outputs page of the Script Transformation Editor dialog box*

The first page of the wizard after the welcome page, the Select a Dimension Table and Keys page, is shown in Figure 7-91. This wizard page requires us to select the Connection Manager that lets us connect to the data mart and to select the table containing the slowly changing dimension. This wizard page also requires us to map the input data flow columns to the fields in the dimension table and to specify which column is the business key column (the unique identifier for the dimension information).

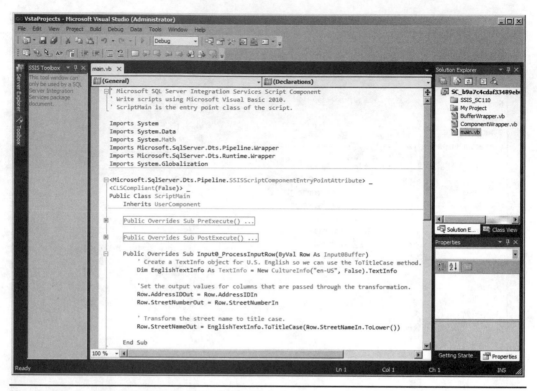

**Figure 7-90**   *The Microsoft Visual Studio for Applications dialog box*

The next page of the wizard, the Slowly Changing Dimension Columns page, is shown in Figure 7-92. This wizard page enables us to specify how each of the nonkey columns in the dimension table should be treated when it changes. A column such as the Sales_Person_Name column is fixed relative to the salesperson ID. A situation should not occur where a different person assumes the use of this salesperson ID. (Yes, names could change due to marriage or other events, but we will conveniently ignore that fact for this example.) This type of column is marked as a fixed attribute.

A column such as the Sales_Person_PhoneNumber column is changeable. We do not need to track previous phone numbers used by the salespeople. This type of column is marked as a changing attribute. A column such as the Sales_Person_Territory column is one whose changes we want to track. This type of column is marked as an historical attribute.

**Figure 7-91**    *The Select a Dimension Table and Keys page of the Slowly Changing Dimension Wizard*

The next page of the wizard, the Fixed and Changing Attribute Options page, enables us to specify the transformation behavior when a fixed or a changing attribute is modified. We can choose to fail the transformation when a fixed attribute is modified. We can also choose to change all historic occurrences of a changing attribute when that attribute is modified.

The Historical Attribute Options page lets us specify the method used to determine which are the historical records and which are the current records. This page is shown in Figure 7-93. The salesperson dimension used in this example has a start date and an end date that determines the current records. We use the system date at the time the new record was created to populate the date fields.

**Figure 7-92** *The Slowly Changing Dimension Columns page of the Slowly Changing Dimension Wizard*

The Inferred Dimension Members page lets us specify whether we can infer information for dimension members that do not yet exist. When the wizard completes, it adds a number of transformations to the package, as shown in Figure 7-94. These additional transformations provide the functionality to make the slowly changing dimension update work properly.

**Sort** The *Sort* transformation enables us to sort the rows in a data flow. The Sort Transformation Editor dialog box is shown in Figure 7-95. In the example in this figure, the data flow is being sorted first by the StreetType column, and then by the StreetName column. The AddressID and StreetNumber columns are not used as sort columns, but are passed through from the input data flow to the output data flow. The Sort transformation can remove rows with duplicate sort keys if Remove Rows with Duplicate Sort Values is checked.

**Figure 7-93**    *The Historical Attribute Options page of the Slowly Changing Dimension Wizard*

**Term Extraction**    The *Term Extraction* transformation lets us extract a list of words and phrases from a column containing freeform text. The Term Extraction transformation identifies recurring nouns and/or noun phrases in the freeform text, along with a score showing the frequency of occurrence for each word or phrase. This information can then be used to help discover the content of unstructured, textual data.

The Term Extraction transformation has two limitations. First, it only works with Unicode data (the DT_WSTR or DT_NTEXT Integration Services data types). This limitation is easily overcome by using the Data Conversion transformation to convert single-byte strings to Unicode. The second limitation is that the Term Extraction transformation only works with English-language text. The term extraction algorithms require knowledge of the structure and syntax of the language they are parsing. Currently, this intelligence is only available for English.

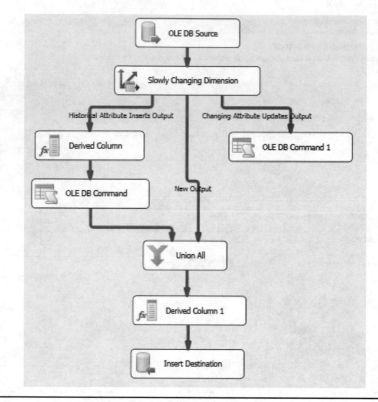

**Figure 7-94** *The results of the Slowly Changing Dimension Wizard*

On the Term Extraction tab of the Term Extraction Transformation Editor dialog box, we simply select the column that contains the freeform text, and then specify the name of the term and score output columns. The Exclusion tab enables us to specify a database table or view that contains a list of words or phrases to exclude from the term list. The Advanced tab, shown in Figure 7-96, lets us configure the operation of the term extraction, including whether nouns, noun phrases, or both are included in the extraction and the number of occurrences that must be found before a word or phrase is added to the list.

**Term Lookup**  The *Term Lookup* transformation enables us to look for occurrences of a set of words or phrases in a data flow column containing freeform text. The Term Lookup transformation functions almost identically to the Term Extraction transformation. The big difference is this: the Term Lookup transformation starts with a table of terms to look for in the freeform text, whereas the Term Extraction transformation creates its own list on-the-fly.

**Figure 7-95**    *The Sort Transformation Editor dialog box*

The Term Lookup transformation creates one row in the output data flow for each term found in the table of terms and in the text column. If the text column contains more than one term, more than one output row is created. For example, if a text column contains three of the terms from the lookup table, three rows are created in the output data flow. The same restrictions of Unicode text only and English only that applied to the Term Extraction transformation also apply to the Term Lookup transformation. The Term Lookup tab of the Term Lookup Transformation Editor dialog box is shown in Figure 7-97.

**Figure 7-96**   *The Advanced tab of the Term Extraction Transformation Editor dialog box*

**Union All**   The *Union All* transformation lets us merge several data flows into a single data flow. Any number of data flows can be unioned together. The only limitation is they all must be able to contribute fields to all of the columns defined in the output. The data flows used as inputs to the Union All transformation do not need to be sorted, as with the Merge and Merge Join transformations. Consequently, the output data flow is not sorted. The Union All Transformation Editor dialog box is shown in Figure 7-98.

**Figure 7-97**    *The Term Lookup Transformation Editor dialog box*

**Unpivot**    The *Unpivot* transformation enables us to take a denormalized data flow and turn it into normalized data. The example shown in Figure 7-99 takes a denormalized table that contains several phone number columns—one for home phone, one for work phone, one for cell phone, and so forth—and changes it

**Figure 7-98** *The Union All Transformation Editor dialog box*

into a normalized table, with one record for each phone number. If the input data flow for our example contains the following rows:

| CustomerID | HomePhone | WorkPhone | CellPhone | Fax |
|---|---|---|---|---|
| 3843 | 891-555-2443 | 891-555-9384 | | 891-555-2923 |
| 4738 | 891-555-9384 | | 891-555-3045 | |

The output data flow would contain the following rows:

| CustomerID | PhoneNumberType | PhoneNumber |
|---|---|---|
| 3843 | HomePhone | 891-555-2443 |
| 3843 | WorkPhone | 891-555-9384 |
| 3843 | Fax | 891-555-2923 |
| 4738 | HomePhone | 891-555-9384 |
| 4738 | CellPhone | 891-555-3045 |

| Available Input Columns | | |
|---|---|---|
| ☑ | Name | Pass Through |
| ☐ | CustomerID | ☑ |
| ☑ | HomePhone | ☑ |
| ☑ | WorkPhone | ☑ |
| ☑ | CellPhone | ☑ |
| ☑ | Fax | ☑ |

| Input Column | Destination Column | Pivot Key Value |
|---|---|---|
| HomePhone | CustomerIDNumber | HomePhone |
| WorkPhone | CustomerIDNumber | WorkPhone |
| CellPhone | CustomerIDNumber | CellPhone |
| Fax | CustomerIDNumber | Fax |

Pivot key value column name: PhoneNumberType

**Figure 7-99**    *The Unpivot Transformation Editor dialog box*

## Data Flow Destinations

Now that we have all this data transformed into exactly the right format, we need to do something with it. This is the job of the data flow destinations. Let's take a look at these options for storing our data.

**ADO.NET Destination**    The *ADO.NET destination* enables us to use ADO.NET to connect to a data destination. We need to create an ADO.NET Connection Manager in the Connections tray for use with this data destination. Once the ADO.NET Connection Manager is created and selected, we can map the columns of the data flow to the fields in the data destination.

**Data Mining Model Training Destination**    The *Data Mining Model Training destination* lets us use a data flow to train a data mining model. Training a data mining model prepares the model for making predictions by gaining knowledge from a set of sample data. We discuss data mining models and their care, feeding, and training in Part V of this book.

**DataReader Destination**    The *DataReader destination* exposes the data in a data flow to external consumers using the ADO.NET Datareader interface. This allows, for example, a SQL Server Reporting Services report to use an Integration Services package data flow as a data source. We can configure which data flow columns are exposed through the datareader interface and what alias is used for each of those output columns.

**Dimension Processing Destination**    The *Dimension Processing destination* lets us send a data flow to process a dimension. By using this destination, we can provide new values for a dimension in an Analysis Services cube. Columns from the data flow are mapped to the dimension and its attributes.

**Excel Destination**    The *Excel destination* enables us to send a data flow to an Excel spreadsheet file. We need to create an Excel Connection Manager in the Connections tray for use with this data destination. Once the Excel Connection Manager is created and selected, we can map the columns of the data flow to the fields in the data destination.

**Flat File Destination**    The *Flat File destination* lets us send a data flow to a text file. We need to create a Flat File Connection Manager in the Connections tray and define the columns that are in the text file. Once the Flat File Connection Manager is created and selected, we can map the columns of the data flow to the fields in the data destination.

**ODBC Destination**    The *ODBC destination* enables us to send a data flow to an ODBC data source. We need to create an ODBC Connection Manager in the Connections tray for use with this data destination. Once the ODBC Connection Manager is created and selected, we can map the columns of the data flow to the fields in the data destination.

**OLE DB Destination**    The *OLE DB destination* enables us to send a data flow to an OLE DB–compliant database. We need to create an OLE DB Connection Manager in the Connections tray for use with this data destination. Once the OLE DB Connection Manager is created and selected, we can map the columns of the data flow to the fields in the data destination.

**Partition Processing Destination**    The *Partition Processing destination* lets us send a data flow to process a partition. By using this destination, we can provide new values for a partition in an Analysis Services cube. Columns from the data flow are mapped to the items in the partition. We discuss Analysis Services partitions in Chapter 10.

**Raw File Destination**    The *Raw File destination* enables us to write a data flow to a raw data file. The Raw File format is the native format for Integration Services. Because of this, raw files can be written to disk and read from disk rapidly. One of the goals of Integration Services is to improve processing efficiency by moving data from the original source to the ultimate destination without making any stops in between. However, on some occasions, the data must be staged to disk as part of an Extract, Transform, and Load process. When this is necessary, the Raw File format provides the most efficient means of accomplishing this task.

**Recordset Destination**    The *Recordset destination* lets us send a data flow to a record set. The record set is then stored in a package variable, which is visible outside of the current data flow. This allows the record set to be used by other items within the package.

**SQL Server Compact Destination**    The *SQL Server Compact destination* enables us to send a data flow to a SQL Server Compact database. We need to create a SQL Server Compact Connection Manager in the Connections tray for use with this data destination. Once the SQL Server Compact Connection Manager is created and selected, we can map the columns of the data flow to the fields in the data destination.

**SQL Server Destination**    The *SQL Server destination* lets us quickly insert records from a data flow into a SQL Server table or view. The SQL Server destination is the equivalent of using the Bulk Insert task with a data flow, rather than a text file, as the source of the data. Because of this, it results in a shorter load time than is required for the same load into SQL Server using the OLE DB destination.

The Bulk Insert task is extremely fast, but it can only use text files for the data source and it does not allow any transformations to the data. The SQL Server destination enables us to pull data from any of the supported data sources, apply transformations, and then do a fast insert into a SQL Server table or view. We need to create an OLE DB Connection Manager in the Connections tray for use with this data destination. Once the OLE DB Connection Manager is created and selected, we can map the columns of the data flow to the fields in the data destination.

The SQL Server destination achieves its speed by using special hooks into the SQL Server database engine itself. For this reason, the SQL Server destination can only be used in SSIS packages that are run on the same server where the destination SQL Server instance is executing.

## Destination Assistant

As with the Source Assistant, the *Destination Assistant* aids you in the creation of OLE DB, Excel, and flat file data sources. The dialog box for the Destination Assistant is shown in Figure 7-100. The Select destination type area has entries for Excel and flat file data destinations as well as an entry for each type of OLE DB provider installed. When "Show only installed destination types" is unchecked, entries for some of the

**Figure 7-100**  *The Destination Assistant dialog box showing Excel, flat file, and installed OLE DB providers*

other supported OLE DB drives appear in the Select destination type area. When one of these types is highlighted, information on where to obtain this OLE DB driver is displayed, just as with the Source Assistant.

The Select connection managers area shows existing Connection Managers of the selected type. Figure 7-100 shows four existing Connection Managers for SQL Server. This can prevent you from creating a duplicate Connection Manager when one already exists for the desired data destination. To use an existing Connection Manager, select that Connection Manager in the Select connection managers area and click OK. To create a new Connection Manager of the desired type, select "<New>" in the Select connection managers area and click OK. When creating a new Connection Manager, the Connection Manager dialog box for the selected connection type will be displayed.

When the Destination Assistant has completed the process of guiding you through the creation of a data destination, the data destination item will appear on the Data Flow Designer tab.

# Getting Under the Sink

This chapter provides a basic understanding of Integration Services package structure and content. In Chapter 8, we will look at how all of this is used to actually get data to flow from one location to another. We will play plumber and get under the sink to connect up these pipes and fittings.

# Chapter 8

# Fill 'er Up—Using Integration Services for Populating Data Marts

## In This Chapter

▶ **Package Development Features**

▶ **Change Data Capture**

▶ **Loading a Fact Table**

▶ **Putting Integration Services Packages into Production**

▶ **Meanwhile, Back at the BI Semantic Model**

*To change and to improve are two different things.*

–Anonymous

We have become familiar with the structure and components of Integration Services. Now it is time to begin putting the tool to use. We will take a more in-depth look at Integration Services packages and how they are produced. We will also utilize several Learn By Doing activities to gain experience in Integration Services package development.

# Package Development Features

Now you have seen all the wonderful tasks and transformations provided by Integration Services. However, just as with all those gadget commercials on TV, you need to wait, because there's more. Integration Services also provides a number of features to aid in the package development process. In this section, we explore a number of features that make Integration Services packages easy to program and easy to debug.

## Give It a Try

Before we begin to discover additional features of Integration Services, let's actually give it a try. We begin with a Learn By Doing exercise.

### Learn By Doing—Using Integration Services to Populate the Maximum Miniatures Manufacturing Data Mart Dimensions

#### Feature Highlighted

▶ Creating an Integration Services package for loading data into a data mart

**Business Need**   In Chapter 6, we created a relational database to hold the information for the Maximum Miniatures Manufacturing data mart. Now it is time to copy information from the Maximum Miniatures online transaction processing (OLTP) systems and load it into the relational database tables. We need to create two processes: one to initially populate all of the dimensional tables and one to add new manufacturing information to the fact table.

**NOTE**

*To complete this Learn By Doing activity, you need the Maximum Miniatures Accounting database. If you have not done so already, go to www.mhprofessional.com and search for the book's page using the ISBN, which is 0071759387. Use the "Code Download" link to download the Zip file containing the book's material. Follow the instructions within the zipped folders in the Zip file to install the Maximum Miniatures Accounting database.*

### Steps to Create the Integration Services Project

1. Open SQL Server Data Tools.
2. Click the New Project button on the toolbar.
3. Make sure Business Intelligence is selected from the Installed Templates, and then select Integration Services Project in the center of the screen.
4. Enter **MaxMinManufacturingDMLoad** for Name, and set the Location to the appropriate folder. The Create directory for solution check box should be unchecked.
5. Click OK to create the project.
6. Once the project is open, right-click the Package.dtsx entry in the Solution Explorer window and select Rename from the context menu. Enter **DimensionLoad.dtsx** for the package name and press ENTER.

### Steps to Create the Data Source for the Load ProductType Data Flow

1. Drag the Data Flow Task item from the SSIS Toolbox and drop it on the Control Flow tab.
2. Right-click the Data Flow Task item you just created and select Rename from the context menu. Enter **Load ProductType** and press ENTER. (You can also single-click the Data Flow Task item to edit the name of the item.)
3. Double-click the Load ProductType item. This takes you to the Data Flow tab.
4. Right-click in the Connections tray and select New ADO.NET Connection from the context menu. Click New in the Configure ADO.NET Connection Manager dialog box to create a new data connection.
5. Enter the name of the server where the MaxMinAccounting database was created in Server name. Select the appropriate method for accessing this server in the Log On to the Server section. Enter credentials if necessary. Select MaxMinAccounting from the Select or enter a database name drop-down list. Click OK to return to the Configure ADO.NET Connection Manager dialog box. Click OK again to exit this dialog box.
6. Drag an ADO.NET Source item from the SSIS Toolbox and drop it on the Data Flow tab.

7. Double-click the ADO.NET Source item you just created. The ADO.NET Source Editor dialog box appears.

8. Select the MaxMinAccounting data connection that you just created in the ADO.NET connection manager drop-down list, if it is not already selected. (The server name will be in front of the database name.) Leave the Data access mode drop-down list set to Table or view. Select "dbo". "ProductTypes" from the Name of the table or the view drop-down list. Click OK.

### Steps to Create the Data Destination for the Load ProductType Data Flow

1. Right-click in the Connections tray and select New OLE DB Connection from the context menu. Click New in the Configure OLE DB Connection Manager dialog box to create a new data connection.

2. Enter the name of the server where the MaxMinManufacturingDM database was created in Server name. Select the appropriate method for accessing this server in the Log on to the server section. Enter credentials if necessary. Select MaxMinManufacturingDM from the Select or enter a database name drop-down list. Click OK to return to the Configure OLE DB Connection Manager dialog box. Click OK again to exit this dialog box.

3. Drag a SQL Server Destination item from the Other Destinations section of the SSIS Toolbox, and drop it on the Data Flow tab.

4. Click the ADO.NET Source item. Click the blue data flow arrow, drag it on top of the SQL Server Destination item, and drop it on this item. This connects the source to the destination.

5. Double-click the SQL Server Destination item. The SQL Destination Editor dialog box appears.

6. Select the MaxMinManufacturingDM data connection that you just created in the Connection manager drop-down list, if it is not already selected. Select DimProductType from the Use a table or view drop-down list.

7. Click Mappings to view the Mappings page. The columns from the data source (which are Available Input Columns to this data destination item) should be automatically mapped to the columns in the destination (the Available Destination Columns). You see an arrow going from each column name under Available Input Columns to the corresponding column name under Available Destination Columns. The automatic mapping occurs because the column names match. Click OK to exit the SQL Destination Editor dialog box.

### Steps to Create the Load ProductSubtype Data Flow

1. Click the Control Flow tab. Drag a second Data Flow Task item on to the Control Flow tab. Rename this new Data Flow Task item **Load ProductSubtype**.

2. Click the Load ProductType item. Drag the precedence arrow onto the Load ProductSubtype item and drop it there. These two items are now linked by a precedence constraint. The Load ProductType item must complete successfully before the Load ProductSubtype item can execute. This is required because ProductType is a foreign key for ProductSubtype.

3. Double-click the Load ProductSubtype item. This takes you to the Data Flow tab, with Load ProductSubtype selected in the Data Flow Task drop-down list.

4. Drag an ADO.NET Source item from the SSIS Toolbox onto the Data Flow tab. Double-click this item. The ADO.NET Source Editor dialog box appears.

5. The MaxMinAccounting data connection will be selected in the ADO.NET connection manager drop-down list. Leave the Data access mode drop-down list set to Table or view. Select "dbo". "ProductSubtypes" from the Name of the table or the view drop-down list. Click OK.

6. Drag a SQL Server Destination item from the SSIS Toolbox, and drop it on the Data Flow tab.

7. Click the ADO.NET Source item. Click the blue data flow arrow, drag it on top of the SQL Server Destination item, and drop it on this item. This connects the source to the destination.

8. Double-click the SQL Server Destination item. The SQL Destination Editor dialog box appears.

9. The MaxMinManufacturingDM data connection will be selected in the Connection manager drop-down list. Select DimProductSubtype from the Use a table or view drop-down list.

10. Click Mappings to view the Mappings page. The input columns should be automatically mapped to the columns in the destination. Click OK to exit the SQL Destination Editor dialog box.

### Steps to Create Additional Data Flow

1. Repeat the steps of the "Create the Load ProductSubtype Data Flow" section to take data from the AccountingSystem.Products table and copy it to the MaxMinManufacturingDM.DimProduct table. Create the precedence arrow to connect the Load ProductSubtype and Load Product data flow tasks. (The RawMaterial and AmountOfRawMaterial columns in the AccountingSystem.Products table are not mapped to columns in the MaxMinManufacturingDM.DimProduct table.)

2. Repeat the steps of the "Create the Load ProductSubtype Data Flow" section again to take data from the AccountingSystem.Countries table and copy it to the MaxMinManufacturingDM.DimCountry table. Create the precedence arrow to connect the Load Product and Load Country data flow tasks.

### Steps to Create the Load Plant Data Flow

1. Click the Control Flow tab. Drag another data flow task item onto the Control Flow tab. Rename this new data flow task item **Load Plant**.

2. Click the Load Country item. Drag the precedence arrow onto the Load Plant item, and drop it there.

3. Double-click the Load Plant item. This takes you to the Data Flow tab, with Load Plant selected in the Data Flow Task drop-down list.

4. Drag an ADO.NET Source item from the SSIS Toolbox onto the Data Flow tab. Double-click this item. The ADO.NET Source Editor dialog box appears.

5. We only want plant site records from the Locations table. We will use a query with a WHERE clause to filter out the records we don't want. The MaxMinAccounting data connection will be selected in the ADO.NET connection manager drop-down list. Select SQL command from the Data access mode drop-down list. Enter the following for SQL command text:

```
SELECT LocationCode AS PlantNumber,
       LocationName AS PlantName,
       CountryCode
FROM Locations
WHERE LocationType = 'Plant Site'
```

6. Click OK to exit the ADO.NET Source Editor dialog box.

7. Drag a SQL Server Destination item from the SSIS Toolbox, and drop it on the Data Flow tab.

8. Click the ADO.NET Source item. Click the blue data flow arrow, drag it on top of the SQL Server Destination item, and drop it on this item.

9. Double-click the SQL Server Destination item. The SQL Destination Editor dialog box appears.

10. The MaxMinManufacturingDM data connection will be selected in the Connection manager drop-down list. Select DimPlant from the Use a table or view drop-down list.

11. Click Mappings to view the Mappings page. The input columns should be automatically mapped to the columns in the destination. Click OK to exit the SQL Destination Editor dialog box.

### Steps to Create the Load Material-Machine Type-Machine Data Flow

1. Click the Control Flow tab. Drag another data flow task item onto the Control Flow tab. Rename this new data flow task item **Load Material-Machine Type-Machine**.

2. Click the Load Plant item. Drag the precedence arrow onto the Load Material-Machine Type-Machine item and drop it there.

3. Double-click the Load Material-Machine Type-Machine item.

4. Drag an ADO.NET Source item from the SSIS Toolbox onto the Data Flow tab. Double-click this item. The ADO.NET Source Editor dialog box appears.

5. The MaxMinAccounting data connection will be selected in the ADO.NET connection manager drop-down list. Leave the Data Access Mode drop-down list set to Table or view. Select "dbo". "CapitalAssets" from the Name of the table or the view drop-down list.

6. Click OK to exit the ADO.NET Source Editor.

7. Drag a Conditional Split item from the Common section of the SSIS Toolbox, and drop it on the Data Flow tab. Rename this new data flow transformation item **Filter For Molding Machines**.

8. Click the ADO.NET Source item. Click the blue data flow arrow, drag it on top of the Filter For Molding Machines item, and drop it on this item.

9. Double-click the Filter For Molding Machines item. The Conditional Split Transformation Editor dialog box appears.

10. We only want records for molding machines from the CapitalAssets table. We will use the Conditional Split transformation to filter out the records we don't want. Click the cell in the Output Name column, and enter **Molding Machine Records**.

11. Expand the Columns folder in the upper-left corner of the dialog box.

12. Click the AssetType column and drag it to the uppermost cell in the Condition column. This will create an "[AssetType]" placeholder for this column.

13. Complete the expression in the Condition cell so it appears as follows:

```
[AssetType] == "Molding Machine"
```

14. Click OK to exit the Conditional Split Transformation Editor dialog box.

15. Drag a Multicast item from the SSIS Toolbox and drop it on the Data Flow tab.

16. Click the Filter For Molding Machines item. Click the blue data flow arrow, drag it on top of the Multicast item, and drop it on this item. The Input Output Selection dialog box appears. This dialog box appears because the Conditional Split Transformation item has two outputs: one that we created called "Molding Machine Records," containing only those records that satisfy our condition expression, and the "Conditional Split Default Output," containing all other records in the data flow.

17. Select Molding Machine Records from the Output drop-down list. Click OK.

18. Drag an Aggregate item from the SSIS Toolbox and drop it on the Data Flow tab. Rename this new aggregate item **Aggregate by Material**.

19. Click the Multicast item. Click the blue data flow arrow, drag it on top of the Aggregate by Material item, and drop it on this item.

20. Double-click the Aggregate by Material item. This opens the Aggregate Transformation Editor dialog box. Check RawMaterial under Available Input Columns. This groups the data by the RawMaterial column to give you a unique list of materials. You can use this unique list to populate the DimMaterial table. Only the RawMaterial column is included in the output of the Aggregate by Material item.

21. In the Output Alias column, change RawMaterial to Material.

22. Click OK to exit the Aggregate Transformation Editor dialog box.

23. Drag a SQL Server Destination item from the SSIS Toolbox and drop it on the Data Flow tab. Rename this new item **SQL Server Destination-DimMaterial**.

24. Click the Aggregate by Material item. Click the blue data flow arrow, drag it on top of the SQL Server Destination-DimMaterial item, and drop it onto this item.

25. Double-click the SQL Server Destination-DimMaterial item. The SQL Destination Editor dialog box appears.

26. The MaxMinManufacturingDM data connection will be selected in the Connection manager drop-down list. Select DimMaterial from the Use a table or view drop-down list.

27. Click Mappings to view the Mappings page. The single input column should be automatically mapped to the single column in the destination. Click OK to exit the SQL Destination Editor dialog box.

28. Drag another Aggregate item from the SSIS Toolbox and drop it on the Data Flow tab. Rename this new Aggregate item **Aggregate by Machine Type**.

29. Click the Multicast item. Click the unattached blue data flow arrow, drag it on top of the Aggregate by Machine Type item, and drop it on this item.

30. Double-click the Aggregate by Machine Type item. This opens the Aggregate Transformation Editor dialog box. Check AssetClass and RawMaterial in the Available Input Columns. This groups the data by the AssetClass and RawMaterial columns to give you a unique list of machine types and their materials. You can use this unique list to populate the DimMachineType table.

31. In the Output Alias column, change AssetClass to MachineType and change RawMaterial to Material.

32. Click OK to exit the Aggregate Transformation Editor dialog box.

33. Drag a SQL Server Destination item from the SSIS Toolbox and drop it on the Data Flow tab. Rename this new item **SQL Server Destination-DimMachineType**.

34. Click the Aggregate by Machine Type item. Click the blue data flow arrow, drag it on top of the SQL Server Destination-DimMachineType item, and drop it onto this item.

35. Double-click the SQL Server Destination-DimMachineType item. The SQL Destination Editor dialog box appears.

36. Select DimMachineType from the Use a table or view drop-down list.

37. Click Mappings to view the Mappings page. The columns should be mapped automatically. Click OK to exit the SQL Destination Editor dialog box.

38. Drag a SQL Server Destination item from the SSIS Toolbox and drop it on the Data Flow tab. Rename this new item **SQL Server Destination-DimMachine**.

39. Click the Multicast item. Click the unattached blue data flow arrow, drag it on top of the SQL Server Destination-DimMachine item, and drop it on this item.

40. Double-click the SQL Server Destination-DimMachine item. The SQL Destination Editor dialog box appears.

41. Select DimMachine from the Use a table or view drop-down list.

42. Click Mappings to view the Mappings page.

43. Drag AssetCode from the Available Input Columns and drop it on MachineNumber in Available Destination Columns.

44. Drag AssetClass from the Available Input Columns and drop it on MachineType in Available Destination Columns.

45. Drag AssetName from the Available Input Columns and drop it on MachineName in Available Destination Columns.

46. Drag LocationCode from the Available Input Columns and drop it on PlantNumber in Available Destination Columns.

47. Click OK to exit the SQL Destination Editor dialog box.

### Steps to Save and Execute the Integration Services Package

1. Click the Save All button on the toolbar to save the completed package.

2. Click the Control Flow tab.

3. Click the Start Debugging button (the green triangle) on the toolbar to execute the completed package. When the execution is complete, click Stop Debugging or click the Package execution completed link to return to design mode.

Executing the DimensionLoad package copies data from the AccountingSystem database tables into the dimension tables of our MaxMinManufacturingDM database.

**NOTE**

*When package execution is complete, all items should have a green circle with a check mark. If any item has an "X" in a red circle, there has been an error during execution. Recheck the steps in this exercise associated with that item to determine the cause of the error and re-execute the package.*

# Programming in Integration Services Packages

In Data Transformation Services (DTS), creating packages was more like creating jobs in SQL Server Agent than it was like creating programs in Visual Studio. We would string together a series of steps that were to execute as a unit. We could do some programming—scripting, actually—inside a DTS package, but it was not elegant and it certainly was not fast.

Integration Services takes us much closer to the program development paradigm. We can now create variables with strong types and scopes. We can use those variables in expressions throughout our Integration Services packages, while still maintaining speed and scalability. In addition, we can define event handlers to react to certain occurrences within a package.

## Variables

*Variables* are used within Integration Services packages to pass information between the various parts of the package. This could be from one data transformation to another, from a control task to a Connection Manager, and so forth. In prior discussions of tasks, data sources, data transformations, and data destinations, we have already seen several examples of variables in use.

Variables are managed using the Variables window, shown in Figure 8-1. (The Variables window can be opened by selecting View | Other Windows | Variables from the Main menu, by right-clicking the designer area and selecting Variables from the context menu, or by clicking the Variables button in the upper-right corner of the

| Name | Scope | Data type | Value |
|---|---|---|---|
| CustNo | Foreach Loop Container | Int32 | 0 |
| DeleteFlag | File System Task | Boolean | False |
| FilePath | Nightly Transfer | String | |
| UserInfo | Data Flow Task | String | |

**Figure 8-1**   *The Variables window*

designer area.) Variables are added using the Add Variable button in the Variables window toolbar. The variable's name and data type must be specified when the variable is created. In addition, an initial value can be provided, if desired. As opposed to other scripting environments, variables in Integration Services are strongly typed. This allows for memory allocation planning to be done in advance rather than at run time, leading to more efficient operation. A variable's name, data type, and initial value can be edited right in the grid of the Variables window. Variables are deleted using the Delete Variable button in the Variables window toolbar.

Each variable has its own scope, which is displayed in the Scope column in Figure 8-1. The variable's *scope* is the set of locations where the variable can be accessed and utilized. A variable is initially created with its scope set to the entire package. The scope can be changed using the Move Variable button in the Variables window toolbar. A variable can be used in expressions and other code that resides in the item specified in the variable's Scope column. The variable can also be used within any items that are contained inside this item. For example, if a variable called LoopCounter is scoped to a For Loop container, that LoopCounter variable can be used in any task that is placed inside the For Loop container.

The Grid Options button in the Variables window toolbar displays the Variable Grid Options dialog box. The Filter section of the dialog box provides two options that we can use to filter the list of variables being displayed in the Variables window. When the Show system variables option is checked, all of the predefined system variables are added to the list. These system variables let us include information about the package, the user executing the package, and the computer the package is running on in the expressions and code created within the package. When the Show variables of all scopes option is checked, all variable regardless of scope are added to this. When this is unchecked, only those variables that belong to the scope of the object selected in the designer area.

The Columns section of the dialog box enables us to select the columns displayed in the grid. Three columns are not displayed by default: the Namespace column, the Raise event when variable value changes column, and the Description column. A *namespace* simply provides a way to create logical groupings of variables for easier debugging and maintenance. All of the system variables are in the System namespace. By default, all of the variables we create are in the User namespace. We can change the namespace of these user-defined variables by using the Choose Variable Columns dialog box to display the Namespace column and then editing the namespace in the grid.

Using the Raise event when variable value changes column, we can choose to trigger an event each time the value of a variable changes. We can then configure an event handler that executes each time the value changes. This can be done for both system- and user-defined variables. In fact, this is the only property of the system variables that we can edit in the Variables window grid. We talk more about events and event handlers in the section "Event Handlers."

## Expressions

*Expressions* let us modify the behavior of a package by evaluating conditions and changing properties at run time. Integration Services uses an expression syntax that is similar to that of the C# programming language. This is used to provide strongly typed variables. As was mentioned previously, strong typing is necessary to implement the advanced memory management necessary for top performance.

**Literals**    *Literals* are used in expressions to represent values that are known at the time the code is written. Literals can be strings, numerics, or Booleans. *String literals* are enclosed in double quotes ( " " ). The following escape sequences can be used in string literals to represent nonprinting characters:

| Escape Sequence | Character |
|---|---|
| \a | Alert |
| \b | Backspace |
| \f | Form feed |
| \n | New line |
| \r | Carriage return |
| \t | Horizontal tab |
| \v | Vertical tab |
| \" | Double quote |
| \\ | Backslash |
| \xhhhh | Unicode character in hexadecimal notation |

*Numeric literals* can be expressed as integers, as decimal numbers, or as scientific notation. They can include a negative sign, but not a digit grouping symbol (the comma is the digit grouping symbol when using U.S. regional settings). Numeric literals may include a suffix that specifies the data type to assign to it.

Integer values may use the following suffixes:

| Suffix | Description | Integration Services Data Type |
|---|---|---|
| None | Integer | DT_I4 |
| U | Unsigned Integer | DT_UI4 |
| L | Long | DT_I8 |
| UL | Unsigned Long | DT_UI8 |

Real values and scientific notation may use the following suffixes:

| Suffix | Description | Integration Services Data Type |
|--------|-------------|-------------------------------|
| None | Numeric | DT_NUMERIC |
| F | Float | DT_R4 |
| L | Double-precision float | DT_R8 |

The suffixes are not case-sensitive.

*Boolean literals* are simply spelled as true and false. They do not include double quotes. Boolean literals are not case-sensitive.

**Identifiers**   Identifiers are used in expressions to represent values that are not known until run time. Identifiers can represent variables. For example:

```
@FileName
@_LoopCounter
@PackageName
```

Identifiers that represent variables are always preceded by an at sign ( @ ). Identifiers can also represent data flow columns. For example:

```
Customer#
AmountWith6PercentTax
```

Identifiers that fit the following rules are called regular identifiers:

▶  The first character is a letter or an underscore ( _ ).

▶  The remaining characters are letters, numbers, an underscore ( _ ), an at sign ( @ ), a dollar sign ( $ ), or a pound sign ( # ).

The at sign that precedes each variable name is not considered part of the variable name when determining if it is a regular identifier. All of the identifiers in the previous paragraph are *regular identifiers.*

If an identifier does not fit these criteria, it is a *qualified identifier.* All this means is it must be enclosed in square brackets. For example:

```
@[Continue Processing Flag]
[Customer Name]
[12MonthTotal]
```

The first two are qualified identifiers because they contain spaces. The third is a qualified identifier because it does not start with a letter or an underscore. If a variable name is a qualified identifier, the at sign ( @ ) is placed outside of the square brackets.

If two identifiers within a given scope have the same name, we must provide additional information to allow the package to determine which identifier to use. When two variables have the same name, they must have different namespaces. We can then include the namespace with the variable name to make the reference unique. The name resolution operator, ::, is placed between the scope and the variable name. Whenever the name resolution operator is used, the identifier is always placed in square brackets, even if it is a regular identifier. For example:

```
@[User::UserName]
@[System::UserName]
```

When two data flow columns have the same name, we can include the name of the data flow source or transformation item where each column was created. A period is placed between the item name and the column name. For example:

```
FlatFileSource.CustomerName
DataConversion.CustomerName
```

If either the item name or the column name is not a regular identifier, they must be enclosed in square brackets. In all cases, the period is not enclosed in the brackets. For example:

```
FlatFileSource.[Customer Number]
[Character Map].ContactName
[Derived Column].[12MonthTotal]
```

**Operators**   The following operators are supported by expressions:

| Operator | Description | Example |
|---|---|---|
| (data type) | Data type conversion (Cast) | (DT_WSTR)"Acme" |
| ( ) | Grouping | (4+5) * (4+7) |
| + | Addition | 34 + 25 |
| + | (String) Concatenation | "Sally" + " " + "Jones" |
| − | Subtraction | 592 − 96 |
| − | Negative | −234 |
| * | Multiply | 20 * 409 |
| / | Divide | 39 / 3 |
| % | Modulo division (provides the remainder of the division) | 41 % 4 |

| Operator | Description | Example |
|----------|-------------|---------|
| \|\| | Logical OR | @LoopCount < 5 \|\| @Alldone |
| && | Logical AND | @Continue && @ DataIsValid |
| ! | Logical Not | !@InError |
| \| | Bitwise Inclusive OR | @Flags \| @MaskVar |
| ^ | Bitwise Exclusive OR | @Flags ^ @MaskVar |
| & | Bitwise AND | @Flags & @MaskVar |
| ~ | Bitwise Not | ~@MaskVar |
| == | Equality | @Quantity == @MaxValue |
| != | Inequality | @Quantity != @MaxValue |
| > | Greater Than | @Quantity > @MaxValue |
| < | Less Than | @Quantity < @MaxValue |
| >= | Greater Than or Equal To | @Quantity >= @MaxValue |
| <− | Less Than or Equal To | @Quantity <= @MaxValue |
| ?: | Conditional | @Counter == @MaxCount?<br>@DoneFlag:@ContinueFlag |

**Functions**    The following mathematical functions are supported by the expressions:

| Function | Description | Example | Result |
|----------|-------------|---------|--------|
| ABS | Returns the absolute value of a numeric expression | ABS(−235) | 235 |
| EXP | Returns the exponential of a numeric expression | EXP(4) | 54.598150033144236 |
| CEILING | Returns the smallest integer that is greater than or equal to a numeric expression | CEILING(37.483) | 38 |
| FLOOR | Returns the largest integer that is less than or equal to a numeric expression | FLOOR(37.483) | 37 |
| LN | Returns the natural logarithm of a numeric expression | LN(10) | 2.3025850929940459 |
| LOG | Returns the base-10 logarithm of a numeric expression | LOG(20) | 1.3010299956639813 |
| POWER | Returns the result of raising a numeric expression to a power | POWER(10,3) | 1000 |
| ROUND | Returns the numeric expression rounded to the specified number of decimal places | ROUND(87.3863, 2) | 87.39 |
| SIGN | Returns −1 if the number is negative | SIGN(−234) | −1 |
| SQUARE | Returns the square of a numeric expression | SQUARE(5) | 25 |
| SQRT | Returns the square root of a given numeric expression | SQRT(25) | 5 |

The following string functions are supported by expressions:

| Function | Description | Example | Result |
|---|---|---|---|
| CODEPOINT | Returns the Unicode value of the leftmost character of the string expression | CODEPOINT ("Anderson Co.") | 65 |
| FINDSTRING | Returns the one-based index of the second occurrence of a character string within a string expression | FINDSTRING ("ABC XYZ ABC", "ABC", 2) | 9 |
| HEX | Returns a string representing the hexadecimal value of an integer expression | HEX(1583) | 62F |
| LEN | Returns the number of characters in a string expression | LEN("ABC XYZ ABC") | 11 |
| LOWER | Returns the lowercase version of a string expression | LOWER ("Anderson Co.") | anderson co. |
| LTRIM | Returns a string expression with all of the leading blanks removed | LTRIM (" ABC XYZ ") | ABC XYZ |
| REPLACE | Returns a string with a set of characters replaced by another set of characters or with an empty string | REPLACE ("ABC XYZ ABC", "ABC", "DEF") | DEF XYZ DEF |
| REPLICATE | Returns a string copied a specified number of times | REPLICATE ("XYZ", 3) | XYZXYZXYZ |
| REVERSE | Returns a string expression in reverse order | REVERSE ("ABC XYZ") | ZYX CBA |
| RIGHT | Returns the specified number of characters from the end of the string | RIGHT ("Anderson Co.", 7) | son Co. |
| RTRIM | Returns a string expression with all of the trailing blanks removed | RTRIM (" ABC XYZ ") | ABC XYZ |
| SUBSTRING | Returns the specified portion of a string expression | SUBSTRING ("Anderson Co.", 3, 6) | derson |
| TRIM | Returns a string expression with all of the leading and trailing blanks removed | TRIM (" ABC XYZ ") | ABC XYZ |
| UPPER | Returns the uppercase version of a string expression | UPPER ("Anderson Co.") | ANDERSON CO. |

The following date functions are supported by expressions:

| Function | Description | Example | Result |
|---|---|---|---|
| DATEADD | Returns a new date based on a set time period added to a specified date | DATEADD("day", 100, (DT_DBTIMESTAMP) "1/1/2011") | 2011-04-11 00:00:00 |
| DATEDIFF | Returns the time period between two specified dates | DATEDIFF("day", (DT_DBTIMESTAMP) "1/1/2011", (DT_DBTIMESTAMP) "4/11/2011") | 100 |
| DATEPART | Returns an integer representing the selected part of the specified date | DATEPART("day", (DT_DBTIMESTAMP) "4/11/2011") | 11 |
| DAY | Returns an integer that represents the day portion of the specified date | DAY( (DT_DBTIMESTAMP) "4/11/2011") | 11 |
| GETDATE | Returns the current system date and time | GETDATE() | 2011-04-11 11:39:43 |
| GETUTCDATE | Returns the current system date in Universal Time Coordinate (UTC) time | GETUTCDATE() | 2011-04-11 16:39:43 |
| MONTH | Returns an integer that represents the month portion of the specified date | MONTH( (DT_DBTIMESTAMP) "4/11/2011") | 4 |
| YEAR | Returns an integer that represents the year portion of the specified date | YEAR( (DT_DBTIMESTAMP) "4/11/2011") | 2011 |

The following null functions are supported by expressions:

| Function | Description | Example |
|---|---|---|
| ISNULL | Returns true if the expression is null; otherwise, returns false | ISNULL( @FileName) |
| NULL | Returns a null value of the requested data type | NULL(DT_WSTR, 50) |

## Event Handlers

The event handlers within a package enable us to create a control flow that executes in reaction to a certain event. The event could be an error, a warning, or a change to the value of a variable. The event could also be the beginning or the completion of a task within the package.

**NOTE**

*Remember, the Variable Value Changed event is triggered only if you have the Raise Change Event property set to true for one or more variables in the package.*

The control flow that we create to respond to an event looks exactly the same as the control flow created for the package as a whole. While the package control flow is executed exactly once each time the package is run, an event handler control flow may be executed many times or not at all. The execution of the event handler control flow depends on what happens during the running of the package. If no error conditions are encountered, the OnError event is never fired. If 20 error conditions are encountered (and this does not terminate the package as a whole), then the OnError event is executed 20 times.

Error handlers are useful for such things as

▶ Checking the state of the host server to make sure it is appropriate for the Integration Services package to execute

▶ Sending an e-mail to the administrator when an error occurs

▶ Doing any necessary cleanup after a process has completed

To create an event handler, click the Event Handlers tab, shown in Figure 8-2. Use the Executable drop-down list to select an item in the Integration Services package. Use the Event Handler drop-down list to select the event. Now click the blue link to create an error handler for this event. You can drag and drop items from the SSIS Toolbox to create the functionality for this event handler.

## Package Development Tools

The aids to Integration Services package development do not stop with the rich programming environment. Several features help with package creation and testing. These features make Integration Services a truly robust data transformation environment.

### Import/Export Wizard

The *Import/Export Wizard* lets us quickly transfer data from one location to another. After we walk through the pages of the wizard to define the data transfer, the wizard creates an Integration Services package and executes it. The package created by the wizard can also be saved for future use.

To launch the Import/Export Wizard, from SQL Server Data Tools, select Project | SSIS Import and Export Wizard from the Main menu. The Import/Export Wizard can

**Figure 8-2**    *The Event Handlers tab*

also be launched from the SQL Server Management Studio, as shown in Figure 8-3. To accomplish this, right-click a database entry in the Object Explorer window and select either Tasks | Import Data or Tasks | Export Data from the context menu. The only difference between these two menu items is the fact that the Import Data item defaults the destination to the database that was clicked, while the Export Data item defaults the source to the database that was clicked.

When the wizard is launched from the SQL Server Management Studio, we can choose to save the Integration Services package to a SQL server or to a file for future use. When it is launched from SQL Server Data Tools, the package is automatically saved to the Integration Services project. A saved package can be executed again in the future in its current form, or it can be edited in an Integration Services project to serve as the starting point for a more complex data transformation.

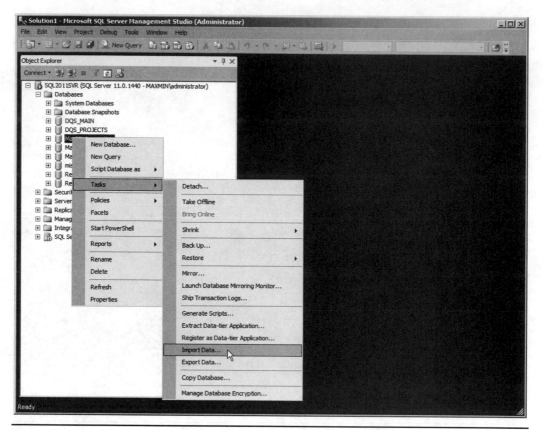

**Figure 8-3**    *Launching the Import/Export Wizard from the SQL Server Management Studio*

## Logging

Because Integration Services packages are, for the most part, designed for unattended operation, it can be extremely important to create a log documenting the execution of the package. This type of execution log can also be helpful for testing and debugging during the creation of the package. We control the logging performed by an Integration Services package using the Configure SSIS Logs dialog box, shown in Figure 8-4.

To display the Configure SSIS Logs dialog box, open an Integration Services package in SQL Server Data Tools and select Logging from the SSIS menu. Use the Providers and Logs tab to determine where the information should be logged.

**Figure 8-4**    *The Providers and Logs tab of the Configure SSIS Logs dialog box*

Select the location for the logging from the Provider Type drop-down list, and then click Add to create a new log. We can create the following types of logs:

▶ Comma-separated values text file

▶ File to be read by the SQL Profiler

▶ SQL Server Table named sysssislog

▶ Windows Event Log

▶ Extensible Markup Language (XML) text file

All of the log types, with the exception of the Windows Event Log, need to be configured to specify exactly where the logged information is to be stored. A Connection Manager is used to determine where each log type will store its entries. Click in the Configuration column to select an existing Connection Manager or create a new one.

In the Containers list, select either the entry for the package itself or an entry for one of the items in the package. Check the check box for an item to enable logging for that item. If a check box is gray, it is being enabled or disabled along with its parent item. You can break this association with the parent by clicking the grayed check box. Once you have enabled logging for an item, click one or more check boxes in the Name column for each of the log types that should be active for that item. Multiple log types can be selected.

Finally, we need to determine which events should be logged for the package or for a package item. On the Details tab, shown in Figure 8-5, check the check boxes for the events that should be logged for this item and any child items that remain associated with it. If no events are checked, only the beginning and ending of an item's execution will be logged.

In addition to the log types discussed, you can view the log entries for a package by using the Log Events window in SQL Server Data Tools. This is located under View | Other Windows or under SSIS in the main menu. Logging must be enabled for the package or for one or more items in the package before log events are displayed

**Figure 8-5**    *The Details tab of the Configure SSIS Logs dialog box*

in the Log Events window. However, you do not need to have any log types enabled for the events to appear in the Log Events window. The Log Events window is cleared each time you run the package.

## Transactions

As with operations in Transact-SQL (T-SQL), we can use transactions in Integration Services packages to ensure that our data remains in a consistent state. By using transactions, we can ensure that a series of items in a package all complete successfully, or the entire process is rolled back to the state where it was prior to the attempted changes. We can even use distributed transactions to commit or roll back changes spread across multiple servers.

Each of the items in the Control Flow SSIS Toolbox and the Integration Services package itself has a TransactionOption property that determines how it deals with transactions. This property has three possible settings:

▶ **Supported**    An item with this property setting joins a transaction if one is already active, but it does not initiate a transaction itself. This is the default setting for the property.

▶ **Required**    An item with this property setting joins a transaction if one is already active and will initiate a transaction if one is not currently active.

▶ **NotSupported**    An item with this property setting does not join a transaction if one is already active and does not initiate a transaction if one is not currently active.

The TransactionOption is set by selecting an item and then modifying this property in the Properties window. This property is not included in the Editor dialog boxes for each item.

Consider the sample Integration Services package with the TransactionOption property settings shown in Figure 8-6. Because the package has its TransactionOption set to Required, a transaction is created when package execution begins. We call this Transaction 1, as shown in Figure 8-7. The File Transfer Protocol task participates in Transaction 1 because its TransactionOption is set to Supported.

The Foreach Loop container does not participate in Transaction 1 because its TransactionOption is set to NotSupported. The data flow task inside the Foreach Loop container cannot participate in Transaction 1, even though its TransactionOption is set to Required. The reason for this is its parent object, the Foreach Loop container, is not participating in Transaction 1. Instead, because its TransactionOption is set to Required, it initiates a second transaction called Transaction 2. All items in the data flow task participate in Transaction 2.

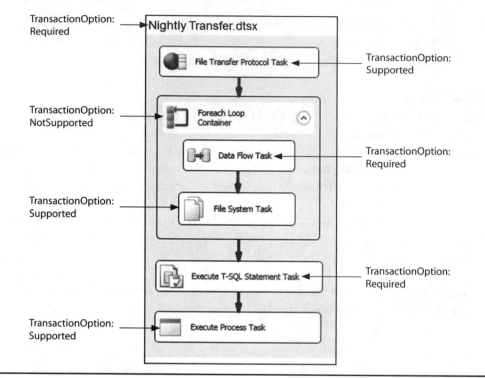

**Figure 8-6**    *Sample Integration Services package*

If any of the items in the data flow task should fail, all of the data changes within Transaction 2 are rolled back. Also, because Transaction 2 is nested within Transaction 1, all of the data changes within Transaction 1 are rolled back as well. If, on the other hand, all of the items in the data flow task complete successfully, the data changes in Transaction 2 are committed as soon as the data flow task completes. In other words, a rollback of Transaction 2 causes a rollback of Transaction 1, but not the other way around.

The File System task in Figure 8-6 and Figure 8-7 has its TransactionOption set to Supported, but there is no transaction for it to join. It is outside of Transaction 2 and it cannot join Transaction 1, because its parent object is not participating in that transaction. Therefore, the File System task is not a member of any transaction. Its success or failure does not affect either Transaction 1 or Transaction 2.

The Execute T-SQL Statement task has its TransactionOption set to Required. It does not need to create a new transaction, however, because it can join the active transaction, Transaction 1. If the Execute T-SQL Statement task should fail, it rolls back all data changes in Transaction 1. As mentioned earlier, the success or failure of the Execute T-SQL Statement task in Transaction 1 has no effect on Transaction 2.

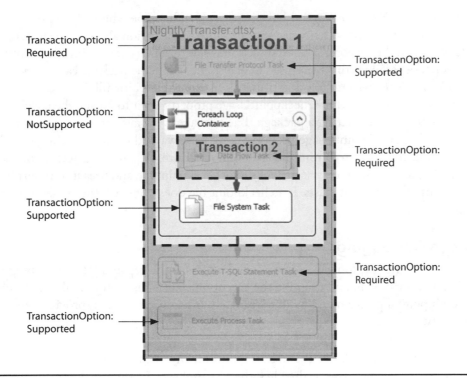

**Figure 8-7**    *Transactions created when executing the sample Integration Services package*

The Execute Process task has its TransactionOption set to Supported. It also joins the active transaction, Transaction 1. Again, its success or failure only affects Transaction 1.

## Checkpoints

There are many situations where an Integration Services package could be restarted at some point in the middle of the control flow after a failure, rather than reexecuting the entire package from the beginning. Perhaps the first portion of a package deletes an old import text file and uses File Transfer Protocol (FTP) to download a new copy of this import file. If the package fails at some point later in the process, it is probably not necessary to perform the file deletion and download again. Checkpoints provide a mechanism for performing this restart in the middle of the package.

The package includes three properties that let us enable checkpoint restarting. These are the SaveCheckpoints property, the CheckpointFilename property, and the CheckpointUsage property. The *SaveCheckpoints property* is a Boolean flag that enables or disables the saving of checkpoint information. This property must be set to true for checkpoint information to be saved.

The *CheckpointFilename property* lets us specify the filename where checkpoint information is to be saved. When a package executes, information about each successfully completed task and each committed transaction is saved to this checkpoint file. In the event of a package failure, this file is used to determine where the package can be restarted.

The *CheckpointUsage property* determines how the checkpoint file is used when a package is executed. When the CheckpointUsage property is set to Never, the checkpoint file is not used when executing a package. The package is always run from beginning to end. When the CheckpointUsage property is set to Always, the package always reads the checkpoint file and starts from the last point of failure. When the CheckpointUsage property is set to IfExists, the package looks for a checkpoint file and uses it to restart from the last point of failure, if it exists. If a checkpoint file does not exist, the package is run from beginning to end.

## Package Debugging

One of the most helpful tools in program development is the capability to pause program execution at a breakpoint and examine the execution state. This feature makes it much easier to pinpoint a problem and fix it. Fortunately, Integration Services provides this functionality.

**Setting Breakpoints**   We can set a breakpoint on any of the control flow tasks in a package. To accomplish this, right-click the task and select Edit Breakpoints from the context menu. The Set Breakpoints dialog box appears as shown in Figure 8-8. A breakpoint can be set on any of the events triggered by that task. We can use the Hit Count Type and Hit Count columns to determine whether execution pauses every time this event is triggered or only after a hit has occurred multiple times.

In addition to these task event breakpoints, breakpoints can be set on any line of code in the Script task. When execution is paused within a script, we may use the Step Into, Step Over, and Step Out features to move through the script code one line at a time. The step features do not function when paused at a task event breakpoint.

**Viewing Package State**   While the package execution is paused at a breakpoint, there are several places to see the current execution state of the package. The windows discussed here are opened using the Debug | Windows menu, the View menu, or the Windows Toolbar button.

▶ **Progress Marks**   As the tasks of a package execute, a symbol appears in the upper-right corner of each item to show the current execution status. A yellow circle containing a timer spinner indicates an item that is currently executing. A green circle containing a white checkmark indicates successfully completed

**Figure 8-8** *The Set Breakpoints dialog box*

execution. A red circle containing a white "X" indicates execution completed with errors. While execution is paused, we can switch between the Control Flow and Data Flow tabs to see the execution status of both.

▶ **Row Counts**   As the data flow tasks of a package execute, the number of rows processed through each data flow is displayed across the data flow arrows.

▶ **Execution Results**   We can switch to the Execution Results tab to see a description of the current execution status in outline form.

▶ **Breakpoints Window**   The Breakpoints window shows all of the breakpoints set in the package and lets us disable or delete breakpoints.

▶ **Output Window**   The Output window displays status messages as the package executes.

▶ **Script Explorer Window**   The Script Explorer window enables us to view the script structure.

- ▶ **Watch Windows**  The Watch windows enable us to examine and modify variable values. Variable names are entered into a Watch window without a leading "@" sign.

- ▶ **Autos Window**  The Autos window shows the value of the variables in the current and the previous line of script code.

- ▶ **Locals Window**  The Locals window displays all of the system and user variables that are currently in scope.

- ▶ **Immediate Window**  The Immediate window is used for evaluating expressions and displaying the value of variables.

- ▶ **Call Stack Window**  The Call Stack window shows the hierarchy of containers around the currently executing task.

- ▶ **Threads Window**  The Threads window shows the threads being used to execute the current package.

- ▶ **Modules Window**  The Modules window lets us view script modules.

- ▶ **Processes Window**  The Processes window shows the currently executing processes.

Several of the debug windows are not used for debugging Integration Services packages. These are the Memory window, the Disassembly window, and the Registers window.

**Viewing Data Flow**  In addition to viewing the doings inside package tasks, it is helpful (perhaps even more helpful) to see what is happening inside the data flow at various steps along the way. We do this by attaching data viewers to the data flow. The data viewer pauses the package execution and enables us to examine the rows in the data flow as it moves from one item to another.

We can attach a data viewer to a data flow from the Data Flow Path Editor dialog box. Open the Data Flow Path Editor dialog box by double-clicking a flow path arrow. The General page of the Data Flow Path Editor dialog box provides general information about this flow path arrow. The Metadata page of this dialog box provides information about the columns in the data flow at that point. This in itself can be helpful when developing and debugging packages. Data viewers are added to the data flow on the Data Viewers page.

On the Data Viewers page of the dialog box, check Enable data viewer to attach a data viewer to the data flow path. By default, all columns in the data flow are displayed in the data viewer. You can change this by moving columns between the Unused columns and the Displayed columns lists. The Data Viewer page of the Data Flow Path Editor dialog box is shown in Figure 8-9

It is also possible to create a data viewer without opening the Data Flow Path Editor dialog. To do this, right-click a flow path arrow and select Enable Data Viewer from

**Figure 8-9**    *The Data Flow Path Editor dialog box*

the context menu. This will enable the data viewer with all columns in the data flow. To remove the data viewer, right-click the flow path arrow and select Disable Data Viewer from the context menu.

Data viewers can be placed on multiple flow path arrows in a data flow, if desired. A data viewer icon is placed on the flow path arrow to show that a data viewer has been attached. When the package executes, the package execution pauses whenever the package reaches a data flow with a data viewer attached. A data viewer window appears for each data viewer, as shown in Figure 8-10.

The data viewers show data one buffer at a time. The number of rows in the buffer depends on the number of columns in the data flow at that point and the width of the data in each column. By default, the buffer will contain either 10,000 rows or 10MB of data, whichever is less.

**Figure 8-10** *A flow path arrow with a data viewer icon and a data viewer window*

When one buffer of data is loaded into the data viewer, the package execution pauses until we click the Continue button (the green triangle) or we detach the data viewer from that data flow. Data viewers are detached by clicking Detach. When data viewers are detached, the data flow resumes without loading data into the data viewer. Data viewers can be reattached by clicking Attach. We can visually inspect the data in the data viewer or click Copy Data to copy the data to the clipboard for saving or analysis in another application.

# Change Data Capture

One of the biggest challenges of the extract, transform, and load (ETL) process is determining which records need to be extracted from the source data and loaded into the data mart. For smaller dimensional tables that are not used to populate slowly changing dimensions, we may choose to truncate the target table and refill it with all of the data from the source with every load. This won't work for fact tables, large dimensional tables, and slowly changing dimensional tables. In these situations, we need to determine what data has changed since the last extract and only grab those records.

There are several methods for determining which data has changed since the last extract. They include

▶ Adding create and last update fields to the database table

▶ Adding flag fields to indicate when records have been extracted

▶ Creating triggers or stored procedures to replicate changes to change capture tables

All of these approaches add overhead to the transactional system and can even require changes to the front-end systems that create the transactions.

If our source data is coming from a SQL Server 2008, SQL Server 2008 R2, or SQL Server 2012 database, we have a feature to make this process much easier. That feature is known as *change data capture*. Rather than working from the tables themselves, change data capture uses the SQL transaction log to capture data modifications. These modifications are then written to a set of change data capture tables. Our ETL process can then read data from the change capture tables to update the data mart.

### NOTE

The Enterprise Edition, or Developer Edition of SQL Server 2012 are required for change data capture.

## Change Data Capture Architecture

As inserts, updates, and delete transactions occur in a SQL Server database table, they are recorded in both the SQL transaction log and in the table itself. While the table contains the net result of these changes, the SQL transaction log contains a record of the changes themselves. This allows the SQL server to maintain data integrity as the modifications are being made and allows for these modifications to be re-created if a log backup is applied as part of database recovery.

The SQL transaction log, therefore, has just the information we need to determine what data changes need to occur in our data mart. Unfortunately, the SQL transaction log is in a format that can only be used internally by the SQL Server database engine. Change data capture provides us with a utility that can harvest the change information from the SQL transaction log and convert it to a format that can be easily understood and used for other purposes. This utility is run as part of a SQL Agent Job, as shown in Figure 8-11.

The transaction information is converted into a more readily usable format and stored in a *change table*. One change table is created for each table that is being tracked by change data capture. The change tables are created in the cdc schema, which is created specifically for that purpose.

**Figure 8-11** *The change data capture architecture*

Change data tracking also provides a method for creating a set of functions to facilitate easy retrieval of the change information from a change table. These functions return a table-valued result containing all of the changes made to a particular table during a specified period. The records in this result set make it possible for a program or an Integration Services package to re-create the changes in another data source, such as a data mart.

## Enabling Change Data Capture

Enabling change data capture is a two-step process. This feature must first be enabled for the database as a whole. Once this is done, change data capture must also be enabled for each table individually.

The following system stored procedure will enable change data capture for a specified database:

```
USE OrderProcessingSystem
EXEC sys.sp_cdc_enable_db
```

This example will enable change data capture in the OrderProcessingSystem database.

> **NOTE**
>
> *The example here is not meant to be a Learn By Doing exercise. If you do choose to restore the OrderProcessingSystem database and try the commands shown here, you will have to run the following before doing any of the other commands:*
> *USE OrderProcessingSystem*
> *Exec sp_changedbowner 'sa'*

In addition to enabling change data capture for each database, it must be enabled for a given table. This is done with a command similar to the following:

```
EXECUTE sys.sp_cdc_enable_table
    @source_schema = N'dbo'
, @source_name = N'Orders'
, @role_name = N'cdc_Admin'
, @supports_net_changes = 1
```

This example will enable change data capture on the dbo.Orders table. The @role_name parameter defines a database role that will be used to establish database rights for the change data capture process. This database role will be created, if it does not already exist in the database.

## All Changes versus Net Changes

As stated, change data capture provides a table-valued function that returns all of the changes made to a table in a given time period. If the same record is updated three times during that time period, the function will return three sets of rows: one set for each change. In some cases, we may care only about the current state of a record at the end of the time period. We may not need to know all of the individual changes along the way.

To support this situation, change data capture has an optional setting to support net changes. When the @supports_net_changes function is set to 1, the change data capture for this particular table will support the net changes feature. This feature provides a second function that returns a single record representing the net effect of the changes made to each record over the given time period.

## The Change Table

One change table is created for each table where change data capture has been enabled. The table is named for the schema and table name of the source table as follows:

```
cdc.schemaname_tablename_CT
```

The cdc tables are found in the System Tables folder in SQL Server Management Studio.

The change table has one column that mirrors each column in the source table where changed data is being captured. These columns have the same name and, in most cases, the same data type as the corresponding column in the source table.

The default, as shown in our previous example of the sys.sp_cdc_enable_table stored procedure, is to capture changes for all of the columns in a table. The sys.sp_cdc_enable_table stored procedure has an optional parameter, @captured_column_list, which enables us to capture changes to only selected columns in a table. Enabling change data capture on selected columns would be done as follows:

```
EXECUTE sys.sp_cdc_enable_table
    @source_schema = N'dbo'
  , @source_name = N'Orders'
  , @role_name = N'cdc_Admin'
  , @captured_column_list = N'OrderID,CustomerAccount,Product,SalesPerson'
```

In addition to the columns that mirror the source table, the change table contains several columns of metadata, as follows:

▶ **__$start_lsn** The log sequence number (LSN) assigned to this change. All changes committed within the same transaction will have the same LSN. The LSN shows the order in which transactions occurred.

▶ **__$end_lsn** This column may be utilized in future versions of SQL Server. In SQL Server 2012, it is always NULL.

▶ **__$seqval** A sequence number used to determine the order of changes that are within the same transaction and thus have the same LSN.

▶ **__$operation** The operation that caused the change as follows:
1 - delete
2 - insert
3 - update (values prior to the update)
4 - update (values after the update)

▶ **__$update_mask** A bit map indicating which columns were affected by an update.

### The Validity Interval

In addition to creating a SQL Agent Job to capture change data from the SQL transaction log, the sys.sp_cdc_enable_db stored procedure creates a SQL Agent Job to remove old change data from the change tables. This prevents the change tables from growing indefinitely. It also means that there is a limited time period during which change data is available. This time period is known as the *validity interval*. By default, the validity interval is three days.

## Loading a Data Mart Table from a Change Data Capture Change Table

In order to utilize the data in the change table, we need to create two Integration Services packages. The first performs the initial load of the data. The second propagates the incremental changes from the source to the destination.

### The CDC Initial Load Package

The Integration Services package for performing the initial load consists of three control flow items. An initial CDC Control Task marks the starting Load Sequence Number (LSN). Next, a control flow copies all of the records from the source table to the destination table. Finally, a second CDC Control Task marks the ending LSN. The CDC initial load package is shown in Figure 8-12.

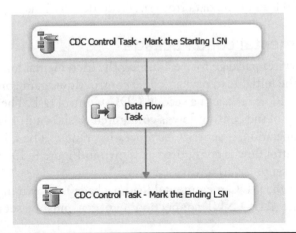

**Figure 8-12**    *The CDC initial load control flow*

In the CDC Control Task Editor dialog box for the task used to mark the starting LSN, the "SQL Server CDC database ADO.NET connection manager" must be set to an ADO.NET connection manager pointing at the source database. This is the database where change data capture is enabled. The "CDC control operation" must be set to "Mark initial load start," which is the default setting.

The "Variable containing the CDC state" is set to an SSIS package variable that is used to hold the CDC state while the package is running. This variable can be created by clicking the New button next to the "Variable containing the CDC state" drop-down list. The data type of this variable must be String.

The "Automatically store state in database table" option must be checked. The "Connection manager for the database where the state is stored" is set to a connection manager pointing at the database which will contain the CDC state table. This is usually the destination database. Use the "Table to use for storing state" drop-down list to select the CDC state table. You will probably want to use the New button next to this drop-down list to have this table created for you in the specified database. (Click New, then click Run in the Create New State Table dialog box.)

Finally, the State name contains a string. This string acts as the key for the CDC state information in the cdc_states table. It defaults to be the same as the CDC state variable. The completed CDC Control Task Editor dialog box for the CDC Control Task used to mark the starting LSN is shown in Figure 8-13.

The CDC Control Task used to mark the ending LSN is configured identical to the CDC Control Task used to mark the starting LSN with one exception. The "CDC control operation" is set to "Mark initial load end." The completed package is run once to perform the initial load of the data from source to destination.

## The CDC Incremental Load Package

The Integration Services package for performing the incremental load is almost as straightforward as the initial load package. The control flow again consists of a CDC Control task, a Data Flow task, and a second CDC Control task. The CDC Control task at the beginning of the control flow is configured as shown in Figure 8-13 *except* the "CDC control operation" is set to "Get processing range." The CDC Control task at the end of the control flow is configured as shown in Figure 8-13 *except* the "CDC control operation" is set to "Mark processed range."

The data flow for the CDC incremental load package is shown in Figure 8-14. In the CDC Source, the "ADO.NET connection manager" must be set to an ADO.NET

**Figure 8-13**    *The CDC Control Task Editor dialog box for the starting LSN CDC Control Task*

**Figure 8-14**    *The CDC incremental load data flow*

connection manager pointing at the source database. The "CDC enabled table" is set to the table from which we are getting our values. This is the table that has change data capture enabled. Selecting this table will also set the "Capture instance" for you. The "CDC processing mode" is set to the desired processing mode. (See the "CDC Source" section of Chapter 7 for more information.) Finally, the Variable containing the CDC state is set to the package variable tracking CDC state.

The CDC Splitter item defaults to the correct configuration. It creates three branches to the data flow: one containing rows to be inserted, one containing rows to be updated, and one containing rows to be deleted. The branch of the data flow containing inserts is connected to an OLE DB Destination pointing at the destination table with the fields mapped to insert the new rows appropriately.

The branch of the data flow containing updates is connected to an OLE DB Command item. The OLE DB Command uses a connection to the destination database and contains a query in the following form:

```
UPDATE {destination_table}
SET {field_0} = ?,
    {field_1} = ?,
        .
        .
        .
    {field_n} = ?
WHERE {PK_field} = ?
```

Each question mark serves as a placeholder for a parameter value. They are numbered from the beginning of the query to the end starting with Param_0 up to Param_n+1. Param_n+1 is used with the primary key field in the WHERE clause. This is shown in Figure 8-15.

The branch of the data flow containing deletes is connected to another OLE DB Command item. This OLE DB Command also uses a connection to the destination database and contains a query in the following form:

```
DELETE FROM {destination_table}
WHERE {PK_field} = ?
```

This time, the single question mark parameter is mapped to the primary key field of the destination table.

**Figure 8-15**    *Mapping fields to parameters in the OLE DB Command for updates*

# Loading a Fact Table

We will next go through two more Learn By Doing exercises. We have populated the dimensional tables in the Manufacturing data mart in a previous Learn By Doing exercise. Now we will populate the fact table in this data mart. In fact, we will add a new wrinkle to the business requirements and populate two fact tables.

## Learn By Doing—Adding a Second Fact Table to the Manufacturing Data Mart

### Features Highlighted

▶ Modifying the structure of a data mart database

▶ Using multiple fact tables in a single data mart

**Business Need**   The vice president of production at Maximum Miniatures, Incorporated would like to be able to view the current inventory amount and the number of backorders pending for products while analyzing manufacturing production. The inventory and backorder amounts are available in the order processing system.

  The inventory and backorder information is added as a second fact table in the data mart. This is done because the inventory information does not relate to all of the same dimensions as the production information. In addition, because the inventory information is populated from a different data source, loading the data mart is easier with two separate fact tables.

### Steps

1. Open the SQL Server Management Studio.
2. Connect to the SQL server where you created the MaxMinManufacturingDM.
3. Expand the Databases folder, and expand the MaxMinManufacturingDM database folder. Right-click the Tables folder, and select New Table from the context menu. A Table Designer tab appears.
4. If the Properties window is not visible, select Properties Window from the View menu.
5. In the Properties window, enter **InventoryFact** for Name and **Inventory Fact populated from the Order Processing System database** for Description.
6. Add the following columns to the table:

| Column Name | Data Type | Allow Nulls |
| --- | --- | --- |
| InventoryLevel | Int | No |
| NumberOnBackorder | Int | No |
| DateOfInventory | Datetime | No |
| ProductCode | Int | No |
| Material | NVarchar(30) | No |

**Figure 8-16**    *The InventoryFact table*

7. Select the DateOfInventory, Product Code, and Material entries in the Table Designer. Click the Set Primary Key button on the toolbar.
8. Click the Save toolbar button to save this table design. The InventoryFact table should appear as shown in Figure 8-16.
9. Close the SQL Server Management Studio.

## Learn By Doing—Populating the Fact Tables in the Manufacturing Data Mart

### Feature Highlighted

▶ Populating a fact table with Integration Services

**Business Need**   Obviously, these data marts don't do Maximum Miniatures any good unless they contain facts! Therefore, we need to populate the fact tables. The information for the Manufacturing fact table is in the BatchInfo.csv file. In an actual production environment, this file would probably have the production results for one day or perhaps one week at the most. The Integration Services package that processes this file would be run daily or weekly. However, because we want to have a good deal of sample data to work from, our copy of BatchInfo.csv has three years' worth of data. The design of the Integration Services package used to import this information remains unchanged.

We also have the little issue of one dimension table that has not been populated. This is the DimBatch table. The only source we have for the batch number information is the BatchInfo.csv file. Therefore, we include a data flow in our Integration Services package to populate the dimension table right before the fact table is populated.

We now have a second fact table in this data mart as well: the Inventory fact table. The information for this fact table comes from the order processing database. Our Integration Services package also includes a data flow to handle this.

**NOTE**

*To complete this Learn By Doing activity, you need the BatchInfo.csv file and the Maximum Miniatures Order Processing database. If you have not done so already, go to www.mhprofessional.com and search for the book's page using the ISBN, which is 0071759387. Use the "Code Download" link to download the Zip file containing the book's material. Follow the instructions within the zipped folders in the Zip file to install the Maximum Miniatures Order Processing database.*

**Steps to Create a Project Connection Manager**

1. Open SQL Server Data Tools.
2. Reopen the MaxMinManufacturingDMLoad project.
3. Open the DimensionLoad.dtsx package, if it is not already open.
4. In the Connections tray, right-click the MaxMinManufacturingDM connection, and select Convert to Project Connection in the context menu. The MaxMinManufacturingDM connection is moved to the Connection Managers folder in the Solution Explorer window. A reference to the project-level MaxMinManufacturingDM connection is placed in the Connection tray. This reference name is preceded by "(project)" to indicate it is a link to a project connection, not a package connection.

**NOTE**

*A project connection can be shared by several packages within the project. A package connection can be promoted to a project connection, as was done in this example. You can also create a project connection directly by right-clicking the Connection Managers folder in the Solution Explorer window and selecting New Connection Manager from the context menu.*

**Steps to Create the Load DimBatch Data Flow**

1. In the Solution Explorer window, right-click the SSIS Packages folder, and select New SSIS Package from the context menu.

2. Right-click the Package1.dtsx entry in the Solution Explorer window, and select Rename from the context menu. Enter **FactLoad.dtsx** for the package name and press ENTER.

3. Drag a Data Flow Task item from the SSIS Toolbox and drop it on the Control Flow tab.

4. Right-click the Data Flow Task item you just created and select Rename from the context menu. Enter **Load DimBatch** and press ENTER. Double-click the Load DimBatch item. This takes you to the Data Flow tab.

5. Right-click in the Connections tray and select New Flat File Connection from the context menu. The Flat File Connection Manager Editor dialog box appears.

6. Enter **BatchInfo.CSV File** for Connection Manager Name. Click Browse. The Open dialog box appears.

7. Select CSV Files (*.csv) in the file type drop-down list in the lower-right corner of the dialog box.

8. Browse to the BatchInfo.csv file that you downloaded from the book's webpage. Select this file and click Open to exit the Open dialog box.

9. Check Column names in the first data row, if it is not checked by default.

10. Select Columns in the page selector on the left side of the dialog box. Note the content of the columns being read from the CSV text file.

11. Select Advanced in the page selector.

12. Change the data type for the BatchNumber, MachineNumber, ProductCode, NumberProduced, and NumberRejected columns to four-byte signed integer [DT_I4]. Change the data type for the TimeStarted and TimeStopped columns to database timestamp [DT_DBTIMESTAMP].

13. Click OK to exit the Flat File Connection Manager Editor dialog box.

14. Drag a Flat File Source item from the Other Sources section of the SSIS Toolbox, and drop it on the Data Flow tab.

15. Double-click the Flat File Source item you just created. The Flat File Source Editor dialog box appears.

16. The BatchInfo.csv File data connection should be selected in the Flat File Connection Manager drop-down list.

17. Select Columns in the page selector on the left side of the dialog box.

18. Uncheck all of the columns in the Available External Columns list except the BatchNumber column.

19. Click OK to exit the Flat File Source Editor dialog box.

20. Drag a Sort item from the Common section of the SSIS Toolbox, and drop it on the Data Flow tab.

21. Click the Flat File Source item. Click the blue data flow arrow, drag it on top of the Sort item, and drop it on this item. This connects the source to the transformation.

22. Double-click the Sort item you just created. The Sort Transformation Editor dialog box appears.

23. Check the box to the left of BatchNumber in the Available Input Columns list.

24. Check Remove rows with duplicate sort values in the lower-left corner of the dialog box. This gives us a distinct list of batch numbers that we can use to populate our dimension table.

25. Click OK to exit the Sort Transformation Editor dialog box.

26. Drag a Derived Column item from the SSIS Toolbox and drop it on the Data Flow tab.

27. Click the Sort item. Click the blue data flow arrow, drag it on top of the Derived Column item, and drop it on this item. This connects the two transformations.

28. Double-click the Derived Column item you just created. The Derived Column Transformation Editor dialog box appears.

29. Enter **BatchName** in the first row under Derived Column Name.

30. Enter the following in the first row under Expression:

```
(DT_WSTR, 50) [BatchNumber]
```

31. Click OK to exit the Derived Column Transformation Editor dialog box.

32. Drag a SQL Server Destination item from the Other Destinations section of the SSIS Toolbox, and drop it on the Data Flow tab.

33. Click the Derived Column item. Click the blue data flow arrow, drag it on top of the SQL Server Destination item, and drop it on this item. This connects the transformation to the destination.

34. Double-click the SQL Server Destination item. The SQL Destination Editor dialog box appears.

35. The MaxMinManufacturingDM connection should already be selected in the Connection manager drop-down list. Select [dbo].[DimBatch] from the Use a table or view drop-down list.

36. Click Mappings to view the Mappings page. The columns from the data source (which are Available Input Columns to this data destination item) should be automatically mapped to the columns in the destination (the Available Destination Columns). The following mappings should be in place:

| Available Input Columns | | Available Destination Columns |
|---|---|---|
| BatchNumber | to | BatchNumber |
| BatchName | to | BatchName |

**Figure 8-17**   *The Data Flow tab for the Load DimBatch Data Flow task*

37.  Click OK to exit the SQL Destination Editor dialog box. The Data Flow tab
     should appear as shown in Figure 8-17.

### Steps to Begin Creating the Load ManufacturingFact Data Flow

1.  Click the Control Flow tab. Drag another Data Flow Task item onto the Control
    Flow tab. Rename this new Data Flow Task item **Load ManufacturingFact**.
2.  Click the Load DimBatch item. Drag the precedence arrow onto the Load
    ManufacturingFact item and drop it there. (The DimBatch table must be loaded
    successfully before the ManufacturingFact table can be loaded.)

3. Double-click the Load ManufacturingFact item. This takes you to the Data Flow tab with Load ManufacturingFact selected in the Data Flow Task drop-down list.

4. Drag a Flat File Source item from the SSIS Toolbox and drop it on the Data Flow tab.

5. Double-click the Flat File Source item you just created. The Flat File Source Editor dialog box appears.

6. The BatchInfo.csv File data connection should be selected in the Flat File Connection Manager drop-down list. Click OK to exit the Flat File Source Editor dialog box.

## Steps to Create a Derived Column Data Flow Item

1. Drag a Derived Column item from the SSIS Toolbox and drop it on the Data Flow tab.

2. Click the Flat File Source item. Click the blue data flow arrow, drag it on top of the Derived Column item, and drop it on this item. This connects the source to the transformation.

3. Double-click the Derived Column item you just created. The Derived Column Transformation Editor dialog box appears.

4. Our flat file does not explicitly provide us with the number of products accepted and the elapsed time of production. Instead, we need to calculate this information from the data that is provided in the flat file. The flat file also includes a time portion on TimeStarted. This causes problems when we use this field to build our time dimension. We can solve these issues by adding three derived columns to the data flow. Enter **AcceptedProducts** in the first row under Derived Column Name. Enter the following in the first row under Expression:

```
[NumberProduced] - [NumberRejected]
```

(You can expand the Columns folder in the upper-left corner of the dialog box, and then drag-and-drop the fields onto the expression, if you like.)

5. Enter **ElapsedTimeForManufacture** in the second row under Derived Column Name. Enter the following in the second row under Expression:

```
(DT_NUMERIC,6,2)DATEDIFF("mi", [TimeStarted], [TimeStopped])
```

(You can expand the Date/Time Functions folder in the upper-right corner of the dialog box, and then drag-and-drop the DATEDIFF function onto the expression. You can also drag-and-drop the fields onto the expression.)

6. Enter **DateOfManufacture** in the third row under Derived Column Name. Enter the following in the third row under Expression:

```
(DT_DBTIMESTAMP)SUBSTRING((DT_WSTR,25)[TimeStarted],1,10)
```

This expression converts TimeStarted into a string and selects the first ten characters of that string (the date portion, but not the time portion). This string is then converted back into a datetime, without the time portion, so time defaults to midnight. (You can expand the Type Casts and String Functions folders in the upper-right corner of the dialog box and drag and drop the (DT_WSTR) type cast, SUBSTRING function, and (DT_DBTIMESTAMP) type cast onto the expression. You can also drag-and-drop the fields onto the expression.)

7. Click OK to exit the Derived Column Transformation Editor dialog box.

## Steps to Create Lookup Data Flow Items

1. Drag a Lookup item from the SSIS Toolbox and drop it on the Data Flow tab.
2. Change the name of this item to **Lookup Batch Number**.
3. Click the Derived Column item. Click the blue data flow arrow, drag it on top of the Lookup Batch Number item, and drop it on this item. This connects the two transformations.
4. Double-click the Lookup Batch Number item. The Lookup Transformation Editor dialog box appears.
5. In the Specify how to handle rows with no matching entries drop-down list, select Redirect rows to no match output.
6. Click Connection to view the Connection page.
7. Select [dbo].[DimBatch] from the Use a table or a view drop-down list.
8. Click Columns to view the Columns page.
9. Click BatchNumber in the Available Input Columns list, and drag-and-drop it on BatchNumber in the Available LookupColumns list.
10. Click OK to exit the Lookup Transformation Editor dialog box.
11. Drag another Lookup item from the SSIS Toolbox and drop it on the Data Flow tab.
12. Change the name of this item to **Lookup Machine Number**.
13. Click the Lookup Batch Number item. Click the blue data flow arrow, drag it on top of the Lookup Machine Number item, and drop it on this item. The Input Output Selection dialog box appears.
14. Select Lookup Match Output from the Output drop-down list and click OK.
15. Double-click the Lookup Machine Number item. The Lookup Transformation Editor dialog box appears.
16. In the Specify how to handle rows with no matching entries drop-down list, select Redirect rows to no match output.
17. Click Connection to view the Connection page.
18. Select [dbo].[DimMachine] from the Use a table or a view drop-down list.
19. Click Columns to view the Columns page.

20. Click MachineNumber in the Available Input Columns list, and drag-and-drop it on MachineNumber in the Available LookupColumns list.

21. Click OK to exit the Lookup Transformation Editor dialog box.

22. Repeat Steps 11 to 21 in this "Steps to Create Lookup Data Flow Items" section to add the following Lookup item to the data flow:

| Item Name | Table | Available Input Column | Available Lookup Columns |
|---|---|---|---|
| Lookup Product | [dbo].[DimProduct] | ProductCode | ProductCode |

### Steps to Create a SQL Server Data Destination Item

1. Drag a SQL Server Destination item from the SSIS Toolbox and drop it on the Data Flow tab.

2. Click the Lookup Product item. Click the blue data flow arrow, drag it on top of the SQL Server Destination item, and drop it on this item. The Input Output Selection dialog box appears.

3. Select Lookup Match Output from the Output drop-down list, and click OK.

4. Double-click the SQL Server Destination item. The SQL Destination Editor dialog box appears.

5. Select [dbo].[ManufacturingFact] from the Use a table or view drop-down list.

6. Click Mappings to view the Mappings page. The columns from the data source (which are Available Input Columns to this data destination item) should be automatically mapped to the columns in the destination (the Available Destination Columns). The following mappings should be in place:

| Available Input Columns | | Available Destination Columns |
|---|---|---|
| BatchNumber | to | BatchNumber |
| MachineNumber | to | MachineNumber |
| ProductCode | to | ProductCode |
| AcceptedProducts | to | AcceptedProducts |
| ElapsedTimeForManufacture | to | ElapsedTimeForManufacture |
| DateOfManufacture | to | DateOfManufacture |

7. Use drag-and-drop to add the following mapping:

| Available Input Columns | | Available Destination Columns |
|---|---|---|
| NumberRejected | to | RejectedProducts |

8. Click OK to exit the SQL Destination Editor dialog box.

**Steps to Create a Data Destination for the Rows in Error**

1. Drag a Union All item from the SSIS Toolbox and drop it on the Data Flow tab.
2. Click the Lookup Batch Number item. Click the unattached blue data flow arrow, drag it on top of the Union All item, and drop it on this item. Note that the Lookup No Match Output is connected to the Union All item. This means the unmatched records are going to follow this data flow.
3. Click the Lookup Machine Number item. Click the unattached blue data flow arrow, drag it on top of the Union All item, and drop it on this item.
4. Repeat this process with the Lookup Product item.
5. Drag a Flat File Destination item from the SSIS Toolbox and drop it on the Data Flow tab.
6. Change the name of this item to **Write Error Records to a Text File**.
7. Click the Union All item. Click the blue data flow arrow, drag it on top of the Write Error Records item, and drop it on this item.
8. Double-click the Write Error Records item. The Flat File Destination Editor dialog box appears.
9. Click New to create a new Flat File Connection Manager. The Flat File Format dialog box appears.
10. Leave the format set to delimited, and click OK. The Flat File Connection Manager Editor appears.
11. Enter **Error Output** for Connection manager name.
12. Click Browse. The Open dialog box appears.
13. Browse to an appropriate location for this error text file. Enter **MfgInfoErrors.txt** for File name.
14. Click Open to exit the Open dialog box.
15. Check the Column names in the first data row check box.
16. Click OK to exit the Flat File Connection Manager Editor.
17. Click Mappings to view the Mappings page of the Flat File Destination Editor dialog box. Mappings have been created for all columns.
18. Click OK to exit the Flat File Destination Editor dialog box. The Data Flow tab should appear as shown in Figure 8-18.
19. Hold down CTRL and click the following items in the data flow:
    Lookup Batch Number
    Lookup Machine Number
    Lookup Product
    Union All
    Write Error Records to a Text File
20. Right-click the Lookup Batch Number item, and select Group from the context menu. The selected items are all placed inside a grouping in the data flow.
21. Click the ^ in the upper-right corner of the Group box to contract the group.

**Figure 8-18** *The data flow to load the Manufacturing fact table*

22. Drag the group so it is between the Derived Column item and the SQL Server Destination item. Position and size the items appropriately.

23. Rename the Group item to **Validate Batch Number, Machine Number, and Product**. The Data Flow should appear similar to Figure 8-19.

### NOTE

*A Group can be used in a control flow or in a data flow to help organize items and improve organization and readability. They do not have any effect on the operation of the SSIS package. You can undo a grouping by right-clicking the group item and selecting Ungroup from the context menu.*

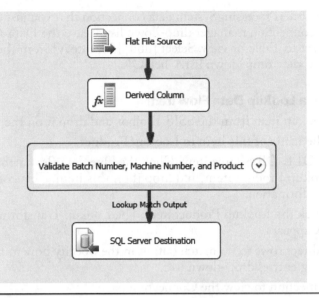

**Figure 8-19**    *The data flow to load the Manufacturing fact table with the Validation Grouping*

## Steps to Begin Creating the InventoryFact Data Flow

1.  Click the Control Flow tab. Drag a third Data Flow Task item onto the Control Flow tab. Rename this new Data Flow Task item **Load InventoryFact**. (You do not need to set precedence between the Load InventoryFact item and the other Data Flow Task items. It does not matter when the InventoryFact table is filled relative to the operations being done on the other tables.)

2.  Double-click the Load InventoryFact item. This takes you to the Data Flow tab.

3.  Right-click in the Connections tray, and select New OLE DB Connection from the context menu. Click New in the Configure OLE DB Connection Manager dialog box to create a new data connection.

4.  Enter the name of the server where the Maximum Miniatures Order Processing database is installed in Server name. Select the appropriate method for accessing this server in the Log on to the server section. Enter credentials if necessary. Select OrderProcessingSystem from the Select or enter a database name drop-down list. (If the drop-down list is empty, either your server name or your login credentials are incorrect.) Click OK to return to the Configure OLE DB Connection Manager dialog box. Click OK again to exit this dialog box.

5.  Drag an OLE DB Source item from the SSIS Toolbox and drop it on the Data Flow tab.

6.  Double-click the OLE DB Source item you just created. The OLE DB Source Editor dialog box appears.

7. Select the OrderProcessingSystem data connection that you just created in the OLE DB connection manager drop-down list. Leave the Data access mode drop-down list set to Table or view. Select [dbo].[Inventory] from the Name of the table or the view drop-down list. Click OK.

### Steps to Create a Lookup Data Flow Item

1. Drag a Lookup item from the SSIS Toolbox and drop it on the Data Flow tab.
2. Change the name of this item to **Lookup Product**.
3. Click the OLE DB Source item. Click the blue data flow arrow, drag it on top of the Lookup Product item, and drop it on this item. This connects the source to the transformation.
4. Double-click the Lookup Product item. The Lookup Transformation Editor dialog box appears.
5. Select Redirect rows to no match output in the Specify how to handle rows with no matching entries drop-down list.
6. Click Connection to view the Connection page.
7. Select the MaxMinManufacturingDM data connection in the OLE DB connection manager drop-down list.
8. Select [dbo].[DimProduct] from the Use a table or a view drop-down list.
9. Click Columns to view the Columns page.
10. Click Code in the Available Input Columns list and drag-and-drop it on ProductCode in the Available LookupColumns list.
11. Click OK to exit the Lookup Transformation Editor dialog box.

### Steps to Create a Data Conversion Data Flow Item

1. Drag a Data Conversion item from the SSIS Toolbox and drop it on the Data Flow tab.
2. Click the Lookup Product item. Click the blue data flow arrow, drag it on top of the Data Conversion item, and drop it on this item. The Input Output Selection dialog box appears.
3. Select Lookup Match Output from the Output drop-down list. Click OK.
4. Double-click the Data Conversion item. The Data Conversion Transformation Editor dialog box appears.
5. Check the check box next to Material in the Available Input Columns area.
6. Enter **Material-Unicode** in the Output Alias column.
7. Select Unicode string [DT_WSTR] from the drop-down list in the Data Type column.
8. Click OK to exit the Data Conversion Transformation Editor dialog box.

## Steps to Create a Data Destination Data Flow Item

1.  Drag a SQL Server Destination item from the SSIS Toolbox and drop it on the Data Flow tab.

2.  Click the Data Conversion item. Click the blue data flow arrow, drag it on top of the SQL Server Destination item, and drop it on this item. This connects the transformation to the destination.

3.  Double-click the SQL Server Destination item. The SQL Destination Editor dialog box appears.

4.  Select the MaxMinManufacturingDM data connection in the OLE DB Connection Manager drop-down list. Select [dbo].[InventoryFact] from the Use a table or view drop-down list.

5.  Click Mappings to view the Mappings page. Delete the line that joins the Material column in both lists.

6.  Use drag-and-drop to add the following mappings:

| Available Input Columns | | Available Destination Columns |
|---|---|---|
| Code | to | ProductCode |
| InventoryDate | to | DateOfInventory |
| AmountOnHand | to | InventoryLevel |
| AmountBackordered | to | NumberOnBackorder |
| Material-Unicode | to | Material |

7.  Click OK to exit the SQL Destination Editor dialog box.

## Steps to Create a Data Destination for the Rows in Error

1.  Drag a Flat File Destination item from the SSIS Toolbox and drop it on the Data Flow tab.

2.  Change the name of this item to **Write Inventory Error Records to a Text File**.

3.  Click the Lookup Product item. Click the blue data flow arrow, drag it on top of the Write Inventory Error Records item, and drop it on this item.

4.  Double-click the Write Inventory Error Records item. The Flat File Destination Editor dialog box appears.

5.  Click New to create a new Flat File Connection Manager. The Flat File Format dialog box appears.

6.  Leave the format set to delimited, and click OK. The Flat File Connection Manager Editor appears.

7.  Enter **Inventory Error Output** for Connection manager name.

8.  Click Browse. The Open dialog box appears.

9. Browse to the same folder you selected for the manufacturing error text file. Enter **InvInfoErrors.txt** for File name.

10. Click Open to exit the Open dialog box.

11. Check the Column names in the first data row check box.

12. Click OK to exit the Flat File Connection Manager Editor.

13. Click Mappings to view the Mappings page of the Flat File Destination Editor dialog box.

14. Click OK to exit the Flat File Destination Editor dialog box. The Data Flow tab should appear as shown in Figure 8-20.

**Figure 8-20**    *The data flow to load the Inventory fact table*

15. Click the Save All button on the toolbar to save the completed package.
16. Click the Start Debugging button on the toolbar to execute the completed package. When the execution is complete, click Stop Debugging or the Package Execution Completed link to return to Design mode.
17. Close the project.

# Putting Integration Services Packages into Production

Integration Services packages can be executed in SQL Server Data Tools. This is convenient for development and debugging, but it probably is not the way you want to use these packages in a production environment. This section looks at how we deploy packages to our servers and execute those packages once they are there.

## Parameters

The Integration Services packages we created in the previous Learn By Doing exercises in this chapter are completely self-contained. We execute the package, and it does its stuff. All of the configuration was done at design time. When we run the package, it requires no further input.

In some situations, however, we may want to have some interaction with the package at run time. For example, a package may be created using databases on a development server, put through quality assurance testing using databases on a test server, and put into production using databases on a production server. It would be nice to move the package through this process without having to open it up in SQL Server Data Tools each time to change the server name. Similarly, server names and data paths change over time as a natural outgrowth of network growth and maintenance. It would be nice to have these items be part of the configuration of the package so they can be managed by an administrator rather than a package developer. This is where parameters come in.

Parameters function similar to variables in an SSIS package. The difference is that *parameters* are exposed outside of the package and can have their value set at run time. This allows us to make our packages configurable.

There are two types of parameters. Project parameters are created in the SSIS project and can be used by any of the packages in that project. This is similar to the project connection manager we encountered in the last Learn By Doing exercise. Package parameters exist within a single package.

When a parameter is created, it is given a value. This value is used for the parameter when the package is run in SQL Server Data Tools. This does not serve as a default value for the parameter when the package is deployed to the server. All parameters have a value of blank (or 0 for parameters with numeric data types) when they are deployed to the server. Therefore, values must be respecified for the parameters on the server.

We will see how to create package and project parameters in the next Learn By Doing exercise.

## Associating Properties with Parameters

Once a parameter has been created, we can use its value to set properties on various items in our package. This can be done in one of two ways. For an item in the control flow, we can right-click the item and select Parameterize from the context menu. This will display the Parameterize dialog box shown in Figure 8-21.

Using the Property drop-down list at the top of the dialog box, we can select a property from this item. The value of the parameter will then be used for this property each time the package is executed. We can then use the "Create new parameter" and "Use existing parameter" radio buttons to determine whether we are associating this property with a parameter that has already been created or we are creating a new parameter.

**Figure 8-21**   *The Parameterize dialog box*

**Figure 8-22**   *Using the Property Expressions Editor dialog box to associate properties with parameters*

If a new parameter is being created, we can specify its name and description. We can also provide a value for the parameter. Remember, this value will be used as the value of the associated item property anytime the package is run within SQL Server Data Tools. Finally, we can specify whether this is a package parameter or a project parameter and whether or not a value is required.

The second method for associating a parameter value with an item property is to use the Expressions property of the item. This can be done for almost any item in an Integration Services package, including Connection Managers. Select the item containing the property that is to be associated, and then select the Expressions property in the Properties window. Click the ellipsis (…) button for the Expressions property to display the Property Expressions Editor dialog box as shown in Figure 8-22.

A property of the item is selected from the drop-down list in the Property column. The ellipsis (…) button is used to display the Expression Builder dialog box. Here we can build the expression that supplies the value for the property. This can simply be the parameter itself or the property used as part of a valid expression, as shown in Figure 8-23.

## The Integration Services Catalog

Integration Services packages can be stored and executed on a server. There is, however, a bit of preparation we must do before this can take place. First, we need to include Integration Services as part of the SQL Server install. After this is done, we also need to create the Integration Services Catalog that will store our packages.

**Figure 8-23** *Using a parameter as part of an expression*

This second step is accomplished using the SQL Server Management Studio. In SSMS, on a server that does not yet have the Integration Services Catalog created, you will see a folder in the Object Explorer window for Integration Services Catalogs with nothing in it. To create the Integration Services Catalog, right-click the Integration Services Catalogs folder and select Create Catalog from the context menu. The Create Catalog dialog box appears as shown in Figure 8-24.

The operation of the Integration Services Catalog requires Common Language Runtime (CLR) integration to be enabled on this SQL Server instance. CLR integration allows SQL Server code to utilize features of the .NET Framework. Check the box to enable CLR integration if it is not enabled on this SQL Server instance. Also, specify a password to be used to protect the encryption key used by the Integration Services Catalog for storing sensitive information. You will see this in action in the next Learn By Doing exercise.

**Figure 8-24**    *The Create Catalog dialog box*

Once the Integration Services Catalog has been created, we can load our Integration Services packages into the catalog. This can be done in two ways. We can push an Integration Services project and its constituent packages to the catalog from SQL Server Data Tools using the deploy process. Alternatively, we can pull a package to the catalog using the import process.

## Deploying SSIS Projects from SQL Server Data Tools

To deploy an Integration Services project from SQL Server Data Tools, right-click the package entry in the Solution Explorer window and select Deploy from the context menu. This launches the Integration Services Deployment Wizard and takes you to the Introduction page. Clicking Next takes you to the Select Source page of the wizard as shown in Figure 8-25. The wizard automatically advances to the next page. You can return to the Select Source by clicking Previous if you wish to modify the default settings.

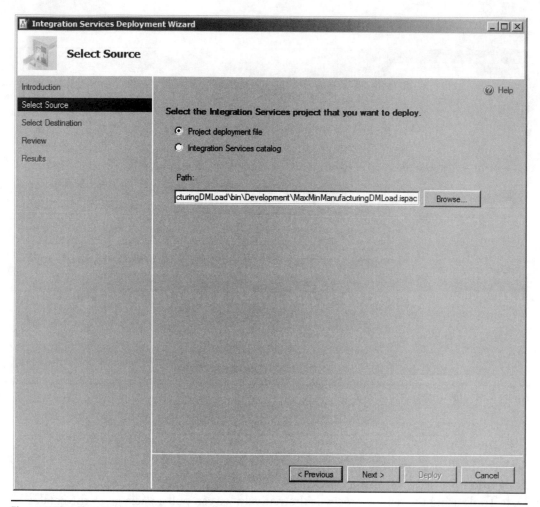

**Figure 8-25** *The Select Source page of the Integration Services Deployment Wizard*

On the Select Source page of the wizard, you can select the Integration Services project you wish to deploy. This can be an SSIS project file (with a .ispac file extension) found in the file system or a package that exists in an Integration Services Catalog on another server. This latter functionality makes it easy to take a package deployed on a development or quality assurance server and promote it to the next server along the develop-test-production progression. The Select Source page defaults to the SSIS project file for the Integration Services project you right-clicked to launch the wizard.

As stated previously, the wizard automatically advances from the Select Source page to the Select Destination page as shown in Figure 8-26. On this page we need to specify the name of the server where we are going to deploy the project along with

**Figure 8-26**    *The Select Destination page of the Integration Services Deployment Wizard*

the path within the Integration Services Catalog on that server where the project will reside. A Browse button is provided to enable us to select from available servers. A second Browse button is provided so we can select an existing path within the chosen Integration Services Catalog. We can also specify a new path, which will be created as part of the deployment process.

Clicking Next on the Select Destination page takes you to the Review page of the wizard. Here you can review the choices made and launch the deployment process by clicking Deploy. The results of the deployment are shown on the Results page. You will see this in the Learn By Doing exercise later in this chapter.

## Importing Packages into the SSIS Catalog

Importing packages is done from SQL Server Management Studio. In order to import a package, we must first have a folder created in the SSIS Catalog. To do this, launch SQL Server Management Studio and expand the Integration Services Catalogs folder in the Object Explorer window. Right-click the SSISDB entry and select Create Folder from the context menu. In the Create Folder dialog box, specify the folder name and a folder description, if desired, and click OK.

The import process itself is a two-step process. The selected SSIS package must be migrated to an Integration Services project deployment (.ispac) file. Then the project deployment file can be deployed to the server. This is accomplished through two wizards that are executed one after the other for us. The Integration Services Project Conversion Wizard creates the Integration Services project deployment file, and the Integration Services Deployment Wizard (the same wizard we discussed in the previous section) deploys the file to the server.

In the Object Explorer window, expand the folder entry that is to contain the imported package. The folder will contain a Projects folder and an Environments folder by default. Right-click the Projects folder and select Import Packages from the context menu. This launches the Integration Services Project Conversion Wizard and takes you to the Introduction page. Clicking Next takes you to the Locate Packages page of the wizard as shown in Figure 8-27.

On the Locate Packages page, you select a folder containing Integration Services packages. This can be a folder in the file system or in a previous version of Integration Services. After selecting the appropriate folder, clicking Next takes you to the Select Packages page of the wizard as shown in Figure 8-28.

The Select Packages page enables you to select one or more packages for import. After checking the packages you would like to import, click Next. This takes you to the Select Destination page of the wizard shown in Figure 8-29. On this page, you specify the path and the file name of the interim Integration Services project deployment file that will be created as part of this process. Remember, this file is only needed by the Integration Services Deployment Wizard, which will run next. Once the package has been deployed, the Integration Services project deployment file can be deleted.

The next four pages of the wizard pertain to migrating older-version Integration Services packages to the current deploy format. Click Next to move through these pages. The Review page of the wizard allows you to view the decisions made. Click Convert to migrate the package to the Integration Services project deployment file. The progress of the migration is shown on the Results page.

When you click Close on the Results page, the Integration Services Deployment Wizard is automatically launched to complete the deployment. Click Next on the Introduction page to move to the Select Destination page. This is shown in Figure 8-26.

**Figure 8-27**    *The Locate Packages page of the Integration Services Project Conversion Wizard*

The folder from which you launched the import process will be selected by default. Click Next to move to the Review page, and click Deploy to complete the process. The status of the deployment will be shown on the Results page. When complete, click Close to exit the wizard.

An entry for the package name that you specified as part of the import process appears in the Projects folder. If it does not appear there, right-click and select Refresh from the context menu. Expanding the package entry reveals a Packages folder, which, in turn, contains the imported package.

**Figure 8-28** *The Select Packages page of the Integration Services Project Conversion Wizard*

## Learn By Doing—Deploying the Packages to a Server

### Features Highlighted

▶ Creating an Integration Services Catalog

▶ Creating parameters

▶ Creating an environment

▶ Deploying packages to a server

**Figure 8-29**    *The Select Destination page of the Integration Services Project Conversion Wizard*

**Business Need**    Now that we have packages created to load data into our manufacturing data mart, we need to put those packages in a production server environment for regular use.

### Steps to Create an Integration Services Catalog

1. Open the SQL Server Management Studio.
2. Connect to the SQL Server that will host your Integration Services Catalog.
3. In the Object Explorer window, right-click the Integration Services Catalogs entry and select Create Catalog from the context menu. The Create Catalog dialog box appears.
4. Check the Enable CLR Integration check box.
5. Enter a password for the SSIS Catalog encryption key.

6. Retype the SSIS Catalog encryption key password.

7. Click OK. The SSIS Catalog, called SSISDB, is created.

### Steps to Create a Project Parameter

1. Open SQL Server Data Tools.

2. Reopen the MaxMinManufacturingDMLoad project.

3. In the Solution Explorer window, double-click the Project.params entry. The Project Parameters (Project.params [Design]) tab opens.

4. Click the Add Parameter button in the Project Parameters tab toolbar. An entry for a new parameter is created.

5. In the Name column, change "Parameter" to **SQLServerName**.

6. Select String from the drop-down list in the Data type column.

7. In the Value column, enter the name of the server hosting the MaxMinAccounting and OrderProcessingSystem databases. (This exercise assumes both of these databases are hosted on the same server.)

8. In the Required column, select True from the drop-down list. You have created a Project Parameter.

### Steps to Create a Package Parameter

1. In the Solution Explorer window, double-click the entry for FactLoad.dtsx. The FactLoad package design (FactLoad.dtsx [Design]) tab is opened and/or is given focus.

2. Select the Parameters tab.

3. Click the Add Parameter button in the Parameters tab toolbar. An entry for a new parameter is created.

4. In the Name column, change "Parameter" to **ErrorFileFolder**.

5. Select String from the drop-down list in the Data type column.

6. In the Value column, enter the Universal Naming Convention (UNC) path to the folder where the error text files are to be stored.

7. In the Required column, select True from the drop-down list. You have created a package parameter.

### Steps to Associate Properties with the ErrorFileFolder Parameter

1. Select the Control Flow tab.

2. Select the Error Output entry in the Connections tray.

3. In the Properties window, select the Expressions item.

4. Click the ellipsis (…) button that appears next to the entry for Expressions. The Property Expressions Editor dialog box appears.

5. Click the blank entry in the Property column. A drop-down list appears.
6. Select ConnectionString from the drop-down list.
7. Click the ellipsis (…) button at the end of the first row. The Expression Builder dialog box appears.
8. Expand the Variables and Parameters entry in the upper-left corner.
9. Drag the $Package::ErrorFileFolder entry and drop it in the Expression area.
10. Type the additional text so the Expression area appears as follows:

```
@[$Package::ErrorFileFolder] + "\\MfgInfoErrors.txt"
```

11. Click Evaluate Expression to make sure the expression is valid. The resulting file path is displayed in the Evaluated value area.
12. Click OK to exit the Expression Builder dialog box.
13. Click OK to exit the Property Expressions Editor dialog box.
14. Select the Inventory Error Output entry in the Connections tray.
15. In the Properties window, select the Expressions item.
16. Click the ellipsis (…) button that appears next to the entry for Expressions. The Property Expressions Editor dialog box appears.
17. Click the blank entry in the Property column. A drop-down list appears.
18. Select ConnectionString from the drop-down list.
19. Click the ellipsis (…) button at the end of the first row. The Expression Builder dialog box appears.
20. Expand the Variables and Parameters entry in the upper-left corner.
21. Drag the $Package::ErrorFileFolder entry, and drop it in the Expression area.
22. Type the additional text so the Expression area appears as follows:

```
@[$Package::ErrorFileFolder] + "\\InvInfoErrors.txt"
```

23. Click Evaluate Expression to make sure the expression is valid. The resulting file path is displayed in the Evaluated value area.
24. Click OK to exit the Expression Builder dialog box.
25. Click OK to exit the Property Expressions Editor dialog box.

## Steps to Associate Properties with the SQLServerName Parameter

1. Select the OrderProcessingSystem entry in the Connections tray.
2. In the Properties window, select the Expressions item.
3. Click the ellipsis (…) button that appears next to the entry for Expressions. The Property Expressions Editor dialog box appears.

4.  Click the blank entry in the Property column. A drop-down list appears.

5.  Select ServerName from the drop-down list.

6.  Click the ellipsis (...) button at the end of the first row. The Expression Builder dialog box appears.

7.  Expand the Variables and Parameters entry in the upper-left corner.

8.  Drag the $Project::SQLServerName entry, and drop it in the Expression area.

9.  Click OK to exit the Expression Builder dialog box.

10. Click OK to exit the Property Expressions Editor dialog box.

11. In the Solution Explorer window, double-click the entry for DimensionLoad. dtsx. The DimensionLoad package design (DimensionLoad.dtsx [Design]) tab is opened and/or is given focus.

12. Select the MaxMinAccounting entry in the Connections tray.

13. In the Properties window, select the Expressions item.

14. Click the ellipsis (...) button that appears next to the entry for Expressions. The Property Expressions Editor dialog box appears.

15. Click the blank entry in the Property column. A drop-down list appears.

16. Select ServerName from the drop-down list.

17. Click the ellipsis (...) button at the end of the first row. The Expression Builder dialog box appears.

18. Expand the Variables and Parameters entry in the upper-left corner.

19. Drag the $Project::SQLServerName entry, and drop it in the Expression area.

20. Click OK to exit the Expression Builder dialog box.

21. Click OK to exit the Property Expressions Editor dialog box.

22. Click the Save All button on the toolbar to save the project.

### Steps to Deploy the Project

1.  In the Solution Explorer window, right-click the entry for the MaxMinManufacturingDMLoad project, and select Deploy from the context menu. The Introduction page of the Integration Services Deployment Wizard appears.

2.  Click Next. After validating the project, the Select Destination page of the Integration Services Deployment Wizard appears.

3.  For Server name, enter the name of the SQL Server where you created the SSIS Catalog (SSISDB) earlier in this Learn By Doing exercise.

4.  Click the Browse button next to the Path text box. The Browse for Folder or Project dialog box appears.

5.  Click New Folder. The Create New Folder dialog box appears.

6.  Enter **BI Book** for Name.

7. Click OK to exit the Create New Folder dialog box.

8. Select the BI Book folder you just created in the Browse for Folder or Project dialog box. Click OK to exit this dialog box.

9. Click Next. The Review page of the Integration Services Deployment Wizard appears.

10. Click Deploy. The two packages in the project will be deployed to the server.

11. Click Close when the deployment is complete.

### Steps to Configure the Project

1. Select the SQL Server Management Studio application.

2. In the Object Explorer window, expand the SSISDB entry under Integration Services Catalogs. You will see the BI Book folder created by our project deployment.

3. Expand the BI Book folder.

4. Expand the Projects folder.

5. Right-click the MaxMinManufacturingDMLoad entry, and select Configure from the context menu. The Configure - MaxMinManufacturingDMLoad dialog box appears.

6. Click the ellipsis (…) button in the SQLServerName row. The Set Parameter Value dialog box appears.

7. In the Edit value text box, enter the name of the SQL Server that is hosting the MaxMinAccounting and OrderProcessingSystem databases.

8. Click OK to exit the Set Parameter Value dialog box.

9. Click the ellipsis (…) button in the ErrorFileFolder row. The Set Parameter Value dialog box appears.

10. In the Edit value text box, enter the UNC path to the folder that should contain the error text files.

11. Click OK to exit the Set Parameter Value dialog box.

12. Click OK to exit the Configure - MaxMinManufacturingDMLoad dialog box.

# Managing Packages in the Integration Services Catalog

Once our packages are in the Integration Services Catalog, we can manage them using the SQL Server Management Studio. In the last section of the Learn By Doing exercise, you saw how to configure a package on the server. We can also save configuration settings that can be shared by several packages. These settings are saved in an environment.

After looking at environments, we'll take a quick look at setting security for Integration Services packages on the server.

## Utilizing Environments

An *environment* is a set of values that can be shared among several packages. This can be useful when a number of packages rely on the same information for their parameters. For example, you may have a number of packages that use one set of servers and file paths when they are undergoing quality assurance testing and another set of servers and file paths when they are in production. We can create one environment called "QA Test" that holds the appropriate parameter settings for a package undergoing quality assurance testing. We can create another environment called "Production" that holds the appropriate parameter settings for a package operating in production.

To create an environment, right-click the Environments folder and select Create Environment from the context menu, as shown in Figure 8-30. This will take you to the Create Environment dialog box. Enter a name and description, as shown in Figure 8-31. Click OK to create the environment.

Once the environment is created, right-click the environment and select Properties from the context menu. This displays the Environment Properties dialog box. Select

**Figure 8-30**   *Creating a new environment*

**Figure 8-31**    *The Create Environment dialog box*

the Variables page of the dialog box. Create variables to correspond to each of the parameters that should be controlled by this environment. This is shown in Figure 8-32. Once the variables are created, click OK to exit the Environment Properties dialog box.

Environments are associated with projects and packages using the configuration settings. Right-click a project or package and select Configure from the context menu. This displays the Configure dialog box. Select the References page of the dialog box. Add a reference to each of the environments that may be used by this project or package, as shown in Figure 8-33.

Once the references are added, select the Parameters page of the Configure dialog box. Use the ellipsis (…) button for each of the parameters to associate it with a variable in the environments. This is shown in Figure 3-34.

When the package is run from the server, you have an opportunity to select an environment to use for this execution as shown in Figure 8-35. The values in the selected environment's variables are used for the associated parameters for this execution of the package.

**Figure 8-32** *The Variables page of the Environment Properties dialog box*

**Figure 8-33** *The References page of the Configure dialog box*

**Figure 8-34**    *The Set Parameter Value dialog box used to associate an environment variable*

**Figure 8-35**    *Selecting an environment in the Run Package dialog box*

## Setting Permissions

Security for Integration Services packages on the server can be set at the folder and project levels. To modify security settings, right-click a folder or project and select Properties from the context menu. Go to the Permissions page of the Project Properties dialog box. The Permissions page of a project is shown in Figure 8-36.

The following permissions can be set for projects:

▶ Read

▶ Modify

▶ Execute

▶ Manage Permission

**Figure 8-36** *The Permissions page of the Project Properties dialog box*

The following permissions can be set for a folder:

- ▶ Read
- ▶ Modify
- ▶ Manage Permissions
- ▶ Create Objects
- ▶ Modify Objects
- ▶ Execute Objects
- ▶ Read Objects
- ▶ Manage Object Permissions

The following permissions can be set for an environment:

- ▶ Read
- ▶ Modify
- ▶ Manage Permissions

## Executing Packages from the SSIS Catalog

Now that we have all of the configuration completed, our packages are ready to be run from the server. To execute a package from the server, right-click the package entry in the Object Explorer window and select Execute from the context menu. The Execute Package dialog box appears.

The Execute Package dialog box enables us to make any final changes to the parameter values before the package is executed. If environments are associated with the package, we can select an environment to use for this execution, as shown in Figure 8-35.

**NOTE**

*If you wish to try executing either the DimensionLoad package or the FactLoad package from the server, you will first need to remove the existing data from the tables they populate. If you do not do so, the package execution will fail with duplicate primary key errors—we are attempting to load the same data more than once. Prior to running the DimensionLoad package, truncate the following tables:*
*DimCountry*
*DimMachine*
*DimMachineType*
*DimMaterial*
*DimPlant*

*DimProduct*
*DimProductSubtype*
*DimProductType*
*Prior to running the FactLoad package, truncate the following tables:*
*DimBatch*
*InventoryFact*
*ManufacturingFact*

In the Execute Package dialog box, click OK to begin package execution. When you do this, you will receive a dialog box explaining that package execution has begun and to see execution status you should use the Integration Services Dashboard report. In most cases, you'll want to click Yes to have this report opened for you.

## Execution Dashboard Reports

The Integration Services Dashboard reports provide information on the execution of an Integration Services package from the server. An example of a Dashboard report is shown in Figure 8-37. Any text that is blue and underlined provides a drillthrough

**Figure 8-37** *The Integration Services Dashboard report*

**Figure 8-38** *The Execution Performance Dashboard report*

link to another report that provides additional detail information. For example, the Execution Performance report is shown in Figure 8-38. Once you have navigated to a drillthrough report, use the Navigate Backward button in the upper-left corner to return to the parent report.

You can view the Integration Services Dashboard reports at any time by right-clicking any item under Integration Services in the Object Explorer window and selecting from the Reports submenu in the context menu.

# Meanwhile, Back at the BI Semantic Model

As we have seen, there is a great deal of capability and flexibility in Integration Services. We can use Integration Services to cleanse data and load it into our data marts, but that is only the beginning. Now that we have a handle on Integration Services, we can return to looking more in-depth at working with the BI Semantic Model in the next chapter.

# Part III

# Working with a Multidimensional BI Semantic Model

# Chapter 9

# Cubism—Measures and Dimensions

## In This Chapter

▶ **Building a Multidimensional BI Semantic Model**
▶ **Measures**
▶ **Dimensions**
▶ **You Are Special**

*There is a fifth dimension beyond those known to man. It is a dimension vast as space and timeless as infinity.*

–Rod Serling
Introduction to *The Twilight Zone*

We have looked at the basics of cubes, with their measures, dimensions, and attributes. We also examined the means of getting information from transactional and other data sources into our data marts. Now let's take a closer look at the way measures and dimensions are implemented in a Multidimensional BI Semantic Model.

The Multidimensional BI Semantic Model lets us group measures together. It also enables us to create different types of dimensions. This classification and differentiation make it easier for users to analyze the data in our cubes. It also makes the cubes easier for us to manage.

# Building a Multidimensional BI Semantic Model

In Chapter 6, we created two data mart structures for our sample company, Maximum Miniatures, Inc. We called these the Manufacturing data mart and the Sales data mart. These data marts serve as repositories for business information that is not available elsewhere from a single source. In this chapter, we will look at completing the Manufacturing data mart by creating a Multidimensional BI Semantic Model.

## Creating a Cube

Now that the Manufacturing data mart contains data, let's go ahead and define an online analytical processing (OLAP) cube on top of the data mart relational database. In Chapter 6, we defined one OLAP cube at the same time we created the Sales data mart relational database. This time around, we approach things from a different direction. We already have the Manufacturing data mart relational database. What we need to do is define our OLAP cube on top of that existing database.

Once the OLAP cube is defined, we use it to help us learn more about measures in the following section of this book.

### Learn By Doing—Building a Multidimensional BI Semantic Model for the Manufacturing Data Mart

#### Feature Highlighted

▶ Creating Multidimensional BI Semantic Model on top of an existing data mart

**Business Need**   The vice president of production wants to perform multidimensional analysis on the information in the Manufacturing data mart. To let him do that, we need to define an OLAP cube on top of that database.

**Steps**

1. Open SQL Server Data Tools.
2. Click the New Project button on the toolbar.
3. Select Business Intelligence | Analysis Services in the Installed Templates area, and then select Analysis Services Multidimensional and Data Mining Project from the templates.
4. Enter **MaxMinManufacturingDM** for the Name and set the Location to the appropriate folder.
5. Click OK to create the project.
6. Right-click the Data Sources folder in the Solution Explorer window, and select New Data Source from the context menu. The Data Source Wizard appears.
7. Click Next on the Welcome page. The Select how to define the connection page appears.
8. Select the data connection to the MaxMinManufacturingDM you previously created. Click Next. The Impersonation Information page appears.

**NOTE**

*Analysis Services needs to access the data mart relational database to populate and update the information in the OLAP cube. This is done using the information in the data connection selected in Step 8. The Analysis Services updates run as a background process. This can be an issue if the data connection specifies Windows Authentication or if the connection is to a file-based database, such as Microsoft Access. In these situations, Analysis Services needs to know what Windows credentials to use when accessing the data source. In other words, Analysis Services needs to impersonate a Windows identity while accessing the data.*

9. On the Impersonation Information page, if you are using Windows Authentication in your data connection, select Use a specific Windows user name and password, and then enter a valid Windows user name and password for database access. If you entered a specific SQL Server login in the data connection, you do not need to worry about impersonation. (If you cannot remember how the data connection was configured, select Use a specific Windows user name and password, and then enter valid Windows credentials, just to be on the safe side.) Click Next. The Completing the Wizard page appears.
10. Enter **Max Min Manufacturing DM** for Data Source Name, if it is not already there. Click Finish.
11. Right-click the Data Source Views folder in the Solution Explorer window, and select New Data Source View from the context menu. The Data Source View Wizard appears.

**NOTE**

*A data source view enables us to specify the subset of the tables and their fields from the data source that should be included in the OLAP cube. We can also define table relationships and calculated fields that do not exist in the underlying database. In this case, we are accessing a data mart that was architected with the cube in mind. Therefore, we use all of the tables and fields in the data mart database and we do not need to specify additional relationships. However, we do use the data source view to define three calculated fields that let us easily create a time dimension hierarchy from the single datetime field that exists in the fact table.*

12. Click Next on the Welcome page. The Select a Data Source page appears.
13. The Max Min Manufacturing DM data source that you just created should be selected. Click Next. The Name Matching page appears.
14. This page appears because we do not have foreign key constraints defined in our database. We will allow the wizard to create logical foreign keys in the data source view. Leave the Create logical relationships by matching columns check box checked. Also, leave the Same name as primary key option selected.
15. Click Next. The Select Tables and Views page appears.
16. Move all of the dimension and fact tables to the Included objects list. (Remember, there are two fact tables now.) Click Next. The Completing the Wizard page appears.
17. Enter **Max Min Manufacturing DM** for Name, if it is not already there. Click Finish. The Data Source View Design tab appears.

**NOTE**

*The Data Source View Design tab shows a diagram of the data source view we just created. This looks similar to a database diagram. This is to be expected, because a data source view is simply a view into the underlying database. The data source view gives us the chance to add items that are required by or remove items that are irrelevant to the cube we are creating.*

18. Find the ManufacturingFact table in the data source view diagram. Right-click the title bar of this table, and select New Named Calculation from the context menu. The Create Named Calculation dialog box appears.
19. Enter **YearOfManufacture** for Column Name.
20. Enter the following for Expression:

```
CONVERT(char(4), YEAR(DateOfManufacture))
```

This creates a character field containing the year corresponding to the date of manufacture.

**NOTE**

*The data source view is interacting with the underlying database to create the named calculation. Therefore, the expression language of that database must be used to define the expression. In this case, the underlying database is SQL Server, so the expression language is T-SQL. The expression is evaluated by sending this SELECT statement to the underlying database:*

```
SELECT {Table Name in Data Source View}.*,
{Named Calculation Expression} AS {Named Calculation Name}
FROM {Table in Data Source} AS {Table Name in Data Source View}
```

*For the named calculation we are creating here, the SELECT statement would be:*

```
SELECT ManufacturingFact.*,
CONVERT (char(4), YEAR(DateOfManufacture))
AS YearOfManufacture

FROM ManufacturingFact AS ManufacturingFact
```

*Any T-SQL expression that is valid in this context, including subqueries (when explicitly surrounded by parentheses), is valid as a named calculation.*

21. Click OK to exit the Create Named Calculation dialog box.

22. Create a second named calculation called **QuarterOfManufacture** with the following expression to contain the year and quarter corresponding to the date of manufacture:

```
CONVERT(char(4), YEAR(DateOfManufacture)) +
CASE
WHEN MONTH(DateOfManufacture) BETWEEN 1 AND 3 THEN 'Q1'
WHEN MONTH(DateOfManufacture) BETWEEN 4 AND 6 THEN 'Q2'
WHEN MONTH(DateOfManufacture) BETWEEN 7 AND 9 THEN 'Q3'
ELSE 'Q4'
END
```

23. Create a third named calculation called **MonthOfManufacture** with the following expression to contain the year and month corresponding to the date of manufacture:

```
CONVERT(char(4), YEAR(DateOfManufacture)) +
RIGHT('0'+CONVERT(varchar(2), MONTH(DateOfManufacture)),2)
```

24. Create **YearOfInventory**, **QuarterOfInventory**, and **MonthOfInventory** named calculations in the InventoryFact table. Use the same T-SQL expressions, substituting DateOfInventory for DateOfManufacture. When completed (and with a little rearranging), the Data Source View Design tab should appear similar to Figure 9-1.

25. Right-click the Cubes folder in the Solution Explorer window, and select New Cube from the context menu. The Cube Wizard appears.

26. Click Next on the Welcome page. The Select Creation Method page appears.

27. Use existing tables should be selected by default. Click Next. The Select Measure Group Tables page appears.

28. The Max Min Manufacturing DM data source view that you just created should be selected. Check ManufacturingFact in the Measure group tables area. We initially leave the measures in the InventoryFact table out of the cube and add them in at a later time.

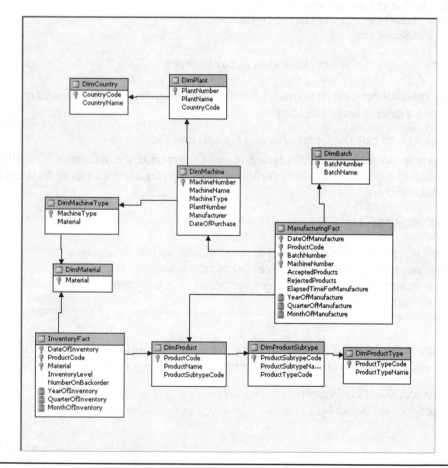

**Figure 9-1**  *The Data Source View Design tab for the Max Min Manufacturing DM data source view*

29. Click Next. The Select Measures page appears.

30. The wizard should have found and checked all of the measure fields in the ManufacturingFact table. The wizard also added a field called Manufacturing Fact Count, which counts the number of records. This does not provide us with any useful information in this data mart, so you should uncheck the Manufacturing Fact Count field.

31. Click Next. The Select New Dimensions page appears.

32. The wizard should have found all of the tables related to the ManufacturingFact table in the data source view. It should also have created hierarchies for the Dim Product and Dim Machine dimensions. Uncheck both ManufacturingFact entries.

33. Click Next. The Completing the Wizard page appears.

34. Enter **Max Min Manufacturing DM** for Cube Name, if it is not already there. Click Finish. The Cube Design tab appears. SQL Server Data Tools windows should appear similar to Figure 9-2.

35. Click the Save All button on the toolbar.

You will notice the wizard did not create our time dimension for us. We will manually create the time dimension later in this chapter.

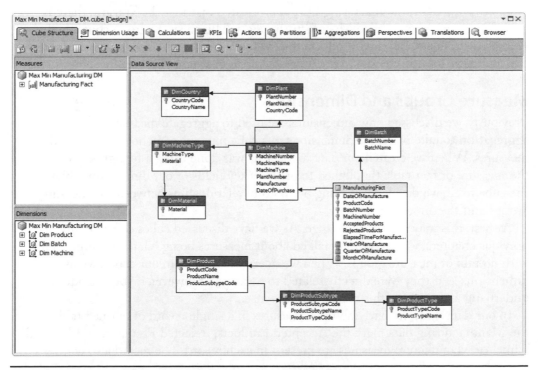

**Figure 9-2**  *SQL Server Data Tools window after the Cube Wizard completes*

# Measures

Now that we have a real live cube in captivity, we can study its basic parts and look at some of its more advanced features. We begin with measures. Measures provide the actual information that the users of our cubes are interested in. *Measures* are the bits of numerical data that we need to aggregate. As we saw in the Cube Wizard, measures come from the fields in the fact tables in the data mart.

The Multidimensional BI Semantic Model provides us with a number of features for managing measures. We can even create new measures that don't exist in the data mart. We can also control the aggregation of the measures along our dimensions.

## Measure Groups

In the Multidimensional BI Semantic Model, measures do not exist on their own inside cubes. Instead, they are clustered together and managed in groupings. These groupings are called measure groups. Each *measure group* in a cube corresponds to a table in the data source view. This table is the measure group's source for its measure data. The measure group is said to be bound to this table. Each record in the table becomes a different member of the measure group.

In the Max Min Manufacturing DM cube created by the Cube Wizard, there is a single measure group called Manufacturing Fact. This measure group contains the Accepted Products, Rejected Products, and Elapsed Time for Manufacture measures. This measure group is bound to the ManufacturingFact table in the data source view.

### Measure Groups and Dimensions

Previously, we discussed how dimensions are used to aggregate measures. For this aggregation to take place, the dimensions in a cube must be somehow related to the measures. When we created our data marts, this was done using a foreign key field in the measure or fact table that linked to primary key fields of our dimension tables. In the cube itself, we do the same thing by creating relationships between the measure groups and the dimensions.

At first, this may seem a bit strange. As we have discussed cubes conceptually in previous chapters, we have always talked about measures being related to dimensions, with no talk of measure groups. When we query the data from our cubes, we use dimensions as if they were directly related to measures. However, if you consider the underlying architecture, this makes perfect sense.

In our data mart, we have multiple measures in a single record of our fact table. In the Manufacturing data mart, the Accepted Products, Rejected Products, and Elapsed Time for Manufacture measures are present in each record. The record also contains the foreign key fields linking it to the lowest-level dimension tables in each of the hierarchies. Again, in the Manufacturing data mart, these are DimProduct, DimBatch, and DimMachine (along with the time dimension that will be created virtually from the DateOfManufacture field).

All of the measures in the ManufacturingFact record (a single row of data) depend on all of the foreign key fields in that record. Therefore, if a given Accepted Products measure and Rejected Products measure reside in the same record, it is impossible for them to relate to two different records in the DimProduct table (see Figure 9-3). Only one foreign key field in their record can be used to link to the DimProduct table, so they must both link to the same product. That's the way well-normalized relational databases work.

We just said that measure groups correspond to a table in the data source view. Just as all of the measures in a given record in the fact table must relate to the same dimension table records, it follows that all of the measures in a given member group must relate to the same members in the cube dimensions.

We look at the technique for creating relationships between measure groups and dimensions in the section "Role Playing Dimensions."

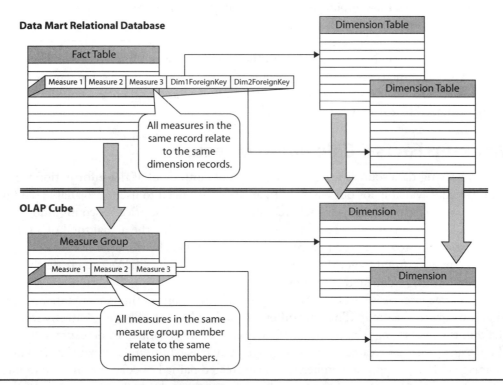

**Figure 9-3**    *Measure groups and dimensions*

## Granularity

The lowest level of a particular dimension hierarchy that is related to a given measure group determines the granularity of that measure group for that dimension. Analysis can only be done on a measure along a certain dimension down to the granularity of its measure group for that dimension. Because measures are related to dimensions through their measure group, all of the measures in a measure group have the same granularity. Two different measure groups (and their constituent measures) in the same cube can have different granularity.

All of this can sound a bit like double-speak, so let's look at a couple of examples. The Manufacturing Fact measure group is related to the machine dimension at the lowest level, the machine number level. Therefore, the Manufacturing Fact measure group has a granularity of machine number for the machine dimension. We can drill down through the machine hierarchy from material to machine type, all the way to the machine number level, and get information for all of the measures in the Manufacturing Fact measure group.

The Inventory Fact measure group, once we create it, will be related to the machine dimension at the material level. The Inventory Fact measure group has a granularity of material for the machine dimension. We can only perform analysis at the material level for measures in the Inventory Fact measure group.

Granularity is important for the analysis, but remember, there will be facts with some values missing or null. Not all materials in the complete list of dimension members are made on all machine types and on all machines in the factory on the same day. SQL Server 2012 Analysis Services continues the tradition of assuring proper handling of null data started by earlier versions of Analysis Services.

## Made-up Facts—Calculated Measures

The underlying data sources for our cubes may not contain all of the information we want to make available for our users. In many cases, we need to use the available data to calculate new measures that our users require. Perhaps the list price, discount amount, and sales tax amount need to be added together to determine the actual total of a sale. Perhaps we want to divide the number of rejected products by the total number of products manufactured to get the percentage of rejects produced. We can create this information using calculated measures.

A *calculated measure* is part of a measure group. It functions in the same manner as any other measure in the group. The only difference is this: Instead of coming directly from a field in the underlying data source, a calculated measure is defined by an expression. These expressions are created using a language known as Multidimensional Expression Language (MDX) script. Remember, when we created named calculations in a data source view, we used the language of the underlying data source. In our case, it was T-SQL.

It would certainly be easier if we could use the same language here to define calculated measures. Unfortunately, that is not the case. *MDX* is a special language with features designed to handle the advanced mathematics and formulas required by OLAP analysis. MDX also includes features for navigating through the dimensions and hierarchies of OLAP cubes. These features are not found in T-SQL, so we need to use MDX script.

In the "Learn By Doing" section for measures and measure groups, we create some straightforward calculated measures. These calculated measures do not require an in-depth knowledge of the MDX script language. We get into the details of MDX script in Chapter 11.

The definition of a calculated measure is stored in the OLAP cube itself. The actual values that result from a calculated measure are not calculated, however, until a query containing that calculated measure is executed. The results of that calculation are then cached in the cube. The cached value is delivered to any subsequent users requesting the same calculation.

## Creating Calculated Measures

Calculated measures are managed on the Calculations tab of the Cube Design tab. A new calculated measure is created by clicking the New Calculated Member toolbar button, shown in Figure 9-4. This opens the Calculated Member form view, shown in Figure 9-5.

The name of the calculated measure is entered in Name. If the name contains one or more spaces, it must be enclosed in square brackets. Likewise, if the name contains one or more of the following characters:

```
! @ # $ % ^ & * ( ) - + = / ? : ; " ' { } \ < >,
```

it must be enclosed in square brackets.

**Figure 9-4**  *Creating a new calculation on the Calculations tab*

**Figure 9-5**    *The Calculated Member form view*

Thus far, we have talked of calculated measures. However, it is possible to calculate members for dimensions as well. In fact, both calculated measures and calculated dimension members are referred to as calculated members, which is why the entry form is called the Calculated Member form. To specify that we are creating a calculated measure, MEASURES must be selected from the Parent hierarchy drop-down list.

The actual definition of the calculated measure is entered in Expression. As mentioned earlier, this expression uses the MDX script language. The expression can be typed by hand, or it can be built using the existing measures, MDX script functions, and templates found in the Calculation Tools window. This window can be seen in the lower-left area of Figure 9-5.

The Format string drop-down list enables us to select the formatting to be applied to the calculation results. We can either select from one of the numeric formatting strings in the drop-down list or type in a custom format string. In most cases, one of the formatting strings from the drop-down list can do the job. The format string must be enclosed in double quotes.

As we study MDX queries in Chapter 12, we learn about MDX queries that ask for only non-empty values from a measure. Rather than evaluating a calculated measure

**Figure 9-6** *The Script view*

expression repeatedly to determine if it is non-empty, we can specify the conditions under which the calculation can produce a non-empty result. In most cases, this depends on whether one or more of the measures used in the calculation is non-empty.

The Non-empty behavior drop-down list lets us select one or more measures in the cube. If any one of the selected measures is non-empty, the expression is executed to determine whether the resulting calculated measure is non-empty. When all of the selected measures are empty, the calculated measure is assumed to be empty without ever executing the expression.

In addition to the form view shown in Figure 9-5, we can look at the underlying MDX script that completely defines the calculated measure. This is shown in Figure 9-6. Again, we explore the MDX script language more completely to understand this code in Chapter 11.

We can use the measures in a cube in the expressions that define calculated measures in that cube. We can also use calculated measures in the expressions that define other calculated measures. This lets us break up complex calculations into much simpler building blocks that are easier to create and maintain.

## It Doesn't Add Up—Measure Aggregates Other Than Sum

We have already discussed how measures are aggregated along dimension hierarchies. By default, the Sum aggregate function is used for each measure. Measures that use the Sum function for their aggregation are *additive measures*.

In some cases, however, things just don't add up. In other words, there may be some measures that should not be summed along dimension hierarchies. For example, taking the sum of an average results in a number that is total nonsense. Instead, we always

**Figure 9-7**   *Setting the aggregate function for a measure*

want to recalculate the average from the granular data. In other situations, we may want to use the maximum or minimum value for a measure along a dimension, rather than taking the sum. These measures are *nonadditive measures.*

The aggregate function used by a particular measure is controlled by the Aggregate property from that measure. Select the measure in the Measures window of the Cube Structure tab, and then use the Properties window to set the AggregateFunction property for this measure. This is shown in Figure 9-7.

## Semiadditive Measures

Certain measures may be added along some dimensions, but not along others. For example, the inventory level measure can be added along the product dimension. The sum of the inventory amounts for each product yields the total number of products in the warehouse. However, the sum of the first three months' inventory amounts does not give the inventory amount at the end of the first quarter. This is shown in Figure 9-8.

Measures such as inventory level are said to be semiadditive. These measures must use a *semiadditive measure* to achieve the proper results when aggregating. Measures that use a semiadditive aggregate function must be related to a time dimension.

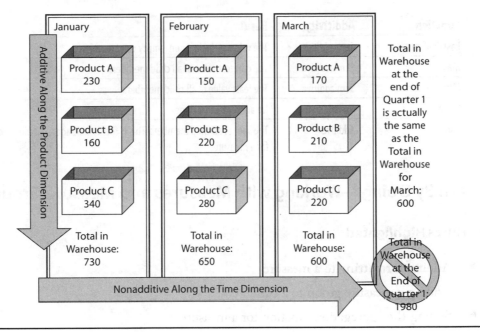

**Figure 9-8**    *Inventory level is a semiadditive measure*

Semiadditive measures require the Enterprise Edition, Business Intelligence Edition, or Developer Edition of SQL Server Analysis Services 2012. Semiadditive measures are not supported by the Standard Edition or other editions.

## Aggregate Functions

Analysis Services provides a number of aggregate functions for use with measures in an OLAP cube.

| Function | Additivity | Result |
|---|---|---|
| AverageOfChildren | Semiadditive | The average of all non-empty child members. |
| ByAccount | Semiadditive | Uses the aggregate function specified by an account dimension in the cube. If the cube does not include an account dimension, this aggregate function works the same as the None aggregate function. |
| Count | Additive | A count of the number of child members. |
| DistinctCount | Nonadditive | A count of the number of unique child members. |
| FirstChild | Semiadditive | The value of the first child member. |
| FirstNonEmpty | Semiadditive | The value of the first non-empty child member. |
| LastChild | Semiadditive | The value of the last child member. |

| Function | Additivity | Result |
|---|---|---|
| LastNonEmpty | Semiadditive | The value of the last non-empty child member. |
| Max | Semiadditive | The greatest value of all child members. |
| Min | Semiadditive | The least value of all child members. |
| None | Nonadditive | No aggregation is done. |
| Sum | Additive | The sum of all child members. This is the default aggregate function for a measure. |

## Learn By Doing—Working with Measures and Measure Groups

### Features Highlighted

▶ Adding formatting to a measure

▶ Adding a measure group to a cube

▶ Setting the aggregation function for a measure

▶ Creating calculated measures

**Business Need**  We have not yet completed the vice president of production's change request for inventory and backorder information in the Max Min Manufacturing DM cube. We added a table for this information into the data mart and we populated that table from the Order Processing database. We now need to add these measures to the cube in a new measure group.

Once the inventory level measure is added to the cube, we need to specify the correct aggregate function for this measure. As noted earlier, inventory level is not additive. The inventory level for a given period is not the sum of the inventory levels within the period. Instead, inventory level is semiadditive. The inventory level for a given period is the inventory level at the end of that period.

In addition, the vice president of production has come up with another change. He would like to see not only the number of accepted products produced and the number of rejected products produced, but also the total number of products produced. This, of course, is the sum of the number of accepted products, plus the number of rejected products. He also wants to see the number of rejected products produced as a percentage of the total number of products produced. We can implement these requests using calculated measures.

**Steps**

1. Open SQL Server Data Tools.
2. Open the MaxMinManufacturingDM project.
3. In the Solution Explorer window, double-click the entry for Max Min Manufacturing DM.cube to display the Cube Design tab, if it is not already visible.
4. Expand the Manufacturing Fact measure group in the Measures window.
5. Select the Accepted Products measure.
6. In the Properties window, select Standard from the FormatString drop-down list.
7. Select the Rejected Products measure in the Measures window.
8. In the Properties window, select Standard from the FormatString drop-down list.
9. Select the Elapsed Time For Manufacture measure in the Measures window.
10. In the Properties window, select Standard from the FormatString drop-down list.
11. Right-click in the Measures window, and select New Measure Group from the context menu. The New Measure Group dialog box appears.
12. Select InventoryFact from the Select a table from the data source view list, and click OK to exit the New Measure Group dialog box. The InventoryFact table is added to the cube, and the Inventory Fact measure group appears in the Measures window.

**NOTE**

*A red, wavy line may appear under the entry for the Inventory Fact measure group in the Measures window. The reason for this error notification is because we have not related this new measure group to any dimensions. We take care of this in a later Learn By Doing exercise titled "Relating Dimensions in the Max Min Manufacturing DM Cube."*

13. Expand the Inventory Fact measure group in the Measures window.
14. Select the Inventory Level measure.
15. If you are not using the Enterprise Edition, Business Intelligence Edition, or Developer Edition of SQL Server 2012, skip to step 16. In the Properties window, select LastNonEmpty from the drop-down list for the AggregateFunction property. The LastNonEmpty aggregate function is now used when aggregating this measure.

**NOTE**

*The Enterprise Edition, Business Intelligence Edition, or Developer Edition of SQL Server 2012 are required by the LastNonEmpty aggregate function. If you are not using one of these editions, ignore Step 15 and Step 18, as well as the aggregate numbers that result from these measures. If you use the LastNonEmpty aggregate function with the Standard Edition or other edition of SQL Server 2012, you will receive an error when you try to deploy the cube definition to the server.*

16. In the Properties window, select Standard from the FormatString drop-down list.

17. Select the Number On Backorder measure in the Measures window.

18. If you are not using the Enterprise Edition, Business Intelligence Edition, or Developer Edition of SQL Server 2012, skip to step 19. In the Properties window, select LastNonEmpty from the drop-down list for the AggregateFunction property.

19. In the Properties window, select Standard from the FormatString drop-down list.

20. Right-click the Inventory Fact Count measure in the Measures window, and select Delete from the context menu. The Delete Objects dialog box appears.

21. Click OK to confirm the deletion. The Cube Design tab should appear similar to Figure 9-9.

### NOTE

*A count of the number of members in the measure group is automatically created when a new measure group is created. In this case, a count of the number of inventory entries is not a helpful measure, so it can be deleted.*

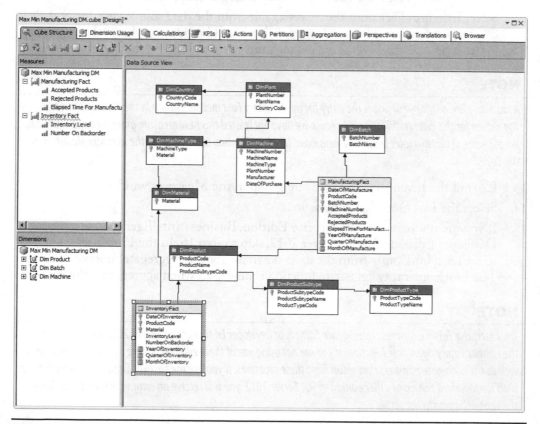

**Figure 9-9**    *The Max Min Manufacturing DM cube with the Inventory Fact measure group*

22. Select the Calculations tab of the Cube Design tab to create calculated measures.

23. Click the New Calculated Member button on the Calculations tab toolbar. The Calculated Member form view appears.

24. Enter [**Total Products**] for Name. Enter the following for Expression:

```
[Accepted Products] + [Rejected Products]
```

25. Select Standard from the Format string drop-down list.

26. Check the Accepted Products and Rejected Products measures in the Non-empty behavior selection window, and click OK.

27. Click the New Calculated Member button on the Calculations tab toolbar. The Calculated Member form returns to the default values.

28. Enter [**Percent Rejected**] for Name. Enter the following for Expression:

```
[Rejected Products] / [Total Products]
```

29. Select Percent from the Format String drop-down list.

30. Check the Accepted Products and Rejected Products measures in the Non-empty behavior selection window, and click OK.

31. Click the Save All button on the toolbar.

# Dimensions

After taking a good look at measures, let's move on to another part of the OLAP cube—namely, the dimensions. As we have seen, dimensions are what give cubes their true analytical power. They enable us to slice and dice the measures in the cube until we find the meaningful business intelligence hidden among all of the numbers. Dimensions provide understandable phrases in business language to define what may be cryptic in a transactional database system.

Just as there is more to measures than initially meets the eye, dimensions, too, come in a number of different varieties. We will examine their various classifications and capabilities, but first, let's look at the way dimensions are related to measure groups.

## Managing Dimensions

Dimensions are managed using the Dimension Design tab. To display this tab, double-click a dimension in the Solution Explorer window. The Dimension Design tab is shown in Figure 9-10 displaying the Dim Product dimension.

**Figure 9-10** *The Dimension Design tab with the Dim Product dimension*

The Dimension Design tab includes the entire structure of the dimension. The Dim Product dimension in Figure 9-10 has a three-level hierarchy. The Dimension Design tab contains information about all three levels: the product level, the product subtype level, and the product type level.

The left-hand column of the Dimension Design tab shows all of the attributes for the entire dimension. The center column shows the structure of the dimension hierarchy. The right-hand column shows the tables from the data source view that define this dimension.

Notice the blue squiggly under the dimension name. This indicates the development environment has some dimensional design suggestions to make. Hover over the squiggle to view these suggestions. We will look at implementing some of this advice in the following Learn By Doing exercise.

We will begin working with dimensions by creating a time dimension in the Max Min Manufacturing DM cube. We will also create hierarchies for two of our dimensions. Finally, we will do some additional clean-up to make our dimensions easier to use when we start to query data from the Max Min Manufacturing DM cube.

## Learn By Doing—Cleaning Up the Dimensions in the Max Min Manufacturing DM Cube

### Features Highlighted

▶ Creating a time dimension

▶ Creating dimensional hierarchies

▶ Hiding unneeded attribute hierarchies

**Business Need**  We need to have the dimensions in the Max Min Manufacturing DM cube related to the measure groups to perform any meaningful analysis on this cube.

### Steps

1. Open SQL Server Data Tools.
2. Open the MaxMinManufacturingDM project.
3. Right-click the Dimensions entry in the Solution Explorer window, and select New Dimension from the context menu. The Dimension Wizard dialog box appears.
4. Click Next on the Welcome page. The Select Creation Method page of the wizard appears.
5. Leave the Use an existing table item selected and click Next. The Specify Source Information page appears.
6. The Max Min Manufacturing DM data source view is already selected. Select ManufacturingFact from the Main table drop-down list. Even though this is a fact table, it is also the table that contains the date information, so it will serve double duty.
7. DateOfManufacture is selected as the first Key column, which is correct. However, the other columns selected in the Key columns area do not apply to our time dimension. Select the blank entry from each of the drop-down lists so DateOfManufacture is the only key column selected.
8. Select DateOfManufacture from the Name column drop-down list. The Specify Source Information page of the wizard should appear as shown in Figure 9-11.
9. Click Next. The Select Related Tables page appears.
10. Uncheck all items in the Related tables area.
11. Click Next. The Select Dimension Attributes page appears.
12. Uncheck Product Code, Batch Number, and Machine Number.
13. Leave Date Of Manufacture checked and also check Year Of Manufacture, Quarter Of Manufacture, and Month Of Manufacture.

**Figure 9-11** *Creating the Time dimension*

14. Click in the Attribute Type column across from Date Of Manufacture.
15. Click the drop-down arrow.
16. Expand the Date entry.
17. Expand the Calendar entry.
18. Select Date and click OK.
19. Click in the Attribute Type column across from Year Of Manufacture.
20. Click the drop-down arrow.
21. Expand the Date entry.
22. Expand the Calendar entry.
23. Select Year and click OK.
24. Repeat Steps 14–18 for Quarter Of Manufacture, selecting Quarter.
25. Repeat Steps 14–18 for Month Of Manufacture, selecting Month.
26. Click Next. The Completing the Wizard page appears.

27. Change the name to **Dim Time**.

28. Click Finish. The Dimension Design tab appears with the Dim Time dimension.

29. Right-click the entry for Date of Manufacture in the Attributes area, and select Rename from the context menu.

30. Enter **Date** for the name of this attribute, and press ENTER.

31. Repeat Steps 29 and 30 to rename the other attributes as follows:

| Old Name | New Name |
| --- | --- |
| Month Of Manufacture | Month |
| Quarter Of Manufacture | Quarter |
| Year Of Manufacture | Year |

32. Drag the Year item from the Attributes column, and drop it in the Hierarchies area.

33. Drag the Quarter item from the Attributes column, and drop it on <new level> in the Hierarchies area.

34. Repeat Step 33 for Month and Date.

35. Right-click the word "Hierarchy" in the Hierarchies area, and select Rename from the context menu.

36. Enter **Date Hierarchy** and press ENTER.

37. Click Date in the Attributes area. Hold down SHIFT and click Year in the Attributes area. All four attributes should be selected.

38. In the Properties window, change the AttributeHierarchyVisible property to False.

**NOTE**

*These attributes can show up individually in the dimension as their own attribute hierarchies, as well as members of the Date Hierarchy we just created. This gets a bit confusing for the user querying data from the cube. To cut down on this confusion, we told the individual attribute hierarchies to be hidden. Only the Date Hierarchy will be visible to the user.*

39. Click the Attribute Relationships tab. Note the Date is related to the other three items, but the relationship structure does not mirror the hierarchy we just created.

40. Select the Month and drop it on the Quarter.

41. Select the Quarter and drop it on the Year.

42. Right-click each of the relationship arrows, and select Relationship Type | Rigid from the context menu. The Attribute Relationships tab should appear as shown in Figure 9-12.

**Figure 9-12**   *The Attribute Relationships tab*

**NOTE**

*A flexible attribute relationship may change between full processes of the dimension. A rigid attribute relationship does not change. For example, 8/1/2011 will always be in August, 2011. It is a rigid relationship. Attribute relationships default to flexible. They should be set to rigid wherever appropriate to increase cube processing efficiency.*

43. Click the Save All button on the toolbar.

44. Close the Dim Time dimension tab.

45. In the Solution Explorer window, double-click the Dim Machine dimension entry. The Dim Machine dimension tab appears.

46. Create a new hierarchy and name it **Material Hierarchy**. This hierarchy should have the following levels:
    Material
    Machine Type
    Machine Number

47. Create a second hierarchy and name it **Plant Hierarchy**. This hierarchy should have the following levels:
    Country Code
    Plant Number
    Machine Number

48. Set the AttributeHierarchyVisible property for all of the attributes to False.

49. Select the Attribute Relationships tab.

50. Change all of the relationship types to rigid.

51. Click the Save All button on the toolbar.

52. Close the Dim Machine dimension tab.

53. In the Solution Explorer window, double-click the Dim Product dimension entry. The Dim Product dimension tab appears.

54. Create a new hierarchy and name it **Product Hierarchy**. This hierarchy should have the following levels:
Product Type Code
Product Subtype Code
Product Code

55. Set the AttributeHierarchyVisible property for all of the attributes to False.

56. Select the Attribute Relationships tab.

57. Change all of the relationship types to rigid.

58. Click the Save All button on the toolbar.

59. Close the Dim Product dimension tab.

## Relating Dimensions to Measure Groups

In the previous Learn By Doing activity, we got our dimensional structure in shape. However, we still have one issue with the Dim Time dimension we created. This dimension is not related to either of the measure groups. A dimension must be related to a measure group before we can use it to analyze data from the cube.

We can solve this situation right now with another Learn By Doing activity.

## Learn By Doing—Relating Dimensions in the Max Min Manufacturing DM Cube

### Feature Highlighted

▶ Relating dimensions to measure groups

**Business Need**   We need to have the Dim Time dimension in the Max Min Manufacturing DM cube related to the measure groups to perform any meaningful analysis on this cube.

## Steps

1. Double-click the entry for Max Min Manufacturing DM.cube to display the Cube Design tab.

2. Select the Dimension Usage tab of the Cube Design tab.

3. Right-click in the empty area of the tab, and select Add Cube Dimension. The Add Cube Dimension dialog box appears.

4. Select the Dim Time dimension, and click OK.

5. The Dim Time dimension is added to the cube. SQL Server Data Tools figures out how to relate the Dim Time dimension to the Manufacturing Fact group. (Not too difficult, considering they are both defined from the same table.) We will need to relate the Inventory Fact group ourselves.

6. Click the entry in the Inventory Fact column and the Dim Time row. An ellipsis (…) button appears.

7. Click the ellipsis button. The Define Relationship dialog box appears.

8. Select Regular in the Select relationship type drop-down list. We are specifying that the Dim Time dimension relates to the Inventory Fact measure group as a regular dimension.

9. Select Date from the Granularity attribute drop-down list. This is the attribute in the dimension that defines the granularity of the dimension for this measure group. We can either select the primary key of the table that defines the dimension or we can select one of the attribute fields in this table.

10. In the Relationship grid, select DateOfInventory from the drop-down list under Measure Group Columns. This creates a relationship between the DateOfManufacture column in the table that defines the dimension and the DateOfInventory column in the table that defines the measure group.

11. Click OK to exit the Define Relationship dialog box. Once completed, the Dimension Usage tab should appear as shown in Figure 9-13.

12. Click the Save All button on the toolbar.

**Figure 9-13**　*The Dimension Usage tab of the Max Min Manufacturing DM cube*

# Types of Dimensions

Dimensions can be placed in a number of classifications. These classifications tell us something about the way a dimension is created and managed. They can also shed some light on how a dimension is utilized.

## Fact Dimensions

In most cases, the information used to populate a dimension resides in a dimension table. DimProduct and DimMachine are examples from our Manufacturing data mart. However, when we created the Dim Time dimension, we used data from the DateOfManufacture field and the YearOfManufacture, QuarterOfManufacture, and MonthOfManufacture named calculations in the ManufacturingFact table.

Dimensions created from attributes in a fact table are known as *fact dimensions*. They are also known in the "biz" as degenerate dimensions. (This seems like a highly slanderous name, if you ask me.)

Fact dimensions follow a few simple rules in Analysis Services:

▶ At most, one fact dimension can be in a measure group.

▶ A fact dimension must be defined by one and only one measure group.

▶ A fact dimension can have a fact relationship with only one measure group. It can, however, have a regular relationship with additional measure groups.

The Define Relationship dialog box for a fact dimension is shown in Figure 9-14.

## Parent-Child Dimensions

A *parent-child dimension* is built on a table that contains a self-referential relationship. An employee table that contains a supervisor field is a good example. Figure 9-15 shows a table with a Supervisor field. The Supervisor field contains the employee number of the person to whom the employee reports. This field is a foreign key field that points back to the same table.

When a table, such as the Employee table in Figure 9-15, is used to define a dimension, the Supervisor field becomes an attribute. This is a special type of attribute known as a *parent attribute*. A parent attribute is created by right-clicking an attribute in the Attributes column of the Dimension Design tab and selecting Set Attribute Usage | Parent from the context menu.

A parent-child dimension creates its own hierarchy. Each step from child to parent creates another level in that hierarchy. What is unique about this is there are an undetermined number of levels to the hierarchy. The number of hierarchy levels depends on the number of links in the parent-child chain you are following.

**Define Relationship**

Select relationship type: `Fact`

The dimension table is the fact table.

Granularity attribute: `Date`

Dimension table: `ManufacturingFact`

Measure group table: `ManufacturingFact`

OK    Cancel    Help

**Figure 9-14**  *The Define Relationship dialog box for a fact dimension*

In the Employee dimension shown in Figure 9-15, we can start at Eva, the developer, and follow the chain of supervisors up to Maya, the CEO. There are six levels to the hierarchy along this path. If, however, we start at Juan, the system administrator, and follow the chain of supervisors up to Maya, there are four levels to the hierarchy.

**Employees**

| EmpNum | Name | Position | Supervisor |
|--------|------|----------|------------|
| 129 | Sandra | Team Leader | 239 |
| 235 | Eva | Developer | 129 |
| 239 | Peter | Development Manager | 303 |
| 293 | Maya | CEO | |
| 303 | Frank | IT Director | 470 |
| 470 | Tia | CFO | 293 |
| 487 | Juan | System Administrator | 303 |

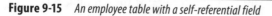

**Figure 9-15**  *An employee table with a self-referential field*

## Role Playing Dimensions

A *role playing dimension* is a dimension that is related to the same measure group multiple times. Each relationship represents a different role the dimension plays relative to the measure group. One of the best examples of this is a time dimension and a sales measure group. The time dimension is related to the sales measure group once for the date of the sale, another time for the date of shipment, and a third time for the date of payment. In this case, the time dimension plays three different roles—date of sale, date of shipment, and date of payment—relative to the sales measure group.

To create a role playing dimension, add the dimension to the Dimension Usage tab multiple times. Each instance of the dimension should be renamed to reflect one of the roles it is playing for this measure group. Then, create a relationship between each instance of the dimension and the measure group.

## Reference Dimensions

A reference dimension is not related directly to the measure group. Instead, a *reference dimension* is related to another regular dimension, which is, in turn, related to the measure group. This is referred to as the intermediate dimension. Reference dimensions are created by selecting Referenced from the Select relationship type drop-down list in the Define Relationship dialog box.

## Data Mining Dimensions

We can include information discovered by data mining algorithms in our cubes for analysis. This is done through the creation of data mining dimensions. We discuss data mining in Chapters 15, 16, and 17. *Data mining dimensions* are created by selecting Data Mining from the Select relationship type drop-down list in the Define Relationship dialog box.

## Many-to-Many Dimensions

*Many-to-many dimensions,* as the name implies, support many-to-many relationships between dimension members and measure group members. For example, if an e-commerce site allows an order to have multiple ship-to addresses, there is a many-to-many relationship. An order can have multiple addresses and, of course, an address can be used by more than one order.

In a relational database, a many-to-many relationship is implemented by creating an intermediate linking table. When a many-to-many relationship is implemented in an Analysis Services cube, the intermediate linking table becomes an intermediate fact table. Many-to-many dimensions are created by selecting Many-to-Many from the Select relationship type drop-down list in the Define Relationship dialog box.

## Slowly Changing Dimensions

For our cubes to provide meaningful information from year to year, we need to have dimensions whose members are fairly constant. If the dimensions are changing drastically month to month, our analysis across the time dimension becomes worthless. Therefore, we need mainly static dimensions.

Some dimensions, however, change over time. Salespeople move from one sales territory to another. The corporate organizational chart changes as employees are promoted or resign. These are known as Slowly Changing Dimensions (SCD).

SCDs come in three varieties: Type 1, Type 2, and Type 3, as defined by the Business Intelligence community. Not exciting names, but they didn't ask for my input, so it's what we are stuck with! Anyway, let's look at what differentiates each type of SCD.

## Type 1 Slowly Changing Dimensions

When a dimension is implemented as a Type 1 SCD, we don't keep track of its history as it changes. The members of the dimension represent the way things are right now. With a *Type 1 SCD*, it is impossible to go back and determine the state of the dimension members at any time in the past.

In actuality, all dimensions in Analysis Services cubes are allowed to change. Some dimensions track that change so a previous state of that dimension's members can be reconstructed during analysis. These are the Type 2 SCD and Type 3 SCD, which we discuss in the sections "Type 2 Slowly Changing Dimensions" and "Type 3 Slowly Changing Dimensions." If a dimension does not track this change, it is a Type 1 SCD. In most cases, the majority of the dimensions in your cubes are going to be Type 1 SCD.

Let's consider a situation where we have four salespeople—Jackie, Andy, Sam, and Mollie—in four sales territories: A, B, C, and D. (All right, so maybe my naming isn't always that creative either!) Figure 9-16 shows the situation in May. Jackie is in sales

**Figure 9-16**   *The state of the salesperson Type 1 SCD in May*

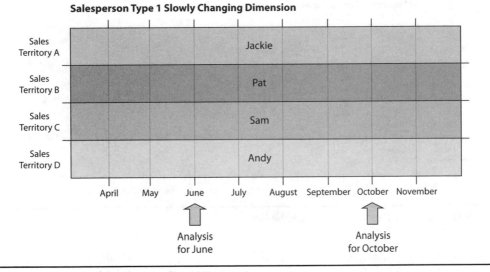

**Figure 9-17**    *The state of the salesperson Type 1 SCD after July*

territory A, Andy is in sales territory B, Sam is in sales territory C, and Mollie is in sales territory D. The figure reflects the fact that the four salespeople are expected to remain in their territories through the rest of the year.

Now, let's suppose at the beginning of July, 2010, Mollie is promoted to sales manager. Andy is moved to Mollie's former sales territory (sales territory D), and a new salesperson, Pat, is hired to take over Andy's former territory (sales territory B). The state of the salesperson dimension after the shuffling is shown in Figure 9-17. Because this is a Type 1 SCD, we do not track any history. We just overwrite the previous dimension information with the current dimension information.

If we perform analysis on sales information using this cube, it will look like Andy has always been in sales territory D and Pat has always been in sales territory B. This is true if we look at sales measures for June or if we look at sales information for October. The history is lost.

## Type 2 Slowly Changing Dimensions

When a dimension is implemented as a *Type 2 SCD*, four supplementary attributes are added to the dimension to track the history of that dimension. These four attributes are:

▶ **SCD Original ID**    The unique identifier from the transactional system

▶ **SCD Start Date**    The date this dimension member became active

▶ **SCD End Date**    The date this dimension member ceased being active

▶ **SCD Status**    The current state of this dimension member, either active or inactive

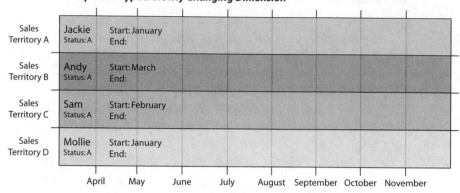

**Figure 9-18**　*The state of the salesperson Type 2 SCD in May*

Let's return to our salesperson dimension example. Figure 9-18 shows the state of the dimension in May. Three of the four new fields are shown in the figure: Start Date, End Date, and Status. Because none of the dimension members has an end date filled in, they are expected to remain active indefinitely into the future.

After the changes to the sales territories occur at the beginning of July, you can see how the new fields are used to track both the previous state and the current state of the sales territory assignments. This is shown in Figure 9-19. Now, by using the Start Date and End Date attributes, when we perform analysis for May, we see how the salespeople were arranged in May. When we do analysis for October, we see how the

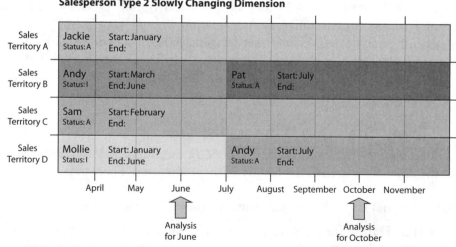

**Figure 9-19**　*The state of the salesperson Type 2 SCD after July*

salespeople were arranged in October. When we want to find the current state of the dimension, we can use the Status attribute to quickly locate the active members rather than doing a lot of date comparisons.

The Original ID attribute holds a unique identifier that was used as the primary key for the dimension members in the original transactional system. This is used to help tie fact information coming from the transactional system to the appropriate dimension member. This Original ID cannot be used as the primary key in our dimension. Because a salesperson can appear in the dimension more than once, the Original ID associated with that salesperson would appear more than once. Therefore, we need to create an alternate key to be used as the primary key to prevent duplicate key violations.

In the Type 1 SCD example, each employee can only appear once in the Salesperson dimension. Therefore, the salesperson's Original ID can be used as the primary. This is not the case with the Type 2 SCD.

In the Type 2 SCD, a salesperson can appear in the dimension more than once. You can see this with Andy in Figure 9-19. Andy has two dimension members: the member with an effective start date in March and the member with the effective start date in July. If we defined a primary key using the Original ID, we would receive an error when we tried to insert the second entry into this dimension. When the alternate key is used as the primary key, there are no run-time errors because the alternate key is unique to each record in the dimension.

When we use the alternate key as the primary key, we also have to use it in the foreign key fields in the fact tables. That way we can tell which measures are linked to Andy when he was in sales territory B and which measures are linked to Andy when he was in sales territory D.

## Type 3 Slowly Changing Dimensions

A Type 3 SCD is similar to a Type 2 SCD with one exception. A Type 3 SCD does not track the entire history of the dimension members. Instead, a *Type 3 SCD* tracks only the current state and the original state of a dimension member.

A Type 3 SCD is implemented using two additional attributes:

▶ **SCD Start Date**   The date the current state of this dimension member became active

▶ **SCD Initial Value**   The original state of this attribute

## Loading the Max Min Sales DM Data Mart

In addition to the Manufacturing data mart, we created another data mart back in Chapter 6. This is the Sales data mart. You will recall that we created both the database schema for the data mart and the OLAP cube definition at the same time using the Cube Wizard. This data mart may have a cube, but it has even less data than the Manufacturing data mart. It is completely empty. We can remedy this situation as well.

The cube we created for the Sales data mart includes an SCD to track the salespeople as they moved from job to job. You can see how we load data into an SCD by using the MaxMinSalesDMLoad project to populate the Sales data mart. In fact, you need to execute the Integration Services package in this project in order to load data into your copy of the MaxMinSalesDM data mart. Alternately, you can restore the back up of the MaxMinSalesDM database, which has already been loaded with data. It is necessary for you to do one or the other in order to have a populated database to use with Learn By Doing exercises later in this book. The Integration Services project and the database backup are included in the Zip file download for this book. Follow the directions that come along with this project or with the database backup.

## You Are Special

In this chapter, we looked deeper into what makes an OLAP cube in a Multidimensional BI Semantic Model tick. We examined the cube's basic parts: measures and dimensions. In Chapter 10, we move from the basics to what makes Microsoft SQL Server Analysis Services such an outstanding tool. We examine many of the special features available to us as we work with our OLAP cubes.

# Chapter 10

# Bells and Whistles— Special Features of OLAP Cubes

## In This Chapter

- ▶ **Where No Cube Has Gone Before**
- ▶ **Additional Cube Features**
- ▶ **More Sophisticated Scripting**

*I do not like poems that resemble hay compressed into a geometrically perfect cube.*

—Yevgeny Yevtushenko

Thus far, we have created two data marts for our sample company, Maximum Miniatures, Incorporated. Both data marts are full of data (assuming you used the MaxMinSalesDMLoad project to populate the Sales data mart as directed at the end of Chapter 9). We also have an online analytical processing (OLAP) cube built on top of each of these data marts. You may think our work is almost done. On the contrary, it is just beginning!

We have data sitting in data marts in relational databases. We have cube definitions that exist as Extensible Markup Language (XML) definition documents in our development environments. What we do not have are multidimensional cubes filled with preprocessed aggregates waiting to help us create business intelligence. (In case you forgot after reading the first few chapters, that is why we are here.)

We begin by taking care of this very issue. We can deploy our cubes to SQL Server Analysis Services databases. We can then begin querying aggregates from the cubes and see benefit from our labors.

Once the cubes are deployed, we examine many of the special features available in these OLAP cubes. We move between SQL Server Data Tools and the SQL Server Management Studio to view the data and try out the development tools at our disposal.

# Where No Cube Has Gone Before

We begin this chapter by taking our cubes where they have not gone before: to a Multidimensional SQL Server Analysis Services server. Up to this point, when we have worked with dimensions and measures, it has been as definitions in SQL Server Data Tools. This environment is great for creating and refining these objects. Unfortunately, dimensions and measures cannot do much when they only exist here. To put them to work, we must deploy them to an Analysis Services server.

Our Analysis Services projects in SQL Server Data Tools contain several properties that control deployment of the content of a project. Once these properties are set correctly, deploying the project content is a snap. All it takes is one selection from a context menu.

Alternatively, we can turn the entire definition of the project into an XML for Analysis (XML/A) script. This is done using the Analysis Services Deployment Wizard. As the script is generated by the Deployment Wizard, we have the ability to change some of the configuration information, such as server names and credentials, so the scripts function on different servers. Your environment may require slightly different configurations for development, quality assurance, and production. Once the script is generated with the appropriate configuration settings, it can be loaded into a SQL Server Management Studio query window and executed on an Analysis Services server.

# Deploying and Processing

We need to complete two steps before our cubes become useful. First, we need to deploy the structures to the Analysis Services database. Second, we need to process those structures in the Analysis Services database.

## Deploying

Deploying is the first step to creating a useful Analysis Services structure. When we *deploy* an Analysis Services project, we move that project's definition from the development environment to a server environment. In a development environment, the developer is the only one who has access to the objects in a project. In the server environment, those objects are exposed to any users with the appropriate access rights.

The objects in a project cannot reside on an Analysis Services server on their own. They must be contained within an Analysis Services database. The name of the database is specified in the project definition. If the specified database is not present, it is created as part of the deployment process.

Deploying a project results in an exact copy of that project's measures and dimensions on the server. Deploying a project does not result in any members being placed in those dimensions or any facts being placed in those measures. For this to happen, we need to process the Analysis Services database.

## Processing

*Processing* is the procedure that pumps the database full of the good stuff. When an Analysis Services database is processed, it reads data from its data source. Dimensions are populated with members. Measures are populated with facts. Then the aggregates for all the combinations within the dimensional hierarchy are calculated.

Dimensions are processed first. Data is read from the dimension tables in the data source and used to create dimension members. After all of the dimension members are loaded, map files that contain all of the possible dimension and hierarchy member combinations are created. These map files are used for calculating aggregates.

Measures are processed after the dimension processing is complete. Data is read from the fact tables in the data source and used to create measures. The map files are used to ensure that aggregations are created for the entire cube.

When processing is complete, the Analysis Services database is ready for analysis to begin.

# Deploying from SQL Server Data Tools

We first look at the steps necessary to deploy from SQL Server Data Tools. This method is certainly the most straightforward of our two options. However, as we see shortly, it does not provide the flexibility of the Analysis Services Deployment Wizard.

We begin with an Analysis Services project in SQL Server Data Tools. Several properties of this project must be set before the deployment can take place. These properties are found on the Deployment page of the Project Property Pages dialog box, shown in Figure 10-1.

Let's go through the properties starting at the bottom of the dialog box and working our way to the top. The *Database property* is the name of an Analysis Services database. This database is created on the server, if it does not already exist there. The *Server property* contains the name of a Multidimensional SQL Server Analysis Services server instance where the project is to be deployed.

The *Deployment Mode property* controls how the project is deployed; either all of the project is deployed or only the changed objects are deployed. The *Transactional Deployment property* determines whether the project is deployed as a single transaction or as multiple transactions. When this property is set to True, the project is deployed as a single transaction. If the project is deployed as multiple transactions, the deploying is done in one transaction and each processing operation done as part of the deployment is done in its own transaction.

The *Processing Option parameter* establishes what cube processing is done as part of the deployment. If Default is selected, the deployment includes whatever processing is necessary to bring the deployed objects to a fully processed state. If Do Not Process

**Figure 10-1** *The Project Property Pages dialog box*

is selected, no processing is done. If Full is selected, all of the data is deleted from the deployed objects and all values are reloaded or recalculated.

The information entered on the Deployment page of the Project Property Pages dialog box is stored in two different configuration files. These files are located in the bin folder inside of the folder created for your project. The configuration settings are stored in the *{project name}*.deploymentoptions file. The deployment target settings are stored in the *{projectname}*.deploymenttargets file. Note, the bin folder and these deployment files are created as part of the deployment process, so they will not be present until you have tried to deploy the project.

Once the properties on the Deployment page are set, we can perform the actual deployment. This can be done by selecting Build | Deploy *{project name}* from the Main menu or by right-clicking the project entry in the Solution Explorer window and selecting Deploy from the context menu. The progress of the deployment is displayed in the Output window and the Deployment Progress window, as shown in Figure 10-2.

**Figure 10-2**   *Deploying an Analysis Services project from SQL Server Data Tools*

SQL Server Data Tools begins the deployment by creating a script. This script contains commands to create the specified Analysis Services database, if necessary, and to create each of the objects in the project. If a processing option is selected for the project, the script also includes commands to process each object. This script is then executed on the specified server. We see what one of these scripts looks like in the next section of this book.

## Learn By Doing—Deploying the MaxMinManufacturingDM Project Using SQL Server Data Tools

### Features Highlighted

▶ Deploying an Analysis Services project using SQL Server Data Tools

▶ Using the Browse window in the SQL Server Management Studio to browse the content of a cube

**Business Need**   To have an OLAP cube we can finally put to use, we must deploy and process this project.

### Steps

1. Open SQL Server Data Tools.
2. Open the MaxMinManufacturingDM project.
3. Select Project | MaxMinManufacturingDM Properties from the Main menu. The MaxMinManufacturingDM Property Pages dialog box appears.
4. For the Server property on the Deployment page, enter the name of a test or development server running a Multidimensional instance of SQL Server 2012 Analysis Services. (Do *not* perform this or any other Learn by Doing activity on a server used for production operations!)
5. MaxMinManufacturingDM should already be entered for Database.
6. Click OK to exit the MaxMinManufacturingDM Property Pages dialog box.
7. Select Build | Deploy MaxMinManufacturingDM from the Main menu. Provide a set of credentials for completing this deployment, if prompted to do so. Monitor the progress of the deployment in the Output and Deployment Progress windows until the Deployment Completed Successfully message appears.
8. To prove that we actually did something, we use the SQL Server Management Studio to browse the cube in our newly created Analysis Services database. Open the SQL Server Management Studio.

9.  Select Analysis Services for Server type, and connect to the Analysis Services server where you deployed the project.

10. Expand the Databases folder under this server in the Object Explorer window.

11. Expand the entry for the MaxMinManufacturingDM database, and then expand the Cubes folder under this database.

12. Right-click the Max Min Manufacturing DM cube, and select Browse from the context menu. You see a Browse window, as shown in Figure 10-3.

13. Expand the Measures entry in the Metadata area of the Browse window. Drag the Total Products calculated member, and drop it on "Drag levels or measures here to add to the query." You see the total products calculated for the entire cube.

**Figure 10-3**    *The Browse window in the SQL Server Management Studio*

14. Expand the Dim Product entry in the Metadata area of the Browse window. Expand the Product Hierarchy entry beneath it. Drag the Product Type Code level, and drop it to the left of the Total Products column in the main area of the Browse window. You see the total products calculation spread across each of the product types. The product type code numbers are shown. We will modify the cube to display the product type names in Chapter 11.

15. Expand the Dim Time entry in the Metadata area of the Browse window. Expand the Date Hierarchy entry beneath it. Drag the Month level, and drop it between the Product Type Code and Total Products columns. You see the total products calculation spread across the product types and months of the year. This is shown in Figure 10-4.

**Figure 10-4**    *Browsing the Max Min Manufacturing DM cube*

**Figure 10-5**  *Two levels from the Dim Time dimension in the Browse window*

16. Drag the Year level, and drop it between the Product Type Code and Month columns. This is shown in Figure 10-5.

**NOTE**

*We are able to skip levels in the hierarchy when we use the Browse window. In this example, we use the Year and Month levels of the Dim Time dimension without using the Quarter level.*

17. Drag the Month heading off the query result until the mouse pointer includes an *X*, as shown in Figure 10-6. Drop the heading any time the mouse pointer includes the *X*, and this dimension is then removed from the query.

18. Continue to experiment with the Browse window as long as you like.

**Figure 10-6**   *Dragging an item off the pivot table*

Congratulations! You have just created and browsed your first bit of honest-to-goodness business intelligence (BI). It only took us ten chapters to get here! SQL Server 2012 greatly simplifies the creation of business intelligence, but it still takes some work. Don't worry: This gets easier and goes faster each time you repeat the process from here on.

**NOTE**

*We have loaded the detail-level data into our cube, but we have not yet created the preprocessed aggregates we have been talking about. We are able to get relatively quick results in the Browse window because the amount of data in our cube is relatively small. We discuss how to control the aggregation setting for the cube and create preprocessed aggregates in the "Aggregation Design" section of this chapter. Completing the aggregation design is essential to creating a cube that provides aggregated measures efficiently.*

# Deploying from the Analysis Services Deployment Wizard

Deploying the Analysis Services project from SQL Server Data Tools works great when we have access to the target Analysis Services server. At times, however, this may not be the case. And, at other times, we need to make changes to the configuration of the project when it is moved from the development environment into production. Fortunately, we have a second method for deploying that handles both of these needs: deploying from the Analysis Services Deployment Wizard.

The Analysis Services Deployment Wizard can deploy a project directly to a server, just like SQL Server Data Tools. However, it can also examine the definition of a project and create an XML/A script that can re-create the items on a server. The XML/A script is written to a file. It is up to us to execute that file on the server to complete the deployment.

To use the wizard, we need to develop an Analysis Services project in SQL Server Data Tools. Once the project is developed, we need to perform a build operation on the project to create the files necessary for the wizard. This is done by selecting Build | Build {*project name*} from the Main menu. Once the project builds successfully, it is ready to deploy.

The wizard is a stand-alone program, separate from SQL Server Data Tools. The Analysis Services Deployment Wizard is launched from the SQL Server 2012 entry in the Windows Start menu. To launch the wizard, select Start | All Programs | Microsoft SQL Server 2012 | Analysis Services | Deployment Wizard.

After the welcome page, the wizard prompts you for the path and name of an Analysis Services database file on the Specify Source Analysis Services Database page, shown in Figure 10-7. This database file is created when we build the Analysis Services project. It has a file extension of .asdatabase and is located in the bin folder inside of the folder created for your project (for example, C:\...\Myproject\bin\MyAnalSrvcsProj.asdatabase).

The Installation Target page, shown in Figure 10-8, asks for the Analysis Services server and Analysis Services database this project is to be deployed to. Remember, the wizard does not perform the deployment; it only creates a script for the deploy step. Therefore, the wizard does not need access to the server you specify.

The Specify Options for Partitions and Roles page enables us to determine how partitions and security entities are to be handled by the deployment. We discuss partitions in the section "Partitions" in this chapter. We discuss security in Chapter 11. This page asks us to specify whether existing objects are overwritten or retained. Therefore, it only applies to situations where we are deploying updates to an existing database. The Specify Options for Partitions and Roles page is shown in Figure 10-9.

The Specify Configuration Properties page, shown in Figure 10-10, collects a number of pieces of configuration information. First, it lets us specify whether the configuration

**Figure 10-7** *The Specify Source Analysis Services Database page of the Analysis Services Deployment Wizard*

**Figure 10-8** *The Installation Target page of the Analysis Services Deployment Wizard*

**Figure 10-9** *The Specify Options for Partitions and Roles page of the Analysis Services Deployment Wizard*

**Figure 10-10** *The Specify Configuration Properties page of the Analysis Services Deployment Wizard* and optimization settings for existing objects are retained or overwritten. Next, it enables us to modify the connection strings used by the data sources in this project. This may be necessary as projects are moved from a development environment to a production environment. We can also configure the impersonation settings, error log file locations, and the path to the database file being created.

The Data Source Impersonation Information entry specifies the Windows credentials that are to be impersonated by this data source while accessing the underlying database. The Default Data Source Impersonation Information entry specifies the Windows credentials that are impersonated if the data source's impersonation is set to default. Somewhere in this chain, we need an actual set of credentials to use during data processing. For this reason, you may need to select the service account for either the Data Source Impersonation Information or the Default Data Source Impersonation Information to deploy and process the script correctly.

The Select Processing Options page lets us select the type of processing we would like to occur as part of the deployment. It also enables us to configure the writeback options. We discuss writeback in the section "Writeback." This page also lets us choose whether the processing is done in one transaction or in multiple transactions. This page is shown in Figure 10-11.

**Figure 10-11** *The Select Processing Options page of the Analysis Services Deployment Wizard*

**Figure 10-12** *The Confirm Deployment page of the Analysis Services Deployment Wizard*

The Confirm Deployment page, shown in Figure 10-12, is where we start the deployment process, either deploying to a server or creating a deployment script. The Create Deployment Script check box enables us to create a deployment script, rather than having the wizard deploy directly to the server. We need to specify the path and name if the script file option is selected.

Clicking Next on the Confirm Deployment page causes the wizard either to deploy the project to the server or to create the deployment script. Once either of these processes is completed, the page appears similar to Figure 10-13. The Deploying database page is followed by the Deployment Complete page, which confirms the deployment process, or at least the script generation, is complete.

If a script is generated by the wizard, we need to execute that script on the SQL Server 2012 Analysis Services server. If the server is not directly connected to the development environment where it was created, the script file can be copied and transferred as needed. When the script is in a location that can be accessed by the Analysis Services server, it can be opened and executed in the SQL Server Management Studio.

After starting the SQL Server Management Studio, select File | Open | File from the Main menu or use the Open File button on the toolbar to load the deployment script.

**Figure 10-13** *The Deploying database page of the Analysis Services Deployment Wizard*

Loading the script causes the SQL Server Management Studio to open an XML/A query window and prompt you to connect to an Analysis Services server, if you are not already connected to one. Once the script is loaded and this connection is made, the SQL Server Management Studio appears similar to Figure 10-14.

Execute the script by selecting Query | Execute from the main menu. The script creates all of the items in your project and performs processing as you instructed in the Deployment Wizard. When the script is completed, you see the "Query executed successfully" message below the Query window.

## Learn By Doing—Deploying the MaxMinSalesDM Project Using the Analysis Services Deployment Wizard

### Feature Highlighted

▶ Deploying an Analysis Services project using the Analysis Services Deployment Wizard

**Figure 10-14**  *The Deployment Script loaded in a SQL Server Management Studio XML/A Query window*

**Business Need**    To have a second OLAP cube ready to go, we must deploy and process the MaxMinSalesDM project.

### NOTE

*You need to either execute the MaxMinSalesDMLoad Integration Services package or restore the MaxMinSalesDM database from the materials provided for this book. If you do not, your cube will not contain data after processing.*

### Steps

1. Open SQL Server Data Tools.
2. Open the MaxMinSalesDM project.
3. Open the MaxMinSalesDM.dsv data source view.
4. Right-click anywhere in the unoccupied area of the data source view diagram, and select Refresh from the context menu. This will determine the differences between the structures in the data source view and the underlying relational tables. The Refresh Data Source View dialog box appears listing these differences.

These are the fields we manually added to the tables near the end of Chapter 6. We need to manually add these changes into the appropriate dimensions.

5.  Click OK to incorporate these changes into the data source view. If you receive an error message, click OK.

6.  Click the Save All button on the toolbar.

7.  Close the data source view design tab.

8.  Open the Customer dimension.

9.  In the Data Source View pane of the Customer dimension design tab, select the PK_Customer field.

10. Drag it to the Attributes pane.

11. Repeat this process with the Address, City, State, ZipCode, Homeowner, MaritalStatus, NumCarsOwned, and NumChildrenAtHome fields.

12. In the Attributes pane, rename the PK Customer attribute to **Account Num**.

13. With Account Num still selected, change the OrderBy property in the Properties window to Key.

14. Click the Save All button on the toolbar.

15. Close the Customer design tab.

16. Open the Product dimension.

17. Drag the RetailPrice and Weight fields from the Data Source View pane to the Attributes pane.

18. Click the Save All button on the toolbar.

19. Close the Product design tab.

20. Repeat steps 16–19 to add the Sales_Person_Territory field to the Sales Person dimension.

21. Repeat steps 16–19 to add the Store_Type field to the Store dimension.

22. Select Build | Build MaxMinSalesDM from the Main menu.

23. Click the Save All button on the toolbar.

24. Close SQL Server Data Tools.

25. From the Windows desktop, select Start | All Programs | Microsoft SQL Server 2012 | Analysis Services | Deployment Wizard. The Analysis Services Deployment Wizard Welcome page appears.

26. Click Next on the Welcome page. The Specify Source Analysis Services Database page of the wizard appears.

27. Click the ellipsis button (…). The Open dialog box appears.

28. Browse to the location of the bin directory under the MaxMinSalesDM project. Select the MaxMinSalesDM.asdatabase file and click Open. Click Next. The Installation Target page of the wizard appears.

29. For the Server property, enter the name of a test or development server running a Multidimensional instance of SQL Server 2012 Analysis Services. (Do *not* perform this or any other Learn by Doing activity on a server used for production operations!)

30. MaxMinSalesDM should already be entered for Database. Click Next. The Specify Options for Partitions and Roles page of the wizard appears.

31. Leave the default settings on this page. Click Next. The Specify Configuration Properties page of the wizard appears.

32. Click the word "Default" under Default Data Source Impersonation Information. An ellipsis (…) button appears. Click the ellipsis button. The Impersonation Information dialog box appears.

33. Select Use a specific Windows user name and password. Enter the User name and Password for an account that has administrative rights on the selected Analysis Services server. Click OK.

34. Click Next. The Select Processing Options page of the wizard appears.

35. Leave the default settings on this page. Click Next. The Confirm Deployment page of the wizard appears.

36. Check Create deployment script. Click the ellipsis (…) button. The Save As dialog box appears. Browse to a folder that is accessible from the test or development Analysis Services server you are using. Enter **MaxMinSalesDM Script.xmla** for File name. Click Save, and then click Next. The Deploying database page of the wizard appears as the wizard creates the deployment script.

37. When the script creation is done, click Next. The Deployment Complete page of the wizard appears. Click Finish.

38. Open the SQL Server Management Studio and connect to a Multidimensional instance of Analysis Services.

39. Click the Open File button on the toolbar. The Open File dialog box appears.

40. Browse to the location where you created the MaxMinSalesDM Script.xmla file. Select this file and click Open. The script is loaded into an XML/A Query window.

41. If prompted, enter the server name and appropriate credentials for the Analysis Services server, and then click Connect.

42. Click the Execute button on the toolbar.

43. The SQL Server Management Studio executes the script and creates the MaxMinSalesDM Analysis Services database. Some "Error Code" messages may appear in the Results area. These can be ignored.

44. When the Query executed successfully message appears below the Query window, right-click the Databases folder entry in the Object Explorer window, and select Refresh from the context menu. The MaxMinSalesDM database appears in the Object Explorer window.

45. Expand the MaxMinSalesDM database and the Data Sources folder.

46. Double-click the Max Min Sales DM data source. The Data Source Properties dialog box appears.

47. Click the Impersonation Info item to select it. Click the ellipsis (...) button. The Impersonation Information dialog box appears.

48. Enter the password for this user name and click OK.

49. Click OK to exit the Data Source Properties dialog box.

50. Right-click the MaxMinSalesDM database and select Process from the context menu. The Process Database dialog box appears.

51. Click OK to begin processing the database.

52. Click Close when processing is complete. Feel free to browse the MaxMinSales cube, just as we did with the Max Min Manufacturing DM cube.

**NOTE**

*We have loaded the detail-level data into our cube, but we have not yet created the preprocessed aggregates we have been talking about. We are able to get relatively quick results in the Browse window because the amount of data in our cube is relatively small. We discuss how to control the aggregation setting for the cube and create preprocessed aggregates in the "Aggregation Design" section of this chapter. Completing the aggregation design is essential to creating a cube that provides aggregated measures efficiently.*

# Additional Cube Features

Throughout the past few chapters, we have learned how to create and, most recently, deploy Analysis Services cubes. I know you are all ready to rush off and create data marts and cubes to start analyzing your own data. This is when I need to be like the knife salesperson on late-night TV and say, "But wait, there's more!"

SQL Server 2012 offers a number of special features in its OLAP cubes. These features enable us to provide our users with more meaningful, better organized, and more secure business intelligence. Space does not permit a detailed examination of each of these features. Instead, the goal here is to give you a basic understanding of each item so you can do additional exploration on your own. SQL Server 2012 has online documentation called Books Online. Refer to this documentation for a more detailed explanation.

## Linked Objects

Depending on the intricacy of your organization and its data processing structure, you may end up creating a number of different Analysis Services cubes from a number of different data sources. Odds are there will be measures in two or three different cubes that a user wants to analyze together. We could solve this problem by duplicating the measures in several cubes. Duplicating data is not a great option, especially if we are preprocessing hundreds of thousands, or even millions, of aggregate values in each cube. Fortunately, we have a better alternative: using linked objects.

By linking objects, we can take measures and their related dimensions from one cube and allow them to be referenced through another cube. This solves our problem without creating maintenance nightmares. Once created, these linked measures and dimensions look to the end user like any other measure or dimension in the cube.

## Creating a Linked Measure

Linked objects are created on the Cube Structure tab of the Cube Design tab in SQL Server Data Tools. We open the project for the cube that will contain the linked objects. Right-click in the Measures or Dimensions area, and select New Linked Object from the context menu, as shown in Figure 10-15, to launch the Linked Object Wizard.

After the introductory page, the Select a Data Source page of the wizard is displayed. Here, we can select an existing Analysis Service data source, if one exists, or create a new data source using the New Data Source button. If the New Data Source button is clicked, the Data Source Wizard appears. This wizard walks us through the creation of a new data source as we have done previously. The only difference is we are creating a connection to an Analysis Services database, rather than to a transactional database.

**Figure 10-15** *Creating a linked object*

**Figure 10-16** *The Select Objects page of the Linked Object Wizard*

Once a data source is created, we are returned to the Linked Object Wizard. Clicking Next takes us to the Select Objects page of the wizard. On this page, we can select the dimensions and measures we want to utilize from this cube to link back into the cube open in SQL Server Data Tools. This is shown in Figure 10-16.

The next page of the wizard lets us review our selections and complete the process. After we click Finish, the selected items are added to the cube definition open in SQL Server Data Tools, as shown in Figure 10-17. The linked items appear in the Measures and Dimensions areas with a chain link added to their icons. These items must still be maintained through their original cube. This is why the source tables for these dimensions are not added to the Data Source View in this cube.

# The Business Intelligence Wizard

A number of complex business intelligence concepts can be applied to cubes in SQL Server 2012 Analysis Services. SQL Server Data Tools wraps a number of these concepts into the Business Intelligence Wizard. You can think of this as being eight wizards wrapped into one.

**Figure 10-17**  *A cube definition with linked objects*

The Business Intelligence Wizard enables us to do any of the following:

▶  **Define time intelligence**    Adds time-related calculated measures to the cube. This includes period-to-date calculations, rolling averages, and period-over-period growth.

▶  **Define account intelligence**    Identifies a dimension and its attributes that define a chart of accounts. Once the chart of accounts is defined, additional calculated values can be created using the account definition.

▶ **Define dimension intelligence**   Identifies a dimension and its attributes as being of a certain type, such as products, customers, rates, time, and so forth. Once the dimension type is defined, additional calculated values can be created using the dimension definition.

▶ **Specify a unary operator**   Specifies the operator to be used instead of the default aggregation in a dimension with a parent-child hierarchy.

▶ **Create a custom member formula**   Creates a calculation to be used instead of the default aggregation in a hierarchy.

▶ **Specify attribute ordering**   Specifies how the members of a particular attribute are to be sorted. The default order is by name.

▶ **Define semiadditive behavior**   Defines the semiadditive behavior of a measure.

▶ **Define currency conversion**   Defines the rules for converting currency and analyzing other multinational information.

The Business Intelligence Wizard is launched by clicking the Add Business Intelligence button on the Cube Structure tab of the Cube Design tab toolbar or by right-clicking a cube or a dimension in the Solution Explorer window and selecting Add Business Intelligence from the context menu. This is shown in Figure 10-18.

## Key Performance Indicators

A key performance indicator (KPI) lets us define a simple, graphic method for analyzing business intelligence that is important to our organization. *KPIs are meant to enable a decision maker to monitor a number of key aspects of the organization's operations at a single glance. KPIs are often used as part of a concept called a digital dashboard.

The *digital dashboard* is modeled after the dashboard in your car: On the car's dashboard, a number of gauges and lights enable you to easily monitor the status of your car's operation. When you want to know what speed you are traveling at, you don't need to wade through an output of the tire's rotational speed over the past few minutes or perform a calculation to determine the tire's circumference. All of the intelligence is built into the dashboard. You simply look down at the speedometer, and the needle tells you what your speed is.

The same is true with the digital dashboard. The decision maker doesn't need to plow though voluminous reports or crunch numbers in a spreadsheet to determine how the organization is doing against specified goals. This business intelligence is in the digital dashboard. A set of electronic gauges and other symbols provides the necessary status information at a single glance.

**Figure 10-18** *Launching the Business Intelligence Wizard*

In SQL Server 2012 Analysis Services, a KPI can reflect five different status levels:

▶ Very Good

▶ Good

▶ Fair

▶ Bad

▶ Very Bad

## Creating a Key Performance Indicator

Key performance indicators are created using the KPIs tab on the Cube Design tab shown in Figure 10-19. On this tab, we define each property of the KPI:

▶ **Name** A unique name for this KPI.

▶ **Associated Measure Group** The measure group being used to calculate the values for this KPI. This can be a single measure group in the cube or all measure groups in the cube.

▶ **Value Expression** An MDX expression used to calculate the current value of the KPI. This may be as simple as a single measure or a calculated member from the cube, or it may be a complex MDX expression looking at the interaction of several measures.

▶ **Goal Expression** An MDX expression used to express the current goal for the KPI. If the goal is a set value, this is a constant value. In other cases, the goal may need to reflect cyclic trends or it may need to vary, depending on dimensional members. The goal could even come from a dimensional attribute. For example, the production goal for each product could be an attribute in the product dimension.

**Figure 10-19** *The KPIs tab on the Cube Design tab*

▶ **Status Indicator**  The graphical representation to be used with this KPI. SQL Server Data Tools and its KPI viewer support nine different graphics. Be aware, however: The graphics available to the user depend heavily on the client tool being used to browse and analyze the cube.

▶ **Status Expression**  An MDX expression used to translate the current value of the KPI into a graphic representation. As noted previously, the KPI can support five different status levels. These equate to five different numeric values: 1 for Very Good, 0.5 for Good, 0 for Fair, –0.5 for Bad, and –1 for Very Bad. The MDX expression must calculate the appropriate value for each status.

Beyond these required items, we can define the following to give the KPI additional functionality:

▶ **Trend Indicator**  The graphical representation to be used when expressing the direction in which the KPI value is trending. SQL Server Data Tools and its KPI viewer support four different graphics. As with the Status Indicator, the graphics available to the user depend heavily on the client tool being used to browse and analyze the cube.

▶ **Trend Expression**  An MDX expression used to translate the trend of the KPI value into a graphic representation. The KPI supports five trend states: 1 for an upward trend, 0.5 for a mildly upward trend, 0 for a flat trend, –0.5 for a mildly downward trend, and –1 for a downward trend. The MDX expression must calculate the appropriate value for each trend situation.

▶ **Display Folder**  The grouping folder for this KPI. This property can be used to collect KPIs into groupings. KPIs that are related can be placed in the same display folder. The client tool used to browse and analyze the cube should then present all of the KPIs in a display folder as a single grouping.

▶ **Parent KPI**  The KPI that serves as a rollup for this and other child KPIs. KPIs can be created in a hierarchical structure, where one KPI displays the status of a rollup value and its child KPIs display the status of the more detailed indicators that make up this value.

▶ **Current Time Member**  An MDX expression defining the current time member. We discuss the concept of a current member of a dimension in Chapter 11.

▶ **Weight**  An MDX expression that expresses the emphasis given to this KPI relative to other KPIs in the group. This expression usually returns a numeric value.

▶ **Description**  A textual description of the KPI.

## Key Performance Indicators and Client Software

We can define KPIs in our cubes and even suggest the graphics we would like used to present those KPIs. However, it is up to the client software used to browse and analyze the cube to display the KPI. Therefore, the client software must not only have the same graphics available, but also honor our suggested graphic for each KPI for the KPIs to appear as we designed them.

You should look at the capabilities of the client tools being used in your organization before spending a lot of time defining KPIs. Make sure KPIs are supported, and determine which parts of the KPI definition the client tools can utilize.

## Learn By Doing—Adding a KPI to the Max Min Manufacturing DM Cube

### Feature Highlighted

► Defining a key performance indicator

**Business Need**    Maximum Miniatures is contemplating the creation of a digital dashboard using KPIs. An initial KPI should be created showing the status of the Percent Rejected calculated measure. This KPI will be used as part of a proof-of-concept project.

The Percent Rejected KPI should reflect status as follows:

► Values less than 1.03 percent should get a Very Good status.

► Values greater than or equal to 1.03 percent but less than 1.04 percent should get a Good status.

► Values greater than or equal to 1.04 percent but less than 1.05 percent should get a Fair status.

► Values greater than or equal to 1.05 percent but less than 1.06 percent should get a Bad status.

► Values greater than or equal to 1.06 percent should get a Very Bad status.

### Steps

1. Open SQL Server Data Tools.
2. Open the MaxMinManufacturingDM project.

3. Double-click the entry for Max Min Manufacturing DM.cube in the Solution Explorer window. The Cube Design tab appears.

4. Select the KPIs tab. Click the New KPI button on the KPIs tab toolbar.

5. Enter **Percent Rejected** for Name.

6. Select Manufacturing Fact from the Associated Measure Group drop-down list.

7. Enter the following for Value Expression:

```
[Measures].[Percent Rejected]
```

8. Enter the following for Goal Expression:

```
"1.02% or less"
```

9. Leave Status indicator set to the default of Gauge.

10. Enter the following MDX expression for Status Expression:

```
Case
    When ROUND([Measures].[Percent Rejected],4) <.0103
        Then 1
    When ROUND([Measures].[Percent Rejected],4) >= .0103 AND
        ROUND([Measures].[Percent Rejected],4) < .0104
        Then .5
    When ROUND([Measures].[Percent Rejected],4) >= .0104 AND
        ROUND([Measures].[Percent Rejected],4) < .0105
        Then 0
    When ROUND([Measures].[Percent Rejected],4) >= .0105 AND
        ROUND([Measures].[Percent Rejected],4) < .0106
        Then -.5
    Else -1
End
```

We discuss MDX expressions in detail in Chapter 11.

11. Click the Save All button on the toolbar. The KPIs tab should appear similar to Figure 10-19.

12. We now want to use SQL Server Data Tools's KPI browser to look at the result of our efforts. To do this, we need to deploy these modifications to the Analysis Services database. Select Build | Deploy MaxMinManufacturingDM from the Main menu.

13. Enter the appropriate credentials, if prompted for them.

14. When the Deployment Completed Successfully message appears in the Deployment Progress window, click the Browser View button on the KPIs tab toolbar, as shown in Figure 10-20. The KPI browser appears.

**Figure 10-20** *The Browser View toolbar button*

The KPI browser shows us the Percent Rejected KPI we just created, as shown in Figure 10-21. The value shown represents the value for the Percent Rejected calculated measure across the entire cube. Our KPI translates this value to a status of Bad (between the red and yellow areas on the gauge).

The upper portion of the KPI browser allows us to filter the information we are sending to the KPI. We use the filter to look at the KPI for some specific dates of production, rather than across the entire cube.

15. Click the cell containing <Select dimension> in the upper portion of the KPI browser. A dimension drop-down list appears. Select Dim Time from this drop-down list. (If <Select dimension> does not appear in the upper portion of the KPI browser, click the Reconnect button on the toolbar of the KPIs tab.)

16. Click the cell immediately below the Hierarchy heading. The hierarchy drop-down list appears. Select Date Hierarchy from this drop-down list.

17. Click the cell immediately below the Filter Expression heading. The Filter Expression drop-down window control appears. Click the down arrow to display the drop-down window.

18. Expand the All entry on the drop-down window. Next expand the 2009 entry, the 2009Q1 entry, and the 200901 entry. Check 2009-01-02 0:00:00.000 and click OK.

**Figure 10-21** *The KPI browser with the Percent Rejected KPI for the entire cube*

**Figure 10-22** *The KPI browser with the Percent Rejected KPI for January 2, 2009*

19. Click anywhere on the KPI browser so the Filter Expression cell loses focus. This causes the KPI to refresh. The KPI browser now has a value of 1.04 percent, which translates to a status of Fair (straight up in the yellow), as shown in Figure 10-22.

20. Try this process again for the following dates:

| Date | Value | Status |
|------|-------|--------|
| 2009-01-07 00:00:00.000 | 1.06% | Very Bad |
| 2009-01-17 00:00:00.000 | 1.03% | Good |
| 2009-01-29 00:00:00.000 | 1.02% | Very Good |

Be sure to uncheck one date before checking another to see the results described here.

21. You can experiment with additional analysis. Try adding a second filter to see the KPI for a single product or a single product type.

# Actions

Actions allow the OLAP cubes to "reach out and touch someone." They enable us to define commands, statements, and directives that are to be executed outside of the cube. In fact, Actions are designed to be executed outside of the Analysis Services environment altogether.

Actions are instructions that are defined and stored inside the cube itself. They are linked to certain objects in the cube. When the user is browsing a certain object in the client software, that software can look for any Actions related to the object. These Actions are then displayed to the user as menu items or Action buttons on the client screen. The user can select one of these Actions to launch separate, but related, applications or interfaces to accomplish related tasks.

For example, suppose a user is browsing a cube that analyzes changing stock prices. This cube may include an action for navigating to a website that contains up-to-the-minute market analysis. If the stock symbol for the company is stored as an attribute in the cube, the Action could pass this along as a parameter in the Uniform Resource Locator (URL).

In another case, a user may be browsing a cube that contains information on purchasing. The cube could include an Action that would launch the organization's document management system and take the user to the folder containing scanned copies of the hardcopy purchase orders. Then, when a questionable purchase is spotted, the user can launch the document management program and examine the paper trail for the purchase.

## Types of Actions

Three different types of Actions are available:

- ▶ **Action** The generic Action type, which has a number of subtypes:
  - ▶ **Dataset** Retrieves a dataset.
  - ▶ **Proprietary** A proprietary action defined by the client software.
  - ▶ **Rowset** Retrieves a rowset.
  - ▶ **Statement** Runs an OLE DB command.
  - ▶ **URL** Displays a page in a browser.
- ▶ **Drillthrough Action** Defines a dataset to be returned as a drillthrough to a more detailed level.
- ▶ **Reporting Action** Launches a SQL Server 2012 Reporting Services report.

## Creating an Action

*Actions* are created on the Actions tab on the Cube Design tab shown in Figure 10-23. On this tab, we define each property of the action:

- ▶ **Name** A unique name for this Action.
- ▶ **Target type** The type of object with which this Action is associated.
- ▶ **Target object** The specific objects of the selected Target type to which this Action is associated.
- ▶ **Condition** An MDX expression defining a condition that would further limit the objects to which this Action is associated.
- ▶ **Type** The type of Action (Dataset, Proprietary, Rowset, Statement, or URL).

**Figure 10-23** *The Actions tab on the Cube Design tab*

▶ **Action expression**   The command that is executed to carry out the Action.

▶ **Invocation**   How the command is executed: Batch, Interactive, On Open.

▶ **Application**   The application used to carry out the Action.

▶ **Description**   A description of the Action.

▶ **Caption**   A caption for this Action.

▶ **Caption is MDX**   A flag showing whether the caption is a string constant or an MDX expression to be evaluated.

## Creating Drillthrough Actions

For the most part, Drillthrough Actions have the same properties as Actions. *Drillthrough Actions* do not have Target Type, Target Object, Type, or Action expression properties. In their place, the Drillthrough Action has the following:

▶ **Measure Group Members**   Defines the measure groups to which this drillthrough action applies.

▶ **Drillthrough Columns**   Defines the objects to be included in the drillthrough dataset.

- ► **Default** A flag showing whether this is the default Drillthrough Action.
- ► **Maximum Rows** The maximum number of rows to be included in the drillthrough dataset.

## Creating Reporting Actions

For the most part, Reporting Actions have the same properties as Actions. *Reporting Actions* do not have Type or Action Content properties. In their place, the Reporting Action has the following:

- ► **Server name** The name of the report server.
- ► **Report path** The path to the report sever.
- ► **Report format** The format of the report to be returned (HTML, Excel, PDF).
- ► **Parameters** The parameter values to be passed to the report.

## Actions and Client Software

We can define Actions in our cubes. However, it is up to the client software used to browse and analyze the cube to display and implement the Action. You should look at the capabilities of the client tools being used in your organization before spending a lot of time defining Actions. Make sure Actions are supported, and determine which parts of the Action definition the client tools can utilize.

# Partitions

We have deployed and processed our cubes to databases on the SQL Server Analysis Services server. We now have, as we have seen, cubes full of information that can be browsed and analyzed. What we have not discussed up to this point is exactly how and where the information in the databases is stored. Let's take care of that deficiency right now.

## Measure Groups and Partitions

When we created the measure groups in our cubes, SQL Server Data Tools created something else for us behind the scenes. It created one partition for each of our measure groups. These partitions are where all of the measure group information is stored. We can view the partitions defined in a cube by using the Partitions tab on the Cube Design tab, as shown in Figure 10-24.

In Figure 10-24, you can see the partitions that were created for each of the measure groups in the Max Min Manufacturing DM cube. The partitions were given the same

**Figure 10-24**  *The Partitions tab on the Cube Design tab*

name as the measure group they are tied to. The *Source column* on this tab tells us where each partition and, therefore, each measure group, gets its fact data. Each partition is tied to a fact table in the data mart. The *Aggregation Design column* tells us how each partition is configured for storing aggregate data.

## Multiple Partitions for a Measure Group

Although we start out with one partition for each measure group, that does not mean we have to keep it that way. We can assign a number of partitions to a single measure group. Each partition has its own data source table. The Standard Edition of SQL Server 2012 allows us to create up to three partitions per measure group. The Business Intelligence Edition, Enterprise Edition, and Developer Edition support this feature without a limitation on the number of partitions per measure group.

This is similar to the concept of partitioned views on the relational side of SQL Server. With partitioned views, we distribute the data from what would be a large table among a number of smaller tables, as shown in Figure 10-25. Sales data from 2008 is in one table. Sales data from 2009 is in another table, and so on. These tables are presented to the client application as if they were a single table by combining them together in a partitioned view. This is done for ease of management and for better performance.

We can essentially do the same thing with partitions and measure groups, as shown in Figure 10-26. Our data can be divided among a number of tables. These tables could be in the same data source or in different data sources. Because they can be in different data sources, the tables could even be on different database servers. We can define multiple partitions, each one pulling data from one of the data source tables. These multiple partitions are then brought together in a single measure group.

**Figure 10-25** *A partitioned view*

As with a partitioned view in a relational database, all of the partitions combined in a single measure group must have the same structure. They must have the same measures and the same relationships to dimensions. If the measures and dimensional relationships don't match, we cannot make the partitions into a single measure group.

It is also possible to create multiple partitions from a single table. We may want to do this because our source data works just fine in a single table, but we can better manage it as a number of separate partitions in Analysis Services. This is shown in Figure 10-27.

We do this by creating a number of views in the relational database or named queries in the data source view. You can think of named queries as equivalent to views.

**Figure 10-26** *A measure group with multiple partitions from multiple relational tables*

**Figure 10-27**  *A measure group with multiple partitions from a single relational table*

They are defined in the data source view of a cube. We try creating a few named queries in the section "Learn By Doing—Creating Multiple Partitions from a Single Table." Each view or named query becomes the data source for a single partition. The partitions are joined together again by the measure group.

Any time we use multiple partitions in a single measure group, but especially when using named queries with a single table, we must be careful not to get the same data in two partitions. If this occurs, the information in our measure group will be incorrect. To prevent this, it is important to strictly define the criteria for membership in each view or named query. In many cases, dividing data by time is wise, as is shown in Figure 10-25, Figure 10-26, and Figure 10-27.

## Learn By Doing—Creating Multiple Partitions from a Single Table

### Features Highlighted

► Creating named queries in a data source view

► Creating multiple partitions for a single measure group

**Business Need**    To better manage the Manufacturing Fact information in Analysis Services, this measure group should utilize three partitions. One partition should contain data from 2009, one partition should contain data from 2010, and one partition should contain data from 2011.

### Steps

1. Open SQL Server Data Tools.
2. Open the MaxMinManufacturingDM project.
3. Double-click the entry for the Max Min Manufacturing DM.dsv data source view. The Data Source View Design tab appears.
4. Right-click any place there isn't a table in the data source diagram area. Select New Named Query from the context menu. The Create Named Query dialog box appears, as shown in Figure 10-28.
5. Enter **ManufacturingFact_2009** for Name.
6. Enter the following query in the SQL pane:

```
SELECT *
FROM ManufacturingFact
WHERE YEAR(DateOfManufacture) = 2009
```

The Create Named Query dialog box appears, as shown in Figure 10-29.

7. Click OK.
8. Create a second named query called **ManufacturingFact_2010**, which includes only 2010 data.
9. Create a third named query called **ManufacturingFact_Current** using the following query:

```
SELECT *
FROM ManufacturingFact
WHERE YEAR(DateOfManufacture) > 2010
```

Obviously, some annual maintenance is required at the beginning of each year. At least, by keeping our final named query open-ended, using > 2010 rather than = 2011, we do not run the risk of leaving out data.

**Figure 10-28** *Creating a new named query*

10.  Click the Save All button on the toolbar, and close the Data Source View Design tab.
11.  Double-click the entry for Max Min Manufacturing DM.cube in the Solution Explorer window. The Cube Design tab appears.
12.  Select the Partitions tab.
13.  Click the New Partition link or the New Partition button on the Partitions tab toolbar. The Welcome page of the Partition Wizard dialog box appears.

**Figure 10-29**  *The ManufacturingFact_2009 Named Query definition*

14. Click Next on the Welcome page. The Specify Source Information page of the wizard appears. Select the Manufacturing Fact measure group and the Max Min Manufacturing DM data source view if they are not already selected. Click the Find Tables button, and check ManufacturingFact_2009 in the Available tables list.

15. Click Next. The Restrict Rows page of the wizard appears. Here, we can further filter the rows in the selected table or named query to ensure no overlap exists between partitions. Our named queries are structured such that no overlap occurs, so we do not need to specify a filter here.

**Figure 10-30**  *The Manufacturing Fact measure group with three partitions*

16. Click Next. The Processing and Storage Locations page of the wizard appears. This page enables us to specify which Analysis Services server is to be used to calculate the aggregates and where the resulting data should be stored. You can see, if we needed a great deal of computing power to calculate a large set of aggregates, we could have a separate server for calculating each partition! If we needed a large amount of storage space, we could have a separate drive system to store the data from each partition! We don't have those types of requirements, so we can leave the defaults.

17. Click Next. The Completing the Wizard page appears. This page lets us choose when and how to design aggregations. We discuss the Aggregation Design Wizard later in this chapter. For now, select Design aggregations later.

18. Click Finish. The new partition appears under the Manufacturing Fact measure group.

19. Repeat Steps 13–18 for the ManufacturingFact_2010 named query.

20. Repeat Steps 13–18 for the ManufacturingFact_Current named query.

21. Right-click the original Manufacturing Fact partition, and select Delete from the context menu. The Delete Objects dialog box appears.

22. Click OK to confirm the deletion. Click the Save All button on the toolbar. The Partitions tab should appear as shown in Figure 10-30.

## Partitions and Storage Options

In Chapter 4 of this book, we discussed the different types of OLAP architectures: Relational OLAP (ROLAP), Multidimensional OLAP (MOLAP), and Hybrid OLAP (HOLAP). Refer to Figure 4-4 if you need a refresher. We are now going to discuss these storage options with regard to our partitions.

**Figure 10-31** *The Partition Storage Settings dialog box*

As we have said, the aggregates in our partitions are going to be preprocessed. Once the preprocessing is completed, all of that data needs to be stored somewhere. SQL Server 2012 Analysis Services provides us with a number of options here, enabling us to select the best mix of query speed versus data latency.

If we click the Storage Settings link or the Storage Settings button on the Partitions tab toolbar, we see the Partition Storage Settings dialog box, as shown in Figure 10-31. This dialog box presents a continuum of storage choices on the Standard Setting slider. These are preconfigured storage options that Analysis Services makes available to us. You can also create your own custom storage settings, but leave that alone for the moment.

The options on the left side of the slider represent the lowest latency but the slowest query speed. The options on the right side of the slider represent the highest latency but the fastest query speed. We need to determine the best choice for each partition.

The predefined options control the following characteristics:

▶ **Storage location for the detail data and the preprocessed aggregates** The detail data and preprocessed aggregates can be stored in one of the following three ways:

- ▶ **ROLAP**   The detail data and the preprocessed aggregates are both stored in a relational format.

- ▶ **HOLAP**   The detail data is stored in a relational format and the aggregates are stored in a multidimensional format.

- ▶ **MOLAP**   The detail data and the preprocessed aggregates are both stored in a multidimensional format.

▶ **How Analysis Services finds out a data source has changed**   Analysis Services can discover data source changes in the following ways:

- ▶ **SQL Server Notification**   The SQL Server relational database engine notifies Analysis Services when changes are made to a data source table. When the partition is linked to a view or a named query, we must specify a SQL table that will cause the notification when it is changed. This is known as a *tracking table*.

- ▶ **Client Initiated Notification**   The client software that is responsible for updating the relational data source sends a NotifyTableChangeCommand to Analysis Services to let it know that data has been changed. Of course, this only works if the data source is modified exclusively through this client software.

- ▶ **Scheduled Polling**   Analysis Services periodically runs a query to determine if the data has changed. This query must return a single value that is compared with the value saved from the previous query execution. This value could be the MAX() of an identity field in the fact table that catches adds, but not edits and deletes. This could also be a MAX() of a last updated date/time stamp, which would catch inserts and edits, but still miss deletes.

▶ **Enable Proactive Caching**   Whether proactive caching is used. This feature requires the Business Intelligence Edition, Enterprise Edition, or Developer Edition of SQL Server 2012. (See Chapter 4 for more information on proactive caching.)

▶ **Silence Interval**   The length of time the data must go without a change before processing begins. The thinking here is that data updates often come in bursts. We don't want to start processing the cube if another ten data changes are coming down the pike. We can wait until things settle down and then start processing.

▶ **Silence Override Interval**   The length of time we wait for a silence interval before we go ahead and initiate processing without one. This prevents the data in the cube from getting too old while waiting for the data changes to die down.

▶ **Drop Outdated Cache Latency**   This is the maximum amount of time we permit outdated aggregates to live in proactive cache while we are waiting for processing to complete. When this time period is reached, the cache is dropped and querying is directed to the relational data source.

▶ **Update Cache Periodically** This is a schedule for updating the proactive cache, even if we have not received a notification that it is out-of-date. This is often used when no notification mechanism is in place.

Let's look at each of the predefined settings in a bit more detail.

**Real-Time ROLAP** All detail data and aggregates are queried directly from the relational data source. No notification is necessary. No proactive caching is used. This may result in slow query performance, but data is always current.

This setting is best for data that is changing frequently, leaving no time for cube processing, and that must always be up-to-date.

**Real-Time HOLAP** Detail data remains in the relational data source. Aggregates are in multidimensional storage. When Analysis Services is notified that the aggregates are out-of-date, it processes the cube. It does not wait for a silence interval. While the aggregates are out-of-date or being processed, queries are sent directly to the relational data source. No proactive cache is used. This provides better performance for queries when the aggregates are up-to-date, but reverts to slow performance while processing.

This setting is best for data that is also changing frequently, but provides some intervals for processing.

**Low-Latency MOLAP** Detail data and aggregates are in multidimensional storage. When Analysis Services is notified that the aggregates are out-of-date, it waits for a silence interval of ten seconds before beginning processing. It uses a silence override interval of ten minutes. While the cube is processing, queries are sent to a proactive cache. If processing takes longer than 30 minutes, the proactive cache is dropped and queries are sent directly to the relational data source. This provides fast query response, unless processing takes longer than 30 minutes. Maximum latency is 30 minutes.

This setting is best in situations where query performance is important but data must remain fairly current.

**Medium-Latency MOLAP** Detail data and aggregates are in multidimensional storage. When Analysis Services is notified that the aggregates are out-of-date, it waits for a silence interval of ten seconds before it starts processing. It uses a silence override interval of ten minutes. While the cube is processing, queries are sent to a proactive cache. If processing takes longer than four hours, the proactive cache is dropped and queries are sent directly to the relational data source. This provides fast query response, unless processing takes longer than four hours. Maximum latency is four hours.

This setting is best in situations where query performance is important and a bit more latency can be tolerated.

**Automatic MOLAP**    Detail data and aggregates are in multidimensional storage. When Analysis Services is notified that the aggregates are out-of-date, it waits for a silence interval of ten seconds before it starts processing. It uses a silence override interval of ten minutes. While the cube is processing, queries are sent to a proactive cache. The proactive cache is not dropped, no matter how long processing takes. This provides fast query response at all times, but it can lead to a large latency if processing is long-running.

This setting is best in situations where query performance is the most important factor and a potentially large latency can be tolerated.

**Scheduled MOLAP**    Detail data and aggregates are in multidimensional storage. Analysis Services does not receive notification of data source changes. Instead, it processes automatically every 24 hours. While the cube is processing, queries are sent to a proactive cache. The proactive cache is not dropped, no matter how long processing takes. This provides fast query response at all times, but it has a maximum latency of 24 hours, plus the time required for processing.

This setting is typically used in situations where a notification mechanism is not available or where data updates occur nightly.

**MOLAP**    Detail data and aggregates are in multidimensional storage. Analysis Services does not receive notification of data source changes. Instead, processing is initiated manually by an administrator. No proactive caching is used, so queries cannot be run while processing is occurring.

This setting is typically used in situations where data is changing rarely or for development and testing environments.

## Learn By Doing—Setting Storage Options for a Cube Partition

### Features Highlighted

- ▶  Setting storage options for a cube
- ▶  Enabling SQL Notification when using named queries

**Business Need**    Before we put the Max Min Manufacturing DM cube into production, we need to revise the storage settings so it keeps itself up-to-date without having to be manually processed. The vice president of production at Maximum Miniatures has asked that this cube have a maximum latency of four hours.

**NOTE**

*The Business Intelligence Edition, Enterprise Edition, or Developer Edition of SQL Server 2012 is required for proactive caching. If you are not using one of these editions, skip Step 7 of this Learn By Doing exercise. If you use proactive caching with the Standard Edition or another edition of SQL Server 2012, you will receive an error when you try to deploy the cube definition to the server.*

**Steps**

1. Open SQL Server Data Tools.
2. Open the MaxMinManufacturingDM project.
3. Double-click the entry for Max Min Manufacturing DM.cube in the Solution Explorer window. The Cube Design tab appears.
4. Select the Partitions tab.
5. Select the Manufacturing Fact 2009 partition.
6. Click the Storage Settings link or the Storage Settings button on the Partitions tab toolbar. The Partition Storage Settings – Manufacturing Fact 2009 dialog box appears.
7. Move the slider to the Medium-latency MOLAP setting. Note the warning message at the bottom of the screen telling us that the default notification method does not work with a named query as a data source.
8. Click the Options button. The Storage Options dialog box appears, as shown in Figure 10-32.
9. Select the Notifications tab.
10. Check Specify tracking tables. This lets us specify a table whose changes cause changes to our named queries. In other words, when this table changes, the data in our named queries changes and the cube needs to be processed.
11. Click the ellipsis (…) button to the right. The Relational Objects dialog box appears.
12. Check the box next to the ManufacturingFact table. Changes to this table cause the SQL Server relational database engine to notify Analysis Services that the cube must be processed.
13. Click OK to exit the Relational Objects dialog box. The Notifications tab of the Storage Options dialog box should appear as shown in Figure 10-33.
14. Click OK to exit the Storage Options dialog box. Click OK to exit the Partition Storage Settings dialog box.

**Figure 10-32** *The General tab of the Storage Options dialog box*

15. Repeat Steps 5–14 for the Manufacturing Fact 2010 partition.
16. Repeat Steps 5–14 for the Manufacturing Fact Current partition.
17. Click the Save All button on the toolbar.

**Figure 10-33** *The Notifications tab of the Storage Options dialog box*

18. Select Build | Deploy MaxMinManufacturingDM from the Main menu. The cube is deployed to the server and processed.
19. Now let's test our notification mechanism. Select the Browser tab on the Cube Design tab.

20. Expand the Measures entry, drag the Total Products calculated member, and drop it in the "Drag levels or measures here to add to the query" area. The total should be 10,296,577.

21. Open the SQL Server Management Studio (leave SQL Server Data Tools open as well) and connect to the SQL Server database engine hosting the MaxMinManufacturingDM relational database.

22. Expand the items in the Object Explorer window until you can see the ManufacturingFact table in the MaxMinManufacturingDM database.

23. Right-click the ManufacturingFact table, and select Edit Top 200 Rows from the context menu.

24. Change the AcceptedProducts field at the top of the grid from 3875 to 4875.

25. Move your cursor off the modified row and wait about a minute.

26. Return to SQL Server Data Tools.

27. Click the Execute Query button on the Browser tab toolbar. If everything is working properly, the total should change to 10,297,577.

28. Go back to the SQL Server Management Studio and change the AcceptedProducts field back to 3875.

29. Move your cursor off the modified row, and then close the SQL Server Management Studio.

## Writeback

Many times, while a user is analyzing data in a cube, they discover data that needs to be adjusted for one reason or another. It may be too time-consuming to make the change in the data source and then wait for it to be processed into the cube. Also, in some situations, business reasons may make it impossible to make the adjustment in the data source. This is where writeback comes in.

*Writeback* enables us to make adjusting entries to the cube data. These entries are stored in a special table that is added to the data source. This table then shows up as an additional partition in the measure group. The adjusting entries are incorporated into queries from this measure group in the same way that data from all of the other partitions is combined.

Writeback is enabled by right-clicking a partition on the Partitions tab and selecting Writeback Settings on the context menu. This displays the Enable Writeback dialog box shown in Figure 10-34. We can specify the name of the writeback table being created and the data source it is created in. We can also specify the storage mode used for the writeback data.

**Figure 10-34** *The Enable Writeback dialog box*

Once writeback is enabled, the writeback partition can be seen on the Partitions tab, as shown in Figure 10-35. Clicking Writeback Settings on the context menu of the writeback partition when writeback is enabled lets you disable this feature.

As with a number of other cube features, the client software used to browse and analyze the cube must support writeback for this feature to be put to use. Microsoft's Office Tools, Excel 2000, XP, 2003, 2007, and 2010 all support this writeback function.

**Figure 10-35** *The Partition tab with a writeback partition*

# Aggregation Design

Previously, we discussed preprocessing all of the aggregates in a cube and putting the results in a multidimensional storage. This is a bit of an overstatement. In fact, Analysis Services determines a pattern of aggregates within the partition that strikes a balance between storage requirements and query speed. This is called an *aggregation design*. This process determines key aggregates and then calculates and stores them. Other aggregations are calculated from the key aggregates at the time a query is submitted.

Aggregations can be designed in two different ways: based on usage or manually. With usage-based aggregation design, the Usage-Based Optimization Wizard uses information from the Analysis Services query log to determine the best aggregation design for a partition. When aggregations are designed manually, the Aggregation Design Wizard guides us through the manual design process. Both wizards are launched from the Aggregations tab on the Cube Design tab.

## Manual Aggregation Design

Here, we look at a few of the screens from the Aggregation Design Wizard. After the Welcome page, the wizard allows you to select which partitions within a measure group you wish to work with. The next page of the wizard is the Review Aggregation Usage page, shown in Figure 10-36.

As we have discussed previously, the dimensional attributes in the cube are used to slice and dice the fact data during analysis. It is the various combinations of these attributes that define the multitude of aggregations that could be created in advance. The aggregation designer looks at each attribute in the cube and makes a determination on how it should be used for preprocessed aggregations. The Review Aggregation Usage page of the wizard allows us to make that determination for the aggregation designer by selecting one of the following:

▶ **Default**   The default aggregation rule is used for this dimensional attribute.

▶ **Full**   Every preprocessed aggregate must include either this attribute or a lower attribute in the same hierarchy. This forces every precalculated aggregate to be sliced by this dimensional attribute. This should not be selected for dimensional attributes that have a large number of members.

▶ **None**   None of the preprocessed aggregates will include this attribute. It will be ignored when designing preprocessed aggregates.

▶ **Unrestricted**   No restrictions are placed on the consideration of this attribute for use when designing preprocessed aggregates.

**Figure 10-36** *The Review Aggregation Usage page of the Aggregation Design Wizard*

The next page of the wizard is the Specify Object Counts page, shown in Figure 10-37. When the Count button is clicked, the wizard counts the number of members in each of the dimensions, including the fact dimension. If you are working with a large cube and do not want to wait for the wizard to do all of this counting, you can enter the member counts manually. You may also want to manually enter counts if you have a small set of data in the cube for testing, but know that a much larger set of data with a different count distribution will be processed into the cube at a later date.

**Figure 10-37**  *The Specify Object Counts page of the Aggregation Design Wizard*

The following page is the Set Aggregation Options page. This is shown in Figure 10-38. On this page, we tell the wizard how to optimize the aggregation design. We can specify a maximum amount of storage we want to allow for aggregates, a maximum performance gain we require, or choose not to design aggregations at all. A fourth option allows the optimization process to run until we tell it to stop. With this last option, the optimizer continues running until it has the best solution or until you get tired of waiting for it and stop it manually. As the optimizer runs, it shows you a graph of its progress.

The last page of the wizard enables us to either deploy and process the changes immediately or save them for later processing. Once the aggregation design has been

**Figure 10-38** *The Set Aggregation Options page of the Aggregation Design Wizard*

completed, the Aggregations tab displays the number of aggregations being preprocessed for each partition. This is shown in Figure 10-39.

Be sure to complete the aggregation design before putting your cubes into production to ensure you get the query performance you expect.

**Figure 10-39** *The Aggregations tab with aggregation design completed*

# Perspectives

In real life, many objects look different, depending on how you look at them—depending on your perspective. In the same way, we can define different perspectives so our cubes look different to different users. By using perspectives, we can provide our users with what they need and not overwhelm them with things they don't. The Business Intelligence Edition, Enterprise Edition, or Developer Edition of SQL Server 2012 is required to use perspectives.

## Creating Perspectives

Perspectives are created on the *Perspectives tab*. This tab lists all of the items in our cube, as shown in Figure 10-40. We can then determine which items are visible in each perspective.

New perspectives are added by clicking the New Perspective button on the Perspectives tab toolbar. Each perspective is given a unique name to identify it. When the perspective is first created, it includes all of the items in the cube. We can remove (uncheck) the items that are not needed or that should not be viewed by people who are going to use that perspective to access the cube.

**Figure 10-40** *The Perspectives tab*

Figure 10-40 shows two perspectives in the Max Min Manufacturing DM cube. The Inventory Monitoring perspective is for users who will be looking at the Inventory Fact measures. They do not need access to the Manufacturing Fact measures or other items that apply only to those measures. The Highlevel Mfg Info perspective is for users who are only interested in the KPI and the two calculated members we have created in our cube. Therefore, only those items and the dimensions are included in this perspective.

## Translations

We live in a global society. More and more, we are required to work internationally to get things done. Business intelligence is certainly no exception to this trend.

To help this along, Analysis Services provides us with the means to localize the metadata contained in our cubes. This is done using the *Translations tab*. The Translations tab is shown in Figure 10-41.

### Creating Translations

New translations are created by clicking the New Translation button on the Translations tab toolbar. First, we must pick the language for the translation. The Select Language dialog box, shown in Figure 10-42, enables us to select the language and country

**Figure 10-41** *The Translations tab*

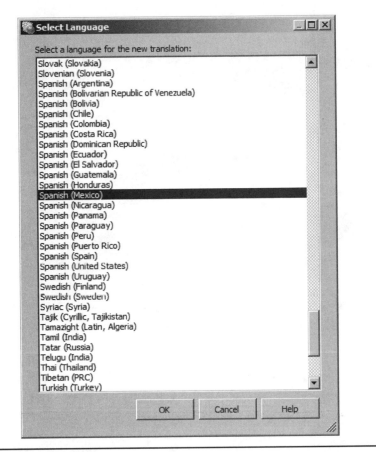

**Figure 10-42** *The Select Language dialog box*

designation for this translation. Next, we can fill in the appropriate translation for each of the metadata items in the cube.

The translations entered in the Translations tab only apply to metadata in the cubes, not to the data in each of the dimensions. To implement multilingual support for the dimensional members, each dimension must have an attribute for each language supported. These attributes then contain the appropriate translations for each member.

# More Sophisticated Scripting

We have used some basic scripting to define objects in Chapters 9 and 10. In Chapter 11, we add to your ability to write MDX script expressions. As a result, we enhance your ability to manipulate and analyze the information in your OLAP cubes.

# Chapter 11

# Writing a New Script— MDX Scripting

## In This Chapter

▶ **Terms and Concepts**
▶ **Putting MDX Scripting to Work**
▶ **Extracting Data from Cubes**

*The world is a stage and most of us are desperately unrehearsed.*

—Sean O'Casey, Playwright

We have already used some basic MDX script expressions to create calculated members in Chapter 9 and to define key performance indicators (KPIs) and Actions in Chapter 10. To complete these tasks, we used the basics of MDX scripting. You probably need to employ more complex MDX scripts to meet the needs of your organization. Thus, we have Chapter 11.

In this chapter, we work to get a handle on the power of MDX scripts. We see how they can be used to perform powerful analysis on your organization's information. In addition to data analysis, we use MDX scripts to set up security restrictions on a cube.

## Terms and Concepts

Before we begin doing all of this good stuff, we need to cover some basics. Up to this point, we have looked at cube concepts and definitions, with the goal of cube creation and population. Now, we need to shift gears a bit and look at the concepts and definitions required for extracting and analyzing the information residing in our cubes.

Let's use an analogy from the relational database world. When we are defining and populating a relational database, we need to know about normalization, constraints, and foreign keys. When we are querying data from a relational database, we need to know about INNER and OUTER JOINS, ORDER BY, and GROUP BY.

As we move to extracting and analyzing information in the cube, we need to learn how to move through our dimensional hierarchies to address a particular location or set of locations in the cube. We need to know how to select a particular measure and combine that with other measures in complex calculations. In short, we need to know how to navigate our cubes without getting lost or, worse yet, without returning utter nonsense to our users.

## Where Are We?

We live in an age of many electronic wonders: computers, of course, but also cell phones, digital cameras, and global positioning satellite (GPS) receivers. With a GPS receiver, we can tell exactly where we are on the planet to within a few feet, perhaps even to within a few inches! The question is this: Will we men now be too stubborn to consult our GPS receivers for directions?

In the world of online analytical processing (OLAP) cubes, we need the equivalent of a GPS system. We need a means to uniquely specify any location within a cube. Fortunately, MDX scripting provides just such a mechanism.

## Cells

The first question might be: Just what are we trying to locate? The answer is: We are trying to locate cells. Fortunately, we do not need a microscope to find these cells. (I never was very good at biology.) These cells are located right inside of our cubes.

Figure 11-1 shows a simplified version of our Max Min Manufacturing DM cube with three dimensions: Dim Machine, Dim Product, and Dim Time. The dimensions divide the cube up into smaller sections. These are cells.

In our cubes, cells contain the values for our measures. In Figure 11-1, the highlighted cell contains the measures for the Woodland Creatures product type produced on the Clay Molder machine type for all of 2010. We can see that 951,959 products were accepted while 10,143 products were rejected and 89,720 minutes were spent in this manufacturing process. If cells contain the measures in a cube, then it is important that we know how to properly address them.

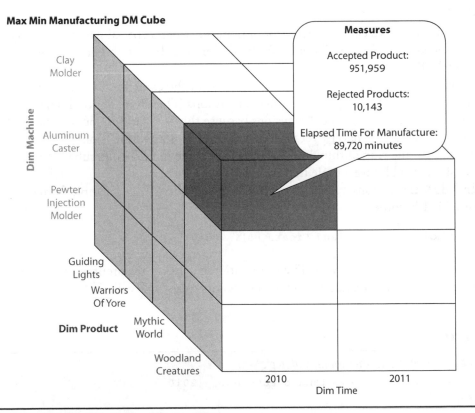

**Figure 11-1**    *A simplified Max Min Manufacturing DM cube*

Identifying the location of a cell in a cube is similar to identifying the location of a point on a three-dimensional graph. On a 3-D graph, we specify the value from each axis (or dimension) that corresponds to the point's location along that axis. Our cube works the same way. We specify the member from each dimension that identifies the cell's location along that dimension. So the cell in Figure 11-1 has a location of

```
[Clay Molder], [Woodland Creatures], [2010]
```

**NOTE**

*Identifiers in MDX—member names, dimension names, hierarchy levels, and so forth—must be enclosed in square brackets ( [ ] ) when they contain a space or other special character or start with a numeral. Because we often have one or more spaces in our identifiers and they often start with numerals, it is a good idea to always enclose identifiers in square brackets, whether they need them or not. This saves trouble down the road.*

## Tuples

The cell location we came up with from Figure 11-1 has a special name. It is a tuple (pronounced *to-pull*). A *tuple* is a list of dimension members with one member present from each dimension.

In our example from Figure 11-1, and in most of the examples in this chapter, we are going to look at examples with three dimensions. Therefore, our tuples have three members. We are using three dimensions because this is easier for you to grasp and for me to illustrate. (I haven't yet mastered drawing in four-dimensional space!) Just don't fall into the trap of thinking all tuples have three members. A cube with 100 dimensions would have a tuple that includes 100 members.

In MDX expressions, tuples are enclosed in parentheses. So our tuple from Figure 11-1 becomes

```
([Clay Molder], [Woodland Creatures], [2010])
```

You can think of it this way: The information between the parentheses, no matter if it is three members or a hundred members, points to a single cell.

**NOTE**

*MDX expressions are not case-sensitive. The tuple*
```
([clay molder], [woodland creatures], [2010])
```
*is also valid.*

## Levels

You are probably thinking: What's the big deal about locating cells? Creating tuples seems pretty straightforward. Well, it would be except for one little detail. Many of our dimensions contain hierarchies. We have to take those hierarchies into account as we create our tuples.

Figure 11-2 shows the structure and the members of the Dim Product hierarchy in the Max Min Manufacturing DM cube. In this hierarchy, we created three levels: the product type, the product subtype, and the product. In addition to the levels we defined, Analysis Services automatically adds another level at the top of the dimension. In Figure 11-2, this upper level is given the same name as the dimension itself: Dim Product. The upper level always contains a single element called All. This element contains all of the dimension members from the lower levels.

Suppose we want to specify the location of the cell containing measures for the Dragon with Knight product. Figure 11-3 shows the path we must follow from the

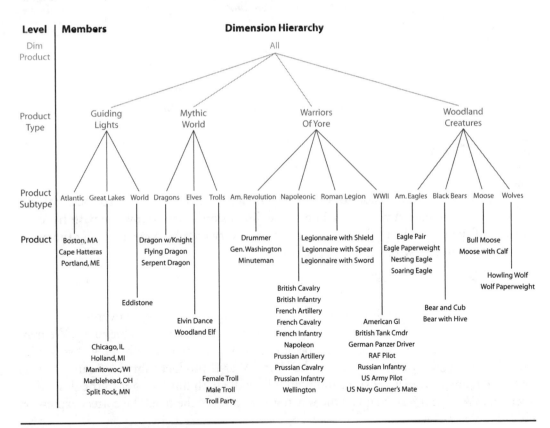

**Figure 11-2**    *The Dim Product dimension*

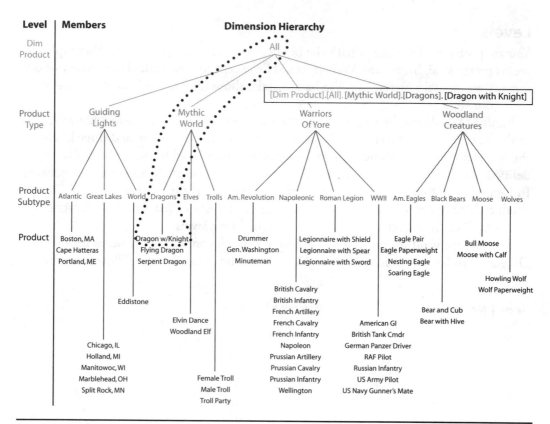

**Figure 11-3**   *The path to the Dragon with Knight product*

highest level of the dimension to reach this product at the lowest level. To specify this location in a tuple, start with the name of the dimension. Then follow the path from the top of the hierarchy to the bottom, including every member we pass along the way.

What we end up with is this:

```
[Dim Product].[All].[Mythic World].[Dragons].[Dragon with Knight]
```

Of course, dimensions with more hierarchies are going to have longer expressions.

We do not always want to retrieve measures at the lowest level of a hierarchy. We may want to see figures for a product subtype or even a product type. Figure 11-4 shows this situation. Here, we want measures for the World War II product subtype. Again, we start with the name of the dimension, and then follow the path until we get to the desired member. We do not have to go all the way to the bottom of the tree. The correct expression from Figure 11-4 is

```
[Dim Product].[All].[Warriors Of Yore].[World War II]
```

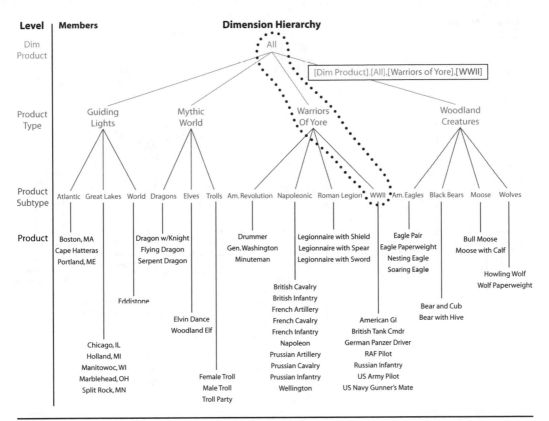

**Figure 11-4**   *The path to the World War II product subtype*

## NOTE

*The figures use the abbreviation for World War II (WWII) because of the need to fit in a large amount of information. The data in our cube uses the longer form of the name. Therefore, the examples in the text will use the longer form as well.*

## Shortcuts

You can see these expressions tend to get long rather quickly. Fortunately, MDX scripting provides some shortcuts for us. Figure 11-5 illustrates one of these shortcuts. Instead of following the chain of members all the way down, we specify the name of the dimension, as before, but then add the name of the hierarchy level we are interested in and, finally, the member of that hierarchy. So, the expression becomes

```
[Dim Product].[Product Subtype].[World War II]
```

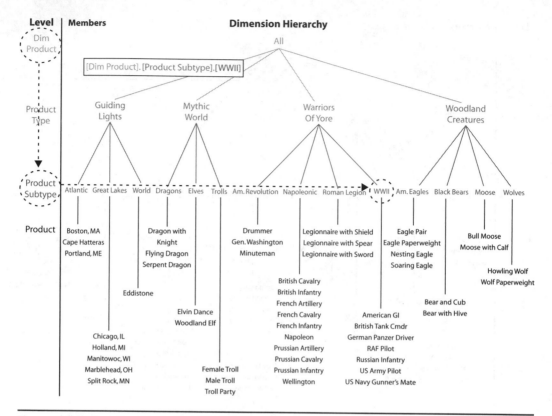

**Figure 11-5** *A shortcut path to the World War II product subtype*

Using this shortcut, it is possible to specify any dimension member with only three items. In a hierarchy with a large number of levels, this can save a lot of typing. However, this is not the only way we can save keystrokes.

It is possible to leave out additional pieces of this path. We can drop the name of the dimension, the dimension level, or both. The key is this: We always have to end up with a nonambiguous location in the dimension. In our Max Min Manufacturing DM cube, any of the following expressions are valid references to the World War II member:

```
[Product Subtype].[World War II]
[Dim Product].[World War II]
[World War II]
```

Because World War II is a unique member name across all levels of all dimensions in our cube, that's all we need to uniquely identify the dimension member.

Even if we are using our original method from Figure 11-3 and Figure 11-4, we can take some shortcuts. First, we can leave out the All member. Thus, our expression from Figure 11-3 becomes

```
[Dim Product].[Mythic World].[Dragons].[Dragon with Knight]
```

The name of the dimension can be removed as well:

```
[Mythic World].[Dragons].[Dragon with Knight]
```

We can also trim off members from the top of the hierarchy, so this still works:

```
[Dragons].[Dragon with Knight]
```

The one thing we cannot do is drop members out of the middle of the path. Therefore, this expression will not work:

```
[Mythic World].[Dragon with Knight]
```

## Expression Errors

If we inadvertently enter an expression for a dimension member that is incorrect, we do not receive an error message. Instead, we end up with nothing for this dimension. The tuple that included the errant dimension is not included in the final result.

This is both a benefit and a problem. It is a benefit because an invalid path expression does not bring everything to a screeching halt. It is a problem because our expression may return information that appears good, but is missing something we expected!

## Default Members

Now that we know how to specify expressions for hierarchical dimensions, let's go back to building tuples. Figure 11-6 shows a more complex, but still watered-down, representation of the Max Min Manufacturing DM cube. This cube includes two-level hierarchies on all three of its dimensions.

Figure 11-6 has one cell highlighted in the cube. The tuple identifying this location is also shown in the figure. Here we are using a shortcut and omitting the dimension names from our path expressions. We could even shorten this up a bit more:

```
([Machine #1], [Wolves], [2010].[Q1])
```

As the dimension members are shown in the figure, we could *not* use the following:

```
([Machine #1], [Wolves], [Q1])
```

There is a Q1 member under 2010 and under 2011, so this last path expression would result in an ambiguous reference.

**Max Min Manufacturing DM Cube**

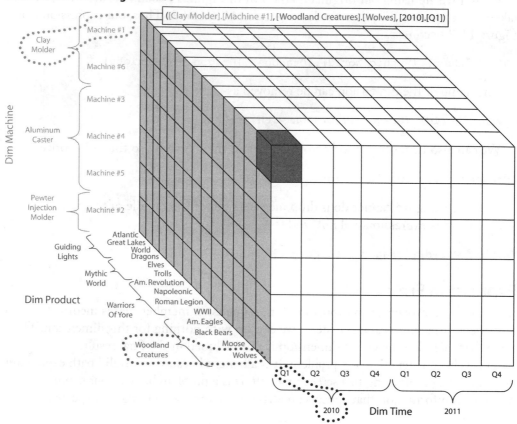

([Clay Molder].[Machine #1], [Woodland Creatures].[Wolves], [2010].[Q1])

**Figure 11-6**  *A more complex version of the Max Min Manufacturing DM cube*

## NOTE

*In the actual Max Min Manufacturing DM cube we created, we use the form 2010Q1 for quarters and 201001 for months, so there is no problem with ambiguous references, even if we use only a single member name.*

What happens if we leave one of the dimensions out of a tuple? Figure 11-7 shows the result. The tuple in this figure includes a member from the Dim Product dimension and the Dim Time dimension. It does not include a member from the Dim Machine dimension.

In this situation, Analysis Services supplies the member for the missing dimension. It does this by using the default member. In this case, the *default member* for the Dim Machine dimension is All. (The All member is not shown in the dimensional hierarchies

**Max Min Manufacturing DM Cube**

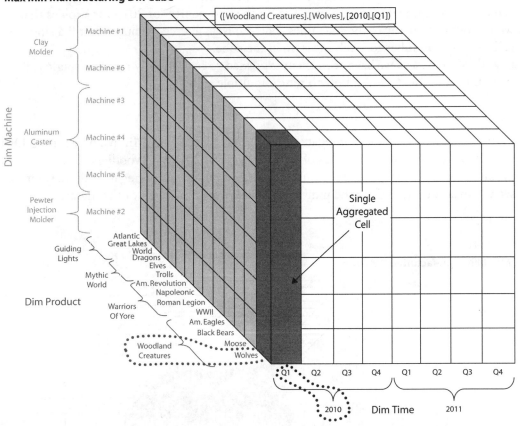

**Figure 11-7**   *A tuple with one dimension omitted*

in Figure 11-7, but is there at the top of each hierarchy by default.) The path expression shown in Figure 11-7 is the equivalent of

```
([Dim Machine].[All], [Woodland Creatures].[Wolves], [2010].[Q1])
```

Each dimension in the cube has a default member. In almost all cases, the All member is most appropriate for the default member. For some dimensions, however, a different member makes more sense. For instance, it may be reasonable to have the Dim Time dimension default to the current year or current quarter. We set the default member of the Dim Time dimension in the Max Min Manufacturing DM cube to 2011 in our next Learn By Doing activity.

The result of this tuple in Figure 11-7 is not six cells. Instead, it is a single cell. This cell contains aggregates of each measure for the first quarter of 2010 for Wolves that were produced on any of the machines. The cell is an aggregate, but it is still a single cell—a single number for each measure in the cube.

Indeed, tuples, as we have seen them expressed so far, can only return a single cell from the cube. Next, we see how to return multiple cells.

## Sets

Figure 11-8 shows another aggregate cell in our simplified Max Min Manufacturing DM cube. This cell contains aggregates of each measure for 2010 for Woodland Creatures produced on any of the machines. Suppose, instead of a single aggregate cell, we want to see the measures from all of the individual cells at the lower levels of the hierarchy.

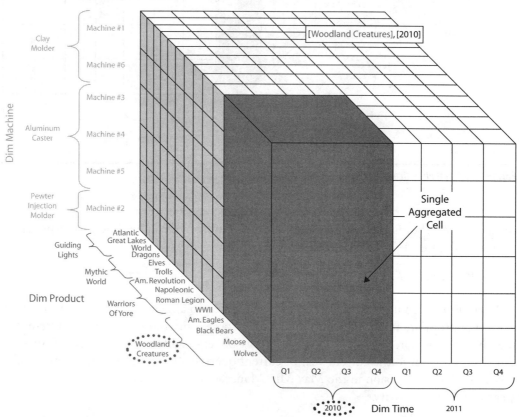

**Figure 11-8**   *Another aggregate cell in the Max Min Manufacturing DM cube*

What we want is the *set* of cells shown in Figure 11-9. To do this, we need to use a group of tuples to specify each of the cells in our set. We express this set of tuples as follows:

```
{([American Eagles], [2010].[Q1]), ([American Eagles], [2010].[Q2]),
([American Eagles], [2010].[Q3]), ([American Eagles], [2010].[Q4]),
([Black Bears], [2010].[Q1]), ([Black Bears], [2010].[Q2]),
([Black Bears], [2010].[Q3]), ([Black Bears], [2010].[Q4]),
([Moose], [2010].[Q1]), ([Moose], [2010].[Q2]),
([Moose], [2010].[Q3]), ([Moose], [2010].[Q4]),
([Wolves], [2010].[Q1]), ([Wolves], [2010].[Q2]),
([Wolves], [2010].[Q3]), ([Wolves], [2010].[Q4])}
```

Note the curly brackets ( { } ) surrounding the entire set in addition to the parentheses around each tuple.

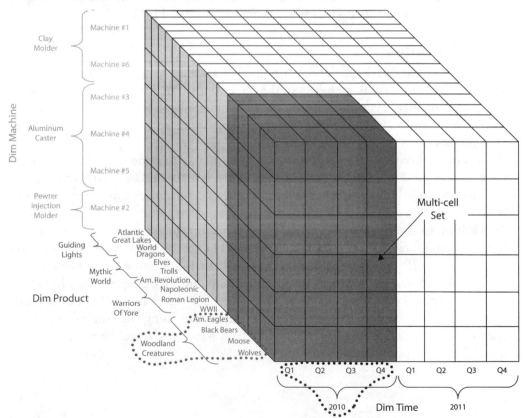

**Max Min Manufacturing DM Cube**

**Figure 11-9**    *A multicell set*

This notation gets the job done, but it is inefficient. Let's look at another way to specify a set that requires fewer keystrokes.

## Range Operator

Excel is another Microsoft product that deals with cells. This program has a special syntax for specifying a range of cells. This is the colon ( : ) operator. To specify cells A1 through A15, for example, we enter **A1:A15** in an Excel expression.

The same is true in Analysis Services. We can use the colon operator to specify a range of members in a tuple. To specify the set shown in Figure 11-9, we can use the range operator as follows:

```
([American Eagles]:[Wolves], [2010].[Q1]:[2010].[Q4])
```

This may not be quite as self-documenting as the set notation, but it is more efficient.

Of course, some groupings cannot be specified by a range. One such grouping is shown in Figure 11-10. Because these cells are not contiguous, we cannot use a range.

We can also combine ranges and sets, as shown in Figure 11-11.

## Name Attributes

When we set up the MaxMinManufacturingDM data mart relational database, we used integer key fields to identify members in the dimensions. The foreign key relationships we created in the data mart are all based on these integer keys. When the OLAP cube was created on top of this data mart, the integer keys were used as the unique identifiers for our members.

This is not convenient. We don't want our users to have to remember that the Wolf Paperweight is product 21 and the plant in Mumbai is plant 6. As a matter of fact, we would not like to have to remember this stuff either. Fortunately, we and our users don't have to.

In addition to having integer key fields in our relational data mart, we have text fields that contain names for each member value. The text fields became attributes in our OLAP cube. If we tell Analysis Services which attribute contains the name for each dimension hierarchy, we can use those names in our MDX expressions. In fact, we have anticipated this by using names rather than key values in all of the examples in this chapter. We see how to specify the name attributes using the NameColumn property in the section "Learn By Doing—Default Members, Level Names, and the NameColumn Property."

**Max Min Manufacturing DM Cube**

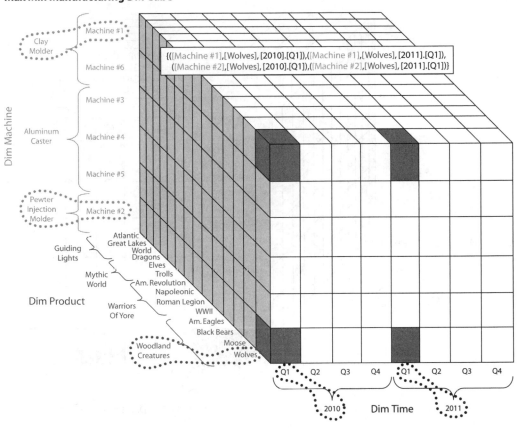

**Figure 11-10**  *A cell group requiring a set*

At times, we may need to reference a member by its key value rather than its name. We can do this by putting an ampersand ( & ) in front of the member key. For example:

```
[Dim Product].[Product].&[21]
```

is the same as

```
[Dim Product].[Product].[Wolf Paperweight]
```

**Max Min Manufacturing DM Cube**

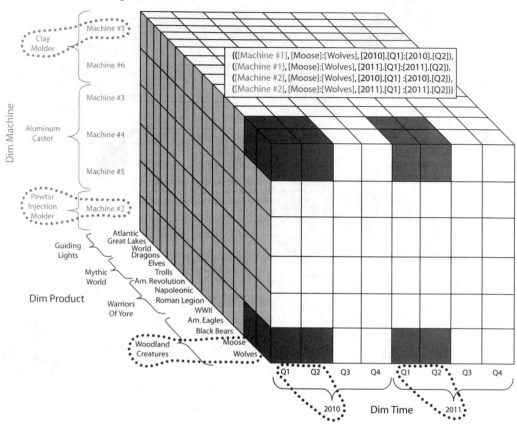

{([Machine #1], [Moose]:[Wolves], [2010].[Q1]:[2010].[Q2]),
([Machine #1], [Moose]:[Wolves], [2011].[Q1]:[2011].[Q2]),
([Machine #2], [Moose]:[Wolves], [2010].[Q1] :[2010].[Q2]),
([Machine #2], [Moose]:[Wolves], [2011].[Q1] :[2011].[Q2])}

**Figure 11-11**   *A cell group using a set with ranges*

## Learn By Doing—Default Members, Level Names, and the NameColumn Property

### Features Highlighted

▶  Providing user-friendly hierarchy level names

▶  Specifying a name column for hierarchy levels

**Business Need**    To make it easier for our users to query the Max Min Manufacturing DM cube, we need to provide more user-friendly names for our hierarchy levels. We should also specify which attribute holds the name for each hierarchy level. In addition, we can set the sort order of the hierarchies. Finally, we can set the default member for our Dim Time dimension to 2011.

### Steps

1. Open SQL Server Data Tools.
2. Open the MaxMinManufacturingDM.sln solution.
3. Double-click the Dim Time.dim dimension in the Solution Explorer. The Dimension Design tab appears.
4. Select the Year entry in the Attributes area.
5. In the Properties Window, click the DefaultMember property. An ellipsis (...) button appears. Click the ellipsis button. The Set Default Member dialog box appears.
6. Select Enter an MDX expression that specifies the default member.
7. Enter **[Dim Time].&[2011]**. The Set Default Member dialog box appears, as shown in Figure 11-12.

**Figure 11-12**  *The Set Default Member dialog box*

8. Click OK to exit the Set Default Member dialog box.

9. Click the Save All button on the toolbar.

10. Close the Dimension Design tab.

11. Double-click the Dim Product.dim dimension in the Solution Explorer. The Dimension Design tab appears.

12. Select the Product Subtype Code entry in the Attributes area.

13. In the Properties window, click the ellipsis (...) button for the NameColumn property. The Name Column dialog box appears.

**NOTE**

*Don't confuse this with the Name property. We are working with the NameColumn property here.*

14. Select ProductSubtypeName in the Source column list.

15. Click OK to exit the Name Column dialog box.

16. In the Properties window, select Name from the OrderBy drop-down list.

17. Select the Product Type Code entry in the Attributes area.

18. In the Properties window, click the ellipsis (...) button for the NameColumn property. The Name Column dialog box appears.

19. Select ProductTypeName in the Source column list.

20. Click OK to exit the Name Column dialog box.

21. In the Properties window, select Name from the OrderBy drop-down list.

22. Select the Product Code entry in the Attributes area.

23. In the Properties window, click the ellipsis (...) button for the NameColumn property. The Name Column dialog box appears.

24. Select ProductName in the Source column list.

25. Click OK to exit the Name Column dialog box.

26. Again, in the Properties window, select Name from the OrderBy drop-down list.

27. Rename the items in both the Attributes and the Hierarchies areas as follows:

| Old Name | New Name |
| --- | --- |
| Product Type Code | Product Type |
| Product Subtype Code | Product Subtype |
| Product Code | Product |

The Dimension Design tab should appear as shown in Figure 11-13.

28. Click the Save All button on the toolbar.

29. Close the Dimension Design tab.

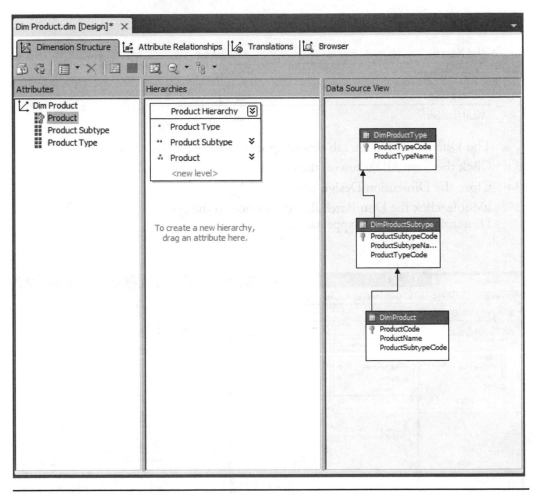

**Figure 11-13** *The Dim Product dimension with revised hierarchy level names*

30. Double-click the Dim Machine.dim dimension in the Solution Explorer. The Dimension Design tab appears.

31. Set the NameColumn property and the OrderBy property for the following items in the Attributes area:

| Item | NameColumn | OrderBy |
|------|------------|---------|
| Country Code | CountryName | Name |
| Machine Number | MachineName | Name |
| Plant Number | PlantName | Name |

32. Rename the items in both the Attributes and the Hierarchies areas as follows:

| Old Name | New Name |
|---|---|
| Machine Number | Machine |
| Country Code | Country |
| Plant Number | Plant |

The Dimension Design tab should appear as shown in Figure 11-14.

33. Click the Save All button on the toolbar.
34. Close the Dimension Design tab.
35. Double-click the Dim Batch.dim dimension in the Solution Explorer. The Dimension Design tab appears.

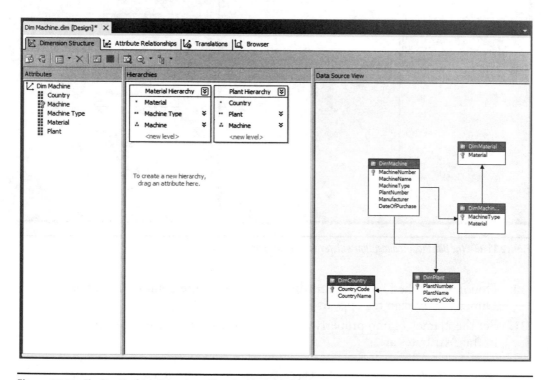

**Figure 11-14** *The Dim Machine dimension with revised hierarchy level names*

**36.** Set the NameColumn property and the OrderBy property for the following item in the Attributes area:

| Item | NameColumn | OrderBy |
|------|-----------|---------|
| Batch Number | BatchName | Name |

The Dimension Design tab should appear as shown in Figure 11-15.

**37.** Click the Save All button on the toolbar.

**38.** Close the Dimension Design tab.

**Figure 11-15**  *The Dim Batch dimension*

39. Select Build | Deploy MaxMinManufacturingDM from the Main menu.
40. Enter the appropriate credentials, if you are prompted to do so.

## Getting There from Here

We now know how to address any cell or group of cells in the cube. This type of absolute navigation is important as we move toward being able to manipulate and extract information from our cubes. We need to master one other skill, which is the skill of relative navigation. *Relative navigation* is the capability to start from a given location and move to another location based on that starting point.

For example, suppose we are examining measures for Wolves produced on Machine #6 in Q1, 2011. This is the Current Cell in Figure 11-16. We may want to look at those

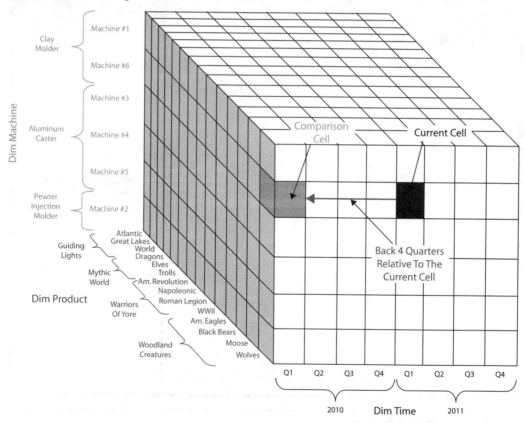

**Figure 11-16** *Comparing measures from two cells using relative location*

same measures from one year ago. This is designated as the Comparison Cell in the figure. We need to know how to find the position of the Comparison Cell relative to the Current Cell.

Of course, we could do this using the absolute navigation we already know. We know the tuple for the Comparison Cell is

```
([Machine #6], [Wolves], [2010].[Q1])
```

This works fine until we move on to look at the measures for Q2, 2011. Now we have to figure out the tuple for the Comparison Cell all over again. Perhaps we are looking at measures in a set of cells—say Q1, 2011 through Q4, 2011. Now it becomes even more tedious to manually determine the tuples for all of the Comparison Cells.

Even more helpful would be a way to identify one cell by its relative position to another cell. Fortunately, MDX scripting provides a way for us to do this: through the use of MDX functions. But, before we look at functions that help us determine the tuple for the Comparison Cell, we need a function that helps us determine the tuple for the Current Cell.

## The Starting Point—The CurrentMember Function

Like any other cell, the Current Cell can be identified by a tuple. This tuple contains the current member from each hierarchy in the cube. But how can we determine what those current members are?

The answer is through the use of the CurrentMember function. For example, we can use the following expression to find out the current member of the Time Hierarchy dimension:

```
[Dim Time].CurrentMember
```

In the example in Figure 11-16, this expression would return the [2011].[Q1] member.

As with any function, the CurrentMember function takes input and returns output. In MDX expressions, the function's input is whatever precedes the function. In this case, that input is the [Dim Time] hierarchy. In fact, the Current Member function requires either a hierarchy or a dimension as its input. This makes sense, because only hierarchies and dimensions have members.

The *CurrentMember function* returns a member. The CurrentMember function does not return a string containing the name of the member. Instead, it returns a reference to the member itself. This distinction is important as we begin to apply other MDX functions to the result returned by the CurrentMember function.

| Function | Input | Output | Description |
|---|---|---|---|
| CurrentMember | Hierarchy or Dimension | Member | Returns the current member of the specified hierarchy or dimension |

## Relative Position Within a Hierarchy Level—The Lag, Lead, NextMember, and PrevMember Functions

A number of MDX functions enable us to select a member relative to a specified member within the same hierarchy. These are shown in Figure 11-17. Assuming the [Dim Time].CurrentMember is [2011].[Q1], the expressions corresponding to the figure are shown here:

| Expression | Resulting Member |
|---|---|
| [Dim Time].CurrentMember.Lag(4) | [2010].[Q1] |
| [Dim Time].CurrentMember.Lead(-4) | [2010].[Q1] |
| [Dim Time].CurrentMember.PrevMember | [2010].[Q4] |
| [Dim Time].CurrentMember.NextMember | [2011].[Q2] |
| [Dim Time].CurrentMember.Lead(3) | [2011].[Q4] |
| [Dim Time].CurrentMember.Lag(-3) | [2011].[Q4] |

As you can see, the PrevMember function takes us to the member immediately preceding the current member. The NextMember function takes us to the member immediately after the current member. These functions are useful for looking at the way measures are trending from one period to the next.

The Lag and Lead functions require an additional parameter. This is an integer representing the number of members to lag or lead. This second parameter is passed in parentheses immediately after the function name.

The *Lag function* moves us backward by the specified number of members. The *Lead function* moves us forward by the specified number of members. Using a negative integer for the number of members parameter reverses the natural direction of each function.

| Function | Input | Output | Description |
|---|---|---|---|
| Lag(N) | Member, $N$ = number of members | Member | Returns the member that is $N$ *before* the specified member. (A negative value for $N$ reverses the direction of the function.) |
| Lead(N) | Member, $N$ = number of members | Member | Returns the member that is $N$ *after* the specified member. (A negative value for $N$ reverses the direction of the function.) |
| NextMember | Member | Member | Returns the member that is immediately after the specified member. |
| PrevMember | Member | Member | Returns the member that is immediately before the specified member. |

**Max Min Manufacturing DM Cube**

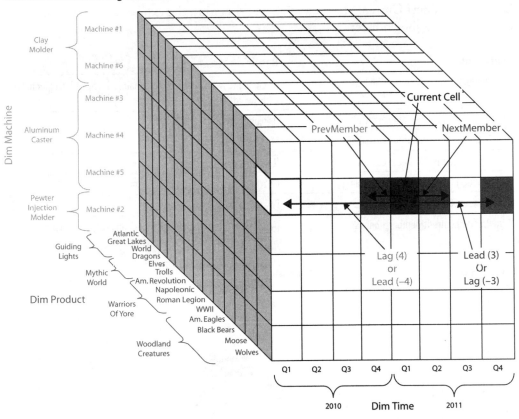

**Figure 11-17**  *Comparing measures from two cells using relative location*

## Immediate Relative Position Between Hierarchy Levels— The Children, FirstChild, FirstSibling, LastChild, LastSibling, Parent, and Siblings Functions

Just as we may want to move across a hierarchy level, we may want to move up and down between hierarchy levels. A number of MDX functions can help us here as well. We begin by looking at the functions that deal with the immediate family in the hierarchy, and then look at functions that return more distant relations.

The functions dealing with immediate relatives are shown in Figure 11-18. Assuming the [Dim Product].CurrentMember is [Roman Legion], the expressions corresponding to the figure are shown here:

| Expression | Resulting Member(s) |
|---|---|
| [Dim Product].CurrentMember.Children | [Legionnaire with Shield], [Legionnaire with Spear], [Legionnaire with Sword] |
| [Dim Product].CurrentMember.FirstChild | [Legionnaire with Shield] |
| [Dim Product].CurrentMember.FirstSibling | [Am. Revolution] |
| [Dim Product].CurrentMember.LastChild | [Legionnaire with Sword] |
| [Dim Product].CurrentMember.LastSibling | [WWII] |
| [Dim Product].CurrentMember.Parent | [Warriors Of Yore] |
| [Dim Product].CurrentMember.Siblings | [Am. Revolution], [Napoleonic], [Roman Legion], [WWII] |

**Figure 11-18**  *MDX immediate relative position functions within the same hierarchy*

Most of the functions are self-explanatory, but a word about the Siblings functions may be helpful. If you look at the list of members returned by the Siblings function, you see that the Roman Legion member is included. This is true even though Roman Legion is the current member when we call the function. The member itself is always included in a list of its siblings.

| Function | Input | Output | Description |
|---|---|---|---|
| Children | Member | Set | Returns the set of members from the hierarchy level immediately below the specified member that is related directly to the specified member |
| FirstChild | Member | Member | Returns the first member from the hierarchy level immediately below the specified member that is related directly to the specified member |
| FirstSibling | Member | Member | Returns the first member that shares the same parent with the specified member |
| LastChild | Member | Member | Returns the last member from the hierarchy level immediately below the specified member that is related directly to the specified member |
| LastSibling | Member | Member | Returns the last member that shares the same parent with the specified member |
| Parent | Member | Member | Returns the member from the hierarchy level immediately above the specified member that is related directly to the specified member |
| Siblings | Member | Set | Returns the set of members that shares the same parent with the specified member |

## Distant Relative Position Between Hierarchy Levels— The Ancestor, Cousin, and Descendants Functions

In addition to the functions that return the close relatives of a member, a number of MDX functions let us select more distant relatives. These are shown in Figure 11-19. The expressions corresponding to the figure are shown here:

| Expression | Resulting Member |
|---|---|
| Ancestor([2009].[Q3].[Jul], [Dim Time] .[Year]) or Ancestor ([2009].[Q3].[Jul], 2) | [2009] |
| Cousin([2009].[Q2].[Apr], [2009].[Q4]) | [2009].[Q4].[Oct] |
| Descendants([2011], [Month]) or Descendants([2011], 2) | [2011].[Q1].[Jan], [2011].[Q1].[Feb], [2011].[Q1].[Mar], [2011].[Q2].[Apr], [2011].[Q2].[May], [2011].[Q2].[Jun], [2011].[Q3].[Jul], [2011].[Q3].[Aug], [2011].[Q3].[Sep], [2011].[Q4].[Oct], [2011].[Q4].[Nov], [2011].[Q4].[Dec] |

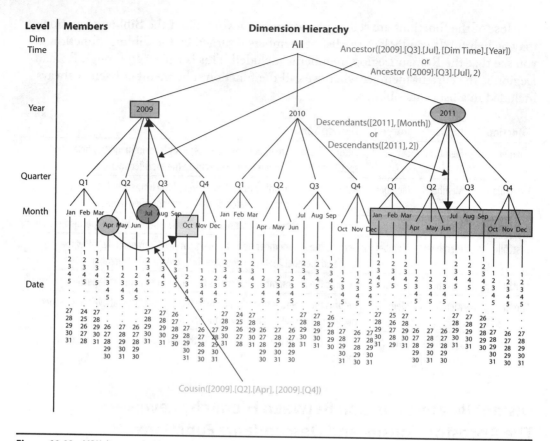

**Figure 11-19** *MDX distant relative position functions within the same hierarchy*

The Ancestor function returns the parent, grandparent, great-grandparent, and so forth of the specified member. The Ancestor function requires two parameters, both of which must be placed within the parentheses. The first parameter is the member that serves as the starting point for the function. The second parameter is either the hierarchy level where the ancestor is to be found or an integer specifying the number of levels to move upward to find the ancestor.

The Cousin function finds the equivalent member at the same level of the hierarchy, but down a different branch of the hierarchy structure. For example, January is the first month of Q1. Its cousins would be the first months in the other three quarters of the year—namely, April, July, and October. Likewise, Q2 is the second quarter in 2009. Its cousins would be Q2, 2010 and Q2, 2011. Obviously, this is extremely helpful when we are trying to compare like periods in the time dimension.

The Cousin function requires two parameters, both of which must be placed within the parentheses. The first parameter is the member whose cousin is to be found. The second parameter is a member at a higher level in the hierarchy under which the cousin is to be found.

The Descendants function returns the children, grandchildren, great-grandchildren, and so forth of the specified member. The Descendants function requires two parameters, both of which must be placed within the parentheses. The first parameter is the member that serves as the starting point for the function. The second parameter is either the hierarchy level where the descendants are to be found or an integer specifying the number of levels to move downward to find the descendants.

| Function | Input | Output | Description |
|----------|-------|--------|-------------|
| Ancestor | Member, Hierarchy Level, or number of levels to go up | Member | Returns the member that is a parent, grandparent, and so forth of the specified member at the specified level |
| Cousin | Member, Member | Member | Returns the member that is in the same sibling position as the specified member |
| Descendants | Member, Hierarchy Level, or number of levels to go down | Set | Returns a set of members that are the children, grandchildren, and so forth of the specified member |

# Putting MDX Scripting to Work

Now that you have a basic understanding of MDX scripting, we can take a look at some of the places it is used in Analysis Services. We do this by completing two Learn By Doing exercises. First, we define a security role in an Analysis Services database. Second, we create additional calculated members in the Max Min Manufacturing DM cube. Along the way, we utilize three additional MDX functions to get the job done.

## Cube Security

In Chapter 10, we saw how to create perspectives that can divide a cube into more manageable pieces for our users. Perspectives are helpful for organizing information in a cube, but they do not limit users' access to only those items in a particular perspective. To secure portions of a cube from unwanted access, we need to use security roles.

Security roles enable us to restrict or permit access to items within the cube, measures, dimensions, and dimensional members. We can also allow or prevent users from doing certain administrative tasks, such as processing the cube or viewing the definition of its structure. The roles are associated with Windows logins and Windows groups to provide access to the cube information.

## Learn By Doing—Setting Security Within an OLAP Cube

### Features Highlighted

▶ Creating a security role

▶ Using an MDX expression to limit access to cube members

**Business Need**  Maximum Miniatures would like to provide access to the Max Min Manufacturing DM cube to the plant manager at the Kawaguchi plant. The plant manager should be given access to the Total Products and Percent Rejected calculated members, but none of the other measures in the cube. This plant only produces products from the Guiding Lights and Woodland Creatures product types. Therefore, access should be limited to these two product types.

### Steps

1. Open SQL Server Data Tools.
2. Open the MaxMinManufacturingDM project.
3. Right-click the Roles folder in the Solution Explorer window, and select New Role from the context menu. The Role Design tab and a Role.role entry in the Solution Explorer window appear.
4. Double-click the Role.role entry in the Solution Explorer window.
5. In the Properties window, enter **Kawaguchi Plant** for Name. On the General tab of the Role Design tab, enter an appropriate description for Role Description.
6. The items under Set the database permissions for this role determine whether members of this role can perform these administrative tasks or read the definition of the cube. Uncheck any of these check boxes that are checked by default. The General tab of the Role Design tab is shown in Figure 11-20.
7. Select the Membership tab. This is the place where the Kawaguchi plant manager's Windows login would be added to this role. If you have a test Windows login that you can use for testing this role, click Add and add the login to the role. Otherwise, move on to Step 8. The Membership tab of the Role Design tab is shown in Figure 11-21.

**Figure 11-20** *The General tab of the Role Design tab*

8. Select the Data Sources tab. Here, we control the access to each data source. Select Read from the Access drop-down list for the Max Min Manufacturing DM data source. We do not want this role to be able to read the definition of the data source, so leave Read Definition unchecked. The Data Sources tab of the Role Design tab is shown in Figure 11-22.

**Figure 11-21** *The Membership tab of the Role Design tab*

**Figure 11-22** *The Data Sources tab of the Role Design tab*

9. Select the Cubes tab. Select Read from the Access drop-down list for the Max Min Manufacturing DM cube. We do not need to allow drillthrough or rights to process this cube, so do not make any changes to these two items. The Cubes tab of the Role Design tab is shown in Figure 11-23.

**Figure 11-23** *The Cubes tab of the Role Design tab*

10. Select the Cell Data tab. This is where we restrict access to the measures in the cube cells. Make sure the Max Min Manufacturing DM cube is selected at the top of the tab.

11. Check Enable read permissions.

12. Enter the following MDX expression for Allow reading of cube content:

```
[Measures].CurrentMember IS [Measures].[Total Products] OR
[Measures].CurrentMember IS [Measures].[Percent Rejected]
```

When creating expressions here, you can click the button next to Edit MDX to use the MDX Builder dialog box for assistance in building your MDX expressions. The Cell Data tab of the Role Design tab should appear as shown in Figure 11-24.

**NOTE**

*This MDX expression used the CurrentMember function along with Measures. This syntax uses Measures as a pseudodimension in the cube. The current member of the Measures pseudodimension is whatever measure we are trying to query information from. We are also using the IS operator to determine if the current member is the specified member. The expression here will return true and, thus, allow access only if we are querying information from the Total Products measure or the Percent Rejected measure. If any other measure is queried, the current member of the measure will not be equal to either of the two we have specified and the MDX expression will return false. When the MDX expression is false, access is denied.*

| Role.role [Design]* × |
|---|

General | Membership | Data Sources | Cubes | Cell Data | Dimensions | Dimension Data | Mining Structures

Cube: `Max Min Manufacturing DM` ▾    Test cube security

☑ Enable read permissions

Allow reading of cube content:    Edit MDX: `...`

`[Measures].CurrentMember IS [Measures].[Total Products] OR [Measures].CurrentMember IS [Measures].[Percent Rejected]`

☐ Enable read-contingent permissions

Allow reading of cell content contingent on cell security:    Edit MDX: `...`

☐ Enable read/write permissions

Allow reading and writing of cube content:    Edit MDX: `...`

Check

**Figure 11-24**  *The Cell Data tab of the Role Design tab*

13. Select the Dimensions tab. On this tab, we set the access rights for the dimensions. Leave the Access drop-down lists set to Read for all of the dimensions. Do not allow this role to read the definitions or process any of the dimensions. The Dimensions tab of the Role Design tab is shown in Figure 11-25.

14. Select the Dimension Data tab. Here is the place to limit access to members of a particular dimension. The Basic tab enables us to use the brute-force method and check or uncheck dimension members to determine access. Expand the Dimension drop-down window at the top of the tab. Select the Dim Machine dimension under the Max Min Manufacturing DM cube and click OK. (Select the Dim Machine dimension in the cube, not the Dim Machine dimension definition in the project. The dimension you want is probably the second occurrence of Dim Machine in the drop-down window.)

15. Select Plant from the Attribute Hierarchy drop-down list. Click the Deselect all members radio button on the left side of the tab. Check the Maximum Miniatures—Kawaguchi member. The Basic tab of the Dimension Data tab is shown in Figure 11-26.

16. Expand the Dimension drop-down window at the top of the tab. Select the Dim Product dimension under the Max Min Manufacturing DM cube, and click OK.

17. Select the Advanced tab on the Dimension Data tab. Here, we can create MDX expressions to determine access.

18. Select Product Type from the Attribute drop-down list.

| Dimension Name | Access | Read Definition | Process |
|----------------|--------|-----------------|---------|
| Dim Product | Read | ☐ | ☐ |
| Dim Batch | Read | ☐ | ☐ |
| Dim Machine | Read | ☐ | ☐ |
| Dim Time | Read | ☐ | ☐ |

**Figure 11-25** *The Dimensions tab of the Role Design tab*

**Figure 11-26**  *The Basic tab of the Dimension Data tab of the Role Design tab*

**19.** Enter the following expression for Allowed member set:

```
{[Dim Product].[Product Type].[Guiding Lights],
[Dim Product].[Product Type].[Woodland Creatures]}
```

Here, we have created a set containing the two allowed members. The Advanced tab of the Dimension Data tab should now appear as shown in Figure 11-27.

**NOTE**

*As shown in Figure 11-27, a user in the Kawaguchi Plant role will be able to see the totals for product types when the query result is at the All level of the Product Hierarchy. Only when the user drills down to the Product Type level of the hierarchy will they be limited to just the totals for the Guiding Lights and Woodland Creatures product types. If you would like to limit the user to seeing totals for only the allowed members no matter what level of the hierarchy is being queried, check the Enable Visual Totals check box.*

**20.** Select the Mining Structures tab. We do not have any data mining structures defined in this cube, so we do not need to make any entries here. Click the Save All button on the toolbar. Close the Role Design tab.

**21.** Select Build | Deploy MaxMinManufacturingDM from the Main menu to deploy the changes to the Analysis Services server.

**Figure 11-27**   *The Advanced tab of the Dimension Data tab for the Dim Product dimension*

22. Next, we use the Browser tab to test our security settings. Double-click the entry for Max Min Manufacturing DM.cube in the Solution Explorer window. The Cube Design tab appears.

23. Select the Browser tab on the Cube Design tab. You are browsing the cube with your credentials, which have administration rights.

24. Expand Measures, and then expand the Manufacturing Fact measure group.

25. Drag the Accepted Products measure, and drop it on the Drag levels or measures here to add to the query target.

26. Drag the Total Products calculated member and drop it next to the Accepted Products measures.

27. Expand the Dim Product dimension, and then expand the Product Hierarchy.

28. Drag the Product Type hierarchy level and drop it on the query area to the left of the Accepted Products column. Notice all four product types are present.

29. Expand the Dim Machine dimension, and then expand the Plant Hierarchy.

30. Drag the Plant hierarchy level, and drop it on the query area between the Product Type and Accepted Products columns. Notice there are three plants present at least once in the query result.

31. The Browser tab appears as shown in Figure 11-28.

**Figure 11-28** *The Browser tab using administrative credentials*

32. Click the Change User button on the Browser tab toolbar. The Security Context dialog box appears.

33. Select the Roles radio button. In the Roles drop-down window, check the Kawaguchi Plant Role. (The All Roles item is also checked.) Click OK to exit the drop-down window. The Security Context dialog box appears as shown in Figure 11-29.

34. Click OK to exit the Security Context dialog box. The Browser tab resets. A message under the Browser tab toolbar informs us that we are browsing while using the credentials of the Kawaguchi Plant security role.

35. We can build the same query as we did before. Expand Measures, and then expand the Manufacturing Fact measure group. All of the measures still appear in this list. However, watch what happens when we try to query from a restricted measure.

36. Drag the Accepted Products measure and drop it on the Drag levels or measures here to add to the query target. We receive a (null) result because our security role does not allow querying from this measure.

37. Drag the Total Products calculated member and drop it next to the Accepted Products measures. Our security role does allow querying from this calculated member, so we do receive our results.

**Figure 11-29** *The Security Context dialog box*

**NOTE**

*You may recall that the Total Products calculated member is the sum of the Accepted Products measure and the Rejected Products measure. Even though our security role does not provide access to these two measures, the calculated member still works. This lets us provide a user with calculated members without having to expose the underlying data.*

38. Expand the Dim Product dimension, and then expand the Product Hierarchy.
39. Drag the Product Type hierarchy level and drop it on the query area to the left of the Accepted Products column. As our security role stipulates, only two product types are present.
40. Expand the Dim Machine dimension, and then expand the Plant Hierarchy.
41. Drag the Plant hierarchy level and drop it on the query area between the Product Type and Accepted Products columns. Again, as expected, only one plant is present. The Browser tab appears as shown in Figure 11-30.

## This Year-to-Last Year Comparisons and Year-to-Date Rollups

Two bits of business intelligence are often requested by users. The first is the comparison of a value from this year with the same value from one year ago. It is a natural desire to

**Figure 11-30** *The Browser tab using the Kawaguchi Plant security role*

know how the organization is doing versus where it was one year ago. In many cases, this is also a telling statistic, providing beneficial insight into the organization's health and performance.

The second bit of business intelligence that is often requested is the year-to-date total. Monthly and quarterly figures are fine, but users also want to know the grand totals as we move through the year. If the year-to-date numbers are not monitored, the year-end figures could be a big surprise to management, which is usually not a good thing!

In this section, we add two calculated members to the Max Min Manufacturing DM cube. One calculated member returns the Percent Rejected from the previous year. The other calculated member returns the year-to-date amount for the Total Products calculated member. To create these calculated members, we use three new functions: ParallelPeriod, YTD, and SUM.

## The ParallelPeriod Function

The *ParallelPeriod function* returns the member from the time dimension that corresponds to a specified member. For example, if we ask for the time dimension member parallel to

Q1, 2011 from one year earlier, we would get Q1, 2010. If we ask for the time dimension member parallel to August 2010 from one year earlier, we would get August 2009.

The ParallelPeriod function has the following format:

```
ParallelPeriod(TimeHierarchyLevel, NumberOfPeriodsBack,
    TimeDimensionMember)
```

*TimeHierarchyLevel* is the level in the Time Dimension Hierarchy that we are using to move backward. The most common hierarchy level to use here is the year level. *NumberOfPeriodsBack* is the number of the TimeHierarchyLevels to move backward. *TimeDimensionMember* is the Time Dimension Member that serves as the starting point.

Consider the following example:

```
ParallelPeriod([Date Hierarchy].[Year], 1,
                        [Date Hierarchy].[Month].[201103])
```

This function starts at the March 2011 member and moves backward one year to return the March 2010 member. In this example:

```
ParallelPeriod([Date Hierarchy].[Quarter], 1,
                        [Date Hierarchy].[Month].[201109])
```

the function starts at the September 2011 member and moves backward one quarter to return the June 2011 member.

## The YTD Function

The *YTD function* returns a set of members from a time hierarchy level that represents the beginning of the year, up to and including the specified member. If the specified member is Q3, 2011, the members Q1, 2011, Q2, 2011, and Q3, 2011 are returned in the set. If the specified member is April 2011, the members January 2011, February 2011, March 2011, and April 2011 are returned in the set.

The YTD function has the following format:

```
YTD(TimeDimensionMember)
```

*TimeDimensionMember* is a member from the time dimension. For example:

```
YTD([Date Hierarchy].[Month].[201103])
```

returns a set of [201101], [201102], and [201103].

## The SUM Function

The *SUM function* adds together the values in a set of measures to create an aggregate value. The SUM function has the following format:

```
SUM(SetOfMeasures)
```

*SetOfMeasures* is a set of measures. For example:

```
SUM({([201104], [Measure].[Total Products]),
                        ([201105], [Measure].[Total Products])})
```

adds the total products produced in April 2011 to the total products produced in May 2011.

## Learn By Doing—Time-Based Analytics

### Features Highlighted

▶ Creating a calculated member to return a value from the previous year

▶ Creating a calculated member to return a year-to-date value

**Business Need**    To make analysis easier, the vice president of production would like to have calculated members for the Percent Rejected in the parallel period of the previous year and for the Year-To-Date Total Products produced.

### Steps

1. Open SQL Server Data Tools.
2. Open the MaxMinManufacturingDM project.
3. Double-click the Max Min Manufacturing DM.cube in the Solution Explorer. The Cube Design tab appears.
4. Select the Calculations tab.
5. Click the New Calculated Member button on the Calculations tab toolbar. A blank Calculated Members form appears.
6. Enter **[Prev Year Percent Rejected]** for Name.
7. Enter the following for Expression:

```
(ParallelPeriod([Date Hierarchy].[Year], 1,
[Date Hierarchy].CurrentMember), [Measures].[Percent Rejected])
```

8. Select Percent from the Format string drop-down list.

9. Check the Accepted Products and Rejected Products measures in the Non-empty behavior selection window, and click OK. The Calculations tab should appear as shown in Figure 11-31.

10. Click the New Calculated Member button on the Calculations tab toolbar to add a second calculated member.

11. Enter [**Year-To-Date Total Products**] for Name.

12. Enter the following for Expression:

```
SUM(YTD([Date Hierarchy].CurrentMember),
[Measures].[Total Products])
```

13. Select Standard from the Format string drop-down list.

14. Check the Accepted Products and Rejected Products measures in the Non-empty behavior selection window, and click OK. The Calculations tab will appear as shown in Figure 11-32.

15. Click the Save All button on the toolbar.

16. Select Build | Deploy MaxMinManufacturingDM from the Main menu. The cube definition is deployed to the Analysis Services server.

**Figure 11-31**  *The Prev Year Percent Rejected calculated measure*

**Figure 11-32**  *The Year-To-Date Total Products calculated measure*

17. When the deploy is complete, select the Browser tab.

18. If dimensions and measures are still on the browser from the previous Learn By Doing exercise, click the Reconnect button on the Browser tab toolbar.

19. Click the Change User button on the Browser tab toolbar. The Security Context dialog box appears.

20. Select Current user and click OK.

21. Expand the Dim Time dimension and the Date Hierarchy.

22. Drag the Year hierarchy level and drop it on the Drag levels or measures here to add to the query target. The column will be added, but no data will appear. This is because we do not yet have any measures added to our query.

23. Expand Measures. Drag the Percent Rejected calculated member and drop it to the right of the Year column.

24. Drag the Prev Year Percent Rejected calculated member and drop it to the right of the Percent Rejected calculated member.

25. Drag the Total Products calculated member and drop it to the right of the two calculated members already in the browser.

**Figure 11-33** *Browsing the calculated members*

26. Drag the Year-To-Date Total Products calculated member and drop it with the other three.

27. Drag the Quarter hierarchy level and drop it between the Year and Percent Rejected columns of the query.

28. You can try adding other levels of the Date Hierarchy to the query as well to confirm the calculations are working as they should. The Browser tab appears similar to Figure 11-33.

# Extracting Data from Cubes

Up to this point, we have been concentrating on building our OLAP cubes. Here, at the end of this last Learn By Doing exercise, we can begin to see some of the potential for getting data out of these cubes and analyzing it to gain business intelligence. In the next chapter, we concentrate on this aspect of Analysis Services as we explore MDX queries.

## Chapter 12

# Pulling It Out and Building It Up—MDX Queries

## In This Chapter

▶ **The MDX SELECT Statement**
▶ **Additional MDX Syntax**
▶ **Tabling the Matter**

*I've never been convinced that experience is linear, circular, or even random. It just is. I try to put it in some kind of order to extract meaning from it, to bring meaning to it.*

–Toni Cade Bambara
U.S. fiction writer

We now turn our attention from building and maintaining online analytical processing (OLAP) cubes in a Multidimensional BI Semantic Model to extracting the information resting within them. After all, this is the whole reason these cubes exist. To do this extraction, we utilize MDX queries. As a reminder, the acronym MDX stands for Multidimensional Expression Language.

We have been looking at MDX expressions since Chapter 9. In this chapter, we look at MDX statements. An MDX statement, specifically the *SELECT statement*, provides the mechanism for querying information. We look at other MDX statements in addition to the SELECT statement. These statements enable us to manipulate the data in an OLAP cube.

Many visual tools are available for extracting information from a cube. We worked with one of these when we used the Browser tab in SQL Server Data Tools in Chapter 10. This tool enables us to drag-and-drop dimensions and measures to pull data from the cube. Of course, SQL Server Data Tools is one big visual tool for defining and managing OLAP cubes (among other things).

Why, when we have such capable tools for defining cubes and extracting their information, do we need to learn anything about MDX statements? The answer is this: It creates character, and helps build strong bones and muscles. Well, perhaps not. The real answer is: It gives us a deeper understanding of how these visual tools operate. After all, SQL Server Data Tools creates MDX statements behind the scenes to perform the information extraction and cube management activities we ask of it.

In addition, at times, it is more convenient and, perhaps, even faster to use an MDX statement to accomplish a goal, rather than using a visual interface. When we are first creating or deploying a cube, we need to verify that everything is set up correctly. At these times, we want to look at the raw information and not have a visual tool adding layers between us and the cube.

With that in mind, let's begin with the MDX SELECT statement.

# The MDX SELECT Statement

The MDX SELECT statement is our means of extracting information from OLAP cubes. In the same way the T-SQL SELECT statement produces a result set from a relational database, the MDX SELECT statement produces a result set from a multidimensional database. The first major difference between the two statements is the *T-SQL SELECT statement* returns rows and columns, while the *MDX SELECT statement* returns a multidimensional result set that can contain rows and columns, but it also can contain things called pages, sections, and chapters. More on that in the "Additional Dimensions" section of this chapter.

The other difference between the T-SQL SELECT statement and the MDX SELECT statement is the MDX SELECT statement is easier. That may be hard for many of you relational database jockeys to believe, but it is true. Just work through this section and see if you don't agree.

When I say "work through this section," I mean it. This section is not labeled "Learn By Doing," but it might as well be. You can gain a better understanding if you read this in front of a running copy of SQL Server Management Studio and try out each query as you go. By the time you're done, you'll agree this multidimensional analysis is no trouble at all.

## The Basic MDX SELECT Statement

We begin with the most basic MDX SELECT statement and gradually add complexity. When we are done, you should have a good understanding of the statement and be ready for almost any data analysis challenge. We begin with some brief instructions for opening an MDX Query window so you can play along at home.

### Opening a SQL Server Management Studio MDX Query Window

To open a SQL Server Management Studio MDX Query window pointing to the Max Min Manufacturing DM cube, do the following:

1. Open SQL Server Management Studio.
2. Connect to the Analysis Services server hosting the MaxMinManufacturingDM database.
3. Expand the entry for this server in the Object Explorer window, and then expand the Databases Folder under this server.
4. Right-click the entry for the MaxMinManufacturingDM database, and select New Query | MDX from the context menu. The MDX Query window displays, as shown in Figure 12-1.
5. The Cube drop-down list shows the cubes and perspectives available in the MaxMinManufacturingDM database. This database contains one cube.

**NOTE**

*You can save your entries in the SQL Server Management Studio Query window by selecting the Save button on the toolbar or by selecting File | Save **filename** from the Main menu.*

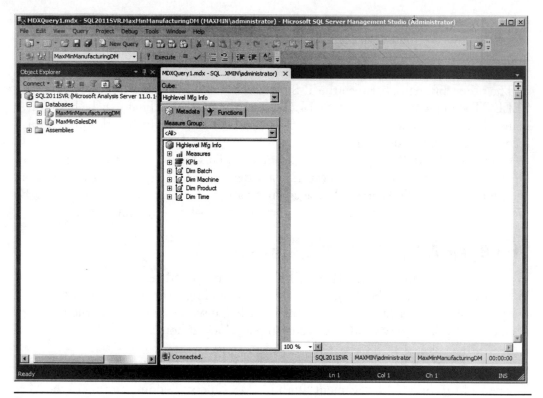

**Figure 12-1** *The SQL Server Management Studio with an MDX Query window*

## The Very Basics

We begin with the most basic MDX SELECT statement possible:

```
SELECT FROM [Cube Name]
```

For example:

```
SELECT FROM [Max Min Manufacturing DM]
```

SELECT identifies this as a SELECT statement. The FROM clause identifies the cube or partition the information is selected from. This is known as the cube context for the SELECT statement. The result of this SELECT statement is shown in Figure 12-2.

**Figure 12-2**    *The most basic MDX SELECT statement*

---

**NOTE**

*You can type **SELECT FROM** in the Query window, and then drag the name of the cube from the Metadata tab and drop it after the word "FROM" in the Query window. If you do this, make sure you unhighlight the cube name before executing the query. If any text is highlighted in the Query window, only that text is executed. This means you can have several query statements in the Query window at the same time and highlight the single query you want to execute. To execute the query, click the Execute button on the toolbar or press F5.*

When a SELECT statement executes, it creates a set of tuples and then returns the value of one or more measures for each of those tuples. Remember, a tuple must contain one member from each dimension in the cube. This includes one of the measures in the cube that is considered part of the Measures dimension. A tuple from the Max Min Manufacturing DM cube includes the following dimensions:

```
(Dim Batch Hierarchy Member,
Dim Machine Hierarchy Member,
Dim Product Hierarchy Member,
Dim Time Hierarchy Member,
Measures Member)
```

In our basic MDX SELECT statement, we are not specifying the members of any dimensions to be included in the result. As we learned in Chapter 11, when a member is not explicitly specified for a dimension, the default member is used. Therefore, our query must be using the default members for all of the dimensions, including the Measures dimension, to get the result.

The tuple that defines our result is

```
([Dim Batch].[Batch Number].DefaultMember,
[Dim Machine].[Material Hierarchy].DefaultMember,
[Dim Product].[Product Hierarchy].DefaultMember,
[Dim Time].[Time Hierarchy].DefaultMember,
[Measures].DefaultMember)
```

The default member for most of the dimensions is All. Recall we set the default member for the Time dimension to 2011. The default member for the Measures dimension is the first measure we defined—namely, the Accepted Products measure. So, the equivalent tuple is

```
([Dim Batch].[Batch Number].[All],
[Dim Machine].[Material Hierarchy].[All],
[Dim Product].[Product Hierarchy].[All],
[Dim Time].[Time Hierarchy].[2011],
[Measures].[Accepted Products])
```

By executing our basic MDX SELECT statement, we learned that for all batches, all materials, and all products for the year 2011, a total of 3,418,942 products were accepted.

## Query Dimensions

As you might expect, we need to be able to specify members other than the default members in our MDX SELECT statements for those statements to be of much interest. We do this by including query dimensions. An MDX SELECT statement with one query dimension has the following format:

```
SELECT {set of dimension members} ON COLUMNS
FROM [Cube Name]
```

For example:

```
SELECT { [Guiding Lights],
         [Mythic World],
         [Warriors Of Yore],
         [Woodland Creatures]} ON COLUMNS
FROM [Max Min Manufacturing DM]
```

Remember, a set is enclosed in curly brackets ({ }). The results of this statement are shown in Figure 12-3.

```
MDXQuery1.mdx - SQL2011SVR.MaxMinManufacturingDM (MAXMIN\administrator)*          S W O R D   ▾ ◻ ✕
Cube:                                  ⊟SELECT {[Guiding Lights],                        ✚
Highlevel Mfg Info                  ▾               [Mythic World],                        ▲
  ⊞ Metadata  ⚡ Functions                            [Warriors Of Yore],
Measure Group:                                       [Woodland Creatures]} ON COLUMNS
<All>                               ▾      FROM [Max Min Manufacturing DM]
  ⬚ Highlevel Mfg Info
  ⊞ ▥ Measures
  ⊞ ▦ KPIs
  ⊟ 📇 Dim Batch                      100 %  ▾ ◂                                          ▶
    ⊞ ▦ Batch Number
  ⊞ 📇 Dim Machine                    ▥ Messages   ▦ Results
  ⊞ 📇 Dim Product               Guiding Lights | Mythic World | Warriors of Yore | Woodland Creatures
  ⊟ 📇 Dim Time                    386,461.00    | 961,734.00   | 1,092,912.00     | 977,835.00
    ⊞ ⬚ Date Hierarchy


  ⊘ Query executed successfully.        SQL2011SVR | MAXMIN\administrator | MaxMinManufacturingDM | 00:00:01
```

**Figure 12-3**  *An MDX SELECT statement with a query dimension*

**NOTE**

*As with the cube name, you can locate the dimension members in the Metadata tab and then drag-and-drop them into the query. If you do this, the query designer will use the key value to identify the dimension member rather than the name. Spaces, tabs, and new lines can be used interchangeably in MDX queries. The new lines are used in the code listing and figures to display the SELECT statements conveniently in the space allowed. Also, the query editor does syntax checking via Intellisense to give you cues if your query is not in proper form.*

If you are paying attention, you realize we can save ourselves some typing and enter this query as follows:

```
SELECT [Product Type].Members ON COLUMNS
FROM [Max Min Manufacturing DM]
```

This gives us the same result but with the All member thrown in as well. When a set of members is specified in this manner, the curly brackets are optional.

Figure 12-4 illustrates how the COLUMNS query dimension is used to create the result set of the SELECT statement. A tuple is created using each member of the COLUMNS query dimension. A value is then retrieved for the member of the Measures dimension in each tuple.

**NOTE**

*The All member of the dimension is included in the query result, but is not included in the figures in order to simplify the diagrams.*

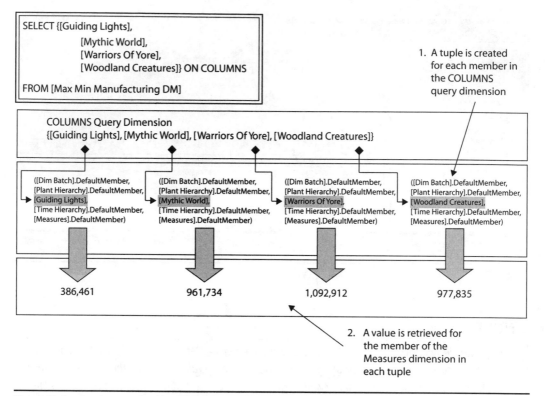

**Figure 12-4** *Creating a result with a COLUMNS query dimension*

Let's add a second query dimension to our MDX SELECT statement. With two query dimensions, the MDX SELECT statement has the following format:

```
SELECT {set of dimension members} ON COLUMNS,
       {set of dimension members} ON ROWS
FROM [Cube Name]
```

For example:

```
SELECT [Product Type].Members ON COLUMNS,
       [Year].Members ON ROWS
FROM [Max Min Manufacturing DM]
```

The results of this statement are shown in Figure 12-5.

Figure 12-6 illustrates how the COLUMNS query dimension and the ROWS query dimension are used to create the result set of the SELECT statement. A tuple is created combining each member of the COLUMNS query dimension with each member of the ROWS query dimension. A value is then retrieved for the member of

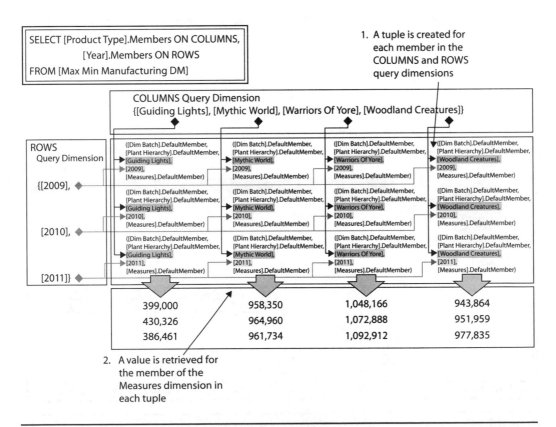

**Figure 12-5**    *An MDX SELECT statement with two query dimensions*

**Figure 12-6**    *Creating a result with two query dimensions* the Measures dimension in each tuple. We can go beyond two query dimensions in an MDX SELECT statement, but we save that discussion for the section "Additional Dimensions."

Because Measures is considered another dimension of our cube, we can use a set of dimension members for a query dimension. For example:

```
SELECT {[Measures].[Accepted Products], [Measures].[Total Products]}
                                                      ON COLUMNS,
       [Year].Members ON ROWS
FROM [Max Min Manufacturing DM]
```

This MDX SELECT statement uses a set containing the Accepted Products measure and the Total Products calculated member for the COLUMNS query dimension. The result is shown in Figure 12-7. We end up with the total of all accepted products and the total of all production for each year.

## Slicer

Using members of the Measures dimension in a query dimension is one way to view different measures in the result set. Using a slicer is another. When using a *slicer*, the MDX SELECT statement has the following format:

```
SELECT {set of dimension members} ON COLUMNS,
       {set of dimension members} ON ROWS
FROM [Cube Name]
WHERE [Measures dimension member]
```

**Figure 12-7**   *Measures dimension members in the COLUMNS query dimension*

For example:

```
SELECT [Product Type].Members ON COLUMNS,
       [Year].Members ON ROWS
FROM [Max Min Manufacturing DM]
WHERE [Measures].[Total Products]
```

The results of this statement are shown in Figure 12-8. Remember, the default measure is Accepted Products. Now in this result set, we get the total products for each product type for each year.

In addition to specifying the measure used in the result set, we can use the slicer to do a bit more. We can specify dimension members to use in place of our default members for dimensions not included in the query dimensions. The format for this type of MDX SELECT statement is

```
SELECT {set of dimension members} ON COLUMNS,
       {set of dimension members} ON ROWS
FROM [Cube Name]
WHERE ([Measures dimension member], [dimension member])
```

The WHERE clause now contains a tuple, rather than a single Measures dimension member. This tuple can include as many dimension members as you like. The rule is this: A dimension can only appear in one place in the MDX SELECT statement: either on one of the query dimensions or in the slicer.

**Figure 12-8**   *An MDX SELECT statement with a slicer*

This sounds confusing, but an example clears things up. Suppose we want to see the total products for our product types for each of the years in the cube, but we only want to see those numbers as they pertain to the Maximum Miniatures plant in Fridley (Plant #3). We can use the following MDX SELECT statement to get this information:

```
SELECT [Product Type].Members ON COLUMNS,
       [Year].Members ON ROWS
FROM [Max Min Manufacturing DM]
WHERE ([Measures].[Total Products], [Plant].&[3])
```

The result of this query is shown in Figure 12-9.

Figure 12-10 illustrates how the tuple in the slicer affects the result set. Each member of the COLUMNS query dimension is combined with each member of the ROWS query dimension. These combinations are then combined with the members of the slicer tuple. The default member is used for any dimension not represented in the COLUMNS query dimension, the ROWS query dimension, or the slicer tuple.

## Filtering with the FILTER Function

Many times, as we are creating MDX SELECT statements, the set of members we want to see on a dimension is dependent on the content of the data. For example, the production manager at Maximum Miniatures may want to see the number of accepted

**Figure 12-9**   *An MDX SELECT statement with a tuple in the slicer*

**Figure 12-10**  *Creating a result with a slicer tuple*

products manufactured for those products that had an increase in their backorder amounts during the month. The production manager does not want to see all of the products in the dimension, only those with a higher amount on backorder. It is not possible to manually type a set of products to satisfy this query from month to month. A product that may have an increasing backorder from May to June may not be in that same state from June to July. It all depends on the data.

Fortunately, the *FILTER function*, which is an MDX function, lets us determine the content of a set using a condition expression. The FILTER function starts with a set of members as a parameter. Then it removes members from the set that do not satisfy the condition expression. Let's see if we can come up with a FILTER condition that can satisfy the production manager. We can compare the backorder amounts for November 2011 and December 2011.

If you switch to the Functions tab, you find the FILTER function in the Set folder because it returns a set. Drag the FILTER function and drop it on the Query window to use it as the content of one of the query dimensions. You see the following:

```
FILTER ( «Set», «Search Condition» )
```

The syntax tells us we need to supply the FILTER function with two parameters: a set and a search condition.

The set should be all members of the Product dimension at the product level. The FILTER function then removes those products that do not meet the search condition. The expression [Product] provides a list of all products.

For the search condition, we use an expression comparing two values with a Boolean operator. The values we are creating come from two tuples. The first tuple is composed of the December 2011 member of the Month hierarchy along with the Accepted Products measure. The second tuple is composed of the November 2011 member of the Month hierarchy along with the Accepted Products measure.

These two tuples are evaluated by including each member of the set of Products (the first parameter of the function) one at a time. The function evaluates

```
([Product].[American GI], [Month].[201112],
                     [Measures].[Number On Backorder]) <
([Product].[American GI], [Month].[201111],
                     [Measures].[Number On Backorder])
```

and then it evaluates

```
([Product].[Bear and Cub], [Month].[201112],
                     [Measures].[Number On Backorder]) <
([Product].[Bear and Cub], [Month].[201111],
                     [Measures].[Number On Backorder])
```

Any members of the set of products that result in an expression evaluating to true are included in the set returned as the FILTER function's result. The result is then used by the SELECT statement to create columns. The MDX SELECT statement and its result are shown in Figure 12-11.

Note, a number of products show "(null)" for the number of accepted products in December 2011. This occurs because this product was not manufactured in December 2011. No data exists to report for this measure in this timeframe, which probably explains why the number of backorders increased for these products!

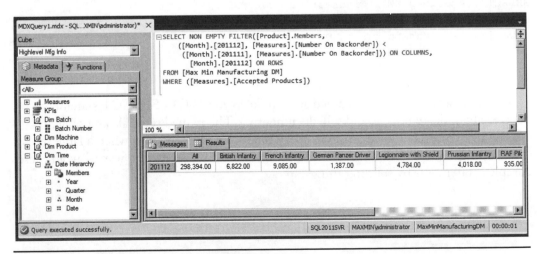

**Figure 12-11**   *An MDX SELECT statement using the FILTER function*

## The NON EMPTY Statement

In the sample query in Figure 12-11, the data for many of the products was (null). These cells in our results set are really empty. The "(null)" string is put there as a placeholder so we can tell the difference between an empty cell and a cell that might happen to contain an empty string ("").

In many situations, we are only interested in the items that actually have data. We only want to see the non-empty cells in our result. We can achieve this by adding the NON EMPTY clause at the beginning of any query dimension statement. This is shown in Figure 12-12.

**Figure 12-12**   *An MDX SELECT statement with a NON EMPTY statement*

## Additional Tools for Querying

We have now covered the basics of the MDX SELECT statement. You've seen how to quickly assemble dimensions, hierarchies, and measures to analyze the cube data and discover business intelligence (BI). However, a few more tools can help take the query process one step further.

## The WITH Statement

In the previous section, we used the FILTER function to create the desired set for one of our query dimensions. But there may be times when the desired set cannot be defined by an expression in a FILTER function. Perhaps we want to look at the production of American World War II figures. There is nothing that lets us create this set using a filter (at least, not a straightforward filter). We need to build this set manually.

Rather than putting this manually created set in the MDX SELECT statement itself, we can use the WITH statement to define a *named set*. Once the named set is defined, it can be used in the MDX SELECT statement. The format for a WITH statement creating a named set is

```
WITH SET [named set name] AS
{set definition}
```

Here is the WITH statement and an MDX SELECT statement that uses it:

```
WITH SET [American WWII Figures] AS
{[American GI], [US Army Pilot], [US Navy Gunner's Mate]}

SELECT {[American WWII Figures]} ON COLUMNS,
        [Year].Members ON ROWS
FROM [Max Min Manufacturing DM]
WHERE [Measures].[Total Products]
```

The results are shown in Figure 12-13.

The main advantage of the named set is to keep your MDX SELECT statements neat, easily understandable, and self-documenting. The named set is also reusable. As we saw in Figure 12-3, even a simple query can look rather complex when a large set is specified right in one of the query dimensions. Named sets provide a way to avoid these complex statements by splitting things up.

**Figure 12-13**  *An MDX SELECT statement using a named set*

We can also use the WITH statement to define temporary calculated members. These can be members of one of our dimensional hierarchies or members of the Measures dimension. The format for a WITH statement that defines a temporary calculated member is

```
WITH
  MEMBER [parent member].[calculated member name] AS
    {member definition}
```

Let's expand on our American World War II Figures set and create calculated members that create rollups for each nationality in the World War II product subtype. Here is the code:

```
WITH
  MEMBER [World War II].[American Figures] AS
    [American GI]+[US Army Pilot]+[US Navy Gunner's Mate]
  MEMBER [World War II].[British Figures] AS
    [British Tank Commander]+[RAF Pilot]
  MEMBER [World War II].[Russian Figures] AS
    [Russian Infantry]+[Russian Tank Commander]
  MEMBER [World War II].[German Figures] AS
    [German Panzer Driver]
```

```
SELECT {[American Figures],
          [British Figures],
          [Russian Figures],
          [German Figures]} ON COLUMNS,
       [Year].Members ON ROWS
FROM [Max Min Manufacturing DM]
WHERE [Measures].[Total Products]
```

The results are shown in Figure 12-14.

The difference between the named set and the calculated member can seem a bit subtle at first glance. The named set is just that—a set of individual members. When we used the set in Figure 12-13, each of the individual members appeared in the result set.

Each calculated member is a new individual member that is composed of the aggregation of information from other members. When the calculated members are used in Figure 12-14, only the newly defined calculated members, not their constituent parts, appear in the result set.

While we are at it, let's define a temporary member of the Measures dimension. Suppose we want to know what percentage of total products our members of the

**Figure 12-14**  *An MDX SELECT statement using temporary calculated members*

product hierarchy accounted for. We can define a temporary calculated member of the Measures dimension and use it as follows:

```
WITH
  MEMBER [Measures].[Percent Of Parent] AS
    CStr(ROUND((([Product Hierarchy].CurrentMember,
                      [Measures].[Total Products])*100/
       ([Product Hierarchy].CurrentMember.Parent,
                      [Measures].[Total Products]),2) )+"%"
SELECT [Product Type].Members ON COLUMNS,
  [Year].Members ON ROWS
FROM [Max Min Manufacturing DM]
WHERE [Measures].[Percent Of Parent]
```

The expression used to define the temporary calculated member is somewhat complex: It consists of two tuples. The first tuple:

```
([Product Hierarchy].CurrentMember, [Measures].[Total Products])
```

returns the value of the total products measure for the current member of the product dimension. The second tuple:

```
([Product Hierarchy].CurrentMember.Parent, [Measures].[Total Products])
```

returns the value of the total products measure for the parent of the current member of the product dimension. We multiply the total products value from the current member by 100, and then divide it by the total products value from the parent member. The resulting decimal number is rounded to two decimal places and converted to a string. Finally, we concatenate the percent sign on the end. There you have it.

The results are shown in Figure 12-15. Note, we get a divide-by-zero error for the All products column, but we can ignore this and analyze the valid data for each product.

## CROSSJOIN

Up to this point, our MDX SELECT statements have been limited to one dimension on each query dimension. Given that they are called query dimensions, it does make sense that would be the case. However, at times, we would like to break what seems an obvious correlation and put two dimensions on a single query dimension. Fortunately, MDX provides a way to do just that. (Of course it does; otherwise, I wouldn't have brought it up!)

We use the *CROSSJOIN function* to combine sets from two dimensions into a single joined set. This joined set can then be placed on a query dimension. If you are familiar

**Figure 12-15** *An MDX SELECT statement using a temporary calculated member of the Measures dimension*

with the cross join in T-SQL, you have a pretty good idea how this is going to work. Our new set is going to be made out of tuples, which combine every member of one set with every member of the other set.

If you switch to the Functions tab, you find the CROSSJOIN function in the Set folder because it returns a set. Drag the CROSSJOIN function and drop it on the Query window. You see the following:

```
CROSSJOIN( <<Set1>>, <<Set2>> )
```

The syntax tells us we need to supply the CROSSJOIN function with two parameters: both sets. Let's look at an example.

Suppose we want to see the total products by product type, by plant, by year. We have three dimensions to work with. Here is what it looks like using the CROSSJOIN function:

```
SELECT CROSSJOIN([Product Type].Members,
                             [Plant].Members) ON COLUMNS,
       [Year].Members ON ROWS
FROM [Max Min Manufacturing DM]
WHERE [Measures].[Total Products]
```

In this query, we are taking all of the members of the product type hierarchy and cross-joining them to all of the members in the plant hierarchy. With four product types plus the All member and five plants plus the All member, we end up with

30 tuples in the cross-joined set and 30 columns in the result set. The result is shown in Figure 12-16.

If you look at the result set in Figure 12-16, you see a number of (null) entries. This indicates a particular product type was not manufactured at a particular plant during that year. For example, there have never been any products from the Guiding Lights product type manufactured at the Hamburg plant.

Let's make our result set easier to analyze by eliminating columns with null values in every row. Again, we do that by adding the NON EMPTY statement to the MDX SELECT statement. With the NON EMPTY keyword included, our query looks like this:

```
SELECT NON EMPTY CROSSJOIN([Product Type].Members,
                           [Plant].Members) ON COLUMNS,
       [Year].Members ON ROWS
FROM [Max Min Manufacturing DM]
WHERE [Measures].[Total Products]
```

The results, with the empty columns removed, are shown in Figure 12-17.

## TOPCOUNT/BOTTOMCOUNT

Often during analysis, we want to see the highest or the lowest values for a given measure. Of course, we can manually scan the rows and columns of numbers to make this determination. However, the more information we need to sift through, the more

**Figure 12-16** *An MDX SELECT statement using the CROSSJOIN function*

**Figure 12-17** *An MDX SELECT statement using the NON EMPTY keyword*

this becomes an arduous and error-prone task. Instead, we should have our MDX SELECT query do this analysis for us.

This is where the TOPCOUNT and BOTTOMCOUNT functions come in. These functions return the select set of the members with the highest or lowest values for a specified measure. The TOPCOUNT and BOTTOMCOUNT functions are found in the Set folder because they each return a set. Drag the TOPCOUNT function and drop it on the Query window. You see the following:

```
TOPCOUNT( <<Set>>, <<Count>>[, <<Numeric Expression>>])
```

The first parameter is the set we are to select from. The second parameter is the number of members to include in our result set. The third parameter is the numeric expression, usually a measure, which is used to rank the set members before taking the requested number of members off the top. The syntax of the BOTTOMCOUNT function is identical to that of the TOPCOUNT function. The only difference, of course, is the BOTTOMCOUNT function is pulling from the bottom of the ranking rather than the top.

Let's begin by looking for the five products we have manufactured the most in 2011. To accomplish this, we use the TOPCOUNT function in the following query:

```
SELECT TOPCOUNT([Product].Members, 5,
       [Measures].[Total Products]) ON COLUMNS
FROM [Max Min Manufacturing DM]
```

The results are shown in Figure 12-18. Note, we now only have five products in the result set, including the All member, but the products are in their ranking order.

To find the three machines that have manufactured the least amount of product in 2011, we can use the following query:

```
SELECT BOTTOMCOUNT([Machine].Members, 3,
            [Measures].[Total Products]) ON COLUMNS
FROM [Max Min Manufacturing DM]
```

The results are shown in Figure 12-19.

Remember, the TOPCOUNT and BOTTOMCOUNT functions simply create a set to use in one of the query dimensions. Let's look at another example to illustrate this point:

```
SELECT TOPCOUNT([Product].Members, 5,
            [Measures].[Total Products]) ON COLUMNS,
      [Year].[2010] ON ROWS
FROM [Max Min Manufacturing DM]
```

The results are shown in Figure 12-20.

At first, a problem seems to exist with the result set shown in Figure 12-20. The products do not appear in the proper rank order. Maximum Miniatures made more Bear and Cub than Dragon with Knight, yet Dragon with Knight is second in the

**Figure 12-18**  *An MDX SELECT statement using the TOPCOUNT function*

**Figure 12-19** *An MDX SELECT statement using the BOTTOMCOUNT function*

result set and Bear and Cub is third. We need to look at exactly what our MDX SELECT statement is doing.

The TOPCOUNT function executes first to create the set for the COLUMNS query dimension. Because we have not specified a member of the Time dimension, the function uses the default member of 2011. It finds the five products with the

**Figure 12-20** *An MDX SELECT statement using the TOPCOUNT function along with a ROWS query dimension*

largest production in 2011. Using this set of five products for the COLUMNS query dimension, the SELECT statement combines it with the 2010 member from the ROWS query dimension to get the total products for our five products in 2010. Dragon with Knight production may have exceeded Bear and Cub production in 2011, but it did not in 2010. As with most computer code, you usually get exactly what you ask for. The trick is asking for the correct thing!

## Aggregates

We have looked at aggregate functions with respect to the rollup done for hierarchy members in the cube. MDX also offers aggregation functions that may be used for creating calculations in MDX SELECT statements. We examine two of these functions here.

First, the SUM function adds the values of a numeric expression for all of the members in a set. The format of the SUM function is

```
SUM( <<Set>> [, <<Numeric Expression>>] )
```

Second, the COUNT function counts the number of items in a set. The COUNT function has the following format:

```
COUNT( <<Set>> [, EXCLUDEEMPTY | INCLUDEEMPTY] )
```

The optional second parameter to the COUNT function determines whether empty cells are counted.

Let's use these two aggregate functions to calculate the average amount produced per month for each product. We use the following query:

```
WITH
     MEMBER [Measures].[Avg per Month] AS
     'ROUND(Sum(Descendants([Date Hierarchy].CurrentMember, [Date]),
                              [Measures].[Total Products]) /
     Count(Descendants([Date Hierarchy].CurrentMember, [Date]))),0)'

SELECT [Year].Members ON COLUMNS,
       [Product Type].Members ON ROWS
FROM [Max Min Manufacturing DM]
WHERE [Measures].[Avg per Month]
```

In our temporary calculated member, we first find the descendants of the current time hierarchy member at the day level. We then take the SUM of the Total Products measure to determine the number produced for this time period. We also take the COUNT of the number of days in the current time hierarchy member. We can then

**Figure 12-21**   *An MDX SELECT statement using SUM and COUNT aggregates*

divide the sum of the total products produced by the count of the number of days in the time period to get the average. Add a Round function to get rid of the fraction amount, and we are done. The results are shown in Figure 12-21.

**NOTE**

*MDX also includes a DISTINCTCOUNT function that has the same structure and function as the COUNT function. The only difference is the DISTINCTCOUNT function counts multiple occurrences of a member in the set only once.*

## Additional Dimensions

To this point, we have worked only with the COLUMNS and ROWS query dimensions. We did hint that more dimensions were possible. Indeed, though it is hard for our brains to visualize in more than three dimensions, Analysis Services can provide many more.

### Pages, Sections, and Chapters

Five named query dimensions are supported by the MDX SELECT statement. They are

- ► COLUMNS
- ► ROWS

▶ PAGES

▶ SECTIONS

▶ CHAPTERS

These query dimensions must be used in the order they are presented here. You cannot have a ROWS query dimension in your MDX SELECT statement unless a COLUMNS query dimension is also present. You cannot have a PAGES query dimension in your MDX SELECT statement unless ROWS and COLUMNS query dimensions are also present, and so on.

## AXIS($n$)

The MDX SELECT statement supports a number of query dimensions beyond the five named query dimensions. Indeed, it is possible to define up to 128 query dimensions. Once we move beyond five, we refer to the query dimensions as AXIS($n$). In fact, we can use AXIS(0) in place of COLUMNS and AXIS(1) in place of ROWS, like so:

```
SELECT [Product Type].Members ON AXIS(0),
       [Year].Members ON AXIS(1)
FROM [Max Min Manufacturing DM]
WHERE [Measures].[Total Products]
```

The results are shown in Figure 12-22.

**Figure 12-22**  *An MDX SELECT statement using AXIS(0) and AXIS(1)*

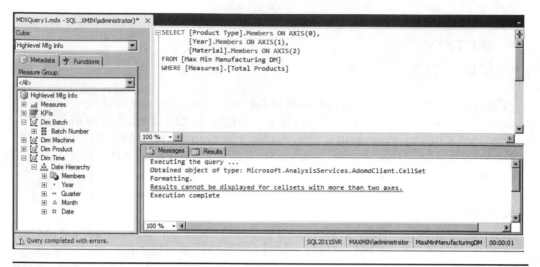

**Figure 12-23**   *A front-end Query window error when trying to use three query dimensions*

Unfortunately, the Query window in the SQL Server Management Studio does not display more than two query dimensions. When we try, we receive an error message, as shown in Figure 12-23. This is an error from the front-end Query window, not from the Analysis Services server. Other front-end tools allow for more dimensions in our queries.

# Additional MDX Syntax

Up to this point in the chapter, we have looked at the ins and outs of the MDX SELECT statement. This statement is extremely important to cube analysis. For the remainder of this chapter, we touch on some additional MDX that is useful in both the MDX SELECT statement and in MDX syntax scripts.

## Operators

First, we take a look at the operators available in MDX.

## Comment

| Item | Description |
|---|---|
| /*...*/ | Multiline comment |
| -- | Single-line comment |
| // | Single-line comment |

If you save your MDX queries for use by others or for your own reuse later, documenting what the query is for and exactly what it returns is important. With some of the more intricate MDX statements, it is not always easy to decipher the statement's purpose. A comment or two can be a lifesaver in these situations.

Multiline comments can span several lines and are not terminated until a */ is encountered. Single-line comments are terminated at the end of the line. Any of the comment types can begin at the beginning or in the middle of a line. Comments are completely ignored during MDX processing.

Here is an example of all three types of comments:

```
/* This is an MDX SELECT statement from the
   "Delivering Business Intelligence with SQL
   Server 2012" book. */
SELECT [Product Type].Members ON COLUMNS, -- the COLUMNS dimension
       [Year].Members ON ROWS                // the ROWS dimension
FROM [Max Min Manufacturing DM]
WHERE [Measures].[Total Products]       /* The slicer */
```

## Numeric

| Item | Description |
|------|-------------|
| + | Positive |
| + | Addition |
| − | Negative |
| − | Subtraction |
| * | Multiplication |
| / | Division |

The numeric operators function as we would expect.

## String

| Item | Description |
|------|-------------|
| + | Concatenation |

String concatenation is performed with the plus (+) sign, as in T-SQL.

## Logical

| Item | Description |
| --- | --- |
| < | Less than |
| <= | Less than or equal to |
| <> | Not equal to |
| = | Equal |
| > | Greater than |
| >= | Greater than or equal to |
| AND | Logical and |
| IS | Tuple equality |
| NOT | Logical not |
| OR | Logical or |
| XOR | Logical exclusive or |

The logical operators perform as expected.

## Set

| Item | Description |
| --- | --- |
| — | Except |
| * | Crossjoin |
| + | Union |
| : | Range |

The except (–) and union (+) operators only work with sets from the same dimension. The crossjoin (*) operator requires two sets from different dimensions. The Range operator was covered in Chapter 11. The crossjoin operator functions in the same manner as the CROSSJOIN function covered in the section "CROSSJOIN" in this chapter.

If Set 1 is

```
{[Bear and Cub], [Bear with Hive], [Bull Moose]}
```

and Set 2 is

```
{[Bull Moose], [Eagle Pair], [Howling Wolf]}
```

then

```
[Set 1] - [Set 2]
```

is

```
{[Bear and Cub], [Bear with Hive]}
```

In other words, it is the members in Set 1 that are not in Set 2.

```
[Set 1] + [Set 2]
```

is

```
{[Bear and Cub], [Bear with Hive], [Bull Moose],
                    [Eagle Pair], [Howling Wolf]}
```

Items found in both sets appear only once in the resulting concatenated set.

# Functions

We look at some additional MDX functions that may be of use.

## Dimensional

These functions return a dimension, a hierarchy, or a level.

**Dimension**    Returns the dimension to which the given object belongs.

```
[Bear and Cub].Dimension
```

returns

```
[Dim Product]
```

**Hierarchy**    Returns the hierarchy to which the given object belongs.

```
[Bear and Cub].Hierarchy
```

returns

```
[Product Hierarchy]
```

**Level**    Returns the level to which the given object belongs.

```
[Bear and Cub].Level
```

returns

```
[Product]
```

## Logical

These functions return either true or false.

**IsAncestor(member1, member2)**    Returns true if *member1* is an ancestor of *member2*.

```
IsAncestor([Woodland Creatures], [Bear and Cub])
```

returns true.

**IsEmpty(MDXexpression)**    Returns true if *MDXexpression* results in an empty cell.

```
IsEmpty(([Warriors Of Yore],[Maximum Miniatures—Mumbai]))
```

returns true because the cell represented by this tuple has no data.

**IsGeneration(member1, numeric expression)**    Returns true if *member1* is a member of the generation represented by *numeric expression*. The lowest level, or leaf level, of a hierarchy is level 0.

```
IsGeneration([Black Bears],1)
```

returns true.

**IsLeaf(member1)**    Returns true if *member1* is at the lowest level of its hierarchy.

```
IsLeaf ([Bear and Cub])
```

returns true.

**IsSibling(member1, member2)**    Returns true if *member1* is a sibling of *member2*.

```
IsSibling ([Bear and Cub], [Bear with Hive])
```

returns true.

**IIF(logical expression, expression1, expression2)**   The IIF function may return a type, logical, set, dimensional, and so on. The reason the IIF function is here is because it requires a logical expression as its first parameter. Therefore, the IIF function is a likely place to find one of these other logical expressions.

If the *logical expression* evaluates to true, *expression1*, the second parameter, is evaluated and the result returned by the IIF function. If the *logical expression* evaluates to false, *expression2*, the third parameter, is evaluated and the result returned. For example:

```
IIF(IsLeaf([Product Hierarchy].CurrentMember),
    [Product Hierarchy].CurrentMember,
    [Product Hierarchy].CurrentMember.FirstChild)
```

In this example, if the current member of the product hierarchy is a leaf member, the current member of the product hierarchy is returned. This is the content of the second parameter passed to the IIF function. If the current member of the product hierarchy is not a leaf member, the first child of the current member of the product hierarchy is returned. This is the content of the third parameter passed to the IIF function.

## Member

These functions return a member.

**ClosingPeriod(level, member)**   Returns the member at the level of *level* that represents the last item in the period occupied by *member*.

```
ClosingPeriod([Month], [2011Q3])
```

returns [201109], the last month member in Q3, 2011.

**Item(n)**   Returns the *n*th member of the tuple. Note, the index is zero-based.

```
([2010], [Bear and Cub], [Clay]).Item(1)
```

returns [Bear and Cub].

**OpeningPeriod(level, member)**   Returns the member at the level of *level* that represents the first item in the period occupied by *member*.

```
OpeningPeriod([Month], [2011Q3])
```

returns [201107], the first month member in Q3, 2011.

## The AGGREGATE Function

When we used the SUM function to aggregate values to calculate the average production per month, we forced an aggregation on the rollup. All of the items were added together to create the aggregate. In some cases, this may not have been appropriate.

If we were working with sales figures, we could have inadvertently added in return amounts that should have been subtracted. If we were working with financial data, we could have added in credits that should have been subtracted. (In these days of Sarbanes-Oxley, that can get a company in real trouble, real fast!)

Instead of forcing an aggregation by using a function like the SUM function, we can use the AGGREGATE function. The AGGREGATE function works just like the SUM function, with one major exception. The *AGGREGATE function* uses the default aggregation operator for a measure, rather than forcing one on it. This helps ensure the data resulting from an aggregation is correct.

## Data Analysis

MDX provides a number of numerical functions to assist in the analysis of OLAP cube data. We do not have space here to treat each in detail. We'll provide a list of these functions here to make you aware of their existence. Then, if you or one of your users has need of a particular type of data or statistical analysis, you can track down the details for the function or functions that fit the bill.

| Function | Description |
| --- | --- |
| Covariance | Returns the population covariance of two series evaluated over a set, using the biased population formula. |
| CovarianceN | Returns the sample covariance of two series evaluated over a set, using the unbiased population formula. |
| LinRegIntercept | Calculates the linear regression of a set and returns the value of $b$ in the regression line $y = ax + b$. |
| LinRegPoint | Calculates the linear regression of a set and returns the value of $y$ in the regression line $y = ax + b$. |
| LinRegR2 | Calculates the linear regression of a set and returns R2 (the coefficient of determination). |
| LinRegSlope | Calculates the linear regression of a set and returns the value of $a$ in the regression line $y = ax + b$. |
| LinRegVariance | Calculates the linear regression of a set and returns the variance associated with the regression line $y = ax + b$. |
| LookupCube | Returns the value of an MDX expression evaluated over another specified cube in the same database. |
| Max | Returns the maximum value of a numeric expression evaluated over a set. |
| Median | Returns the median value of a numeric expression evaluated over a set. |
| Min | Returns the minimum value of a numeric expression evaluated over a set. |

| Function | Description |
|----------|-------------|
| Stddev, Stdev | Returns the sample standard deviation of a numeric expression evaluated over a set, using the unbiased population formula. |
| StddevP, StdevP | Returns the population standard deviation of a numeric expression evaluated over a set, using the biased population formula. |
| Var, Variance | Returns the sample variance of a numeric expression evaluated over a set, using the unbiased population formula. |
| VarP, VarianceP | Returns the population variance of a numeric expression evaluated over a set, using the biased population formula. |

# Tabling the Matter

The Multidimensional BI Semantic Model provides a very powerful and, perhaps more importantly, a very mature technology for managing and storing large amounts of data for creating business intelligence. In the next section, we take a look at the new kid on the block, the Tabular BI Semantic Model. While this new technology has some limitations, it does offer some advantages when it comes to simplicity.

So, come on! You've got a place at the table.

# Part IV

# Working with a Tabular BI Semantic Model

# Chapter 13

# Setting the Table—Creating a Tabular BI Semantic Model

## In This Chapter

▶ **Preparation for Creating Tabular Models**
▶ **Creating a Tabular Model**
▶ **A Second Tabular Model**
▶ **Putting More on the Table**

*I drink to the general joy o' the whole table.*

—*Macbeth. Act iii. Sc. 4,* William Shakespeare

In Chapter 6, we built our first Multidimensional BI Semantic Model for use by our sample company, Maximum Miniatures, Inc. This was the MaxMin-SalesDM. In Chapter 9, we built our second Multidimensional BI Semantic Model—MaxMinManufacturingDM. We then spent Chapters 10 through 12 making enhancements to that model and learning about the MDX language used by Multidimensional models.

Now we are going to shift gears and look at the Tabular BI Semantic Model. In essence, we are going to duplicate, as much as possible, what we have done in the MaxMinSalesDM and MaxMinManufacturingDM Multidimensional models. In this chapter, we will create a Tabular version of MaxMinSalesDM and MaxMinManufacturingDM. In Chapter 14, we will explore the Data Analysis Expressions (DAX) language used by Tabular models.

This parallel between our Multidimensional model examples and our Tabular model examples is being done purposefully. It will give you the opportunity to gauge the relative effort in creating Multidimensional and Tabular models. It will also allow you to compare the capabilities of the two types of models.

# Preparation for Creating Tabular Models

Before we begin creating Tabular models, we need to do a bit of preparation. When we build our Multidimensional models, we can happily work in SQL Server Data Tools without worrying about the Analysis Services server where the model will live. With Multidimensional models, the Analysis Services server doesn't come into play until it is time to deploy and process. As we build the Tabular model, however, SQL Server Data Tools will be in constant communication with the Analysis Services server to give us immediate feedback on what the data looks like in the model. Therefore, we need to have our Tabular instance of Analysis Services available right from the start.

## SQL Server Analysis Services Tabular Instance

A particular instance of SQL Server Analysis Services 2012 is installed to support a specific type of BI Semantic Model. An Analysis Services instance can support Multidimensional models or it can support Tabular models, but not both. In order for you and your organization to work with both Multidimensional models and Tabular models, you will need at least two instances of Analysis Services.

In Chapters 10 through 12, we worked with Multidimensional models deployed to an instance of Analysis Services. This instance of Analysis Services cannot be used as the deployment server for the Learn By Doing exercises in this and the following chapter. You must have a second, Tabular instance of Analysis Services available to you to complete these exercises. As always, a development or test instance of Analysis Services should be used. Do not use a production instance of Analysis Services when completing the exercises in this book.

### NOTE

*Creating a Tabular instance of Analysis Services requires the Business Intelligence Edition, Enterprise Edition, or Developer Edition of SQL Server Analysis Services 2012. Tabular instances of Analysis Services are not supported by the Standard Edition or other editions. If you are not working with a Business Intelligence Edition, Enterprise Edition, or Developer Edition of SQL Server Analysis Services 2012, you will not be able to complete the Learn By Doing exercises in this chapter and in Chapter 14.*

It is recommended that the Tabular instance of Analysis Services that hosts your workspace databases be on the same computer where you are running SQL Server Data Tools to design your model. Having this "local" setup will give you the best performance as you work with the data in the model. Having your workspace database on a remote server can introduce delays and slow down your design process.

There are also a couple of restrictions when you host your workspace databases on a remote server. You cannot set the Data Backup property to "Backup to Disk." Also, you cannot import data from a PowerPivot workbook using the "Import from PowerPivot" project template. Both of these items are discussed later.

## Managing the Workspace Database

As was mentioned previously, SQL Server Data Tools is going to be in constant communication with Analysis Services as we define our Tabular model. In fact, as soon as we create an Analysis Services Tabular project, SQL Server Data Tools creates a workspace database in Analysis Services. This *workspace database* hosts the data in our model to give us a real-time view of the model as we create it.

The location and behavior of the workspace database is controlled by three properties of the Tabular model. These are

- ▶ Workspace Server
- ▶ Workspace Retention
- ▶ Data Backup

Because the values found in these properties are used to instantiate the workspace database as the model is first created, we must provide meaningful default values for these items.

The default values for these properties come from three SQL Server Data Tools options settings. They are

▶ **Default workspace server** The server name found in this option setting is assigned to the model's Workspace Server property, and a workspace database is immediately created on that server. This must be a Tabular instance of SQL Server 2012 Analysis Services. It is recommended that this Tabular instance be running on the same computer where you are executing SQL Server Data Tools for optimum performance.

▶ **Workspace database retention after the model is closed** The selection made for this option is assigned to the model's Workspace Retention property. This determines what happens to the workspace database when the model project is closed in SQL Server Data Tools. The options are

   ▶ **Keep workspace in memory** This option keeps the workspace database loaded in the Analysis Services memory space. The model is still available for querying and browsing through the server.

   ▶ **Keep workspace databases on disk but unload from memory** This option unloads the workspace database from the Analysis Services memory space. However, it persists a copy of the database on disk. This allows the database to be quickly reloaded into the Analysis Services memory space the next time the model project is opened, without having to reload the data from the data sources. (This option is selected by default.)

   ▶ **Delete workspace** This option unloads the workspace database from the Analysis Services memory space and does not persist the database on disk. The next time the model project is opened, the workspace database is re-created and its data is reloaded from the data sources.

▶ **Data backup** Specifies whether the data is backed up to disk (to an .abf file) each time the model definition is saved. This data backup is used if you cancel the changes made to the model. Therefore, having the backup of the data on disk will make canceling changes go faster. However, creating the backup of the data on disk will increase the time required each time the model is saved. Options are

   ▶ Keep backup of data on disk

   ▶ Do not keep backup of data on disk. (This is selected by default.)

## Learn By Doing—Preparing SQL Server Data Tools for Tabular Model Development

### Feature Highlighted

▶ Set SQL Server Data Tools default to a Tabular instance of Analysis Services

**Business Need**   In order for SQL Server Data Tools to function properly as we create Tabular BI Semantic Models, it needs to point to a Tabular instance of Analysis Services by default.

### Steps

1. Open SQL Server Data Tools.
2. Select Tools | Options from the main menu. The Options dialog box appears.
3. Scroll down in the pages area until you see the section for Analysis Services.
4. Expand the Analysis Services entry and select Data Modeling. The Data Modeling page of the Options dialog box appears.
5. For Default workspace server, enter the name of a Tabular instance of SQL Server Analysis Services where you have rights to create databases. (Do *not* perform this or any other Learn By Doing activity on a server used for production operations!)
6. Click Test Connection to make sure you can connect to the Tabular instance of Analysis Services you entered. If the test does not succeed, check the following:

    ▶ The name of the Analysis Services instance is entered correctly. If this is a named instance of Analysis Services, ensure the instance name is included along with the server name.

    ▶ You have the appropriate rights to interact with this instance of Analysis Services.

    ▶ You are entering the name of a Tabular instance of Analysis Services, not a Multidimensional instance of Analysis Services. If you receive an error message telling you the workspace database server is not running in VertiPaq mode, then you entered the name of a Multidimensional instance of Analysis Services.

    ▶ If you are using a named instance of SQL Server Analysis Services, make sure the SQL Server Browser service is running.

    You need to make a successful connection before proceeding with the other activities in this chapter. The Options dialog box is shown in Figure 13-1 with the Default workspace server set to a named instance of Analysis Services called "TABULAR" running on the local computer. The name of your Analysis Services server will likely be something different.

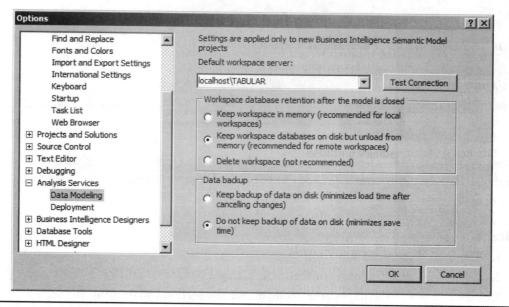

**Figure 13-1**    *The Data Modeling page of the Options dialog box*

7.  We will use the default settings for Workspace database retention after the model is closed and Data backup. Click OK to exit the Options dialog box.

With this, we are ready to begin. Let's create a Tabular model.

# Creating a Tabular Model

We are now ready to create our first Tabular model. As we did with the Multidimensional models, we will create a Tabular version of the Maximum Miniatures sales data first. We will follow that up by creating a Tabular version of the Maximum Miniatures Manufacturing data.

## Data Sources for Our Tabular Models

We could certainly create our Tabular models from the data that is loaded in the MaxMinSalesDM database and the MaxMinManufacturingDM database. In some ways, this might make it easier for us to create neat, clean models for our users to explore. It certainly wouldn't be wrong to create a Tabular model using data that has been copied from transactional systems into a reporting warehouse or relational data mart.

However, for our Learn By Doing exercises, we are going to load our Tabular models directly from the original source systems. That would be the MaxMinAccounting and

OrderProcessingSystem databases in SQL Server and the BatchInfo comma-separated value (CSV) text file. This will give you a better feel for what is required when loading transactional data into a Tabular model.

## Learn By Doing—Creating the Maximum Miniatures Sales Tabular BI Semantic Model

### Features Highlighted

- ▶ Creating a Tabular BI Semantic Model project
- ▶ Importing SQL Server tables into the model
- ▶ Importing a query result set into the model

**Business Need**    The VP of sales for Max Min, Inc., would like to analyze sales information. The VP of sales and several of his managers would like to use the Power View tool in SQL Server 2012. Therefore, a Tabular model should be created for this information.

The VP of sales would like to be able to analyze the following numbers:

- ▶ Dollar value of products sold
- ▶ Number of products sold

These numbers should be viewable by

- ▶ Store
- ▶ Sales promotion
- ▶ Product
- ▶ Day, month, quarter, and year
- ▶ Customer
- ▶ Salesperson

### Steps to Create the Analysis Services Tabular Project

1. Open SQL Server Data Tools.
2. Click the New Project button in the toolbar.

**Figure 13-2** *The New Project dialog box creating a Tabular model project*

3. Make sure Business Intelligence | Analysis Services is selected in the Installed Templates area, and then select Analysis Services Tabular Project from the center area.

4. Enter **MaxMinSalesTabular** for Name and set the Location to the appropriate folder. Make sure Create directory for solution is not checked. The New Project dialog box is shown in Figure 13-2.

5. Click OK to exit the New Project dialog box and create the Tabular model project.

**NOTE**

*A blank Model.bim tab should open in the main design area of SQL Server Data Tools screen. If this does not open, you do not have the Default workspace server option set properly and need to redo the "Learn By Doing— Preparing SQL Server Data Tools for Tabular Model Development" exercise.*

**Steps to Create a Data Source in the Model**

1. Select Model | Import From Data Source from the main menu. The Table Import Wizard dialog box appears with the Connect to a Data Source page visible.

2. Scroll through the list and note all of the different types of data sources that may be used to provide data for a Tabular model. Scroll back to the top and ensure the Microsoft SQL Server entry is selected in the Relational Databases section of the list as shown in Figure 13-3.

3. Click Next. The Connect to a Microsoft SQL Server Database page of the Table Import Wizard appears.

4. In the Server name field, enter the name of the SQL Server relational database server where you restored the OrderProcessingSystem database.

**Figure 13-3**  *The Connect to a Data Source page of the Table Import Wizard*

5. Enter the appropriate credentials for accessing this server.

6. Select OrderProcessingSystem from the Database name drop-down list. The Connect to a Microsoft SQL Server Database page of the wizard should appear as shown in Figure 13-4.

7. Click Next. The Impersonation Information page of the Table Import Wizard appears.

8. Enter a Windows user name and password that can be used to connect to the OrderProcessingSystem database. These credentials will be used when the Analysis Services server imports and refreshes the data in the model. This is shown in Figure 13-5.

**Figure 13-4** *The Connect to a SQL Server Database page of the Table Import Wizard*

**Table Import Wizard** ? X

**Impersonation Information**
Specify the credentials used by the Analysis Services server to connect to the data source. These credentials are used by the server when importing and refreshing data.

⊙ Specific Windows user name and password

Connects to the data source using the credentials of the user named below.

User Name:  MAXMIN\Administrator

Password:  ●●●●●●●●●●

○ Service Account

Connects to the data source using the credentials of the user running the Analysis Service server.

< Back    Next >    Finish    Cancel

**Figure 13-5**   *The Impersonation Information page of the Table Import Wizard*

## NOTE

*If you enter a specific user name on the Impersonation Information page, you must include the domain name along with the user name.*

### Steps to Import Tables into the Model

1. Click Next. The Choose How to Import the Data page of the Table Import Wizard appears as shown in Figure 13-6.

2. Ensure the Select from a list of tables and views to choose the data to import option is selected, and click Next. The Select Tables and Views page of the Table Import Wizard appears.

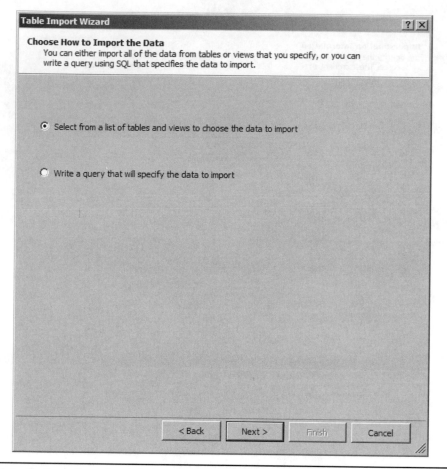

**Figure 13-6**    *The Choose How to Import the Data page of the Table Import Wizard*

3.  Check the following tables:
    ▶  Customers
    ▶  Discounts
    ▶  Products
    ▶  SalesLocations
4.  Change the Friendly Name for Discounts to **Promotions**.
5.  Change the Friendly Name for SalesLocation to **Stores**.

6. Select the Customers row.

7. Click Preview & Filter in the lower-right corner of the dialog box. A new dialog box appears showing the Preview Selected Table page of the Table Import Wizard with the Customers table data.

8. Uncheck the following columns to exclude them from the model:

   ► MiddleInitial

   ► NumberOfCarsOwned

   ► HomeOwnerFlag

   ► Married

   ► NumberOfChildren

   The Preview Selected Table page of the Table Import Wizard appears as shown in Figure 13-7.

9. Click OK to return to the Select Tables and Views page of the Table Import Wizard. Note the Applied filters link, which now appears in the Customers row. This link allows us to modify the column filtering for this table.

**Figure 13-7**   *The Preview Selected Table page of the Table Import Wizard*

**Figure 13-8** *The Select Tables and Views page of the Table Import Wizard*

10. Repeat Steps 19 through 22 to remove the following field from the Products table:

    ▶ TypeCode

    Upon completion of this step, The Select Tables and Views page of the Table Import Wizard will appear similar to Figure 13-8.

11. Click Finish. Data from the selected tables will be imported into the model. Upon completion of the data import, the Importing page of the Table Import Wizard will appear as shown in Figure 13-9.

**Figure 13-9**  *The Importing page of the Table Import Wizard*

12.  Click Close. Each imported table will appear as a tab across the bottom of the model design area as shown in Figure 13-10.

### Steps to Import a Query Result Set into the Model

1.  We still need to add orders and salespeople to our model. Tabular models do not directly accommodate slowly changing dimensions, so we are going to create a query that will combine this information into a single table in the model. Select Model | Existing Connections from the main menu. The Existing Connections dialog box appears.

**Figure 13-10** *The model with imported data*

### NOTE

*When going back to pull additional data from a data source already used in a Tabular model, it is important to launch the Table Import Wizard from the Existing Connections dialog box rather than creating a new connection. Creating multiple connections to the same data source within a single model generates unnecessary overhead and causes problems for future maintenance of the model.*

2. The connection we created for the OrderProcessingSystem should be the only connection in the list. With this connection selected, click Open. This launches the Table Import Wizard starting at the Choose How to Import the Data page.
3. Select Write a query that will specify the data to import.
4. Click Next. The Specify a SQL Query page of the Table Import Wizard appears.
5. Change Friendly Query Name to **Orders**.
6. Enter the following for SQL Statement:

```
SELECT
    o.*,
    ISNULL(s1.Name, s2.Name) AS SalesPersonName
FROM
    Orders o
LEFT OUTER JOIN
    SalesStaffJanuary2009 s1 ON o.SalesPerson = s1.SalesTerritory
                            AND o.OrderDate < '7/1/2010'
LEFT OUTER JOIN
    SalesStaffJuly2010 s2 ON o.SalesPerson = s2.SalesTerritory
                            AND o.OrderDate >= '7/1/2010'
```

7. Click Validate to ensure the query was entered correctly. The dialog box should appear as shown in Figure 13-11.

**Figure 13-11**  *The Specify a SQL Query page of the Table Import Wizard*

8. Click Finish. This causes the query to be executed and the resulting data to be imported into the model. The Orders table is fairly large, so this import will take a bit. Still, you should get over 3 million rows imported into the model in a minute or less.

9. Click Close.

### Steps to Rename Columns in the Model

1. Click the Customers tab to select the Customers table.
2. Right-click the AccountNumber column heading and select Rename Column from the context menu.
3. Replace the column name with **Account Number**.
4. Press ENTER.
5. Repeat Steps 2 through 4 to rename the following columns.

| Old Column Name | New Column Name |
|---|---|
| FirstName | First Name |
| LastName | Last Name |
| ZipCode | Zip Code |

6. Click the Promotions tab to select the Promotions table.
7. Rename the following columns.

| Old Column Name | New Column Name |
|---|---|
| Code | Promotion Code |
| Name | Promotion |

8. Click the Products tab to select the Products table.
9. Rename the following columns.

| Old Column Name | New Column Name |
|---|---|
| Code | Product Code |
| Description | Product |
| TypeDescription | Product Type |
| RetailPrice | Retail Price |

10. Click the Stores tab to select the Stores table.

11. Rename the following columns.

| Old Column Name | New Column Name |
| --- | --- |
| Code | Store Code |
| Name | Store |
| StoreType | Store Type |

12. Click Save All in the toolbar.

# Measures in a Tabular Model

A measure is a quantity that can be aggregated across groups of records. This is the same for Tabular models as it was for the Multidimensional models we created in previous chapters. In our Multidimensional models, a measure could be aggregated across sets defined by dimensions and hierarchies. A property existed for each measure defining an aggregation method for that measure. Precalculated aggregates could then be created using that aggregation method.

In the Tabular model we just created, the StoreSales and UnitSales fields are quantities we wish to analyze. However, in some client tools, we cannot use those fields by themselves as measures. A field, in and of itself, does not have an aggregation method associated with it.

To create a measure in our Tabular model, we define a formula in the Measure Grid that associates a field with an aggregate function. Once this is in place, the Tabular model knows how to deal with that quantity in grouping situations. The Tabular model does not precalculate aggregations. Instead, it uses the measure's aggregate function to quickly calculate aggregations from the data stored in memory.

## Learn By Doing—Adding Measures to the Maximum Miniatures Sales Tabular BI Semantic Model

### Features Highlighted

▶  Adding measures to the model

▶  Hiding fields in the model

**Business Need**   We need to continue our work on the MaxMinSalesTabular model to meet the requirements set by the VP of sales.

### Steps to Add Measures to the Model

1. Click the Orders tab to select the Orders table.
2. Click the StoreSales column title to select the entire column.
3. Click the sigma (Σ) in the toolbar. This creates a measure in the Measure Grid at the bottom of the design area. This is shown in Figure 13-12. (The column has been widened to show the entire column content.)
4. The cell containing the new Sum of StoreSales measure should be selected. In the Properties window, enter **Sales in Dollars** for Measure Name property.
5. Also in the Properties window, select Currency for the Format property.
6. Click the UnitSales column title to select the entire column.
7. Click the sigma in the toolbar to create a measure for this column in the measure grid. The cell containing the new Sum of UnitSales measure should be selected.
8. In the Properties window, enter **Sales in Units** for Measure Name property.
9. Select Whole Number for the Format property.
10. Select True for the Show Thousands Separator property.

**Figure 13-12**  *A column with a sum measure in the Measure Grid*

### Steps to Hide Columns in the Model

1. Click the OrderID column title to select the entire column.

2. Hold down the SHIFT key and click the UnitSales column title. This will select all of the columns from OrderID to UnitSales. The columns contain foreign key IDs that will be used to create relationships within the model, but should not be exposed to the business user. The StoreSales and UnitSales columns will be exposed through the measures you just created, so these fields should be hidden as well.

3. In the Properties window, set the Hidden property to True. The Orders table will appear similar to Figure 13-13.

4. Click Save All in the toolbar.

## Manually Creating a Time Table

When we created the MaxMinSalesDM data mart earlier in this book, we had SQL Server Data Tools create a time table for us. We specified start and end dates, and SQL Server Data Tools populated the time table with records for every day in this date range. We then used that time table to create our Time dimension in the Multidimensional BI Semantic Model.

**Figure 13-13** *The Orders table with hidden columns*

We are going to do something similar for the Tabular version. This time, however, SQL Server Data Tools won't do the work for us. Instead, we are going to create the basis for the Time table ourselves using Microsoft Excel 2010. We will then import that table into our Tabular model.

## Learn By Doing—Adding a Time Table to the Maximum Miniatures Sales Tabular BI Semantic Model

### Features Highlighted

▶ Manually creating a time table in Excel

▶ Importing data from an Excel workbook

**Business Need**   Additional work on the MaxMinSalesTabular model is needed to meet the requirements set by the VP of sales.

### Steps to Create the Time Table in Microsoft Excel 2010

1. Open Microsoft Excel 2010.
2. Type the following headings in the specified cells:

| Cell | Heading |
|------|---------|
| A1 | Date |
| B1 | Year |
| C1 | Quarter |
| D1 | Month |
| E1 | MonthSort |
| F1 | DayOfYear |
| G1 | DayOfQuarter |
| H1 | DayOfMonth |
| I1 | MonthOfYear |
| J1 | MonthOfYearSort |
| K1 | MonthOfQuarter |
| L1 | QuarterOfYear |

**Figure 13-14**  *The Fill button in Excel 2010*

3. In cell A2, type **1/1/2009** and press ENTER.

4. Click cell A2 so it has focus.

5. On the Home tab of the ribbon, click the Fill button as shown in Figure 13-14.

6. Select Series from the drop-down menu. The Series dialog box appears.

7. Select Columns for Series in.

8. Type should default to Date, Date unit should default to Day, and Step value should default to 1. For Stop value, enter **12/31/2011**. The Series dialog box appears as shown in Figure 13-15.

9. Click OK. Date values from 1/1/2009 to 12/31/2011 will be created in column A of our spreadsheet.

**Figure 13-15**  *The Series dialog box*

10. Enter the following formulas in the specified cells:

| Cell | Formula |
| --- | --- |
| B2 | =YEAR(A2) |
| C2 | =YEAR(A2)& "-" & CHOOSE(MONTH(A2),"Q1", "Q1", "Q1", "Q2", "Q2", "Q2", "Q3", "Q3", "Q3", "Q4", "Q4", "Q4") |
| D2 | =TEXT(A2,"MMMM, YYYY") |
| E2 | =TEXT(A2, "YYYYMM") |
| F2 | =A2-DATE(YEAR(A2),1,0) |
| G2 | =A2 - DATE(YEAR(A2), CHOOSE(MONTH(A2), 1, 1, 1, 4, 4, 4, 7, 7, 7, 10, 10, 10), 0) |
| H2 | =DAY(A2) |
| I2 | =TEXT(A2,"MMMM") |
| J2 | =RIGHT("0" & MONTH(A2), 2) |
| K2 | =CHOOSE(MONTH(A2), 1, 2, 3, 1, 2, 3, 1, 2, 3, 1, 2, 3) |
| L2 | =CHOOSE(MONTH(A2),"Q1", "Q1", "Q1", "Q2", "Q2", "Q2", "Q3", "Q3", "Q3", "Q4", "Q4", "Q4") |

11. Select cell B2.
12. While holding down CTRL and SHIFT, press END. All of the cells in the table, except for the first column, are selected.
13. On the Home tab of the ribbon, click the Fill button.
14. Select Down from the drop-down menu. All of the selected cells are populated with the appropriate formulas.
15. Click Save in the upper-left corner of the Excel window. The Save As dialog box appears.
16. Enter **MaxMinSalesTimeTable** for File name.
17. Navigate to the folder where you would like to save this workbook. We will import the workbook into the MaxMinSalesDM Tabular BI Semantic Model from this location.
18. Click Save.
19. Close Excel.

### Steps to Import the Time Table into the Model

1. Return to the copy of SQL Server Data Tools with the MaxMinSalesTabular model.
2. From the main menu, select Model | Import from Data Source. The Connect to a Data Source page of the Table Import Wizard appears.
3. Scroll down to the Text Files section of the list, and select Excel File.
4. Click Next. The Connect to a Microsoft Excel File page of the Table Import Wizard appears.

5. Click Browse. The Open dialog box appears. Browse to the location where you saved the MaxMinSalesTimeTable.xlsx file.

6. Select the MaxMinSalesTimeTable.xlsx file and click Open. You return to the Connect to a Microsoft Excel File page of the Table Import Wizard.

7. Check the Use first row as column headers check box.

8. Click Next. The Impersonation Information page of the Table Import Wizard appears.

9. Enter a Windows user name and password that can be used to obtain rights to the MaxMinSalesTimeTable.xlsx file. These credentials will be used when the Analysis Services server imports and refreshes the data in the model.

10. Click Next. The Select Tables and Views page of the Table Import Wizard appears.

11. Check the check box for the Sheet1$ row.

12. Enter **Time** for Friendly Name.

13. Click Finish. The Importing page of the Table Import Wizard appears.

14. When the import is complete, click Close to exit the Table Import Wizard.

15. Make sure the Time table is selected, and then select Table | Date | Mark As Date Table from the main menu. The Mark as Date Table dialog box appears as shown in Figure 13-16.

16. The Date field should be selected as the unique identifier for the table. This is correct. Click OK to exit the Mark as Date Table dialog box.

**Figure 13-16** *The Mark as Date Table dialog box*

**NOTE**

*If the incorrect field is selected as the unique identifier for the Date Table, you can select Table | Date | Date Table Settings from the main menu to modify this value.*

**17.** Click Save All in the toolbar.

## Relationships and Hierarchies

We now have all of the data we need imported into the MaxMinSalesTabular model. Unfortunately, our model still isn't very useful. We have a collection of tables in our model, but these tables are not related to each other in any way. We can't really query the model in a meaningful way until relationships are created between the tables.

**NOTE**

*If the source database contains foreign key constraints, these are brought into the model as relationships. This was not the case with our source database.*

Our users would also like to drill down to view different periods of time in the same way they can in the Multidimensional model. They want to go from viewing a particular year to seeing the data by quarter, by month, or even by day. To facilitate this, we need to create a hierarchy in our Time table.

### Learn By Doing—Adding Relationships and a Time Hierarchy to the Maximum Miniatures Sales Tabular BI Semantic Model

#### Features Highlighted

▶ Using the diagram view

▶ Creating relationships in our model

▶ Creating a time hierarchy

**Business Need**  A final set of modifications to the MaxMinSalesTabular model is needed to meet the requirements set by the VP of sales.

#### Steps to Add Relationships to the Model

**1.** In the lower-right corner of the design area, click the Diagram button as shown in Figure 13-17. The design area will change from grid view to diagram view.

**Figure 13-17** *Switching to diagram view*

2. The set of controls in the upper-right corner of the diagram view manages our view of the diagram. Click the four-headed arrow button to open the minimap.

3. Try clicking and dragging the black box around the minimap to view different parts of the diagram. You can use this to move around a large diagram and quickly locate specific content, as shown in Figure 13-18.

4. Click the four-headed arrow button again to close the minimap

5. Click the Fit to Screen button to view all of the tables.

6. Arrange the tables into a more compact formation. Because the Orders table links to the other five tables, place the Orders table in the middle of the formation with the other five tables around it. You may also want to resize the Customers, Orders, and Time tables so all of the fields are visible.

7. Click the Fit to Screen button again. If you have done a good job of arranging the tables, you should now see a much larger view with all six tables remaining in view. You can experiment with different arrangements to determine what gives you the best layout to work with.

8. Drag the OrderDate field from the Orders table and drop it on the Date field in the Time table as shown in Figure 13-19. (The OrderDate field is supposed to be grayed out, because it is not visible to the business user in the model. This will not prevent you from completing this step.) If you receive an error dialog box after attempting this step, click OK and try again.

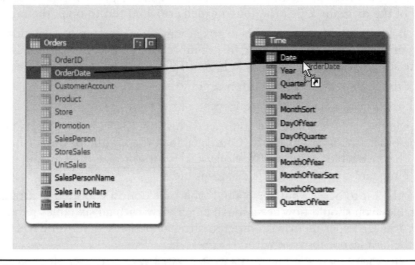

**Figure 13-18** *Using the minimap to explore a model in diagram view*

**Figure 13-19** *Creating a relationship in diagram view*

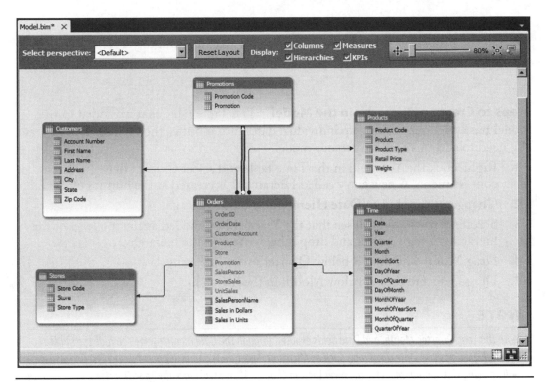

**Figure 13-20**  *Relationships in the diagram view*

9.  Drag the CustomerAccount field from the Orders table and drop it on the Account Number field in the Customers table. This will create a relationship between Orders and Customers.

10. Drag the Product field from the Orders table and drop it on the Product Code field in the Products table.

11. Drag the Store field from the Orders table and drop it on the Store Code field in the Stores table.

12. Drag the Promotion field from the Orders table and drop it on the Promotion Code field in the Promotions table. The diagram should appear similar to Figure 13-20.

**Steps to Set the Sort By Columns**   The values in the Month and MonthOfYear fields will not sort correctly. That was why we created the MonthSort and MonthOfYearSort fields. We need to set the model to use our sort columns for proper sorting.

1.  Click the Month field in the Time table.

2.  In the Properties window, select the Sort By Column property. From the drop-down list for this property, select MonthSort.

3. Click the MonthOfYear field in the Time table.

4. In the Properties window, select the Sort By Column property. From the drop-down list for this property, select MonthOfYearSort.

**Steps to Create a Hierarchy in the Model** The Time table that we added to the model has a hierarchy rolling up individual dates into months, then quarters, then years. We need to add this hierarchy to our model.

1. Right-click the Year field in the Time table and select Create Hierarchy from the context menu. A new entry called Hierarchy1 is created at the bottom of the table.

2. Change Hierarchy1 to **Date Hierarchy** and press ENTER.

3. Scrolling down, you will see that the Year field was added as the top level of the hierarchy. Drag Quarter and drop it below Year in the hierarchy.

4. Drag Month and drop it below Quarter in the hierarchy.

5. Drag Date and drop it below Month in the hierarchy.

**NOTE**

*With the Year, Quarter, Month, and Date fields exposed through the Date hierarchy, we can hide the fields themselves. However, some client tools such as Microsoft Power View do not support hierarchies. Because we will be using this Tabular model with Power View in Chapter 18, we will leave the Year, Quarter, Month, and Date fields exposed to use in that tool.*

6. The MonthSort and MonthOfYearSort fields are used for sorting purposes only and are not needed for any client tool. We will go ahead and hide these fields. Right-click the MonthSort field and select Hide from Client Tools in the context menu. MonthSort is now grayed out in the table.

7. Right-click the MonthOfYearSort field and select Hide from Client Tools in the context menu. When sized to show all fields, the Time table appears as shown in Figure 13-21.

8. Click Save All in the toolbar.

## Validating the Model Using the Analyze in Excel Feature

We now have all of the requested information assembled in our model with the correct relationships and hierarchies. Next we need to validate the model to ensure things are set up correctly. This is done using the Analyze in Excel feature.

**Figure 13-21** *The Time table with the Date hierarchy*

## Learn By Doing—Viewing the Model

### Feature Highlighted

▶  Using the Analyze in Excel feature

### Business Need  We need to validate the data in our MaxMinSalesTabular model.

### Viewing the Model

### NOTE

*Microsoft Excel 2010 must be installed on the computer where you are running SQL Server Data Tools in order for you to use the Analyze in Excel feature demonstrated here. If you do not have Microsoft Excel 2010 installed on this computer, skip this part of the Learn By Doing exercise.*

**Figure 13-22**   *The Analyze in Excel dialog box*

1.  Click the Analyze in Excel button in the toolbar. The Analyze in Excel dialog box appears as shown in Figure 13-22.

2.  You can use the options in this dialog box to view the model as another user or to select a specific perspective. We'll cover model perspectives in Chapter 14. We'll use the default settings for now. Click OK to continue. Excel will open with our model active in a PivotTable designer.

3.  In the PivotTable Field List window, click the Sales in Dollars and Sales in Units measures. Each measure will be selected and placed in the Values area of our pivot table.

4.  Scroll down to find the Product field in the Products table. Drag the Product field and drop it in the Row Labels area.

5.  Scroll down to find the Date Hierarchy in the Time table. Expand the Date Hierarchy, drag the Year level, and drop it in the Column Labels area above the Values entry.

6.  In the pivot table, click the plus sign next to 2010 to drill down to the quarter level of the hierarchy. Your PivotTable should appear similar to Figure 13-23 with a little sizing.

7.  Close Excel. When asked to save changes, click Don't Save.

Congratulations! You have created your first Tabular BI Semantic Model and used the Analyze in Excel feature to show the model can be used for data analysis.

**Figure 13-23** *The PivotTable in Excel*

# A Second Tabular Model

In our previous work in this chapter, we have seen how quickly a basic Tabular model can be created. We have also seen how quickly and efficiently a Tabular model can deal with fairly large amounts of data. Now let's further explore Tabular model creation by replicating the MaxMinManufacturingDM cube in tabular form.

# Data Persistence

In Chapter 6, we discussed the fact that a relational data mart was needed when one of the data sources for your BI Semantic Model (BISM) is an XML or text file. Let's consider the scenario for the Maximum Miniatures Manufacturing data. The data on the performance of the manufacturing equipment is saved to a comma-separated value (CSV) text file.

In the following Learn By Doing exercise, we will import that text file directly into our Tabular BI Semantic Model. This will work just fine in this learning exercise. We will end up with the data from the manufacturing process available for analysis. This works in our situation for one specific reason—we only have a single text file. In a real-world scenario, the manufacturing machinery is going to spit out a text file at the end of every day, or maybe even at the end of each shift.

Each time we load data into a table in our Tabular model, the existing data is dumped from the table and it is loaded from scratch. If we did indeed try to load manufacturing information directly from daily text files, it would mean that we would only have the last day's worth of data to analyze. Each time the current day's text file is loaded, data from any previous days would be lost. Probably not an acceptable scenario for your users.

It will work to continually reload data from a text or XML file, if the content of that file is always comprehensive. Perhaps the text file contains fairly static list look-up values, like state names and abbreviations. Or perhaps the text file always has a complete list of all customers from your CRM system. In these cases, it is acceptable to completely refresh the table in the model each time. No history is lost in the process.

If, however, your text or XML file contains transactional information, odds are you are going to need to persist that data in a data mart. It won't easily persist across multiple table refreshes in the Tabular model. So, in this exercise we will take advantage of the limitations of our sample data to enable you to try loading data from a text file. When you design your real-world solutions, be sure to take into account the real-world data persistence needs required for your data.

## Learn By Doing—Creating the Maximum Miniatures Manufacturing Tabular BI Semantic Model

### Features Highlighted

▶   Importing data from a CSV file

▶   Using the Create Relationship dialog box

**Business Need**   The vice president (VP) of production for Max Min, Inc., wants to analyze the statistics available from the manufacturing automation system. Again, the new ad hoc reporting tool in SQL Server 2012 is to be used to analyze this data. For this reason, a Tabular model should be created.

### Steps to Create the Analysis Services Tabular Project and Import MaxMinAccounting Tables

1. Create an Analysis Services Tabular project called **MaxMinManufacturingTabular**.
2. Select Model | Import From Data Source from the main menu. The Table Import Wizard dialog box appears with the Connect to a Data Source page visible.
3. Ensure the Microsoft SQL Server entry is selected and click Next.

4. Enter the name of the SQL Server relational database server where you restored the MaxMinAccounting database.

5. Enter the appropriate credentials for accessing this server.

6. Select MaxMinAccounting from the Database name drop-down list.

7. Click Next. The Impersonation Information page of the Table Import Wizard appears.

8. Enter a Windows user name and password that can be used to connect to the MaxMinAccounting database. These credentials will be used when the Analysis Services server imports and refreshes the data in the model.

9. Click Next. The Choose How to Import the Data page of the Table Import Wizard appears.

10. Ensure the Select from a list of tables and views to choose the data to import option is selected, and click Next.

11. Click the check box in the upper corner of the grid to select all of the tables in the database.

12. Enter **Machines** for the Friendly Name of the CapitalAssets table.

13. With the CapitalAssets row selected, click the Preview & Filter button. The Preview Selected Table dialog box appears.

14. Click the drop-down arrow for the AssetType column heading. The sorting and filtering menu box appears.

15. Click (Select All) in the Text Filters area to uncheck all of the items.

16. Check the Molding Machine entry in the Text Filters area. Only records with a value of "Molding Machine" in the AssetType column will be imported for this table. The sorting and filtering menu box appears as in Figure 13-24.

**Figure 13-24** *The sorting and filtering menu box*

17. Click OK to exit the sorting and filtering menu box. The filtered data is displayed in the grid.

18. Click the check box in the upper-left corner of the grid to uncheck all columns.

19. Check the following columns:

    ▶ AssetCode

    ▶ AssetClass

    ▶ AssetName

    ▶ LocationCode

    ▶ RawMaterial

20. Click OK to exit the Preview Selected Table dialog box.

21. Select the Locations row and click the Preview & Filter button.

22. Click the drop-down arrow for the LocationType column heading. The sorting and filtering menu box appears.

23. Click (Select All) in the Text Filters area to uncheck all of the items.

24. Check the Plant Site entry in the Text Filters area. Only records with a value of "Plant Site" in the LocationType column will be imported for this table.

25. Click OK to exit the sorting and filtering menu box. The filtered data is displayed in the grid.

26. Click the check box in the upper-left corner of the grid to uncheck all columns.

27. Check the following columns:

    ▶ LocationCode

    ▶ LocationName

    ▶ CountryCode

28. Click OK to exit the Preview Selected Table dialog box.

29. Select the Products row and click the Preview & Filter button.

30. Click the check box in the upper-left corner of the grid to uncheck all columns.

31. Check the following columns:

    ▶ ProductCode

    ▶ ProductName

    ▶ ProductSubtypeCode

32. Click OK to exit the Preview Selected Table dialog box.
33. Click Finish. The Importing page will be displayed, and the table data will be imported into the model.
34. When the import is complete, click Close.

## Steps to Import the BatchInfo.csv File

1. Select Model | Import from Data Source from the main menu. The Connect to a Data Source page of the Table Import Wizard appears.
2. Scroll down in the list and select Text File.
3. Click Next. The Connect to Flat File page of the Table Import Wizard appears.
4. Enter **BatchInfo.CSV** for Friendly connection name.
5. Click Browse. The Open dialog box appears.
6. In the lower-right corner, change the file type to Comma Separated File (*.csv).
7. Browse to and select the BatchInfo.CSV file, and then click Open.
8. Make sure the "Use first row as column headers" check box is checked.
9. Click Next. The Impersonation Information page of the Table Import Wizard appears.
10. Enter a Windows user name and password that can be used to access this text file. These credentials will be used when the Analysis Services server imports and refreshes the data in the model.
11. Click Finish. The Importing page will be displayed, and the data from the text file will be imported into the model.
12. When the import is complete, click Close. The data is imported into a table called BatchInfo.
13. Right-click the BatchInfo tab and select Rename from the context menu.
14. Change the name to **Manufacturing Info** and press ENTER.

**Steps to Add Relationships to the Model**   When we created the MaxMinSalesTabular BI Semantic Model, we created table relationships on the diagram view using drag-and-drop. This time around, we are going to use the Manage Relationships dialog box. Both methods produce exactly the same result, so use whichever works best for you.

1. Select Table | Manage Relationships from the main menu. The Manage Relationships dialog box appears.
2. Click Create. The Create Relationship dialog box appears.

**Figure 13-25**  *The Create Relationship dialog box*

3.  Select Manufacturing Info from the table drop-down list.
4.  Select MachineNumber from the Column drop-down list.
5.  Select Machines from the Related Lookup Table.
6.  Select AssetCode from Related Lookup Column. The Create Relationship dialog box appears as shown in Figure 13-25.
7.  Click Create to create the relationship and exit the Create Relationship dialog.
8.  Use the same method to add these relationships:

| Table | Column | Related Lookup Table | Related Lookup Column |
|---|---|---|---|
| Machines | LocationCode | Locations | LocationCode |
| Locations | CountryCode | Countries | CountryCode |
| Manufacturing Info | ProductCode | Products | ProductCode |
| Products | ProductSubtypeCode | ProductSubtypes | ProductSubtypeCode |
| ProductSubtypes | ProductTypeCode | ProductTypes | ProductTypeCode |

The Manage Relationships dialog box appears as shown in Figure 13-26.

**Figure 13-26** *The Manage Relationships dialog box*

9. Click Close to exit the Manage Relationships dialog box.
10. Click the tab for the Machines table. Notice two new relationship column icons have shown up in the column headings as indicated in Figure 13-27. The icon next to the AssetCode heading indicates this column is being used as a lookup column. In other words, it is being used as the primary key in the relationship. The icon next to the LocationCode heading indicates this column is being used as a foreign key column in a relationship.
11. Click Save All in the toolbar.

**Figure 13-27** *The relationship column icons*

## Calculated Columns

When we created our Multidimensional BI Semantic Models, we discovered that not all of the quantities our business users want to analyze are available directly from the source data. In some cases, we need to combine items in arithmetic expressions to come up with the answers our users are looking for. We need to create calculations.

In a Tabular BI Semantic Model, this is done by adding calculated columns to our tables. This is done in a manner similar to the way calculated columns are added in Excel. A formula is added in an empty cell. As soon as we press ENTER, the formula is evaluated and the resulting value is displayed. What is different about the Tabular model environment is the formula is automatically spread to all of the rest of the rows in the table. (Even if there are millions of rows in that table!)

In the Learn By Doing exercises that follow, we will use calculated columns for three different purposes. In the first exercise, we will calculate new quantities and use those quantities to create measures. This is probably the first purpose most of us would think of when it comes to calculated columns, but it is by no means their only use.

We will also create calculated columns to help us define elements for our time-based analysis in the model. We are not creating our own custom Time table for this model, so we need to use calculated columns to determine month, quarter, etc. In the final Learn By Doing exercise in the chapter, we will use calculated columns to assist with the creation of two hierarchies within the model.

So, let's make a calculated effort to learn how to work with calculated columns.

## Learn By Doing—Using Calculated Columns

### Feature Highlighted

▶ Creating calculated columns in the model

**Business Need**   Additional work on the MaxMinManufacturingTabular model is needed to meet the requirements set by the VP of production.

### Steps to Add Calculated Columns to the Manufacturing Info Table

1. Select the Manufacturing Info tab and scroll to the right until you see the "Add Column" column heading.
2. Click the cell below the Add Column heading.
3. Type the following formula:

```
=[NumberProduced] - [NumberRejected]
```

As soon as you type the equal sign, the character shows up in the formula area with the text cursor there ready for more.

**TIP**

*Use the chevron button to the right of the formula entry area to expand the formula entry area when entering long formulas.*

4. Press ENTER. The formula you entered is evaluated for all of the rows in the table. The column heading is changed to CalculatedColumn1 and a new "Add Column" column is added to the table.

5. In the Properties window, enter **NumberAccepted** for Column Name.

6. Repeat this process to add the following calculated columns to the Manufacturing Info table with the specified column names.

| Column Name | Formula |
|---|---|
| ElapsedTime | =HOUR([TimeStopped] - [TimeStarted]) * 60 + MINUTE([TimeStopped] - [TimeStarted]) |
| Date of Manufacture | =DATEVALUE(FORMAT([TimeStarted], "MM/DD/YYYY")) |
| Year of Manufacture | =YEAR([Date of Manufacture]) |
| Quarter of Manufacture | =YEAR([Date of Manufacture]) & "-" & SWITCH(MONTH([Date of Manufacture]), 1, "Q1", 2, "Q1", 3, "Q1", 4, "Q2", 5, "Q2", 6, "Q2", 7, "Q3", 8, "Q3", 9, "Q3", 10, "Q4", 11, "Q4", 12, "Q4") |
| Month of Manufacture | =YEAR([Date of Manufacture]) & "-" & RIGHT("0"&MONTH([Date of Manufacture]),2) |

**NOTE**

*The formula for the Date of Manufacture calculated column uses the FORMAT() function to convert the date/time value in the TimeStarted field to text without including the time portion. It then uses the DATEVALUE() function to convert that text back to a date/time value. This causes all of the date/time values to have midnight as their time portion, essentially eliminating time from consideration.*

### Steps to Add Measures and Hide Columns

1. Add measures to the following columns with the specified measure names. Each measure should use the SUM() aggregation. (If you need help with this, see the "Steps to Add Measures to the Model" section earlier in this chapter.)

| Column Name | Measure Name |
|---|---|
| NumberProduced | Total Products |
| NumberRejected | Rejected Products |
| NumberAccepted | Accepted Products |
| ElapsedTime | Elapsed Time For Manufacture |

2. Hide the following columns in the Manufacturing Info table. (If you need help with this, see the "Steps to Hide Columns in the Model" section earlier in this chapter.)

| Column Name |
| --- |
| MachineNumber |
| ProductCode |
| TimeStarted |
| TimeStopped |

The Manufacturing Info table will appear as shown in Figure 13-28 and Figure 13-29.

3. Click Save All in the toolbar.

**Figure 13-28**   *The left seven columns of the Manufacturing Info table*

**Figure 13-29** *The right six columns of the Manufacturing Info table*

# Hierarchies Spanning Multiple Tables

When we created the Date Hierarchy, all of the fields that made up the levels of our hierarchy were in the same table. This makes hierarchy creation very easy. It turns out, it is also a requirement in the Tabular model.

This presents a problem for us in the MaxMinManufacturingTabular model. We wish to duplicate the Plant Hierarchy and Product Hierarchy that we created in the MaxMinManufacturingDM Multidimensional model. The fields needed for those hierarchies happen to be spread across multiple tables. Fortunately, we can consolidate that information into a single table using calculated columns. There are two different functions we can use for this purpose.

## The LOOKUPVALUE Function

The LOOKUPVALUE()function allows us to look up a value in one table, the lookup table, and pull it into another table. In its simplest form, the LOOKUPVALUE() function has three parameters: ResultColumnName, SearchColumnName, and SearchValue. The ResultColumnName is the name of the field in the lookup table where we find the value we wish to return. The SearchColumnName is the name of the field in the lookup table where we will look for a matching value—in other words, the key field of the lookup table. The SearchValue is the value we are looking for in the lookup table.

Here is an example of this form of the LOOKUPVALUE() function:

```
=LOOKUPVALUE(States[StateName], [StateKey], "MN")
```

In this example, we want to return a value from the StateName field of the States table. We are looking for a value of "MN" in the StateKey field of the States table. The value we are looking for can come from a field in the table that is hosting the LOOKUPVALUE() function. For example, we can look for a match to the content of the StateAbbrv field:

```
=LOOKUPVALUE(States[StateName], [StateKey], [StateAbbrv])
```

The LOOKUPVALUE() function can also handle situations where our lookup table has several fields that make up its key. We can specify multiple SearchColumnName and SearchValue pairs as function parameters. For example, we can look up the ItemQuantity from an invoice line item where that line item is uniquely identified by the invoice number and the line number as follows:

```
=LOOKUPVALUE(LineItem[ItemQuantity], [InvoiceNumber], "MM12943",
                                      [LineNumber], 4)
```

## The RELATED Function

The RELATED() function provides us with another way to do a similar type of lookup. The difference is the RELATED() function leverages the relationships already defined in the model (thus, the name). With the LOOKUPVALUE() function, we had to specify the fields that were being matched between the two tables. The RELATED() function, by contrast, uses the relationship defined in the model to determine this link.

The RELATED() function takes a single parameter. That parameter is a fully qualified reference to a field in another table. "Fully qualified" means we need to specify both the name of the table and the name of the field. A relationship must exist in the model between the table that contains the calculated column using the RELATED() function and the table referred to by the fully qualified parameter.

For example, in our model we have a relationship between the Products table and the ProductSubtypes table. The relationship in the model specifies that the ProductSubtypeCode field in the Products table is a foreign key reference to the ProductSubtypeCode field in the ProductSubtypes table. Because of this relationship, we can create the following calculated column in the Products table:

```
=RELATED(ProductSubtypes[ProductSubtypeName])
```

This returns the content of the ProductSubtypeName field in the ProductSubtypes table that is related to the given row in the Product table.

Let's try out these functions to create the hierarchies in the MaxMinManufacturingTabular model.

## Learn By Doing—Using the LOOKUPVALUE() and RELATED() Functions

### Features Highlighted

▶ Using the LOOKUPVALUE() function

▶ Using the RELATED() function

**Business Need**   A final set of modifications to the MaxMinManufacturingTabular model is needed to meet the requirements set by the VP of production.

### NOTE

*Because of the relationships that exist in the model, it would be proper to use the RELATED() function for all of the calculated columns in this Learn By Doing exercise. We are using the LOOKUPVALUE() function here to allow you to gain some familiarity with both of these functions.*

### Steps to Create Calculated Columns Using the LOOKUPVALUE() Function

1. Select the Locations table.
2. Add the following calculated column:

| Column Name | Formula |
|---|---|
| CountryName | =LOOKUPVALUE(Countries[CountryName], [CountryCode], [CountryCode]) |

3. Select the Machines table.
4. Add the following calculated columns:

| Column Name | Formula |
|---|---|
| LocationName | =LOOKUPVALUE(Locations[LocationName], [LocationCode], [LocationCode]) |
| CountryName | =LOOKUPVALUE(Locations[CountryName], [LocationCode], [LocationCode]) |

### Steps to Create Calculated Columns Using the RELATED() Function

1. Select the ProductSubtypes table.
2. Add the following calculated column:

| Column Name | Formula |
|---|---|
| ProductTypeName | =RELATED(ProductTypes[ProductTypeName]) |

3. Select the Products table.
4. Add the following calculated columns:

| Column Name | Formula |
|---|---|
| ProductSubtypeName | =RELATED(ProductSubtypes[ProductSubtypeName]) |
| ProductTypeName | =RELATED(ProductSubtypes[ProductTypeName]) |

### Steps to Create Hierarchies in the Model

1. Click the Diagram button in the lower-right corner of the design area.
2. Rearrange the tables in the diagram, if you wish.
3. Locate the Machines table.
4. Right-click the RawMaterial field and select Create Hierarchy from the context menu.
5. Change Hierarchy1 to **Material Hierarchy** and press ENTER.
6. Scrolling down, you will see that the RawMaterial field was added as the top level of the hierarchy. Right-click this entry and select Rename from the context menu.
7. Type **Material** and press ENTER.
8. Drag AssetClass and drop it below Material (RawMaterial) in the hierarchy.
9. Rename AssetClass to **Machine Type** in the hierarchy.
10. Drag AssetName and drop it below Machine Type (AssetClass) in the hierarchy.
11. Rename AssetName to **Machine**.
12. Right-click CountryName and select Create Hierarchy from the context menu.
13. Change Hierarchy1 to **Plant Hierarchy** and press ENTER.
14. Rename CountryName to **Country** in the hierarchy.
15. Drag LocationName and drop it below Country (CountryName) in the hierarchy.
16. Rename LocationName to **Plant** in the hierarchy.
17. Drag AssetName and drop it below Plant (LocationName) in the hierarchy.
18. Rename AssetName to **Machine**.
19. Select AssetCode.

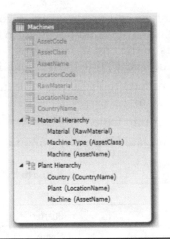

**Figure 13-30**  *The Machines table with hierarchies*

20.  Hold down the SHIFT key and click CountryName. The seven fields in the table should be selected.

21.  Right-click these fields and select Hide from Client Tools in the context menu. The Machines table should appear as shown in Figure 13-30.

22.  Because the location and country information is now exposed through the Plant Hierarchy, we do not need to expose the Locations and Countries tables to the end user. Right-click the heading of the Locations table and select Hide from Client Tools from the context menu. The entire table will be grayed out.

23.  Right-click the heading of the Countries table and select Hide from Client Tools from the context menu.

24.  Locate the Products table.

25.  Create a hierarchy named **Product Hierarchy** using the following fields:

| Field Name | Name in Hierarchy |
|---|---|
| ProductTypeName | Product Type |
| ProductSubtypeName | Product Subtype |
| ProductName | Product |

26.  Hide the following fields in the Products table:
ProductCode
ProductName
ProductSubtypeCode
ProductSubtypeName
ProductTypeName

27. Because the product subtype and product type information is now exposed through the Product Hierarchy, we do not need to expose the ProductSubtypes and ProductTypes tables to the end user. Right-click the heading of the ProductSubtypes table and select Hide from Client Tools from the context menu.

28. Right-click the heading of the ProductTypes table and select Hide from Client Tools from the context menu.

29. Locate the Manufacturing Info table.

30. Create a hierarchy named **Date Hierarchy** using the following fields:

| Field Name | Name in Hierarchy |
| --- | --- |
| Year of Manufacture | Year |
| Quarter of Manufacture | Quarter |
| Month of Manufacture | Month |
| Date of Manufacture | Date |

31. Hide the following fields in the Products table:
    Date of Manufacture
    Year of Manufacture
    Quarter of Manufacture
    Month of Manufacture

    Your model should appear similar to Figure 13-31.

32. Click Save All in the toolbar.

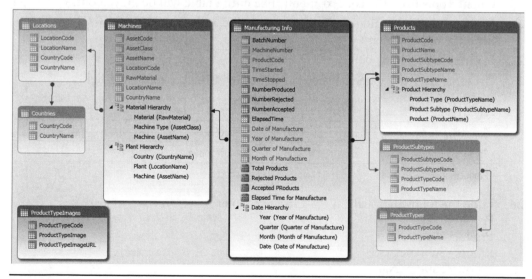

**Figure 13-31** *The completed MaxMinManufacturingTabular model*

## Putting More on the Table

We have created two Tabular models. We have seen how quickly these models can be created and how effectively they can deal with large sets of data. In the next chapter we will explore a few more features in the Tabular model and explore more of the DAX query language.

The table has been set. Let's dig in!

# Chapter 14

# A Fancy Table—Tabular BI Semantic Model Advanced Features

## In This Chapter

*I don't set a fancy table, but the kitchen's awful homey.*
—Anthony Perkins as Norman Bates in *Psycho*

In Chapter 13, we created two Tabular BI Semantic Models. We saw that Tabular models are quick and easy to create. Even so, they provide a powerful analysis environment.

In this chapter, we add to our Tabular models as we look at some of the more advanced features of this architecture. Some of these features, such as perspectives, KPIs, partitions, and role-based security, are analogous to features in the multidimensional models. One feature, image support, is unique to the Tabular world.

Next, we look at the DAX language. In Chapter 13, we used DAX functions to define measures and to create the members of our time hierarchy in the MaxMinManufacturingTabular model. In this chapter, we examine DAX functions that assist us with more sophisticated time analytics.

Finally, we deploy our model to a "production" environment. Even though the workspace database provides a fully functioning Tabular model, this is not a database we want to expose to our end users. Instead, we will deploy the models to a secure production environment for general use.

Without further ado, let's take our simple table and make it fancy!

# Enhancing Our Tabular Model

One of the main reasons we utilize BI Semantic Models is to capture an organization's business logic in a central location. This allows for business rules to be used in a consistent manner across reporting and analysis tasks. Once this business logic is collected in the model, we need to make it quick and easy to use. In the next few sections of this chapter, we look at ways to do just that.

## Table and Column Properties

Our BI Semantic Models, whether they are Tabular models or Multidimensional models, are only useful if they are utilized by our business decision makers. One of the keys to having this happen is to make our models as well organized, as self-documenting, and as efficient as possible. The Tabular model provides a number of table-level and column-level properties we can utilize to work toward these goals.

Those properties are

▶ **Table Description** The Table Description property provides an explanation of the content of the table for the end user. In the Microsoft Tabular model query tools, the Table Description appears as a ToolTip when the user hovers over the name of the table.

▶ **Description**    The Description property of a column provides an explanation of the content of the column. The property does not apply to hierarchy members based on the column. In the Microsoft Tabular model query tools, the Column Description appears as a ToolTip when the user hovers over the name of the column.

▶ **Row Identifier**    The Row Identifier property signifies the column that serves as the primary key for that table. The values in this column must be unique. Only one column in a table can be set as the Row Identifier.

▶ **Default Label**    The Default Label property identifies a column to serve as the default value for each row in the table. The value in this column is then used by client tools as a label or heading for the row. Only one column in a table can be set as the Default Label.

▶ **Default Image**    The Default Image property identifies an image column to serve as the default image for each row in the table. The image is then used by client tools as a representation for the row. Only one column in a table can be set as the Default Image.

▶ **Default Field Set/Table Detail Position**    The Default Field Set/Table Detail Position properties determine which columns should be included as the default detail columns for this table. In a client tool, when the table is selected, the default columns are placed in the visualization being created. Default Field Set is a property of the table. Table Detail Position is a property of a column. Each property provides access to the same Default Field Set dialog box used to select which fields are default fields and what order they should appear in the client tool.

▶ **Data Format/Format**    The Data Format/Format property applies formatting to a set of values. A column has a Data Format property. A measure has a Format property.

## Adding Images to a Tabular Model

One capability not present in the Multidimensional model is the ability to have images in the model. There are a number of situations where it can be beneficial to have images associated with the rows in a table. You could have a picture of each employee in a personnel table, an illustration of each item in a product table, or a map of each sales territory in the sales region table.

Client tools that support images can then display these pictures, illustrations, or maps along with data being analyzed. As noted in the prior section, you can use the Default Image property to identify an image column. The client tool will then display that image with each row.

## Images Stored in a Table

Images can be utilized in two different ways. The first method utilizes images stored as binary large objects (BLOBs) in the database table. Images stored in this manner are imported right into the model along with the rest of the data in the table.

Images pulled into the model in this way may take up large amounts of memory. They may negatively affect the performance and the capacity of the model. Having the images in the model does, however, ensure those images are always available with the model data.

After the table containing the images is imported into the model, the BLOB field appears as a binary data field. We must change the data type of the field to Image. We can also identify the field as a Default Image, if desired.

## Images Referenced as URLs

Images can also be accessed through URLs stored in a field. The images, of course, must be available on a web server for this architecture to be used. That web server must be accessible to any client tool that will explore the model.

This architecture makes it very easy to update an image. The new image file simply replaces the old one on the web server. In addition, the same image can be referenced from multiple tables in multiple models. This makes storage much more efficient.

To use URLs to reference images, we create a string field in the source table. This string field contains the URL for each image. Each row can contain a different URL so each row points to a unique image. Alternatively, several rows can contain the same URL so groups of rows point to the same image.

The URL field is imported into the model along with the other fields. Once the table is imported, we must change the data type of the URL field to Image URL. We can also identify the field as a Default Image, if desired.

## Learn By Doing—Enhancing the Maximum Miniatures Manufacturing Tabular BI Semantic Model

### Features Highlighted

► Setting model properties to improve user friendliness

► Adding images to a model

**Business Need**   The VP of production for Max Min, Inc., would like to have an image in the model to identify each product type. In addition, we need to provide a well-organized and self-documenting reporting model.

**Steps to Set Table and Column Properties**

1. Open SQL Server Data Tools.
2. Open the MaxMinManufacturingTabular model.
3. Change to the grid view of the model if it opens in diagram view.
4. Click the Machines table tab.
5. In the Properties window, enter **This table contains the Material/MachineType hierarchy and the Plant/Country hierarchy** for Table Description.
6. Click the Default Field Set property. An ellipsis (…) button appears.
7. Click the ellipsis button. The Default Field Set dialog box appears.
8. Select the AssetClass field in the Fields in the table area and click Add.
9. Select the AssetName field in the Fields in the table area and click Add. The Default Field Set dialog box appears as shown in Figure 14-1.
10. Click OK to exit the Default Field Set dialog box.

**Figure 14-1**   *The Default Field Set dialog box*

11. Right-click the AssetCode column heading and select Freeze Columns. The AssetCode column becomes the leftmost column in the grid and will stay on the screen when scrolling the grid to the right. (This does not help the user of the model, but it can help us by keeping the unique identifier for each row in view as we work with the data in the table.)

12. With the AssetCode column still selected, change the following property settings in the Properties window:

| Property | Value |
|---|---|
| Description | The unique identifier for each machine |
| Row Identifier | True |

13. Click the AssetName column heading.

14. In the Properties window, change the following property settings:

| Property | Value |
|---|---|
| Description | The make and model of the manufacturing machine |

15. Click the AssetClass column heading.

16. In the Properties window, change the following property settings:

| Property | Value |
|---|---|
| Description | The machine type |

17. Click the Manufacturing Info table tab.

18. Click the NumberProduced column heading.

19. In the Properties window, change the Data Format property to Whole Number.

20. Repeat Steps 18 and 19 for the NumberRejected and Number Accepted columns.

21. Click the cell containing the Total Products measure in the Measures Grid.

22. In the Properties window, change the Format property to Whole Number.

23. Repeat Steps 21 and 22 for the Rejected Products, Accepted Products, and Elapsed Time For Manufacture measures.

### Steps to Add Images to the Model

1. Switch to the diagram view.
2. Move the ProductTypeImages table so it is next to the ProductTypes table.
3. Drag the ProductTypeCode field from the ProductTypeImages table and drop it on the ProductTypeCode field in the ProductTypes table. This will create a relationship between these two tables.
4. Switch to the grid view.
5. Select the ProductTypeImages table and scroll right so Add Column is visible.
6. Add the following calculated column:

| Column Name | Formula |
| --- | --- |
| ProductTypeName | =RELATED(ProductTypes[ProductTypeName]) |

7. Click Save All.

# Parent/Child Relationships

In Chapter 9, we talked about parent/child relationships and their support in the Multidimensional BI Semantic Model. If you need to review the definition of a parent/child relationship, see the "Types of Dimensions" section of Chapter 9. We'll use the same structure that was illustrated in Chapter 9 for our discussion of parent/child relationships here. That illustration is repeated here in Figure 14-2.

Once the table containing the records shown in Figure 14-2 is imported into the model, we use three DAX functions to turn the parent/child relationship into a hierarchy.

**Employees**

| EmpNum | Name | Position | Supervisor |
| --- | --- | --- | --- |
| 129 | Sandra | Team Leader | 239 |
| 235 | Eva | Developer | 129 |
| 239 | Peter | Development Manager | 303 |
| 293 | Maya | CEO | |
| 303 | Frank | IT Director | 470 |
| 470 | Tia | CFO | 293 |
| 487 | Juan | System Administrator | 303 |

**Figure 14-2**   *An employee table with a self-referential field*

### Path(PrimaryKeyField, ParentForeignKeyField)

The Path function uses the primary key field and the parent foreign key field to traverse up the parent/child relationship. As it does, it builds a list of each of the primary key values it encounters along the way. The primary key values are delimited by the "|" character.

In the structure shown in Figure 14-2, we could use the following Path function:

```
= PATH([EmpNum], [Supervisor])
```

In the record for Eva, this function returns the following path:

```
293|470|303|239|129
```

This path results because Eva's supervisor is employee number 129—Sandra. Sandra's supervisor is employee number 239—Peter. Peter's supervisor is employee number 303—Frank. Frank's supervisor is employee number 470—Tia. Tia's supervisor is employee number 293—Maya. Maya is the CEO, so her supervisor field is empty.

### PathItem(PathField, PathLevel)

The PathItem function extracts one of the primary key values from the delimited list created by the Path function. To use the PathItem function, a calculated field must first be created using the Path function. The "path field" can then be referenced as the first parameter (PathField) of the PathItem function.

The value extracted from the list is determined by the second parameter (PathLevel) of the PathItem function. A PathLevel value of 1 extracts the leftmost primary key value in the path. A PathLevel of 2 extracts the primary key value that is second from the left, and so on.

If we use the Path function to create a calculated field called SupervisorPath for our structure in Figure 14-2, we can then use the following PathItem function:

```
=PATHITEM ([SupervisorPath], 3)
```

In the record for Eva, this function returns the following foreign key value:

```
303
```

This is the third item from the left in the list created by the Path function.

### LookUpValue(ReturnValueField, PrimaryKeyField, PrimaryKeyValue)

In most cases, finding the primary key value at a certain level in the parent/child relationship is not enough. In our example here, we probably want to know the name of the supervisor or their position. We do this with the LookUpValue function we encountered in Chapter 13.

Again, using the sample from Figure 14-2, we use the following expression to get the name of the person at the third level in the relationship:

```
= LOOKUPVALUE ([Name], [EmpNum], PATHITEM ([SupervisorPath], 3))
```

In the record for Eva, this function returns:

```
Frank
```

because Frank is the name corresponding to the employee number found at the third level of the path.

## Creating a Parent/Child Hierarchy

Using the LookUpValue function and the PathItem function together as shown in the preceding example, we create a calculated column for each possible level of the parent/child relationship. This does require that we know the maximum number of levels that are possible in the parent/child relationship. The resulting table in the model is shown in Figure 14-3.

Many of the calculated columns will have blank values for some records. This is expected based on that record's level in the parent/child relationship. A record will have values for the calculated column showing its level in the hierarchy and for all levels above that level. It will be blank for all levels in the hierarchy below its level.

**Figure 14-3**  *A parent/child relationship table in a Tabular model*

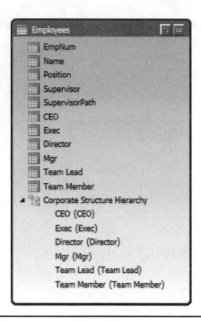

**Figure 14-4** *The hierarchy created from the parent/child relationship*

Finally, we use these calculated columns to create a hierarchy within our model. This is shown in Figure 14-4. This hierarchy allows aggregations to provide the appropriate values at any desired level.

## Multiple Relationships Between the Same Tables

In our Multidimensional model, we were able to have more than one relationship between a measure group and a given dimension. We called these role-playing dimensions. The most common occurrence of this situation is with the time dimension. Our measure group may contain an order date and a delivery date, both linked to the time dimension.

We can implement the same situation in our Tabular model, but in a little different manner. In the Tabular model, we can define these multiple relationships, but only one of the relationships can be active. This is shown in Figure 14-5.

This figure shows relationships between both the OrderDate and the DeliveryDate in the Orders table and the Time table. The active relationship is shown as a solid line. The inactive relationship is shown as a dashed line. The active relationship is used with any Related functions defined between the two tables. Therefore, the content of a calculated column using a Related function can change depending on which relationship is active.

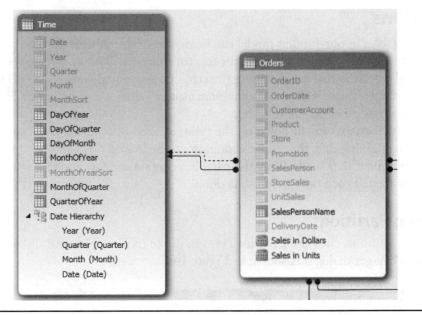

**Figure 14-5**  *Multiple relationships between two tables*

You can modify the active status of a relationship using the Active property in the Properties window or in the Edit Relationship dialog box. This is shown in Figure 14-6. You must set the currently active relationship as inactive before you can set another relationship as active.

**Figure 14-6**  *Modifying the active status of a relationship*

## Partitions

The larger tables in our Tabular model can be divided into multiple partitions. This allows us to better manage the refresh process for this table. The partitions should be constructed so values that are changing (inserts, updates, and deletes) will end up in a single partition. Values that are not changing, usually values from further back in time, should end up in other partitions.

In this manner, we can cut down on the time required to refresh a large table. The partitions containing data that is not changing can be loaded once and not touched during subsequent data loads. Only the partition containing new and changing data needs to be loaded each time a refresh is done.

### Defining Partitions

To define partitions, click the Partitions button in the toolbar. This will display the Partition Manager dialog box shown in Figure 14-7.

**Figure 14-7**    *The Partition Manager dialog box*

Select the table you wish to partition from the Table drop-down list. Use the New button or the Copy button to define new partitions. Give each partition a descriptive name. You can populate each partition from a different relational database table.

Alternatively, you can use WHERE clauses to divide the content of a single relational database table amongst several partitions. This is done by using the Query Editor button to change to the Query Editor and adding a WHERE clause to each query. Using either method, multiple tables or WHERE clauses, all of the partitions in a single table must utilize the same connection.

## Processing Partitions

To load data for a selected partition rather than an entire table, use the Process Partitions option on the toolbar as shown in Figure 14-8. This will display the Process Partitions dialog box. This is shown in Figure 14-9.

The Process Partitions dialog box enables you to choose one or more partitions to be refreshed. Once you click OK, the selected partitions are refreshed. The refresh status and the number of rows loaded are shown in the Data Refresh dialog box as shown in Figure 14-10.

## Perspectives

Not all of your users need to utilize all of the information in your model. To make the model more user friendly for those users, it would be helpful to limit their view of the model. This is done by creating one or more perspectives within the model.

**Figure 14-8**   *The Process Partitions option*

**Figure 14-9** *The Process Partitions dialog box*

A perspective limits the tables, fields, and measures that can be seen by the user. These limits correspond to the needs of a particular set of business users. This allows a decision maker to focus on what they care about to make efficient use of the model.

**Figure 14-10**  *The Data Refresh dialog box*

## Creating Perspectives

Perspectives are created by clicking the Perspectives button in the toolbar. This will display the Perspectives dialog box. This is shown in Figure 14-11. Clicking the New Perspective button creates a column for a new perspective. Rename the new perspective, and then select items that should be visible through this perspective.

**Figure 14-11** *The Perspectives dialog box*

# DAX Functions

Entire books could be written, and have been written, about the functions in the DAX language. We encountered some of those functions in Chapter 13 and earlier in this chapter. In this section, we look at some additional DAX functions useful for creating analytics in measures and calculated columns.

## The Context for Measures and Calculated Columns

As we look at measures and calculated columns, it is important to keep in mind the context in which these calculations occur. A solid understanding of this is needed in order to create the appropriate expression for the calculation desired. This context changes depending on where and how you are creating the expression.

## The Default Context for Calculated Columns

For calculated columns, the default context of the calculation is the row itself. In Chapter 13, we created a calculated column to give us the number of accepted products using the following expression:

```
[NumberProduced] - [NumberRejected]
```

This expression is evaluated for each row in the table. As this is done, the values for NumberProduced and NumberRejected from each row are used to create a result for that row. We saw this in the previous chapter in Figure 13-29.

## The Default Context for Measures

Measures are not created as a table row. Instead, they are created below the table in the Measure Grid. This difference in location provides a reminder of the measure's context.

The default context for a measure is the entire table. For this reason, we must utilize aggregate functions when creating measures. We need to give the model a way to take values from multiple rows in the table and calculate a single result. We saw this in the previous chapter in Figure 13-12.

## Aggregate Functions in Calculated Columns

While aggregate functions are required in measures, they can also be used in calculated columns. The default context for an aggregate function is the entire table. This is shown in Figure 14-12. When evaluating the expression for the row indicated by the large white arrow, the SUM() function adds together the values in the NumberProduced column from all of the rows in the table to get the total of 725.

**Manufacturing Info**  =Sum([NumberProduced])

| Date Of Manufacture | Product Code | Machine Number | Number Produced | Calculated Column1 |
|---|---|---|---|---|
| 1/1/2009 | 11 | 1 | 100 | 725 |
| 1/1/2009 | 11 | 2 | 50 | 725 |
| 1/1/2009 | 12 | 1 | 200 | 725 |
| 1/2/2009 | 11 | 1 | 150 | 725 |
| 1/2/2009 | 12 | 1 | 125 | 725 |
| 1/3/2009 | 11 | 1 | 75 | 725 |
| 1/3/2009 | 11 | 2 | 25 | 725 |

**Figure 14-12**  *An aggregate function in a calculated column*

**Manufacturing Info**

=[NumberProduced] / Sum([NumberProduced])

100/ 725 = .1379

| Date Of Manufacture | Product Code | Machine Number | Number Produced | Calculated Column1 |
|---|---|---|---|---|
| 1/1/2009 | 11 | 1 | 100 | 13.79% |
| 1/1/2009 | 11 | 2 | 50 | 6.90% |
| 1/1/2009 | 12 | 1 | 200 | 27.59% |
| 1/2/2009 | 11 | 1 | 150 | 20.69% |
| 1/2/2009 | 12 | 1 | 125 | 17.24% |
| 1/3/2009 | 11 | 1 | 75 | 10.34% |
| 1/3/2009 | 11 | 2 | 25 | 3.45% |

**Figure 14-13**  *Calculating percent of total*

**NOTE**

*If you add the calculated column shown in Figure 14-12 to the Manufacturing Info table in your model, you will get a result much larger than 725. Figure 14-12 and those that follow are using a simplified version of the Manufacturing Info data for clarity and simplicity of illustration.*

This difference in default context can be useful. We can calculate things such as percent of total. This is done using the following expression:

```
=[NumberProduced]  /  SUM([NumberProduced])
```

as shown in Figure 14-13.

The first reference to the NumberProduced column is in the default context of the calculated column so, when evaluating the value for the row indicated by the large white arrow, it will return the value for the NumberProduced column in that row. The second reference to the NumberProduced column is in the default context of the aggregate function, so the result of the aggregate function will be the sum of all the values in the NumberProduced column for all the rows. When we take the first and divide it by the second, and then format as a percentage, we get the percent of total.

## Filtering Aggregates

Being able to use aggregate functions to produce values across the entire table is useful in some circumstances, as we just saw. However, in many situations, we want to use aggregate functions on a subset of the rows in the table. We, along with our end users, can create these subsets in a couple of different ways. First, we can use functions to modify the context of an aggregation. Second, our end users can filter the data as they perform their analysis using a front-end tool.

## CALCULATE(Expression, Filter1, Filter2, ...)

We first explore modifying the context of an aggregate by using functions. This is a two-step process. First, we use one function to create a framework for applying filters. Then, we add one or more filter functions.

The function that creates the framework is the CALCULATE() function. The CALCULATE() function provides a mechanism for executing an expression in a context other than its default context. The first parameter is a valid DAX expression. The second and following parameters are DAX filters. The DAX expression is executed in the context resulting from the application of the filters. The filter parameters are optional.

Let's look at what happens when we use the CALCULATE() function without any filter parameters. We can wrap the CALCULATE() function around the SUM() function used in Figure 14-12 to get the result shown in Figure 14-14. With the CALCULATE() function in place, the context of the SUM() function becomes the current row. When evaluating the SUM() function for the row indicated by the large white arrow, only the value for NumberProduced in that row is used. The value in the calculated column is 100.

## ALLEXCEPT(TableName, TableFieldReference1, TableFieldReference2, ...)

The first filter function we are going to look at is the ALLEXCEPT() function. TableName specifies the name of the table whose rows we are filtering. The second parameter is the table name and field name combination identifying the field used as the filter. It is necessary to supply a table name as part of the second parameter, because we could filter on a field in the table being filtered or we could filter on a field in a related table.

**Manufacturing Info**

=CALCULATE(Sum([NumberProduced]))

| Date Of Manufacture | Product Code | Machine Number | Number Produced | Calculated Column1 |
|---|---|---|---|---|
| 1/1/2009 | 11 | 1 | 100 | 100 |
| 1/1/2009 | 11 | 2 | 50 | 50 |
| 1/1/2009 | 12 | 1 | 200 | 200 |
| 1/2/2009 | 11 | 1 | 150 | 150 |
| 1/2/2009 | 12 | 1 | 125 | 125 |
| 1/3/2009 | 11 | 1 | 75 | 75 |
| 1/3/2009 | 11 | 2 | 25 | 25 |

**Figure 14-14** *The CALCULATE() function with no filter parameters*

**Manufacturing Info**

=CALCULATE(SUM([NumberProduced]),
ALLEXCEPT('Manufacturing Info','Manufacturing Info'[DateOfManufacture]))

| Date Of Manufacture | Product Code | Machine Number | Number Produced | Calculated Column1 |
|---|---|---|---|---|
| 1/1/2009 | 11 | 1 | 100 | 350 |
| 1/1/2009 | 11 | 2 | 50 | 350 |
| 1/1/2009 | 12 | 1 | 200 | 350 |
| 1/2/2009 | 11 | 1 | 150 | 275 |
| 1/2/2009 | 12 | 1 | 125 | 275 |
| 1/3/2009 | 11 | 1 | 75 | 100 |
| 1/3/2009 | 11 | 2 | 25 | 100 |

**Figure 14-15** *The ALLEXCEPT() function based on the DateOfManufacture field*

You can think of the ALLEXCEPT() function working in this way, "Use ALL rows in the *TableName* table, EXCEPT those rows with a different value in the *TableFieldReference* field." Let's look at an example to make this a bit more concrete. In Figure 14-15, we use the ALLEXCEPT() function as the second parameter for the CALCULATE() function. The ALLEXCEPT() function says, "Use ALL rows in the Manufacturing Info table, EXCEPT those rows with a different value in the Manufacturing Info table's DateOfManufacture field."

When evaluating the calculated column expression for the row indicated by the large, white arrow, the ALLEXCEPT() filter function must be considered first. For the indicated row, this function translates to, "Use ALL rows in the Manufacturing Info table, EXCEPT those rows with a value in the DateOfManufacture field different from 1/1/2009." To simplify a bit, we only include rows that have a matching value for DateOfManufacture. Thus, the first three rows become the context for the aggregate function. The sum of the values in the NumberProduced field for these three rows is the result in the calculated column for the indicated row.

Let's look at another example. In Figure 14-16, the ALLEXCEPT() function says, "Use ALL rows in the Manufacturing Info table EXCEPT those rows with a different value in the Products table's ProductName field." For the row indicated by the large, white arrow, we only include rows in the Manufacturing Info table that have a value of "Soaring Eagle" in the related Products table's Product Name field. The sum of the values in the NumberProduced field for these five rows is the result in the calculated column for the indicated row.

The example shown in Figure 14-17 utilizes two table field references. This can be interpreted as, "Use ALL rows in the Manufacturing Info table EXCEPT those rows with a different value in the DateOfManufacture field or the Products table's ProductName field." For the row indicated by the large, white arrow, we only

**Manufacturing Info**

=CALCULATE(SUM([NumberProduced]),
ALLEXCEPT('Manufacturing Info','Products'[ProductName]))

| Date Of Manufacture | Product Code | Machine Number | Number Produced | Calculated Column1 |
|---|---|---|---|---|
| 1/1/2009 | 11 | 1 | 100 | 400 |
| 1/1/2009 | 11 | 2 | 50 | 400 |
| 1/1/2009 | 12 | 1 | 200 | 325 |
| 1/2/2009 | 11 | 1 | 150 | 400 |
| 1/2/2009 | 12 | 1 | 125 | 325 |
| 1/3/2009 | 11 | 1 | 75 | 400 |
| 1/3/2009 | 11 | 2 | 25 | 400 |

**Products**

| Product Code | Product Name |
|---|---|
| 11 | Soaring Eagle |
| 12 | Eagle Pair |

**Figure 14-16**   *The ALLEXCEPT() function based on the Products table's ProductName field*

include rows in the Manufacturing Info table that have a value of 1/1/2009 in the
DateOfManufacture field and a value of "Soaring Eagle" in the related Products table's
Product Name field. The sum of the values in the NumberProduced field for these two
rows is the result in the calculated column for the indicated row.

**Manufacturing Info**

=CALCULATE(SUM([NumberProduced]),
ALLEXCEPT('Manufacturing Info','Manufacturing Info'[DateOfManufacture],
'Products'[ProductName]))

| Date Of Manufacture | Product Code | Machine Number | Number Produced | Calculated Column1 |
|---|---|---|---|---|
| 1/1/2009 | 11 | 1 | 100 | 150 |
| 1/1/2009 | 11 | 2 | 50 | 150 |
| 1/1/2009 | 12 | 1 | 200 | 200 |
| 1/2/2009 | 11 | 1 | 150 | 150 |
| 1/2/2009 | 12 | 1 | 125 | 125 |
| 1/3/2009 | 11 | 1 | 75 | 100 |
| 1/3/2009 | 11 | 2 | 25 | 100 |

**Products**

| Product Code | Product Name |
|---|---|
| 11 | Soaring Eagle |
| 12 | Eagle Pair |

**Figure 14-17**   *The ALLEXCEPT() function using two TableFieldReference parameters*

## ALL(TableNameOrTableFieldReference1, TableFieldReference2, ...)

We saw how the ALLEXCEPT() function applies a filter to define a subset of rows in a table. The ALL() function is used to override the subset of rows created by a filter to create a different subset. This is best illustrated by exploring the model in a front-end tool. Figure 14-18 shows the Manufacturing Info table viewed in an Excel PivotTable.

A measure called Total Number Produced has been defined in the model using the SUM() aggregate function. The pivot table groups the rows by ProductCode. The user has added a filter to the pivot table so only rows with a DateOfManufacture of 1/1/2009 are included. The resulting pivot table shows 150 of ProductCode 11 and 200 of ProductCode 12 were produced on that date.

Figure 14-19 shows a second measure added to the pivot table. This measure was defined using the same SUM() aggregate function. However, that SUM() function is now placed inside a CALCULATE() function and an ALL() function is included. The ALL function can be read as, "Use ALL rows no matter what value they contain in the DateOfManufacture field." This overrides the user's filter on the pivot table. For the row indicated by the large, white arrow, rows for ProductCode 11 from all dates are included to calculate the sum of NumberProduced.

Figure 14-20 shows a different measure added to the pivot table. This measure is similar to that shown in Figure 14-19 except that the ALLEXCEPT() function is used in place of the ALL() function. We can interpret this in the same manner we have previously: "Use ALL rows in the Manufacturing Info table, EXCEPT those rows with a different value in the Manufacturing Info table's DateOfManufacture field."

The ALLEXCEPT() function has the effect of overriding the grouping that is being applied by the pivot table. Instead of showing the total for just a single ProductCode, the total is for all ProductCodes. The user's filter is not being overridden, so the total

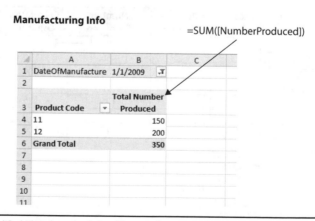

**Figure 14-18**  *Our simplified Manufacturing Info table viewed in an Excel PivotTable*

**Manufacturing Info**

=CALCULATE(SUM([NumberProduced]), ALL('Manufacturing Info'[DateOfManufacture]))

**Figure 14-19**   *An ALL() function overriding a user filter in an Excel PivotTable*

**Manufacturing Info**

=CALCULATE(SUM([NumberProduced]),
    ALLEXCEPT('Manufacturing Info','Manufacturing Info'[DateOfManufacture]))

**Figure 14-20**   *An ALLEXCEPT() function overriding the grouping in an Excel PivotTable* is for the filtered date only. For the row indicated by the large, white arrow, rows for all ProductCodes on 1/1/2009 are included to calculate the sum of NumberProduced.

# Table-Valued Functions

In the next section of this chapter, we are going to look at the aggregate functions available in the DAX language. Before we do that, however, we need to look at another group of DAX functions—those that return a table. These table-valued functions are used as input to some types of aggregate functions, thus our need to consider the table-valued functions first.

A table-valued function takes a table as its input. It applies a filter to that table or in some other way manipulates the rows in that table and, in turn, produces a table as its output. That resulting table cannot be displayed directly. It can only be used as the input to another function that requires a table as one of its input parameters.

## RELATEDTABLE(TableExpression)

The RELATEDTABLE() function is similar to the RELATED() function we saw in Chapter 13. It makes use of a one-to-many relationship between the table where the function is used and the table specified by the TableExpression parameter. The RELATED() function takes a foreign key and uses the relationship to find the record containing the matching primary key. The RELATEDTABLE() function takes a primary key and uses the relationship to find all the rows containing a matching foreign key. Where the RELATED() function works from the "many" side of the relationship to find the "one," the RELATEDTABLE() function works from the "one" side of the relationship to find the "many."

The following example can be used in the Products table to create a table of all the rows in the Manufacturing Info table related to each product:

```
RELATEDTABLE('Manufacturing Info')
```

As we will see in the next section of this chapter, we can then use the table that results from the RELATEDTABLE() function as a parameter to an aggregate function. This enables us to sum a field or count rows in a related table.

## CALCULATETABLE(TableExpression, Filter1, Filter2)

The CALCULATETABLE() function is almost identical to the RELATEDTABLE() function. Even though the word "RELATED" is not present in the name of the function, the CALCULATETABLE() function utilizes any relationship that exists between the table where the function is used and the table specified by the TableExpression parameter. The only difference is the CALCULATETABLE() function allows you to add filters by specifying additional filter parameters.

The following example can be used in the Products table to create a table of all the rows in the Manufacturing Info table related to each product where the MachineNumber is 1:

```
CALCULATETABLE('Manufacturing Info',
                        'Manufacturing Info'[MachineNumber] = 1)
```

# Aggregate Functions

Now that you know a bit about table-valued functions, let's take a look at some of the basic aggregate functions available in the DAX language. The aggregate functions come in several varieties. Standard aggregate functions calculate their aggregation on a field found in the table where they are used.

Aggregate functions with an "X" appended to their name require a table as their first parameter. (This is where the RELATEDTABLE() and CALCULATETABLE() functions come into play.) These "X" functions calculate their aggregation in the context of the table passed as that first parameter. The standard and "X" aggregate functions are able to perform aggregations on fields with numeric and date types only.

Aggregate functions with an "A" appended to their name will work with additional types of data. They will work with Boolean values and with text values. When working with Boolean values, TRUE is considered to be 1 and FALSE is considered to be 0. A text value is always considered to be 0.

The final type of aggregate functions have an "AX" appended to their name. These functions combine the characteristics of both the "X" and "A" aggregate functions. They require a table as their first parameter and calculate in the context of that table. They handle Boolean and text values as described earlier.

## AVERAGE(Field)

Calculates the mean of the values in the specified field. Works with numeric and date types only.

Example:

```
=AVERAGE([Accepted Products])
```

## AVERAGEA(Field)

Calculates the mean of the values in the specified field. Handles Boolean and text data types as well as numeric and date.

Example:

```
=AVERAGEA([Accepted Products])
```

## AVERAGEX(Table, Expression)

Calculates the mean of the values yielded by the expression in the context of the specified table.

Example:

```
=AVERAGEX(RELATEDTABLE('Manufacturing Info'),
                        'Manufacturing Info'[Accepted Products])
```

## COUNT(Field)

Counts the number of rows in which the specified field contains a numeric or date value.

Example:

```
=COUNT([Accepted Products])
```

## COUNTA(Field)

Counts the number of rows in which the specified field contains a value.

Example:

```
=COUNTA([Accepted Products])
```

## COUNTAX(Table, Expression)

Counts the number of rows in which the expression yields a value in the context of the specified table.

Example:

```
=COUNTAX(RELATEDTABLE('Manufacturing Info'),
                        'Manufacturing Info'[Accepted Products])
```

## COUNTBLANK(Field)

Counts the number of rows in which the specified field is blank. If no rows have a blank value, a blank is returned by the function.

Example:

```
=COUNTBLANK([NumberRejected])
```

## COUNTROWS(Table)

Counts the number of rows in the specified table.
   Example:

```
=COUNTROWS(RELATEDTABLE('Manufacturing Info'))
```

## COUNTX(Table, Expression)

Counts the number of rows in which the expression yields a numeric or date value in the context of the specified table.
   Example:

```
=COUNTX(RELATEDTABLE('Manufacturing Info'),
                         'Manufacturing Info'[Accepted Products])
```

## DISTINCTCOUNT(Field)

Counts the number of distinct values in the specified field.
   Example:

```
=DISTINCTCOUNT([ProductTypeName])
```

## MAX(Field)

Returns the maximum of the values in the specified field. Works with numeric and date types only.
   Example:

```
=MAX([Accepted Products])
```

## MAXA(Field)

Returns the maximum of the values in the specified field. Handles Boolean and text data types as well as numeric and date.
   Example:

```
=MAXA([Accepted Products])
```

## MAXX(Table, Expression)

Returns the maximum of the values yielded by the expression in the context of the specified table.

Example:

```
=MAXX(RELATEDTABLE('Manufacturing Info'),
                         'Manufacturing Info'[Accepted Products])
```

## MIN(Field)

Returns the minimum of the values in the specified field. Works with numeric and date types only.

Example:

```
=MIN([Accepted Products])
```

## MINA(Field)

Returns the minimum of the values in the specified field. Handles Boolean and text data types as well as numeric and date.

Example:

```
=MINA([Accepted Products])
```

## MINX(Table, Expression)

Returns the minimum of the values yielded by the expression in the context of the specified table.

Example:

```
=MINX(RELATEDTABLE('Manufacturing Info'),
                         'Manufacturing Info'[Accepted Products])
```

## SUM(Field)

Calculates the total of the values in the specified field.

Example:

```
=SUM([Accepted Products])
```

## SUMX(Table, Expression)

Calculates the total of the values yielded by the expression in the context of the specified table.

Example:

```
=SUMX(RELATEDTABLE('Manufacturing Info'),
                    'Manufacturing Info'[Accepted Products])
```

# DAX Functions for Time Analytics

One of the reasons we create a model is to capture time analytics within the model. We do this in a Tabular model through the use of DAX functions. Here is a basic overview of a few of the time analytic functions available to us.

## CLOSINGBALANCEMONTH(Expression, Dates, Filter)
## CLOSINGBALANCEQUARTER(Expression, Dates, Filter)
## CLOSINGBALANCEYEAR(Expression, Dates, Filter, YearEndDate)

The CLOSINGBALANCE*period*() functions enable us to perform calculations with semi-additive measures. As was discussed in Chapter 9, certain measures may be added along some dimensions, but not along others. Inventory levels are the classic example. The sum of the inventory amounts for each product yields the total number of products in the warehouse. However, the sum of the first three months' inventory amounts does not give the inventory amount at the end of the first quarter. It is the inventory amount for the last month of the quarter, the "closing balance for the quarter," that is the inventory amount for the quarter. You can refer back to Figure 9-8 for an illustration of this.

The CLOSINGBALANCE*period*() functions provide a way to find these end-of-period amounts. Three different periods are supported. There are functions for end of month, end of quarter, and end of year.

The Expression parameter must return a numeric value. This is the quantity we want to find the closing balance for. In the example discussed earlier, this would be the number of products in the warehouse.

The Dates parameter must be one of the following:

▶ A reference to a field containing date/time values

▶ A table-valued function call that returns a table with a single column of dates

▶ A Boolean expression that defines a single-column table of date/time values

This field is used to determine which numeric quantity is the one for the end of the period. The Filter parameter is optional. It is a filter expression used to modify the context of the function.

Example:

```
=CLOSINGBALANCEMONTH(SUM('Inventory Info'[InventoryLevel]), 'Time'[Date])
```

## DATESMTD(Dates)
## DATESQTD(Dates)
## DATESYTD(Dates, [YearEndDate])

In the discussion of the CLOSINGBALANCE*period*() functions, one possibility for the second parameter was a table-valued function returning a single column of dates. The DATES*period*() functions do just that. Given a column containing dates, these functions return a table of dates up to and including the current date in the context. There are functions for month to date, quarter to date, and year to date.

The Dates parameter must be one of the following:

▶ A reference to a field containing date/time values

▶ A table-valued function call that returns a table with a single column of dates

▶ A Boolean expression that defines a single-column table of date/time values

For example, suppose the DATESMTD() function is called in a column containing a reference to January 15, 2009. January 15, 2009, becomes the context for the function call. The function would return a table with rows for January 1, 2009, through January 15, 2009.

```
=CALCULATE(SUM('Manufacturing Info'[NumberAccepted]),
  ALLEXCEPT('Manufacturing Info', 'Manufacturing Info'[ProductCode]),
  DATESYTD('Manufacturing Info'[Date of Manufacture]))
```

## PARALLELPERIOD(Dates, NumPeriods, Period)

The PARALLELPERIOD() function also returns a table of dates. It takes the dates passed as the first parameter and shifts those dates by the specified number of periods. The PARALLELPERIOD() function always returns all of the dates in the specified period. For example, if the Dates parameter contains dates from June 10, 2011, through June 20, 2011, the NumPeriods is -1, and the Period parameter is month, the PARALLELPERIOD() function will return a table of dates from June 1, 2010, to June 30, 2010.

The Dates parameter must be one of the following:

▶ A reference to a field containing date/time values

▶ A table-valued function call that returns a table with a single column of dates

▶ A Boolean expression that defines a single-column table of date/time values

A period can be any of the following:

▶ Month

▶ Quarter

▶ Year

The period value is not put in quotes.

Example:

```
=CALCULATE(SUM('Manufacturing Info'[NumberAccepted]),
  ALLEXCEPT('Manufacturing Info', 'Manufacturing Info'[ProductCode]),
  PARALLELPERIOD('Manufacturing Info'[Date of Manufacture], -1, month))
```

## SAMEPERIODLASTYEAR(Dates)

The SAMEPERIODLASTYEAR() function is similar to a call to the PARALLELPERIOD() function with the NumPeriods parameter set to -1 and the Periods parameter set to year. The difference is the SAMEPERIODLASTYEAR() function returns one and only one date in the output table for each date in the Dates parameter. It does not fill in the entire period as the PARALLELPERIOD function does.

The Dates parameter must be one of the following:

▶ A reference to a field containing date/time values

▶ A table-valued function call that returns a table with a single column of dates

▶ A Boolean expression that defines a single-column table of date/time values

Example:

```
=CALCULATE(SUM('Manufacturing Info'[NumberAccepted]),
  ALLEXCEPT('Manufacturing Info', 'Manufacturing Info'[ProductCode]),
  SAMEPERIODLASTYEAR('Manufacturing Info'[Date of Manufacture]))
```

## TOTALMTD(Expression, Dates, Filter)
## TOTALQTD(Expression, Dates, Filter)
## TOTALYTD(Expression, Dates, Filter,[YearEndDate])

The TOTAL*period*() functions enable us to total a numeric quantity to get a period-to-date value. There are functions for month to date, quarter to date, and year to date. The Expression parameter must return a numeric value.

The Dates parameter must be one of the following:

▶ A reference to a field containing date/time values

▶ A table-valued function call that returns a table with a single column of dates

▶ A Boolean expression that defines a single-column table of date/time values

The Filter parameter is optional. It is a filter expression used to modify the context of the function.

Example:

```
=TOTALYTD(SUM('Manufacturing Info'[NumberAccepted]),
    'Manufacturing Info'[Date of Manufacture])
```

# Putting DAX Functions to Use

Now that you have been introduced to some of the basic DAX concepts and functionality, we look at two ways to put DAX, and the calculations it creates, to use. First, we examine the process for creating KPIs in a Tabular model. Second, we see how to create security roles.

## Creating a Key Performance Indicator

As we have stated previously, one of the goals of our models is to capture business logic within the model. A key performance indicator (KPI) is an excellent way to accomplish this goal. The key performance indicator takes a measure and adds a target along with information on how to interpret the measure's performance against that target.

In the Multidimensional model, we needed to create a number of MDX expressions to define a KPI. In the Tabular model, KPI creation is more straightforward. Once the DAX expression to create the measure is defined, the rest is easy.

**Figure 14-21** *The Create KPI button in the toolbar*

KPIs in a Tabular model include the following information:

▶  The measure the KPI is based upon

▶  A target value, either defined by another measure or entered as a constant value

▶  Threshold values

▶  An icon style

▶  Descriptions of the value, the status, the target, and the KPI itself

To create a KPI in a Tabular model, select an existing measure in the grid view of the model. With the measure selected, click the Create KPI button in the toolbar as shown in Figure 14-21. This will open the Key Performance Indicator dialog box.

Either click Absolute value and type in the target value for this measure, or leave Measure selected and pick the Measure that defines the target value from the drop-down list. Next, set the values to denote the transitions between the red, yellow, and green areas for the KPI. Also select how many thresholds there should be and how they should be arranged—red to yellow to green, green to yellow to red, red to yellow to green to yellow to red, or green to yellow to red to yellow to green.

Select the style of icon you would like the KPI to use. Finally, fill in the desired description text for each of these items as desired. Simple as that. The Create KPI dialog box is shown in Figure 14-22. We will give this a try in the Learn By Doing exercise later in this chapter.

## Role-Based Security

In many cases, we may want to limit the access certain individuals or groups have within a Tabular model. This is done by creating one or more roles within the model. A role is created by clicking the Roles button in the toolbar as shown in Figure 14-23. This displays the Role Manager dialog box.

**Figure 14-22** *The Create KPI dialog box*

Using the Role Manager dialog box, we can define new security roles within the Tabular model. For each role, we can use DAX expressions to filter the rows of a given table that are visible to members of this role. In the example shown in Figure 14-24, the members of the Kawaguchi Plant role can only see rows in the Locations table where the LocationName is "Maximum Miniatures - Kawaguchi."

**Figure 14-23** *The Roles button in the toolbar*

**Figure 14-24**  *The Role Manager dialog box*

The Members tab of the Role Manager dialog box enables us to specify Active Directory users or Active Directory groups that are members of a particular role.

# Deploying a Tabular Model

In the beginning of Chapter 13, we discussed the fact that any time you have a Tabular model open in SQL Server Data Tools, it creates a workspace database on the specified Tabular instance of SQL Server Analysis Services. It may be tempting to have users access this workspace database from a front-end tool for their analysis needs. However, there are several problems with this approach.

First, because the workspace database is an extension of the development environment, it should not be placed on a production server. It should reside on a workstation or a development server that is not generally available to your users. Second, the names assigned to workspace databases are long and cumbersome. Finally, a given workspace database exists on the Analysis Services server only when the associated Tabular model is open for modification in SQL Server Data Tools. As soon as the model project is closed, the workspace database disappears—a situation most users won't put up with.

When we are ready for users to access a Tabular model, we need to use the deploy process to create an instance of that model on a production Analysis Services server.

## Deployment Configuration

Before deploying, however, we must specify the name and location of the Analysis Services database where the model will reside. This is done on the Properties dialog box for the project as shown in Figure 14-25.

Under the Deployment Options section, we can set the following properties for the model in the server environment:

▶ **Processing Option**   Determines the type of processing the model receives after it is deployed. Options are Full, Do Not Process, or Default.

▶ **Transactional Deployment**   Determines whether the deployment process is completed as a single transaction. If not transactional, completed portions of the deployment will persist on the server even if a subsequent step in the deployment fails.

**Figure 14-25**   *The Properties dialog box for a Tabular model project*

▶ **Query Mode**  Determines whether the model will operate in In-memory or DirectQuery mode on the server. In In-memory mode, the data is loaded into memory for enhanced query performance, as was discussed in Chapter 13. In DirectQuery mode, no data is loaded into memory. Instead, all data is queried directly from the data sources as it is needed. Options are

   ▶ **DirectQuery**  All data is queried from the data sources.

   ▶ **DirectQuery with In-memory**  Data is queried from the data sources unless specified in the connection string.

   ▶ **In-memory**  All data is stored in memory.

   ▶ **In-memory with DirectQuery**  Data is stored in memory unless specified in the connection string.

Under the Deployment Server section, we can set the following properties for the server environment:

▶ **Server**  The name of a Tabular instance of SQL Server Analysis Services.

▶ **Edition**  The edition of SQL Server this model is targeted for. Options are

   ▶ Business Intelligence

   ▶ Developer

   ▶ Enterprise

   ▶ Evaluation

   ▶ Standard

▶ **Database**  The name of the Analysis Services database where this model will be deployed.

▶ **Cube Name**  The name of the cube shown in client tools when connecting to this model.

▶ **Version**  This is a read-only property showing the version of the SQL Server Analysis Services instance.

Under the DirectQuery Options section, we can set one property to control DirectQuery operation:

▶ **Impersonation Settings**  Specifies the credentials used when accessing data sources in DirectQuery mode. These credentials are not used for In-memory mode.

## Completing the Deployment

Once the deployment configuration is set, we can complete the deployment to the Analysis Services server. This is done using the Deploy dialog box, which can be launched from the Deploy menu choice on the Build menu. It can also be done by selecting Deploy from the context menu for the project in the Solution Explorer window.

This will initiate the deploy process. If the model has been set to process automatically as part of the deployment process, the status of that processing will be shown on the Deploy dialog box as seen in Figure 14-26.

**Figure 14-26** *The Deploy dialog box*

# Learn By Doing—Enhancing the Maximum Miniatures Manufacturing Tabular BI Semantic Model

## Features Highlighted

- ▶ Using DAX functions
- ▶ Adding time analytics to a model
- ▶ Creating a KPI
- ▶ Deploying a model

**Business Need**   The VP of production for Max Min, Inc., has asked for the following additions to the MaxMinManufactuingTabular model:

- ▶ Products accepted for a day as a percentage of total number of that product accepted over all time
- ▶ Total products accepted year-to-date
- ▶ Total accepted on the same day last year
- ▶ A KPI of products rejected as a percentage of total products

The VP also wants to begin using the model as soon as possible.

## Steps to Add Calculations to the Model

1. Open SQL Server Data Tools.
2. Open the MaxMinManufacturingTabular model.
3. Change to the grid view of the model, if it opens in diagram view.
4. Click the Manufacturing Info tab.
5. Scroll to the right until you see the "Add Column" column heading.
6. Click the cell below the Add Column heading.
7. Type the following formula:

```
=CALCULATE(SUM([NumberAccepted]),
  ALLEXCEPT('Manufacturing Info','Manufacturing Info'[ProductCode]))
```

8. Press ENTER.

9. In the Properties window, enter **Total Products Accepted** for Column Name.

10. Repeat this process to add the following calculated columns to the Manufacturing Info table with the specified column names.

| Column Name | Formula |
|---|---|
| Percent of Products | =[NumberAccepted]/[Total Products Accepted] |
| Total Accepted YTD | =CALCULATE(SUM('Manufacturing Info'[NumberAccepted]), ALLEXCEPT('Manufacturing Info', 'Manufacturing Info'[ProductCode]), DATESYTD('Manufacturing Info'[Date of Manufacture])) |
| Total Accepted Same Day Last Year | =CALCULATE(SUM([NumberAccepted]), ALLEXCEPT('Manufacturing Info', 'Manufacturing Info'[Date of Manufacture]), SAMEPERIODLASTYEAR('Manufacturing Info'[Date of Manufacture])) |

## Steps to Add a KPI to the Model

1. Click an empty cell in the Measure Grid.

2. Enter the following formula:

```
=SUM([NumberRejected]) / SUM([NumberProduced])
```

3. Press ENTER.

4. Modify the following properties in the Properties window:

| Property | Value |
|---|---|
| Measure Name | Percent Rejected |
| Format | Percentage |

5. With the newly created Percent Rejected measure still selected, click the Create KPI button in the toolbar. The Key Performance Indicator (KPI) dialog box appears.

6. Click the Absolute value radio button.

7. Replace "100" with **.0102**.

8. Find the group of four color bars in the lower-right corner of the Define status thresholds area. Click the bar with green on the left, yellow in the middle, and red on the right.

9. Again in the Define status thresholds area, click the double-headed arrow at the far right end of the color bar. Drag the double-headed arrow to the left slightly. This will shift the position of the two threshold indicators on the color bar.

10. Click the double-headed arrow at the far left end of the color bar and drag it slightly to the left. Repeat this process until the color bar appears as shown in Figure 14-27.

11. Replace "0.0001" with **0.0104**.

12. Press TAB. The entry area containing "0.0104" moves to the right.

13. Replace "0" with **0.0102**.

14. Press TAB, and then use the double-headed arrows at the ends of the color bar to again have it divided into three equal sections—one-third green, one-third yellow, and one-third red.

15. In the Select icon style area, click the set of icons with the red diamond/yellow triangle/green circle.

16. Click OK to exit the Key Performance Indicator (KPI) dialog box.

**Figure 14-27** *Adjusting the threshold points on the color bar*

### Steps to Deploy the MaxMinManufacturingTabular Model

1. Select Project | MaxMinManufacturingTabular Properties from the main menu. (The menu choice may just say "Properties" depending on what is selected at the time.) The MaxMinManufacturingTabular Property Pages dialog box appears.

2. Make sure "In-memory" is selected for Query Mode.

3. For the Server property, enter the name of a Tabular instance of SQL Server Analysis Services where you have rights to create databases. (Do *not* perform this or any other Learn By Doing activity on a server used for production operations!)

4. For the Database property, enter **Max Min Manufacturing.**

5. For the Cube Name property, enter **Max Min Manufacturing.**

6. Click OK to exit the MaxMinManufacturingTabular Property Pages dialog box.

7. Select Build | Deploy MaxMinManufacturingTabular from the main menu. The Deploy dialog box appears.

8. Enter the impersonation credentials password for each connection, if prompted, and click OK.

9. When the deploy and processing complete, click Close to exit the Deploy dialog box.

### Steps to Deploy the MaxMinSalesTabular Model

1. Click Save All in the toolbar.

2. Close the MaxMinManufacturingTabular model and open the MaxMinSalesTabular model.

3. Select Project | MaxMinSalesTabular Properties from the main menu. (The menu choice may just say "Properties" depending on what is selected at the time.) The MaxMinSalesTabular Property Pages dialog box appears.

4. Make sure "In-memory" is selected for Query Mode.

5. For the Server property, enter the name of a Tabular instance of SQL Server Analysis Services where you have rights to create databases. (Do *not* perform this or any other Learn By Doing activity on a server used for production operations!)

6. For the Database property, enter **Max Min Sales.**

7. For the Cube Name property, enter **Max Min Sales.**

8. Click OK to exit the MaxMinSalesTabular Property Pages dialog box.

9. Select Build | Deploy MaxMinSalesTabular from the main menu. The Deploy dialog box appears.

10. Enter the impersonation credentials password for each connection, if prompted, and click OK.

11. When the deploy and processing complete, click Close to exit the Deploy dialog box.

12. Close SQL Server Data Tools.

## Can You Dig It?

We have now built and deployed Multidimensional models and Tabular models. Now it is time to move on to another aspect of business intelligence. We are moving on to data mining. We dig in (pun intended) to the topic to learn how to set up structures that enable us to unlock secrets buried deep within our data.

So, don your hard hat and grab your pick. We're off to the mines!

# Part V

# Mining

# Chapter 15

# Panning for Gold— Introduction to Data Mining

## In This Chapter

▶ **What Is Data Mining?**
▶ **Data Mining Algorithms**
▶ **Grab a Pick Axe**

*People who want milk shouldn't sit on a stool in the middle of a field in the hopes that a cow will back up to them.*

—Curtis Grant, author

A s the previous quote states so vividly, we should not sit around and wait for good things to drop into our milk pails. However, in Part V of this book, we are talking about a technique that can, at first blush, sound like sitting and waiting for good things to drop out of your data and into your milk p…er, into your lap. We are talking about a technique called data mining.

In Chapter 2, we defined *data mining* as the use of a complex mathematical algorithm to sift through detail data to identify patterns, correlations, and clustering within the data. Does that mean we simply turn one of these complex mathematical algorithms loose on our data, and nuggets of business intelligence (BI) wisdom will pour forth? Not exactly.

In this chapter, we learn more about what data mining is and how it is used. We look at the work we have to do to gain business intelligence using data mining and what things the data mining algorithms can do for us. Finally, we look at the nine data mining algorithms provided in SQL Server 2012 and discover what each one is good at.

# What Is Data Mining?

If data mining is not something akin to magic, just what is it and why should we care? Data mining enables us to put computing power to work, combing through mounds of data to find meaningful bits of information. Data mining takes this number-crunching responsibility out of our hands. We do, however, need to follow a number of steps to prepare the data and the algorithm for the mining process. We also need to evaluate the result to find the gold among the slag produced.

## Order from Chaos

Relational database systems are great at piling up mounds of data as they record day-to-day business transactions. Multidimensional systems summarize that data with their aggregations, but they also multiply it along a myriad of dimensions and hierarchies. All this data can be a bit overwhelming. In many cases, this much data is so overwhelming, it is dumped onto backup tapes or placed in archives and forgotten.

The problem, from a business perspective, is that this data is the life story of your organization. It contains the entire record of where your organization has been and, more importantly, it may be able to provide some clues as to where your organization is going. This information could be helpful in your organization's management. The problem lies in making sense of all this data.

| | | | | | | | | | | | | | | | | | | | | | | | |
|---|---|---|---|---|---|---|---|---|---|---|---|---|---|---|---|---|---|---|---|---|---|---|---|
| 798 | 799 | 799 | 799 | 799 | 799 | 799 | 800 | 800 | 800 | 800 | 799 | 799 | 799 | 798 | 798 | 798 | 798 | 797 | 797 | 797 | 797 | 797 | 796 |
| 799 | 800 | 800 | 800 | 800 | 800 | 800 | 800 | 803 | 803 | 800 | 800 | 800 | 799 | 798 | 800 | 800 | 800 | 800 | 800 | 800 | 800 | 797 | 796 |
| 799 | 800 | 803 | 805 | 805 | 805 | 805 | 805 | 805 | 805 | 805 | 805 | 805 | 800 | 800 | 805 | 805 | 805 | 805 | 805 | 805 | 803 | 800 | 798 |
| 800 | 801 | 803 | 805 | 808 | 808 | 808 | 808 | 808 | 808 | 808 | 808 | 807 | 805 | 805 | 805 | 808 | 808 | 808 | 807 | 806 | 805 | 800 | 800 |
| 800 | 802 | 804 | 805 | 806 | 809 | 810 | 810 | 810 | 810 | 810 | 810 | 810 | 810 | 810 | 810 | 810 | 810 | 807 | 805 | 804 | 802 | 800 | |
| 800 | 802 | 804 | 805 | 806 | 808 | 810 | 811 | 811 | 812 | 812 | 812 | 812 | 811 | 811 | 811 | 811 | 810 | 808 | 806 | 805 | 803 | 800 | 800 |
| 800 | 803 | 804 | 805 | 806 | 808 | 809 | 810 | 810 | 810 | 810 | 810 | 810 | 810 | 810 | 811 | 811 | 810 | 808 | 806 | 805 | 803 | 800 | 798 |
| 799 | 800 | 803 | 804 | 805 | 806 | 808 | 809 | 809 | 809 | 809 | 809 | 809 | 809 | 809 | 810 | 810 | 810 | 808 | 806 | 805 | 803 | 800 | 798 |
| 799 | 800 | 803 | 804 | 805 | 806 | 807 | 808 | 808 | 808 | 808 | 808 | 808 | 808 | 808 | 809 | 809 | 809 | 807 | 806 | 805 | 803 | 800 | 798 |
| 799 | 800 | 802 | 803 | 804 | 805 | 805 | 806 | 805 | 805 | 805 | 805 | 805 | 805 | 807 | 808 | 808 | 807 | 806 | 806 | 805 | 803 | 800 | 798 |
| 799 | 800 | 802 | 802 | 803 | 804 | 804 | 805 | 804 | 804 | 803 | 803 | 803 | 804 | 805 | 805 | 805 | 805 | 805 | 805 | 805 | 802 | 800 | 798 |
| 799 | 800 | 801 | 801 | 802 | 803 | 804 | 804 | 803 | 803 | 802 | 802 | 802 | 803 | 804 | 804 | 804 | 804 | 804 | 804 | 804 | 802 | 800 | 798 |
| 799 | 800 | 800 | 801 | 802 | 802 | 803 | 803 | 802 | 802 | 801 | 801 | 801 | 802 | 803 | 803 | 803 | 803 | 803 | 803 | 802 | 801 | 800 | 798 |
| 799 | 799 | 799 | 800 | 801 | 801 | 801 | 801 | 800 | 800 | 800 | 800 | 800 | 801 | 802 | 802 | 802 | 802 | 802 | 802 | 802 | 801 | 800 | 798 |
| 798 | 798 | 798 | 799 | 800 | 800 | 800 | 800 | 799 | 799 | 798 | 799 | 799 | 800 | 800 | 801 | 801 | 801 | 801 | 801 | 801 | 801 | 800 | 798 |
| 797 | 797 | 797 | 798 | 799 | 799 | 799 | 799 | 798 | 798 | 797 | 798 | 798 | 799 | 800 | 800 | 800 | 800 | 800 | 800 | 800 | 800 | 800 | 798 |

**Figure 15-1**   *Topographic information data overload*

We can compare the task of comprehending these mounds of data with understanding the topography of a patch of land we are preparing to hike across. Each point has a certain elevation above sea level. We could print the elevation of each of these points on our map, as shown in Figure 15-1. The result does, indeed, represent the topography of the land, but it is nearly incomprehensible. This is the same problem we face when we are overwhelmed by transactional and multidimensional data.

## Making Connections

In the world of topography, we have the simple, yet powerful, tool of contour lines to help us distill the data down to something understandable. One contour line connects all the points at 800 feet above sea level. Another line connects all the points at 805 feet above sea level. And, yet another, at 810 feet. The remaining values are removed from the map, as shown in Figure 15-2.

The resulting contour map, with its concentric curves, provides almost as much information as the printout of the elevation for every point. The advantage is the contour map is immediately understandable with a little training and experience.

**Figure 15-2**   *A topographic map*

With the topographic map, we can plan our route in a matter of minutes, as shown in Figure 15-3, and still have confidence we will not walk off a cliff. With the printout of elevations shown in Figure 15-4, darkness would probably fall before we could figure out which way to go!

Data mining works in a manner similar to our topographic map. It makes connections within the data that may not be readily apparent to the human observer. These connections make the data easier to understand. Using this new understanding, we can efficiently analyze the data and set direction so our organizations do not tumble over a cliff.

**Figure 15-3**   *Planning a route using a topographic map*

| 798 | 799 | 799 | 799 | 799 | 799 | 799 | 800 | 800 | 800 | 800 | 799 | 799 | 799 | 798 | 798 | 798 | 798 | 797 | 797 | 797 | 797 | 797 | 796 |
|---|---|---|---|---|---|---|---|---|---|---|---|---|---|---|---|---|---|---|---|---|---|---|---|
| 799 | 800 | 800 | 800 | 800 | 800 | 800 | 800 | 803 | 803 | 800 | 800 | 800 | 799 | 798 | 800 | 800 | 800 | 800 | 800 | 800 | 800 | 797 | 796 |
| 799 | 800 | 803 | 805 | 805 | 805 | 805 | 805 | 805 | 805 | 805 | 805 |  | 800 | 800 | 805 | 805 | 805 | 805 | 805 | 805 | 803 | 800 | 798 |
| 800 | 801 | 803 | 805 | 808 | 808 | 808 | 808 | 808 | 808 | 80? |  | 805 | 805 | 808 | 808 | 808 | 807 | 806 | 805 | 800 | 800 |
| 800 | 802 | 804 | 805 | 806 | 809 | 810 | 810 | 810 | 810 | 810 | 810 |  | 810 | 810 | 810 | 810 | 810 | 807 | 805 | 804 | 802 | 800 |
| 800 | 802 | 804 | 805 | 806 | 808 | 810 | 811 | 811 | 812 | 812 | 81? |  | 811 | 811 | 811 | 811 | 810 | 808 | 806 | 805 | 803 | 800 | 800 |
| 800 | 803 | 804 | 805 | 806 | 808 | 809 | 810 | 810 | 810 | 810 | 81? |  | 810 | 810 | 811 | 811 | 810 | 808 | 806 | 805 | 803 | 800 | 798 |
| 799 | 800 | 803 | 804 | 805 | 806 | 808 | 809 | 809 | 809 | 809 | 80? |  | 809 | 809 | 810 | 810 | 810 | 808 | 806 | 805 | 803 | 800 | 798 |
| 799 | 800 | 803 | 804 | 805 | 806 | 807 | 808 | 808 | 808 | 808 | 808 | 808 | 808 | 809 | 809 | 809 | 807 | 806 | 805 | 803 | 800 | 798 |
| 799 | 800 | 802 | 803 | 804 | 805 | 805 | 806 | 805 | 805 | 805 | 805 | 805 | 807 | 808 | 808 | 807 | 806 | 806 | 805 | 803 | 800 | 798 |
| 799 | 800 | 802 | 802 | 803 | 804 | 804 | 805 | 804 | 804 | 803 | 803 | 803 | 804 | 805 | 805 | 805 | 805 | 805 | 805 | 805 | 802 | 800 | 798 |
| 799 | 800 | 801 | 801 | 802 | 803 | 804 | 804 | 805 | 803 | 802 | 802 | 802 | 803 | 804 | 804 | 804 | 804 | 804 | 804 | 804 | 802 | 800 | 798 |
| 799 | 800 | 800 | 801 | 802 | 802 | 803 | 803 | 802 | 802 | 801 | 801 | 801 | 802 | 803 | 803 | 803 | 803 | 803 | 803 | 802 | 801 | 800 | 798 |
| 799 | 799 | 799 | 800 | 801 | 801 | 801 | 801 | 800 | 800 | 800 | 800 | 800 | 801 | 802 | 802 | 802 | 802 | 802 | 802 | 802 | 801 | 800 | 798 |
| 798 | 798 | 798 | 799 | 800 | 800 | 800 | 800 | 799 | 799 | 798 | 799 | 799 | 800 | 800 | 801 | 801 | 801 | 801 | 801 | 801 | 801 | 800 | 798 |
| 797 | 797 | 797 | 798 | 799 | 799 | 799 | 799 | 798 | 798 | 797 | 798 | 798 | 799 | 800 | 800 | 800 | 800 | 800 | 800 | 800 | 800 | 800 | 798 |

**Figure 15-4**  *Data overload leads to confusion.*

## Making Predictions

The topographic map holds another advantage for us. Looking at the data shown on the map, we can make predictions of what lies beyond. Judging from the patterns appearing in the contour lines of the map, we can extrapolate to infer the topography of areas beyond the map. This is shown in Figure 15-5.

With any prediction of the unknown, we have a risk of being incorrect. Still, we have a much better chance of being correct when we work with the patterns provided by the topographic map. Of course, the more data we have to extrapolate from, the better chance we have of making the correct prediction.

Data mining provides us with a similar capability. We can use the patterns found in our data to make predictions of what will happen next. Data mining may find patterns in the way our clients make use of our services. Based on these patterns, we can predict which clients may need additional services in the future. Data mining may find patterns in the valid data entered for a particular screen. Based on these patterns, we can predict whether a newly entered set of data is accurate or contains a data entry error.

**Figure 15-5**   *Making predictions from the topographic map*

## Tasks Accomplished by Data Mining

In our topographic map analogy, we touched on a couple of the benefits of data mining. Let's look more specifically at the various tasks data mining can help us accomplish.

### Classification

*Classification* enables us to fit items into slots, as shown in Figure 15-6. Perhaps we have a customer we would like to classify as a good credit risk or a bad credit risk. Or, we may need to classify a potential customer as someone who is likely to need our services or someone who is not. If we know how to classify an individual, an entity, or a thing, we can make more intelligent decisions as we deal with that individual, entity, or thing.

We begin our classification process by selecting the classification we want to make. In other words, we select an attribute whose value we want to predict as part of future transactions. Once we make this selection, we look at the past data. In this data, we already know the value of our prediction attribute. Next, we determine, in the past data, which attributes most distinguish the customers with one value for our prediction attribute from customers with a different value. These distinguishing attributes are then used to forecast the value of the prediction attribute in future transactions.

Let's look at an example. Maximum Miniatures is having a problem with some wholesale customers not paying their invoices in a timely manner. Therefore, we want

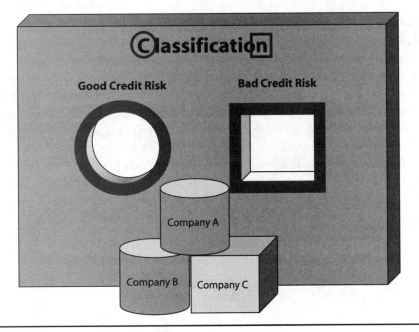

**Figure 15-6**  *Classification*

a way to predict the credit risk of prospective customers. Credit risk is our prediction attribute. We look at the past data, where we already know the value of the credit risk attribute. We know who paid their bills on time and who had to be taken to collections. We can examine the past data and determine the attributes that most distinguish the customers that were good credit risks from those that were bad credit risks. These are the distinguishing attributes. This sounds like an easy thing to do, but if we have millions of records in our past data, it can be a daunting task.

This is where data mining proves its worth. Data mining is excellent at plowing through millions of records to find correlations. It can process the past data and determine whether it is net assets, annual revenue, invoice payment history, or a CEO's favorite color that is a distinguishing attribute for credit risk.

Perhaps customers with over ten million dollars in assets and three million dollars in annual revenue are almost always good credit risks, while customers that don't meet these criteria are almost always bad credit risks. These become our distinguishing attributes: the measures we can apply to prospective customers to determine what their credit risk is likely to be. Using the distinguishing attributes, we can identify bad credit-risk prospects and ask for cash in advance, before they have thousands of dollars' worth of overdue invoices.

## Regression

Classification is used to predict the value for a discrete attribute, meaning an attribute that has one of a set number of distinct values. *Regression,* on the other hand, is used to predict a continuous value. (It would seem the opposite of discrete values would be indiscrete values, but that doesn't sound too good, so we will use the term "continuous values" instead.) The measures that we have been talking about since the beginning of this book are all continuous values. Sales is a good example, as shown in Figure 15-7. Sales can be any number from $0 to $1,000,000,000 (or maybe more).

To predict a continuous value, regression looks at trends likely to continue and repeat over time. Perhaps our sales are seasonal, with peaks in August and December. The regression algorithm discovers these peaks while looking at sales figures from past years and continues those trends when predicting future years.

**Figure 15-7**   *Regression*

Like classification, regression also looks at relationships between the value being predicted and other continuous values available in the data. In our example, perhaps the price of gasoline has a big effect on sales. (This is certainly true of anyone trying to sell sport utility vehicles!) Our regression algorithm may factor in the price of gasoline at the beginning of the month as it predicts the sales amount for that month.

## Segmentation

Segmentation is the "divide and conquer" approach to data analysis. *Segmentation* divides data into groups with similar characteristics. We can then analyze the characteristics of each group for insights. This is shown in Figure 15-8.

For example, a service company can apply segmentation to divide its clients into groups. One group might be companies with over 1,000 employees. Another group might be companies with 500 to 999 employees, and so on. The analyst for the service company can then look at each group to see how much revenue they have generated, what types of needs they have, how much management time they have required, and other factors.

When looking at groups of companies, insights can be gained that would not have been apparent when looking at one company at a time. Using this information, the service company can determine which types of companies should be the focus of its sales and marketing efforts. The service company can also create policies on project management approaches at various types of companies.

**Figure 15-8**  *Segmentation*

## Association

*Association* requires we have some type of grouping in our data. Multiple items could be grouped together in a single sales transaction. Multiple services could be provided to a single family unit. Multiple classes could be taken by a student. This is shown in Figure 15-9.

The association algorithm examines the groups found in past data to find patterns in the group membership. For example, items *A, B,* and *C* may occur together in a large number of groupings. Based on the patterns found, predictions can be made on the makeup of future groups. If items *A* and *B* are in a group, there is a strong possibility that item *C* will be added as well.

We are all familiar with the buying suggestions generated by association. When I have *Delivering Business Intelligence with Microsoft SQL Server 2012* and *Microsoft SQL Server 2012 Reporting Services* from McGraw-Hill Professional in my online shopping cart, the website informs me that a number of people who bought these books also purchased *Visualizing Data with Microsoft Power View* from McGraw-Hill Professional. (How's that for a subtle product plug?)

Classification, segmentation, and association can sometimes run together. They seem similar. The difference is this: With classification, we pick the attribute that defines the grouping and the algorithm determines what most distinguishes those groupings. With segmentation, the algorithm itself creates the grouping, based on what it determines as distinguishing characteristics. With association, the underlying data already contains some type of grouping. The algorithm makes determinations about items likely to be in the group, rather than attributes they are likely to have in common.

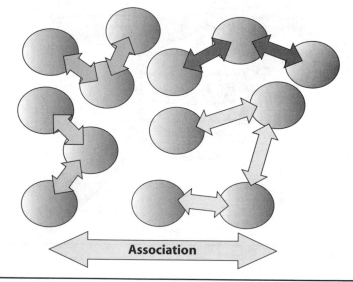

**Figure 15-9** *Association*

## Sequence Analysis

*Sequence analysis* is used to examine ordered stops along a route, as shown in Figure 15-10. Data on past routes is processed by the algorithm. Then, the algorithm can predict future routes. Given the current stop, the algorithm can determine the probability of navigating a given route.

Sequence analysis is often applied to navigation on a website. A user is on Page *A*. The user is then most likely to navigate to Page *B*, with a somewhat smaller probability of navigating to Page *C*.

Of course, sequence analysis can be applied to other types of events occurring in a sequence. Customers may buy products or utilize services in a particular sequence. We can analyze this data and determine the likely products or services the customer will be interested in next.

## Probability Predictions

As stated earlier, data mining is not magic. It cannot see into the future to predict events. Instead, it mathematically analyzes what has occurred in the past and determines what is most probable to occur if present trends continue. A chance always exists that some outside force could cause present trends not to continue. The user, buyer, or prospect we are trying to analyze may be the anomaly that doesn't follow the present trends, even when everyone else does.

At least with data mining, we can determine, with some confidence, what the present trends are. We can then make intelligent decisions based on those trends. Without data mining, we don't know what the trends and associations are, so we are left operating on gut feelings alone.

**Figure 15-10** *Sequence analysis*

## Steps for Data Mining

Now that you know what data mining can do for you, the next logical question is this: How do I make data mining do all that great stuff for me? Data mining is a multistep process. As with all of the business intelligence approaches we cover in this book, it takes some time and preparation. Despite the complex mathematics data mining algorithms bring to the table, utilizing data mining is not all that complex. This is especially true in SQL Server 2012 and SQL Server Data Tools.

In this section, we introduce the steps required for data mining in the abstract. This lets you gain some familiarity with the general process, without being overwhelmed by the specifics. In Chapter 16, we work through the specific tasks that must be accomplished in SQL Server Data Tools.

## Problem Definition

The first step for a data mining solution is to define the problem we are trying to solve. Data mining is great at finding patterns and relationships that are not apparent to human eyes. However, it cannot solve problems unless we point that analytical power in a specific direction.

We need to define the business goal we are working toward. Perhaps we want to do a better job at identifying perspective customers who are a bad credit risk. Perhaps we want to identify customers who are likely to switch to our competitor's products or services. Perhaps we want to predict future sales to put in place the capacity to meet those needs.

Once the business goal is defined, we determine what we need data mining to do for us. We select which of the five data mining tasks we are looking to accomplish:

▶ Classification

▶ Regression

▶ Segmentation

▶ Association

▶ Sequence analysis

Our choice of task influences our choice of data mining algorithm.

SQL Server 2012 provides a number of algorithms to perform each task. Often, we try several algorithms capable of accomplishing our selected task. We can then determine which algorithm proves most accurate for our purpose. We discuss the algorithms provided by SQL Server 2012 and their appropriate tasks in the section "Data Mining Algorithms." With one or more algorithms selected, we determine what data we need to feed into those algorithms.

## Data Preparation

When we learned about BI Semantic Model design, one of our main concerns was where the data to populate the model was going to come from. With data mining, we have the same concern: Where are we going to get the data to be fed into our data mining algorithms?

Data mining in SQL Server 2012 uses the same data sources and data source views we used in our Analysis Services cube projects in SQL Server Data Tools. This gives us great flexibility in where we get our data for data mining. The data source may be tables in a relational database or an OLAP cube in an Analysis Services database. It can also come from one of the OLE DB or other data sources supported by SQL Server Data Tools.

If the data is not readily accessible, we can use the power of SQL Server Integration Services to extract the data, cleanse it, and put it in a location where it can be utilized. You may recall from Chapter 7 a special data flow destination called Data Mining Model Training, which loads data from an Integration Services data flow directly into a data mining model. We talk about data mining models in Chapter 16.

## Training

With algorithms selected and our data in place, we begin the process of working with the data mining model. You can think of a data mining model as the combination of one or more data mining algorithms with some real, live data. The model applies the algorithms to the data and creates the classifications, associations, regression formulas, and so forth that we use to solve our business problem.

This step is known as training the data mining model. We provide our data to the data mining algorithms so they can be trained on a particular aspect of our organization. They "learn" what is unique about our data, as well as the operations and entities, customers, products, and sales transactions that produced that data.

## Testing

We spoke previously in this chapter about providing a data mining algorithm with past data so it could find the classifications, associations, and so forth contained within. In actuality, we often divide our past data into two sets. One set of data is used to train the data model. The second set is used to test the model after it is trained. Let's return to our credit risk example for an illustration.

We have historical data containing a number of attributes for our customers, including whether they turned out to be a good credit risk or a bad credit risk. To create and test a data mining model, we divide this data into two sets. One serves to train the model, as we discussed. The second, testing data set is used to validate the results from each of the data mining algorithms.

The data in the training data set is fed into the data mining model, and we ask the model to predict which customers will be good credit risks and which will be bad credit risks. Remember, this is historical data, so we already know whether the customers in this set of data were good or bad credit risks.

Each algorithm makes a prediction for each customer in the testing data set. Next, we compare the predictions against the known reality for each customer. We can then select the data mining algorithm to use in our production solution based on which had the highest percentage of correct predictions. This algorithm should do the best job of predicting which customers will be good or bad credit risks in the future.

As we separate data into training and testing data sets, it is important we do not do the separation in such a way as to skew the results. For example, taking the first 100,000 records is not a good way to separate the data, especially if we are dealing with transactional records in chronological order. Some event or circumstance may have affected the data during the time the first 100,000 records were generated that was not present when the rest of the data was generated or as future records are generated. For example, your business may be seasonal. Using a training data set from a time when the seasonal cycle is at its peak can make the data model a poor predictor of outcomes during those times when the cycle is at its nadir.

A random sampling is often a good way to ensure impartiality. Data selected from across business cycles can provide the best training and testing for the model. The SQL Server Integration Services row sampling data flow task is excellent for creating random samples for training and testing data mining models.

## Deployment

Once we test the data mining model and determine which data mining algorithm gives us the most accurate information, we can put it to work. We place the model where it can be accessed by the front-end tools that will utilize it. We use the Data Mining Extensions (DMX) query language to feed new records to our algorithm and have it generate information. We discuss the DMX query language in Chapter 17.

# Data Mining Algorithms

SQL Server 2012 provides us with nine data mining algorithms. Most of these algorithms perform several different tasks. Having a detailed understanding of the inner workings of each algorithm is unnecessary. Instead, this section provides a brief explanation of each to give you some background information. More important is the knowledge of what each can be used to accomplish.

## Microsoft Decision Trees

The *Microsoft Decision Trees algorithm* is one of the easiest algorithms to understand because it creates a tree structure during its training process. (You probably already guessed that from the name.) The tree structure is then used to provide predictions and analysis.

### Function

Figure 15-11 shows a sample decision tree created by the Microsoft Decision Trees algorithm. In this tree, we are analyzing the relationship between various product attributes and likelihood to be a high seller. Each new attribute the algorithm processes adds a new branch to the tree. In the diagram, we have a binary tree. But, using an attribute with more than two values, it is possible to have a fork with more than two branches—an *N*-ary tree, if you like the lingo.

As each node in the tree is created, the attribute we will be predicting is examined in the training data set. In Figure 15-11, 75% of products made from clay were high sellers in the training data. Further down the tree, 93% of clay products costing $25 or less were top sellers. If you were a member of the Maximum Miniatures planning team, what types of new products would you emphasize? (If you said clay products costing under $25, all this talk about mathematical algorithms has not yet put you in a stupor and you are definitely catching on.)

**Figure 15-11** *The Microsoft Decision Trees algorithm*

## Tasks

The main purpose of the Microsoft Decision Trees algorithm is

▶   Classification

It can also be used for

▶   Regression
▶   Association

# Microsoft Linear Regression

The *Microsoft Linear Regression algorithm* is a specialized implementation of the Microsoft Decision Trees algorithm. As the name suggests, this algorithm is used to model a linear relationship between two numeric variables. Using that linear relationship, if we know the value of one variable, called the *independent variable*, we can predict the value of the other variable, called the *dependent variable*.

## Function

The Microsoft Linear Regression algorithm begins with a set of known points, as shown in Figure 15-12. The algorithm works to find the line that will best model these known points. The distance of any given point from the line is the error of that point in the current model. The sum of the errors for all of the points is the error of the model.

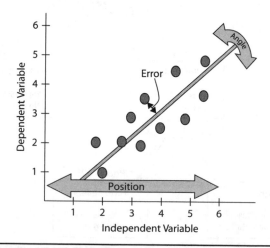

**Figure 15-12**   *Creating a linear model with the Microsoft Linear Regression algorithm*

The model is adjusted by changing both the position and the angle of the line until the model with the smallest error is found.

Once we have established a linear model, we can use that model to make predictions. Let's assume the line shown in Figure 15-12 represents the model with the smallest error. Then, using that model, we can predict the value of the dependent variable for any value of the independent value.

If we have an independent value of 5, we move straight up from 5 on the independent axis until we intersect the line created by the linear model. Next, we move to the left until we reach the dependent axis. Using this method, our linear model predicts the dependent value will be 4 when the independent value is 5.

Obviously, this is a very simplified view of how the Microsoft Linear Regression algorithm functions. A decision tree structure is created to assist in the development of the linear model. Also, the predictions are done algebraically rather than in the graphical manner just described. Still, you get the idea of the basic concepts.

The Microsoft Linear Regression algorithm requires that both the independent and the dependent variables be continuous, numeric data types.

## Tasks

As the name implies, the Microsoft Linear Regression algorithm can only be used for

▶   Regression

# Microsoft Naïve Bayes

Donald Farmer, a former Principal Program Manager for Microsoft Data Mining, claimed because there is a Naïve Bayes algorithm, there must be a "deeply cynical" Bayes algorithm out there somewhere in data mining land. I guess it is needed to bring balance to data mining's version of the "force." We will try not to be too naïve as we explore the benefits and shortcomings of this algorithm.

## Function

The *Microsoft Naïve Bayes algorithm* looks at each attribute of the entity in question and determines how that attribute, on its own, affects the attribute we are looking to predict. Figure 15-13 shows a Naïve Bayes algorithm being used to predict whether a customer is a good credit risk. One by one, the Naïve Bayes algorithm takes a single attribute of a customer—size of company, annual revenue, and so forth—and looks at the training data to determine its effect on credit risk.

In our diagram, 57% of companies with a size attribute of small are bad credit risks. Only 14% of companies with a size attribute of large are bad credit risks. In this particular

**Customer Attributes**

| Name | Values |
|------|--------|
| Size of Company | Small |
| | Medium |
| | Large |
| Revenue | < $1M |
| | $1M to $3M |
| | $3M to $5M |
| | > $5M |
| Profit | <= $0 |
| | $1 to $100K |
| | $100K to $500K |
| | > $500K |

**Credit Risk**

| Attribute | % Bad Credit |
|-----------|--------------|
| Small Company | 57% |
| Medium Company | 38% |
| Large Company | 14% |
| Revenue < $1M | 41% |
| Revenue $1M to $3M | 33% |
| Revenue $3M to $5M | 21% |
| Revenue > $5M | 9% |
| Profit <= $0 | 72% |
| Profit $1 to $100K | 64% |
| Profit $100K to $500K | 28% |
| Profit > $500K | 6% |

**Figure 15-13**  *The Naïve Bayes algorithm*

example, it looks pretty cut and dried: We should never extend credit to small companies and we should always extend credit to large companies.

What the Naïve Bayes algorithm does not tell us is what the results might be if we consider more than one attribute at a time. Are small companies with annual profits of more than $500,000 a bad credit risk? Are large companies with annual profits in the negative a good credit risk? The Naïve Bayes does not consider combinations of attributes, so it simply doesn't know. This is why our Naïve Bayes algorithm is so naïve!

## Tasks

The Naïve Bayes algorithm can only be used for

▶   Classification

# Microsoft Clustering

Next on our list is the Microsoft Clustering algorithm.

## Function

The *Microsoft Clustering algorithm* builds clusters of entities as it processes the training data set. This is shown in Figure 15-14. Once the clusters are created, the algorithm analyzes the makeup of each cluster. It looks at the values of each attribute for the entities in the cluster.

When we view the Microsoft Clustering algorithm in SQL Server Data Tools, we see a diagram similar to Figure 15-14. By entering the attribute value we want, we can have the clusters color-coded according to the concentration of our desired value.

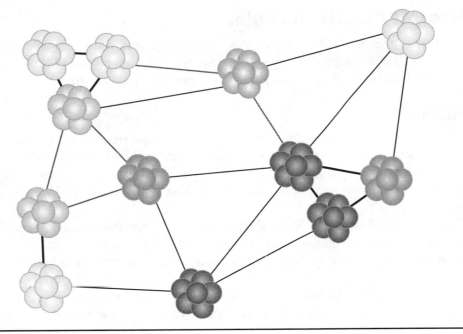

**Figure 15-14**  *The Microsoft Clustering algorithm*

For example, say we are trying to determine the distinguishing characteristics of customers who are likely to go to the competition in the next two months. We create our clusters of customers from the training data. Next, we ask SQL Server Data Tools to show us the concentration of customers from the training data set who did leave within two months. The darker the cluster, the more departed customers it contains. Finally, we can examine what attributes most distinguish the high-concentration clusters from the others.

## Tasks

The main purpose of the Microsoft Clustering algorithm is

▶   Segmentation

It can also be used for

▶   Regression

▶   Classification

# Microsoft Association Rules

As the name suggests, the *Microsoft Association Rules algorithm* is used for association. Therefore, to use this algorithm, we must have entities that are grouped into sets within our data. Refer to the section "Association" if you need more information.

## Function

The Microsoft Association Rules algorithm creates its own sets of entities and then determines how often those sets occur in the training data set. This is shown in Figure 15-15. In this set, we are looking at groupings of products purchased together in a single purchase transaction. To simplify our example, we are only looking at products in the World War II product subtype.

The Microsoft Association Rules algorithm begins by creating one-item sets. You may think it takes more than one item to make a set, but just put that aside for a moment. This algorithm then looks at how many times a purchase included the item in each one-item set.

Next, the algorithm determines which sets were popular enough to go on to the next level of analysis. For this, a particular threshold, or *minimum support*, is used.

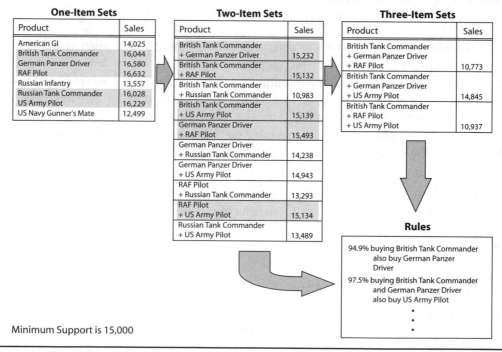

**One-Item Sets**

| Product | Sales |
| --- | --- |
| American GI | 14,025 |
| British Tank Commander | 16,044 |
| German Panzer Driver | 16,580 |
| RAF Pilot | 16,632 |
| Russian Infantry | 13,557 |
| Russian Tank Commander | 16,028 |
| US Army Pilot | 16,229 |
| US Navy Gunner's Mate | 12,499 |

**Two-Item Sets**

| Product | Sales |
| --- | --- |
| British Tank Commander + German Panzer Driver | 15,232 |
| British Tank Commander + RAF Pilot | 15,132 |
| British Tank Commander + Russian Tank Commander | 10,983 |
| British Tank Commander + US Army Pilot | 15,139 |
| German Panzer Driver + RAF Pilot | 15,493 |
| German Panzer Driver + Russian Tank Commander | 14,238 |
| German Panzer Driver + US Army Pilot | 14,943 |
| RAF Pilot + Russian Tank Commander | 13,293 |
| RAF Pilot + US Army Pilot | 15,134 |
| Russian Tank Commander + US Army Pilot | 13,489 |

**Three-Item Sets**

| Product | Sales |
| --- | --- |
| British Tank Commander + German Panzer Driver + RAF Pilot | 10,773 |
| British Tank Commander + German Panzer Driver + US Army Pilot | 14,845 |
| British Tank Commander + RAF Pilot + US Army Pilot | 10,937 |

**Rules**

94.9% buying British Tank Commander also buy German Panzer Driver

97.5% buying British Tank Commander and German Panzer Driver also buy US Army Pilot

•
•
•

Minimum Support is 15,000

**Figure 15-15**   *The Microsoft Association Rules algorithm*

In Figure 15-15, the minimum support required is 15,000. In other words, a particular set must be present in at least 15,000 purchases in the training data set to move on. In our example, British Tank Commander, German Panzer Driver, RAF Pilot, Russian Tank Commander, and U.S. Army Pilot have the minimum support required.

The algorithm now repeats the process with two-item sets. The 5 one-item sets that had the minimum support at the previous level are combined to create 10 two-item sets. Now, the algorithm examines the training data set to determine how many purchases included both items in each two-item set. Again, a minimum level of support is required. In Figure 15-15, you can see we have 5 two-item sets with the minimum support required.

Items from the two-item sets are now combined to form three-item sets. This process continues until there is either one or zero sets with the minimum support. In Figure 15-15, no three-item sets have the minimum support required so, in this case, the algorithm does not continue with four-item sets.

Once the sets are created, the algorithm creates membership rules based on the result. The algorithm determined that 16,044 purchases included the British Tank Commander. Of those purchases, 15,232, or 94.9%, also included the German Panzer Driver. This becomes a rule for predicting future associations. In the future, when someone puts the British Tank Commander in their shopping cart, 95 times out of 100, they will also include the German Panzer Driver in the same purchase.

## Tasks

The Microsoft Association Rules algorithm can only be used for

▶   Association

# Microsoft Sequence Clustering

The Microsoft Sequence Clustering algorithm was developed by Microsoft Research. As the name implies, the *Microsoft Sequence Clustering algorithm* is primarily used for sequence analysis, but it has other uses as well.

## Function

The Microsoft Sequence Clustering algorithm examines the training data set to identify transitions from one state to another. The training data set contains data, such as a web log showing navigation from one page to another, or perhaps routing and approval data showing the path taken to approve each request. The algorithm uses the training data set to determine, as a ratio, how many times each of the possible paths is taken.

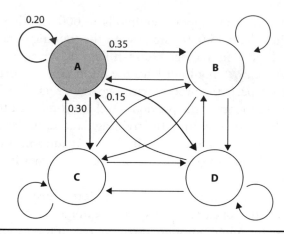

**Figure 15-16**  *The Microsoft Sequence Clustering algorithm*

Figure 15-16 shows an example of the sequence cluster diagram that results. In the diagram, we can see that if in state *A*, 35 times out of 100 there will be a transition to state *B*, 30 times out of 100 there will be a transition to state *C*, and 15 times out of 100 there will be a transition to state *D*. The remaining 20 times out of 100, it remains in state *A*. These ratios discovered by the algorithm can be used to predict and model behavior.

## Tasks

The main purposes of the Microsoft Sequence Clustering algorithm are

▶ Sequence analysis

▶ Segmentation

It can also be used for

▶ Regression

▶ Classification

# Microsoft Time Series

The *Microsoft Time Series algorithm* is used for analyzing and predicting time-dependent data. It is actually a combination of two algorithms in one: the ARTxp algorithm developed by Microsoft and the industry-standard ARIMA algorithm, which was developed by Box and Jenkins.

## Function

The ARTxp algorithm has proved to be very good at short-term prediction. The ARIMA algorithm is much better at longer-term prediction. By default, the Microsoft Time Series algorithm blends the results of the two algorithms to produce the best prediction for both the short and long term.

The Microsoft Time Series algorithm starts with time-related data in the training data set. In Figure 15-17, this is sales data for each month. To simplify things, we are only looking at data for two products in our example.

The sales data is pivoted to create the table at the bottom of Figure 15-17. The data for case 1 is for March 2008. The sales amounts in the (t0) columns for this case come from the March 2008 sales figures. The sales amounts in the (t-1), or time minus one month, columns come from February 2008, and the sales amounts in the (t-2) columns come from January 2008. Case 2 shifts the months ahead one, so (t0) becomes April, (t-1) becomes March, and (t-2) becomes February.

The algorithm then uses the data in this pivot table to come up with mathematical formulas that use the numbers from the (t-1) and (t-2) columns to calculate the number in the (t0) column for each product. In fact, it uses both the ARTxp and

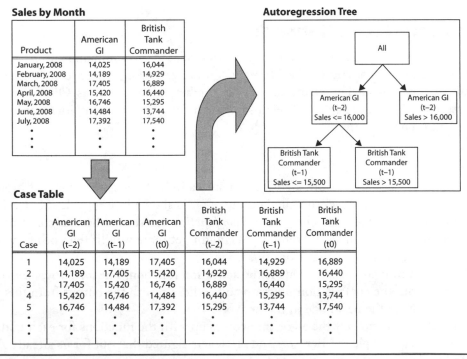

**Figure 15-17**  *The Microsoft Time Series algorithm*

ARIMA algorithms to do this calculation and comes up with a blended result. Using these formulas, we can predict the sales values for a product into the future.

With something as complex as predicting the future, you can understand that a single formula for each product is probably not going to do the trick. This is where the autoregression tree comes into play. The autoregression tree is shown in the upper-right corner of Figure 15-17. The *autoregression tree* allows the algorithm to set up conditions for choosing between multiple formulas for making a prediction. Each node in the autoregression tree has its own formula for making a prediction. In the figure, we have one formula when sales for the American GI at (t-2) are less than or equal to 16,000 and another formula where sales are over 16,000.

Don't worry; we don't need to know how to create autoregression trees or the formulas they contain. All we need to know is how to use them. We will see how to do this in Chapter 16 and Chapter 17.

### Tasks

The Microsoft Time Series algorithm can only be used for

▶   Regression

## Microsoft Neural Network

Neural networks were developed in the 1960s to model the way human neurons function. Microsoft has created the *Microsoft Neural Network algorithm* so we can use neural networks for such mundane activities as predicting product sales. Of course, predicting product sales might not seem so mundane if your future employment is dependent on being correct.

### Function

The Microsoft Neural Network algorithm creates a web of nodes that connect inputs derived from attribute values to a final output. This is shown in Figure 15-18. Each node contains two functions. The *combination function* determines how to combine the inputs coming into the node. Certain inputs might get more weight than others when it comes to affecting the output from this node.

The second function in each node is the activation function. The *activation function* takes input from the combination function and comes up with the output from this node to be sent to the next node in the network.

Again, don't ask me how the algorithm comes up with the functions for each node. Some very smart people at Microsoft and elsewhere figured that out for us already. All we need to do is use the algorithm and reap the rewards.

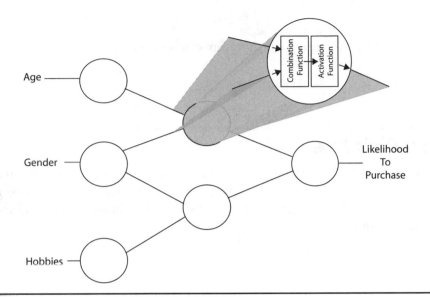

**Figure 15-18**  *The Microsoft Neural Network algorithm*

## Tasks

The main purposes of the Microsoft Neural Network algorithm are

▶    Classification

▶    Regression

# Microsoft Logistic Regression

The Microsoft Logistic Regression algorithm is a special form of the Microsoft Neural Network algorithm. Logistic regression is used to model situations where there is one of two possible outcomes. A customer will or will not buy a given product. A person will or will not develop a certain medical condition.

## Function

The *Microsoft Logistic Regression algorithm* uses a neural network to model the influence of a number of factors on a true/false outcome. The magnitude of the various influences is weighed to determine which factors are the best predictors of a given outcome. The "logistical" part of the name comes from a mathematical transformation, called a logistic transformation, which is used to minimize the effect of extreme values in the model.

## Tasks

The Microsoft Logistic Regression algorithm can be used for

▶ Regression

# Grab a Pick Axe

Now that you are familiar with data mining procedures, tasks, and algorithms, it's time to put all of this to work. In the next chapter, we create data mining models and go through the process of creating, training, and testing data mining solutions. Let's see what we can dig up!

# Chapter 16

# Building the Mine—Working with the Data Mining Model

## In This Chapter

- ▶ Data Mining Structure
- ▶ Mining Model Viewer
- ▶ Reading the Tea Leaves

*We shall not cease from exploration*
*And the end of all our exploring*
*Will be to arrive where we started*
*And know the place for the first time.*

—"Little Gidding"
T. S. Eliot

You have learned some of the basics of data mining in Chapter 15. Now it is time to dive into the specifics of the data mining process in SQL Server 2012. We use SQL Server Data Tools to create, train, and test data mining models. This tool provides all we need to quickly get the job done.

The examples in this chapter utilize the MaxMinSalesDM BI Semantic Model. You should have created this model as part of the Learn By Doing exercises earlier in this book. If you have not done this, you may download the model definition and its underlying relational data mart from the book's website.

# Data Mining Structure

As we work with data mining in SQL Server Data Tools, we use a data mining structure to contain everything we develop. The data mining structure enables us to define the data we will use, either from a relational database or from an online analytical processing (OLAP) cube, as the source for the mining. It also lets us define one or more data mining algorithms to apply to that data.

## Data Columns

The first step in doing any mining is to select the data being mined. We select a data source: either relational data or an OLAP cube. Once this is done, we need to select a table, if this is a relational data source, or a dimension, if this is an OLAP data source. Finally, we must select the table columns or dimension attributes to be used as the data columns for our data mining.

Although an initial table or dimension must be selected for data mining, it is possible to select additional related tables or dimensions for inclusion. These are known as *nested tables*. If a relational database is being used, the initial table and the nested table must be linked by a foreign key relationship (or a chain of foreign key relationships). If a cube is being used, the initial dimension and the nested dimension must be linked through the fact table.

## Data Mining Model

The data mining model combines the data columns with a data mining algorithm. As part of this process, we must determine how each data column should be used by the data mining algorithm. This determines how the data mining algorithm functions and what it predicts.

### Data Column Usage

Each column in the data mining structure must have one of the following usages:

▶ **Key** The *key* is the unique identifier for a table or a dimension. The key is not used by the data mining algorithm to predict values.

▶ **Input** An *input* is a data column used by the data mining algorithm when making a prediction. The *input values* are the values that influence the prediction made by the algorithm.

▶ **Predict** A *predict* is a data column whose value is being predicted by the data mining algorithm. This column can also be used as an input column. If data column *A* and data column *B* are both predict, then data column *A* will serve as an input when the algorithm is predicting data column *B,* and vice versa.

▶ **Predict Only** A *predict only* is a data column whose value is being predicted by the data mining algorithm. This column cannot be used as an input column when predicting other columns.

▶ **Ignore** This data column is not used by the data mining algorithm.

## Training Data Set

In Chapter 15, we discussed the fact that data must be divided into training and testing data sets. For the exercises in this book, we will use an OLAP cube as our data source. If we were to use a relational data source, the data would need to be split up elsewhere. It is a bit more challenging to divide the data when it resides in a single OLAP cube. To accomplish this division, we use the cube slice.

### Cube Slice

The *cube slice* enables us to specify an expression that divides the cube into two parts. The portion of the data that satisfies the expression is fed into the data mining algorithm for training. The rest of the data will be the testing data set.

## Learn By Doing—Defining a Data Mining Model

### Features Highlighted

▶ Creating a data mining structure based on an OLAP cube

▶ Defining data mining models

▶ Slicing the source cube

**Business Need**    The Maximum Miniatures Marketing Department wants to do a targeted mailing promoting the Mythic World line of figurines. Previous research has shown that the vast majority of buyers of the Mythic World product line do not have any children living at home. Unfortunately, the list of addresses and demographics purchased for the Mythic World mailing does not include a statistic on the number of children living at home. It does include the following facts about each household:

▶ Number of cars owned

▶ Marital status

▶ Whether the address is a rental property or occupied by the owner

The marketing department would like to find a way, using the three facts included in the mailing list data and the information known about current customers, to predict which households have no children living at home. The mailing will then be sent only to those households likely to have no children living at home.

Wholesale customers have customer numbers below 5000. Retail customers have customer numbers of 5000 and above. Of course, we should only use retail customers as our data for this mining operation.

### Steps to Deploy from SQL Server Data Tools

1. Look at the business requirements and determine which data mining task we need to accomplish. In this case, we want to classify the households in the new mailing list as either having no children living at home or having children living at home.

2. Select the data mining algorithms to perform this task. Four algorithms perform classification: Microsoft Decision Trees, Microsoft Naïve Bayes, Microsoft Clustering, and Microsoft Neural Network.

3. Determine where the data for the mining operation will come from. We have an OLAP cube full of customer data. This can provide an efficient source for our mining operation.

4.  Open SQL Server Data Tools.

5.  Open the MaxMinSalesDM project. In Chapter 10, we deployed this cube using the Deployment Wizard. Now, we will deploy it directly from SQL Server Data Tools.

6.  Select Project | Properties from the main menu. (The menu choice may say MaxMinSalesDM Properties, depending on what currently has focus.) The MaxMinSalesDM Property Pages dialog box appears.

7.  On the Deployment page, for the Server property, enter the name of the Analysis Services server instance where the MaxMinSalesDM database resides. Click OK.

8.  Select Build | Deploy MaxMinSalesDM from the main menu to deploy the latest version of the cube to the server. If you receive a prompt concerning overwriting the existing MaxMinSalesDM database, click Yes to overwrite it.

9.  If prompted for credentials, provide the appropriate credentials to complete the deployment.

10. When the deployment is complete, right-click the entry for the MaxMinSalesDM project in the Solution Explorer window. Select Process from the context menu. The Process Database—MaxMinSalesDM dialog box appears.

11. Click Run. The Process Progress dialog box appears.

12. When the process has succeeded, click Close to close the Process Progress dialog box. Click Close to close the Process Database—MaxMinSalesDM dialog box.

### Steps to Create a Mining Structure with One Mining Model

1.  Right-click the Mining Structures folder in the Solution Explorer window and select New Mining Structure from the context menu. The Data Mining Wizard appears.

2.  Click Next on the Welcome page. The Select the Definition Method page of the wizard appears, as shown in Figure 16-1.

## NOTE

*Data mining structures can use both relational databases and OLAP cubes for data. We could just as easily have used the MaxMinSalesDM relational database as the source for this cube. Relational databases designed for transactional operations, rather than for a data mart, can also be used.*

3.  Select the From existing cube radio button. Click Next. The Create the Data Mining Structure page of the wizard appears as shown in Figure 16-2.

4.  Select Microsoft Decision Trees from the drop-down list. Click Next. The Select the Source Cube Dimension page of the wizard appears, as shown in Figure 16-3.

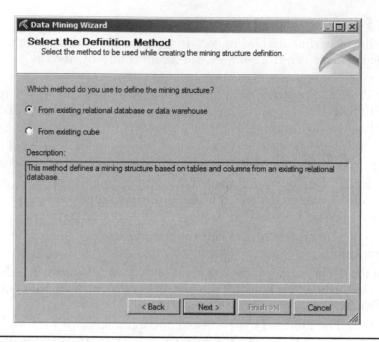

**Figure 16-1** *The Select the Definition Method page of the Data Mining Wizard*

**Figure 16-2** *The Create the Data Mining Structure page of the Data Mining Wizard*

**Figure 16-3**    *The Select the Source Cube Dimension page of the Data Mining Wizard*

5.  Select the Customer dimension. This is the main source of information for this mining operation. Click Next. The Select the Case Key page appears as shown in Figure 16-4.

6.  Leave the Customer attribute selected. This attribute serves as the primary key for the mining operation. Click Next. The Select Case Level Columns page of the wizard appears.

7.  The columns selected here serve as the input and predictable columns in our model. Check the following attributes:

    ▶  Homeowner

    ▶  Marital Status

    ▶  Num Cars Owned

    ▶  Num Children At Home

    The Select Case Level Columns wizard page appears as shown in Figure 16-5.

8.  Click Next. The Specify Mining Model Column Usage page of the wizard appears.

9.  Uncheck the check box in the Input column for Num Children At Home. Check the check box in the Predictable column for Num Children At Home. The Specify Mining Model Column Usage page appears as shown in Figure 16-6.

**Figure 16-4**    *The Select the Case Key page of the Data Mining Wizard*

**Figure 16-5**    *The Select Case Level Columns page of the Data Mining Wizard*

**Figure 16-6**  *The Specify Mining Model Column Usage page of the Data Mining Wizard*

10. Click Next. The Specify Columns' Content and Data Type page of the wizard appears.

11. Change the Content Type for Num Cars Owned to Discrete. Change the Content Type for Num Children At Home to Discrete. The Specify Columns' Content and Data Type page appears as shown in Figure 16-7.

## NOTE

*In Chapter 15, we said that some data mining algorithms can predict discrete values, while others can predict continuous values. In this case, we are using algorithms that require discrete values. Even though the Num Cars Owned and Num Children At Home have long integer data types, we know, in reality, that they have only a few discrete values. Therefore, we can change their Content Type to Discrete. It is possible to force a continuous set of values to be discrete. We do this by choosing Discretized as the Content Type, and then selecting a method that groups continuous values into a discrete number of buckets (that is, ages 11–15, ages 16–20, and so on). Often, it is much easier to do analysis on discretized values than on continuous values. For the purposes of a given analysis, the buying habits of 16–20-year-olds may be similar enough so that we can study them as a group in one discretized bucket.*

**Figure 16-7** *The Specify Columns' Content and Data Type page of the Data Mining Wizard*

12. Click Next. The Slice Source Cube page of the wizard appears.

13. We need to use only retail customers for our data mining (Account Num attribute of 5000 and above). Select Customer from the drop-down list in the first row of the Dimension column.

14. Select Account Num from the drop-down list in the first row of the Hierarchy column.

15. Select Range (Inclusive) from the drop-down list in the first row of the Operator column.

16. Click in the first row of the Filter Expression column. Two drop-down lists appear. Activate the drop-down list on the left.

17. Expand the All entry, select 5000 from the list, and click OK.

18. Activate the drop-down list on the right. Scroll to the bottom of the list.

19. Click the Filter Members link. The Filter Members – Children of All dialog box appears.

20. Select Name in the drop-down list under Property.

21. Select Begins with in the drop-down list under Operator.
22. In the Value area, enter **444**.
23. Click Test. The Filter Members dialog box appears, as shown in Figure 16-8.
24. Click OK to exit the Filter Members dialog box.
25. Select 44496 in the list and click OK. The Slice Source Cube page appears, as shown in Figure 16-9.

**Figure 16-8**  *The Filter Members dialog box*

**Figure 16-9** *The Slice Source Cube page of the Data Mining Wizard*

26. Click Next. The Create Testing Set page appears. We need to split our data into a training data set and a testing data set. We will split our data down the middle.

27. Change the Percentage of data from testing to **50%**. The Create Testing Set page appears as shown in Figure 16-10.

28. Click Next. The Completing the Wizard page appears.

29. Enter **Classification—Children At Home** for Mining structure name.

30. Enter **Decision Trees—Children At Home** for Mining model name. The Completing the Wizard page appears as shown in Figure 16-11.

31. Click Finish. The data mining structure containing our new data mining model is created, and the Data Mining Design tab appears as shown in Figure 16-12.

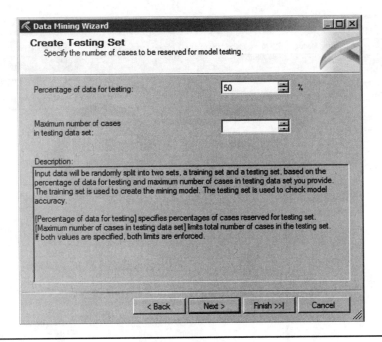

**Figure 16-10** *The Create Testing Set page of the Data Mining Wizard*

**Figure 16-11** *The Completing the Wizard page of the Data Mining Wizard*

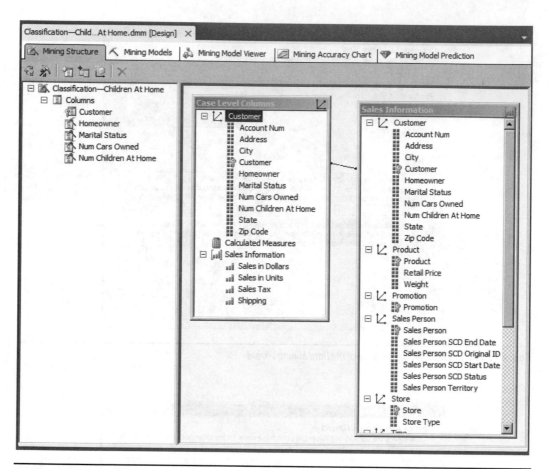

**Figure 16-12** *The Mining Structure tab on the Data Mining Design tab*

### Steps to Add Mining Models to the Mining Structure

1. Select the Mining Models tab on the Data Mining Design tab.

**NOTE**

*If needed, we can change the column usage right on the Mining Models tab, as shown in Figure 16-13. However, we do not need to make any changes here for our model.*

2. Click the Create a related mining model button on the Mining Models tab toolbar. The New Mining Model dialog box appears.

3. Enter **Naive Bayes—Children At Home** for Model name.

**Figure 16-13** *Changing the column usage*

4. Select Microsoft Naive Bayes from the Algorithm name drop-down list. The New Mining Model dialog box appears as shown in Figure 16-14.

5. Click OK.

6. Again, click the Create a related mining model button on the Mining Models tab toolbar. The New Mining Model dialog box appears.

7. Enter **Clustering—Children At Home** for Model name.

8. Select Microsoft Clustering from the Algorithm name drop-down list.

9. Click OK.

10. Once more, click the Create a related mining model button on the Mining Models tab toolbar. The New Mining Model dialog box appears.

**Figure 16-14**  *The New Mining Model dialog box*

11.  Enter **Neural Network—Children At Home** for Model Name.
12.  Select Microsoft Neural Network from the Algorithm name drop-down list.
13.  Click OK. The Mining Models tab appears as shown in Figure 16-15.
14.  Click the Save All button on the toolbar.
15.  Click the Process the mining structure and all its related models button on the Mining Models tab toolbar. A dialog box informs you the server content appears to be out-of-date.
16.  Click Yes to deploy the project. If prompted to overwrite the database, click Yes to continue.

**Figure 16-15**  *The Mining Models tab on the Data Mining Design tab*

17. When the deployment is complete, the Process Mining Structure dialog box appears, as shown in Figure 16-16. Click Run. The Process Progress dialog box appears.

18. When the models have all been trained and the process has been completed successfully, the Process Progress dialog box appears as shown in Figure 16-17. Click Close to exit the Process Progress dialog box.

19. Click Close to exit the Process Mining Structure dialog box.

**Figure 16-16** *The Process Mining Structure dialog box*

**Figure 16-17**  *The Process Progress dialog box*

# Mining Model Viewer

Now that we have several data mining models created and trained, let's look at how we begin to analyze the information. We do this by using the data mining model viewers, which are found on the Mining Model Viewer tab on the Data Mining Design tab.

Each data mining algorithm has its own set of viewers, enabling us to examine the trained data mining algorithm. These viewers present the mining information graphically for ease of understanding. If desired, we can also use the Microsoft Generic Content Tree Viewer to look at the raw data underlying the graphical presentations.

We will not do a specific Learn By Doing activity in this section. Really, the whole section is a Learn By Doing exercise. Please feel free to follow along on your PC as we explore the data models created in the previous Learn By Doing activity.

# Microsoft Decision Trees

Recall from Chapter 15, the Microsoft Decision Trees algorithm creates a tree structure. It would make sense, then, to view the result graphically as a tree structure. This is exactly what is provided by the Decision Tree tab of the Microsoft Tree Viewer. We can also determine how much each input attribute affects the result using the Dependency Network tab of the Microsoft Tree Viewer.

## Microsoft Tree Viewer—Decision Tree Tab

To use the Decision Tree tab of the Microsoft Tree Viewer, select the Mining Model Viewer tab on the Data Mining Design tab. (I know this "tab on tab within tabs" stuff sounds rather confusing. As strange as it sounds, the description here is correct!) Select Decision Trees—Children At Home from the Mining Model drop-down list. The Microsoft Tree Viewer appears with the Decision Tree tab selected, as shown in Figure 16-18. To duplicate

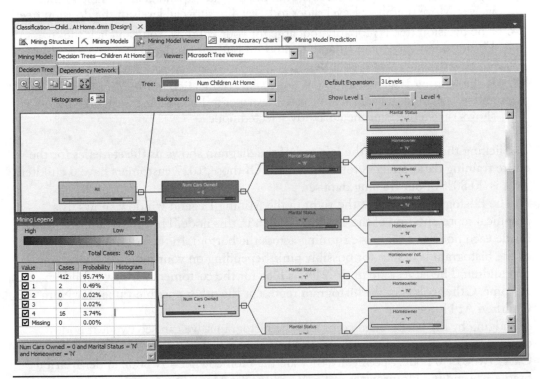

**Figure 16-18** *The decision tree view for the Microsoft Decision Tree algorithm*

this figure on your PC, adjust the following settings *after* you reach the Decision Tree tab and have the Decision Trees—Children At Home mining model selected:

1. The Tree drop-down list lets us select the predictable column to view. In this case, there is only one predictable column, Num Children At Home, so it is already selected for us.

2. By default, the background color of the tree nodes reflects the distribution of the cases throughout the tree. In our example, 4938 customers are in our training data. Nodes representing a larger percentage of those 4938 customers are darker than those representing a smaller percentage. The All node represents all 4938 customers, so it is the darkest. We can change the meaning of the node shading using the Background drop-down list. From the Background drop-down list, select 0. The background color now represents the percentage of customers with 0 children at home in each node. In other words, the color now represents how many customers with no children at home are represented by each group.

3. The Default Expansion drop-down list and the Show Level slider control work together to determine the number of nodes that are expanded and visible in the viewer. Move the Show Level slider to Level 4 to show all levels of the decision tree.

4. The decision tree is probably too large for your window. You can click the Size to Fit button or the Zoom In and Zoom Out buttons on the Decision Tree tab to size the decision tree appropriately.

5. If the Mining Legend window is not visible, right-click in the Decision Tree tab and select Show Legend from the context menu. The Mining Legend window shows the statistics of the currently selected node.

Clicking the All node on the left end of the diagram shows us the statistics for the entire training data set: 4938 total customers. Of those, 1027 customers have 0 children. This is 20.80% of our training data set.

The Histogram column at the right in the Mining Legend window shows us a graphical representation of the case breakdown in this node. The histogram is repeated inside each node as a rectangle running across the bottom. In the All node, 20.80% of the histogram is orange (or possibly pink, depending on your monitor), signifying no children. The largest group, 26.91%, is blue for the customers with two children at home. Other colors in the histogram represent the other possible values for Num Children At Home.

Judging by the background color and the histograms, we can see two leaf nodes contain the most customers with no children at home. Both of these are under the Num Cars Owned = 0 node. Specifically, they are the Homeowner = *N* node under Marital Status = *N* and the Homeowner not = *N* node under Marital Status = *Y*. In Figure 16-18, one of these two nodes is highlighted. This is the node with the most customers with no children at home. The bottom of the Mining Legend window shows the path through the decision tree to get to this node. This can also be thought of as the rule that defines this decision tree node. From this, we can see that someone who owns no cars, is unmarried, and does not own a home is likely to have no children at home.

## Microsoft Tree Viewer—Dependency Network Tab

Switching to the Dependency Network tab brings up a screen similar to Figure 16-19. This screen shows how each of the attributes included in the data mining model affect the other attributes. We can see which attributes predict other attributes. We can also see the strength of these interactions.

Clicking an attribute activates the color coding on the diagram. The selected node is highlighted with aqua green. The attributes predicted by the selected attribute are blue. The attributes that predict the selected attribute are light brown. If an attribute is predicted by the selected attribute but also can predict that attribute, it is shown in purple. The key for these colors is shown below the diagram.

The arrows in Figure 16-19 also show us which attributes predict other attributes. The arrow goes from an attribute that is a predictor to an attribute it predicts. Num Cars Owned, Marital Status, and Homeowner all predict Num Children At Home.

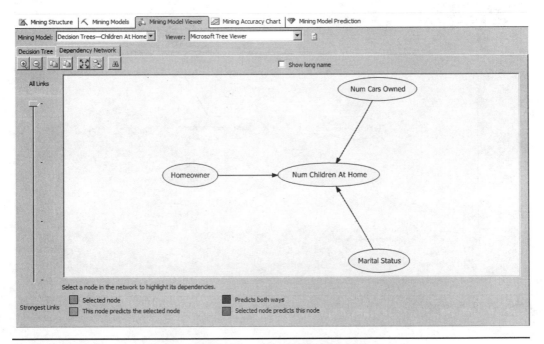

**Figure 16-19** *The Dependency Network tab for the Microsoft Decision Tree algorithm*

The slider to the left of the diagram controls which arrows are displayed. When the slider is at the top, as shown in Figure 16-19, all arrows are visible. As the slider moves down, the arrows signifying weaker influences disappear. Only the stronger influences remain. In Figure 16-20, we can see that the capability of the Num Cars Owned to predict Num Children At Home is the strongest influence in the model.

We have a simple dependency network diagram because we are only using a few attributes. It is possible to have diagrams with tens or even hundreds of attribute nodes. To aid in finding a node in such a cluttered diagram, the viewer provides a search feature. To use the search feature, click the Find Node button (the binoculars icon).

## Microsoft Generic Content Tree Viewer

If, for some reason, we need to see the detailed data underlying the diagrams, it is available using the Microsoft Generic Content Tree Viewer. This is selected using the Viewer drop-down list. The Microsoft Generic Content Tree Viewer is shown in Figure 16-21.

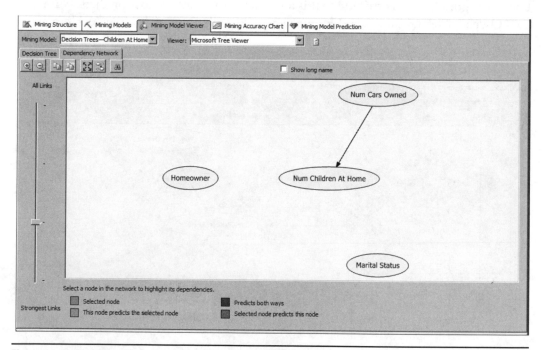

**Figure 16-20**  *The strongest influence in this data mining model*

**Figure 16-21** *The Microsoft Generic Content Tree Viewer*

## Microsoft Naïve Bayes

We look next at the tools available for reviewing the results of the Naïve Bayes algorithm. Recall from Chapter 15, the Naïve Bayes algorithm deals only with the influence of each individual attribute on the predictable value. Let's see how this is represented graphically.

### Microsoft Naïve Bayes Viewer—Dependency Network

Selecting the Naïve Bayes—Children At Home mining model from the Mining Model drop-down list displays the Microsoft Naïve Bayes Viewer—Dependency Network. This looks a lot like the Dependency Network Viewer we just saw for the Decision Trees algorithm, as shown in Figure 16-22. (Does this look like a Klingon starship to you, too?) In fact, it functions in an identical manner. Using the slider to the left of the diagram, we can see the Num Cars Owned attribute is also the best predictor of Num Children At Home for this model. This is shown in Figure 16-23.

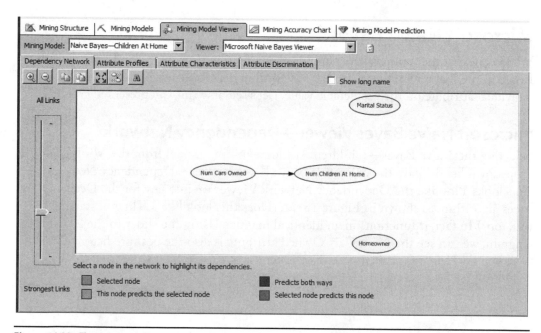

**Figure 16-22** *The Dependency Network Viewer for the Microsoft Naïve Bayes algorithm*

**Figure 16-23** *The strongest influence in this mining model*

## Attribute Profiles

Next, select the Attribute Profiles tab. We can select the predictable we want to analyze using the Predictable drop-down list. Num Children At Home is our only predictable in this model, so it is already selected. The diagram shows the distribution of each attribute value for the various predictable values. This is shown in Figure 16-24.

Again, we have a Mining Legend window to provide more detailed information. Selecting a cell in the Attribute Profiles grid shows, in the Mining Legend, the numbers that underlie the histogram for that cell. The cell for the Num Cars Owned where Num Children At Home is 0 is selected and pointed to by the mouse cursor in Figure 16-24.

## Attribute Characteristics

Select the Attribute Characteristics tab. Num Children At Home is already selected in the Attribute drop-down list, and 0 is already selected in the Value drop-down list. We can see the attribute characteristics for the model. In other words, we can see the probability of a particular attribute value being present along with our predictable value. This is shown in Figure 16-25.

**Figure 16-24** *The Attribute Profiles Viewer for the Microsoft Naïve Bayes algorithm*

**Figure 16-25** *The Attribute Characteristics Viewer for the Microsoft Naïve Bayes algorithm*

In this figure, we can see a customer with no cars has a high probability of having no children at home. We can also see a high probability exists that a customer who is not married does not have any children at home. There is a low probability that a person with one car has no children at home.

## Attribute Discrimination

Select the Attribute Discrimination tab. Num Children At Home is already selected in the Attribute drop-down list, and 0 is already selected in the Value 1 drop-down list. All other states is selected in the Value 2 drop-down list. This diagram lets us determine what attribute values most differentiate nodes favoring our desired predictable state from those disfavoring our predictable state. This is shown in Figure 16-26.

From the figure, we can see that not owning a car favors having no children at home. Being married favors having children at home. As with the other diagrams, selecting a cell displays the detail for that cell in the Mining Legend.

# Microsoft Clustering

We move from Naïve Bayes to the Microsoft Clustering algorithm. In Chapter 15, we learned the Clustering algorithm creates groupings, or clusters. We examine the clusters to determine which ones have the most occurrences of the predictable value we are looking for. Then we can look at the attribute values that differentiate that cluster from the others.

**Figure 16-26** *The Attribute Discrimination Viewer for the Microsoft Naïve Bayes algorithm*

## Cluster Diagram

Selecting the Clustering—Children At Home mining model from the Mining Model drop-down list displays the Microsoft Cluster Viewer–Cluster Diagram. We can see the algorithm came up with eight different clusters. The lines on the diagram show how closely related one cluster is to another. A dark gray line signifies two clusters that are strongly related. A light gray line signifies two clusters that are weakly related.

Select Num Children At Home from the Shading Variable drop-down list. The State drop-down list should have the 0 value selected. The shading of the clusters now represents the number of customers with 0 children at home in each cluster. This is shown in Figure 16-27.

In the diagram, Cluster 6 has the highest concentration of customers with no children at home. To make analysis easier on the other tabs, let's rename this cluster. Right-click Cluster 6 and select Rename Cluster from the context menu. The Rename Cluster dialog box appears. Enter **No Children At Home** and click OK.

## Cluster Profiles

Selecting the Cluster Profiles tab displays a grid of cluster profiles, as shown in Figure 16-28. This functions exactly the same as the Naïve Bayes Attribute Profiles tab. We use this tab to examine the characteristics of the clusters that most interest us. In this case, it is easy to pick out the cluster of interest because we named it No Children At Home.

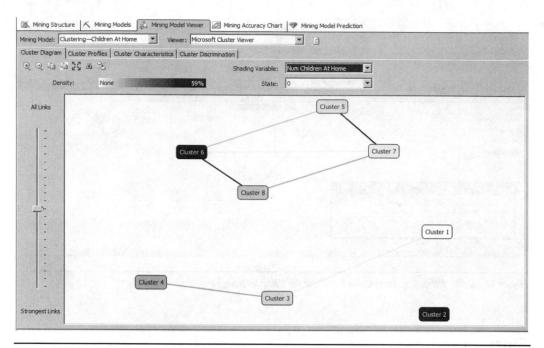

**Figure 16-27** *The Cluster Diagram Viewer for the Microsoft Clustering algorithm*

**Figure 16-28** *The Cluster Profiles Viewer for the Microsoft Clustering algorithm*

## Cluster Characteristics

We next select the Cluster Characteristics tab to display the grid of cluster characteristics. Select No Children At Home from the Cluster drop-down list to view the characteristics of this cluster. The Cluster Characteristics tab functions in the same manner as the Attribute Characteristics tab we encountered with the Microsoft Naïve Bayes algorithm. The Cluster Characteristics tab is shown in Figure 16-29.

## Cluster Discrimination

Select the Cluster Discrimination tab, and then select No Children At Home from the Cluster 1 drop-down list. This diagram enables us to determine what attribute values most differentiate our selected cluster from all the others. This is shown in Figure 16-30.

# Microsoft Neural Network

Selecting the Neural Network—Children At Home mining model from the Mining Model drop-down list displays the Microsoft Neural Network Viewer. The Microsoft Neural Network algorithm uses a Discrimination Viewer similar to those we have seen with other algorithms. This lets us determine the characteristics that best predict our predictable value.

Num Children At Home is already selected in the Output Attribute drop-down list. Select 0 in the Value 1 drop-down list. Select 1 in the Value 2 drop-down list. We can now see what differentiates customers with no children at home from customers with one child at home. The Discrimination Viewer is shown in Figure 16-31.

**Figure 16-29** *The Cluster Characteristics Viewer for the Microsoft Clustering algorithm*

**Figure 16-30** *The Cluster Discrimination Viewer for the Microsoft Clustering algorithm*

**Figure 16-31** *The Discrimination Viewer for the Microsoft Neural Network algorithm*

## Microsoft Association Rules

The Microsoft Association Rules algorithm deals with items that have been formed into sets within the data. In the example here, we look at sets of products that were purchased by the same customer. SQL Server Data Tools provides us with three viewers for examining these sets.

**NOTE**

We did not use the Microsoft Association or the other algorithms that follow in the remainder of this section in our mining structure.

## Itemsets

The Itemsets Viewer is shown in Figure 16-32. The *Itemsets Viewer* shows a textual description of each set. The Support column shows the number of cases supporting the set. For clarity of analysis, we set Minimum Support to require at least 300 occurrences for a set to be displayed. The Size column tells us the number of members in the set.

**Figure 16-32** *The Itemsets Viewer for the Microsoft Association Rules algorithm*

## Rules

The Rules Viewer displays the rules the algorithm created from the sets. This is shown in Figure 16-33. The Probability column shows the probability of a rule being true. In Figure 16-33, we have a number of rules with a 100% (1.000) probability—a sure thing! This means we do not have a single case in our training data set where this rule is not true.

The *Importance column* tells us how useful the rule may be in making predictions. For example, if every set contained a particular attribute state, a rule that predicts this attribute state is not helpful; it is of low importance. The *Rule column,* of course, describes the rule. The rule at the top of Figure 16-33 says a set that contains a British Infantry figure and a Flying Dragon figure also contains a Cape Hatteras, NC Lighthouse.

## Dependency Network

The Dependency Network Viewer functions in the same manner as we have seen with other algorithms. There is a node for each predictable state. In our example, there is a node for each member of the Product dimension. Selecting a product node shows which products it predicts will be in the set and which products predict it will be in the set. The Dependency Network Viewer is shown in Figure 16-34.

**Figure 16-33** *The Rules Viewer for the Microsoft Association Rules algorithm*

**Figure 16-34** *The Dependency Network Viewer for the Microsoft Association Rules algorithm*

## Microsoft Sequence Clustering

The Microsoft Sequence Clustering algorithm is similar to the Microsoft Clustering algorithm. Consequently, these two algorithms use the same viewers. The only difference is the addition of the State Transitions Viewer. This viewer shows the probability of moving from one state in the sequence to another.

## Microsoft Time Series

The Microsoft Time Series algorithm uses a Decision Tree Viewer, as we have seen with other algorithms. Recall from Chapter 15, each node in the decision tree contains a regression formula that is used to forecast future continuous values. The Microsoft Time Series also uses a Chart Viewer, shown in Figure 16-35, to chart these forecast values.

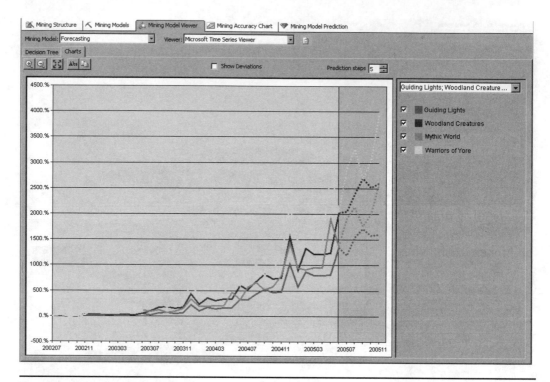

**Figure 16-35** *The Chart Viewer for the Microsoft Time Series algorithm*

# Reading the Tea Leaves

Now that we have built a data mining model and done some preliminary analysis, it is time to put data mining to work. In Chapter 17, we look at ways to combine data mining with applications. This combination can add immense value and functionality to business solutions.

# Spelunking—Exploration Using Data Mining

## In This Chapter

- ▶ **Mining Accuracy Chart**
- ▶ **Mining Model Prediction**
- ▶ **Data Mining Extensions**
- ▶ **Special Delivery**

*All we discover has been with us since the sun began to roll.*

—Herman Melville

In Chapter 15, we learned the five steps for data mining:

▶ Problem Definition

▶ Data Preparation

▶ Training

▶ Testing

▶ Deployment

In Chapter 16, we worked through the first three steps. Now it is time to work on the final two.

In this chapter, we use the Mining Accuracy Chart in SQL Server Data Tools to test the data mining models we created in Chapter 16. Then, we use the Mining Model Prediction tab to make predictions with our mining models. Finally, we look at the Data Mining Extensions (DMX), which enable us to create data mining queries.

# Mining Accuracy Chart

Before we put a data mining model to use in a production environment, we need to ensure the model is making predictions with the desired accuracy. This is done using the Mining Accuracy Chart tab in SQL Server Data Tools. The *Mining Accuracy Chart tab* provides four tools for determining the accuracy of our mining models: the Lift Chart, the Profit Chart, the Classification Matrix, and Cross Validation.

The *Lift Chart* is a line graph showing the performance of our mining models using a test data set. The *Profit Chart* is a line graph showing the projected profitability of a marketing campaign as it relates to the accuracy of our mining models. The *Classification Matrix* provides a chart showing the number of correct predictions and the number of each type of error made by our models. *Cross Validation* provides a technical analysis of the model's performance when making a specified prediction. Before we can use any of these tools, we need to use the Input Selection tab to specify the data to use for testing our models.

## Column Mapping

The *Input Selection tab* lets us determine which models to include in our tests. It also lets us select which prediction we are testing. Finally, it allows us to determine the source for the data we use to do the model validation. The Input Selection tab is shown in Figure 17-1.

## Select the Mining Models and Prediction

The upper portion of the tab is where we select which of the models in the mining structure to include in our accuracy charts. We do this by placing a check mark next to each mining model. We can select from any of the mining models we included in our mining structure.

Our mining models may include more than one predictable column. If that is the case, we need to select which predictable to use for testing. We can test our model on the prediction of all values for the predictable or on its accuracy at predicting a selected value.

We can choose to test the same prediction for all of the selected models by checking the Synchronize Prediction Columns and Values check box. When this box is checked, whatever predictable column and predict value we select for one model is automatically copied to the other models.

**Figure 17-1**   *The Input Selection tab*

### Select the Test Data

The lower portion of the tab is where we select which data to use when testing our model. We have three options: mining model test cases, mining structure test cases, or another data set. Mining model test cases are created as part of defining the training data for a mining model. Mining structure test cases are created as part of defining the mining model structure.

### Viewing the Mining Accuracy Charts

In order to view the mining accuracy charts described in the next section of this chapter, we actually do not need to make any changes on the Input Selection tab. All of the mining models in the mining structure are selected by default, which is exactly what we want. Our models have only one predictable column, so there is nothing to change there. We will begin by looking at all predictable values, so that can also remain at its default setting.

Recall that when we created the mining structure in Chapter 16, we specified retail customers (customers with account numbers of 5000 and above) from the customer dimension were to be used to train the mining models. Actually, we said 50% of those customers should be used to train the models. The other 50% was to be set aside for testing the models. This mining model test case is selected for us by default.

## Lift Chart

The Lift Chart is used to judge the effectiveness of a mining model. It creates a line graph showing the accuracy of each mining model at predicting the selected value. In addition, the Lift Chart contains a line showing the perfect prediction of an ideal model. Finally, when a prediction value is specified, a line showing the prediction accuracy of a random-guess model is added to the chart. Any distance that the graph line has for a particular mining model above the random-guess model is *lift*. The more lift, the closer the mining model comes to the ideal model.

### The Lift Chart with No Prediction Value Specified

Two different types of Lift Charts are available to use. The first type is produced when we do not have a prediction value specified. If we select the Lift Chart tab and then wait a few moments for the chart to be calculated, we see a chart similar to Figure 17-2.

This type of Lift Chart shows how well each mining model did at predicting the correct number of children at home for each customer in the testing data set. The $X$ axis represents the percentage of the testing data set that was processed. The $Y$ axis represents

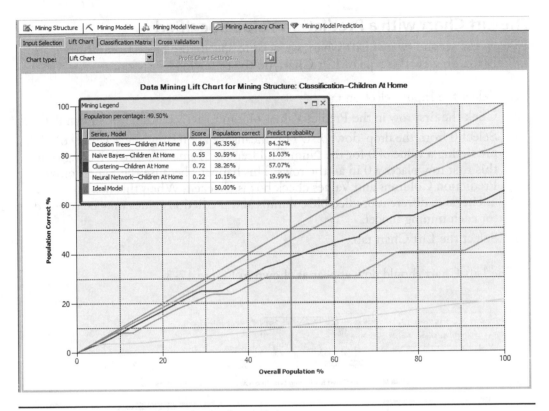

**Figure 17-2**    *The Lift Chart with no prediction value specified*

the percentage of the testing data set that was predicted correctly. The line along the diagonal of the graph shows the ideal prediction model. If 50% of the testing data set has been processed, then 50% of the testing data set has been predicted correctly. This type of Lift Chart does not include a line for a random-guess model.

The *Mining Legend* gives the statistics for each mining model at a certain overall population percentage. This percentage is shown at the top of the Mining Legend window and is represented on the graph by the thicker gray vertical line. This line can be moved to different positions by clicking the desired location on the graph. In Figure 17-2, the Mining Legend contains information for an overall population percentage of 49.50%. We can see that when 49.50% of the population is processed, the Decision Trees mining model will have predicted 45.35% of the values correctly. The Neural Network mining model will have predicted only 10.15% correctly.

## The Lift Chart with a Prediction Value Specified

To view the second type of Lift Chart, we need to specify the prediction value we are looking for. To view this type of Lift Chart, do the following:

1. Select the Input Selection tab.
2. Click the first row in the Predict Value column to activate the drop-down list.
3. Select 0 from the drop-down list. This means we are testing the accuracy of predicting a value of 0 for the Num Children At Home column. Selecting 0 in this first row places a 0 in all the rows. This happens because the Synchronize Prediction Columns and Values check box is checked. When this box is unchecked, different predictable columns and prediction values may be selected for each mining model.
4. Select the Lift Chart tab.

The Lift Chart should now appear as shown in Figure 17-3.

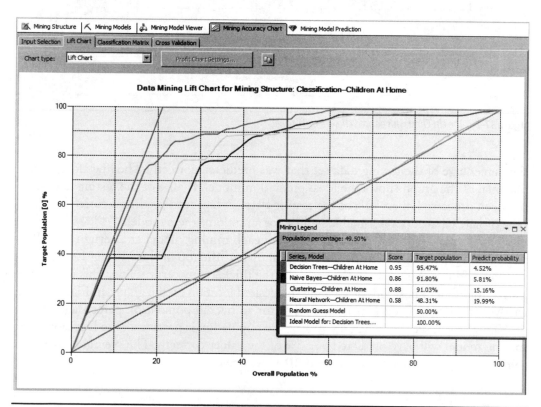

**Figure 17-3**   *The Lift Chart with a predict value of 0*

On this chart, the $X$ axis still represents the percentage of the testing data set that has been processed. The meaning of the $Y$ axis has changed. We now have a target population for our predictions. That target population is customers with no children at home (Num Children At Home = 0).

Of the customers in the testing data set, 21% have no children at home. Therefore, in a perfect world, we only need to process 21% of the testing data set to find all the customers with no children at home. This is why the line for the ideal model reaches 100% on the $Y$ axis at 21% on the $X$ axis. Using the random-guess model, when 50% of the testing data set has been processed, 50% of the target population will have been found.

On this Lift Chart, it is hard to see where some of the lines are because they overlap. This is where the Mining Legend window comes in handy. If we click at about 6% on the $X$ axis, we can see where these overlapping lines are located. This is shown in Figure 17-4. Using the figures in the Mining Legend, we can see the Decision Trees mining model is at 26.90% and the Naïve Bayes mining model is at 26.42% of the target population.

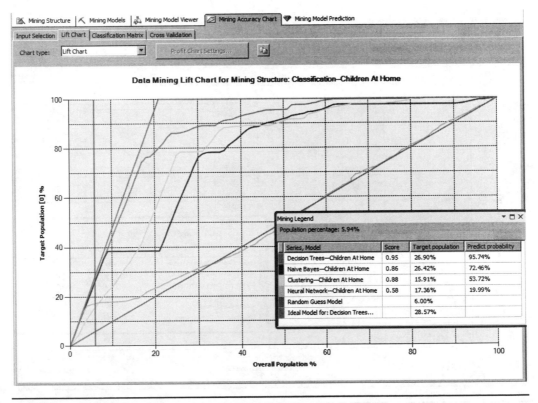

**Figure 17-4**  *The Lift Chart at 6%*

If we jump up to near 20%, as shown in Figure 17-5, we can see things have changed. The Decision Trees mining model has now found 78.30% of the target population. The Naïve Bayes mining model is at 38.48%, hardly any progress over where it was at 6%.

Moving to about 60%, we can see that most of the other mining models have finally caught up to the Decision Trees mining model. This is shown in Figure 17-6. All the models except the Neural Network have found at least 95% of the target population. Some differentiation occurs between the mining models as we move higher than 35%, but the spread is small and we have already identified the vast majority of the target population at this point.

## Profit Chart

The Profit Chart lets us analyze financial aspects of a campaign that depend on the predictive capabilities of our mining models. The information in the Profit Chart can help us determine the size of campaign we should undertake. It can also provide a prediction of the profit we should expect from a campaign (hence, the name).

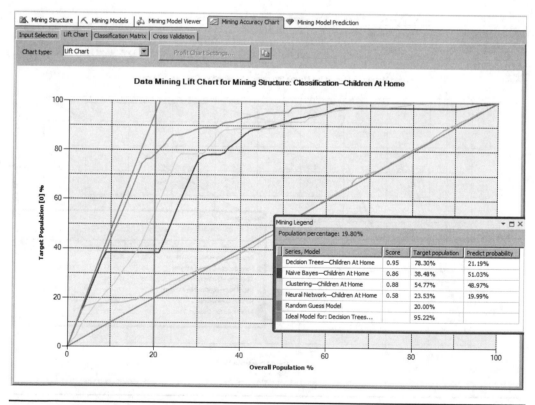

**Figure 17-5** *The Lift Chart at 20%*

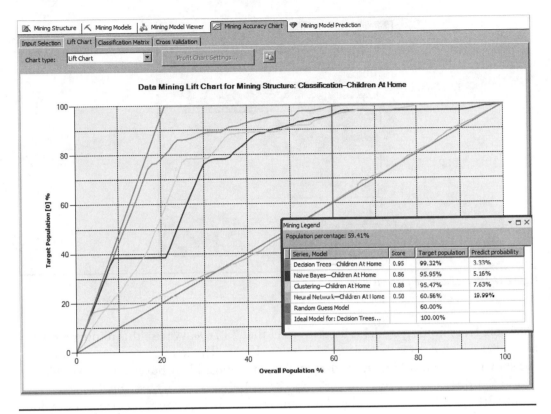

**Figure 17-6**   *The Lift Chart at 60%*

## Creating a Profit Chart

To create a Profit Chart, select Profit Chart from the Chart type drop-down list. This displays the Profit Chart Settings dialog box. We need to enter the population and financial aspects of the campaign we are modeling. In our case, let's suppose Maximum Miniatures has purchased a mailing list with 100,000 names. Enter **100000** for Population in the dialog box. This mailing will have $4,000 of fixed costs—costs that do not change no matter how many items we mail—and $2 per mailing sent. Enter **4000** for Fixed Cost and **2** for Individual Cost. Finally, for each person who receives the mailing and makes a purchase, we are going to receive, on average, $20. Enter **20** for Revenue per individual. The completed Profit Chart Settings dialog box is shown in Figure 17-7. Click OK to produce the Profit Chart.

The resulting Profit Chart is shown in Figure 17-8. We can see from this graph that the maximum profit will come if Maximum Miniatures sends the mailing to 23.76% of the names in the mailing list it purchased. At least, that is the case if the

**Figure 17-7**   *The Profit Chart Settings dialog box*

Decision Trees mining model is used to select that 23.76%. We use this mining model to predict which customers have no children at home. (Remember, previous research has shown Maximum Miniatures that these are the most likely buyers of the Mythic World figurines.) Given this mining model's capability to predict, we should make about $309,758 in profit after the cost of the mailing. Mailing to more people does not significantly improve our chances of getting sales, but it does increase our costs. Because of this, our expected profit goes down if we mail to more people.

## Classification Matrix

We know our mining models are not going to do a perfect job of predicting. They are going to make mistakes. The Classification Matrix lets us see exactly what mistakes our models have made.

### Viewing the Classification Matrix

We view the Classification Matrix by selecting the Classification Matrix tab on the Mining Accuracy Chart tab. The Classification Matrix is shown in Figure 17-9. Using the Classification Matrix, we can see the predictions made by each mining model.

The left-hand column in each grid shows the value predicted by the mining model. In Figure 17-9, this is the number of children at home predicted for each customer in the testing data set. The other columns show the actual value for the number of children at home for each customer.

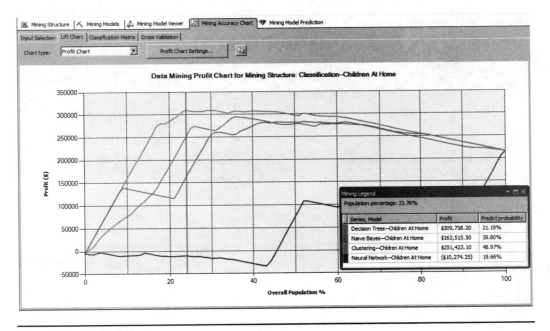

**Figure 17-8**  *The Profit Chart*

In Figure 17-9, the top grid shows the result for the Decision Trees mining model. Looking at the top row in the grid, we can see that in 791 cases, the Decision Trees mining model predicted zero children at home when there were actually zero children at home. These were correct predictions. In ten cases, the Decision Trees mining model predicted zero children at home when there were actually three children at home. These predictions were in error.

The diagonal of the grid shows the correct predictions: predicted zero with actual zero, predicted three with actual three, predicted one with actual one, and so on. We want to have the largest numbers along the diagonal. This is the case for the Decision Trees mining model. We already know this model is accurate. The Naïve Bayes mining model, shown second from the top in Figure 17-9, does not always have the largest numbers along the diagonal. This mining model had a tendency to predict two children at home when there were actually zero children at home. This mistake occurred 392 times during the processing of our testing data set.

**Figure 17-9** *The Classification Matrix*

# Cross Validation

The final tab on the Mining Accuracy Chart tab provides access to the Cross Validation analysis tool. This tool provides one more method for comparing the accuracy of several mining models within a mining structure. Cross Validation provides a grid of technical figures for each mining method tested.

## Viewing the Cross Validation

To view the Cross Validation, select the Cross Validation tab. This tab provides an area at the top for specifying the various parameters required for cross validation. The parameters are as follows:

▶ **Fold Count** The fold count divides the validation data into distinct sets. For each validation, one fold is used to test the model, while the remaining folds are used to first train the model before testing.

▶ **Max Cases**   The max cases signifies the maximum number of cases to use for validation. The cases are then divided evenly among the folds.

▶ **Target Attribute**   The attribute we are trying to predict.

▶ **Target State**   The value of the target attribute we are trying to predict.

▶ **Target Threshold**   The required probability that a prediction is correct. This is a number between 0.0 and 1.0. A number closer to 1.0 represents a higher prediction probability.

The Cross Validation tab is shown in Figure 17-10. Analysis of the cross validation results is beyond the scope of this book. For further information, consult SQL Books Online.

**Decision Trees—Children At Home**

| Partition Index | Partition Size | Test | Measure | Value |
|---|---|---|---|---|
| 1 | 11 | Classification | True Positive | 0.000e+000 |
| 2 | 9 | Classification | True Positive | 0.000e+000 |
| 3 | 10 | Classification | True Positive | 0.000e+000 |
| | | | Average | 0.000e+000 |
| | | | Standard Deviation | 0.000e+000 |
| 1 | 11 | Classification | False Positive | 0.000e+000 |
| 2 | 9 | Classification | False Positive | 0.000e+000 |
| 3 | 10 | Classification | False Positive | 0.000e+000 |
| | | | Average | 0.000e+000 |
| | | | Standard Deviation | 0.000e+000 |
| 1 | 11 | Classification | True Negative | 9 |
| 2 | 9 | Classification | True Negative | 7 |
| 3 | 10 | Classification | True Negative | 8 |
| | | | Average | 8.0667 |
| | | | Standard Deviation | 0.8138 |
| 1 | 11 | Classification | False Negative | 2 |
| 2 | 9 | Classification | False Negative | 2 |
| 3 | 10 | Classification | False Negative | 2 |
| | | | Average | 2 |
| | | | Standard Deviation | 0.000e+000 |

**Figure 17-10**  *The Cross Validation tab*

# Mining Model Prediction

All this training and testing has finally gotten us to a place where we have a mining model ready to make real-world predictions. We have seen how well each of the mining models does at making predictions; now, we can pick one and put it to work. The Mining Model Prediction tab enables us to do just that.

Using the Mining Model Prediction tab, we can create queries that use a mining model to make predictions. Two types of prediction queries are supported: a singleton query and a prediction join. We look at the singleton query first.

# A Singleton Query

A *singleton query* lets us feed a single set of input values to the mining model. We receive a single value for the predictable based on these values. This enables us to manually enter a scenario to see what the mining model will predict.

## Creating a Singleton Query

For both the singleton query and the prediction join, we must first select the mining model to use. When the model is selected, the Singleton Query Input dialog box contains an input field for each input column in the mining model. We can then enter values for each of these input columns.

We then select the columns we would like in the result set. The predictable column should be included in the result set; otherwise, the query isn't doing much for us. We can also include our own custom expressions, as desired.

When the query is designed, we switch to the result view to see the result set. We can also switch to the SQL view to see the DMX query being created for us behind the scenes—more on that in the section "Data Mining Extensions." Queries can be saved to be re-run at a later time.

## Learn By Doing—Creating a Singleton Query

### Feature Highlighted

▶ Creating a singleton query using the Mining Model Prediction tab

**Business Need**   Our business need is simple. We will try out the mining model we have worked so hard to create.

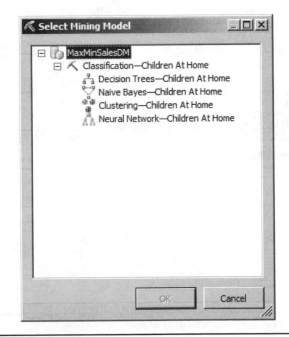

**Figure 17-11** *The Singleton Query toolbar button*

## Steps

1. Open SQL Server Data Tools.
2. Open the MaxMinSalesDM project.
3. If the Data Mining Design tab for the Classification—Children At Home data mining structure is not displayed, double-click the entry for this data mining structure in the Solution Explorer window.
4. Select the Mining Model Prediction tab on the Data Mining Design tab.
5. Click the Singleton Query button on the Mining Model Prediction tab toolbar. This is shown in Figure 17-11.
6. Click Select Model in the Mining Model window. The Select Mining Model dialog box appears, as shown in Figure 17-12.

**Figure 17-12** *The Select Mining Model dialog box*

7. Select the Decision Trees—Children At Home mining model and click OK.

8. In the Singleton Query Input window, select Y from the Homeowner drop-down list in the Value column.

9. Select N from the Marital Status drop-down list.

10. Select 2 from the Num Cars Owned drop-down list.

11. Now select the columns in the result set. In the first row under the Source column, select the Decision Trees—Children At Home mining model from the drop-down list. This is shown in Figure 17-13. Num Children At Home is selected by default in the Field column because it is the only predictable in the mining model.

12. In the second row under the Source column, select Custom Expression from the drop-down list.

13. In the second row under the Field column, enter the following:

```
'Homeowner = Y; Marital Status = N; Num Cars Owned = 2'
```

**Figure 17-13** *Selecting the columns in the singleton query result set*

| Mining Structure | Mining Models | Mining Model Viewer | Mining Accuracy Chart | Mining Model Prediction |

**Mining Model**

☐ 🔲 Decision Trees—Children
   🔲 Customer
   🔲 Homeowner
   🔲 Marital Status
   🔲 Num Cars Owned
   🔲 Num Children At Hom

Select Model...

**Singleton Query Input**

| Mining Model Column | Value |
| --- | --- |
| Homeowner | Y |
| Marital Status | N |
| Num Cars Owned | 2 |
| Num Children At Home | |

| Source | Field | Alias | Show | Group | And/Or | Criteria/Argument |
| --- | --- | --- | --- | --- | --- | --- |
| Decision Trees—Children At Home | Num Children At Home | | ☑ | | | |
| Custom Expression | 'Homeowner = Y; Marital Status = N; Num Cars Owned = 2' | Input Criteria | ☑ | | | |
| | | | ☐ | | | |

**Figure 17-14**  *The completed singleton query*

14. In the second row under the Alias column, enter **InputCriteria**. The Mining Model Prediction tab appears as shown in Figure 17-14.

15. Select Result from the View drop-down list on the Mining Model Prediction tab toolbar, as shown in Figure 17-15.

**Figure 17-15**  *Selecting the result view*

**Figure 17-16**   *The singleton query result set in the result view*

16. The result view is displayed, as shown in Figure 17-16. The model predicts that someone who is a homeowner, is not married, and owns two cars will most likely have four children at home.

17. Select Design from the View drop-down list on the Mining Model Prediction tab toolbar to return to the design view.

## A Prediction Join Query

The singleton query lets us use a single set of inputs to generate a single row result set. The prediction join query enables us to use a tableful of inputs to generate a multiple-row result set. We feed multiple records to the mining model, and it creates a prediction for each of these records.

### Creating a Prediction Join Query

The *prediction join query* functions similarly to the singleton query: The difference is that the Singleton Query Input window is replaced by the Select Input Table(s) window. This window lets us select the table or joined set of tables that will serve as the record source for the prediction join.

## Learn By Doing—Creating a Prediction Join Query

### Feature Highlighted

▶ Creating a prediction join query using the Mining Model Prediction tab

**Business Need**    In a previous Learn By Doing exercise, we discussed a scenario where the Maximum Miniatures Marketing Department purchased a mailing list that they wanted classified into those households likely to have no children at home and those that have one or more children at home. We now have a trained and tested mining model ready to perform that classification.

To keep things simple, we can use the same customer table and a little imagination to pretend this is the newly purchased list. Remember, the whole reason we had to do this classification was because the newly purchased list did not include the number of children at home. Therefore, if we have our existing customer table play the role of the newly purchased list, we must ignore the fact that it already has a number of children at home field.

### Steps

1. Click the Singleton Query button on the Mining Model Prediction tab toolbar to toggle back to the Prediction Join Query mode. Click Yes to continue when warned about losing your query.
2. Click Select Case Table in the Select Input Table(s) window. The Select Table dialog box appears.
3. Select the Customer (dbo) table and click OK. The fields are automatically mapped, based on field names.
4. We are not supposed to have a Num Children At Home field in this table, so we need to delete this mapping and predict this value instead. Click the mapping line going from Num Children At Home to NumChildrenAtHome so it is highlighted.
5. Right-click the mapping line and select Delete from the context menu.
6. In the first row under the Source column, select Decision Trees—Children At Home mining model from the drop-down list. Again, Num Children At Home is selected by default in the Field column because it is the only predictable in the mining model.

7. In the second row under the Source column, select Customer Table from the drop-down list.

8. In the second row under the Field column, select Customer_Name from the drop-down list.

9. In the third row under the Source column, select Customer Table from the drop-down list.

10. In the third row under the Field column, select Address from the drop-down list.

11. Continue this process to include City, State, and ZipCode in the result set. The Mining Model Prediction tab appears as shown in Figure 17-17.

**Figure 17-17**  *The completed prediction join query*

12. Select Result from the View drop-down list on the Mining Model Prediction tab toolbar. The result view is displayed, as shown in Figure 17-18.

13. One issue remains. The Marketing Department only wants to mail to households that are predicted to have no children at home. All of the others should be eliminated from the list. Select Design from the View drop-down list on the Mining Model Prediction tab toolbar to return to the design view.

14. In the first row under the Criteria/Argument column, enter = **0**.

15. We do not need to see the predictable value in our result set, especially now that it will be 0 for every row. Uncheck the check box in the first row of the Show column. The Mining Model Prediction tab appears as shown in Figure 17-19.

| Num Children At Home | Customer_Name | Address | City | State | ZipCode |
|---|---|---|---|---|---|
| 4 | Stanley R Johnson | 135 Waymore Blvd. | Edgeview | ND | 56293 |
| 4 | Henry D Cramer | 9483 49th St. | Appleford | ME | 03904 |
| 4 | Owen N Von Brocken | 2843 Drummin Lane | Foggyville | AK | 99302 |
| 4 | Wilhelm A Hoover | 135 Poplar St. | Parkside | ND | 56293 |
| 4 | Vern Z Von Stubben | 2839 5th Ave. | Yankton | MD | 21201 |
| 4 | Terry K Anthony | 2932 50th St. | Diffley | KS | 58239 |
| 4 | Marian W Smith | 27391 Overton Dr. | Upton | TX | 75201 |
| 4 | Jennifer N Ali | 3489 Waverly St. | Templeton | VA | 23607 |
| 4 | Ramona C Pearl | 2384 Park Ct. | Ivers | OR | 97205 |
| 4 | Walter R Hederson | 2932 Waverly St. | Quincy | KY | 42718 |
| 4 | Winifred S Pearl | 8293 Polar Ave | Karlstown | NM | 88044 |
| 4 | Arun J Anthony | 135 Wicker Way | Upton | ND | 56293 |
| 4 | Jennifer W Mueller | 4839 73rd Ave. | Foggyville | SD | 57049 |
| 4 | Ralph M Pearl | 283 Highview Blvd. | Upton | PA | 19107 |
| 4 | Brad R Taft | 2838 Becker Way | Venice | CT | 06032 |
| 4 | Xia F Goldbloom | 3838 Mortimer Ct. | Appleford | NJ | 09483 |
| 4 | Melissa V Wellington | 2839 Seasame Ln. | Hillburg | CT | 06032 |
| 4 | Henry N Sipulski | 3489 45th St. | Diffley | AK | 99302 |
| 4 | Walter D Winstrom | 2833 39th Ave. | Parkside | IL | 60610 |
| 4 | Douglas E Alvarez | 2843 Waverly St. | Big Fork | MS | 38804 |
| 4 | Cassie N Petrov | 2939 73rd Ave. | Parkside | RI | 02892 |
| 4 | Zeb Y Hoover | 7472 Anchor St. | Lowry | NC | 27412 |
| 4 | Nels E Roosevelt | 135 23rd St. | Orville | MN | 55802 |
| 4 | Nels L Allens | 2839 Hwy 45 | Crawley | WA | 98011 |
| 4 | Ralph J Popovich | 828 Seasame Ln. | Yankton | MI | 48226 |
| 4 | Ramona V Sipulski | 8232 Baker Ave. | Jonesbourgh | OK | 59304 |
| 4 | Edward K Roberts | 2843 Birch St. | Watertown | CA | 94109 |
| 4 | Xia W Popovich | 2843 5th Ave. | Stapleton | AK | 99302 |
| 4 | Ramona K Hokah | 283 Mycroft Ln. | Ivers | MO | 63301 |

Query execution completed with 10000 rows fetched

**Figure 17-18**  *The prediction join query result set in the result view*

**Figure 17-19** *The prediction join query with filter criteria*

16. Select Result from the View drop-down list on the Mining Model Prediction tab toolbar. Now only those households predicted to have no children at home are included in our result set, as shown in Figure 17-20.

17. Now we need to place this result set somewhere where it can be used for the mailing. Click the Save query result button on the Mining Model Prediction tab toolbar. The Save Data Mining Query Result dialog box appears.

18. We save the query result set to a table in the Max Min Sales DM data source. Enter **MythicWorldMailing** for Table Name. We can choose to add the table to a data source view, if desired, but we do not need to do that here. The Save Data Mining Query Result dialog box appears as shown in Figure 17-21.

| Customer_Name | Address | City | State | ZipCode |
|---|---|---|---|---|
| Thomas R Ali | 2839 Park Ct. | Rowley | OR | 97205 |
| Fritz N McCloud | 283 58th Ave. | Newton | CT | 06032 |
| Wilhelm V Trott | 3827 23rd St. | Karlstown | CO | 80203 |
| Valerie N Winstrom | 8438 23rd St. | Yankton | NE | 57203 |
| Valerie F Winstrom | 2838 23rd St. | Appleford | GA | 30308 |
| Xia W Petrov | 2823 28th St. | Jonesbourgh | CO | 80203 |
| Darla D Fulston | 2843 Elm St. | Foggyville | MO | 63301 |
| Zeb X Carson | 823 Angle St. | Zeller | WV | 34898 |
| Gary J Drake | 8293 Small Street | Edgeview | MA | 02139 |
| Greg Z Popovich | 2838 Filborn Ave. | Xavier | AR | 62312 |
| Ralph S Meunsch | 29838 32nd Ave. | Big Fork | CA | 94109 |
| Fritz Z Wong | 2823 Overland Dr. | Crawley | NM | 88044 |
| Lia Z Petrov | 3948 Filborn Ave. | Jonesbourgh | TX | 75201 |
| Melissa C Unger | 14322 32nd Ave. | Jonesbourgh | IN | 46601 |
| Petra Y McCloud | 8293 49th St. | Hillburg | CT | 06032 |
| Wilhelm D Unger | 828 50th St. | Ivers | OR | 97205 |
| Frank W Anthony | 283 Mayfair Ln. | Foggyville | IL | 60610 |
| Winifred M Perkins | 2772 Mortimer Ct. | Newton | WY | 82070 |
| Uma C Taylor | 283 Becker Way | Orville | ND | 56293 |
| Carlos P Carson | 283 Mycroft Ln. | Rowley | MT | 59715 |
| Inga H Elert | 3288 Quay St. | Quincy | KS | 58239 |
| Vern C Zipperer | 9293 Drummin Lane | Yankton | GA | 30308 |
| Quincy D Hoover | 2833 Hwy 45 | Edgeview | NV | 89701 |
| Gary V Frank | 823 Upton Way | Martinsville | VT | 04394 |
| Stanley S Smith | 2838 Polar Ave | Diffley | NY | 10007 |
| Paul R Winstrom | 2823 58th Ave. | Greeley | PA | 19107 |
| Melissa H Olsen | 2839 Mycroft Ln. | Karlstown | IA | 56279 |
| Stanley R Kline | 2839 Polar Ave | Edgeview | NE | 57203 |
| Edward O Petrov | 3827 Birch St. | Ivers | TN | 38103 |

Query execution completed with 1717 rows fetched

**Figure 17-20**  *The prediction join query result set with filter criteria*

**Figure 17-21**  *The Save Data Mining Query Result dialog box*

**NOTE**

*Saving a table such as this one to a data mart database is probably not a great idea, because it is being created for a one-time mailing, not for ongoing analysis. We do this here for demonstration purposes only!*

19. Click Save. A table called MythicWorldMailing is created in the MaxMinSalesDM database, and all the rows of the result set are inserted into that table.

20. Select Query from the View drop-down list on the Mining Model Prediction tab toolbar. The query appears as shown in Figure 17-22. This is the DMX query you created using the graphical tools. We learn more about DMX in the following section.

| Mining Structure | Mining Models | Mining Model Viewer | Mining Accuracy Chart | Mining Model Prediction |

**Mining Model**

- Decision Trees—Children
  - Customer
  - Homeowner
  - Marital Status
  - Num Cars Owned
  - Num Children At Home

**Select Input Table(s)**

- Customer
  - Address
  - City
  - Customer
  - Customer_Name
  - Homeowner
  - MaritalStatus
  - NumCarsOwned

```
SELECT
    t.[Customer_Name],
    t.[Address],
    t.[City],
    t.[State],
    t.[ZipCode]
From
    [Decision Trees—Children At Home]
PREDICTION JOIN
    OPENQUERY([Max Min Sales DM],
        'SELECT
            [Customer_Name],
            [Address],
            [City],
            [State],
            [ZipCode],
            [Homeowner],
            [MaritalStatus],
            [NumCarsOwned]
        FROM
            [dbo].[Customer]
        ') AS t
ON
    [Decision Trees—Children At Home].[Homeowner] = t.[Homeowner] AND
    [Decision Trees—Children At Home].[Marital Status] = t.[MaritalStatus] AND
    [Decision Trees—Children At Home].[Num Cars Owned] = t.[NumCarsOwned]
WHERE
    [Decision Trees—Children At Home].[Num Children At Home] =0
```

**Figure 17-22** *A DMX prediction join query*

# Data Mining Extensions

In previous chapters, we learned about the MDX query language and the DAX query language. Data mining structures also have their own query language, known as Data Mining Extensions (DMX).

In this section, we look at the most prominent aspect of DMX, the prediction query. The *prediction query* provides a means to have a data mining model create predictions based on rows in another table. In fact, you already used DMX prediction queries when you used the Mining Model Prediction tab.

## Prediction Query Syntax

The prediction query looks much like a SELECT statement in T-SQL. In fact, it has many of the same clauses as a SELECT statement. We look at each of those clauses and how they are used.

### SELECT Clause

The SELECT clause in a DMX query serves the same function as the SELECT clause in a T-SQL statement. The *SELECT clause* specifies what fields or calculations are going to be included as columns in the result set. This is done by placing a field list following the word "SELECT." For example:

```
SELECT Fname, Lname, Address1, City, State_Province, Postal_Code
```

The SELECT statement has two special keywords that may precede the field list: FLATTENED and TOP *n*. The *FLATTENED keyword* causes the prediction query to return a flattened result set of rows and columns. When the FLATTENED keyword is not used, the SELECT statement may return a hierarchical result set.

The *TOP* n *keyword* works the same here as it does in the T-SQL SELECT statement: It limits the number of rows in the result set to the number specified for *n*. We can order the result set, perhaps by a probability in descending order, and then use the TOP *n* keywords to include only the rows with the highest probability.

### FROM Clause

The *FROM clause* specifies the mining model being used in the query. For example:

```
FROM [Decision Trees-Children At Home]
```

### PREDICTION JOIN Clause

The *PREDICTION JOIN clause* lets us feed information into the inputs of the mining model. The content or the absence of this clause determines the type of prediction query being run. See the section "Types of Prediction Queries" for details on the syntax of the PREDICTION JOIN clause.

### WHERE Clause

The *WHERE clause* enables us to filter the result of the SELECT statement. The filter conditions in the WHERE clause are applied after the predictions are made by the mining model. Therefore, we can use the prediction result as part of the filter. For example, if the Decision Trees—Children At Home mining model is predicting Num Children At Home, we can create a filter to give us only those records where Num Children At Home was predicted to be 0:

```
WHERE [Decision Trees-Children At Home].[Num Children At Home] = 0
```

### ORDER BY Clause

The *ORDER BY clause* lets us sort the result set: We can sort in either ascending or descending order. Adding DESC to the clause provides a descending sort. Adding ASC to the clause provides an ascending sort. ASC is the default sort order when neither ASC nor DESC is specified.

The ORDER BY clause in T-SQL includes a comma-separated list of fields to provide the sort columns. The ORDER BY clause in DMX is a bit different. It allows only a single expression. If we want to sort by more than one column, we need to create an expression concatenating these two columns, as follows:

```
ORDER BY [Lname] + [Fname] ASC
```

## Types of Prediction Queries

Several types of prediction queries are available to us. As stated earlier, the format or absence of the PREDICTION JOIN clause determines the type of prediction query being created. Let's look at the format and operation of each type.

### PREDICTION JOIN

The standard prediction join query enables us to take records from another data source and feed them into our mining model to create predictions. For this to happen, we must specify where the joined data is coming from. We also need to specify how the columns in the data source are mapped to the input columns of the mining model.

A typical PREDICTION JOIN clause looks like this:

```
PREDICTION JOIN
  OPENQUERY([Max Min Sales DM],
    'SELECT
      [Fname],
      [Lname],
      [Address1],
      [City],
      [State_Province],
      [Postal_Code],
      [Num_Cars_Owned],
      [Homeowner],
      [Marital_Status]
    FROM
      [MaxMinSalesDM].[Customer]
    ') AS t
ON
  [Decision Trees-Children At Home].[Num Cars Owned] = t.[Num_Cars_Owned]
AND
  [Decision Trees-Children At Home].[Homeowner] = t.[Homeowner]
AND
  [Decision Trees-Children At Home].[Marital Status] = t.[Marital_Status]
```

Remember, the DMX query is running on an Analysis Services server. If we want to include data from a relational table in the prediction join, we need to use the appropriate syntax for utilizing data from another server. This is the OPENQUERY() function.

The OPENQUERY() function executes the specified statement on the server indicated. The OPENQUERY() function requires two parameters. The first is the name of the server where the query is to be executed. In the prediction join, this will probably be the name of a data source defined in the Analysis Services database. In the example code, we are using the Max Min Sales DM data source. This data source points to the MaxMinSalesDM relational database.

The second parameter contains the query to be executed. The query is enclosed in single quotes. In our example, we are selecting fields from the Customer table in the MaxMinSalesDM database. The result set from the OPENQUERY() function is given an alias so it can be referred to elsewhere in the prediction join query. The alias is provided by the "AS t" portion of the PREDICTION JOIN clause.

The lines following the ON keyword map columns from the joined data to the input columns of the mining model. This tells the mining model what input values it should use for each prediction. In our example, the Num_Cars_Owned field from the Customer table is used as the Num Cars Owned input column in the mining model. The Homeowner field is used as the Homeowner input, and the Marital_Status field is used as the Marital Status input.

## NATURAL PREDICTION JOIN

The NATURAL PREDICTION JOIN clause works exactly like the PREDICTION JOIN clause, with one convenient exception: It does not include the ON portion. Instead, the *NATURAL PREDICTION JOIN clause* does its mapping of fields to input columns based on the names of each. This can be convenient when working with mining models with a large number of input columns. As you might guess, for this to work, the names of the fields must exactly match the names of the input columns.

We can make our PREDICTION JOIN example work as a NATURAL PREDICTION JOIN, with a slight modification to the query inside the OPENQUERY() function, as follows:

```
NATURAL PREDICTION JOIN
   OPENQUERY([Max Min Sales DM],
     'SELECT
       [Fname],
       [Lname],
       [Address1],
       [City],
       [State_Province],
       [Postal_Code],
       [Num_Cars_Owned] AS [Num Cars Owned],
       [Homeowner],
       [Marital_Status] AS [Marital Status]
    FROM
       [MaxMinSalesDM].[Customer]
     ') AS t
```

By applying aliases to the Num_Cars_Owned and Marital_Status fields, we can make the field names in the OPENQUERY() result exactly match the input column names. Now, no mapping is necessary.

## Empty Prediction Join

The empty prediction join is not a join at all. With an *empty prediction join,* we do not pass any information to the mining model input columns. When we do this, the mining model returns the most likely prediction.

Here is a sample of an empty prediction join:

```
SELECT
    [Num Children At Home]
From
    [Decision Trees-Children At Home]
```

## Singleton Query

Where the prediction join and the natural prediction join enabled us to feed data from another data source into the mining model, the singleton query lets us enter hardcoded values for each input column. For example:

```
SELECT
    [Decision Trees-Children At Home].[Num Children At Home]
From
    [Decision Trees-Children At Home]
NATURAL PREDICTION JOIN
(SELECT 'Y' AS [Homeowner],
    'N' AS [Marital Status],
      '2' AS [Num Cars Owned]) AS t
```

To create our singleton query, we are using a NATURAL PREDICTION JOIN clause and hardcoding the content of the inner SELECT statement. Of course, to make this work with a natural prediction join, we must alias each column in the inner SELECT statement to match the names of the mining model input columns.

## Learn By Doing—Creating a Query in the SQL Server Management Studio

### Feature Highlighted

▶ Creating a DMX query in the SQL Server Management Studio

**Business Need**    One of the power users in the Marketing Department is familiar with DMX queries and wants to be able to create DMX queries against the mining models without the graphical interface. Entering DMX queries into the query view of the Mining Model Prediction tab is possible. However, if we switch back to the design view, we lose everything entered in the query view.

The SQL Server Management Studio provides a better alternative.

**NOTE**

*Always take care when giving users, even power users who seem to know what they are doing, access to tools such as SQL Server Management Studio. Make sure security is set appropriately so the users do not do catastrophic damage, either maliciously or by accident. SQL Server 2012 has expanded its security model. See SQL Books Online for more information.*

**Steps**

1. Open the SQL Server Management Studio.
2. Connect to the Analysis Services server hosting the MaxMinSalesDM database.
3. Expand the Databases folder in the Object Explorer window.
4. Right-click the MaxMinSalesDM database entry in the Object Explorer window and select New Query | DMX from the context menu. A DMX Query window appears.
5. Select Decision Trees—Children At Home from the Mining Model drop-down list.
6. Enter the following in the query area to create an empty prediction query:

```
SELECT
    [Num Children At Home]
From
    [Decision Trees-Children At Home]
```

7. Click the Execute button on the toolbar. The SQL Server Management Studio appears as shown in Figure 17-23.

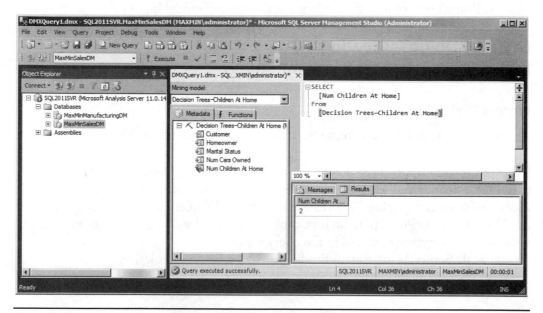

**Figure 17-23** *An empty prediction query in the SQL Server Management Studio*

**Figure 17-24** *A singleton query in the SQL Server Management Studio*

8. Replace the empty prediction query with the following singleton query:

```
SELECT
    [Decision Trees-Children At Home].[Num Children At Home]
From
    [Decision Trees-Children At Home]
NATURAL PREDICTION JOIN
(SELECT 'Y' AS [Homeowner],
 'N' AS [Marital Status],
 '2' AS [Num Cars Owned]) AS t
```

9. Click the Execute button on the toolbar. The SQL Server Management Studio appears as shown in Figure 17-24.

10. If you want to give your fingers a workout, try entering and executing the prediction join query shown in Figure 17-25.

**Figure 17-25**   *Prediction join query*

# Special Delivery

We created Multidimensional and Tabular models along with mining models. We used MDX, DAX, and DMX queries to extract data from these items. However, unlike the power user in our last Learn By Doing exercise, most users will not want to jump into SQL Server Data Tools or the SQL Server Management Studio and start cranking out queries. Most users want the data delivered to them in a polished, prepackaged format that is easy to understand and easy to use.

In Chapter 18, we look at some of the tools provided by Microsoft for delivering the data in these models to end users.

# Part VI

# Delivering

# Special Delivery–
# Microsoft Business
# Intelligence Client Tools

## In This Chapter

▶ **Front-End BI Tools from Microsoft**

▶ **Reporting Services**

▶ **Excel**

▶ **PerformancePoint Services in SharePoint 2010**

▶ **Power View**

▶ **Putting It All Together**

*The two most engaging powers of an author are to make new things familiar, and familiar things new.*

—Samuel Johnson

In the preceding chapters of this book, we discovered ways to create business intelligence (BI). We saw the BI Semantic Models and data mining algorithms dissect and analyze data. The result of this dissection and analysis is the foundational and feedback information needed for business intelligence.

Creating this information is only half the battle. As we discussed in Chapter 1, delivering business intelligence to decision makers in a timely manner is as important as creating that intelligence in the first place. The name of this book begins with the word "delivering" for just that reason.

In this chapter and the next, we examine the tools provided by Microsoft for delivering business intelligence. These are the tools that consume our BI Semantic Models and provide usable business information to our users. In this chapter, we review various Microsoft tools that utilize BI Semantic Models to put business intelligence in the hands of decision makers. In Chapter 19, we work at ways to integrate business intelligence into custom applications.

# Front-End BI Tools from Microsoft

Microsoft provides a rich set of front-end tools for delivering business intelligence to end users. This includes

- ▶  Reporting Services
- ▶  Excel PivotTable
- ▶  Excel PowerPivot
- ▶  SharePoint PerformancePoint Services
- ▶  Power View

It is great to know that as we create these robust Multidimensional and Tabular BI Semantic Models, there is a wide array of capable tools for delivering model content to the business user.

Some might say Microsoft is providing too many tools, making it difficult to know what tool to use when. This decision making is not helped by the fact that there is overlap in the capabilities of each tool. We can create something that looks and performs like a dashboard in Reporting Services, or the Excel PivotTable Wizard, or SharePoint PerformancePoint Services.

It would be great to take the same approach to BI front-end tool selection that we used for data mining algorithm selection—try them all and see which one works the best for a particular need. While it was easy to use that approach within a data mining structure, building out the same solution in multiple front-end BI tools is a bit more complicated. Still, after working through this chapter and gaining a working familiarity with each tool, you may be able to define a limited-scope proof of concept and do just that.

# Selecting a Front-End BI Tool

If building out a proof-of-concept solution using multiple front-end tools is not feasible, here are some guidelines for selecting front-end tools.

## What Can Be Supported in Your Organization?

First, you need to make an honest determination of what can be adequately supported by the IT infrastructure in your organization. If your organization has a larger IT infrastructure, then it is feasible to support a number of these tools, using them in a more specialized manner. Reporting Services is used for reports. PerformancePoint is used for dashboards. Power View is used for ad hoc data exploration. Each front-end tool has its own group within the IT department to support it.

We'll call this the socket set approach. Think of the person with the 200-piece socket set in the big rolling toolbox. Need to tighten a bolt with the 1/4-inch head? There is a 1/4-inch socket for that. Need to loosen that bolt with a 1/2-inch head? Well, then we put away the 1/4-inch socket and get out the 1/2-inch socket for that.

It costs money to buy the 200-piece socket set. It also costs money for the infrastructure for all of those pieces to be properly stored and stay usable. In this case, it takes a big toolbox with lots of little drawers. It also takes the appropriate training to know how and when to use each specialized tool. (Well, maybe it doesn't take specialized training to know the difference between a 1/4-inch socket and a 1/2-inch socket, but throw in a torque wrench, a cone wrench, and a spoke wrench and the analogy holds...mostly.)

While it might be fun to know and work with all of the tools listed, if your organization has an IT department that consists of just a few people, that may not be the best approach. You will probably achieve better results and higher end-user satisfaction supporting a few tools that you know well.

We might call this the adjustable wrench approach. (I could have called this the monkey wrench approach, but throwing a monkey wrench into a process has negative connotations, so we'll go with adjustable wrench.) We select one tool, an adjustable wrench, that will do a good job tightening a bolt with a 1/4-inch head or loosening a bolt with a 1/2-inch head. The tool is flexible, we can keep it in a pocket, and we know how to use it.

## Who Will Be the Primary Developers?

Nowadays, we need to consider who will be using the BI tools we select. We can no longer assume BI will be delivered by a group of techie report developers. It could just as easily be a group of business decision makers doing their own exploration of the data.

More technical users, like those report developers, will want a tool that has a broad range of capabilities to allow them to present the data exactly the way they want it to look. A tool like Reporting Services is a good fit for this group. Less technical users, like the business decision makers, will want a tool that is easy to use and allows them to concentrate on the data rather than on the tool. The Excel PivotTable Wizard or Power View are probably better choices for this group.

## Does the Tool Provide the Necessary Capabilities in an Efficient Manner to Fulfill Current and Likely Future Needs?

While many of the Microsoft front-end BI tools are flexible, they all have their limits. There are things you can do with Reporting Services that cannot be accomplished in Power View. Conversely, there are things that can be done very rapidly in Power View that take much longer to accomplish in Reporting Services.

Going back to our wrench analogy, there are some situations where an adjustable wrench will work, but it is not quite as optimal as a socket set. There are also some situations where an adjustable wrench will not fit, but a socket wrench will work just fine. In those cases, we need to spend the money for the specialized tool and learn how to use it.

This is probably the trickiest question of the three. It is hard to predict what capabilities our business users will need in the future. It may even be hard to know all of their current needs when we are at the initial tool selection stage of a project. Still, we need to make the best determinations we can with the information available.

## A Bit of Knowledge Is a Big Help

The key to selecting one or more front-end BI tools for your organization is having some knowledge of the users' needs and capabilities along with some knowledge of the features of each BI tool. I can't really help you in determining the needs and capabilities of your users. You'll have to determine that. What I hope to do in this chapter, however, is help you get to know enough about the capabilities of each of the tools to do some intelligent decision making.

# Reporting Services

Since before the invention of computers, the primary method for sharing business intelligence has been the report. This is slowly changing as tools that allow interactive exploration of a BI Semantic Model become easier to use and more widely available. In fact, some of the tools and capabilities of SQL Server 2012 encourage this evolution from static reports to interactive exploration, as we will see later in this chapter.

Still, in the business intelligence world, the report is still a staple. That being the case, it is important to have a capable and easy-to-use reporting environment at our disposal. Reporting Services fits that bill.

If Reporting Services were simply a report authoring environment, it would be a good tool. However, Reporting Services has much more to offer beyond just report creation. In fact, *Reporting Services* is a complete, enterprise-wide report management and distribution service. Reporting Services enables us to securely distribute reports throughout an organization using an existing intranet infrastructure, and it provides for the integration of reports with both desktop and web-based applications.

Reporting Services also is a bridge between static, paper reports and interactive data exploration tools with its ability to play both roles. In addition to creating reports for printing, Reporting Services permits users to interact with reports, drilling down from summary to detail information, navigating to related reports, and even jumping to related websites. To use Reporting Services to its fullest extent, we need to create reports that encourage user interaction.

Reporting Services enables both developers and users to create reports. It offers two report authoring tools: the Report Builder and the Report Designer. The tools are very similar, with the main difference being the user interface. The *Report Builder* is geared toward those who are most comfortable in an environment that resembles the Microsoft Office tools. Report Builder utilizes the ribbon-style interface. Creating a report in Report Builder feels a bit like creating a document in Word or a spreadsheet in Excel.

The *Report Designer* environment is part of SQL Server Data Tools. It is a great fit for those who are comfortable working in SQL Server Data Tools, as I trust most of you are by now. For that reason, the sample reports in this chapter will be created using the Report Designer. There is no difference between reports produced by the Report Builder and those produced by the Report Designer.

The following section provides an introduction to Reporting Services and its many capabilities. For a more in-depth and comprehensive exploration of Reporting Services, I recommend *Microsoft SQL Server 2012 Reporting Services* by … well, me … also available from McGraw-Hill Professional.

## Report Structure

A report project can contain a number of reports. Each report contains two distinct sets of instructions that determine what the report will contain. The first is the *data definition*, which controls where the data for the report comes from and what information is to be selected from that data. The second set of instructions is the *report layout*, which controls how the information is presented on the screen or on paper. Both of these sets of instructions are stored using the Report Definition Language (RDL).

Figure 18-1 shows this report structure in a little more detail.

## Data Definition

The data definition contains two parts: the data source and the dataset. The *data source* is the same as we have seen used in Multidimensional BI Semantic Model projects: It is the set of instructions the report needs to gain access to a data source that provides data for the report. The *data source definition* can be created right inside the report definition, or it can be created externally and shared by a number of reports. In most cases, report management is easier when we use external shared data sources.

When the report is executing, it uses the data source instructions to gain access to the data source. It then extracts information from the data source into a new format that can be used by the report. This new format is called a *dataset*. A report may contain multiple datasets from the same data source or even multiple datasets from multiple data sources.

**Figure 18-1**  *Report structure*

The content of the dataset is defined using a tool called the Query Designer. The *Query Designer* helps us build a database query. The database query may be in T-SQL for querying relational data, MDX for querying multidimensional data, or DMX for querying data-mining data. The query provides instructions to the data source, telling it what data we want selected for our report. The query is stored in the report as part of the data definition.

The data selected by the query into the dataset consists of rows and columns. The rows correspond to the records the query selects from the data source. The columns correspond to the fields the query selects from the data source. (Reporting Services does not support hierarchical result sets, so MDX and DMX query results are flattened into a single table of rows and columns.) Information on the fields to be selected into the dataset is stored in the report as part of the data definition. Only the information on what the fields are to be called and the type of data they are to hold is stored in the report definition. The actual data is not stored in the report definition, but instead, is selected from the data source each time the report is run.

**NOTE**

*Reporting Services does have capabilities to cache report data so that reports can be created from the cache rather than the data source. However, by default, Reporting Services always queries the underlying data sources each time a report is run.*

## Report Layout

The data the report has extracted into a dataset is not of much use to us unless we have some way of presenting it to the user. We need to specify which fields go in which locations on the screen or on paper. We also need to add things such as titles, headings, and page numbers. All of this forms the report layout.

In most cases, our report layout will include one or more special areas that interact with the dataset. This special area is known as a data region. A *data region* displays all the rows in the dataset by repeating a section of the report layout for each row.

## Report Definition Language

The information in the data definition and the report layout is stored using the Report Definition Language (RDL). *RDL* is an Extensible Markup Language (XML) standard designed by Microsoft specifically for storing report definitions. This includes the data source instructions, the query information that defines the datasets, and the report layout. When we create a report in the Report Designer, it is saved in a file with a .rdl extension.

## Report Delivery

We have discussed how a report is created by the report author. What we have not discussed is where that report will reside after it is created. To make a report available throughout the organization, that report is deployed to a report server. Once on the report server, the report may be executed by a user through the Report Manager website. It may be sent in response to a web service request that came, not from a user, but from another program. It may also be e-mailed to a user who has a subscription to that report.

### NOTE

*A report server can also be configured to operate in SharePoint Integrated mode. In this case, SharePoint provides the user interface for executing reports. We'll look at Reporting Services running in SharePoint Integrated mode when we discuss Power View later in this chapter.*

### Report Manager Website

One way for users to request a report from the report server is through the Report Manager website. Reports deployed to the report server are organized into folders. The Report Manager website allows users to browse through these folders to find the report they need. They can also search the report titles and descriptions to locate a report.

Security can be applied to folders and to individual reports on the report server. With this security, the site administrator can create security roles for the users who will be accessing the site. These security roles control which folders and reports a user is allowed to access. This ensures that when exploring the report server using the Report Manager, users only see the reports and folders they should.

In the Report Manager, reports are always displayed using the Hypertext Markup Language (HTML) format. Once a report has been displayed as an HTML page, the user can then export it into any of the other available formats.

### Subscription Delivery

If the users do not want to go to the report, Reporting Services can make the report go to them. In other words, users do not necessarily need to come to the Report Manager website to receive a report. They can have the report delivered to them through a subscription service. The Report Manager enables users to locate a report on the site and then subscribe to it so it will be delivered to them in the future.

When users subscribe to a report, they provide an e-mail address to which the report is to be delivered, whether as the body of the e-mail, as an e-mail attachment, or as a

URL link to the report. Users can specify the format for the report at the time they create their subscription.

The site administrator can also set up report subscriptions. These function like a mass mailing, using a list of e-mail addresses. Rather than requiring each user to access the Report Manager to create their own subscription, the site administrator can create one subscription that is delivered to every user in the list.

## Web Service Interface

In addition to delivering reports to humans, either at their request or on a subscription basis, the report server can deliver reports to other software applications. This is done through a series of web services. A program calls a web service on the report server, requesting a particular report in a particular format. The completed report is returned to the program that originated the request as the response to the web service request.

We see an example of this in Chapter 19.

# Data Regions

In this section, we create a report with Reporting Services. This is an introduction to Reporting Services to give you a feel for its capabilities. To really explore the depth and breadth of Reporting Services, you will want to work with other reference materials (such as my book mentioned earlier).

Reports are created using a drag-and-drop approach. Report items are taken from the Toolbox window in Report Designer or the ribbon in Report Builder and placed on the report. The function of some of these report items is not hard to figure out: text boxes contain text; images display image files. Other report items are more complex and vital to the workings of Reporting Services reports.

As mentioned earlier, there are special report items designed specifically for working with datasets. These special report items are called data regions. *Data regions* are able to work with multiple records from a dataset. The data region reads a record from the dataset, creates a portion of the report using the data found in that record, and then moves on to the next record. It does this until all the records from the dataset have been processed.

The tablix is one of these data regions. However, you will not find the tablix in the Toolbox or on the ribbon. Instead, the tablix data region is created through the use of three different templates that are found in the Toolbox. These templates control the default look and behavior of the resulting tablix. The three templates are the table, the matrix, and the list. (The name tablix comes from the combination of "table" and "matrix"—but maybe you guessed that already.) It should be noted that the templates specify the initial state of a tablix added to a report. They do not limit what can be done with the tablix after it exists in the report layout.

## The Table Template for the Tablix

The *table template* creates the traditional-style report with rows and columns. *Rows* are created from the records in the dataset and can be grouped within the tablix as well. *Columns* are created from the fields in the dataset. The table template produces a predefined set of columns and an unknown number of rows; the number of rows depends on the content of the dataset.

The table template creates what is called a *banded report* in some other report authoring environments. The *detail bands* in these reports correspond to the detail rows in the table. The *summary bands* in these reports correspond to the header and footer rows in the table.

The tablix that results from the table template includes a tablix header and footer. The tablix header often contains column headings for the tablix. The tablix footer often contains the grand totals for the entire tablix.

In addition to the tablix header and footer, the tablix data region can include multiple group headers and footers. The group headers often contain the information to identify a grouping. The group footers usually contain totals for the group. Drilldown can be defined in a report so the detail content of a group can be initially hidden and only made visible when the user drills down into the detail for that group.

## The Matrix Template for the Tablix

The *matrix template* does not create a banded report, but it does create what is known as a pivot table or a crosstab report. The matrix template creates both rows and columns based on the content of the dataset. The resulting tablix has groupings on both rows and columns. Drilldown can be defined for both rows and columns.

The data cells created by the matrix template always contain aggregate data. Therefore, the data in the cells is numeric. Because of this, the matrix mirrors the fact and dimension structure of a Multidimensional BI Semantic Model cube and works well for displaying cube data.

## The List Template for the Tablix

The *list template* does not deal in columns and rows at all. Instead, the list template provides a freeform layout area that is repeated for each record in the dataset. This layout may produce a whole section, perhaps a whole page or more, for each record in the dataset. This makes it a good choice for creating a report that is meant to resemble a form.

## The Chart Data Region

The *chart* report item is a data region like the tablix, which means the chart can process multiple records from a dataset. The tablix enables you to place other report items in a row, a column, or a list area that is repeated for every record in the dataset. The chart, on the other hand, uses the records in a dataset to create visuals such as bars, lines, or pie wedges. You cannot place other report items inside a chart item.

## The Map Data Region

The *map* report item is a data region used for presenting geographic and geometric data. We can shade areas on a map to represent data elements associated with a particular country, state, province, or other geographic region. The map report item also allows us to place symbols on a map to represent data or simply show location.

We can utilize SQL Server's geography data type to define our own shapes such as our organization's sales regions or service areas. We can utilize SQL Server's geometry data type to create our representation of an office floor plan or a warehouse layout. By feeding these geography and geometry data types into a map data region, we can incorporate these custom representations into our reports and overlay them with additional data, such as sales by region or inventory level by warehouse location.

## Using Data Regions

Each data region item has a property called DataSetName. This property contains the name of the dataset used by the data region. In most cases, the Report Designer sets this automatically. This property is set to the dataset of the first field placed in the data region.

In many cases, a report includes a single data region to create the body of the report. In other cases, multiple data regions are combined on a single report. This mix and match has no limit. Perhaps a chart data region containing a line graph and a tablix data region containing detail information are placed on the same report. We can mix and match to our hearts' content.

# Creating a Reporting Services Report

In this Learn By Doing exercise, we will create a report using Reporting Services. This exercise will give you a taste of the report creation process. It is in no way a comprehensive look at the features of Reporting Services.

If you have a Reporting Services report server available to you, you can deploy the report created here and utilize it in the Learn By Doing exercises in Chapter 19. Remember, don't use a production server for completing training exercises. Even if you do not have a Reporting Services report server, you can still create and preview the report in SQL Server Data Tools.

## Learn By Doing—Creating a Matrix Report

### Features Highlighted

▶ Using the matrix template

▶ Using aggregate functions

▶ Enabling drilldown

▶ Formatting report items

**Business Need**    The Maximum Miniatures Marketing Department would like to analyze wholesale sales for each store over time. The marketing department wants to be able to select a year and view the quarters within the selected year. They would like to be able to drill down to the month level within a quarter. They would also like to be able to drill down to specific products within a store. In addition to the sales dollar amount, they would like to see the sales as a percent of total sales for the quarter.

We use the Max Min Sales DM cube as the data source for this report.

### Steps to Create a Report Server Project

1. Open SQL Server Data Tools.
2. Click the New Project button on the toolbar. The New Project dialog box appears.
3. In the Installed Templates area, select Reporting Services under Business Intelligence.
4. Select Report Server Project in the center of the dialog box.
5. Enter **MaxMinReports** for Name and set the Location to the appropriate folder. This will be the only project in this solution, so leave Create directory for solution unchecked.
6. Click OK to create the project.

### Steps to Create a Shared Data Source

1. Right-click the Shared Data Sources folder in the Solution Explorer window and select Add New Data Source from the context menu. The Shared Data Source Properties dialog box appears.
2. Enter **MaxMinSalesDMCube** for Name.
3. Select Microsoft SQL Server Analysis Services from the Type drop-down list.
4. Click Edit. The Connection Properties dialog box appears.
5. Enter the name of the Analysis Services server hosting the Max Min Sales DM OLAP cube for Server name.

6. From the Select or enter a database name drop-down list, select MaxMinSalesDM. The Connection Properties dialog box appears as shown in Figure 18-2.

7. Click OK to exit the Connection Properties dialog box.

8. Click OK to exit the Shared Data Source Properties dialog box. The shared data source is created.

### Steps to Create a New Report with a Data Set

1. Right-click the Reports folder in the Solution Explorer window and select Add | New Item. (Selecting Add New Report launches the Report Wizard, which we are not using for this report.) The Add New Item dialog box appears.

2. Select Report in the center area. Enter **Wholesale Sales By Month Report** for Name.

3. Click Add. The Report Design tab appears.

4. In the Report Data window, select New | Data Source from the toolbar. The Data Source Properties dialog box appears.

**Figure 18-2**    *The Connection Properties dialog box*

**NOTE**

*If the Report Data window is not visible, select View | Report Data from the main menu.*

5. Enter **MaxMinSalesDMCube** for Name.

6. Select the Use shared data source reference option.

7. Select the MaxMinSalesDMCube shared data source from the drop-down list. The Data Source Properties dialog box is shown in Figure 18-3.

8. Click OK to exit the Data Source Properties dialog box.

9. Right-click the MaxMinSalesDMCube data source you just created in the Report Data window and select Add Dataset from the context menu. The Dataset Properties dialog box appears.

10. Enter **WholesaleSales** for Name.

11. Click Query Designer. The MDX Query Designer window appears.

12. Expand the Time dimension, and then expand the Year - Quarter - Month - Date hierarchy. Drag the Quarter and Month members of this hierarchy onto the query area. (The area labeled Drag levels or measures here to add to the query.)

13. Expand the Store dimension and drag the Store attribute onto the query area.

**Figure 18-3**   *The Data Source Properties dialog box*

14. Expand the Product dimension and drag the Product attribute onto the query area.

15. Expand Measures and the Sales Information measure group, and drag the Sales in Dollars measure onto the query area. The query executes.

16. Because our business requirements were for wholesale sales only, we need to add a filter to the query to include only wholesale customers (account numbers below 5000). In the filter pane (directly above the query pane), click the cell labeled <Select Dimension>. From the drop-down list, select Customer.

17. For Hierarchy, select Account Num.

18. For Operator, select Range (Inclusive).

19. For Filter Expression, create a range from 4500 to 4996.

20. We need to add a second filter to allow the user to select the year being viewed. In the second row in the Filter pane, click the cell labeled <Select Dimension>. From the drop-down list, select Time.

21. For Hierarchy, select Year.

22. For Operator, select Equal.

23. For Filter Expression, select Calendar 2011.

24. Check the box in the second row of the Parameters column. This will allow the user to select a year when the report is run.

25. The query executes again to apply the filters. With columns expanded appropriately, the MDX Query Designer appears as shown in Figure 18-4.

**Figure 18-4**   *The MDX Query Designer with the query for the Wholesale Sales By Month Report*

26. Click OK to exit the Query Designer window. Click OK to exit the Dataset Properties dialog box.

27. Expand the Parameters folder in the Report Data window.

28. The @TimeYear parameter was created when we placed the check mark in the Parameters column in Step 24. Double-click the entry for the @TimeYear parameter. The Report Parameter Properties dialog box appears.

29. Uncheck the Allow multiple values check box. The Report Parameter Properties dialog box appears as shown in Figure 18-5.

30. Click OK to exit the Report Parameter Properties dialog box.

**NOTE**

*In this example we queried data from one of our Multidimensional BI Semantic Models. We can use a similar approach to connect to a Tabular instance of SQL Server Analysis Services and query data from our Tabular BI Semantic Model for use in a Reporting Services report.*

**Report Parameter Properties**

| General |
| Available Values |
| Default Values |
| Advanced |

Change name, data type, and other options.

Name:
TimeYear

Prompt:
Year

Data type:
Text

☐ Allow blank value ("")
☐ Allow null value
☐ Allow multiple values

Select parameter visibility:
◉ Visible
○ Hidden
○ Internal

Help | OK | Cancel

**Figure 18-5** *The Report Parameter Properties dialog box*

### Steps to Create the Report Layout

1. Click the report design area to activate the Report menu, and then select Report | Report Properties from the main menu. The Report Properties dialog box appears.
2. Select Landscape for Orientation.
3. Click OK.
4. Drag a text box from the Toolbox and drop it on the report body layout area.
5. Using the Properties window, modify the properties of the text box as follows:

| Property | Value |
|---|---|
| Font: FontSize | 16pt |
| Font: FontWeight | Bold |
| Location: Left | 0in |
| Location: Top | 0in |
| Size: Width | 6in |
| Size: Height | 0.375in |

## NOTE

*Several properties, such as the Font property, contain subproperties. The property must be expanded to view the subproperties. These are referred to with the following format: Property: Subproperty.*

6. In the text box, enter **Wholesale Sales By Month Report - .**
7. With the text edit cursor still blinking at the end of the string you just entered, right-click the text edit cursor and select Create Placeholder from the context menu. The Placeholder Properties dialog box appears.
8. Click the *fx* button next to the Value drop-down list. The Expression dialog box appears.
9. Select Parameters in the Category pane.
10. Double-click the TimeYear entry in the Values pane. This will create an expression representing this parameter.
11. In the Set expression for: Value area, replace "Value" with **Label**. The Expression dialog box appears as shown in Figure 18-6.
12. Click OK to exit the Expression dialog box. Click OK to exit the Placeholder Properties dialog box.
13. Drag a matrix from the Toolbox and drop it on the report body layout area below the text box. This will create a tablix data region using the matrix template.
14. From the Report Data window, drag the Month field and drop it in the Columns cell.

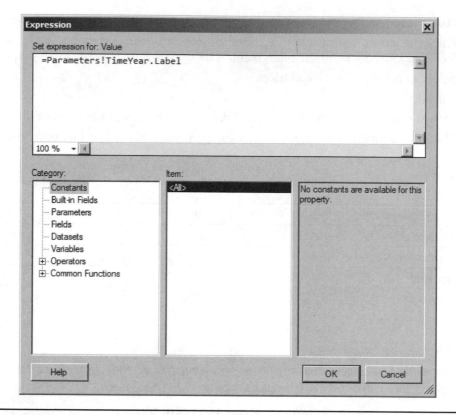

**Figure 18-6**  *The Expression dialog box with a Parameter expression*

15. In addition to dragging fields from the Report Data window, we can use the pop-up field picker to select fields. Hover over the Rows cell until the field picker icon appears as shown in Figure 18-7.

16. Click the field picker icon to display the pop-up field list. Select the Product field from the field list.

17. Select the Sales_in_Dollars field in the Data cell.

18. Drag the Quarter field and drop it on the line forming the top of the Month cell.

19. Drag the Store field and drop it on the line forming the left side of the Product cell. The report layout should appear as shown in Figure 18-8.

### Steps to Enable Drilldown

1. As requested in the business needs, we are going to enable drilldown in this report. Click the drop-down arrow for the Month group in the Column Groups area at the bottom of the screen. Select Group Properties from the drop-down menu. The Group Properties dialog box appears.

2. Select the Visibility page.

**Figure 18-7**    *The pop-up field picker*

3. Select the Hide option under the When the report is initially run prompt.
4. Check the Display can be toggled by this report item check box.
5. Select Quarter from the drop-down list. The Group Properties dialog box appears as shown in Figure 18-9.

**Figure 18-8**    *The report layout*

**Figure 18-9**  *The Group Properties dialog box*

6. Click OK to exit the Group Properties dialog box.
7. Click the drop-down arrow for the Product group in the Row Groups area. Select Group Properties from the menu. The Group Properties dialog box appears.
8. Select the Visibility page.
9. Select the Hide option under the When the report is initially run prompt.
10. Check the Display can be toggled by this report item check box.
11. Select Store from the drop-down list.
12. Click OK to exit the Group Properties dialog box.
13. Click the Preview tab. The report appears as shown in Figure 18-10.

### Steps to Accomplish Additional Report Formatting

1. Click the Design tab. Let's make a few changes to improve the looks and readability of the matrix.

| Wholesale Sales By M...h Report.rdl [Design] ✕ | | | | |

Design | Preview

Year | Calendar 2011 ▾ | | View Report

◀◀ 1 of 1 ▶ ▶◀ | ← ⊗ ⊕ | 🖶 ▢ ▣ ▦ ▾ | 100% ▾ | Find | Next

## Wholesale Sales By Month Report -  Calendar 2011

| Store | Product | ⊞ Quarter 1, 2011 | ⊞ Quarter 2, 2011 | ⊞ Quarter 3, 2011 | ⊞ Quarter 4, 2011 |
|---|---|---|---|---|---|
| ⊞ Online | | 2210493.82 | 2205968.71 | 2244701.60 | 2262913.08 |
| ⊞ Retail-Store 1 | | 86909.04 | 87073.05 | 89627.89 | 78579.39 |
| ⊞ Retail-Store 2 | | 84433.51 | 82211.09 | 72858.25 | 66388.93 |
| ⊞ Retail-Store 3 | | 75468.20 | 71287.71 | 61176.89 | 50700.28 |
| ⊞ Retail-Store 5 | | 152307.18 | 115361.00 | 100142.05 | 90171.51 |
| ⊞ Wholesale | | 7347969.28 | 7487552.77 | 7345023.65 | 6777428.54 |

**Figure 18-10** *The Wholesale Sales By Month Report preview—in progress*

### NOTE

*When selecting cells in a tablix, click near the outside of the cell to avoid entering text edit mode within the cell.*

2. Select the cell containing the Sum of the Sales_in_Dollars field (the detail cell for the matrix). Set the following properties in the Properties window:

| Property | Value |
|---|---|
| Format | C |
| Size: Width | 1.5 in |

The "C" value provides currency formatting for the number in this cell.

3. Select the cell containing the Quarter field. Set the following properties in the Properties window:

| Property | Value |
| --- | --- |
| BackgroundColor | CornflowerBlue |
| Font: FontWeight | Bold |
| TextAlign | Right |

4. Select the cell containing the Month field. Use the toolbar buttons to set the font weight to bold, the background color to PowderBlue, and the alignment to align right. (Hint: Click the More colors link to select the color by name.)

5. Select the cell containing the Store field. Use the toolbar buttons to set the font weight to bold and the background color to CornflowerBlue.

6. Select the cell containing the Product field. Use the toolbar buttons to set the font weight to bold and the background color to PowderBlue.

### Steps to Add a Calculated Column

1. Right-click the detail cell. Select Tablix: Insert Row | Inside Group - Below. A new detail cell is created below the existing detail cell.

2. Right-click the new detail cell and select Textbox: Expression from the context menu. The Expression dialog box appears.

3. Enter the following expression:

```
=Sum(Fields!Sales_in_Dollars.Value) /
                Sum(Fields!Sales_in_Dollars.Value, "Quarter")
```

### NOTE

*The first Sum aggregate function in this expression adds all the sales for the current detail cell. This aggregate function determines what items to add based on the scope of the cell it is in. When no items are expanded in the matrix, the scope of each cell is the year column and product row the cell is in. When we pass a second parameter to the aggregate function, we explicitly specify the scope of the function. In this case, we require the second Sum aggregate function to always add sales for the current quarter column grouping. This enables us to calculate the total for the column to complete the percent of total calculation.*

4. Click OK to exit the Expression dialog box. You will see "<<Expr>>" as a placeholder for the expression.

5. Click to the right of the <<Expr>> placeholder in the new detail cell until you see the blinking edit cursor in the cell.

6. Enter a space followed by **of quarter** in the cell after the placeholder.

7. Click the <<Expr>> placeholder until it is highlighted.

8. Right-click the <<Expr>> placeholder and select Placeholder Properties from the context menu. The Placeholder Properties dialog box appears.

9. Select the Number page.

10. Select Percentage from the Category list.

11. Select the Font page.

12. Check the Bold check box.

13. Click OK to exit the Placeholder Properties dialog box.

### NOTE

*We changed the numeric formatting and the font weight for just the expression portion of the cell content as represented by the placeholder. We did not change the formatting of the text after the placeholder.*

14. Click elsewhere to unselect this cell, and then click this cell again. Now the entire cell is selected, rather than just one portion of the content.

15. Use the toolbar buttons to set the alignment to align right.

16. Drag the right side of the report layout area (report body) as far left as possible.

17. Select the Preview tab. Your report appears as shown in Figure 18-11.

18. Try expanding the quarter columns and the store rows. Click the Save All button on the toolbar when you are done exploring the report.

Wholesale Sales By M...h Report.rdl [Design]   ×

Design   Preview

Year   Calendar 2011 ▾                                                     View Report

◀◀ ◀ 1   of 1 ▶ ▶▮ | ← ⊗ ⊕ | 🖨 ▢ 🖺 🖫▾ | 100%           ▾        Find | Next

**Wholesale Sales By Month Report -    Calendar 2011**

| Store | Product | Quarter 1, 2011 ⊞ | Quarter 2, 2011 ⊞ | Quarter 3, 2011 ⊞ | Quarter 4, 2011 |
|---|---|---|---|---|---|
| ⊞ Online | | $2,210,493.82 | $2,205,968.71 | $2,244,701.60 | $2,262,913.08 |
| | | 22.20% of quarter | 21.95% of quarter | 22.64% of quarter | 24.26% of quarter |
| ⊞ Retail-Store 1 | | $86,909.04 | $87,073.05 | $89,627.89 | $78,579.39 |
| | | 0.87% of quarter | 0.87% of quarter | 0.90% of quarter | 0.84% of quarter |
| ⊞ Retail-Store 2 | | $84,433.51 | $82,211.09 | $72,858.25 | $66,388.93 |
| | | 0.85% of quarter | 0.82% of quarter | 0.73% of quarter | 0.71% of quarter |
| ⊞ Retail-Store 3 | | $75,468.20 | $71,287.71 | $61,176.89 | $50,700.28 |
| | | 0.76% of quarter | 0.71% of quarter | 0.62% of quarter | 0.54% of quarter |
| ⊞ Retail-Store 5 | | $152,307.18 | $115,361.00 | $100,142.05 | $90,171.51 |
| | | 1.53% of quarter | 1.15% of quarter | 1.01% of quarter | 0.97% of quarter |
| ⊞ Wholesale | | $7,347,969.28 | $7,487,552.77 | $7,345,023.65 | $6,777,428.54 |
| | | 73.79% of quarter | 74.51% of quarter | 74.09% of quarter | 72.67% of quarter |

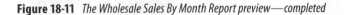

**Figure 18-11**   *The Wholesale Sales By Month Report preview—completed*

# Excel

Most business decision makers are comfortable with the applications that make up Microsoft Office. Spreadsheets were some of the first tools for doing what we now call ad hoc analysis and reporting. In almost every organization, decision makers depend heavily on spreadsheets as data repositories and tools for analysis. Wouldn't it make sense to allow our business intelligence information to be incorporated and manipulated in this comfortable and ubiquitous environment as well? Microsoft provides us the means to do this in Excel with the PivotTable and PivotChart Wizard.

# Creating Pivot Tables and Pivot Charts

The PivotTable and PivotChart Wizard takes us step by step through the process of creating a pivot table and/or pivot chart. It first enables us to set the data source to be used for the pivot items. Fortunately, the data source can be a BI Semantic Model in an Analysis Services database. Once the data source is set, we can either lay out the report while we are still in the wizard or have the wizard create an empty pivot table, and then populate it after the wizard is complete.

## Connecting to the Data

Pivot tables and pivot charts require a data source to work from. One option is to use data from cells right inside the spreadsheet. Pivot tables and pivot charts can also access data from external sources. This second option, of course, is the one we are most interested in. The wizard steps us through the process of setting up access to an external data source, which, in our case, is Analysis Services.

## Layout

The pivot table layout is done in a manner similar to the drag-and-drop approach we saw on the SQL Server Data Tools Design tab. One advantage of the Excel pivot table is that it not only includes row and column dimensions, but it can also include data in the page dimension. We can, therefore, use these tools to look at three dimensions at a time.

As stated earlier, the pivot table layout can be created either as part of the PivotTable and PivotChart Wizard or after the wizard completes. In most cases, the layout is created after exiting the wizard. Waiting until after the wizard is complete provides a cleaner and more capable report creation environment. The one time we may want to create the layout in the wizard is in a situation where the underlying data has gotten large and unwieldy. By creating the layout in the wizard, we can specify a field to serve as the page grouping. Once this is done, data is retrieved one page at a time, eliminating the need to retrieve the entire data set before displaying results.

## Learn By Doing—Creating an Excel Pivot Table

### Feature Highlighted

▶ Creating a pivot table in Microsoft Excel

**Business Need**    The vice president (VP) of production for Maximum Miniatures,
Incorporated would like to do some of his own analysis of the information in the
Max Min Manufacturing DM cube. He is a big Excel user and is comfortable with this
program. To fulfill the VP's needs, we show him how to create a pivot table in Excel,
pulling data from the MaxMinManufacturingDM cube.

**NOTE**

*Pivot tables can be created in Excel 2003, Excel 2007, or Excel 2010. Excel 2010 was used for the Learn By Doing
exercises in this chapter.*

### Steps to Create the Connection to a Cube on Analysis Services

1. Open Microsoft Excel 2010.
2. Select the Insert ribbon and click the PivotTable icon, as shown in Figure 18-12.
   The Create PivotTable dialog box appears.
3. Select the Use an external data source option to use data from outside the
   spreadsheet as shown in Figure 18-13.
4. Click the Choose Connection button. The Existing Connections dialog box appears.
5. Click the Browse for More button. The Select Data Source dialog box appears.
6. Click the New Source button. The Data Connection Wizard dialog box appears,
   as shown in Figure 18-14.

**Figure 18-12** *Creating a pivot table in Excel*

**Figure 18-13**  *The Create Pivot Table dialog box*

7.  Select Microsoft SQL Server Analysis Services from the list of data source types.

8.  Click Next. The Connect to Database Server page of the Data Connection Wizard appears.

9.  Enter the name of the Analysis Services server hosting the MaxMinManufacturingDM database.

**Figure 18-14**  *The Data Connection Wizard dialog box*

10. Enter the appropriate credentials for accessing this server. The Connect to Database Server page of the wizard appears as shown in Figure 18-15.

11. Click Next. The Select Database and Table page of the Data Connection Wizard appears.

12. Select MaxMinManufacturingDM from the database drop-down list, if it is not selected by default.

13. Select the Max Min Manufacturing DM cube from the list of cubes and perspectives. The Select Database and Table page of the wizard appears, as shown in Figure 18-16.

14. Click Next. The Save Data Connection File and Finish page of the Data Connection Wizard appears as shown in Figure 18-17.

15. Enter a description of the data source and click Finish. We return to the Create PivotTable dialog box.

16. Click OK to exit the Create PivotTable dialog box. An empty pivot table is created, as shown in Figure 18-18.

## NOTE

*In this example we queried data from one of our Multidimensional BI Semantic Models. We can use a similar approach to connect to a Tabular instance of SQL Server Analysis Services and query data from our Tabular BI Semantic Model for use in a PivotTable or PivotChart.*

**Figure 18-15**   *The Connect to Database Server page of the Data Connection Wizard*

**Figure 18-16** *The Select Database and Table page of the Data Connection Wizard*

**Figure 18-17** *The Save Data Connection File and Finish page of the Data Connection Wizard*

**Figure 18-18**  *The empty pivot table layout in the Excel spreadsheet*

## Steps to Create the PivotTable Layout

1. In the PivotTable Field List, locate the Date Hierarchy. Drag the Date Hierarchy and drop it on the Report Filter area. This creates a report filter in the upper-left corner of the spreadsheet, as shown in Figure 18-19.

2. Click the filter icon next to 2011 in the upper-left corner of the spreadsheet.

3. Check the Select Multiple Items check box. We can now select multiple dimension members.

4. Expand the 2011 item in the list.

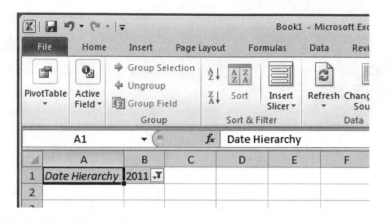

**Figure 18-19** *A filter added to the pivot table layout*

5. Uncheck the 2011Q3 and 2011Q4 items in the list. The Date Hierarchy drop-down window appears as shown in Figure 18-20.

6. Click OK.

7. In the PivotTable Field List, locate the Product Hierarchy. Drag the Product Hierarchy and drop it on the Row Labels area.

**Figure 18-20** *The Date Hierarchy report filter*

8. Rows are created in the pivot table for the highest level in the hierarchy, the Product Type. Click the drop-down arrow next to Row Labels. The Row Labels drop-down menu appears.

9. Uncheck the Woodland Creatures and Warriors of Yore items. The Row Labels drop-down window is shown in Figure 18-21.

10. Click OK.

11. In the PivotTable Field List, locate the Plant Hierarchy. Drag the Plant Hierarchy and drop it on the Column Labels area. Columns are created for the highest level of the Plant Hierarchy, which is the Country level.

**Figure 18-21** *The Row Labels drop-down window*

**Figure 18-22** *A pivot table with a single measure*

12. In the PivotTable Field List, locate the Accepted Products measure. Drag the Accepted Products measure and drop it on the Values area. The Accepted Products measure is added to the pivot table, as shown in Figure 18-22. When a pivot table includes a single measure, the label for that measure appears in the upper-left corner of the pivot table.

13. Drag the Rejected Products measure and drop it in the area where you dropped the Accepted Products measure. Both measures are included in the layout. The labels for the measures are now at the top of each column, as shown in Figure 18-23.

14. Now that we are done placing items on the layout, we can close the PivotTable Field List window. We can close the window or click the Field List button in the Options ribbon, as shown in Figure 18-24. We can bring back the PivotTable Field List window by clicking this ribbon button a second time.

**Figure 18-23** *A pivot table with multiple measures*

15. Select one of the cells containing the Accepted Products measure label. Change the text to **# Accepted**. When we exit the modified cell, all occurrences of the measure label are changed.

16. Change the Rejected Products measure label to **# Rejected**. The completed pivot table appears as shown in Figure 18-25.

17. Save the spreadsheet in an appropriate location.

**Figure 18-24** *The Field List button in the Options ribbon*

**Figure 18-25**   *The completed pivot table*

# Pivot Chart

Now that we have seen how to work with pivot tables, let's try a pivot chart.

## Learn By Doing—Creating a Pivot Chart

### Feature Highlighted

▶  Creating a pivot chart in Microsoft Excel

**Business Need**   Our intrepid VP of production is extremely happy with the information he has been able to discover using the pivot table in Excel. Now, he would like to create a chart from this information to use at an upcoming presentation. We can show him how to create a pivot chart in Excel.

**Steps**

1. Select the Sheet2 tab in the spreadsheet used in the first Learn By Doing exercise in this chapter.

2. Select the Insert ribbon.

3. Select PivotChart from the drop-down list below the PivotTable icon, as shown in Figure 18-26. The Create PivotTable with PivotChart dialog box appears.

4. Select the Use an external data source option to use data from outside the spreadsheet and click Choose Connection. The Existing Connections dialog box appears.

5. Select the connection to the Analysis Services database you created in the previous Learn By Doing exercise.

6. Click Open to return to the Create PivotTable with PivotChart dialog box.

7. Click OK to exit the Create PivotTable with PivotChart dialog box. An empty pivot chart is created, as shown in Figure 18-27.

8. In the PivotTable Field List, locate the Plant Hierarchy. Drag the Plant Hierarchy and drop it on the Report Filter area.

9. Expand the Plant Hierarchy drop-down window in the upper-left corner of the spreadsheet.

10. Expand the All entry, and then expand the United States entry.

11. Select the Maximum Miniatures - Fridley entry.

12. Click OK.

13. In the PivotTable Field List, locate the Date Hierarchy. Drag the Date Hierarchy and drop it on the Row Labels area.

**Figure 18-26** *Creating a pivot chart*

**Figure 18-27** *An empty pivot chart*

14. In the PivotTable Field List, locate the Product Hierarchy. Drag the Product Hierarchy and drop it on the Column Labels area.

15. In the PivotTable Field List, locate the Total Products measure. Drag the Total Products measure and drop it on the Values area. The chart appears as shown in Figure 18-28.

16. Save the spreadsheet.

To format the pivot chart, select a section of the chart you want to format: the axis labels, the legend, or a graph area itself. Right-click and use the context menu to carry out the desired formatting.

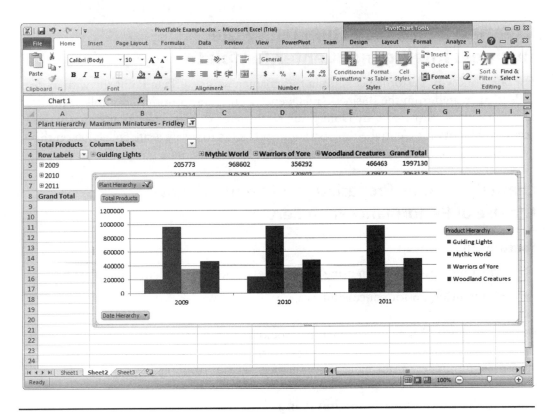

**Figure 18-28**  *A pivot chart*

# PerformancePoint Services in SharePoint 2010

PerformancePoint Services is a business intelligence tool provided as part of SharePoint 2010 Enterprise Edition. It allows us to create visualizations from KPIs defined in our BI Semantic Models. It also allows us to define new KPIs to be used in visualizations. The KPI visualizations can then be incorporated into scorecards and dashboards.

The features of PerformancePoint Services are accessed through a site collection created using the Business Intelligence Center template. A Business Intelligence Center SharePoint site provides access to the Dashboard Designer. Using the Dashboard Designer, we can create scorecards and dashboards to display our KPIs. Look for additional information about PerformancePoint Services in books covering SharePoint 2010.

# Creating a Site Collection Using the Business Intelligence Center Template

For our work with PerformancePoint in this chapter, we use a SharePoint site with a site collection created from the Business Intelligence Center template. You can follow the directions in the next Learn By Doing exercise to create this site collection. You will need access to SharePoint Central Administration and rights to create a site collection on the SharePoint server. As always, do not complete these exercise on a production server.

## Learn By Doing—Preparing SharePoint to Allow the Use of PerformancePoint Services

### Features Highlighted

▶ Creating a site collection using the Business Intelligence Center template

▶ Configuring PerformancePoint Services

**Business Need** Maximum Miniatures would like to create dashboards using PerformancePoint Services. We need to perform the appropriate installations and customization to get PerformancePoint Services up and running.

### Steps to Create the Site Collection Using the Business Intelligence Center Template

1. Open SharePoint Central Administration.
2. Click Application Management on the left side of the page. The Application Management page appears.
3. Under the Site Collections heading, click the Create site collections link. The Create Site Collection page appears.
4. Enter an appropriate title and description for the site collection.
5. Complete the URL for the site collection. Make note of this URL so you can navigate to the site collection later.
6. In the Select a template area, select the Enterprise tab, and then select the Business Intelligence Center template as shown in Figure 18-29.
7. Enter the user name of the Primary Site Collection Administrator.
8. Click OK to create the site collection.

**Figure 18-29** *Creating a site collection using the Business Intelligence Center template*

## Steps to Configure PerformancePoint Services

1. Click OK.
2. Click the Central Administration heading on the left side of the page.
3. Under the Application Management heading, click the Manage service applications link. The Service Applications page appears.
4. Click Application Management on the left side of the page. The Application Management page appears.
5. Click New in the ribbon. A drop-down menu appears.
6. Select PerformancePoint Service Application from the drop-down menu. The New PerformancePoint Service Application page appears.
7. Enter **PPS Service App BI Book** for Name.
8. Check the "Add this service application's proxy to the farm's default proxy list." check box.
9. Scroll down to the Application Pool section.
10. Select the Create new application pool radio button, if it is not already selected.
11. Enter **PPSServiceAppPool** for Application pool name.
12. The Configurable radio button should be selected under "Select a security account for this application pool."

13. Select an appropriate domain account from the Configurable drop-down list or use the "Register new managed account" to specify another domain account to be used by this application pool.

14. Click Create to create the PerformancePoint Services service application.

15. Click OK after the service application is successfully completed. You will be taken to a list of service applications.

16. Scroll down and click the entry for the "PPS Service App BI Book" service application we just created. The Manage PerformancePoint Services: PPS Service App BI Book page appears.

17. Select PerformancePoint Service Application Settings. The PerformancePoint Service Application Settings page appears.

18. Enter a domain user name and password for the Unattended Service Account as shown in Figure 18-30. These credentials are used to authenticate to PerformancePoint data sources. Therefore, this domain account must be granted access rights to those data sources.

19. Click OK to save your changes to the PerformancePoint Services configuration.

**Figure 18-30** *Configuring PerformancePoint Services*

20. Click the System Settings link on the left side of the page. The Systems Settings page appears.
21. Under the Servers heading, click the Manage services on server link. The Services on Server page appears.
22. Scroll down and make sure both the PerformancePoint Service and the Secure Store Service are started. If either is not started, click the link to start that service.

# Creating a Dashboard Using PerformancePoint Services

Now that we have PerformancePoint Services activated and configured on our SharePoint 2010 Enterprise site, we can give it a try. We create a new KPI based on the number of items on backorder. Then we combine this with a chart to create a simple dashboard.

## Learn By Doing—Creating KPIs and a Dashboard Using PerformancePoint Services

### Features Highlighted

▶ Creating a KPI using PerformancePoint Services

▶ Creating a dashboard using PerformancePoint Services

**Business Need** The operations manager at Maximum Miniatures would like a dashboard with a KPI showing items on backorder along with a chart showing the number of products accepted by product type for the past three years. The KPI and the chart need to be created using PerformancePoint Services.

### Steps to Defining a Data Connection

1. Navigate to the site you created from the Business Intelligence Center template. The main page of this site should appear as shown in Figure 18-31.
2. Click the PerformancePoint Content link on the left side of the page. The PerformancePoint Content library appears.
3. Click the Add new item link. The first time you do this, the Dashboard Designer application will download and install. If prompted to run the Dashboard Designer application, click Run. The Dashboard Designer will appear as shown in Figure 18-32.
4. In the Workspace Browser, select the Data Connections item.

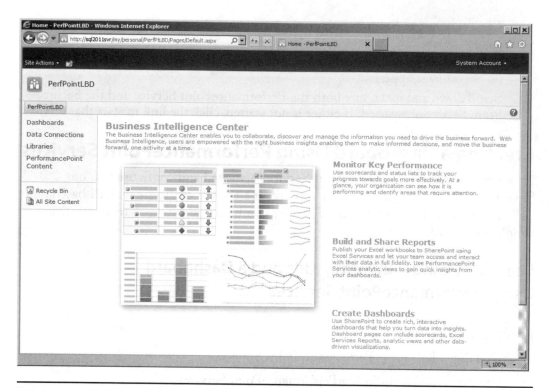

**Figure 18-31** *The main page of the Business Intelligence Center SharePoint Site*

**Figure 18-32** *The Dashboard Designer*

5. Select the Create tab of the ribbon and click Data Source. The Select a Data Source Template dialog box appears as shown in Figure 18-33.

6. Select the Analysis Services template, if it is not already selected, and click OK.

7. A new data source appears in the Workspace Browser area. The center of the screen allows you to fill in the details for this new data source. Replace "New Data Source" with **MaxMinManufacturingDM** for the name of the data source.

8. For Server, enter the name of the server where the Max Min Manufacturing DM cube was deployed.

9. Select MaxMinManufacturingDM from the Database drop-down list.

10. Select Max Min Manufacturing DM from the Cube drop-down list. The Dashboard Designer should appear similar to Figure 18-34.

11. Click the Save button in the upper-left corner of the Dashboard Designer.

**Figure 18-33** *The Select a Data Source Template dialog box*

**Figure 18-34** *The Dashboard Designer with a new data connection*

### Steps to Create a KPI

1. In the Workspace Browser, select the PerformancePoint Content item.
2. Click KPI on the Create tab of the ribbon. The Select a KPI Template dialog box appears as shown in Figure 18-35.
3. Select Blank KPI, if it is not already selected, and click OK.
4. A new KPI appears in the Workspace Browser area. The center of the screen allows you to fill in the details for this new KPI. Replace "New KPI" with **Backorder KPI**.
5. Click the link in the first row under the Data Mappings column. This is the Actual row. The Fixed Values Data Source Mapping dialog box appears.
6. Click Change Source. The Select a Data Source dialog box appears.
7. Select the MaxMinManufacturingDM Analysis Services data source as shown in Figure 18-36.
8. Click OK. The Fixed Values Data Source Mapping dialog box has changed to the Dimensional Data Source Mapping dialog box.
9. Check the Use MDX tuple formula check box.

**Figure 18-35**  *The Select a KPI Template dialog box*

**Figure 18-36**  *The Select a Data Source dialog box*

10. Enter the following in the formula area:

```
ABS(ROUND([Number On Backorder] /
      COUNT(DESCENDANTS([Product Hierarchy].CurrentMember,
                        [Product Hierarchy].[Product])), 0))
```

This MDX expression takes the number on backorder for a given product type, product subtype, or product and divides it by the number of products in that grouping. This gives the average amount on backorder for the grouping. The expression rounds the result to a whole number because you can't really have half of a product on backorder. It also takes the absolute value of the backorder amount to allow us to deal with positive numbers in the KPI. The Dimensional Data Source Mapping dialog box should appear as shown in Figure 18-37.

11. Click OK.

12. Click the link in the second row under the Data Mappings column. This is the Target row. The Fixed Values Data Source Mapping dialog box appears.

13. Replace 1 with **600**.

**Figure 18-37** *The Dimensional Data Source Mapping for the average amount on backorder*

14. Click OK.

15. In the Thresholds area, click the Set Scoring Pattern and Indicator button. The Select the Scoring Pattern page of the Edit Banding Settings dialog box appears. (If the Thresholds area is not visible, click anywhere in the Target row.)

16. Select Decreasing is Better from the Scoring pattern drop-down list. The dialog box should appear as shown in Figure 18-38.

17. Click Next. The Select an Indicator page of the Edit Banding Settings dialog box appears.

18. Leave the default settings and click Next. The Specify the worst value page of the Edit Banding Settings dialog box appears.

19. Leave the default setting and click Finish. The Dashboard Designer should appear similar to Figure 18-39.

20. Click Save.

**Figure 18-38**  *The Select the Scoring Pattern page of the Edit Banding Settings dialog box*

**Figure 18-39** *The Dashboard Designer with a new KPI*

**Steps to Create a Scorecard Using a PerformancePoint KPI**    A PerformancePoint Scorecard combines a KPI with dimensions and filters to produce meaningful information.

1. In the Workspace Browser, select the PerformancePoint Content item.

2. Click Scorecard on the Create tab of the ribbon. The Select a Scorecard Template dialog box appears. Click All in the Category pane to see the various types of scorecards that can be created, as shown in Figure 18-40.

3. Make sure Analysis Services is selected in the Template pane and click OK. The Select a data source page of the Create an Analysis Services Scorecard dialog box appears.

4. Select the MaxMinManufacturingDM Analysis Services data source.

5. Click Next. The Select a KPI Source page of the Create an Analysis Services Scorecard dialog box appears.

6. Make sure the Create KPIs from SQL Server Analysis Services measures radio button is selected and click Next. The Select KPIs to Import page of the Create an Analysis Services Scorecard dialog box appears.

**Figure 18-40** *The Select a Scorecard Template dialog box.*

7.  Click Select KPI. The Select a KPI dialog box appears with our brand-new Backorder KPI as shown in Figure 18-41.

8.  With the Backorder KPI selected, click OK. The Backorder KPI is added to the list on the Select KPIs to Import page.

9.  Click Next. The Add Measure Filters page of the Create an Analysis Services Scorecard dialog box appears. This page allows us to apply filter conditions to the KPI.

10. Click Next. The Add Member Columns page of the Create an Analysis Services Scorecard dialog box appears.

11. Check the Add column members check box.

12. Click Select Dimension. The Select Dimension dialog box appears.

13. Select Dim Product.Product Hierarchy.

14. Click OK.

**Figure 18-41** *The Select a KPI dialog box*

15. Click Select Members. The Select Members dialog box appears.
16. Check Guiding Lights, Mythic World, Warriors of Yore, and Woodland Creatures as shown in Figure 18-42.
17. Click OK.
18. Click Finish.
19. Replace "New Scorecard" with **Backorder Scorecard**. The scorecard appears as shown in Figure 18-43. Try drilling into the Product Subtype and Product levels.
20. Click Save.

### Steps to Create an Analytic Chart

1. In the Workspace Browser, select the PerformancePoint Content item.
2. Click Analytic Chart on the Create tab of the ribbon. The Select a Data Source page of the Create an Analytic Chart Report dialog box appears.
3. Select the MaxMinManufacturingDM Analysis Services data source.
4. Click Finish.

**Figure 18-42** *The Select Members dialog box*

**Figure 18-43** *The Backorder Scorecard*

5. Replace "New Report" with **Accepted Products Chart**.

6. In the Details window to the right, expand the Measures entry.

7. Drag Accepted Products and drop it in the Series area at the bottom of the chart layout.

8. In the Details window, expand the Dimensions entry.

9. Drag the Dim Time hierarchy and drop it in the Bottom Axis area at the bottom of the chart layout. A column chart is created with one column showing the accepted products for 2011 (the default member of the Time dimension, as you might recall).

10. Click the drop-down arrow next to the Dim Time Date Hierarchy entry in the Bottom Axis area. The Select Members dialog box appears.

11. Uncheck Default Member (2011).

12. Check 2009, 2010, and 2011.

13. Click OK.

14. Drag the Dim Product hierarchy and drop it in the Series area below Accepted Products.

15. Click the drop-down arrow next to the Dim Product Product Hierarchy entry in the Series area. The Select Members dialog box appears.

16. Uncheck Default Member (All).

17. Check Guiding Lights, Mythic World, Warriors of Yore, and Woodland Creatures.

18. Click OK. We have a bar chart showing the number of products accepted by product type by year as shown in Figure 18-44.

19. Click Save.

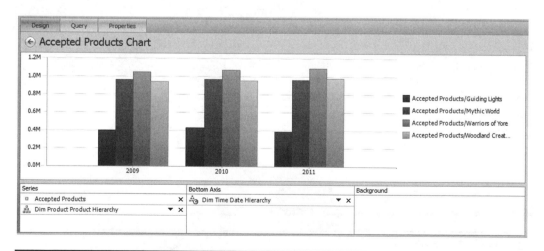

**Figure 18-44** *Analytic chart of products accepted by product type by year*

## Steps to Create a Dashboard

1. In the Workspace Browser, select the PerformancePoint Content item.
2. Click Dashboard on the Create tab of the ribbon. The Select a Dashboard Page Template dialog box appears as shown in Figure 18-45.
3. Select "2 Rows" as shown in Figure 18-45.
4. Click OK.
5. Replace "New Dashboard" with **Manufacturing Dashboard**.
6. In the Details window, expand the Scorecards item.
7. Expand the PerformancePoint Content item under Scorecards.
8. Drag the Backorder Scorecard item from the Details window and drop it in the Top Row zone of the new dashboard.
9. In the Details window, expand the Reports item.
10. Expand the PerformancePoint Content item under Reports.

**Figure 18-45** *The Select a Dashboard Page Template dialog box*

**Figure 18-46** *The Manufacturing Dashboard layout*

11. Drag the Accepted Products Chart from the Details window and drop it in the Bottom Row zone. The dashboard layout appears as shown in Figure 18-46.

12. Click Save All. The Save As dialog box appears.

13. Navigate to an appropriate folder to save the Dashboard Designer workspace.

14. Enter **Max Min PerfPt Dashboard** for File name.

15. Click Save.

16. In the Workspace Browser window, right-click the Manufacturing Dashboard entry and select Deploy to SharePoint from the context menu. The Deploy To dialog box appears with the Dashboards folder selected.

17. Click OK. The Manufacturing Dashboard will be deployed and will display in a new browser tab as shown in Figure 18-47.

18. Hover your mouse over a bar in the chart. A ToolTip will tell you which product type is being represented.

19. We have already explored drilldown in our scorecard. Let's try it in the chart. Right-click any of the green bars showing Warriors of Yore information in the chart.

20. Select Drill Down To | Dim Product | Product Subtype from the context menu as shown in Figure 18-48.

**Figure 18-47**   *The Manufacturing Dashboard after deployment*

**Figure 18-48**   *Drilling down in the chart*

**Figure 18-49** *The Manufacturing Dashboard with drilldown*

21. The chart will drill down to show information for the product subtypes in the Warriors of Yore product type as shown in Figure 18-49.

22. Right-click a bar in the chart and select Drill Up from the context menu to return the chart to its original form.

23. After you have explored the new dashboard, close the browser tab displaying the dashboard.

24. In the original browser tab, select Dashboards from the menu on the left. You see the entry we just created by deploying the dashboard.

25. Click the Manufacturing Dashboard link. You see an entry for page 1 of the dashboard.

26. Click the Page 1 link to display the dashboard.

27. Close the browser and the Dashboard Designer.

# Power View

Power View is a brand-new reporting tool from Microsoft. Where Reporting Services caters to the report authors in the IT department, Power View is aimed at subject matter experts who want a quick, easy, and fun way to explore their data. More specifically, Power View is an ad hoc reporting environment that provides meaningful business information in no more than three clicks. This includes creating tabular-style reports as well as charts and graphs.

The Power View authoring environment is browser-based. No software install is required. It should be noted, however, that Power View leverages the Silverlight environment, so this browser add-in is required. Power View is a part of SQL Server. Similar to PerformancePoint Services, though, it is hosted by SharePoint 2010 as part of Reporting Services operating in SharePoint Integrated mode. The Enterprise version of SharePoint 2010 is required.

In its initial release with SQL Server 2012, Power View only supports the Tabular BI Semantic Model. It is expected that Power View support for Multidimensional BI Semantic Models will follow in a subsequent update. Perhaps, by the time you are reading this book, it is already available.

In addition to Power View's polish and ease of use, its other big selling point is its interactivity. Not only can the user readily interact with the data in the report, but different parts of a report interact with each other. Clicking a bar in a chart causes a table in the same report to be filtered by that bar's context. Graphs come alive as they give an animated replay of values through time.

So, let's have some fun with Power View.

## Setting Up Power View in SharePoint 2010

To use Power View, SQL Server Reporting Services must be installed in SharePoint Integrated mode. To accomplish this, Reporting Services must be installed on your SharePoint application server. This is done using the SQL Server installation software.

On the Feature Selection page of the SQL Server 2012 Setup program, you need to select the "Reporting Services - SharePoint" and "Reporting Services Add-in for SharePoint Products" options under Shared Features. This is shown in Figure 18-50. The appropriate Reporting Services features will be installed on your SharePoint server.

Once the Reporting Services items are installed, they are configured using the SharePoint Central Administration. The following Learn By Doing exercise will take you through this configuration process.

### Learn By Doing—Configuring SQL Server Reporting Services for SharePoint Integrated Mode Operation

#### Feature Highlighted

▶ Configuring SSRS using SharePoint Central Administration

**Business Need**   SQL Server Reporting Services must be configured in SharePoint Integrated mode before Power View can be used.

**Figure 18-50** *Installing Reporting Services for SharePoint Integrated mode operation*

### Steps for Creating a Reporting Services Service Application

1. Open SharePoint Central Administration. The main page of the SharePoint Central Administration site is shown in Figure 18-51.

2. Under the Application Management heading, click the Manage service applications link. The Service Applications page appears.

3. Click the New button in the upper-left part of the page. This will open a drop-down list showing the types of items you can create.

4. Select SQL Server Reporting Services Service Application as shown in Figure 18-52.

5. The Create SQL Server Reporting Services Service Application dialog box appears. Enter **Reporting Services** as the Name for the service application.

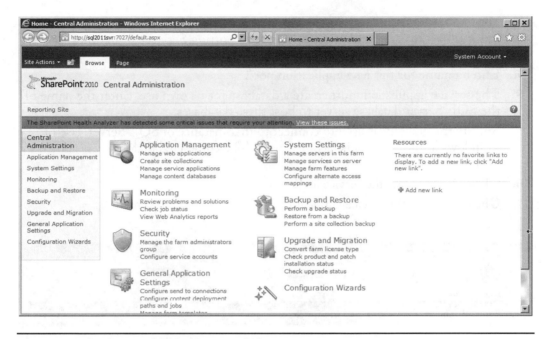

**Figure 18-51**  *The main page of the SharePoint Central Administration site*

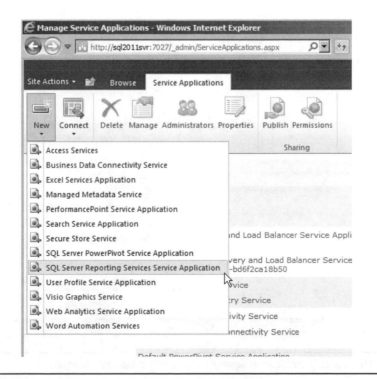

**Figure 18-52**  *Creating a new SQL Server Reporting Services service application*

6. You can select an existing application pool to use for this new service application, but it is best to create a new one to isolate Reporting Services from other web services. Select the Create new application pool radio button.

7. Enter a name for this new application pool.

8. The service application must create a database for its own use. Enter the name of the SQL Server database server to host these databases.

9. Specify the credentials used to connect to that instance of SQL Server. Use of Windows authentication is recommended. The completed dialog box is shown in Figure 18-53.

10. Click OK to create the service application.

11. Click OK after the service application has been successfully created.

**Figure 18-53**  *The completed Create SQL Server Reporting Services Service Application dialog box*

**Steps for Making the Service Application Part of the Default Application Proxy Group**    With the Reporting Services service application created, we must make it a part of the default application proxy group.

1. In the Central Administration menu on the left side of the screen, click Application Management.
2. On the Application Management page, click the Configure service application associations link under Service Applications.
3. On the Service Application Associations page, click the default link under Application Proxy Group. The Configure Service Application Associations dialog box appears.
4. Click to check the box next to SQL Server Reporting Services Service Application. The Configure Service Application Associations dialog box is shown in Figure 18-54.
5. Scroll down, if necessary, and click OK to exit the dialog box.

**Steps for Starting the Reporting Services Service Application**    As our final step, we need to start the Reporting Services Service Application that we just created.

1. In the Central Administration menu on the left side of the screen, click Application Management.

**Figure 18-54**  *The Configure Service Application Associations dialog box*

**Figure 18-55**   *The Start link for the SQL Server Reporting Services Service*

2. On the Application Management page, click the Manage services on server link under Service Applications.

3. On the Services on Server page, scroll down, if necessary, to find the SQL Server Reporting Services Service.

4. Click the Start link next to the SQL Server Reporting Services Service as shown in Figure 18-55. After a few moments, the page should refresh showing the SQL Server Reporting Services Service as Started.

**Steps for Setting Content Types**   Finally, we need to tell the document library being used to store Power View reports to recognize the appropriate content types. This is the regular SharePoint site, not the Central Administration site.

1. Open the SharePoint document library that will be used to store the Power View reports.

2.  Select the Library tab of the ribbon.

3.  On the right side of the ribbon, select Library Settings. The Document Library Settings page appears.

4.  In the General Settings area, click Advanced settings. The Advanced Settings page appears.

5.  In the Content Types area, select Yes to Allow management of content types.

6.  Scroll down and click OK. You will return to the Document Library Settings page.

7.  Scroll down to the Content Types area, and click the "Add from existing site content types" link. The Add Content Types page appears.

8.  In the Select site content types from: drop-down list, select SQL Server Reporting Services Content Types. Three content types are now available for you to select: Report Builder Model, Report Builder Report, and Report Data Source.

9.  Double-click Report Data Source to move it to the Content types to add: list. The Add Content Types page should appear as shown in Figure 18-56.

10. Click OK. You will return to the Document Library Settings page.

Your Reporting Services SharePoint Integrated mode installation is now ready to go.

**Figure 18-56** *The Add Content Types page*

## Creating a Connection to a Tabular BI Semantic Model

To create a Power View report from one of our Tabular BI Semantic Models, we must first have a connection to that model. To do this, we create a Report Data Source. This is why we had to configure the document library to recognize the Report Data Source content type.

**NOTE**

*Power View can be launched from either a Report Data Source or from a BI Semantic Model Connection.*

When creating reports with Reporting Services, it is likely that the report author will create the shared data source as the first report is added to a report project. In the Power View environment, this is less likely to be the case. The Report Data Source is usually created by someone more technical with knowledge of the Analysis Services server instance and Analysis Services database names. Once this Report Data Source is in place in the document library, it is used by subject matter experts who want to get to the data and start exploring.

The following Learn By Doing exercise will guide you through the process of creating a Report Data Source

## Learn By Doing—Creating a Report Data Source

### Feature Highlighted

▶  Creating a Report Data Source

**Business Need**    Several business users at Maximum Miniatures wish to use Power View to explore the Tabular BI Semantic Models. They need the appropriate Report Data Source put in place to allow this to happen.

### Steps for Creating a Reporting Data Source

1. Navigate to the library where you configured the Report Data Source content type.
2. Select the Documents tab of the ribbon.
3. In the ribbon, click the New Document drop-down arrow. The New Document drop-down menu will appear as shown in Figure 18-57.
4. Select Report Data Source. The Data Source Properties page appears.
5. Enter **Max Min Sales Tabular** for Name.
6. Select Microsoft BI Semantic Model for Power View from the Data Source Type drop-down list.

**Figure 18-57** *Creating a new document*

7. Enter the following for Connection string:

```
Data Source={servername};Initial Catalog="Max Min Sales"
```

where *{servername}* is the name of tabular instance of Analysis Services where you deployed the MaxMinSalesTabular BI Semantic Model.

8. Click Test Connection to ensure the Report Data Source has been created correctly. The Data Source Properties page appears as shown in Figure 18-58.

9. Click OK.

**Figure 18-58** *A Report Data Source*

## Creating a Power View Report

We are now ready to create a Power View report.

### Learn By Doing—Creating a Power View Report

#### Feature Highlighted

▶ Creating a Power View report

**Business Need** A business user at Maximum Miniatures wishes to use Power View to explore the sales data.

#### Steps for Creating a Power View Report

1. Hover over the Max Min Sales Tabular Report Data Source created in the previous Learn By Doing exercise. A drop-down arrow appears.
2. Click the drop-down arrow and select Create Power View Report from the drop-down menu as shown in Figure 18-59.
3. The Power View report authoring environment appears with the Max Min Sales Tabular model loaded on the right side of the window. Expand the Products table entry.
4. Click the Product field to create a table in the report layout area as shown in Figure 18-60.

Figure 18-59 *Launching Power View*

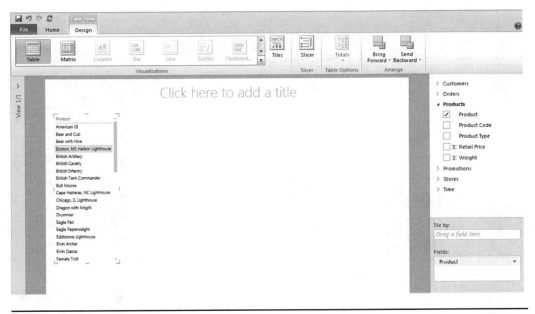

**Figure 18-60** *The products in a Power View table*

5. Expand the Orders table entry and check the Sales in Dollars measure to add it to the table.

**NOTE**

*Be sure the table containing the list of products is still selected when you check the Sales in Dollars measure. This will add the item to the existing table. If the existing table is not selected, a second table will be created when the Sales in Dollars measure is checked.*

6. In the Table Tools Design tab of the ribbon, select the Column visualization. The table is transformed into a column chart as shown in Figure 18-61.

7. Hover over the Product Type field in the Products table in the model area on the right side of the screen. A drop-down arrow appears.

8. Click the drop-down arrow and select Add as Tile By from the drop-down menu. The chart is now tiled by Product Type.

9. Hover your mouse over the chart. An outer set of sizing handles appears.

10. Use the outer sizing handle in the middle of the right side, as shown in Figure 18-62, to make the chart wide enough to see all four product types.

11. Drag the chart wider so it covers all of the area under the Product Type tabs.

12. Click in an empty section in the report layout area to unselect the chart.

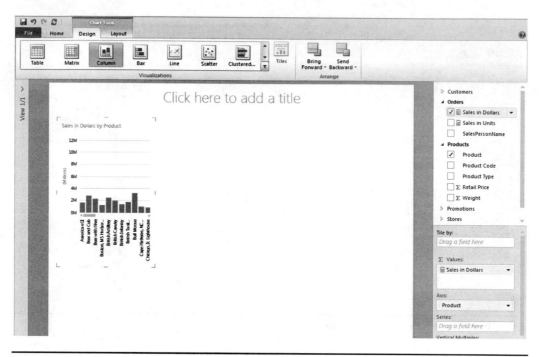

**Figure 18-61**  *Creating a column chart*

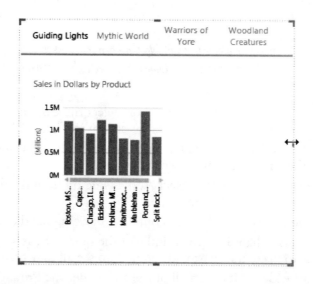

**Figure 18-62**  *Sizing the chart*

13. Expand the Stores table and check the Store field. A new table is created.
14. In the Orders table, check the Sales in Units measure.
15. Click in an empty section in the report layout area to unselect the table.
16. Expand the Promotions table and check the Promotion field. A new table is created.
17. In the Orders table, check the Sales in Dollars measure.
18. Click the "Click here to add title" item and enter **Sales Analysis** for the report title.
19. Let's see how the report works. Click the Product Type tiling tabs to view the various product types in the chart.
20. Click one of the bars in the chart. Notice how the figures in the two tables are now filtered by the selected product. This is shown in Figure 18-63.
21. Click Save in the upper-left corner. The Save As dialog box appears. The folder from which we launched Power View is selected by default.
22. Enter **Sales Analysis Report** for File name.
23. Click Save.
24. Select File | Export to PowerPoint. Another Save As dialog box appears.
25. Enter **Sales Analysis Report from Power View** for File name.

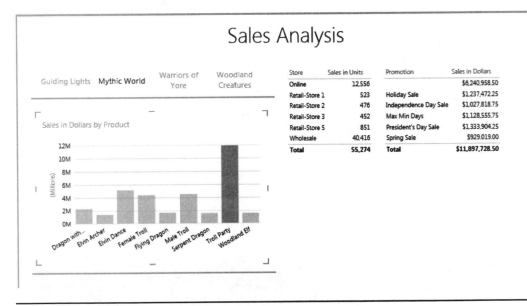

**Figure 18-63** *Filtering the table content by selecting a chart item*

26. Select an appropriate folder for the PowerPoint file and click Save.
27. Click your browser's back arrow to return to the SharePoint library.
28. Click your browser's refresh button so you see the report in the SharePoint library.

## Putting It All Together

Business intelligence that simply sits on a relational or OLAP server without ever getting to the users does no good for anyone. To make a difference, this information must reach its target audience. In many cases, the target audience is too busy with other commitments to seek out the information. It is up to us to put business intelligence at their fingertips.

In this chapter, we saw several tools that can be part of the solution for getting information to the decision makers. In the next chapter, we look at ways developers can integrate business intelligence right into their applications.

# Chapter 19

# Let's Get Together—Integrating Business Intelligence with Your Applications

## In This Chapter

- ► **ADOMD.NET**
- ► **Integrating a Reporting Services Report with an Application**
- ► **Great Capabilities, Great Opportunities**

*If you want to make beautiful music, you must play the black and the white notes together.*

—Richard Milhous Nixon

In the previous chapter, we looked at several tools that make our BI Semantic Models available to business decision makers. In some situations, however, our users don't want a separate tool. At times, our business intelligence must integrate tightly with other programs and solutions.

Once again, SQL Server 2012 provides us with the tools to fulfill this need. The ADOMD.NET data provider enables us to execute queries against BI Semantic Models on Analysis Services servers. Analysis Management Objects (AMO) provides a programming interface for the management of an Analysis Services server and the objects residing on that server. Reporting Services also offers a number of methods for integrating reports with applications.

With these features, we can provide our users with the complete package, the integrated solution, the all-in-one application, the tightly coupled, well-oiled . . . well, you get the picture.

# ADOMD.NET

ADOMD.NET, the multidimensional counterpart to ADO.NET, is our means to programmatically access the wealth of business intelligence we have been creating on the Analysis Services server. With ADOMD.NET, our client applications can query databases on an Analysis Services server. ADOMD.NET also allows these applications to programmatically view and manipulate the structures residing in Analysis Services databases. ADOMD.NET uses XML for Analysis (XML/A) to interact with the Analysis Services server.

## ADOMD.NET Structure

The structure of ADOMD.NET is similar to the structure of ADO.NET. Both use a connection object to manage the connection string and set up access to the server. Both use a command object to execute queries against a database. And both provide structures for connected and disconnected access to data.

### AdomdConnection

The *AdomdConnection* manages the connection between the client application and the Analysis Services server. A connection string similar to the following is used to initiate the connection to a server:

```
Data Source=ServerName;Catalog=AnalSvcsDB;Provider=msolap;
```

The connection to the server is made using either Transmission Control Protocol/ Internet Protocol (TCP/IP) or Hypertext Transfer Protocol (HTTP). This enables connections to be made with a minimum of firewall and network interference.

Once the connection is open, an AdomdCommand object can be used to interact with the Analysis Services database. When the session has concluded, the connection must be explicitly closed with the Close method. An AdomdCommand object does not automatically close the connection when it goes out of scope in your code. (This is done to facilitate connection sharing.)

## AdomdCommand

The *AdomdCommand* manages the execution of queries against a multidimensional server. The query is set using either the CommandText property or CommandStream property. The query itself must be an MDX command or an XML/A-compliant command that is valid on the target server.

AdomdCommand offers the following methods for executing the query:

▶ **Execute**   The Execute method returns the result of the command either as a CellSet or as an AdomdDataReader, depending on the format of the results themselves.

▶ **ExecuteCellSet**   The ExecuteCellSet method returns the result of the command as a CellSet.

▶ **ExecuteNonQuery**   The ExecuteNonQuery method executes a command that does not return a result.

▶ **ExecuteReader**   The ExecuteReader method returns the result of the command as an AdomdDataReader.

▶ **ExecuteXMLReader**   The ExecuteXMLReader method returns the result of the command in the native XML/A format using an XMLReader.

## AdomdDataReader

The *AdomdDataReader* provides a means for reading a forward-only result set from a query. While this result set is being read, the connection to the data source remains busy. This is a connected result set. Connected access requires more server overhead to maintain the active connection.

## CellSet

Unlike the AdomdDataReader, the *CellSet* facilitates a disconnected result set. The CellSet contains the entire structure of the multidimensional result set. Therefore, an application can interact with this result set without having to maintain a connection to the server.

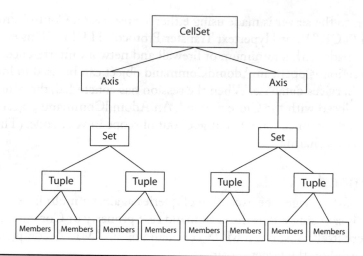

**Figure 19-1**    *A partial view of the CellSet structure*

A portion of the CellSet structure is shown in Figure 19-1. The CellSet contains one or more axis objects. These represent the query dimensions: Column, Row, Page, and so on. Review Chapter 12 if you need a refresher on query dimensions in an MDX query. Each axis contains a set of tuples. A set can have zero, one, or many tuples. As we discussed in Chapter 11, tuples are made up of dimension and hierarchy members.

In addition to the items shown in Figure 19-1, the CellSet contains a collection of cells called Cells. These *cells* contain the measures that are included in the MDX query. The cell collection contains one index for each dimension in the MDX query. For example, if the MDX query contains Column, Row, and Page dimensions, the cell collection will have three indexes and an individual cell would be addressed as shown:

```
CellSet.Cells(x, y, z)
```

The measure calculated for an individual cell is accessed through the Value property, as shown:

```
CellSet.Cells(x, y, z).Value
```

## ADOMD.NET Example

Let's look at an example using ADOMD.NET to incorporate an MDX query result into an application. A Maximum Miniatures developer has created a Windows program for analyzing prospective customers called *Prospect Analyzer*. The method of analysis being used by this program is to take a prospective customer's city of residence and display the buying habits of other residents of that city for the past three years. Many of Max Min's products have regional appeal, so this type of analysis can be helpful when planning a sales approach to a prospective customer.

The program displays the number of product sales by store by year. Because we have three dimensions in the result set, a bit of creativity was required. Two of the three dimensions are represented by the rows and columns of a data grid. Multiple data grids are placed on a set of tab pages to represent the third dimension. The user interface for the Prospect Analyzer is shown in Figure 19-2.

Recall the MDX Query window in SQL Server Management Studio only allows two dimensions in query results. Here, we have an MDX query result viewer that allows three. Your homework is to design your own MDX query result viewer that will display four dimensions.

**NOTE**

*The Prospect Analyzer sample application is included in the Zip file available for download from the publisher's website for this book.*

**Figure 19-2**   *The Prospect Analyzer sample application with a three-dimensional MDX query result viewer*

## Setting a Reference

We can use ADOMD.NET in a number of different .NET project types. But before we can use ADOMD.NET in the project, we must first set a reference to the assembly that implements it. That reference is set, within your Visual Studio project, by doing the following:

1. Right-click the project entry in the Solution Explorer window and select Add Reference from the context menu. The Add Reference dialog box appears.
2. Select the .NET tab.
3. Click the Component Name heading to sort the list by name.
4. Scroll down in the .NET tab, and select the entry for Microsoft.AnalysisServices.AdomdClient. If this entry is not present, select the Browse tab and navigate to the following folder if you are using a 32-bit version of Windows:

   ```
   C:\Program Files\Microsoft.NET\ADOMD.NET\110
   ```

   or to the following folder if you are using a 64-bit version of Windows:

   ```
   C:\Program Files (x86)\Microsoft.NET\ADOMD.NET\110
   ```

   and then select Microsoft.AnalysisServices.AdomdClient.dll.
5. Click OK to exit the Add Reference dialog box and add a reference to this assembly in your project.

If you need to view the references currently set for a project to determine if the ADOMD.NET client has already been referenced, use the following steps:

1. Right-click the project entry in the Solution Explorer window and select Properties from the context menu. The Project Properties tab appears. (This tab will have the name of the project you are working with.)
2. Select the References page of the Project Properties tab. This page appears as shown in Figure 19-3. Notice the entry for Microsoft.AnalysisServices .AdomdClient at the top of the list of references.

We will import AdomdClient so we don't need to use the prefix "Microsoft.AnalysisServices.AdomdClient" in front of every object type. The following line of code must be at or near the beginning of each program:

```
Imports Microsoft.AnalysisServices.AdomdClient
```

**Figure 19-3**    *The References page of the Project Properties tab*

## Retrieving a CellSet

The code to retrieve the CellSet is shown here. This code should look familiar to anyone who has used ADO.NET because it has the same format. We connect to the database server, we create and execute the query on this server, and then we pick up the query result and pass it back:

```
Imports Microsoft.AnalysisServices.AdomdClient


Public Class ADOMDWrapper

    Public Function BuyingByProductByStoreByYearMDX( _
                    ByRef CityName As String) As CellSet
        Dim conn As AdomdConnection
        Dim cmd As AdomdCommand
        Dim cst As CellSet
        Dim strServer As String = "local"
        Dim strDatabase As String = "MaxMinSalesDM"
        Dim strMDXQuery As String
```

```
strMDXQuery = "SELECT [Time].[Year].members ON PAGES, " & _
              "[Store].[Store].members ON ROWS, " & _
              "[Product].[Product].members ON COLUMNS " & _
              "FROM [MaxMinSales] " & _
               "WHERE ([Measures].[Sales in Units], " & _
                  " [Customer].[City].[" & CityName & "])"

' Open the connection to the Analysis Services server
Try
    ' Create a new AdomdConnection object, providing the
    ' connection string.
    conn = New AdomdConnection("Data Source=" & strServer & _
    ";Catalog=" & strDatabase & ";Provider=msolap;")
    ' Open the connection.
    conn.Open ()
Catch ex As Exception
    Throw New ApplicationException( _
        "An error occurred while connecting.")
End Try

' Execute the MDX Query
Try
    ' Create a new AdomdCommand object,
    ' providing the MDX query string.
    cmd = New AdomdCommand(strMDXQuery, conn)
    ' Run the command and return a CellSet object.
    cst = cmd.ExecuteCellSet()

    ' Return the CellSet object
    Return cst

Catch ex As Exception
    Throw New ApplicationException( _
        "An error occurred while opening the cellset.")
End Try

' Release resources.
Try
    conn.Close ()
Catch ex As Exception
    ' Ignore errors
Finally
    cst = Nothing
```

```
            cmd = Nothing
            conn = Nothing
        End Try

    End Function
End Class
```

The next code listing shows how to parse the information into our fancy three-dimensional viewer. First, we loop through the content of Axis(2), the Pages dimension, to create a tab page for each one. Each tab page has a DataGridView control for displaying columns and rows on that tab. Second, we loop through the content of Axis(0), the Column dimension, to create columns in the DataGridView. Third, we loop through the content of Axis(1), the Row dimension, to create row labels in the DataGridView. Finally, we loop through the cells in the CellSet to populate the content of the DataGridView on each tab page:

```
Imports Microsoft.AnalysisServices.AdomdClient

Public Class ProspectAnalyzer

    Private Sub cmdAnalyze_Click(ByVal sender As System.Object, _
            ByVal e As System.EventArgs) Handles cmdAnalyze.Click
        Dim ADOMDBWpr As New ADOMDWrapper
        Dim CSet As CellSet
        Dim i, j, k As Integer
        Dim DataGridView As System.Windows.Forms.DataGridView
        Dim DataGridViewColumn As _
            System.Windows.Forms.DataGridViewTextBoxColumn

        ' Don't do any analysis if there is no city selected
        If String.IsNullOrEmpty(cboCity.Text) Then
            Return
        End If

        ' Set the label on the buying analysis group box
        gbxBuyingAnalysis.Text = "Buying Analysis for " & cboCity.Text

        ' Call the function to get a CellSet
        ' with the results for the specified city
        CSet = ADOMDBWpr.BuyingByProductByStoreByYearMDX(cboCity.Text)

        ' Create a tab for each Page in the resulting CellSet
        TabForPages.TabPages.Clear()
```

```
For i = 0 To CSet.Axes(2).Set.Tuples.Count - 1
    ' Label the tab using the caption for
    ' each Page in the CellSet

    TabForPages.TabPages.Add( _
        CSet.Axes(2).Set.Tuples(i).Members(0).Caption)

    ' Place a DataGridView on the new tab
    DataGridView = New System.Windows.Forms.DataGridView
    DataGridView.ReadOnly = True
    DataGridView.Width = TabForPages.TabPages(i).Width
    DataGridView.Height = TabForPages.TabPages(i).Height
    DataGridView.RowHeadersVisible = True
    DataGridView.RowHeadersWidth = 123

    ' Create a column in the DataGridView for
    ' each Column in the CellSet
    For j = 0 To CSet.Axes(0).Set.Tuples.Count - 1
        DataGridViewColumn = New _
            System.Windows.Forms.DataGridViewTextBoxColumn

        ' The headers for the column is the caption
        ' for each Column in the CellSet
        DataGridViewColumn.HeaderText = _
          CSet.Axes(0).Set.Tuples(j).Members(0).Caption

        DataGridViewColumn.Width = 150

        DataGridView.Columns.Add(DataGridViewColumn)
    Next

    ' Create an empty row in the DataGridView
    ' for each Row in the CellSet
    DataGridView.RowCount = CSet.Axes(1).Set.Tuples.Count

    ' The headers for each row is the caption
    ' for each Row in the CellSet
    For k = 0 To CSet.Axes(1).Set.Tuples.Count - 1
        DataGridView.Rows(k).HeaderCell.Value = _
            CSet.Axes(1).Set.Tuples(k).Members(0).Caption
    Next

    ' Place the values from the CellSet in the DataGridView
    ' cells
```

```
            For j = 0 To CSet.Axes(0).Set.Tuples.Count - 1
                For k = 0 To CSet.Axes(1).Set.Tuples.Count - 1
                    DataGridView(j, k).Value = CSet.Cells(j, k, i).Value
                Next
            Next

            ' Place the DataGridView on the tab page
            TabForPages.TabPages(i).Controls.Add(DataGridView)
        Next

        ' Set the Buying Analysis group box visible
        gbxBuyingAnalysis.Visible = True

    End Sub
End Class
```

# Integrating a Reporting Services Report with an Application

In addition to writing our own code to query a BI Semantic Model and display the result, we can integrate a Reporting Services report with an application. There are several ways to accomplish this, such as using URL links or using the Report Viewer control. In the Learn By Doing exercises in this chapter, we will accomplish this integration using a call to the report server web service.

In order to give this a try, we need to deploy our Reporting Services reports to a report server. First, a little information about the report server. As was discussed in Chapter 18, Reporting Services can operate in either native mode or SharePoint Integrated mode. The discussion and Learn By Doing exercises here pertain to Reporting Services operating in native mode.

## Report Server

The report server is the piece of the puzzle that makes Reporting Services the product it is. This is the software environment that enables us to share our reports with the masses, at least those masses who have rights to the report server. The report server holds a copy of each report that is deployed to it. It then allows users to locate and run those reports in a secure environment.

When a report is deployed to a report server, a copy of the report's RDL definition is put in that server's Report Catalog. The *Report Catalog* is a set of databases used to store the definitions for all the reports available on a particular report server. It also stores the configuration, security, and other information necessary for the operation of that report server.

## Folders

Before we deploy reports to the report server, we need to have an understanding of the way the report server organizes reports in the Report Catalog. In the *Report Catalog*, reports are arranged into a system of folders similar to the Windows file system. Folders can contain reports, supporting files (such as external images and shared data sources), and even other folders. The easiest way to create, view, and maintain these folders is through the Report Manager.

Although the Report Catalog folders look and act like Windows file system folders, they are not actual file system folders. You cannot find them anywhere in the file system on the computer running the report server. *Report Catalog folders* are on-screen representations of records in the databases that hold the Report Catalog.

## The Report Manager

The *Report Manager* application provides a straightforward method for creating and navigating folders in the Report Catalog. When we initially install Reporting Services, the Home folder is created by default. This is the only folder that exists at first.

By default, the Report Manager site is installed in the default website on the server. It is located in a virtual directory called Reports. Therefore, the default URL for the Report Manager is as follows, where *ComputerName* is the name of the computer hosting Reporting Services:

```
http://ComputerName/reports
```

No matter how we get there, the Report Manager appears similar to Figure 19-4.

**NOTE**

*Figure 19-4 shows the Report Manager as it appears for a user with content manager privileges. If you do not see the New Folder, New Data Source, Report Builder, and Upload File buttons on the toolbar, you do not have content manager privileges and will be unable to complete the exercises in this section of the chapter. If possible, log out and then log in with a Windows login that has local administration privileges on the computer running the report server.*

To use the Report Manager, we must be using Microsoft Internet Explorer.

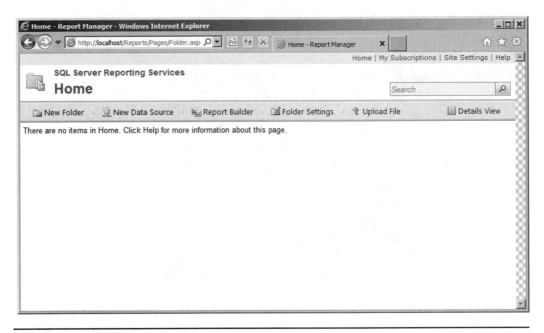

**Figure 19-4**    *The Report Manager with no folders defined*

# Deploying Reports Using SQL Server Data Tools

In the following Learn By Doing exercise, we are going to deploy the report we created in Chapter 18 to a report server. We will deploy the report from the SQL Server Data Tools environment where we originally created it.

## Learn By Doing—Deploying a Report

### Feature Highlighted

▶  Deploying a report from SQL Server Data Tools

**Business Need**    The Maximum Miniatures Marketing Department would like the Wholesale Sales By Month Report integrated with a custom application. The first step toward making that happen is to deploy the report to a report server.

### Steps to Create a Report Server Project

1.  Open SQL Server Data Tools.
2.  Open the MaxMinReports project.

3. Select Project | MaxMinReports Properties from the main menu. The MaxMinReports Property Pages dialog box appears.

4. Enter **MaxMinReports/Data Sources** for TargetDataSourceFolder.

5. Enter **MaxMinReports/Reports** for TargetReportFolder.

6. Type **http://ComputerName/ReportServer** for TargetServerURL, where ComputerName is the name of the computer where the report server is installed. If you are using a secure connection, you should replace http: with https:. The MaxMinReports Property Pages dialog box appears as shown in Figure 19-5.

7. Click OK to exit the MaxMinReports Property Pages dialog box.

8. Right-click the MaxMinReports project entry in the Solution Explorer window and select Deploy from the context menu.

9. The Report Designer builds the report and then deploys it, along with any supporting files, to the report server. (During the build process, the Report Designer checks each report for any errors that would prevent it from executing properly on the report server.) The results of the build and deploy are shown in the Output window seen in Figure 19-6.

10. Open the Report Manager in your browser. Click the MaxMinReports folder to view its content. Click the Data Sources folder. Our MaxMinSalesDMCube shared data source was deployed here.

**Figure 19-5**   *The MaxMinReports Property Pages dialog box*

**Figure 19-6**  *Deploying a report project*

11. Use the breadcrumbs at the top of the page to navigate back to the MaxMinReports folder.
12. Click the Reports folder to view its content. The Wholesale Sales By Month Report was deployed here.
13. Click the Wholesale Sales By Month report. The report displays as shown in Figure 19-7

## Deploying a Single Report

In Step 8, you used the project's context menu to deploy all the items in the project. Alternatively, you could have right-clicked a shared data source or a report and selected Deploy from the context menu. This would have deployed only that item, not the entire project. When deploying individual items, the shared data sources must be deployed before you can deploy reports that depend on them.

On some occasions, you might want to deploy a single report rather than the entire project. At times, one report is going to be completed and ready for deployment, while the other reports in the project are still under construction. At other times, one report is revised after the entire project has already been deployed. In these situations, it is only necessary to redeploy the single revised report.

**Figure 19-7**   *The Wholesale Sales By Month report in the Report Manager*

## Web Service Access

The *Report Manager* provides a nice interface for finding and executing reports, but sometimes, the Report Manager is not the best way to deliver a report to your users. Perhaps the user is browsing your website and needs to view a report. In these situations, we want to provide an integrated approach with reporting available within the application. We want to deliver the report to the user right where they are.

It is possible to access reports programmatically using the Reporting Services web service interface. This is the same interface used by the Report Manager to interact with Reporting Services. This means anything you can do in Report Manager, you can also do through the web service interface.

The *web service interface* enables you to specify a set of credentials to use when executing a report. This allows your custom application to use a set of hard-coded credentials to access reports through the web service interface. This can be a big benefit in situations where you want Reporting Services reports to be exposed on an Internet or extranet site where each user does not have a domain account.

## Learn By Doing—Displaying a Report in an Application

### Feature Highlighted

▶   Using the Reporting Services web service

**Business Need**   With our report deployed to the report server, let's build an application that accesses the report.

### Steps to Create a Project and a Web Reference

1.  Start Visual Studio 2010. (This example also works in earlier versions of Visual Studio.NET.)
2.  Create a new project.
3.  Select Visual Basic | Web in the Installed Templates area.
4.  Select ASP.NET Web Application from the list in the center of the dialog box.
5.  Enter **MaxMinRptFrontEnd** for Name.
6.  Enter an appropriate path for Location.
7.  Click OK.
8.  When the new project has been created, right-click the MaxMinRptFrontEnd project entry in the Solution Explorer and select Add Service Reference from the context menu. The Add Service Reference dialog box appears.
9.  Click Advanced. The Service Reference Settings dialog box appears.
10.  Click Add Web Reference. The Add Web Reference dialog box appears.
11.  Enter the following address for URL:

    ```
    http://localhost/ReportServer/ReportExecution2005.asmx
    ```

> **NOTE**
> _____
>
> *If Reporting Services is not on your computer, replace "localhost" with the name of the computer where Reporting Services is installed.*

12.  Click Go.
13.  When the "ReportExecutionService" Description appears, enter **RptExec** for Web reference name. The completed dialog box is shown in Figure 19-8.
14.  Click Add Reference.

To use a web service, you need to create code that knows how to send data to and retrieve data from that web service. Fortunately, this code is generated for you by Visual Studio through the process of creating a web reference. Once the web reference is in

**Figure 19-8**   *The Add Web Reference dialog box*

place, you can call the methods of the web service the same way you call the methods of a local .NET assembly.

### Steps to Create a Web Form for the User Interface

1. Change the name of Default.aspx to **ReportFrontEnd.aspx**.
2. Click Design near the bottom of the screen to switch to the Design tab.
3. Place two labels, one drop-down list, and a button on the web form, as shown in Figure 19-9.
4. Change the ID property of the drop-down list to **lstYear**.
5. Populate the Items collection as follows:

| Text | Value |
|------|-------|
| 2009 | [Time].[Year].&[2009-01-01T00:00:00] |
| 2010 | [Time].[Year].&[2010-01-01T00:00:00] |
| 2011 | [Time].[Year].&[2011-01-01T00:00:00] |

**Figure 19-9**    *The Report Front End form*

6.  Change the ID property of the button to cmdExecute.

7.  Change the Text property of the button to Display Report.

8.  Double-click the cmdExecute button to open the code window.

9.  Enter the following code for cmdExecute_Click:

```
Private Sub cmdExecute_Click(sender As System.Object,_
                             e As System.EventArgs) _
                             Handles cmdExecute.Click
    Dim report As Byte () = Nothing

    ' Create an instance of the Reporting Services
    ' Web Reference.
    Dim rs As RptExec.ReportExecutionService _
                        = New RptExec.ReportExecutionService

    ' Create the credentials that will be used when accessing
    ' Reporting Services. This must be a logon that has rights
    ' to the Manufacturing By Machine report.
    ' *** Replace "LoginName", "Password", and "Domain" with
    ' the appropriate values. ***
    rs.Credentials = New _
            System.Net.NetworkCredential("LoginName", _
            "Password", "Domain")
    rs.PreAuthenticate = True

    ' The Reporting Services virtual path to the report.
    Dim reportPath As String = _
    "/MaxMinReports/Reports/Wholesale Sales By Month Report"
```

```vb
' The rendering format for the report.
Dim format As String = "PDF"

' The devInfo string tells the report viewer
' how to display with the report.
Dim devInfo As String = _
    "<DeviceInfo>" + _
"<Toolbar>False</Toolbar>" + _
"<Parameters>False</Parameters>" + _
"<DocMap>True</DocMap>" + _
"<Zoom>100</Zoom>" + _
"</DeviceInfo>"

' Create an array of the values for the report parameters
Dim parameters (0) As RptExec.ParameterValue
Dim paramValue As RptExec.ParameterValue _
                            = New RptExec.ParameterValue
paramValue.Name = "TimeYear"
paramValue.Value = lstYear.SelectedValue
parameters (0) = paramValue

' Create variables for the remainder of the parameters
Dim historyID As String = Nothing
Dim credentials () As _
            RptExec.DataSourceCredentials = Nothing
Dim showHideToggle As String = Nothing
Dim encoding As String
Dim mimeType As String
Dim warnings () As RptExec.Warning = Nothing
Dim reportHistoryParameters () As _
            RptExec.ParameterValue = Nothing
Dim streamIDs () As String = Nothing

' Prepare for report execution.
Dim execInfo As New RptExec.ExecutionInfo
Dim execHeader As New RptExec.ExecutionHeader
rs.ExecutionHeaderValue = execHeader
execInfo = rs.LoadReport(reportPath, historyID)
rs.SetExecutionParameters(parameters, "en-us")

Try
    ' Execute the report.
    report = rs.Render(format, devInfo, "", mimeType, _
                                "", warnings, streamIDs)

    ' Flush any pending response.
    Response.Clear ()

    ' Set the HTTP headers for a PDF response.
    HttpContext.Current.Response.ClearHeaders ()
    HttpContext.Current.Response.ClearContent ()
    HttpContext.Current.Response.ContentType = "application/pdf"
```

```
' filename is the default filename displayed
' if the user does a save as.
HttpContext.Current.Response.AppendHeader ( _
    "Content-Disposition", _
    "filename=""WholesaleSalesByMonthReport.pdf""")

' Send the byte array containing the report
' as a binary response.
HttpContext.Current.Response.BinaryWrite(report)
HttpContext.Current.Response.End ()
Catch ex As Exception
    If ex.Message <> "Thread was being aborted." Then
        HttpContext.Current.Response.ClearHeaders ()
        HttpContext.Current.Response.ClearContent ()
        HttpContext.Current.Response.ContentType = _
                "text/html"
        HttpContext.Current.Response.Write ( _
            "<HTML><BODY><H1>Error</H1><br><br>" & _
                                ex.Message & "</BODY></HTML>")
        HttpContext.Current.Response.End ()
    End If
End Try
End Sub
```

10. Replace LoginName, Password, and Domain in the NetworkCredentials() method call with credentials that have rights to execute the Wholesale Sales By Month Reports on the report server.

11. Click Save All on the toolbar.

12. Select Debug | Start Debugging from the main menu. This executes your program.

13. When the browser window appears with the web application front-end page, select a year and click Display Report. The report appears as a PDF document using the year selected on the front-end page.

14. Switch back to Visual Studio and select Debug | Stop Debugging from the main menu.

You can refer to the comments in the code sample for information on the purpose of each section of code.

## Managing Reporting Services Through Web Services

In addition to executing reports through the web service interface, you can manage Reporting Services using the web services. If you choose, you can write an application that completely replaces the Report Manager web application for controlling Reporting Services.

**NOTE**

*You can also integrate reports with .NET applications using the Report Viewer control. The Report Viewer control can be used to display reports rendered by a report server, or it can provide the rendering engine for reports running local to the application.*

# Great Capabilities, Great Opportunities

The business intelligence tools in SQL Server 2012 offer us tremendous capabilities. We can create powerful analysis tools to provide business intelligence to decision makers at every level of our organizations. We can define, construct, deploy, and analyze with greater speed and efficiency than ever before.

The complexity that made data warehousing, data mining, enterprise-wide reporting, and the integration of those items with line-of-business applications a lengthy, expensive, and risky venture has been reduced, if not eliminated.

The reputation of business intelligence projects as not worth the time, money, and headaches involved is widespread and deeply ingrained. Too many times, business intelligence projects delivered less than expected, in a less effective manner than anticipated, over a longer timeline than allowed for, while requiring more money than budgeted. Most small and mid-size organizations would never dream of creating a data mart or using OLAP cubes or data mining. Yet, these are the same organizations that stand to benefit the most from what SQL Server 2012 has to offer. A number of large organizations have been down the business intelligence road with huge, all-encompassing projects that ended up failing miserably. With SQL Server 2012, these large organizations can implement business intelligence with an incremental approach that leads to a much higher success rate.

Those of us working with business intelligence in SQL Server 2012 have a job ahead of us. We need to let organizations of all sizes know that the tools, the architecture, and, indeed, the rules of business intelligence are changing. SQL Server 2012 allows for more of an iterative style and less of the all-or-nothing approach to business intelligence projects of the past. With SQL Server 2012, it is possible to get *more* than you expected in a *more* effective manner than anticipated with a *shorter* timeline than allowed requiring *less* money than budgeted.

Those organizations that hear this message can reap the rewards offered by the business intelligence tools in SQL Server 2012 and the strategic advantages that go along with them. They can efficiently create tools to achieve effective decision making!

# Index

# Master Microsoft® SQL Server® 2012 and Microsoft's Powerful Business Intelligence Tools

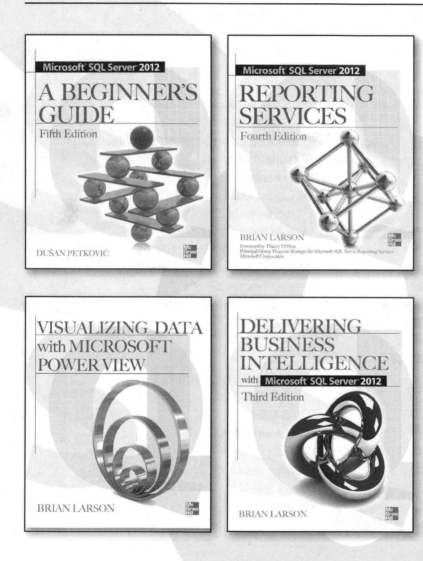

### Microsoft SQL Server 2012: A Beginner's Guide, Fifth Edition
Dušan Petkovic

Filled with real-world examples and hands-on exercises, this book makes it easy to learn essential skills.

### Microsoft SQL Server 2012 Reporting Services, Fourth Edition
Brian Larson

Create, deploy, and manage BI reports using the expert tips and best practices in this hands-on resource.

### Delivering Business Intelligence with Microsoft SQL Server 2012, Third Edition
Brian Larson

Equip your organization for informed, timely decision making with the expert tips in this practical guide.

### Visualizing Data with Microsoft Power View
Brian Larson, Mark Davis, Dan English, and Paul Purington

Unlock the power of Microsoft Power View and build rich BI reports with just a few clicks.

### Microsoft SQL Server 2012 Master Data Services, Second Edition
Tyler Graham and Suzanne Selhorn

Learn best practices for deploying and managing Master Data Services (MDS).

Available in print and e-book format

Follow us 🐦 @MHComputing

 Learn more. Do more:

MHPROFESSIONAL.COM